Mastering Harvard Graphics 3.0

Mastering Harvard Graphics 3.0

Donald Richard Read

Windcrest®/McGraw-Hill

FIRST EDITION
FIRST PRINTING

Published by Windcrest Books, an imprint of TAB Books.
TAB Books is a division of McGraw-Hill, Inc.
The name "Windcrest" is a registered trademark of TAB Books.

Library of Congress Cataloging-in-Publication Data

Read, Donald Richard.
Mastering Harvard graphics 3.0 / by Donald Richard Read.
p. cm.
ISBN 0-8306-3602-1 (pbk.)
1. Harvard graphics (Computer program) I. Title.
T385.R433 1992
006.6′869—dc20 92-2886
CIP

TAB Books offers software for sale. For information and a catalog, please contact TAB Software Department, Blue Ridge Summit, PA 17294-0850.

Director of Acquisitions: Ron Powers
Book Editor: Kellie Hagan
Director of Production: Katherine G. Brown
Cover Design: Sandra Blair Design, Harrisburg, PA
Kaleidoscope photograph courtesty of Van Cort Instruments, Northampton, MA WT1

Contents

Introduction

By acquiring Harvard Graphics 3.0, you've made a valuable addition to your little red tool box. You've added to your potential for jacking up personal productivity, for getting more done in less time at a lower cost, for turning out work that looks professional, and for making points more effectively.

To turn potential into reality, you need to learn to use this shiny new tool. And that's what this book is all about.

How to use the tools

Using Harvard Graphics involves learning to flip the switches, push the buttons, hit the keys, handle the disks, and maneuver the mice—in other words, operate all the things that make the program go. You want to be able to make Harvard Graphics 3.0 sit, stay, fetch, and lie down—and you want to do it with authority and dispatch. Whether you want a pie chart, an animated drawing, a text chart, or a computerized slide show, you want to be able to reach into your grab bag of graphical legerdemain and pull out just the right magic rabbit that will dazzle and convince your audience.

Working your way to proficiency with the mechanics of the program might seem a bit daunting at first, but with the help of this handy guide your learning curve will climb rapidly. You'll learn not only how to make the bells and whistles of the program perform, but how to make them perform melodically, harmonically, and to great effect.

Hardware requirements

Harvard Graphics 3.0 will run on quite a variety of hardware configurations. There are some minimum requirements you have to meet, but the program is designed to permit you great latitude in hardware selection.

Computers

Harvard Graphics 3.0 works on PC-AT class or PS/2 series microcomputers and 100% compatibles that run on the DOS or MS-DOS operating system. This includes all machines with 80286, 80386, or 80486 microprocessors that also meet the criteria below.

DOS (disk operating system)

To run this software, you'll need DOS version 3.0 or higher (DOS 3.10 or higher for networks).

Memory

The minimum memory requirement is 640 K (640,000) bytes of RAM (random-access memory), with at least 438 K available to run the program.

Disk drives

Your computer system must have a hard-disk drive and one floppy drive.

Graphics boards

Harvard Graphics 3.0 requires either an IBM EGA color or monochrome graphics board (with at least 256 K of memory), or a VGA or compatible board.

Printers and plotters

Your software supports a long list of printers, plotters, and other peripheral devices for producing hard copies or other kinds of displays of your charts and graphics. Printer and plotter manufacturers that are either directly supported or supported through VDI include IBM, Hewlett-Packard, NEC, Epson, Okidata, Xerox, Toshiba, Qume, AST, Apple, CalComp, Matrix, and Tektronix.

Film recorders

For producing output on film, you can use film recorders such as the Agfa Matrix ChromaScript, Polaroid Palette Plus, Lasergraphics Rascol II/LFR, PTI Montage FRI, and General Parametrics VideoShow, among others.

Networking

If you're going to share printers or other output devices on a network with other users, you should have the IBM PC-LAN program, Novell ELS, Advanced, SFT Netware, Netware 386, 3Com 3+ Share, Banyan Vines 386, or Harvard Graphics LAN.

And finally, mice

Harvard Graphics 3.0 doesn't require a mouse, but the little devils sure make it a lot more convenient and fun. Any mouse that's compatible with the Microsoft mouse will work with the program.

Part 1
Learning the basics

1
CHAPTER

Getting started

Harvard Graphics 3.0 is wonderfully uncomplicated to operate. The program uses either a mouse or a handful of keys to move among menus and choices, and it uses the function keys in a clear and consistent way. The real beauty of the program design is that you never have to memorize the command structure; you can always tell from the screen what to do and how to do it.

When you load the program by going to the proper directory (probably C:\HG3), and typing:

hg3 Enter

the Harvard Graphics logo appears, and then the Main Menu. The Main Menu and the first set of submenus are shown in Figs. 1-1 through 1-10. You might want

```
Harvard Graphics
F1-Help          F2-Show chart
F6-Main Menu     F7-Spell check                          F10-Continue

  ▸ Create chart        1
    Edit chart          2
    Draw                3
    ─────────────────────
    File                4
    Output              5
    ─────────────────────
    Presentation        6
    ─────────────────────
    Macros              7
    Setup               8
    ─────────────────────
    Applications        9
    ─────────────────────
    Exit                E

      Copyright 1991 Software Publishing Corporation
            Copyright 1991 Bitstream Inc.
```

1-1 The Main Menu.

to photocopy these figures and put them on the wall near you to use as a road map as you work.

The Main Menu offers 10 choices (including Exit). Select among the options by using the up or down arrow keys, the space bar, your mouse, or simply by pressing the number corresponding to the option you want. If you want to create a new chart, for example, press 1 or move the arrow to 1 by using the space bar, the arrow keys, or the mouse. Then press Enter (click the left-hand button on the mouse), and the Create New Chart menu will pop up alongside the Main Menu (see Fig. 1-2). There are seven submenus off the Main Menu:

Submenu	Number	Figure
Create New Chart	1	1-2
File	4	1-5
Output	5	1-6
Presentation	6	1-7
Macros	7	1-8
Setup	8	1-9
Applications	9	1-10

Pressing 2 (Edit chart) from the Main Menu takes you to the data sheet for the chart you're currently working on (see Fig. 1-3). Pressing 3 (Draw) takes you to a graphics screen where you can alter the current chart by drawing on it, erasing, adding text, etc. Or you can create professional-looking graphics from scratch (see Fig. 1-4). And pressing E takes you out of the program.

In addition to the ten options presented in the Main Menu, there are numerous other maneuvers you can perform from the first screen, as described in the following section.

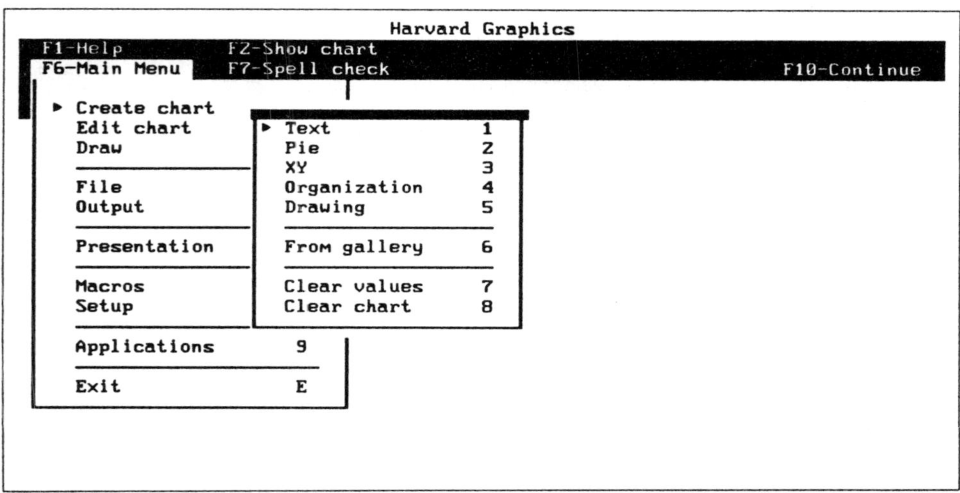

1-2 The Create Chart menu.

ARGOSPIE.CH3 Pie Chart 1

F1-Help F2-Show chart F3-Choices F4-Draw F5-Mark
F6-Main Menu F7-Spell/Text F8-Options F9-Pie data F10-Continue

Title: Foreign Sales
Subtitle: Third Quarter, 1987
Footnote: Figures in thousands of dollars
Pie title:

Slice	Label	Value	Cut	Color	Pattern
1	U.S. Sales	18352	No	Gry DD|S	4
2	Foreign Sales	8245	Yes	Gry |S	8
3			No	Gry L|S	2
4			No	Gry L|S	3
5			No	Gry LL|S	4
6			No	White |S	5
7			No	Gry DD|S	6
8			No	Gry |S	7
9			No	Gry L|S	8
10			No	Gry L|S	9
11			No	Gry LL|S	10
12			No	White |S	11

1-3 The Edit Chart selection takes you to a chart data screen.

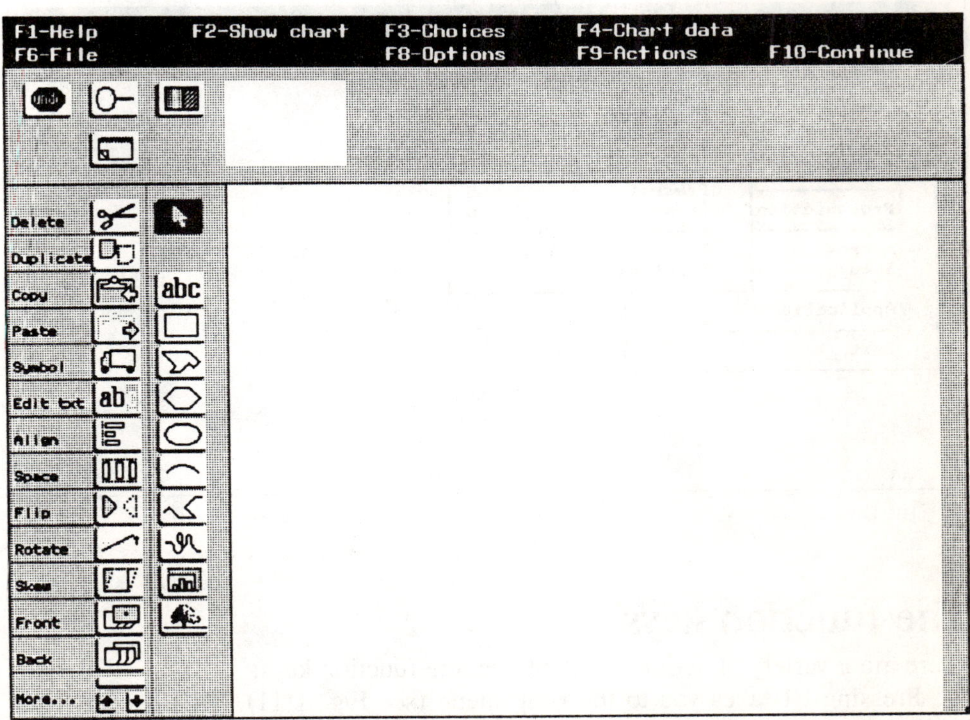

1-4 The Draw selection takes you to the Draw screen.

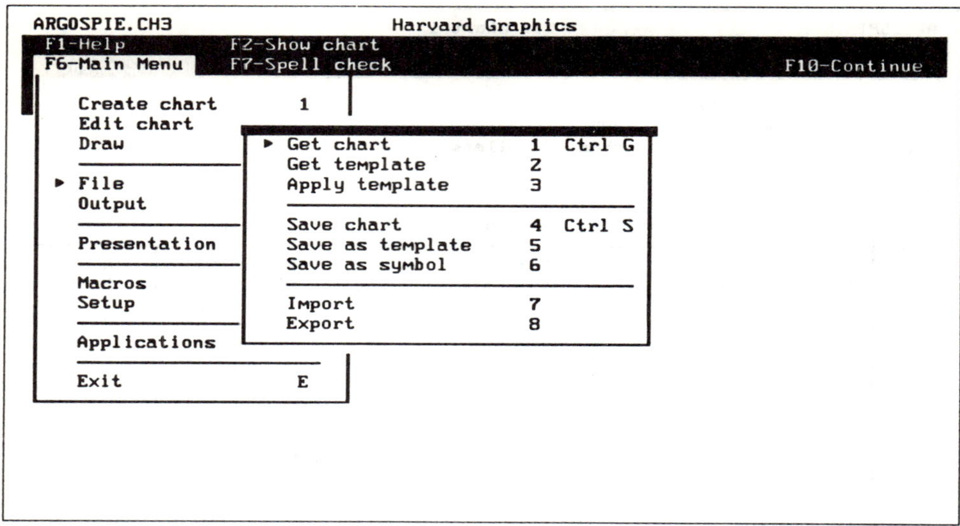

1-5 The File submenu.

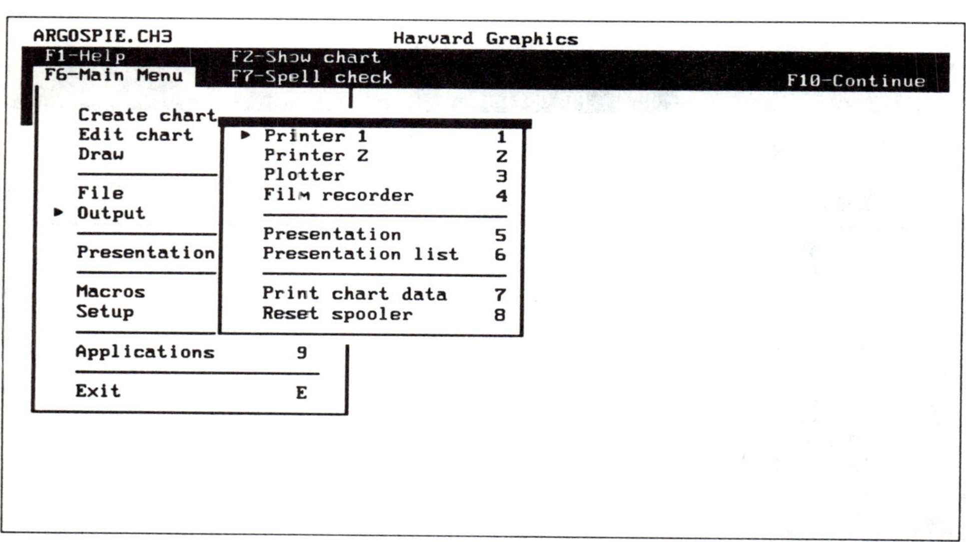

1-6 The Output submenu.

The function keys

There are a variety of actions available via the function keys:

Pressing F1 takes you to the Help menu (see Fig. 1-11). This is called the *context-sensitive* help screen; i.e., pressing F1 at any location in the program

```
ARGOSPIE.CH3                        Harvard Graphics
 F1-Help         F2-Show chart
 F6-Main Menu    F7-Spell check                          F10-Continue

   Create chart        1
   Edit chart          2
   Draw
                 ▸ Create presentation          1
   File            Edit presentation            2
   Output
                   Display ScreenShow           3
 ▸ Presentation
                   Get presentation             4
   Macros          Save presentation            5
   Setup           Spell check presentation     6

   Applications        9

   Exit                E
```

1-7 The Presentation submenu.

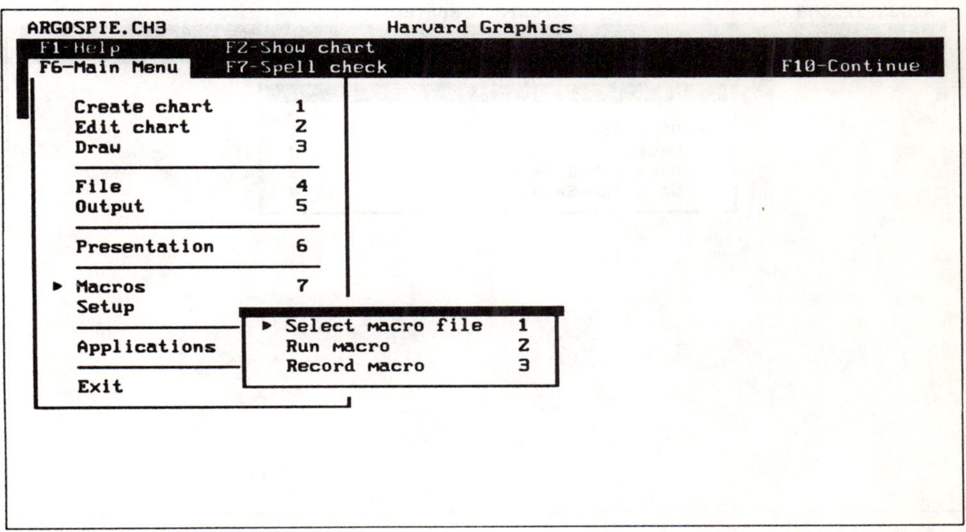

1-8 The Macros submenu.

takes you to a screen that provides help with actions and commands appropriate to that specific point in the program.

Pressing F2 takes you to a full-screen display of the current chart (see Fig. 1-12).

Pressing F3 at many locations in the program will cause a list of choices to

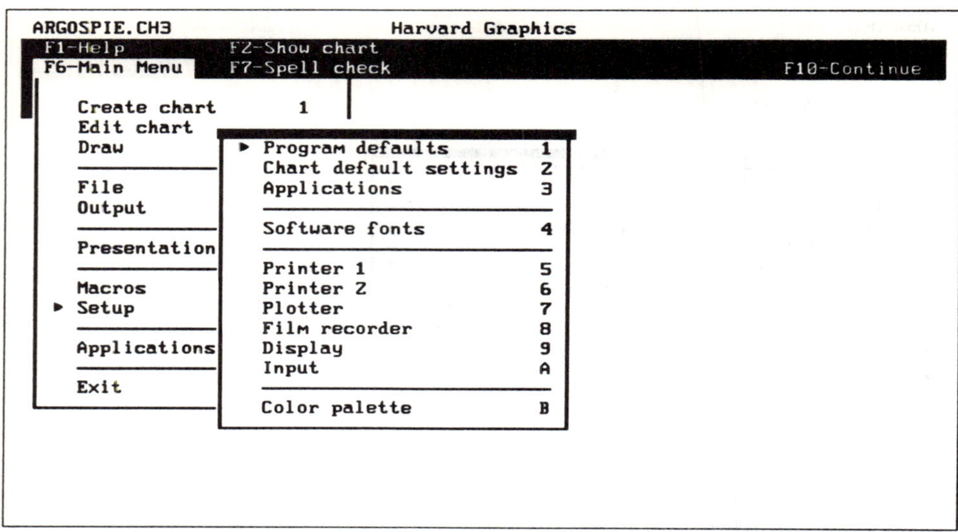

1-9 The Setup submenu.

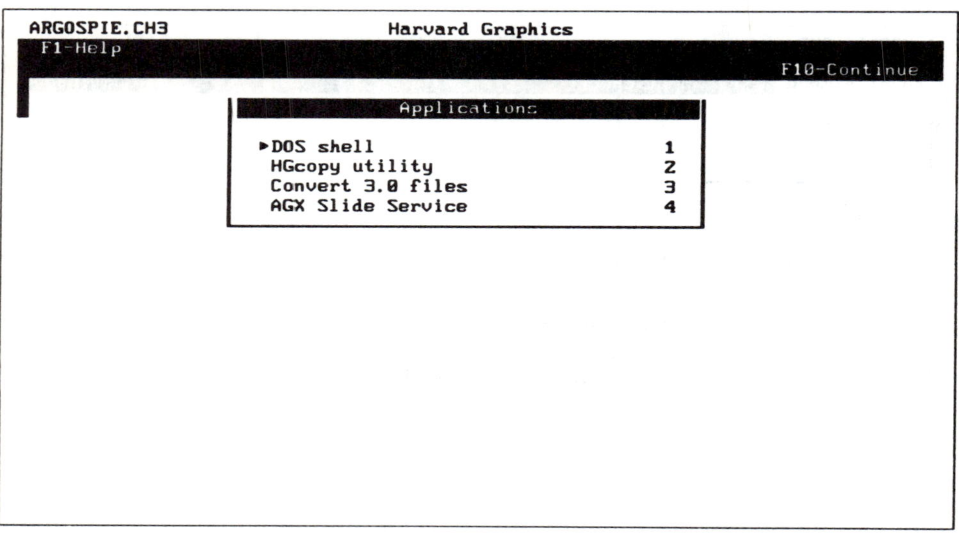

1-10 The Applications submenu.

appear. Because this function doesn't apply to the Main Menu screen, it will be discussed later.

Pressing F7 checks the spelling of any text on your current chart (see Fig. 1-13).

Help

Select Create chart to create a new chart. If you were previously editing a chart, Harvard Graphics displays a warning and gives you a chance to save it.

At the Create chart menu, select the type of chart you want to create:

- Text: title, bullet, and table charts
- Pie: column or pie charts
- XY: bar, line, area, high/low/close, and point charts
- Organization: organization charts
- Drawing: a drawing chart from scratch .

Shift F1-Help Menu — Ctrl F1-Speed keys

1-11 The current Help screen.

1-12 The F2 key takes you to a display of the current chart.

Spell Check Status

Complete

1-13 The F7 key runs a spelling check on your current chart.

Pressing F10 will either move the program to the next step or confirm a choice. For example, in Fig. 1-10, the Applications submenu shows a small arrow to the left of DOS shell, meaning that returning to the DOS shell is the selected action. Pressing F10 will confirm the choice and take you (temporarily) out of Harvard Graphics 3.0.

Pressing Shift – F1 takes you to the Help Topics Index screen (see Fig. 1-14). From that screen you can select a topic with which you need further help, and you'll be guided to further layers of Help menus and information screens.

```
                Help Topics Index

▸Learning the basics
 Creating text charts
 Creating pie and column charts
 Creating XY charts
 Creating organization charts
 Creating presentations
 Producing output
 Using Draw
 Working with color
 Importing and exporting data
 Working with macros
 The Autographix Overnight Slide Service
 About Software Publishing Corporation
```

1-14 Press Shift – F1 to display the Help Topics Index screen.

Harvard Graphics 3.0 has a number of *speed keys*, combinations of the Ctrl key and another key, which provide shortcuts to certain operations. For a listing of these key combinations, press Ctrl – F1 (see Figs. 1-15, 1-16, and 1-17). Of the speed keys listed here, only the following four are available from the Main Menu:

Keys	**Action**
Ctrl – G	Get a chart from a directory (Fig. 1-18)
Ctrl – P	Print the current chart (Fig. 1-19)
Ctrl – S	Save the current chart
Ctrl – V	Display the Harvard Graphics version you're using (Fig. 1-21)

```
                           Help

(I) = Import      (O) = Organization charts
(P) = Presentations

Ctrl-B            Insert special characters
Ctrl-E            Edit current chart data form (P)
Ctrl-G            Get chart
Ctrl-H            Hide subordinates (O)
Ctrl-J            Jump to file #xxx (P)
Ctrl-J            Jump to new location (I)
Ctrl-L            Switch left (O)
Ctrl-M            Activate mouse (P)
Ctrl-N            Edit Notes
Ctrl-P            Print chart
Ctrl-R            Switch right (O)
Ctrl-S            Save file

Shift F1-Help Menu
```

1-15 Press Ctrl – F1 to display a listing of the speed keys.

```
                         Help
Ctrl-T             Display Titles/Footnotes pop-up
Ctrl-U             Show subordinates (O)
Ctrl-V             Display version number
Ctrl-Z             Add text to box (O)

Ctrl-Up Arrow      Move current line up
Ctrl-Up Arrow      Move current file up (P)
Ctrl-Dn Arrow      Move current line down
Ctrl-Dn Arrow      Move current file down (P)
Ctrl-Right Arrow   Move cursor to next word
Ctrl-Left Arrow    Move cursor to previous word

Ctrl-Home          Move cursor to first field
Ctrl-Home          Go to top of file (I)
Ctrl-End           Move cursor to last field
Shift F1-Help Menu
```

1-16 The first screen of the speed key listing.

```
                         Help
Ctrl-Dn Arrow      Move current line down
Ctrl-Dn Arrow      Move current file down (P)
Ctrl-Right Arrow   Move cursor to next word
Ctrl-Left Arrow    Move cursor to previous word

Ctrl-Home          Move cursor to first field
Ctrl-Home          Go to top of file (I)
Ctrl-End           Move cursor to last field
Ctrl-End           Go to end of file (I)
Ctrl-Ins           Insert new line
Ctrl-Ins           Add a new file (P)
Ctrl-Ins           Add subordinate (O)
Ctrl-Del           Delete current line
Ctrl-Del           Delete file (P)
Ctrl-Del           Delete box or group (O)
Shift F1-Help Menu
```

1-17 The second screen of the speed key listing.

```
                              Get Chart
  Directory: C:\HG3\DATA\*.CH*
  Filename:  SYLLABUS.CH3

 ..              <DIR>
►SYLLABUS.CH3    TABLE    Syllabus: English 11-5803
 BLINDS   .CH3   DRAW     Bkg: Horizontal Bands         Use 4,5,7.PL3
 BLUESKY  .CH3   DRAW     Bkg: Sky & Clouds            Use 9 or 10.PL3
 CYLINDER.CH3    DRAW     Bkg: Cylinder blend          Use 3,4,6,7.PL3
 FLOOR    .CH3   DRAW     Bkg: Checkered floor          Use 1ZHDW.PL3
 FRAME1   .CH3   DRAW     Bkg: single line frame          Use any PL3
 FRAMEZ   .CH3   DRAW     Bkg: double line frame          Use any PL3
 LEAVES   .CH3   DRAW     Bkg: Leaves                 Use 7 or 7SHD.PL3
 LOGOBKG1.CH3    DRAW     Bkg: Use your own logo.pcx      Use any PL3
```

1-18 Press Ctrl – G to get a file from the directory.

Output To Printer	
Device	Okidata ML393 (LQ Module)
Port	LPT1
Quality	♦High
Paper size	A (8.5 in. x 11 in.)
Chart size	Full
Copies	1
Output to disk	No
Output filename	C:\HG3\OUTPUT\6QBACKLG.OUT

1-19 Press Ctrl – P to print the current chart.

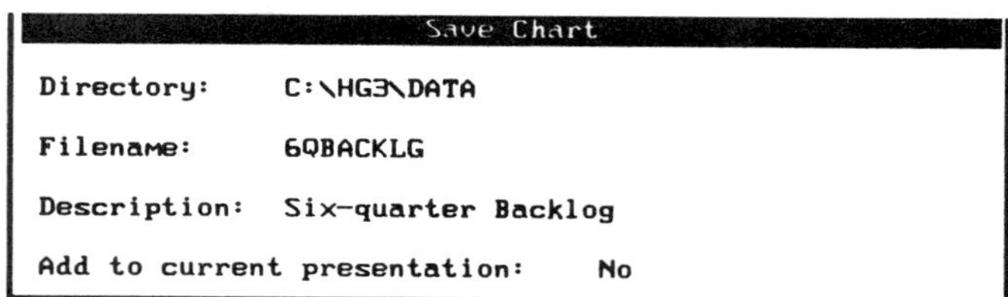
Save Chart

Directory: C:\HG3\DATA

Filename: 6QBACKLG

Description: Six-quarter Backlog

Add to current presentation: No

1-20 When you press Ctrl – S, the Save Chart menu appears.

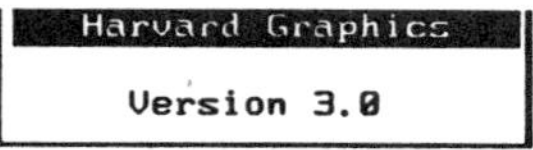

1-21 Pressing Ctrl – V causes the version information to appear.

Using the keyboard

Harvard Graphics 3.0 makes it easy to move around the program. The number of keystrokes you have to remember is kept to a minimum. For moving among menu selections, use the up and down arrows, the space bar, or the mouse.

For choosing a menu option, use the number keys, the Enter key, the F10 key, or the left mouse button. For returning to the previous menu level, use the Esc key or the right mouse button.

That's all you need to know about basic maneuvers. I'll explain other details as you go along. You've slammed the doors, kicked the tires, and pushed a few buttons of this marvelous machine. Time to fasten your seat belt and take a trial spin; let's see how Harvard Graphics 3.0 performs on the road.

2
CHAPTER

Quick charts from the Gallery

Harvard Graphics 3.0 makes it possible for you to construct charts, graphs, and other graphics, and to manipulate them in great detail. The program also assumes, however, that many people are often focused on getting quick results—which means that much of the time we're content to whip out a generic chart or graph without doing a lot of detailed editing or customization.

The folks at Software Publishing Corporation who created Harvard Graphics 3.0 anticipated the need for quick results nicely by creating a collection of generic charts and graphs called the *Gallery*. The Gallery begins with nine types of charts, and then offers you a number of variations within each of the nine types. When you select the variation that best suits your purpose (or your discerning eye), you can then "edit" that chart by substituting your own data for the data in the generic chart.

Using the Gallery

Here's how it works: From the main menu, select Create chart. The Create Chart menu appears, as shown in Fig. 2-1. Go to the Gallery by selecting From Gallery. In a couple of seconds the graphics screen in Fig. 2-2 will appear. This screen, called the *home screen* of the Gallery, displays nine types of basic charts:

Text
Pie
Bar
Line

Area
High/low/close
Organization
Horizontal bar
Combination

By pointing to any of the chart panels, you can go to another screen displaying further variations of the nine basic chart types. For example, if you select panel 1, Text Chart, the program will display a screen of nine variations of text charts (see Fig. 2-3). Figures 2-4 through 2-11 show multiple versions of the other eight types of Gallery charts.

You use the Gallery by selecting a chart that's closest to what you have in mind, and then substituting your own text or data for the sample text and data in the chart. Let's begin with a text chart.

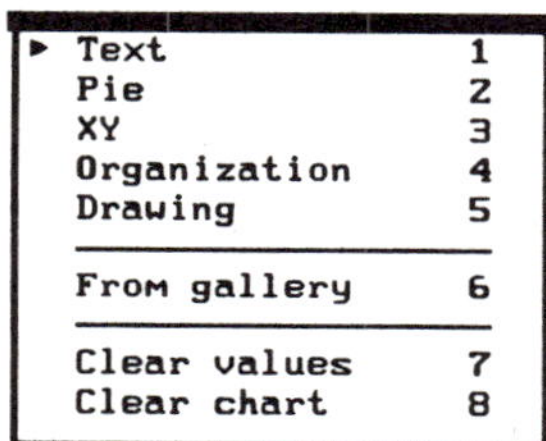

2-1 The Create Chart menu.

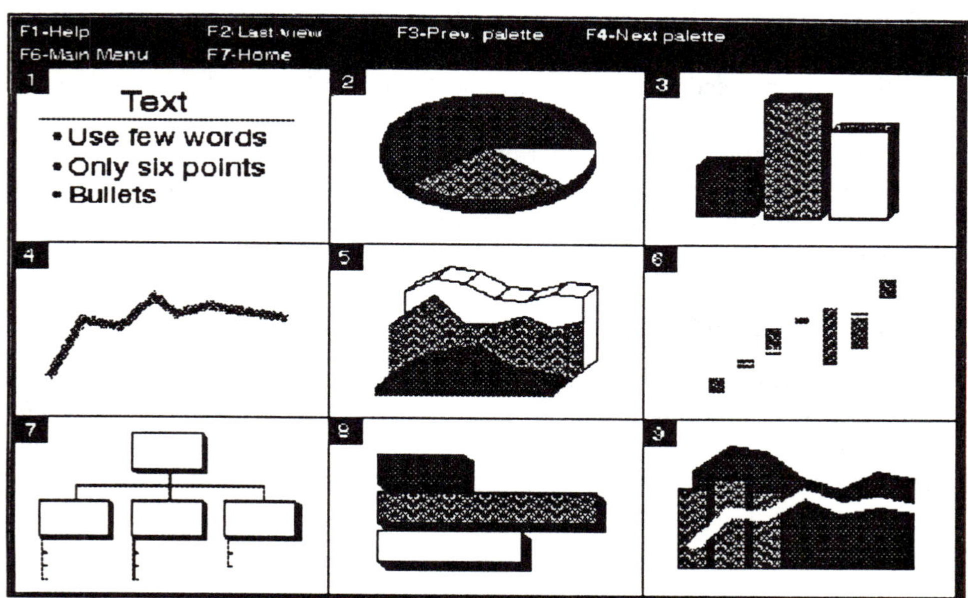

2-2 The Gallery home screen.

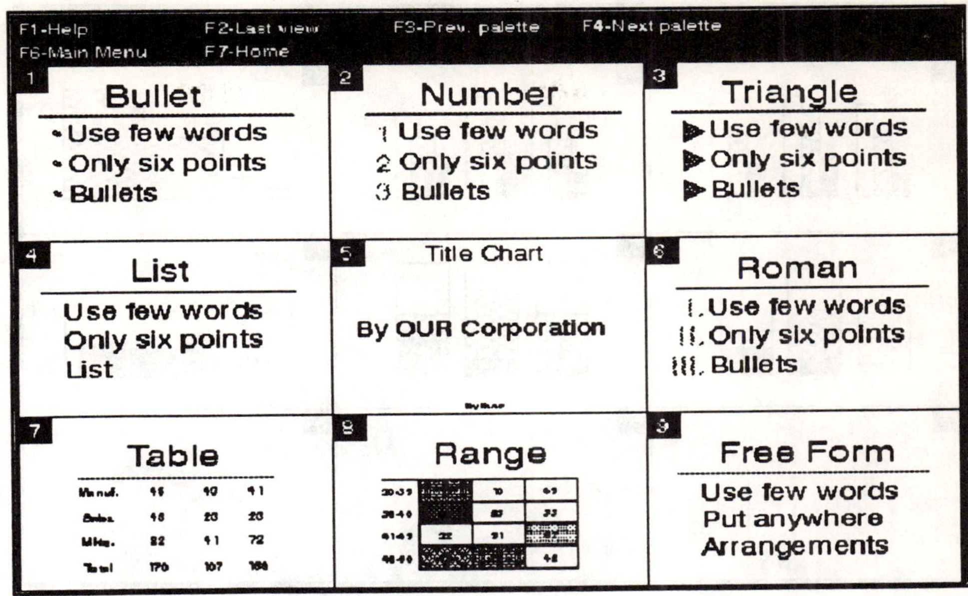

2-3 Nine versions of generic text charts.

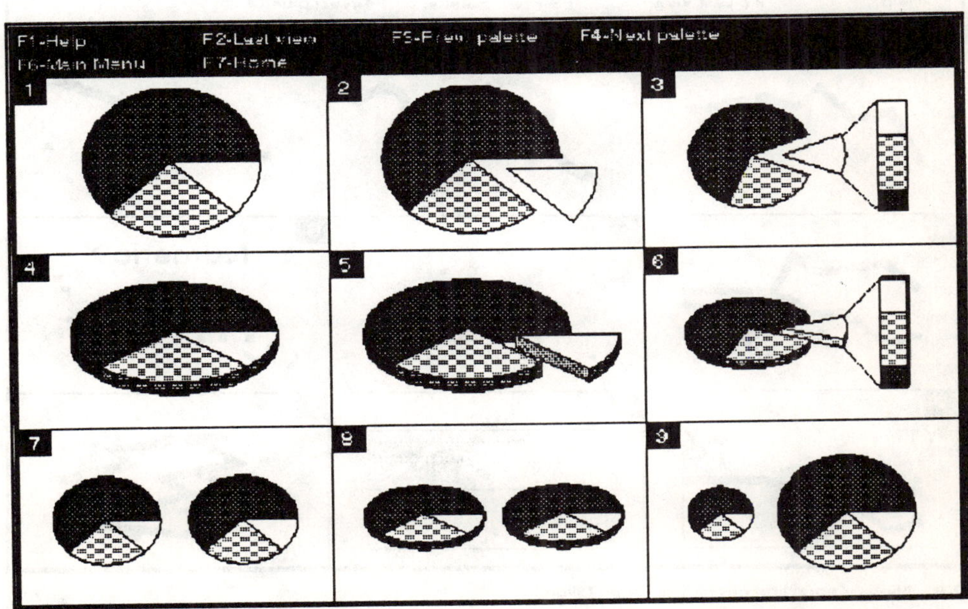

2-4 Nine generic pie charts from the Gallery.

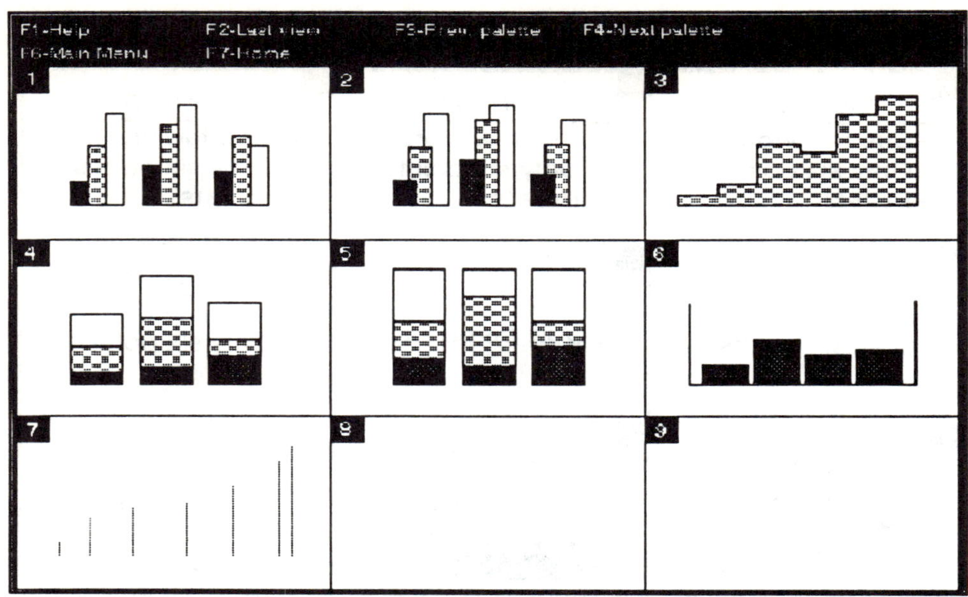

2-5 Seven vertical bar charts from the Gallery.

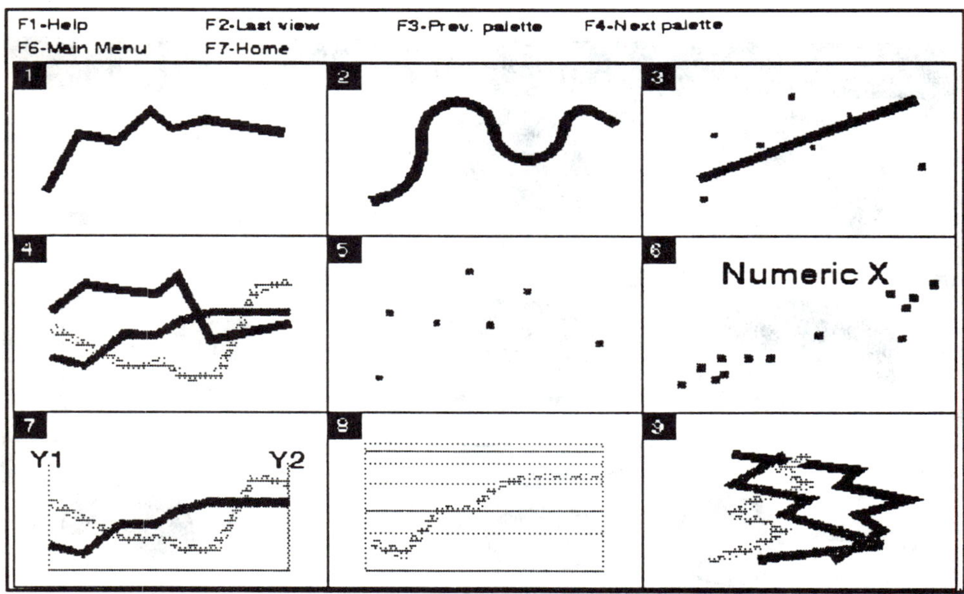

2-6 Nine generic line charts from the Gallery.

2-7 Nine generic area charts from the Gallery.

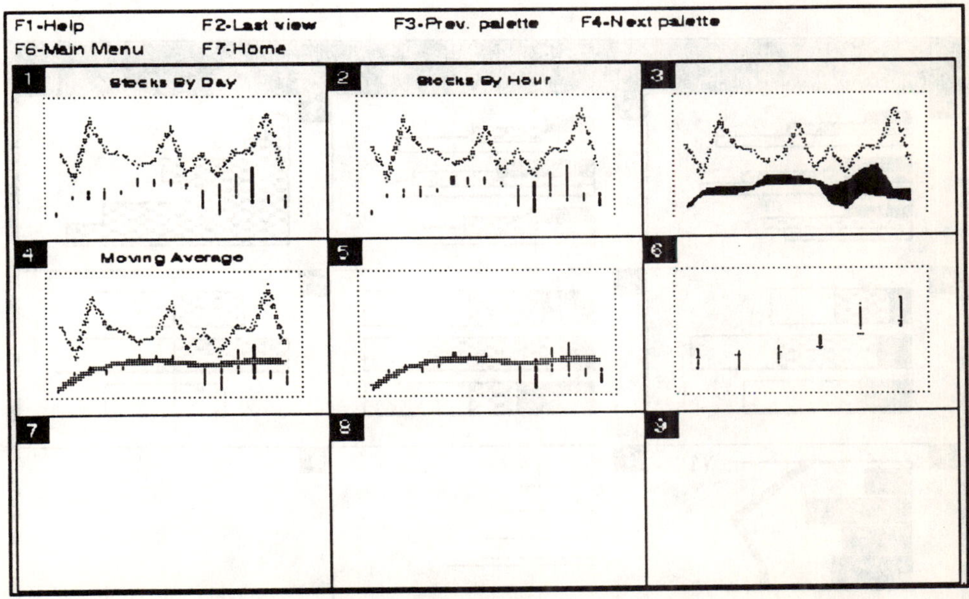

2-8 Six generic high/low/close charts from the Gallery.

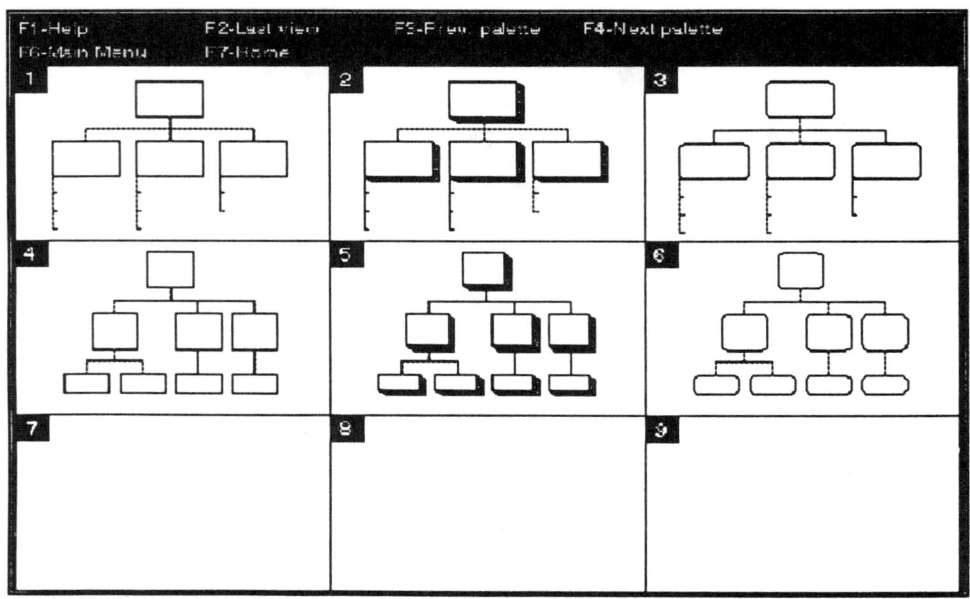

2-9 Six generic organization charts from the Gallery.

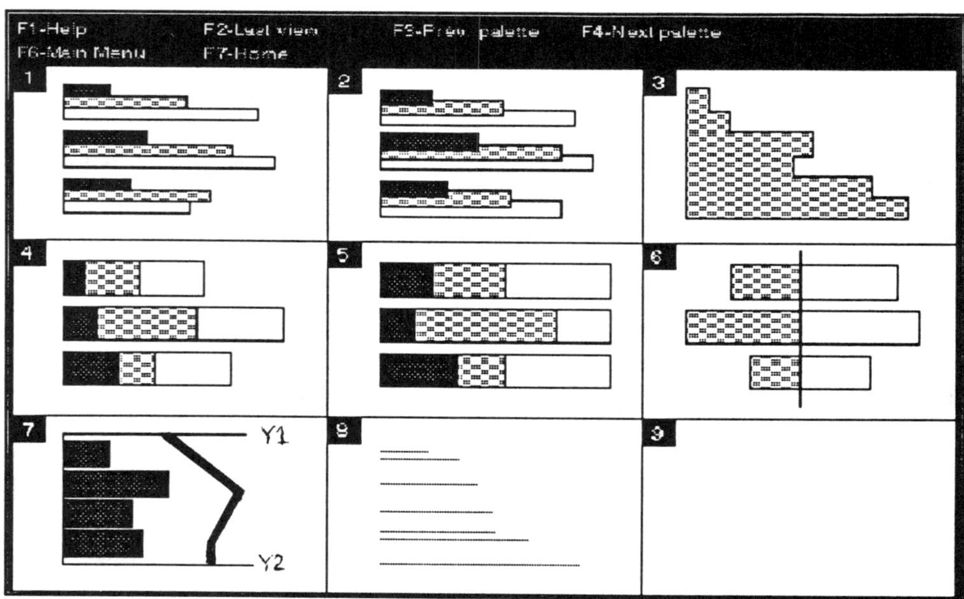

2-10 Eight generic horizontal bar charts from the Gallery.

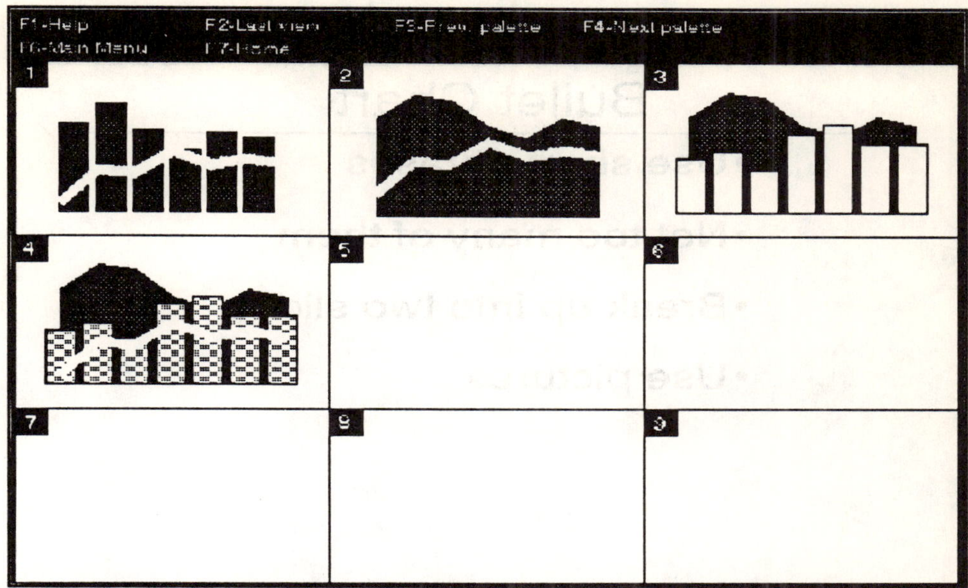

2-11 Four generic combination charts from the Gallery.

Text chart

For this chart—and for many of the sample charts you'll create in this book—you'll be using data from the 1990 annual report of a public company called Compression Labs, Inc. The stock of Compression Labs trades over the counter on the NASDAQ National Market System under the trading symbol CLIX. Their primary business is the manufacture of equipment used to "digitize and compress full-motion color video for economical transmission over land-based or satellite communications networks," and they describe themselves as the world leader in video-conferencing. Because this is all public information, you're free to use it to create real-life examples of Harvard Graphics 3.0 applications.

For a presentation to securities analysts and portfolio managers, you want to create a text chart containing the highlights of the letter to stockholders in the Compression Labs annual report. Begin by selecting a generic text chart that appears to best fit your needs from the Gallery.

1. From the Main Menu, select Create Chart to get that submenu (see Fig. 2-1)
2. Select From gallery to display the Gallery home screen (see Fig. 2-2).
3. Click on the text panel to move to the nine generic text charts (see Fig. 2-3), and select the bullet chart by clicking on that panel or pressing 1. The program will display the generic bullet chart shown in Fig. 2-12.

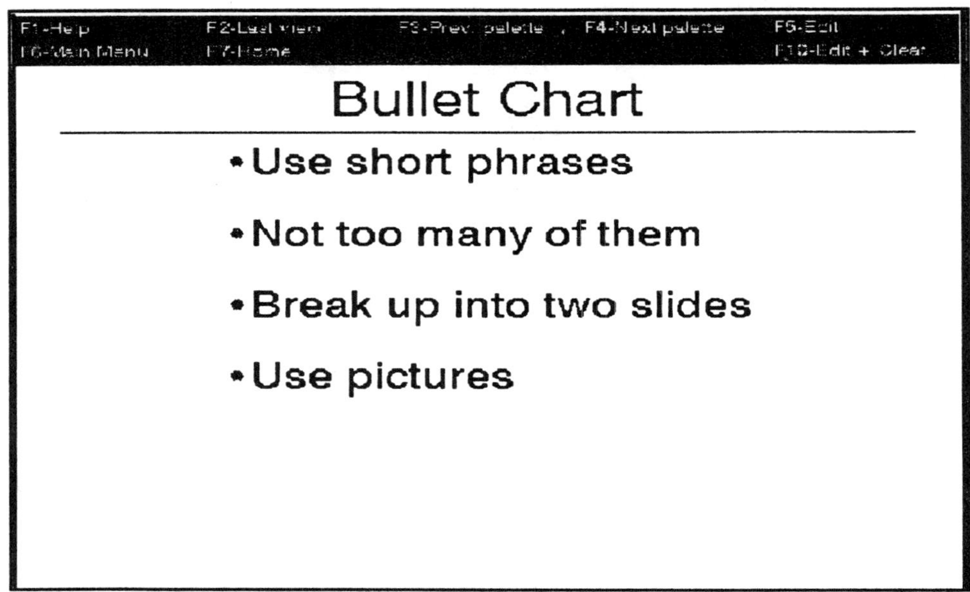

2-12 The generic bullet chart from the Gallery.

Not wasting a word, the generic bullet chart provides a little education about effective text charts, with a brief homily on the virtues of using short phrases and not too many of them, etc. You'll be using the data sheet to substitute your own data (or text, in this case) for the sample text provided in the Gallery. So the next move is to go to the data sheet. Select F5 – Edit to display the data sheet for the bullet chart (see Fig. 2-13).

At this point, you want to substitute your own text for the sample text in the Gallery chart. The title of your new chart will be Annual Highlights, and the six bulleted items will be Growing revenues and earnings, Delivering complete solutions, Penetrating vertical markets, Forging strategic partnerships, Building for the future, and Looking ahead. The cursor is blinking under the B of Bullet Chart.

1. Type Annual Highlights and press the Tab key three times to move down to the first bulleted item (see Fig. 2-14).
2. Type Growing revenues and earnings, and then press Tab twice.
3. Type Delivering complete solutions, and then press Tab twice.
4. Type Penetrating vertical markets, and then press Tab twice.
5. Type Forging strategic partnerships, and then press Tab twice. A new bullet should have appeared when you hit the second Tab (see Fig. 2-15).
6. Now type Building for the future and press Tab twice.
7. Type Looking ahead, but don't press Tab. Your screen should look like the one in Fig. 2-16.

8. Select F2 to view your first text chart (see Fig. 2-17), and then press Esc or the right mouse button to return to the data sheet.
9. Refer to Fig. 1-15; you see that the Speed Key combination for saving a chart is Ctrl−S. Press Ctrl−S; the Save Chart menu will appear with the cursor blinking after Filename (see Fig. 2-18).
10. Type highlite as the filename, then press F10 to complete the action.

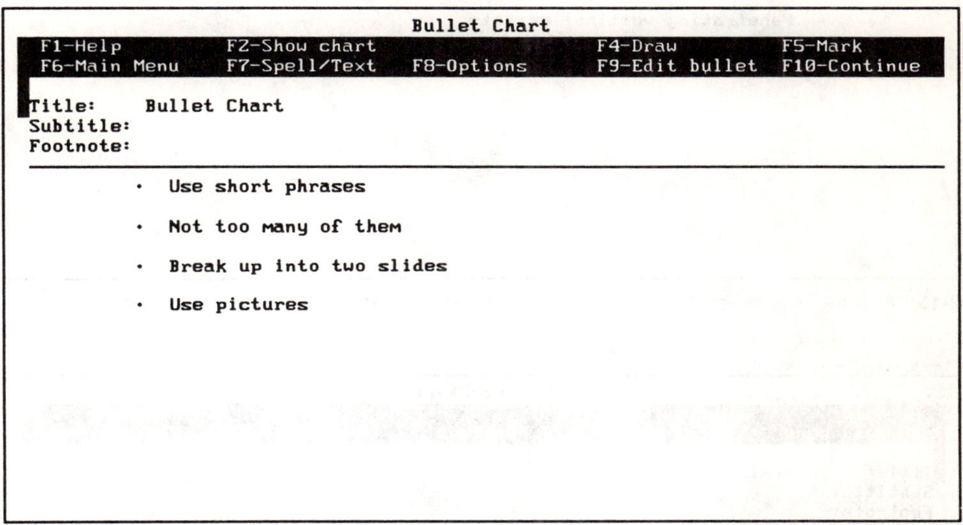

2-13 The data sheet for the bullet chart.

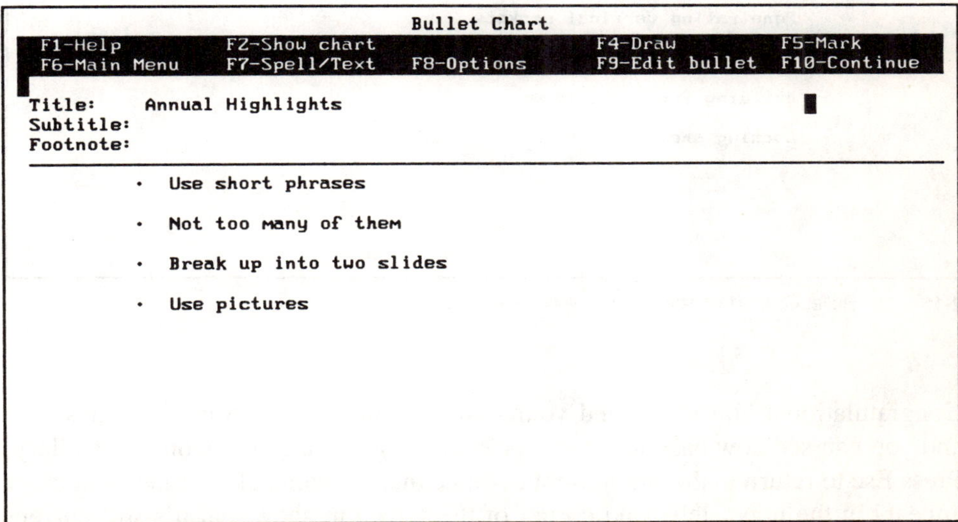

2-14 The Bullet Chart data sheet with the new title.

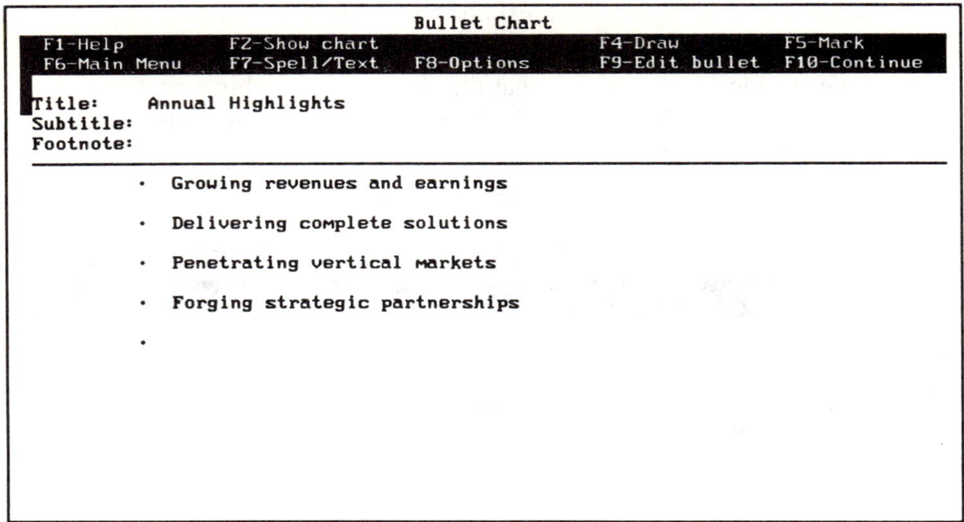

2-15 After the original items are replaced, a new bullet appears.

```
                              Bullet Chart
 F1-Help        F2-Show chart                F4-Draw        F5-Mark
 F6-Main Menu   F7-Spell/Text   F8-Options   F9-Edit bullet F10-Continue

Title:    Annual Highlights
Subtitle:
Footnote:
-----------------------------------------------------------------------
          •  Growing revenues and earnings

          •  Delivering complete solutions

          •  Penetrating vertical markets

          •  Forging strategic partnerships

          •  Building for the future

          •  Looking ahead
```

2-16 The Bullet Chart data screen with all items entered.

Congratulations! You've created your first text file with Harvard Graphics 3.0, and you can see how easy it is to work with the generic charts from the Gallery. Press Esc to return to the Main Menu. Notice that the name of your new text chart appears in the upper left-hand corner of the screen to show that it's still current (see Fig. 2-19).

Annual Highlights

- Growing revenues and earnings
- Delivering complete solutions
- Penetrating vertical markets
- Forging strategic partnerships
- Building for the future
- Looking ahead

2-17 The completed Annual Highlights bullet chart.

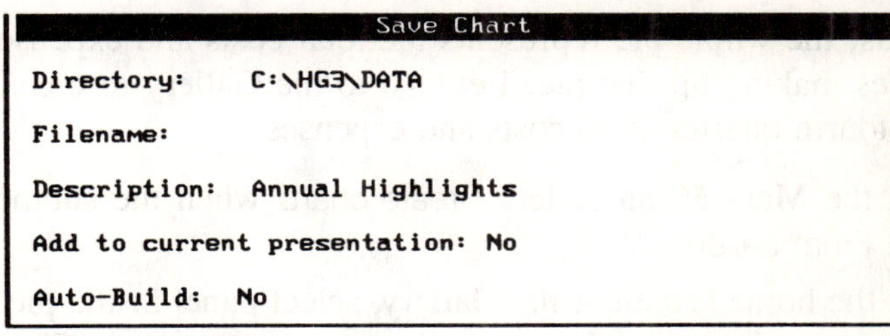

2-18 The Save Chart menu.

Pie chart

Pie charts are useful when you want to show how a total is divided into segments. You might, for example, want to show how total revenues are made up of revenues from a number of sources, i.e., what portion of the total pie is accounted for by the various slices.

Returning to the Compression Labs 1990 annual report, you'll see that the area of costs and expenses has three components: cost of sales, selling and general

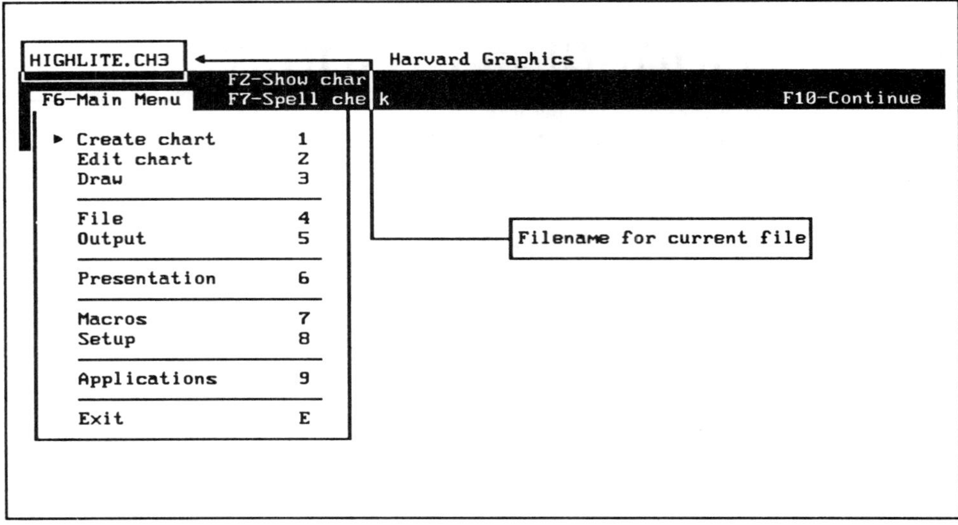

2-19 The filename shows that there is a current chart.

and administrative costs, and research and development costs. In the fourth quarter of 1990, those costs were broken down as follows:

Cost of sales:	$10,134,000
Selling, general and administrative costs:	4,472,000
Research and development costs:	871,000
Total Costs and Expenses:	$15,477,000

In other words, the whole pie represents the total costs and expenses, and there are three slices making up that pie. Let's go to the Gallery to create a pie chart representing fourth quarter 1990 costs and expenses.

1. From the Main Menu, select Create chart; when the submenu appears, select From gallery.
2. From the home screen of the Gallery, select panel 2, the pie chart panel. The screen of generic pie charts appears, as you saw in Fig. 2-4.
3. Select the basic three-dimensional pie chart as shown in panel 4, and the program will display the fruity chart shown in Fig. 2-20.
4. Select F5 to edit the data sheet, i.e., to replace its data with your own (see Fig. 2-21).
5. The cursor is blinking under the P of Pie Chart; replace this title by typing Costs and Expenses, and then press Tab.
6. The cursor moves to the second line, opposite Subtitle. For the subtitle, type Fourth Quarter, 1990, and then press Tab four times until Apples is highlighted opposite Slice 1.

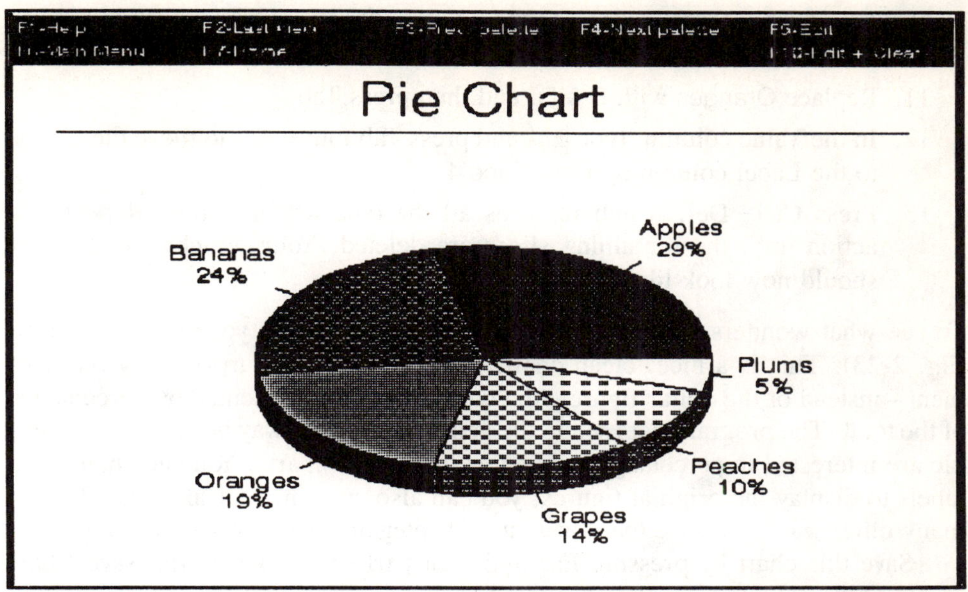

2-20 The basic three-dimensional pie chart from panel 4.

Pie Chart 1

F1-Help F2-Show chart F3-Choices F4-Draw F5-Mark
F6-Main Menu F7-Spell/Text F8-Options F9-Pie data F10-Continue

Title: Pie Chart
Subtitle:
Footnote:
Pie title:

Slice	Label	Value	Cut	Color	Pattern
1	Apples	60	No	Gry DD|S	0
2	Bananas	50	No	Gry |S	1
3	Oranges	40	No	Gry L|S	2
4	Grapes	30	No	Gry L|S	3
5	Peaches	20	No	Gry LL|S	4
6	Plums	10	No	White |S	5
7			No	Gry DD|S	6
8			No	Gry |S	7
9			No	Gry L|S	8
10			No	Gry L|S	9
11			No	Gry LL|S	10
12			No	White |S	11

2-21 The data sheet for the generic pie chart.

7. Type Cost of sales, and press Tab to move the cursor to the Value column.
8. In the Value column opposite Cost of sales, type 10134, then press Tab four times to move the cursor to the Label column opposite Slice 2.
9. Replace Bananas with Selling, G&A (for General and Administrative), and then press Tab.

10. In the Value column, type 4472 and press Tab four times to move the cursor to the Label column opposite Slice 3.
11. Replace Oranges with R & D, and then press Tab.
12. In the Value column, type 871 and press Tab four times to move the cursor to the Label column opposite Slice 4.
13. Press Ctrl−Del, which removes all the data for one slice. Repeat this action until the remaining slices are deleted. Your pie chart data sheet should now look like the one in Fig. 2-22.

To see what wonders you've wrought, select F2 to display your new chart (see Fig. 2-23). This is a nice, clean chart, but you might be surprised by one element—instead of the dollar figures, the cost items are represented by percentages of the total. The programmers set up the generic chart this way because many people are interested in percentages when they create pie charts. You can change the labels to display the original figures; you can also customize or alter the chart in many other ways. I'll save that for a later chapter on advanced pie charting.

Save this chart by pressing Esc and then Ctrl−S to display the Save Chart menu. Opposite Filename, type costs-q4, and then press F10 to finish saving the chart. Return to the Main Menu by selecting F6. That completes the work on your first pie.

Bar chart

Bar charts have many uses. They're especially useful when you want to compare performance over several intervals of time—sales per quarter, net income per

```
                              Pie Chart 1
 F1-Help         F2-Show chart   F3-Choices      F4-Draw         F5-Mark
 F6-Main Menu    F7-Spell/Text   F8-Options      F9-Pie data     F10-Continue

Title:      Costs and Expenses
Subtitle:   Fourth Quarter, 1990
Footnote:
Pie title:
```

Slice	Label	Value	Cut	Color	Pattern
1	Cost of sales	10134	No	Gry DD|S	0
2	Selling, G&A	4472	No	Gry |S	1
3	R & D	871	No	Gry L|S	2
4			No	White |S	5
5			No	Gry LL|S	4
6			No	Gry L|S	3
7			No	Gry DD|S	6
8			No	Gry |S	7
9			No	Gry L|S	8
10			No	Gry L|S	9
11			No	Gry LL|S	10
12			No	White |S	11

2-22 The pie chart data sheet with your new data added.

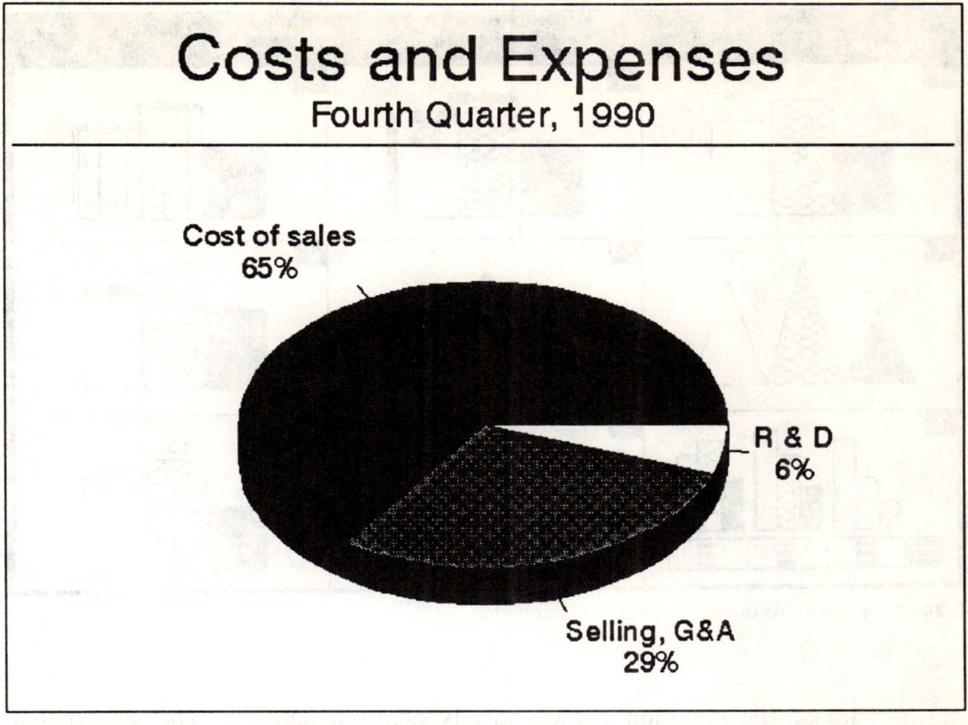

2-23 Your generic Costs and Expenses pie chart.

year, number of shares traded per day, etc. For your first trial run with a vertical bar chart from the Gallery, you can track Compression Labs' revenues over a five-year period, from 1986 through 1990. Here's the data:

Year	Revenue
1986	$15,607,000
1987	$16,690,000
1988	$21,402,000
1989	$29,197,000
1990	$51,754,000

Now you need to find a generic bar chart from the Gallery that will do a good job of representing this data graphically.

1. From the Main Menu, select Create chart, then select From gallery from the submenu.
2. From the home screen, click on the vertical bars in panel 3. The next screen you'll see is the same one as in Fig. 2-5. Select the charts in panel 1; the program will display the nine varieties of bar charts, shown in Fig. 2-24.

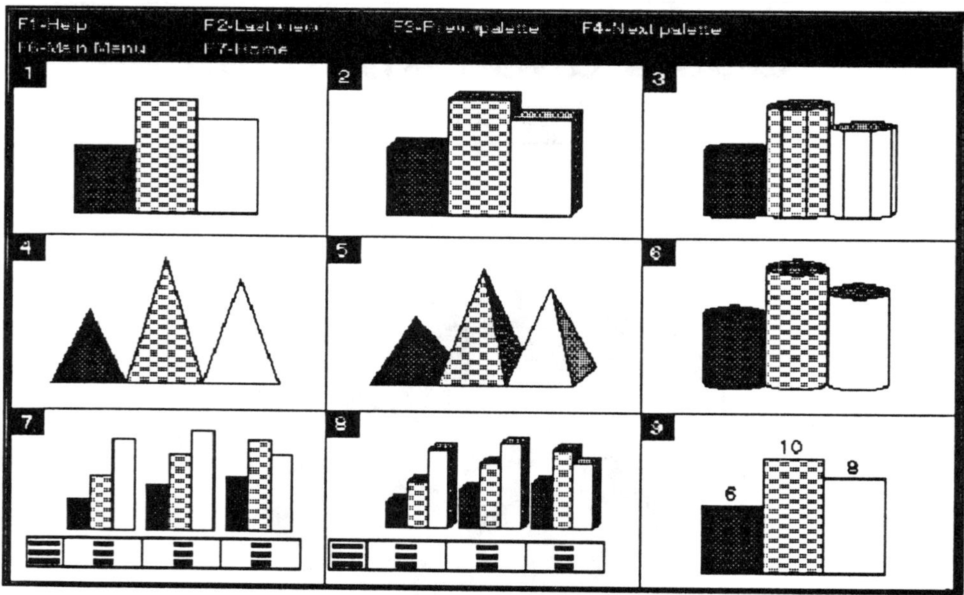

2-24 Nine variations on nonoverlapping bar charts.

3. Choose the common garden variety chart in panel 1. The screen that appears is titled Cluster, and shows a six-series bar chart (see Fig. 2-25). Your own chart will be even simpler than this one, because you're going to plot only one series of data.
4. Select F5 to go to the data sheet for this chart (see Fig. 2-26). Series 1 will be the revenue figures, and will be the only series.
5. With the cursor blinking under Cluster, replace this title by typing Five-year Revenues, then press Tab to move the cursor to the next line.
6. Opposite Subtitle, type 1986 through 1990, then press Enter twice to move the cursor to the X Axis column opposite Data Point 1.
7. Type 1986, then press Tab to move the cursor to the Series 1 column.
8. Type 15607000, and then press Tab to move the cursor to the Series 2 column.

Caramba! That value you entered in the Series 1 column is now 1.5607E+07. Say what? Not to worry—in order to keep you from filling columns with huge multidigit numbers, Harvard Graphics 3.0 switches into scientific notation when numbers get beyond a certain size. 1.5607E+07 simply means 1.5607×10^7. Ten to the seventh power is 10,000,000, and $1.5607 \times 10,000,000$ equals 15,607,000—which is what you entered in the first place.

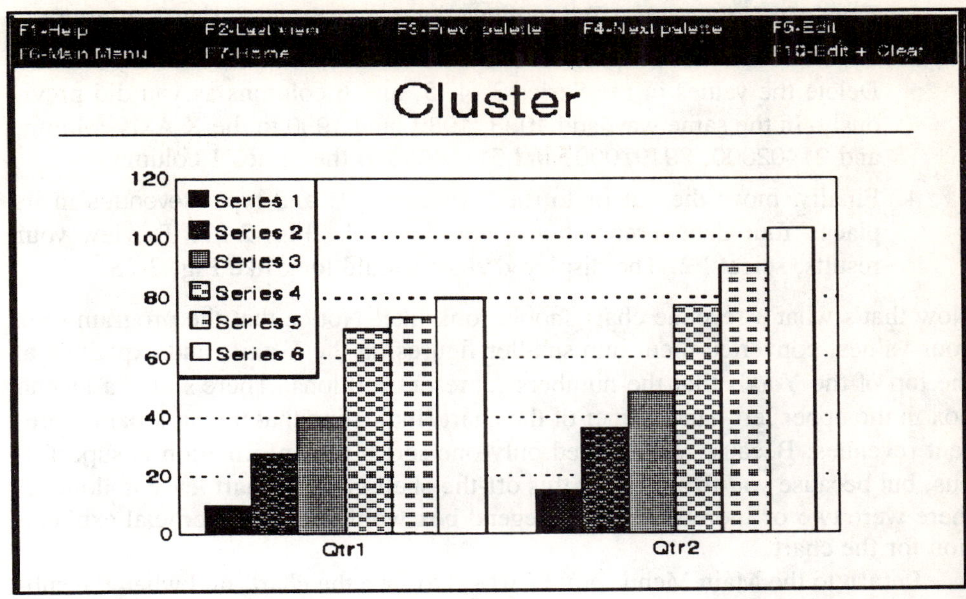

2-25 A two-dimensional bar chart with six data series.

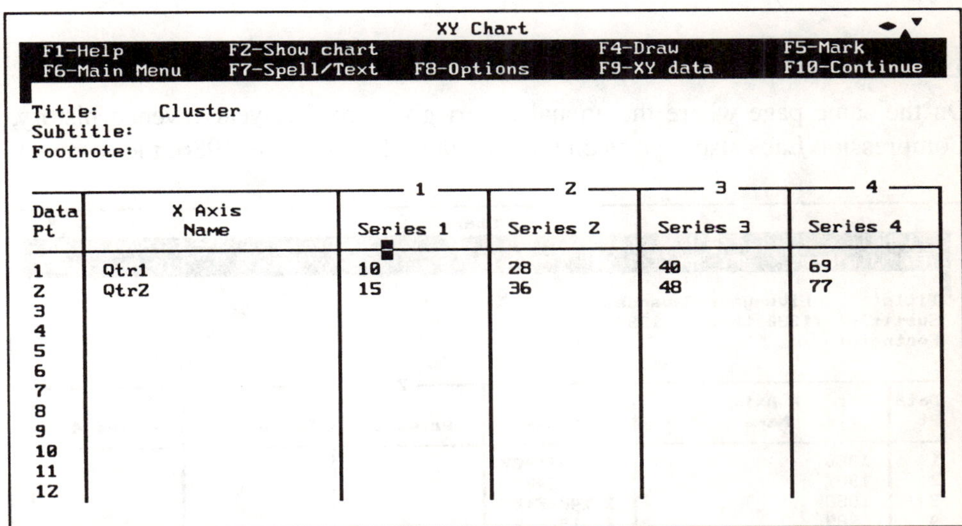

XY Chart

F1-Help F2-Show chart F4-Draw F5-Mark
F6-Main Menu F7-Spell/Text F8-Options F9-XY data F10-Continue

Title: Cluster
Subtitle:
Footnote:

Data Pt	X Axis Name	1 Series 1	2 Series 2	3 Series 3	4 Series 4
1	Qtr1	10	28	40	69
2	Qtr2	15	36	48	77
3					
4					
5					
6					
7					
8					
9					
10					
11					
12					

2-26 The data sheet for the model chart.

1. Use the Del key to delete the value in the Series 2 column, then press Tab to move to the Series 3 column. In the same manner, delete the figures in the Series 3, 4, 5, and 6 columns, and then use the mouse or the arrow keys to return to the X Axis column opposite Data Point 2.

2. Type 1987, then press Tab to move the cursor to the Series 2 column.
3. Type 16690000, then press Tab to move the cursor to the Series 3 column. Delete the values in the Series 3, 4, 5, and 6 columns as you did previously. In the same way, add 1988, 1989, and 1990 to the X Axis column, and 21402000, 29197000, and 51754000 to the Series 1 column.
4. Finally, move the cursor to the S in Series 1, and type Revenues in its place. Your data screen should now look like Fig. 2-27. To view your results, select F2. The displayed chart should look like Fig. 2-28.

Now that's what a revenue chart should look like! Notice that the program took your values, converted them into smaller figures on the Y-axis, and explained at the top of the Y-axis that the numbers represent millions. There's also a legend box in the upper left-hand corner of the chart, indicating that the dark bars represent revenues. Because you entered only one series this information is superfluous, but because you're accepting this off-the-shelf generic chart leave it alone. If there were two or more series, this legend box would provide a crucial explanation for the chart.

Return to the Main Menu, press Ctrl−S to save the chart, and when the submenu appears type revenues. Press F10 to complete the action, and you're ready for a break.

Line chart

On the same page where the annual report gives the five-year revenue history, Compression Labs also reports on the growth of their staff. In 1986, the company

XY Chart

F1-Help F2-Show chart F4-Draw F5-Mark
F6-Main Menu F7-Spell/Text F8-Options F9-XY data F10-Continue

Title: Five-year Revenues
Subtitle: 1986 through 1990
Footnote:

Data Pt	X Axis Name	1 Revenues	2 Series 2	3 Series 3	4 Series 4
1	1986	1.5607E+07			
2	1987	1.669E+07			
3	1988	2.1402E+07			
4	1989	2.9197E+07			
5	1990	5.1754E+07			
6					
7					
8					
9					
10					
11					
12					

2-27 The data sheet filled in with the data for your own chart.

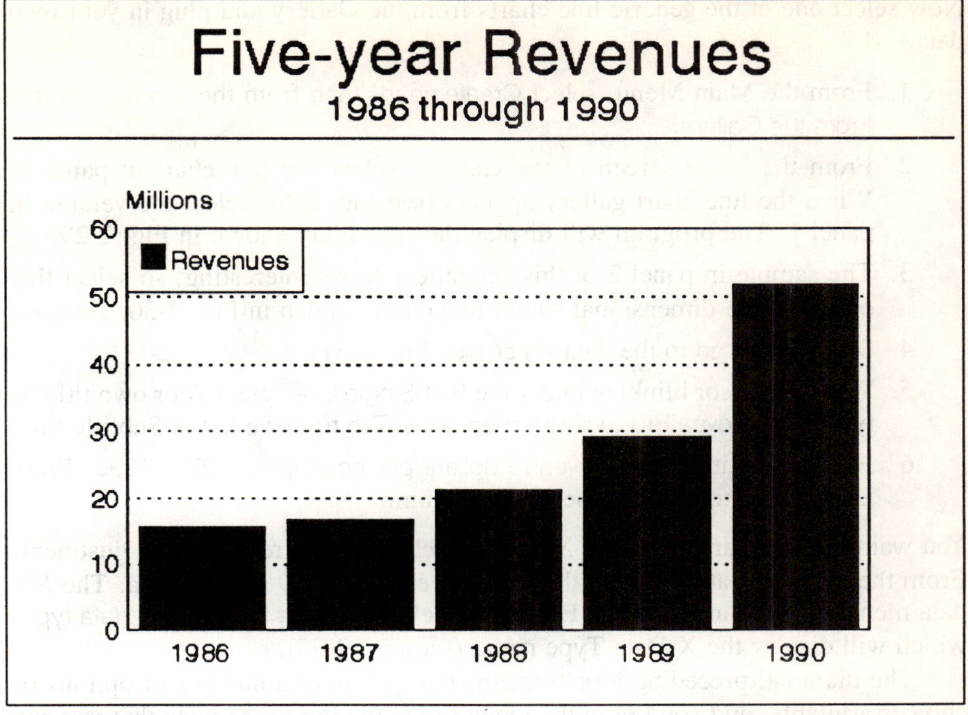

2-28 Your first vertical bar chart.

had 125 employees; by 1990, they had grown to 271. Now, as is the case of many companies, the rate of growth of the staff is greater than the rate of growth of revenues, because a prosperous company will add employees to do jobs that are deemed important though not revenue-producing.

A crude but useful measure of productivity in a company is the rate of revenue per employee, and a helpful way to present that data visually is with a simple line chart. You're going to create a line chart from the Gallery, and as a bonus you'll become acquainted with another Harvard Graphics 3.0 feature—the calculator.

You used the revenue data for the bar chart above; here's the five-year employee history:

Year	No. of employees
1986	125
1987	124
1988	144
1989	173
1990	271

Now select one of the generic line charts from the Gallery and plug in your own data.

1. From the Main Menu, select Create chart, then from the submenu select From the Gallery.
2. From the home screen of the Gallery, select the line chart in panel 4. When the line chart gallery appears (see Fig. 2-6), select the version in panel 1. The program will display the subgallery shown in Fig. 2-29.
3. The sample in panel 2 of this subgallery looks interesting, so select that one. A three-dimensional single-line chart, shown in Fig. 2-30, appears.
4. Select F5 to go to the data sheet (see Fig. 2-31).
5. With the cursor blinking under the S of Single Line, enter your own title by typing Employee Productivity; then press Tab to move to the Subtitle line.
6. For the subtitle, type Revenue dollars per employee, 1986 – 1990. Press Enter twice to move to the X-axis column.

You want to plot years along the X-axis, which will require a minor adjustment. From the menu bar at the top of the data screen, select F9 for XY data. The XY data menu appears, as shown in Fig. 2-32. Select the first item, Set X data type, which will display the X Data Type menu (see Fig. 2-33).

The diamond preceding Month means that you have a number of options or choices available, and you see in the menu bar at the top of the page that you can

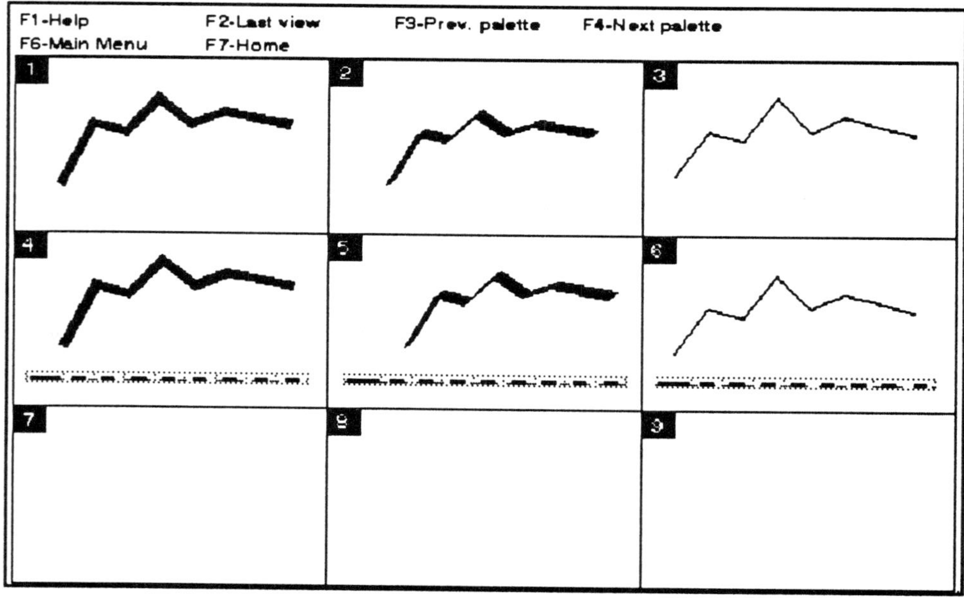

2-29 The subgallery of panel 1 in the line chart gallery.

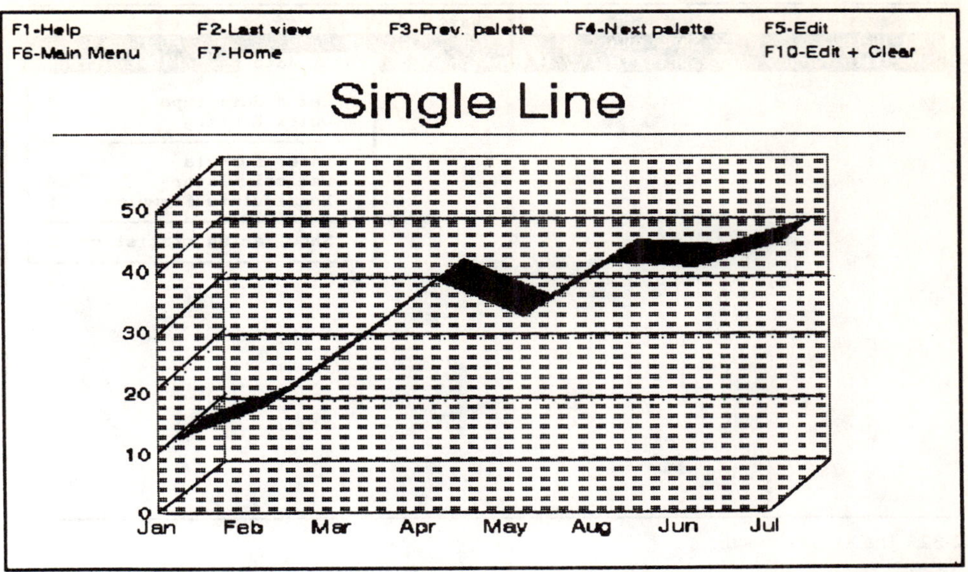

2-30 A generic single-line chart in three dimensions.

XY Chart

F1-Help F2-Show chart F4-Draw F5-Mark
F6-Main Menu F7-Spell/Text F8-Options F9-XY data F10-Continue

Title: Single Line
Subtitle:
Footnote:

Data Pt	X Axis Month	1 Series 1	2 Series 2	3 Series 3	4 Series 4
1	Jan	10			
2	Feb	15			
3	Mar	25			
4	Apr	36			
5	May	30			
6	Aug	39			
7	Jun	38			
8	Jul	42			
9					
10					
11					
12					

2-31 The data sheet for the generic line chart.

move to these choices with the F3 key—which is your key for choices throughout the program.

1. Select F3 to reveal the X data type choices available to you. A submenu will appear, and the up and down arrows at the top of the submenu indicate that further choices are available (see Fig. 2-34).

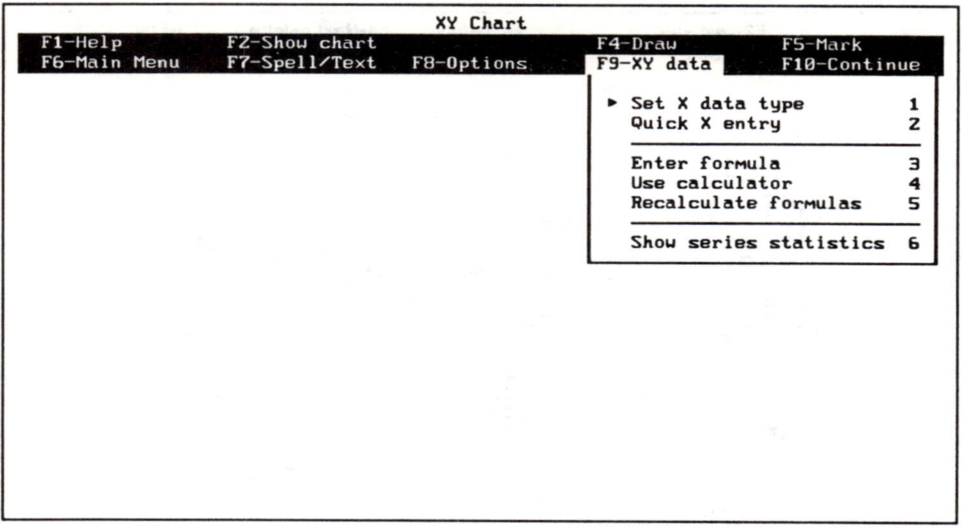

2-32 The XY data menu.

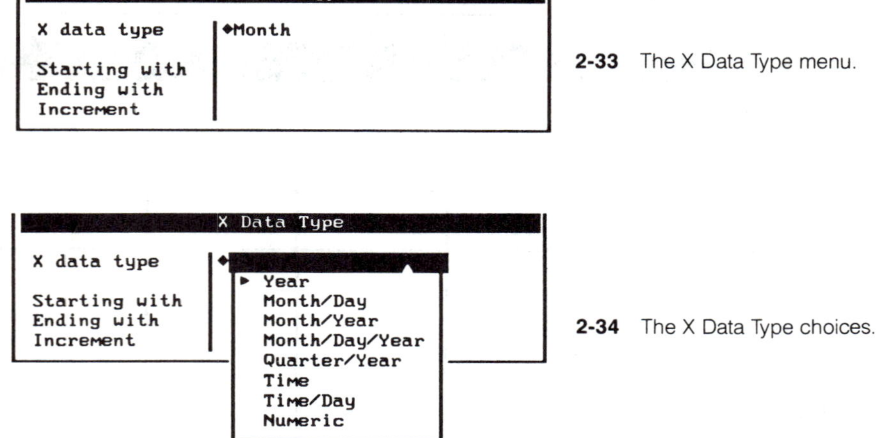

2-33 The X Data Type menu.

2-34 The X Data Type choices.

2. Select Year from the menu of choices. The X Data Type box reappears.
3. In the X Data Type box, press Enter to move the cursor down one line.
4. Opposite Starting with, type 1986 and Enter.
5. Opposite Ending with, type 1990 and Enter.
6. Opposite Increment, type 1 and Enter.

You've now instructed the program to label the X axis from 1986 to 1990, in increments of 1 year. That's exactly what now appears on the data screen. In the

XY Chart

F1-Help	F2-Show chart		F4-Draw	F5-Mark
F6-Main Menu	F7-Spell/Text	F8-Options	F9-XY data	F10-Continue

Title: Employee Productivity
Subtitle: Revenue dollars per employee, 1986-1990
Footnote:

Data Pt	X Axis Year	1 Series 1	2 Series 2	3 Series 3	4 Series 4
1	1986	10			
2	1987	15			
3	1988	25			
4	1989	36			
5	1990	30			
6		39			
7		38			
8		42			
9					
10					
11					
12					

2-35 The X Axis data type changed from Months to Years.

heading for the X-axis column, the word Months has now been replaced with the word Year, and there are now five values in that column—1986 through 1990. The cursor is blinking opposite Data Point 1 (see Fig. 2-35).

Press Tab to move the cursor to the top of the Series 1 column, opposite 1986. You're now going to learn to use a new Harvard Graphics 3.0 feature—the calculator. For the Y-axis data, you want to enter the productivity figure, which is the revenue per employee. You get this figure by dividing the gross revenue for a given year by the number of employees in that same year. You can use the calculator to do the division for you; the program will then enter the result at your cursor position in the Series column.

1. Select F9 to display the XY data menu again. This time, choose item 4 on the menu, Use calculator. The Calculator box will appear (see Fig. 2-36).

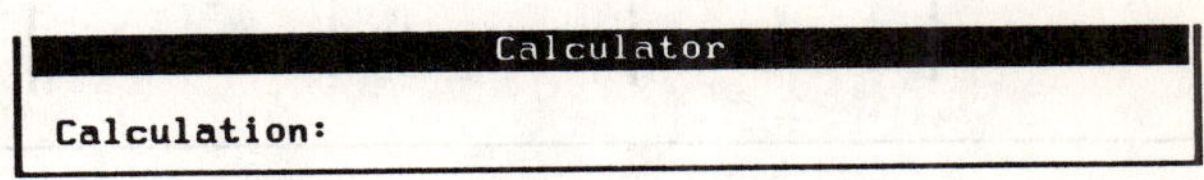
Calculator

Calculation:

2-36 The Calculator box.

2. Type 15607000/125 and press Enter. The result will appear in the first line of the Series 1 column (see Fig. 2-37).
3. In the same way, for data points 2 through 5, calculate 16690000/124, 21402000/144, 29197000/173, and 51754/271.
4. Next, delete all remaining values below data point 5 in the Series 1 column.

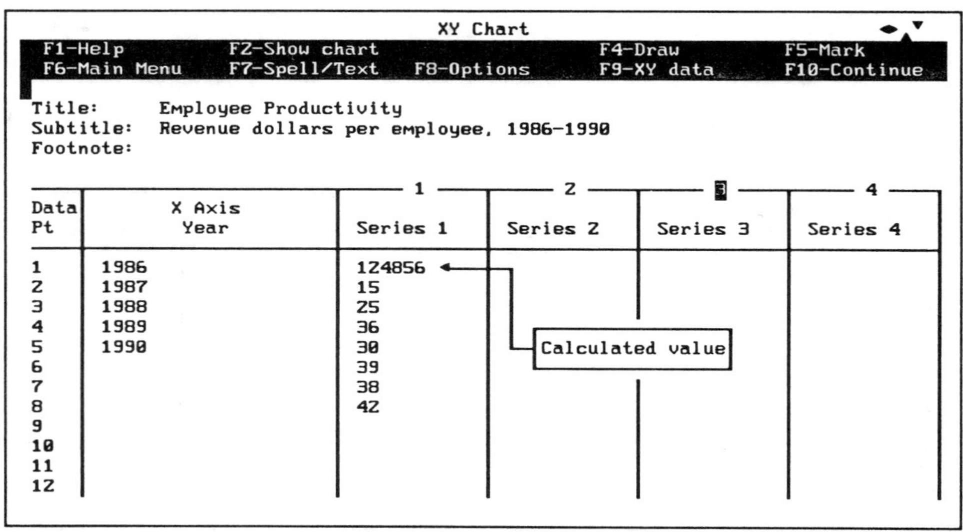
XY Chart

F1-Help F2-Show chart F4-Draw F5-Mark
F6-Main Menu F7-Spell/Text F8-Options F9-XY data F10-Continue

Title: Employee Productivity
Subtitle: Revenue dollars per employee, 1986-1990
Footnote:

Data Pt	X Axis Year	1 Series 1	2 Series 2	3 Series 3	4 Series 4
1	1986	124856			
2	1987	15			
3	1988	25			
4	1989	36			
5	1990	30			
6		39			
7		38			
8		42			
9					
10					
11					
12					

2-37 The calculated productivity value in the Series 1 column.

XY Chart

F1-Help F2-Show chart F4-Draw F5-Mark
F6-Main Menu F7-Spell/Text F8-Options F9-XY data F10-Continue

Title: Employee Productivity
Subtitle: Revenue dollars per employee, 1986-1990
Footnote:

Data Pt	X Axis Year	1 Productivi	2 Series 2	3 Series 3	4 Series 4
1	1986	124856			
2	1987	134596.8			
3	1988	148625			
4	1989	168768.8			
5	1990	190974.2			
6					
7					
8					
9					
10					
11					
12					

2-38 The data screen.

5. Finally, put the cursor under the S of Series 1, type Productivity, and press Enter. When you're finished, your data screen should look like the one in Fig. 2-38.

And now it's magic time. To view the finished chart, select F2 (see Fig. 2-39). That productivity line is ramping up nicely. It's difficult to maintain the upward slope indefinitely, even in a burgeoning market like video-conferencing and other

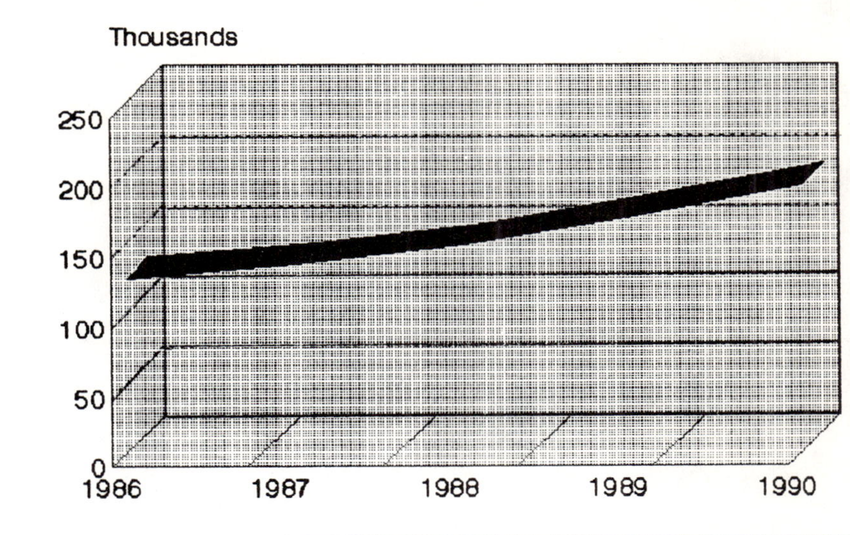

2-39 The completed Employee Productivity line chart.

video-compression applications. It'll be interesting to see how far Compression Labs can go before productivity growth peaks. Press Esc to leave the chart, then Ctrl – S to save the chart. Opposite Filename, type prdctvty, then select F10 to complete the action.

In this chapter you've learned to create, in pretty quick order, four types of charts from the generic versions found in the Gallery: text, pie, vertical bar, and line charts. In the next chapter, you can peruse the Gallery offerings in area, high/low/close, organization, and combination charts.

3
CHAPTER

More quick charts from the Gallery

This chapter continues the lesson begun in the previous chapter, that is, creating quick charts using the Gallery feature of Harvard Graphics 3.0.

Area chart

An area chart is useful when you want to emphasize general trends rather than specific X-axis points. For example, in product sales you might be less interested in the unit sales for a particular time period than in the cumulative direction of sales over a number of time periods.

In the Compression Labs 1990 annual report, the selected financial data information documents the annual sales of codec units over a five-year period. (*Codecs* are coders-decoders that compress video signals for transmission, then decompress them at the receiving end for viewing.) The financial data also reports the history of backlog over the same time period. (*Backlog* refers to orders received but not shipped, and is therefore a strong indicator of revenues in the future.) During the five-year period covered, unit sales of codecs and backlog looked like this:

Year	Codec Units Shipped	Backlog
1986	225	$ 363,000
1987	231	1,762,000
1988	292	2,200,000
1989	478	23,100,000
1990	802	26,400,000

Plot units shipped and backlog as two series on a single area chart.

1. From the Main Menu, select Create chart, and when the first submenu appears select From gallery.
2. The home gallery screen shows area charts in panel 5, so select that one. The area chart gallery appears, with nine generic versions (see Fig. 2-7).
3. Select the three-dimensional charts as shown in panel 4 (see Fig. 3-1).
4. Press F5 to go to the data sheet (see Fig. 3-2) and, like you did for the charts in chapter 2, replace the Overlap title with Codec Units Shipped and Backlog.
5. Next, press Enter to move the cursor to the Subtitle row.
6. Opposite Subtitle, type Five-year growth, 1986 – 1990, then press Enter twice.

There's a lot of data in six different series on this chart, so begin by clearing it all. Your cursor should now be blinking under March in the X-axis column. Press Ctrl – Del seven times; that should clear all values from your data screen and give you a clean slate to work with, as you can confirm by pressing F2 to reveal the blank chart, as shown in Fig. 3-3.

Because the X-axis data type for the chart will be years instead of months, you have to make that change. Follow the same procedure you used in creating the Employee Productivity line chart in chapter 2.

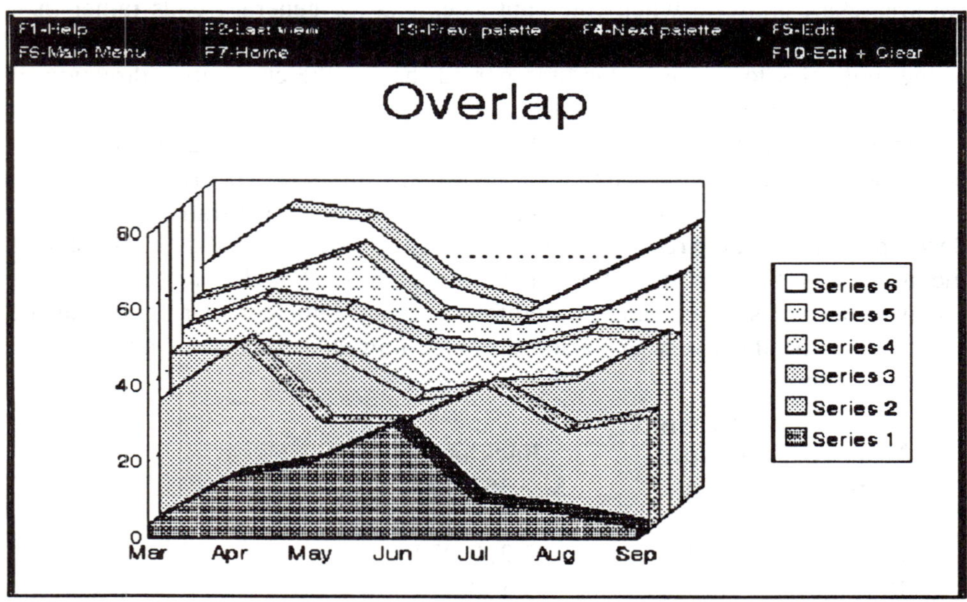

3-1 The generic overlapping area chart in three dimensions.

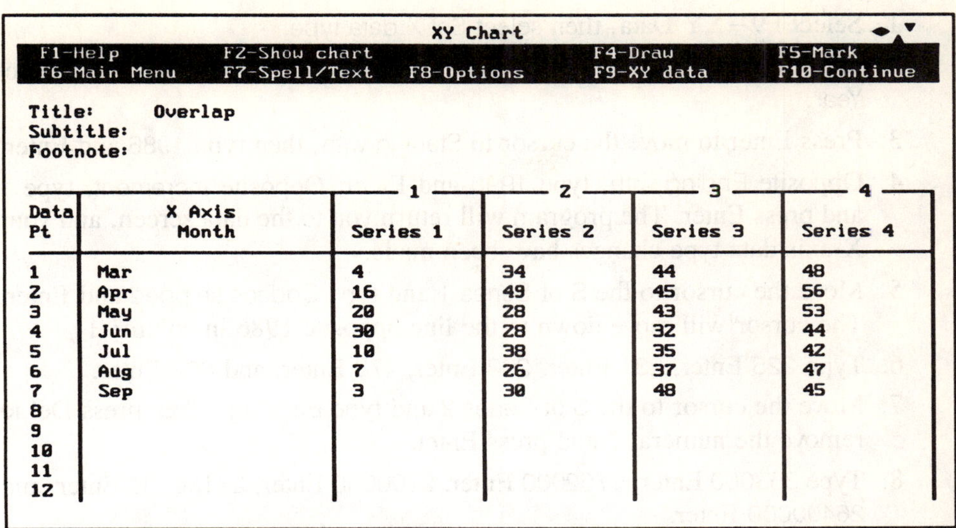

XY Chart

F1-Help F2-Show chart F4-Draw F5-Mark
F6-Main Menu F7-Spell/Text F8-Options F9-XY data F10-Continue

Title: Overlap
Subtitle:
Footnote:

Data Pt	X Axis Month	1 Series 1	2 Series 2	3 Series 3	4 Series 4
1	Mar	4	34	44	48
2	Apr	16	49	45	56
3	May	20	28	43	53
4	Jun	30	28	32	44
5	Jul	10	38	35	42
6	Aug	7	26	37	47
7	Sep	3	30	48	45
8					
9					
10					
11					
12					

3-2 The data sheet for the overlapping area chart.

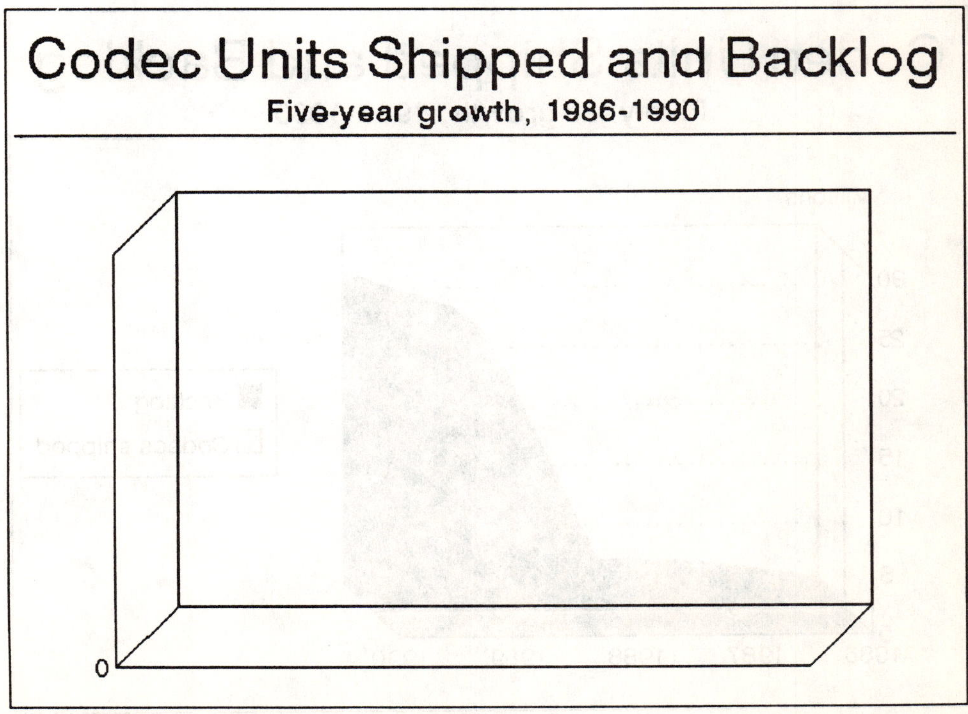

3-3 The blank chart after you've erased all data values.

1. Select F9—XY Data, then select Set X data type.
2. When the X Data Type menu appears, click on F3—Choices, and select Year.
3. Press Enter to move the cursor to Starting with, then type 1986 and Enter.
4. Opposite Ending with, type 1990 and Enter. Opposite Increment, type 1 and press Enter. The program will return you to the data screen, and your X-axis data type changes have been made.
5. Move the cursor to the S of Series 1 and type Codecs shipped and Enter. The cursor will move down to the line opposite 1986 in column 1.
6. Type 225 Enter, 231 Enter, 292 Enter, 478 Enter, and 802 Enter.
7. Move the cursor to the S of Series 2 and type Backlog. Then press Del to remove the numeral 2 and press Enter.
8. Type 363000 Enter, 1762000 Enter, 2200000 Enter, 23100000 Enter, and 26400000 Enter.

At this point, you've entered all of the chart data. Press F2 to have a look at your chart. Well, the backlog chart looks terrific, but the codecs shipped chart looks like part of the floor (see Fig. 3-4). ¿Que pasa?

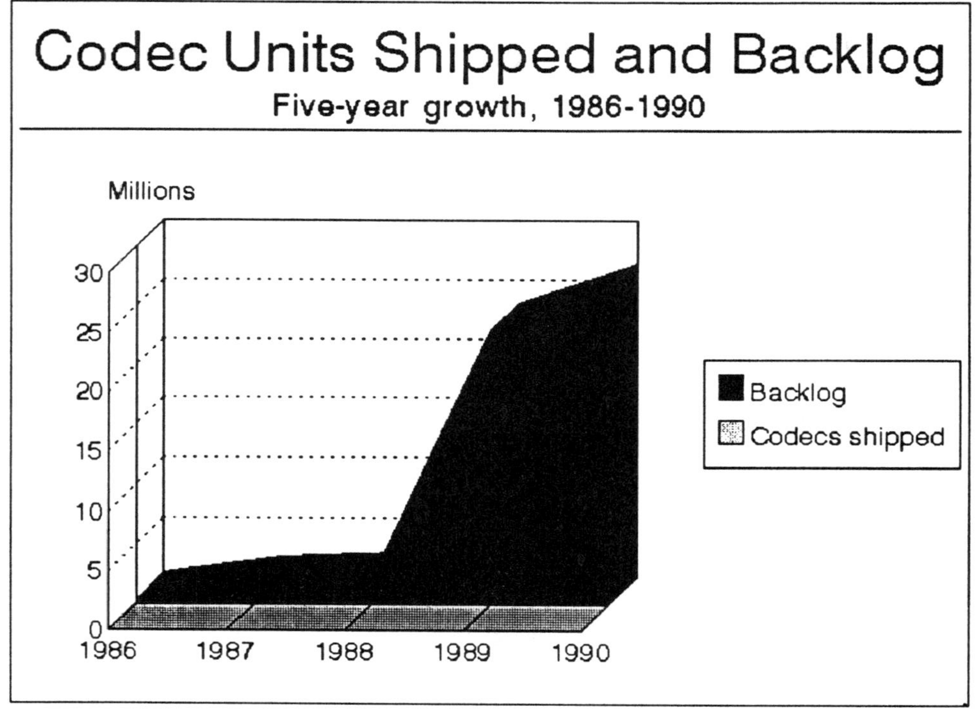

3-4 The first run at the area chart, with a flat Codecs series.

Problem: Both data series are being plotted on same Y axis—but codec shipments are in units of hundreds, while backlog figures are in units of millions. The program has to set up for the larger numbers, so the smaller numbers disappear. Solution: Set up a second Y axis for the second series. But how to do that?

Select F8–Options. The Options menu will appear, as shown in Fig. 3-5. Press 6 or click on Series, and Harvard Graphics 3.0 will display the Series Options menu (see Fig. 3-6). All of a sudden you're confronted with more choices than you might have wanted to deal with—an indication of how rich in features this software is. It also demonstrates why the Gallery is so valuable: it allows you to escape many of these detailed design decisions if you're content with the models supplied with the Gallery.

Because you're working with the Gallery chart, you don't have to get into all of these possible variations right now; save them for the expert-level chapters later on. For now, simply solve your scale problem by referring series 2, or backlog, to a second Y axis. Here's how: In the Series 2 column and the Y-axis row, select Y1. A diamond will appear in front of Y1, indicating that you have choices. Select F3–Choices. A small options box will appear indicating that you can choose between the Y1 and Y2 axes (see Fig. 3-7).

Select Y2, then press F10 to continue. The data sheet is now complete, and looks like the one in Fig. 3-8. Press F2 again to view the chart, and voila! That curve for codec shipments now looks as dramatic as it should (see Fig. 3-9). Part of the backlog curve is hidden behind the codec curve, but its steep rise out of nowhere demonstrates its geometric growth—which will drive future revenues. A footnote explaining that the backlog figures represent dollars might be useful to

```
                                  XY Chart
 F1-Help           F2-Show chart                     F4-Draw          F5-Mark
 F6-Main Menu      F7-Spell/Text     F8-Options      F9-XY data       F10-Continue

                                   ▸ Titles/Footnotes    1  Ctrl-T
                                     Text attributes     2
                                     Appearance          3
                                     Notes               4  Ctrl-N
                                     ─────────────────────────────
                                     Style               5
                                     Series              6
                                     Legend              7
                                     Axis frame          8
                                     Axis options        9
                                     Format              A
                                     Data table/labels   B
```

3-5 The Options menu.

XY Chart

F1-Help F2-Show chart F3-Choices F10-Continue

Series Options

	Series 1	Series 2	Series 3	Series 4
Show series	♦Yes	Yes	Yes	Yes
Show as	Area	Area	Area	Area
Y axis	Y1	Y1	Y1	Y1
Cumulative	No	No	No	No
Data labels	Yes	Yes	Yes	Yes
Data table	Yes	Yes	Yes	Yes
Fill style	Color	Color	Color	Color
Fill pattern	1	2	3	4
Fill color	Gry DD|S	Gry |S	Gry L|S	Gry L|S
Line fit	Normal	Normal	Normal	Normal
Line style	1 ——	1 ——	1 ——	1 ——
Line width	0	0	0	0
Line color	Gry DD|S	Gry |S	Gry L|S	Gry L|S
Marker style	1	2	3	4

3-6 The Series Options menu.

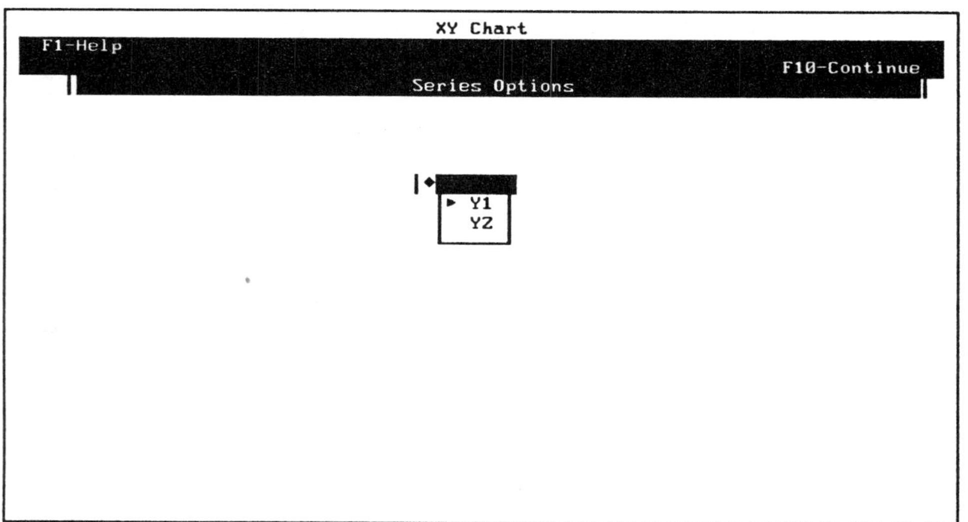

3-7 The Y1/Y2 axis choice box.

your audience, but leave that for future tinkering. You're in the quick-and-dirty demo mode right now.

Press Esc to leave the graphics screen, then Ctrl–S to save the chart. In the Save Chart box, type backlog as the filename, and press F10 to confirm the action. Press Esc again to return to the Main Menu, and your mastery of the generic area chart from the Gallery is complete.

XY Chart

F1-Help F2-Show chart F4-Draw F5-Mark
F6-Main Menu F7-Spell/Text F8-Options F9-XY data F10-Continue

Title: Codec Units Shipped and Backlog
Subtitle: Five-year growth, 1986-1990
Footnote:

Data Pt	X Axis Year	1 Codecs shi	2 Backlog	3 Series 3	4 Series 4
1	1986	225	363000		
2	1987	231	1762000		
3	1988	292	2200000		
4	1989	478	2.31E+07		
5	1990	802	2.64E+07		
6					
7					
8					
9					
10					
11					
12					

3-8 The finished data sheet.

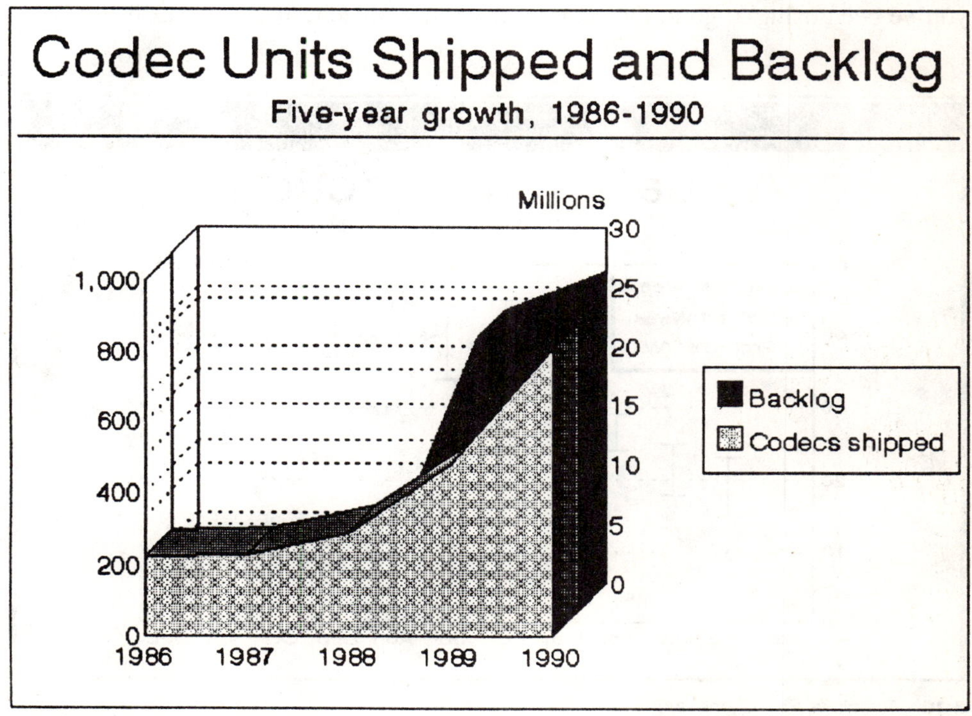

3-9 The complete area chart.

High/Low/Close chart

A High/Low/Close chart is most commonly used to record stock trading—so that's the way you'll demonstrate this variety of chart. The Compression Labs 1990 annual report records eight quarters of stock activity, in 1989 and 1990. The quoted prices, however, include only quarterly highs and lows—no closing prices. You could invent some closing prices, but just to remain true to the published data save that demonstration for later and make this a High/Low chart.

1. From the Main Menu, select Create chart, then from the submenu select From gallery. The Gallery home screen will appear.
2. Select panel 6 from the home screen, and the High/Low/Close subgallery will be displayed (see Fig. 2-8).
3. Select panel 6 from the subgallery, and you'll go to the generic, Actuals vs. Projections, chart (see Fig. 3-10).

In previous chart demonstrations, you've cleared the data from the generic chart screens piecemeal, one data point at a time. There's a quicker way to do it, however, provided you need no guidance from the values and series on the sample data sheet. Notice that, at the right end of the menu bar at the top of the Actuals vs Projections chart on your screen, there are two Edit choices: F3 – Edit, which you've been using to go to the generic chart data screen, and F10 – Edit + Clear.

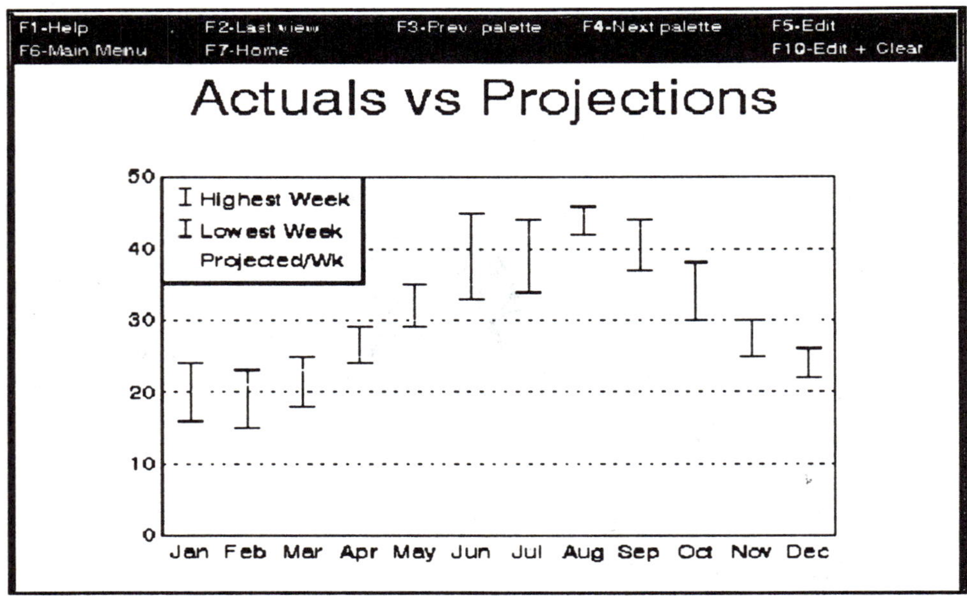

3-10 Actuals vs Projections, a generic high/low/close chart.

If you select F10 – Edit + Clear, you'll go to the data screen, but all values are deleted, and it's easy to start filling in your own.

1. Select F10 – Edit + Clear. The blank data screen will appear, as shown in Fig. 3-11.
2. Opposite Title, type Quarterly Stock Prices and Enter.
3. Opposite Subtitle, type 1989 – 1990 and press Enter twice.
4. The X Axis Data Type is currently Name; you want to change that to Quarter, so select F9 – XY data. The XY data menu will appear (see Fig. 2-32).
5. Select X Data Type, and that box will appear with ♦ Name highlighted (see Fig. 3-12).
6. Select F3 – Choices, and from the Choices menu select Quarter/Year.
7. Press Enter to move to Starting with, and type Q1/89.
8. Press Enter to move to Ending with, and type Q4/90 Enter.
9. Opposite Increment, type 1 and Enter.

Your quarterly data points will appear in the X-axis column (see Fig. 3-13). Place the cursor on the S of Series 1 and type High Price Enter. Here's the Compression

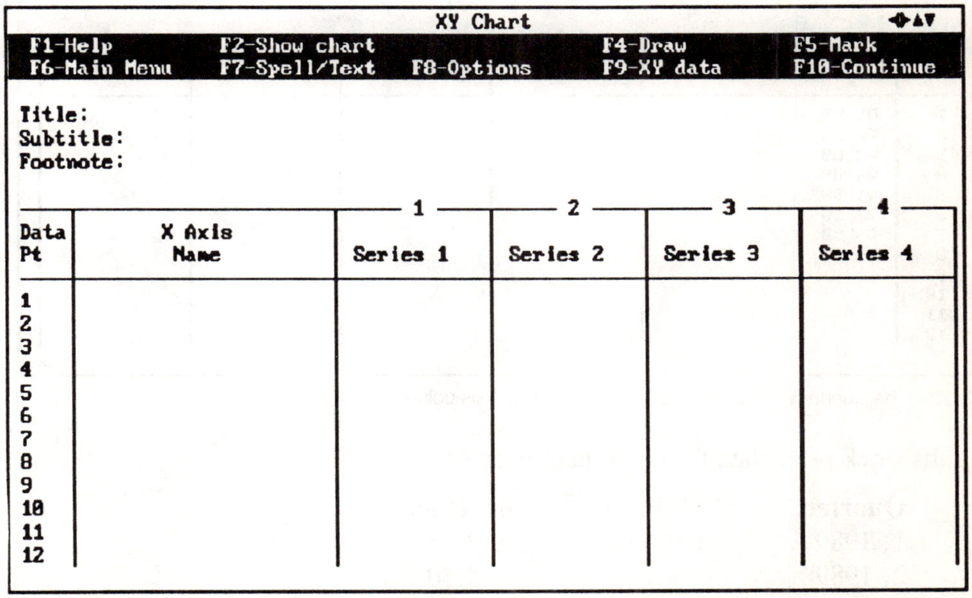

```
                              XY Chart
 F1-Help           F2-Show chart                 F4-Draw        F5-Mark
 F6-Main Menu      F7-Spell/Text    F8-Options   F9-XY data     F10-Continue

Title:
Subtitle:
Footnote:

                              1             2             3             4
Data       X Axis
Pt         Name         Series 1      Series 2      Series 3      Series 4

1
2
3
4
5
6
7
8
9
10
11
12
```

3-11 The generic chart data screen with all values changed.

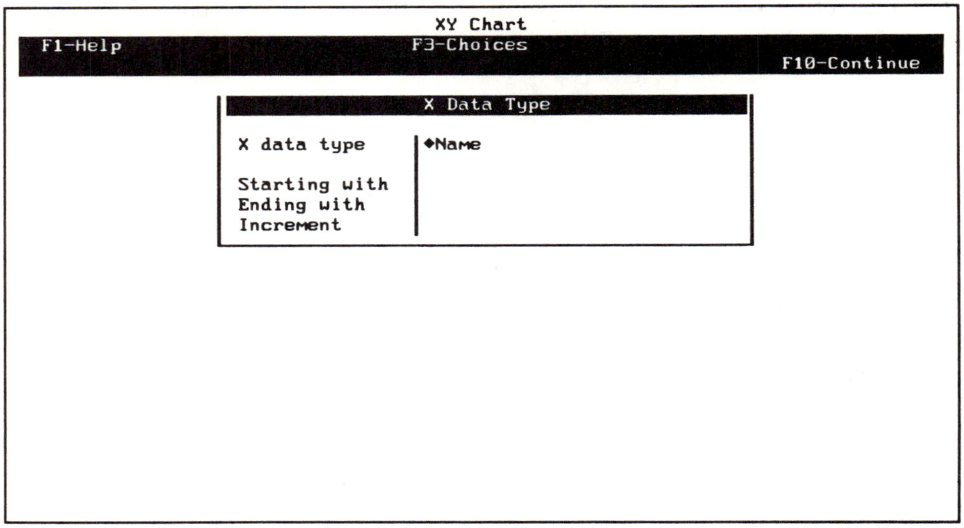

```
                          XY Chart
 F1-Help                 F3-Choices
                                                   F10-Continue

              X Data Type
   X data type       ♦Name

   Starting with
   Ending with
   Increment
```

3-12 The X Data Type box with ♦Name highlighted.

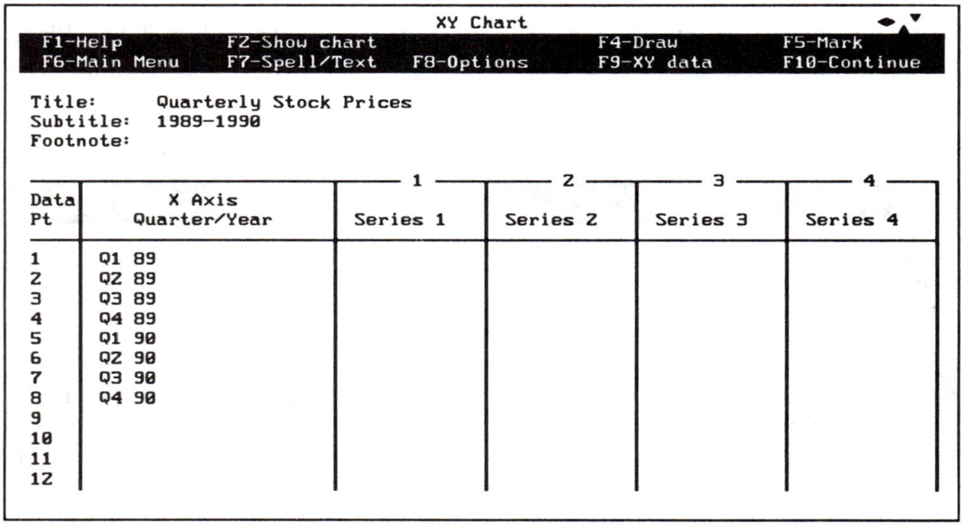

```
                          XY Chart
 F1-Help       F2-Show chart               F4-Draw      F5-Mark
 F6-Main Menu  F7-Spell/Text  F8-Options   F9-XY data   F10-Continue

 Title:     Quarterly Stock Prices
 Subtitle:  1989-1990
 Footnote:

                               1          2          3          4
 Data       X Axis
 Pt      Quarter/Year      Series 1   Series 2   Series 3   Series 4

 1     Q1 89
 2     Q2 89
 3     Q3 89
 4     Q4 89
 5     Q1 90
 6     Q2 90
 7     Q3 90
 8     Q4 90
 9
 10
 11
 12
```

3-13 The quarterly data points displayed in the X Axis column.

Labs stock price data for eight quarters:

Quarter	High Price	Low Price
1, 1989	$ 4.88	$ 3.13
2, 1989	8.75	4.50
3, 1989	11.25	7.13
4, 1989	10.75	7.38

Quarter	High Price	Low Price
1, 1990	14.75	9.25
2, 1990	15.50	10.25
3, 1990	16.38	9.50
4, 1990	16.38	9.00

The cursor should be in the High Price column opposite Q1 89.

1. Type 4.88 Enter, 8.75 Enter, 11.25 Enter, 10.75 Enter, 14.75 Enter 15.50 Enter, 16.38 Enter, and 16.38 Enter.
2. Move the cursor to the S of Series 2.
3. Type Low Price and Enter.
4. With the cursor in the first row of the Low Price column, enter the Low Price data just as you entered the High Price data in column 1. When you've finished, your data screen should look like the one shown in Fig. 3-14.

Select F2—Show chart, and your completed high/low chart should look like the one in Fig. 3-15. Investors responded to the company's good revenues and earnings reports by pushing up the stock prices, but with higher prices they grew less confident and the spread between high and low prices increased, reaching almost $7.00 in the third quarter of 1990. (This quick analysis of stock performance is thrown in at no extra charge. I should probably mention that the high-low spread could also be explained by about 83 other variables.)

```
                              XY Chart
 F1-Help        F2-Show chart                F4-Draw        F5-Mark
 F6-Main Menu   F7-Spell/Text  F8-Options    F9-XY data     F10-Continue

Title:     Quarterly Stock Prices
Subtitle:  1989-1990
Footnote:
```

Data Pt	X Axis Quarter/Year	1 High Price	2 Low Price	3 Series 3	4 Series 4
1	Q1 89	4.88	3.13		
2	Q2 89	8.75	4.5		
3	Q3 89	11.25	7.13		
4	Q4 89	10.75	7.38		
5	Q1 90	14.75	9.25		
6	Q2 90	15.5	10.25		
7	Q3 90	16.38	9.5		
8	Q4 90	16.38	9.88		
9					
10					
11					
12					

3-14 The complete data screen for the high/low chart.

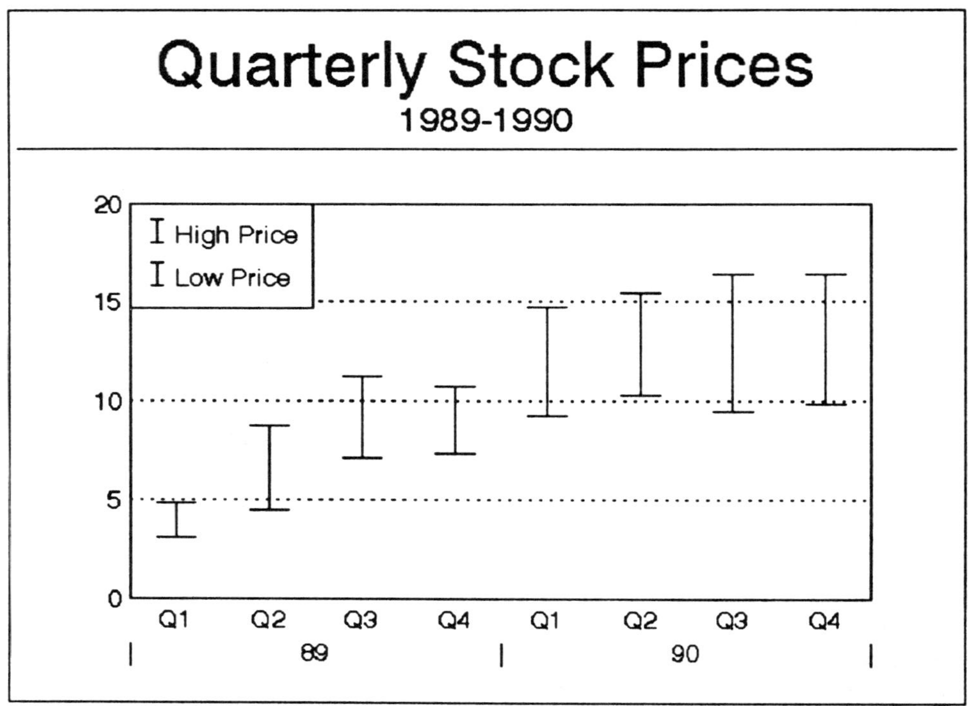

3-15 The complete high/low chart.

Press Esc to leave the chart, and press Ctrl–S to bring up the Save Chart menu. Type stocks as the filename, press F10 to confirm the action, and select F6–Main Menu. Sit back, rest your eyes, and pop the top on a cold Dos Equis. You've earned a break.

Organization chart

As is the case of other programs, Harvard Graphics 3.0 offers several variations of generic organization charts from the Gallery. For your demonstration organization chart, use the listing of corporate officers that appears on page 34 of the Compression Labs 1990 annual report. Here are the names and titles:

John E. Tyson
Chairman of the Board, President, and Chief Executive Officer

Dr. Wen-hsiung Chen
Executive Vice President, Research, and Chief Scientist

Kenneth L. Kenitzer
Executive Vice President, Operations

John J. O'Shea
Executive Vice President, Chief Financial Officer, Secretary, and Treasurer

John J. Walsh
Executive Vice President, Sales and Marketing

Ted S. Augustine
Vice President, North American Sales

Michael W. Glancy
Vice President, Engineering, Videoconferencing Products

Carl M. Marszewski
Vice President, International Sales

Bonnie L. Nunke
Vice President, Human Resources

Todd V. Townsend
Vice President, New Business Development and Advanced Engineering.

I'll have you fill in the reporting relationships as you create the chart. Here you go:

1. From the Main Menu, select Create chart, then when the submenu appears select From gallery.
2. From the home screen of the Gallery, select panel 7 for organization charts (see Fig. 2-9).
3. Select panel 5 of the organization chart subgallery. The generic chart titled Our Corporation will appear (see Fig. 3-16).

Go to the data sheet for the organization chart by selecting F3 – Edit (see Fig. 3-17). Note that one box of the chart is highlighted, and the name, title, and comment that belong to that box appear at the bottom of the screen. Click on any other box and the information for that box will appear. You're going to start at the top and replace the sample information that's in the boxes with your own information.

1. Move the cursor to the first letter of the title, then type Compression Labs, Inc. and Enter.
2. Opposite Subtitle, type Corporate Directory and two Enters. The cursor will move back to the box that was originally highlighted when you selected F5 – Edit.
3. Click on the box at the top of the array. The message at the bottom of the screen should say Name: Sam Nelson, Title: President, Comment: (see Fig. 3-18).
4. To replace the current text with your own, start by selecting F9 – Organization. The Organization menu will drop down (see Fig. 3-19).

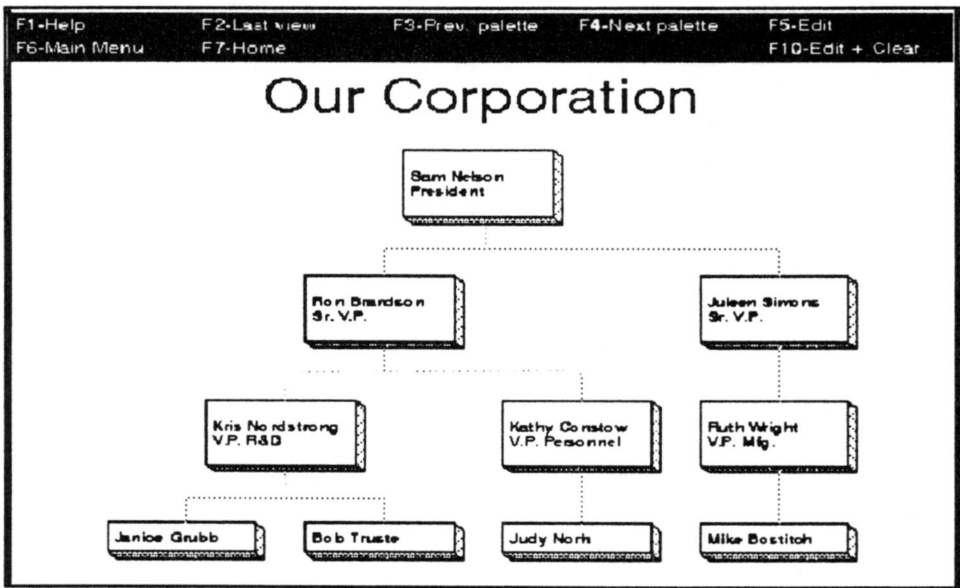

3-16 The organization chart from panel 5 of the subgallery.

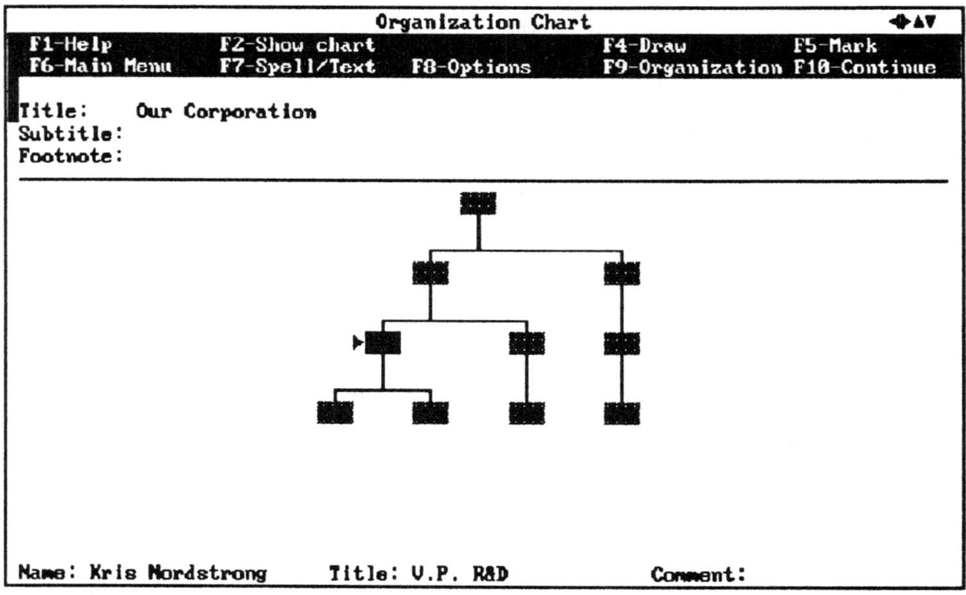

3-17 The data sheet for the organization chart.

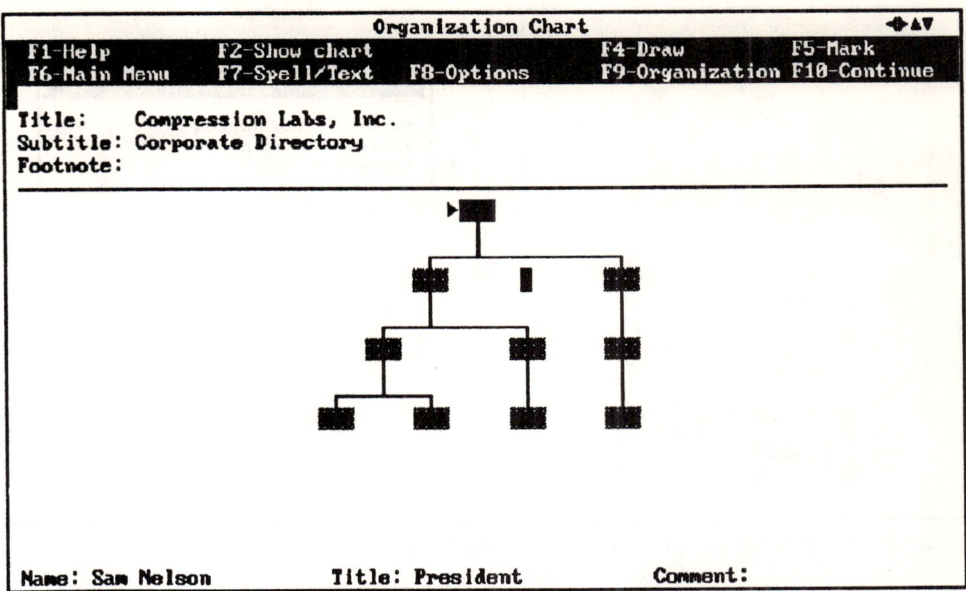

3-18 The top box selected, with its information at the bottom.

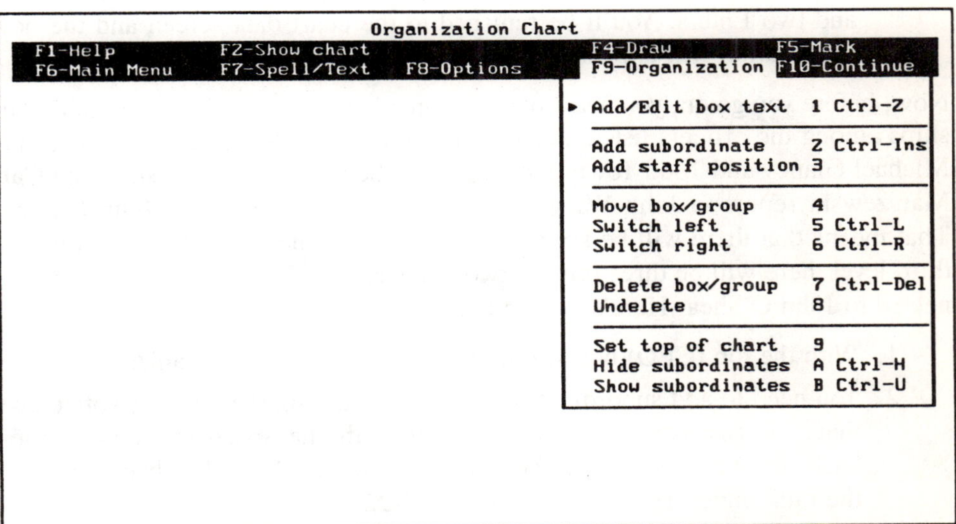

3-19 The Organization menu.

5. Select the first choice: Add/Edit box text. Note that the speed-key combination is Ctrl – Z. The Add/Edit Box Text menu appears, showing the current contents of the top box (see Fig. 3-20). The cursor is blinking under the first character of the president's name.

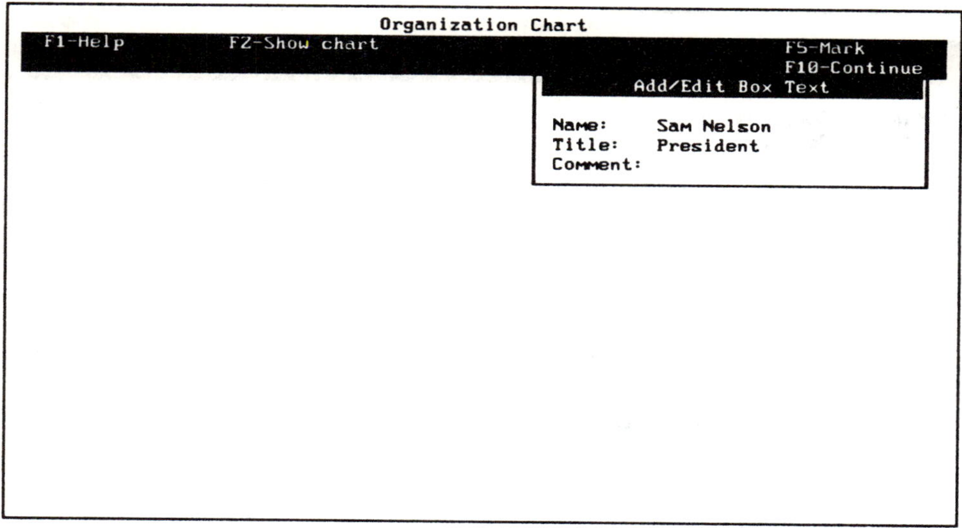

3-20 The Add/Edit Box Text menu for the currently selected box.

6. Press Ctrl – Del to erase Nelson's name, and then type J. Tyson and Enter.
7. Opposite Title, press Ctrl – Del to erase the present text, then type CEO and two Enters. You'll be returned to the chart data screen and the new information will appear at the bottom of the screen (see Fig. 3-21).

Now, before you go on, you need to know something about the reporting relationships among the officers listed above. All of the Executive Vice Presidents, plus Michael Glancy and Todd Townsend, report to the CEO. Ted Augustine and Carl Marszewski report to John Walsh, and Bonnie Nunke reports to John O'Shea. That means that there will be six boxes connected to the Tyson box, then on the third level there will be three boxes—two connected to John Walsh, and one connected to John O'Shea. Here's how to add more:

1. With the top (CEO) box still highlighted, select F9 – Organization.
2. You need to add subordinates, which is item 2 on the menu. (Notice also that you can perform this maneuver with the speed-key combination Ctrl – Ins.) Select Add subordinate. A new, third box has been added to the rank under Tyson's box (see Fig. 3-22).
3. Three more subordinates are needed in this row; press Ctrl – Ins three times. The second row now shows six boxes.
4. Move to the first box (on the left) in the second row. Select that box so that it's highlighted (the information line at the bottom of the screen should say Ron Brandson, Sr. V.P., etc.), then press Ctrl – Z (remember that speed-key combo?). The Add/Edit Box Text menu will drop down.

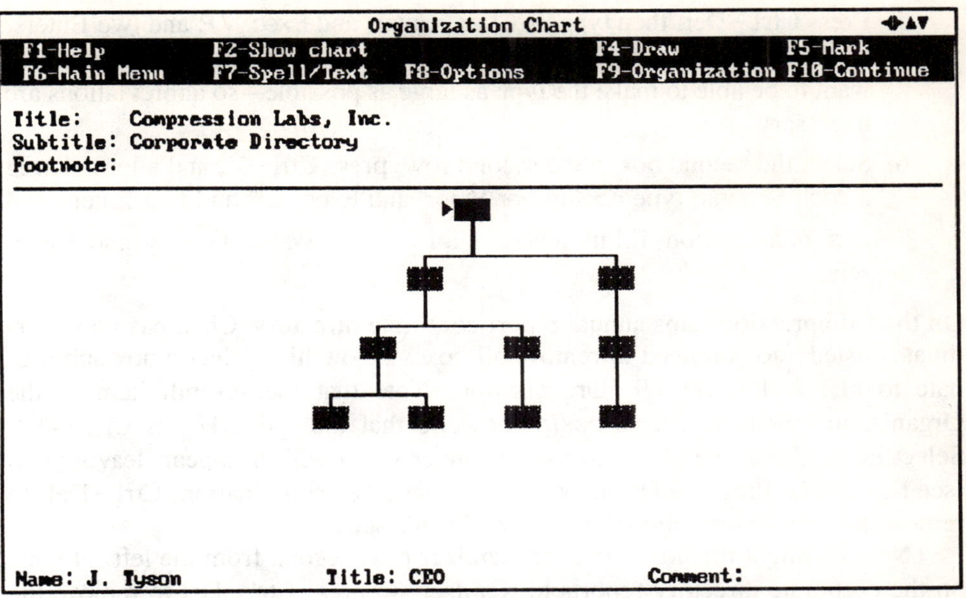

3-21 The new information appears at the bottom of the screen.

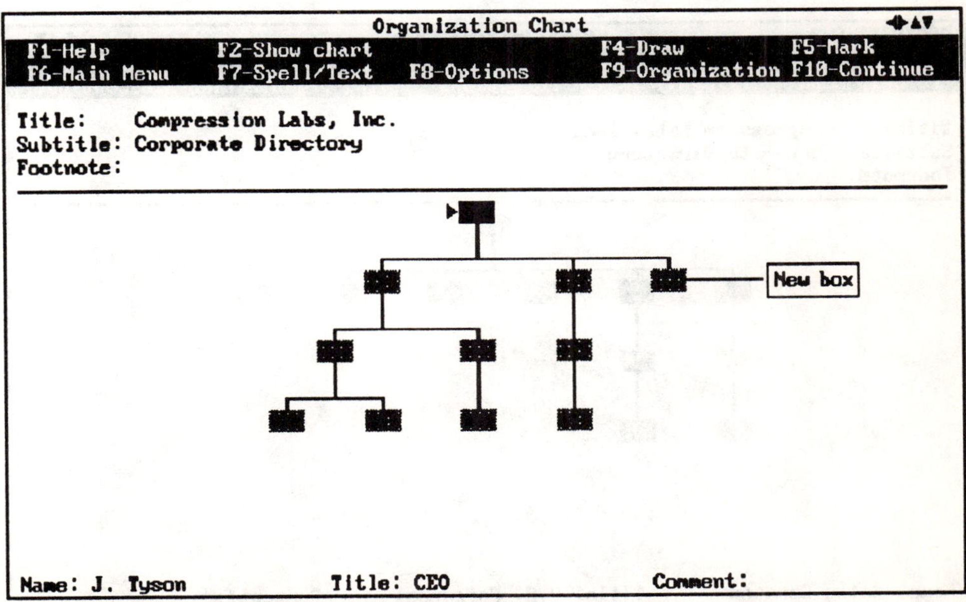

3-22 A new box appears after you select *Add subordinate*.

5. Press Ctrl – Del, then type W. Chen, Enter, and Exec. V.P. and two Enters. There's a limit to the amount of text you can enter on one line, and you want to be able to make the type as large as possible—so abbreviations are necessary.
6. Select the second box in the second row, press Ctrl – Z, and after deleting Juleen Simons, type K. Kenitzer Enter, and Exec. V.P. and two Enters.
7. In similar fashion, fill in the boxes for O'Shea, Walsh, Glancy, and Townsend.

On the Compression Labs annual report corporate directory, Chen has no subordinates listed—so you need to remove all boxes below his. Select a box subordinate to his, and select F9 – Organization. Note that the seventh item in the Organization menu is Delete box/group, and that the speed key is Ctrl – Del. Select item 7, and one of the two boxes under Chen will disappear, leaving two (see Fig. 3-23). Press the Delete box/group speed-key combination, Ctrl – Del, to remove the remaining subordinates from Chen's stack.

Now highlight the box under the Kenitzer box, second from the left. No one on the corporate directory reports to Kenitzer, so press Ctrl – Del to remove the subordinate boxes.

Highlight the O'Shea box, third from left. Because Bonnie Nunke reports to O'Shea, you need to add a subordinate box. Press Ctrl – Ins and a new subordinate box will appear (see Fig. 3-24). Select the new box, press Ctrl – Z, and type B. Nunke Enter, and V.P. and two Enters.

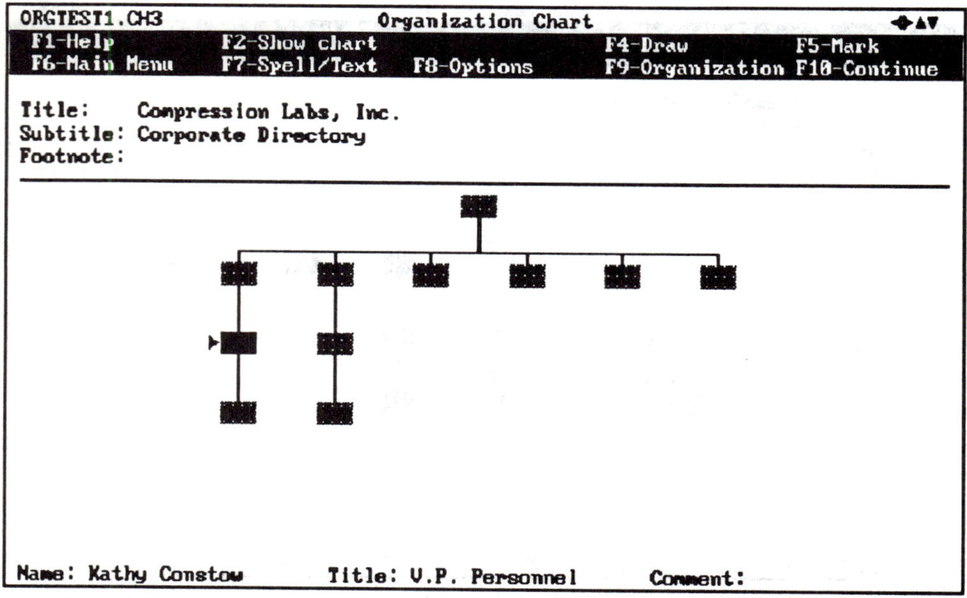

3-23 One of Chen's subordinates has been removed.

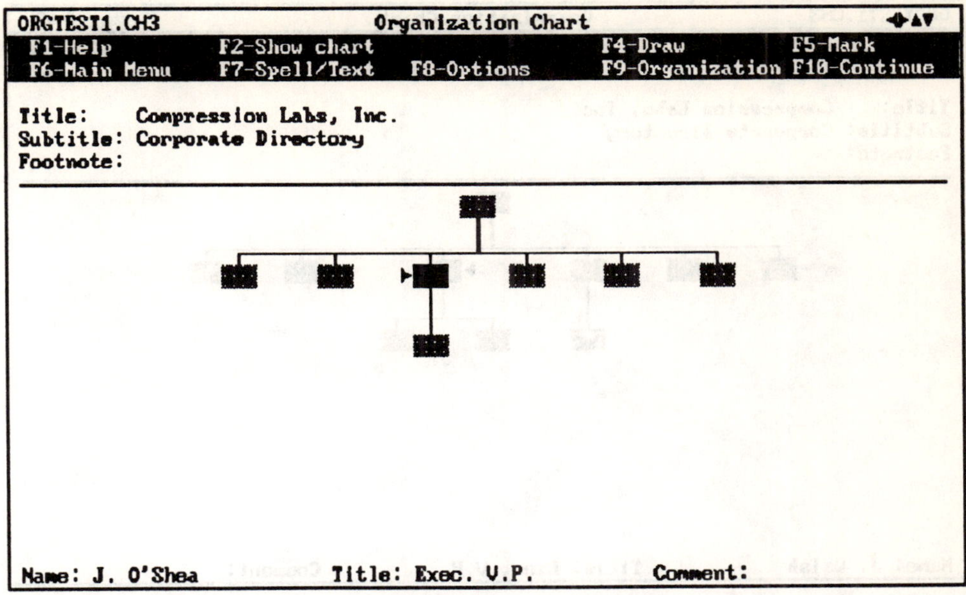

3-24 Pressing Ctrl – Ins adds a new subordinate box below O'Shea.

Highlight the Walsh box, fourth from left. Augustine and Marszewski report to Walsh, so you need to add two subordinate boxes. Press Ctrl – Ins twice, and Walsh now has a little group (see Fig. 3-25). Highlight the left subordinate box under Walsh and press Ctrl – Z. Type T. Augustine Enter, and V.P. and two Enters. Highlight the right subordinate box under Walsh and press Ctrl – Z. Type C. Mars zewski Enter, and V.P. and two Enters.

Select F2 – Show chart to view your accomplishment (see Fig. 3-26). It looks pretty good, except for one small thing—the generic chart has been set up so that the titles of the people at the lowest level are not shown. The chart, unfortunately, is intended to show only reporting relationships, not relative rank. The fact that Glancy and Townsend report directly to Tyson doesn't necessarily mean that they outrank the other vice presidents, so you should be sure that all titles are showing. That's easy to do:

1. Press Esc to go back to the data screen, and select F8 – Options. The Options menu will appear (see Fig. 3-27).
2. Select item 5, Box options and the Box Options menu will drop down (see Fig. 3-28).
3. Near the bottom of the Box Options menu you'll see Last level, and immediately below that you see that the current setting for Show title is No. You'll have to change that.

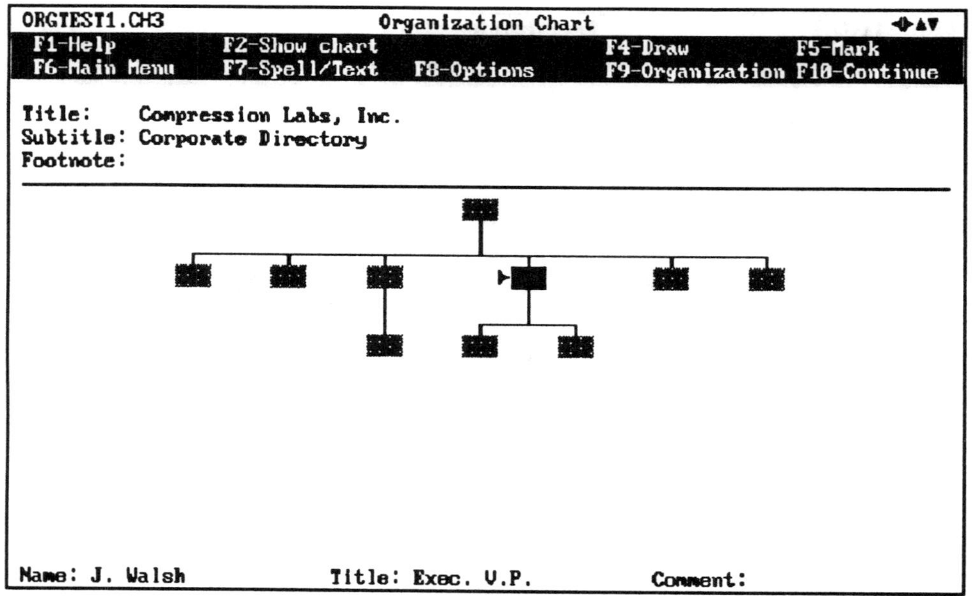

3-25 The chart in progress; Walsh has two subordinate boxes.

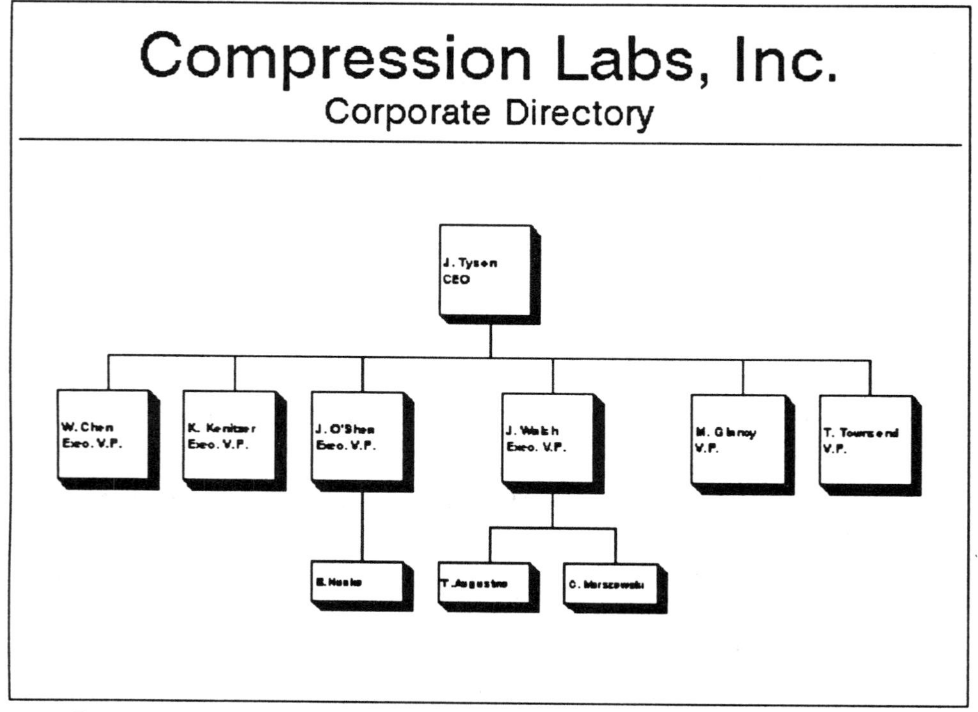

3-26 The completed organization chart, first draft.

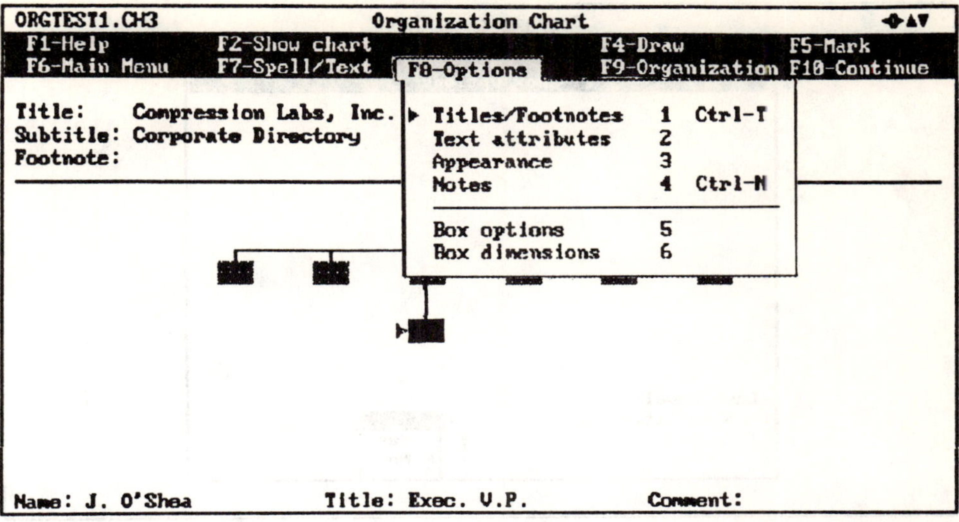

3-27 The Options menu.

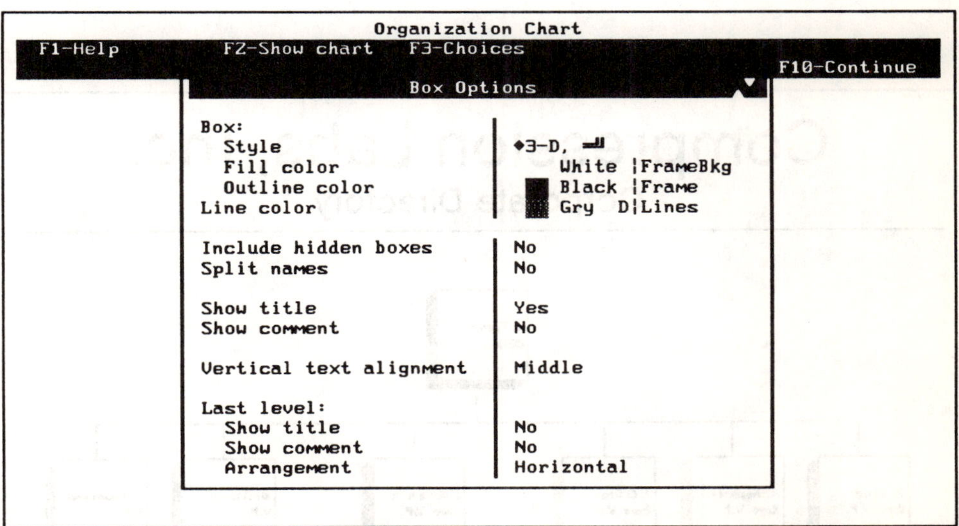

3-28 The Box Options menu.

4. Select the No opposite Show title under Last level; select F3 – Choices, and a little choice box will appear opposite Show title (see Fig. 3-29).
5. Select Yes, then press F10 to continue.
6. Select F2 – Show chart to view your results again, and now you should see that all titles are displayed (see Fig. 3-30).
7. Type orgchart, press F10 to confirm the action, and it's siesta time.

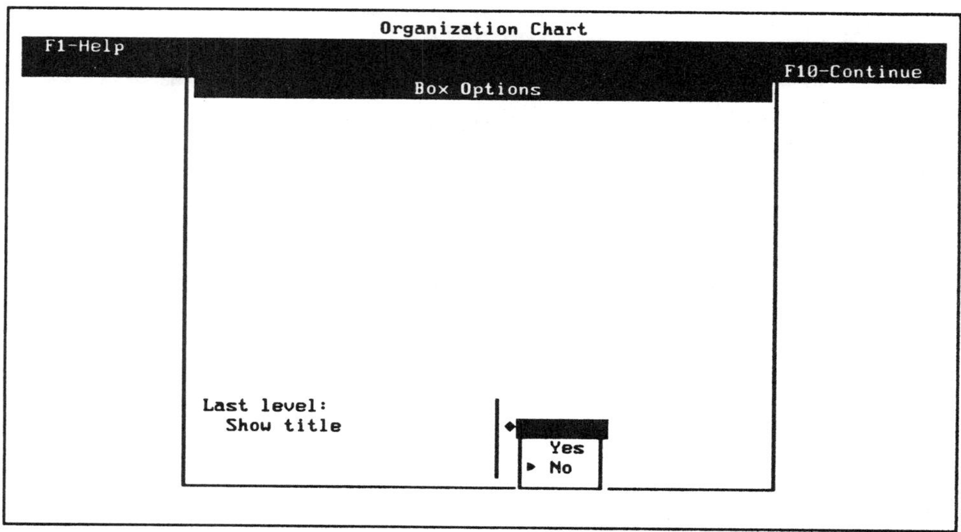

3-29 The choice box opposite *Show title*.

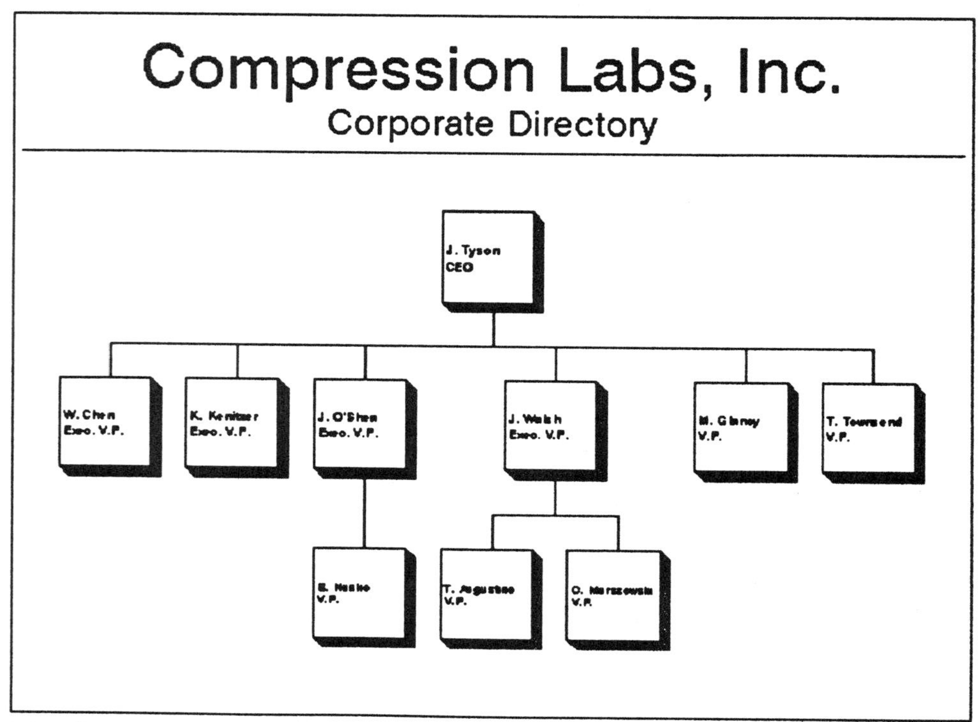

3-30 The revised chart, with all titles displayed.

Combination chart

For your final demonstration of using the generic or sample charts in the Gallery, you'll create a combination chart—in this case, a bar/line chart, which combines a series represented by vertical bars with a series represented by a line. The bar chart will represent Compression Labs' operating income for a five-year period, while the line chart will represent net income for the same period.

1. From the Main Menu, select Create chart, then when the submenu appears select From gallery.
2. At the Gallery home screen, select panel number 9 for combination charts, and the combination chart gallery, with four options, will be displayed (see Fig. 2-11).
3. Use the first of these choices—the combination Bar/Line chart in panel 1. Select that panel, and a nine-panel bar/line subgallery will appear (see Fig. 3-31).
4. From the bar/line subgallery, select the sample chart in panel 9. The bar/line chart shown in Fig. 3-32 will appear.
5. Now you need to clear the values used in this generic chart. Select F10 – Edit + Clear to delete all values and go to the data screen.
6. At the blank data screen, opposite Title, type Five-year Income History and Enter.

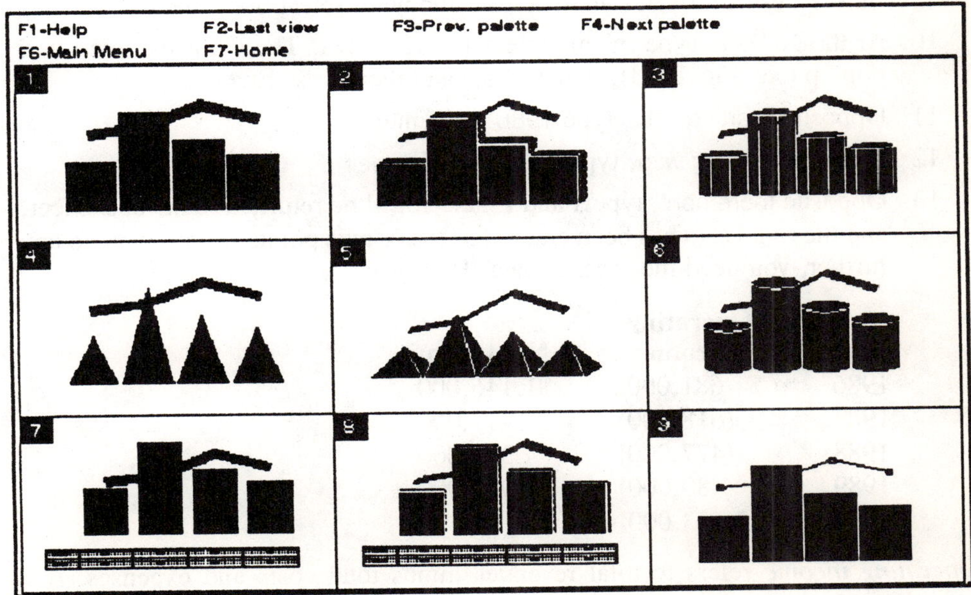

3-31 The Bar/Line subgallery.

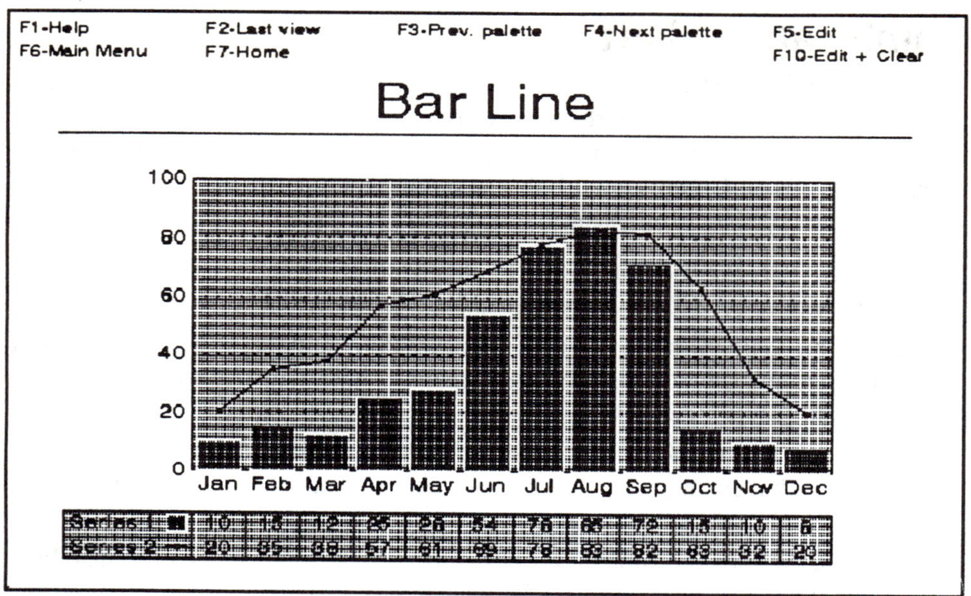

3-32 The generic bar line chart.

7. Opposite Subtitle, type Operating/Net Income, 1986 – 1990 and Enter.
8. Opposite Footnote, type Figures in thousands of dollars and Enter.
9. You've chosen a five-year history, so the X axis will be graduated in years. Select F9 – XY data, then from the submenu select Set X data type.
10. At the X Data Type menu, select F3 – Choices. The Choices menu will pop up (see Fig. 3-33). Select Year, and then press Enter.
11. Opposite Starting with, type 1986 and Enter.
12. Opposite Ending with, type 1990 and Enter.
13. Opposite Increment, type 1 and Enter. You'll be returned to the data sheet, and the five years has been entered as the X-axis points. Before you go any further, you need the income data. Here it is:

Year	Operating Income	Net Income
1986	$ 681,000	$1,146,000
1987	(618,000)	17,000
1988	(477,000)	304,000
1989	(180,000)	901,000
1990	2,453,000	

Operating income refers to total revenues minus total costs and expenses. *Net income* adds interest income and subtracts interest expense from operating

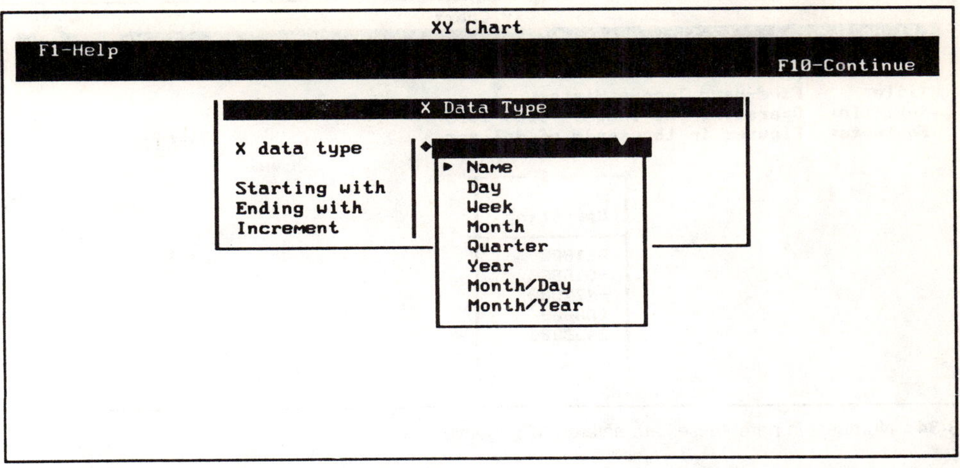

3-33 The menu of choices for the X data type.

income. Because 1987–89 show negative operating income but positive net income, all of the company's earnings for those three years must have been coming from interest. That situation changes dramatically in 1990, with $2.4 million in operating income. End of your business school lesson.

1. Move the cursor to the S of Series 1, and type Operating Income and Enter.
2. For the five data points in the Operating Income series, type 681000 Enter, (618000) Enter, (477000) Enter, (180000) Enter, and 2453000 and Enter. Note that when you enter a number in parentheses, Harvard Graphics 3.0 automatically changes it to a negative number (see Fig. 3-34).
3. You might be interested in having a look at your chart in progress at this point. Select F2–Show chart (see Fig. 3-35).
4. A new feature of this type of chart is the table of values below the chart. Press Esc to return to the data sheet, and move the cursor to the S of Series 2.
5. Type Net Income and Enter.
6. For the five data points in the Net Income series, type 1146000 Enter, 17000 Enter, 304000 Enter, 901000 Enter, and 2600000 and Enter (see Fig. 3-36).
7. Select F2–Show chart. The final result, in all its splendor, should look like Fig. 3-37.
8. Press Esc to leave the graphics screen, and press Ctrl–S to bring up the Save Chart box.
9. Opposite Filename, type income, select F10–Continue to confirm your action, and hit Esc to return to the Main Menu.

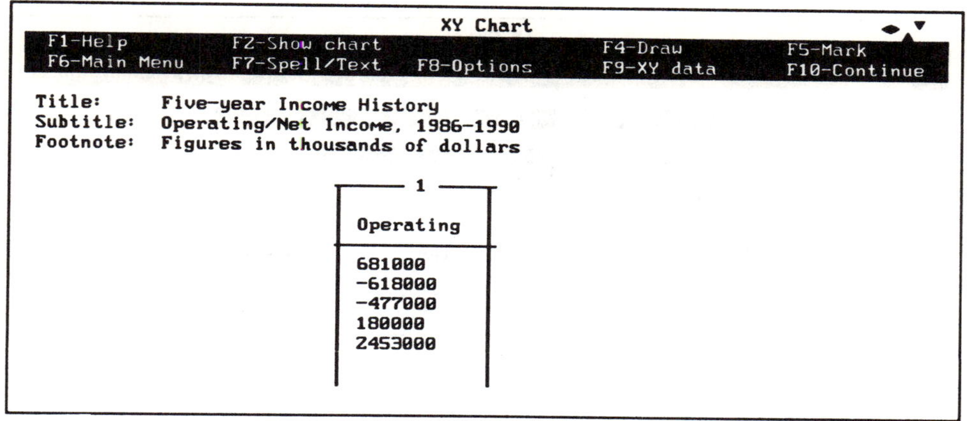

3-34 Numbers in parentheses are entered as negative numbers.

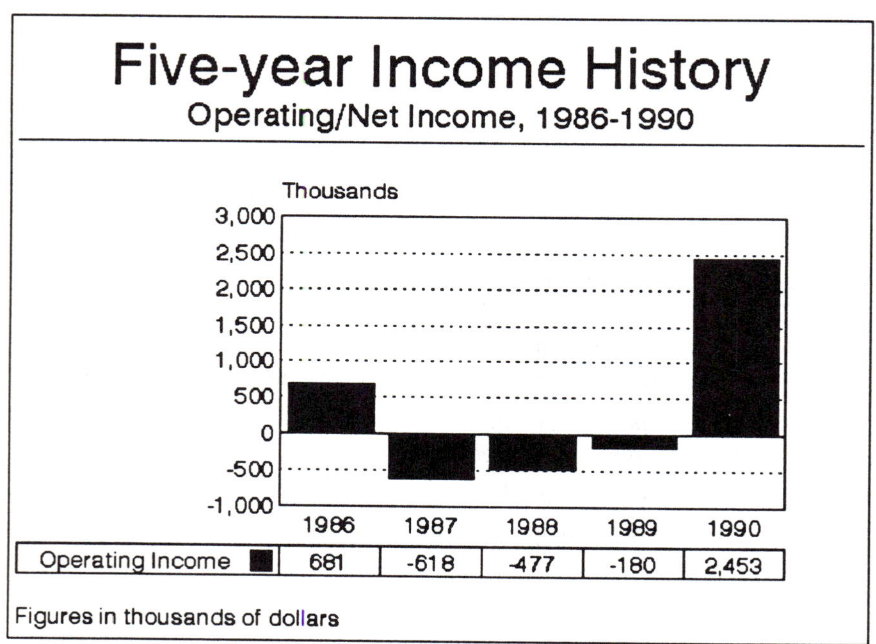

3-35 The chart in progress, showing the Operating Income series.

That wraps up your introductory tour through the Gallery. You've discovered how quick and easy it is to create eight different types of charts using the off-the-shelf models provided by the Gallery. Many, many kinds of alterations to these charts are possible, as you'll discover in the later, more advanced chapters. However, you've now reached at least the intermediate level of chart design, and it's likely that the techniques you've already mastered will be sufficient for most of the chart work you'll ever want to do.

XY Chart

F1-Help	F2-Show chart		F4-Draw	F5-Mark
F6-Main Menu	F7-Spell/Text	F8-Options	F9-XY data	F10-Continue

Title: Five-year Income History
Subtitle: Operating/Net Income, 1986–1990
Footnote: Figures in thousands of dollars

Data Pt	X Axis Year	1 Operating	2 Net Income	3 Series 3	4 Series 4
1	1986	681000	1146000		
2	1987	-618000	17000		
3	1988	-477000	304000		
4	1989	-180000	901000		
5	1990	2453000	2600000		
6					
7					
8					
9					
10					
11					
12					

3-36 The complete data sheet for the bar/line chart.

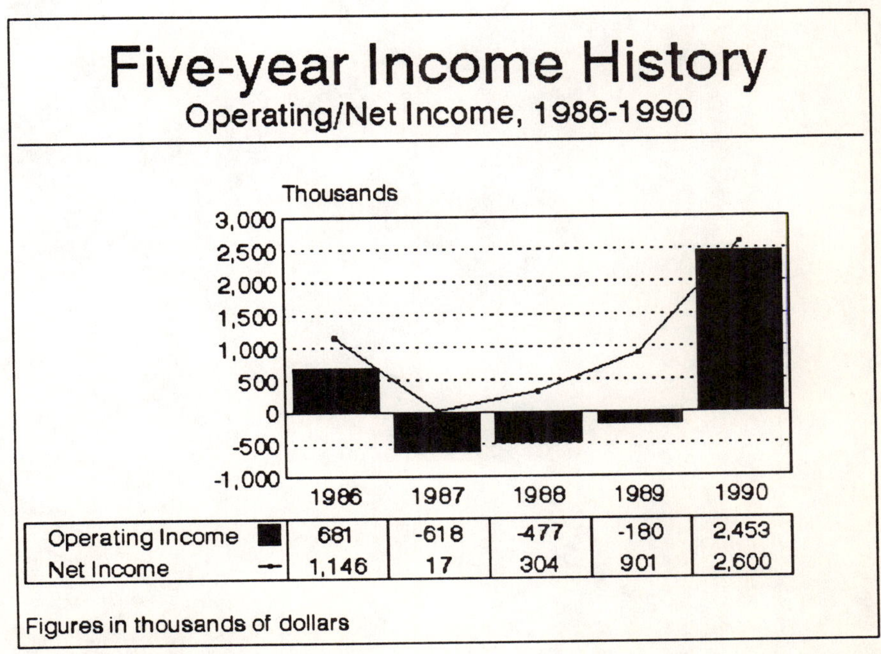

3-37 The finished bar/line chart.

4
CHAPTER

The Draw function

One of the major improvements of Harvard Graphics 3.0 over previous versions of the software is in the Draw function. Users now have a versatile drawing and painting function for enhancing charts or creating original graphics from scratch. With Draw, you can also import graphics files in several formats, including scanned images. In this chapter you'll achieve quick mastery of many of the basic maneuvers of the Draw function.

From the Main Menu, make selection 3, Draw. The Draw screen will appear, as shown in Fig. 4-1. In the chapter on advanced drawing, I'll take you on a comprehensive tour of all the drawing and editing tools. For now, however, you can start with the basics. You'll be able to tell by the little graphics you create what most of the drawing tools can do.

Using the Help function in Draw

Before you continue, it's worth a moment to point out how useful the Help function is. To get Help with any function, simply position the pointer over the icon representing that function and press F1. To demonstrate this, use your mouse or the arrow keys to move the pointer into position over the box tool (see Fig. 4-2). Next, press F1; a Help area will pop up with information specifically about the box tool (see Fig. 4-3). When you're finished, press Esc to return to the Draw screen.

Drawing a box

To make boxes, select the tool with the rectangle. Click on the box tool (see Fig. 4-4). When you do, the tool will be highlighted, a box will appear in the status

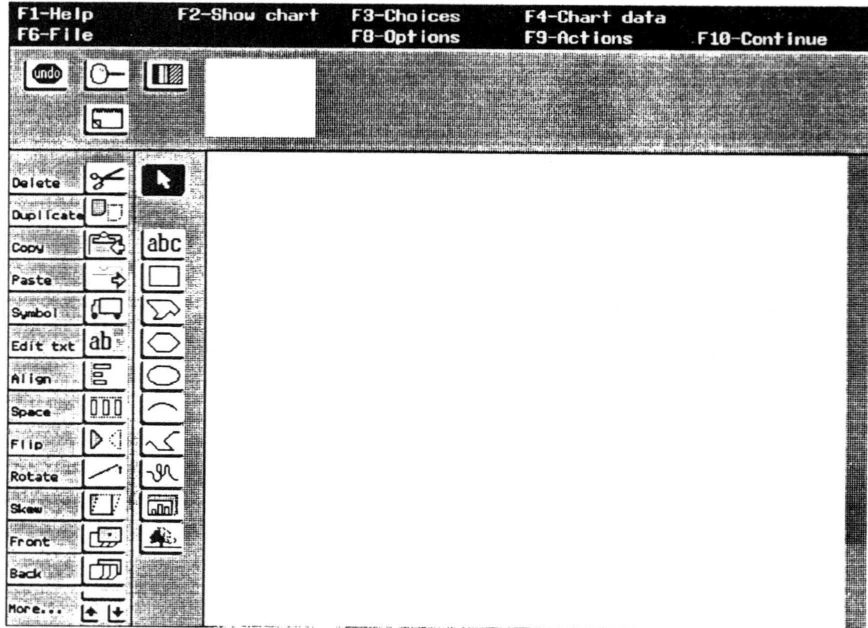

4-1 The Draw screen, with drawings and editing tools.

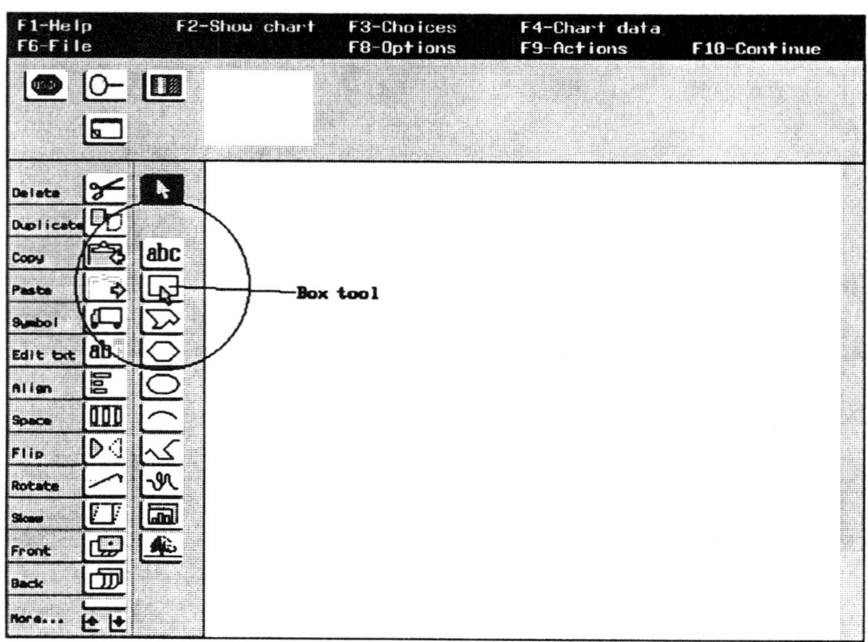

4-2 The pointer in position over the Box tool.

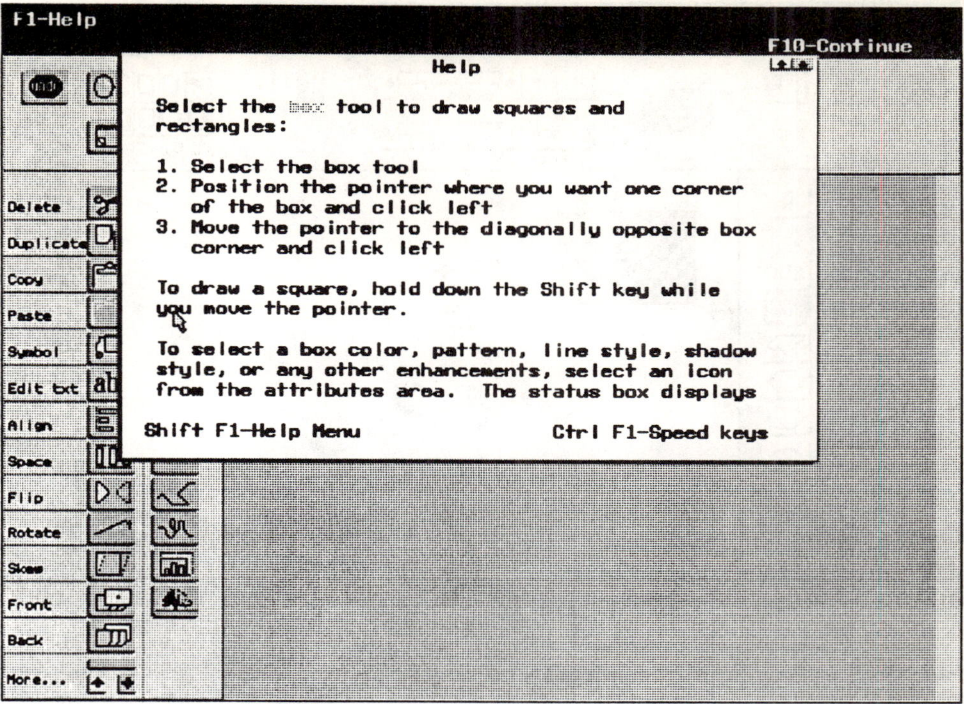

4-3 Pressing F1 displays information about the Box tool.

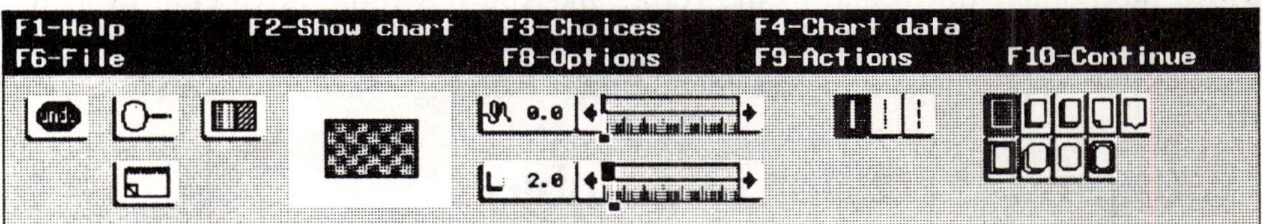

4-4 The top of the Draw screen when you select the Box too.

box, and several new items will be displayed at the top of the screen:

- a line width slider bar
- a box style width slider bar
- a line type icon that lets you select solid, dotted, or dashed lines
- a box style icon that lets you choose among nine types of box styles

For now, however, you're going to use the plain garden variety box—but you get an idea of the array of possible variations.

Position the pointer in the upper left-hand corner of the canvas and click once with the left mouse button (or press Enter) to fix one corner of the rectangle.

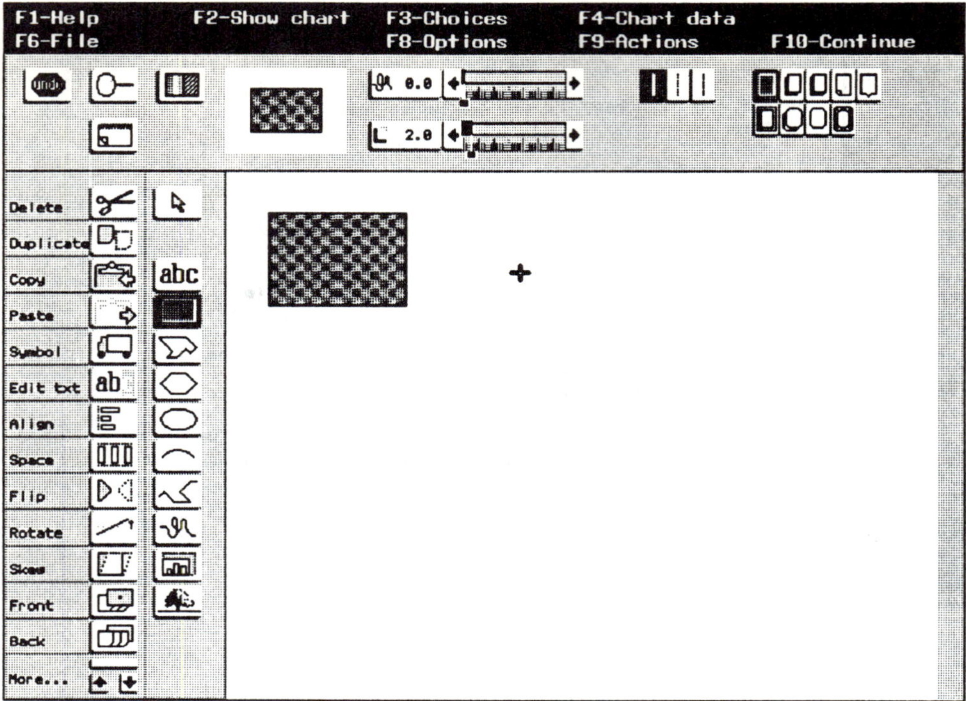

4-5 The completed box.

Move the pointer down and to the right, and you'll see the box begin to form. Click the left button again to fix the opposite corner, and a box will appear. It will be filled or empty, depending on your settings (see Fig. 4-5).

Changing the color of an object

Want to change the color of your box? Fill it with a pattern or gradient or bitmap image? You can perform these actions, and many others, in many variations. First, however, in order to do anything to an existing object on your canvas, you must select it.

Choose the selection tool (see Fig. 4-6). The selection tool will be highlighted, and the status box made blank. Point to the box you drew and click to select it. When you do, an image of the box will appear in the status box, and eight little square handles appear around the periphery of the box (see Fig. 4-7). The box is now ready for modification.

Click on the color icon in the upper left-hand corner (see Fig. 4-8). The appearance of this panel—particularly of the Chart colors section—depends upon the palette that's been selected. (The palette file used for these examples is HG23.PAL.) Because this book is illustrated in black and white, my discussions

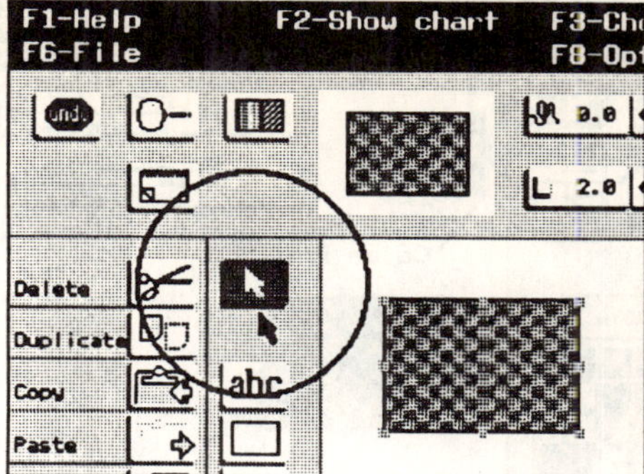

4-6 The selection tool.

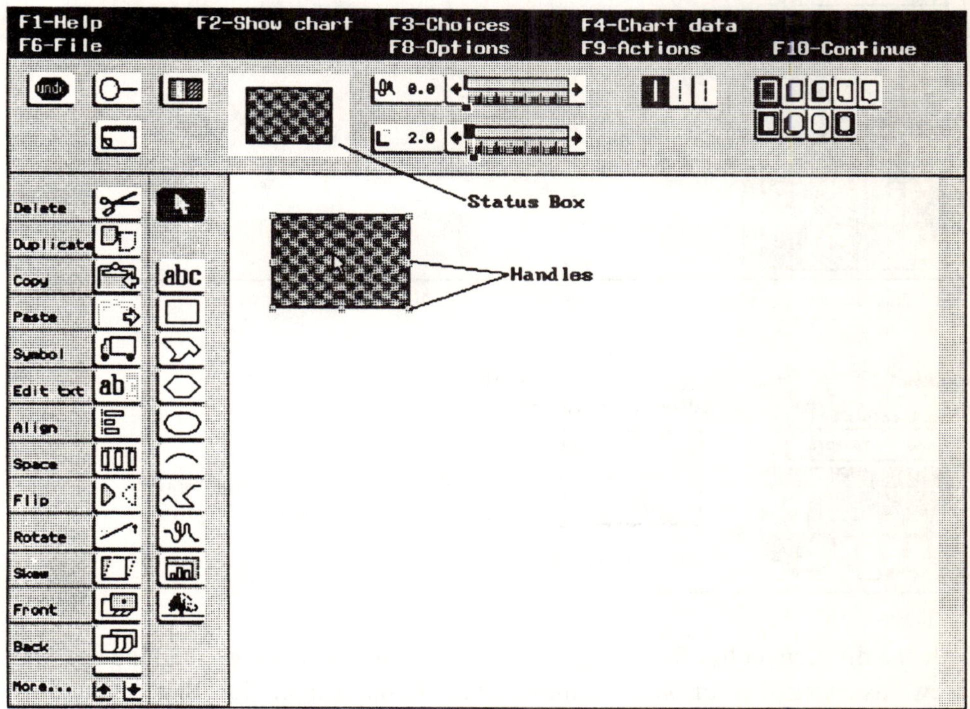

4-7 The selected box, with handles and the status box.

of color have to be limited. From this panel, you can select from existing colors, create your own customized color, choose a fill pattern, and much more. You're going to change the color and choose a pattern.

In the Chart colors section, the current color is highlighted by a white border, and the color is described in the block above the color samples (see Fig. 4-9).

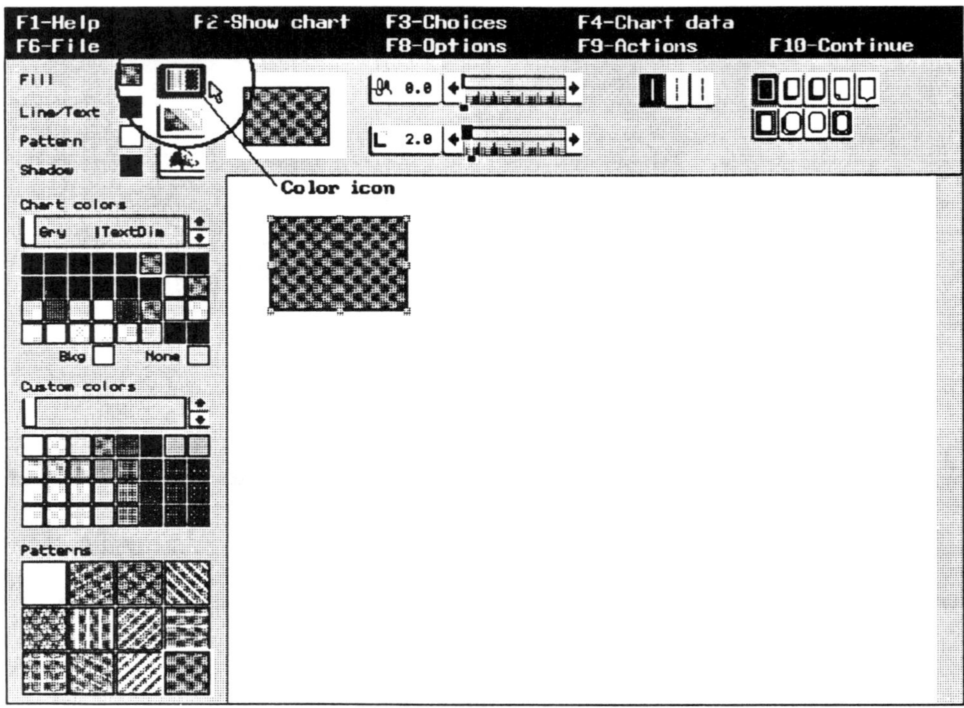

4-8 The Color icon.

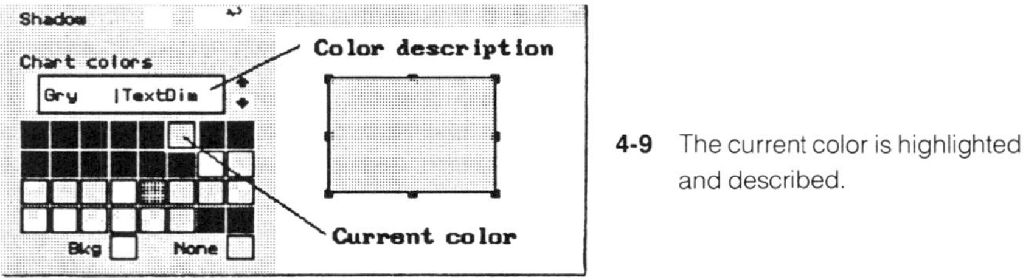

4-9 The current color is highlighted and described.

Select a different color. In Fig. 4-10, a red color has been chosen, and the box you drew has changed color on the canvas and in the status box. Note that the patterns at the bottom of the panel have also changed color.

Adding a pattern

I'll have you make one more change—add a pattern. In the Patterns box, select a crosshatch pattern. When you do, that pattern is highlighted and the pattern appears in the boxes on the canvases and in the status box (see Fig. 4-11). Click the right mouse button or press Esc to return to the main drawing tools panel. Press Esc once more to deselect the box. The handles will disappear.

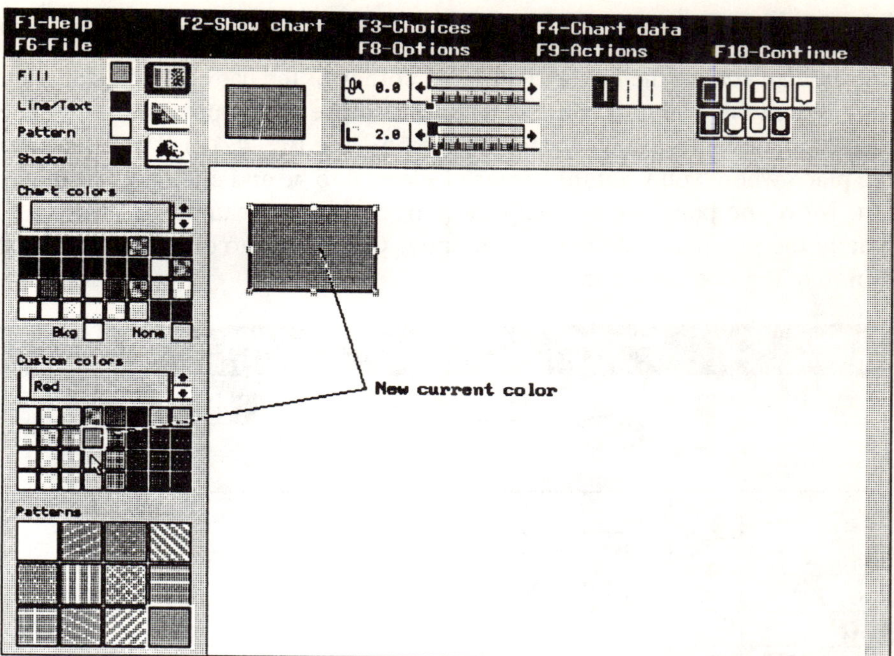

4-10 The tool panel and canvas, with a new color selected.

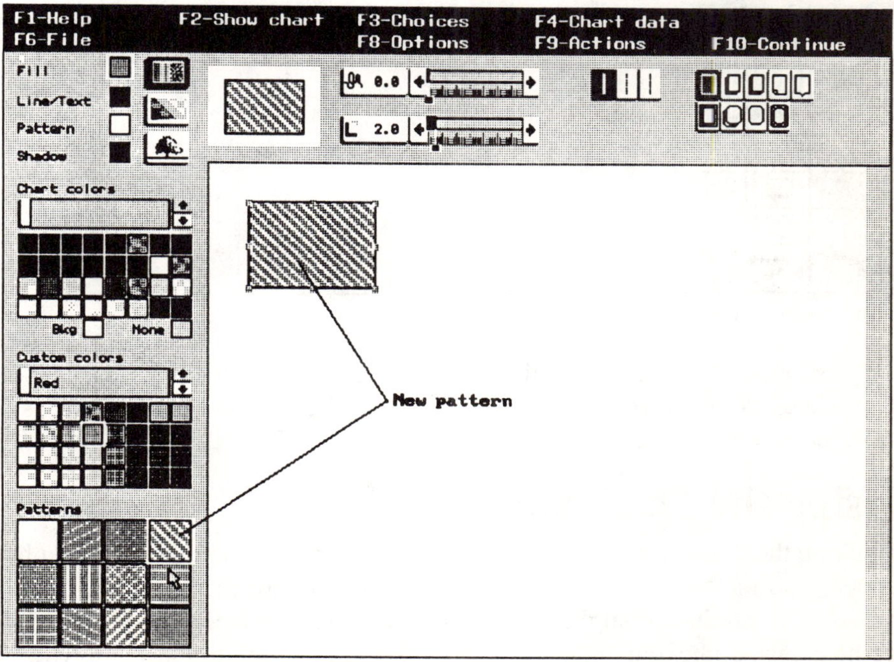

4-11 The selected pattern appears in the box.

Drawing an oval

To draw an oval in the lower right-hand corner of the canvas, first select the oval tool. When the oval tool is highlighted, an ellipse will appear in the status box in the color and pattern you selected for the box (see Fig. 4-12). Move the pointer to the place where you want the center of the oval to be and click the left mouse button. Move the pointer diagonally away from the center until the oval is approximately the same size as the box you drew. Click again to draw the oval. It should look like the one shown in Fig. 4-13.

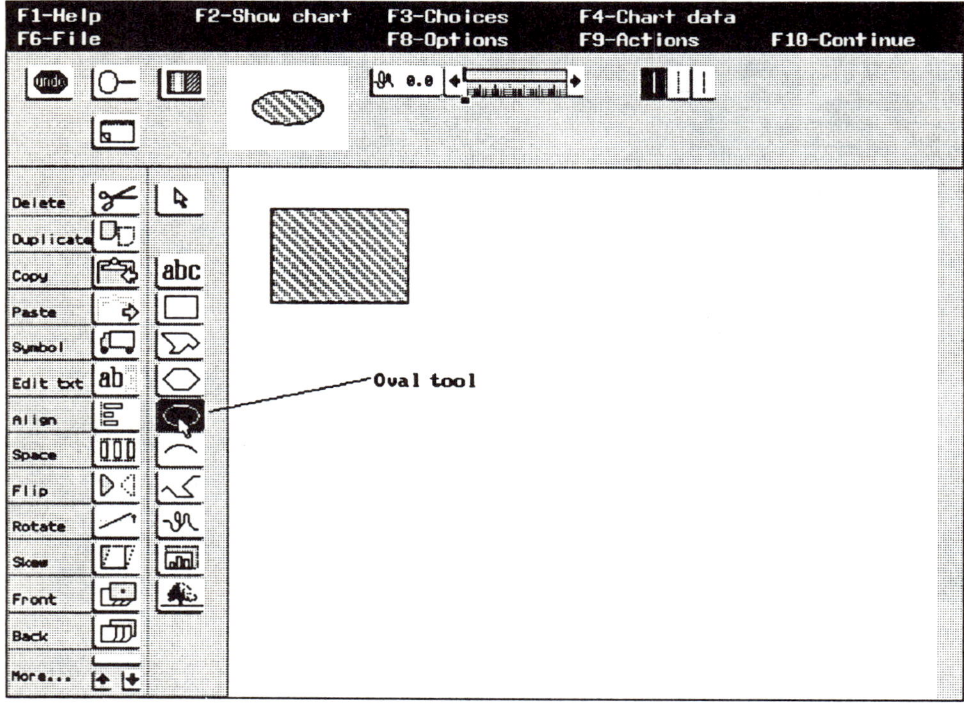

4-12 Select the Oval tool; an oval appears in the status box.

As you can see from the list down the left-hand side of the panel, you can Duplicate, Copy, Paste, Flip, Rotate, Skew, and do many other wondrous things to objects on the canvas.

Using the Duplicate tool

Click on the Select tool, and select the box you drew. When the selection handles appear and the box shows up in the status box, choose Duplicate. A copy of the box will be produced, slightly offset from the original (see Fig. 4-14). Move the pointer inside the duplicate box, and then drag the duplicate downward by depressing the left mouse key and moving the mouse (see Fig. 4-15).

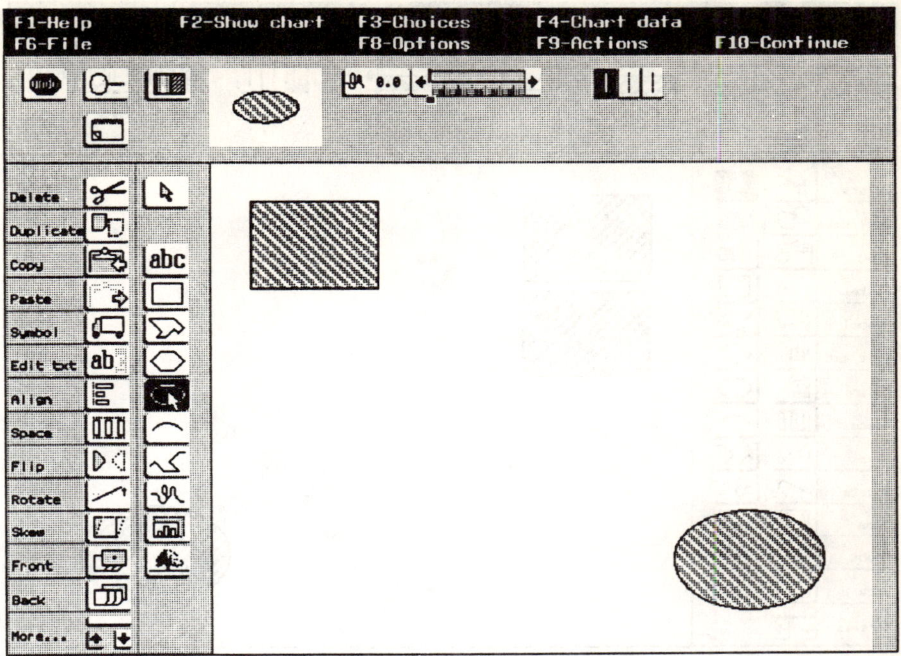

4-13 The finished oval.

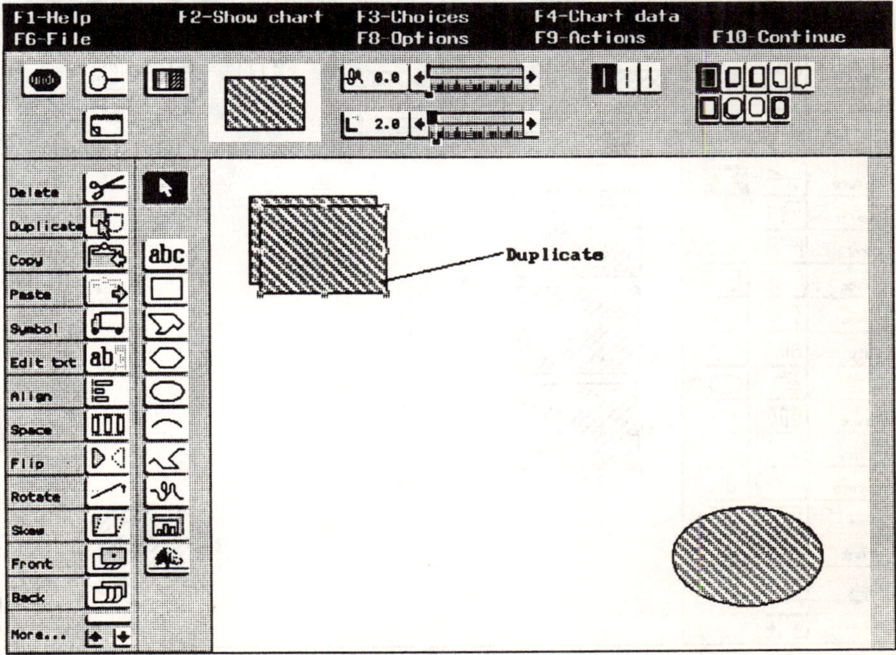

4-14 Selection handles mark the duplicate of the original box.

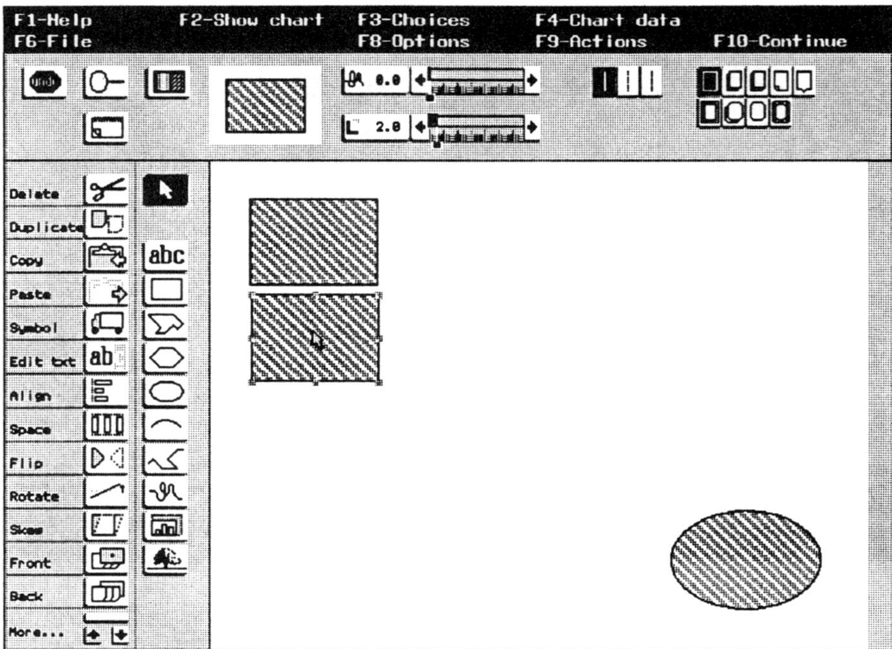

4-15 The duplicate after you've dragged it down.

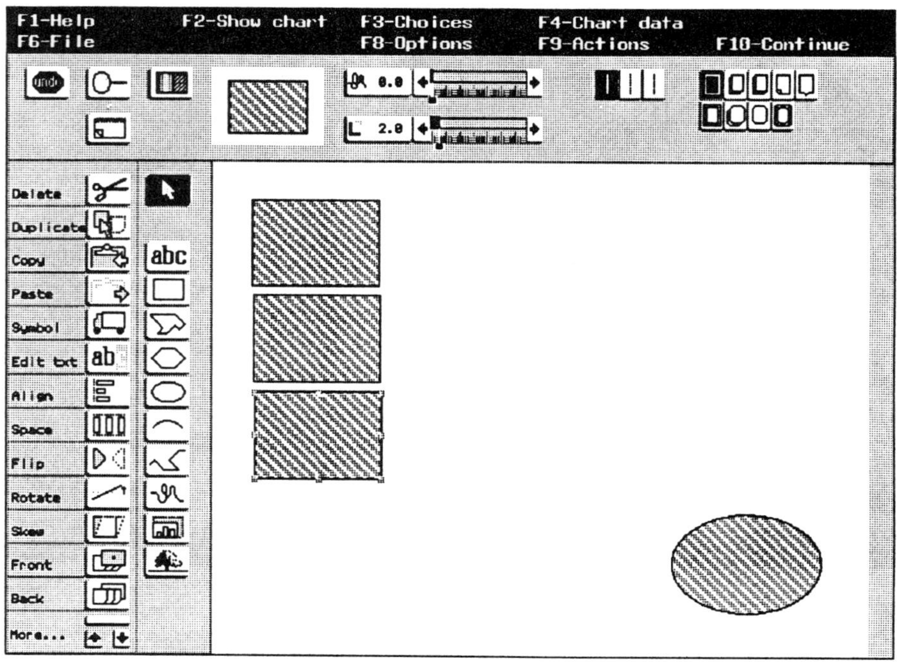

4-16 The second copy, with a new offset distance and direction.

You've now established a new offset direction and distance for the duplicate function. Press the Duplicate tool again, and another clone of the original box will appear, offset below the first one just as the second one is now offset below the first (see Fig. 4-16).

Using the Skew tool

Select the top box again, and click on the Skew tool. A number of skew options will appear at the bottom of the draw tools panel, eight skew directions plus the degree of skew. The options permit you to skew the top or bottom of the box to the right or left, or to skew the left or right side up or down (see Fig. 4-17).

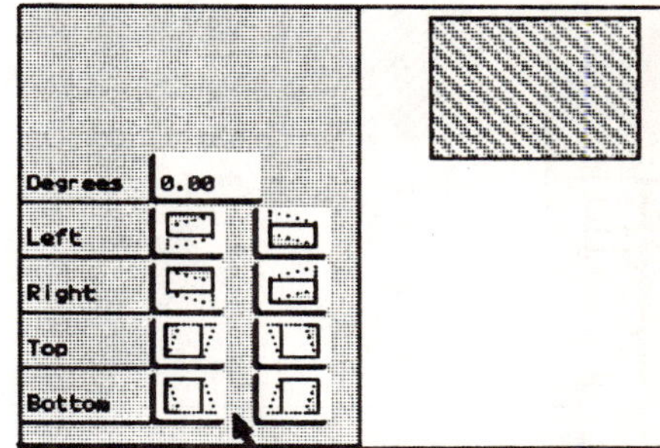

4-17 The skew options.

You're going to skew the top of the box 45 degrees to the right. Select the Degrees box, type 45.00, and press the right mouse key or Esc. Select the Top skew option, and the top box will be skewed to the right, as shown in Fig. 4-18. Esc back to the main tools panel, and select Flip. The program will ask you whether you want to flip horizontally or vertically (see Fig. 4-19). Choose the horizontal option, and the skewed image will flip, as in Fig. 4-20.

Using the Evolve tool

Select Esc to deselect all objects, then select the lower left-hand box. To select the oval shape at the same time, press Shift while selecting the oval. You should now see selection handles on both figures, and both appear in the status box (see Fig. 4-21). To get to it, click on the highlighted down arrow at the bottom of the Tools panel. A new collection of editing tools will appear (see Fig. 4-22).

Choose Evolve (see Fig. 4-23). The panel will display some Evolve options: you can choose whether to evolve in reverse (counter-clockwise) or forward (clockwise), and you can choose the number of steps (between 1 and 50) for the number of images you want to use for the evolution. Accept the default of 10 steps and choose Forward. A number of intermediate images will appear as the rectangular shape of the box is changed step-wise into the oval. Press Esc to turn off the selection handles, and your new creation should resemble Fig. 4-24.

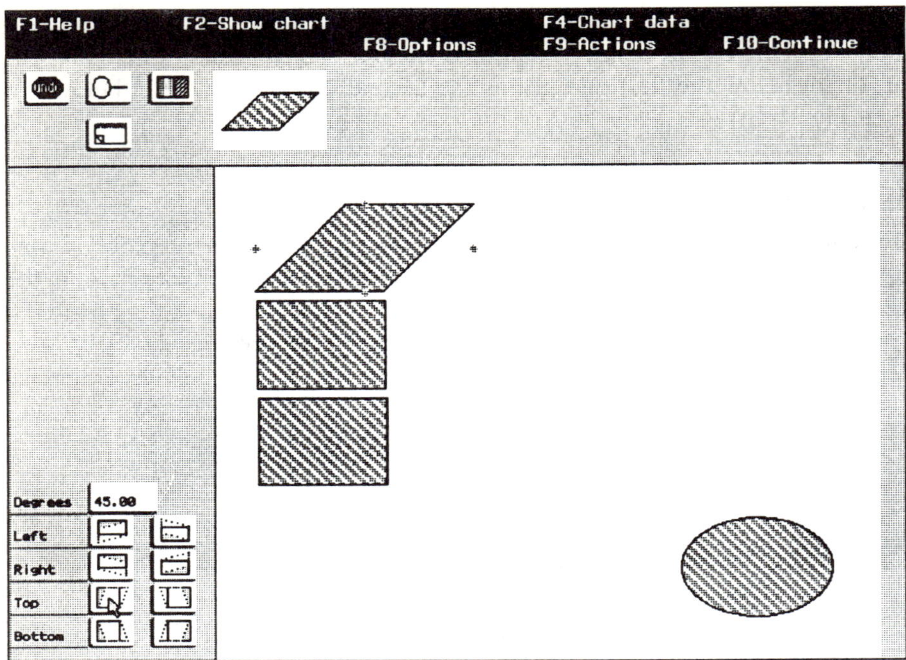

4-18 The top box skewed 45° to the right.

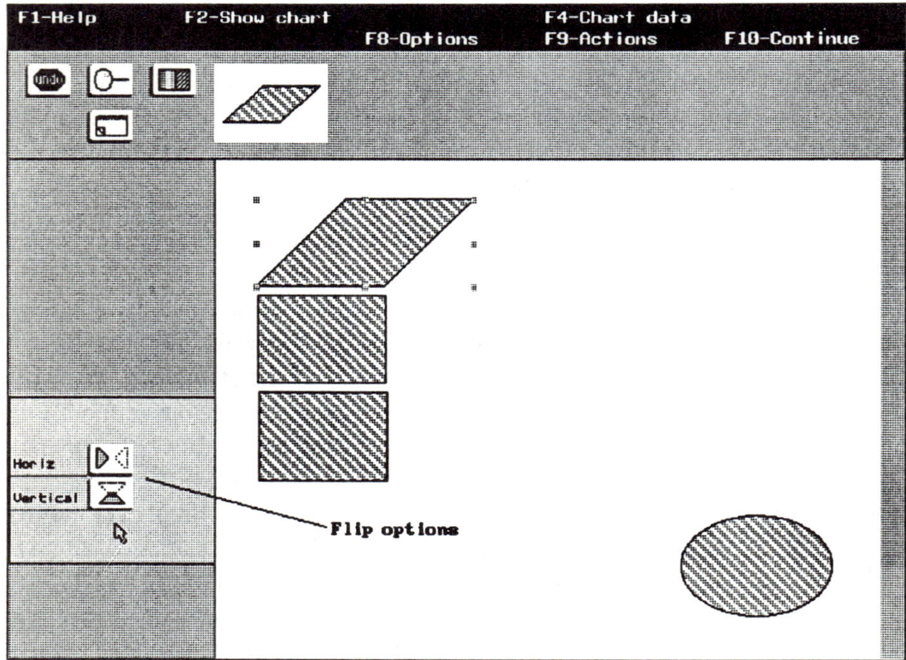

4-19 The horizontal and vertical flip options.

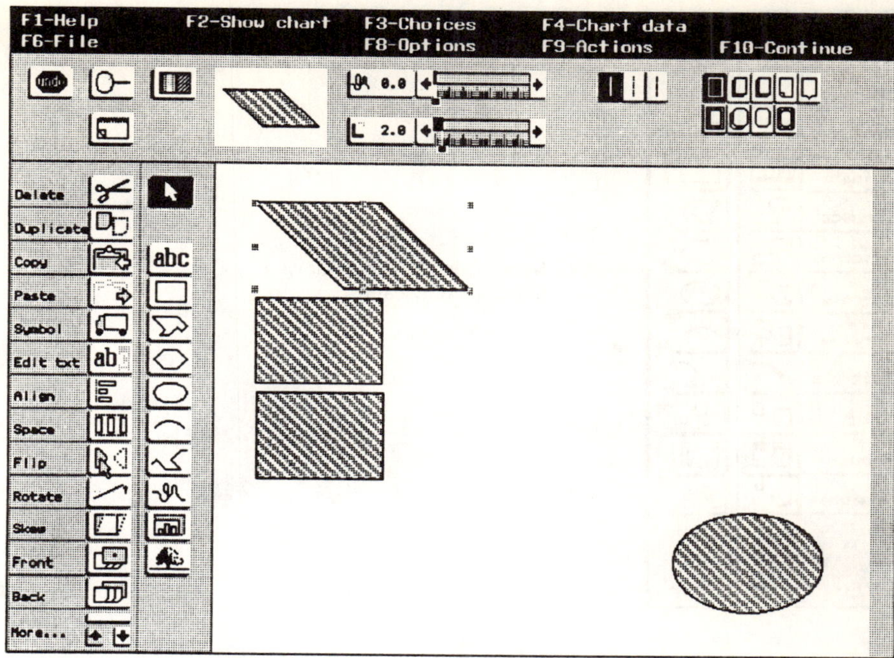

4-20 The old box after being skewed and flipped.

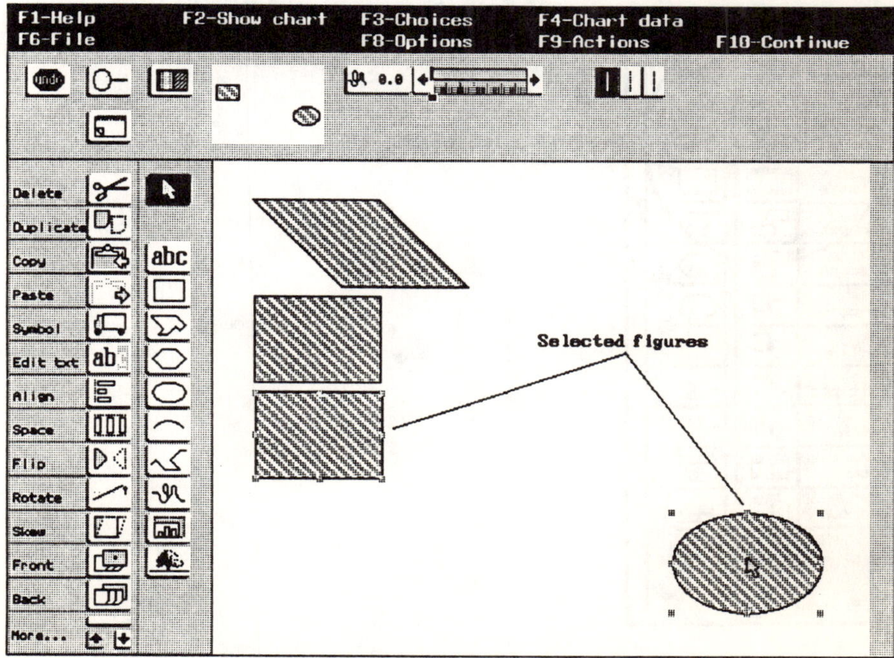

4-21 Two figures selected on the canvas and in the status box.

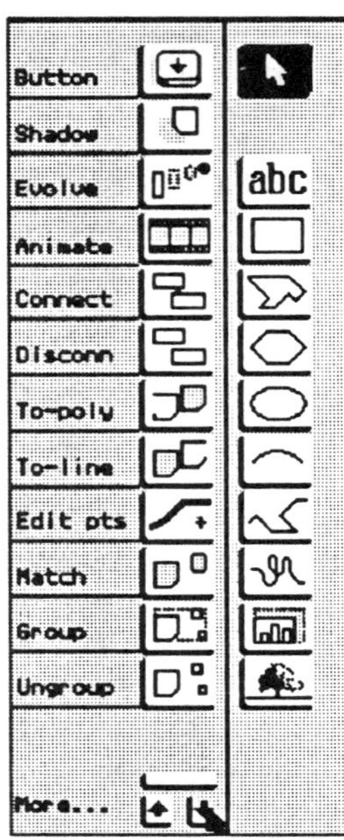

4-22 More editing tools appear when you select the down arrow.

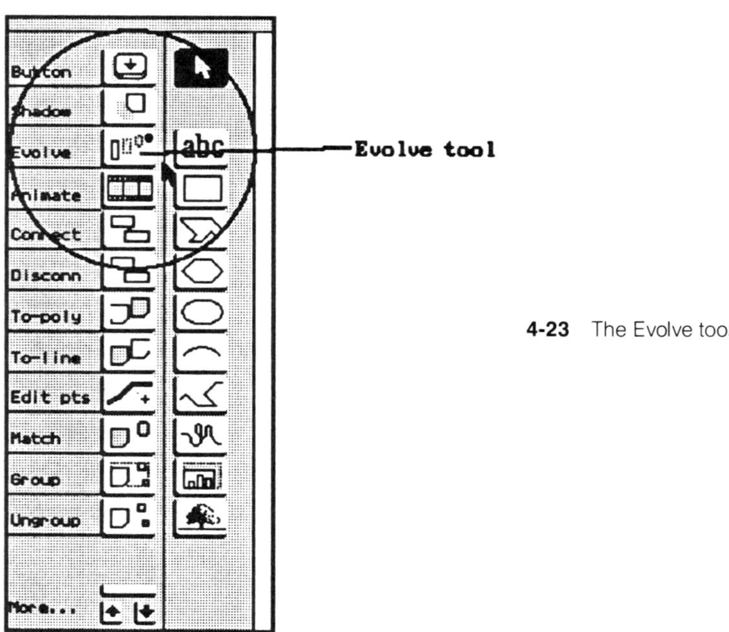

4-23 The Evolve tool.

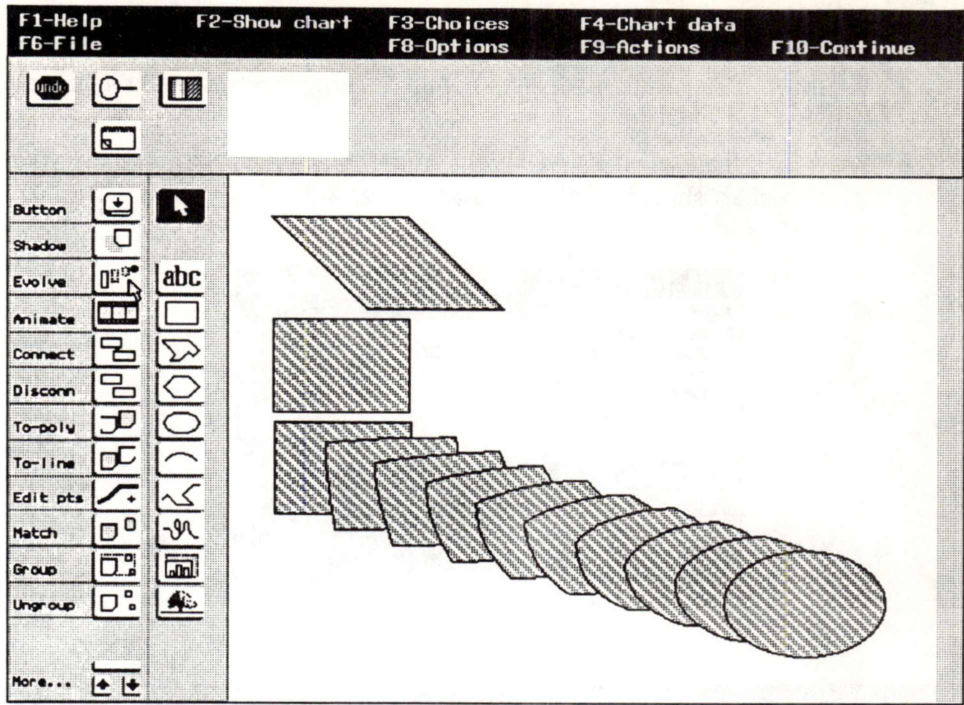

4-24 The completed act of evolution.

Enhancing a chart with Draw

You're likely to find the Draw function especially useful for adding to or dressing up charts that you've created with the charting function of Harvard Graphics 3.0. One obvious way is to add text—and that's the operation I'm going to take you through right now in this introductory cruise of Draw. I'm going to have you load one of those charts you created from the Gallery, shrink it a bit with the editing tools, and add an appropriate block of text.

1. From the Main Menu, select Create chart, then at the submenu select Clear chart so you can go to the drawing canvas with a clean slate.
2. Back at the Main Menu, select Draw.
3. At the top of the screen, select F6 – File and the File menu will drop down (see Fig. 4-25).
4. Select Get chart. (Notice that you could have done this from the Draw screen with the Ctrl – G speed-key combination.)

5. From the Chart directory listing (probably C: \ HG3 \ DATA \ *.CH*), select the file you saved earlier as BACKLOG (the program adds the .CH3 extension). The chart is displayed full screen; to refresh your memory, look back at Fig. 3-9.
6. Press Esc, then select F4—Draw to go to the drawing board, where your backlog chart should be displayed as in Fig. 4-26.

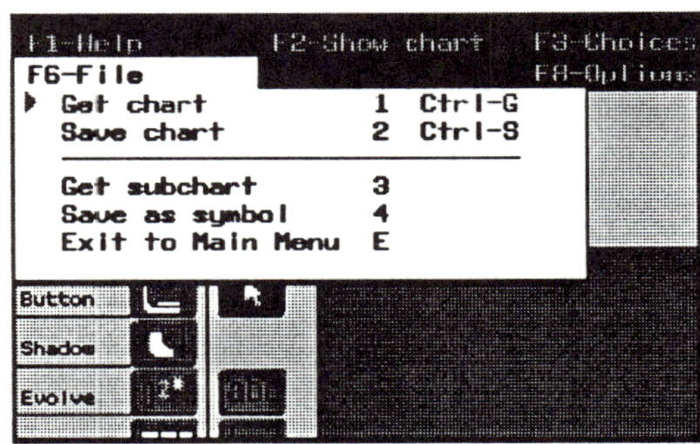

4-25 The File menu.

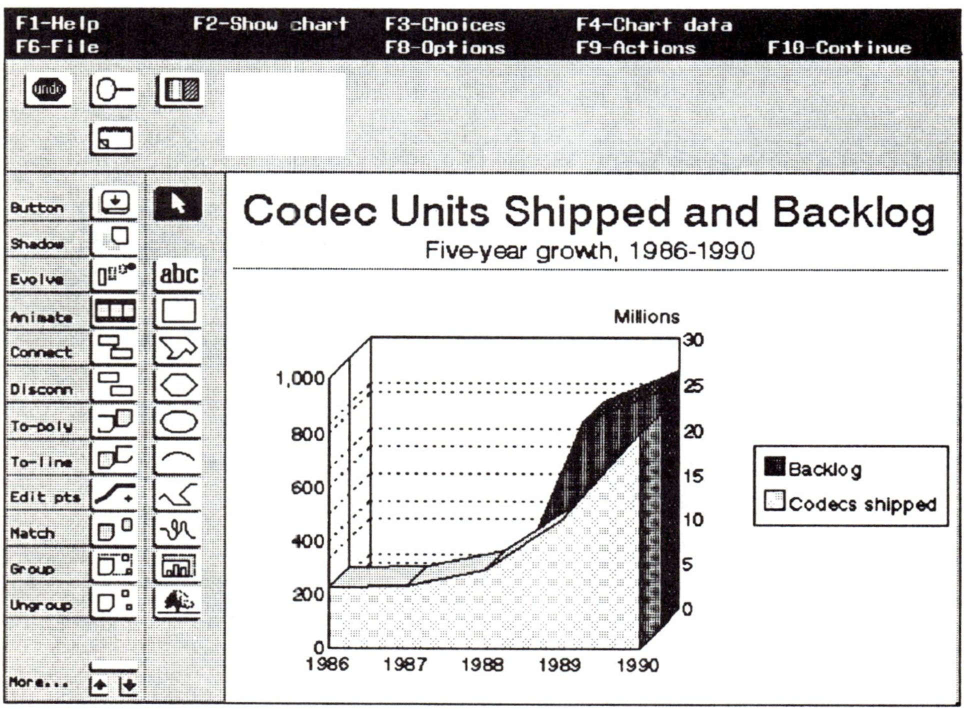

4-26 The backlog chart, displayed on the Draw canvas.

This chart is now a single unit that you can select and manipulate on the canvas much as if it were one of the objects you had drawn with the drawing tools. Click on the selection tool if it's not already highlighted; selection handles will appear around the periphery of the chart, and an image of the chart will appear in the status box (see Fig. 4-27).

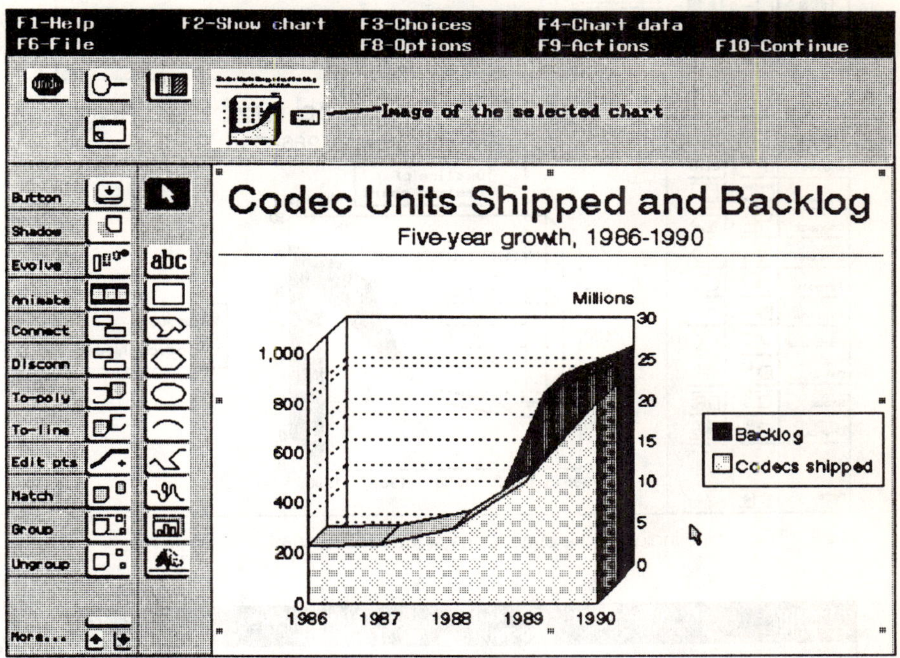

4-27 The chart is selected; its image appears in the status box.

Resizing an object or chart

Now you're going to resize this chart on the canvas. To do that, point to one of the selection handles, press and hold down the left mouse button, and "drag" that handle until the chart's new size suits you. If you drag one of the middle handles on the left or right side, you'll change the width of the chart. If you drag one of the middle handles on the top or bottom, you'll change the height of the chart. If you drag a corner handle, you'll change width and height simultaneously.

If you want to resize a chart (or object) but keep its original proportions, hold down the Shift key while you're dragging a corner handle. That's what you want to do right now. Point to the lower left-hand corner selection handle. Depress the left mouse button and hold down the Shift key. Slide the mouse upward, and the chart will get narrower and shorter while keeping the same ratio of width to height. You'll see an outline indicating the chart's changing dimensions.

Shrink the chart until the left boundary of the chart coincides with the beginning of the U in Units in the chart's title (see Fig. 4-28). Release the Shift key and mouse button, and the chart will be redrawn in its smaller size (see Fig. 4-29).

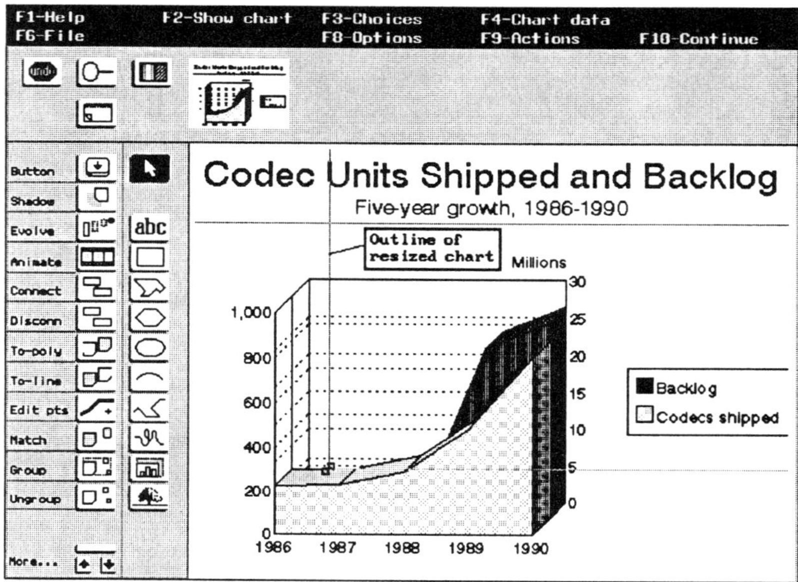

4-28 The outline indicates the dimensions of the resized chart.

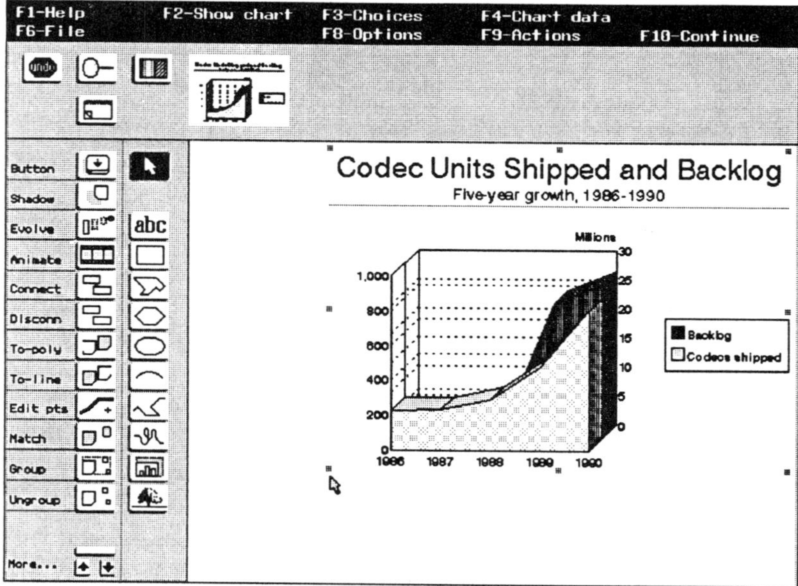

4-29 The reduced chart.

Adding text to a chart

Select the text tool—the one that says ABC. When it's highlighted, the letters Abc will appear in the status box and a group of text editing tools will appear at the top of the screen (see Fig. 4-30).

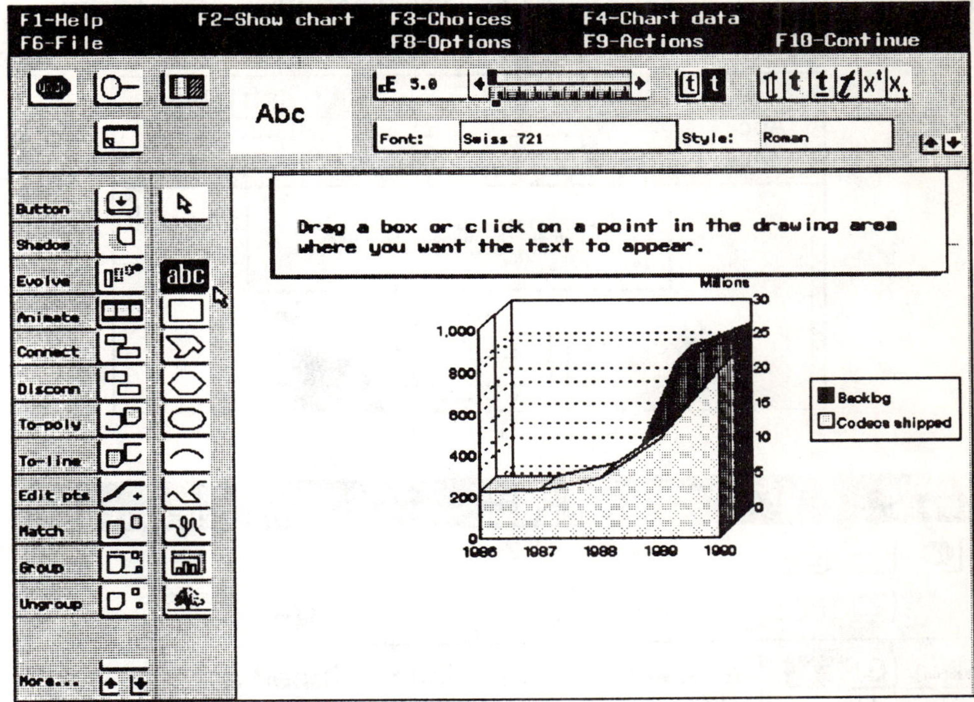

4-30 *Text* is selected; text editing tools appear above the canvas.

4-31 The text pop-up writing area.

To define the area where you want to place the text, drag a box at the left side of the canvas as if you were drawing a box there. When you release the mouse button, a text pop-up appears, waiting for you to start entering text (see Fig. 4-31).

Type the following text, taken from the 1990 Compression Labs annual report: Even with 1990's sales growth, our backlog grew throughout the year, reaching more than $26 million at year-end (see Fig. 4-32). When you select F10–

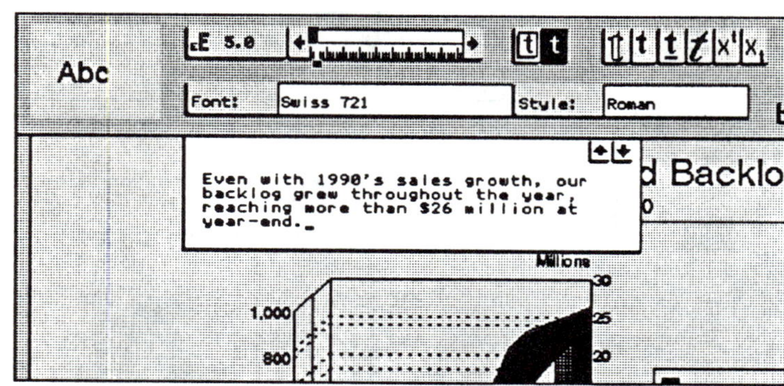

4-32 The text pop-up area, with your new text.

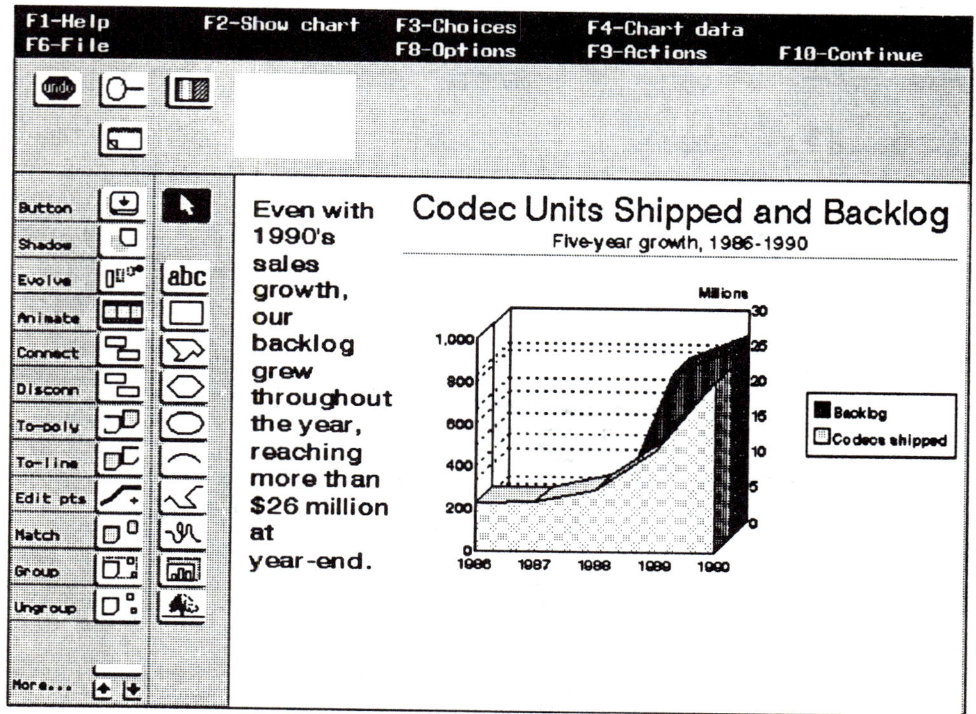

4-33 The new text alongside the chart.

Continue, the new text will appear along the left side of the canvas. You accepted the default text values, which in this case are:

Text size: 5.0
Font: Swiss 721
Style: Roman

If any of your values are different, your results will look somewhat different than the chart in Fig. 4-33. This text somewhat overwhelms the chart, so you might have chosen a different font, type size, etc.—but you get the idea. Save this revised chart by pressing Ctrl–S and typing backlog2 opposite Filename. Select F10–Continue to end this session.

You've only scratched the surface, but by now you should have had enough practice with the Draw function to use most of its separate operations. When you come back to the "drawing board" in a later chapter, you can get into some of the maneuvers in more detail.

5
CHAPTER

Working with color

Harvard Graphics 3.0 offers powerful resources for the color user. It's possible to do an infinite amount of tinkering with the colors in your charts and graphs. In this chapter you'll be introduced to the major types of color adjustments that are available in the program. The illustrations that I provide in this book are limited because they're in shades of gray—and if you have a monochrome monitor, you'll experience the same limitation with the program. The software still provides great versatility, however, as you'll see.

Changing the colors in Gallery charts

Harvard Graphics 3.0 supplies you with a large assortment of off-the-rack charts from the Gallery; the program also makes it just as easy to change the colors of those Gallery charts via a number of ready-to-use palettes. You simply load the chart type you want to use, then cycle through the available palettes until you find the one that suits you.

Before you begin, it helps to know what colors you're starting with. This is determined by the chart palette that's selected as part of the Setup program. Let's begin there. At the Main Menu, select item 8, Setup. The Setup submenu will be displayed (see Fig. 5-1). From that submenu, select the second item, Chart default settings (see Fig. 5-2).

As you see, this screen permits you to set the automatic, or default settings for your charts right at the beginning. In other words, unless and until you give differ-

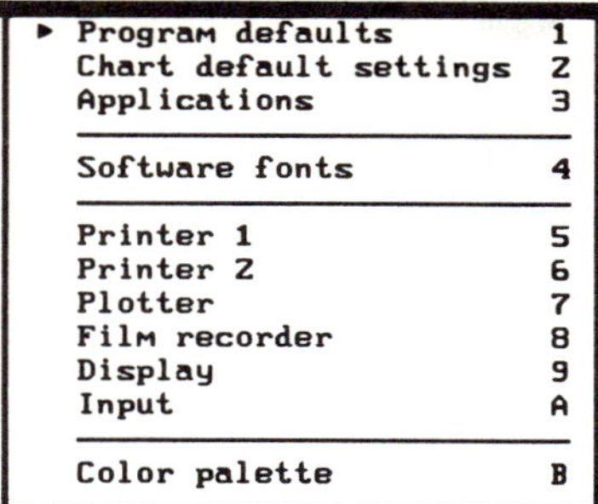

5-1 The Setup submenu.

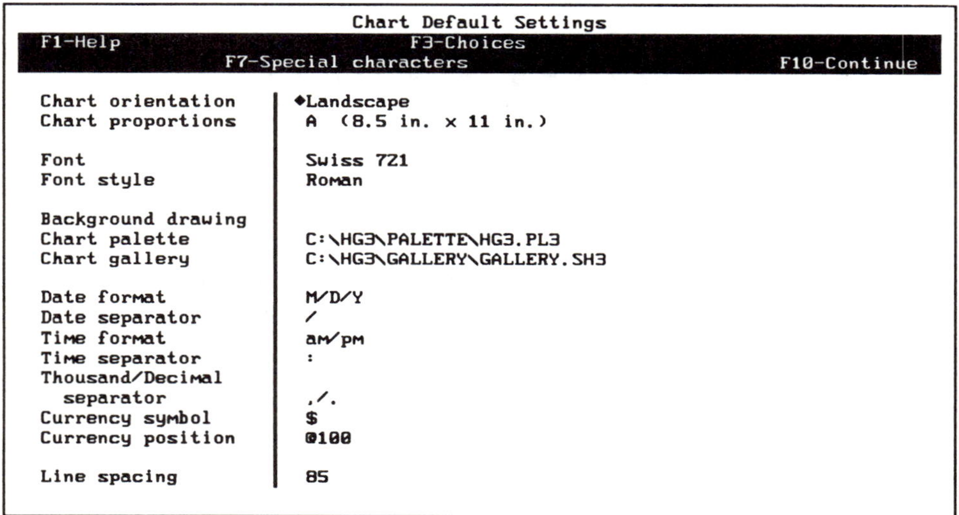

5-2 The Chart Default Settings screen.

ent instructions, the next chart you create (based on the settings you see in Fig. 5-2) will have the following characteristics:

- It will be in landscape orientation
- The printed chart will be 8.5×11 inches
- The font for added text will be Swiss 721
- The font style will be Roman
- There will be no background drawing, unless you select one
- The chart palette will be C: \ HG3 \ PALETTE \ HG3.PL3 (Some other palette file may be showing on your own Chart Default Setting screen.)

To change the chart palette, select it and the palette filename will be highlighted and preceded by a diamond, indicating that you have choices available. Select F3–Choices, and the Get Chart Palette directory listing will appear (see Fig. 5-3).

```
                         Get Chart Palette
  Directory: C:\HG3\PALETTE\*.*
  Filename:  HG3.PL3

 ..                 <DIR>
►HG3       .PL3     PALETTE    Bkg Black        :Cyn, Blu D, Blu, Cyn
 16COLOR   .PL3     PALETTE    Bkg Black        :Pure bright colors
 8COLOR    .PL3     PALETTE    Bkg White        :Fast for color printing
 1SHD      .PL3     PALETTE    Bkg Blu to Blk   :Cyn, Blu D, Blu, Cyn
 2         .PL3     PALETTE    Bkg Blu          :Blu D, BluGry, Blu, Blu
 2SHD      .PL3     PALETTE    Bkg Blu to Gry   :Blu D, BluGry, Blu, Blu
 3         .PL3     PALETTE    Bkg Blu          :Blu D, Blu, Cyn, Red D
 3SHD      .PL3     PALETTE    Bkg Blu to Blu   :Blu D, Blu, Cyn, Red D
 4         .PL3     PALETTE    Bkg Blu          :Blu D, Gry D, Red, Orn
```

5-3 The Get Chart Palette directory lists all the chart palette files.

There are 32 options here, each with a characteristic background and color mix. The files with SHD in the filename have shaded backgrounds—usually from some color to black. I'll have you use 16COLOR.PL3 for this chapter because it usually makes workable monochrome illustrations.

If it's not already visible, click on the down arrow of the Get Chart Palette listing until the 16COLOR.PL3 file appears, then select it by pointing to it and clicking the left mouse button. You'll be returned to the Chart Default Settings screen, where the chart palette is now indicated as C:\HG3\PALETTE\16COLOR.PL3.

Select F10 – Continue, then Esc, to return to the Main Menu. From the Main Menu, select Create chart, then From gallery. The Gallery home screen will be displayed (see Fig. 5-4).

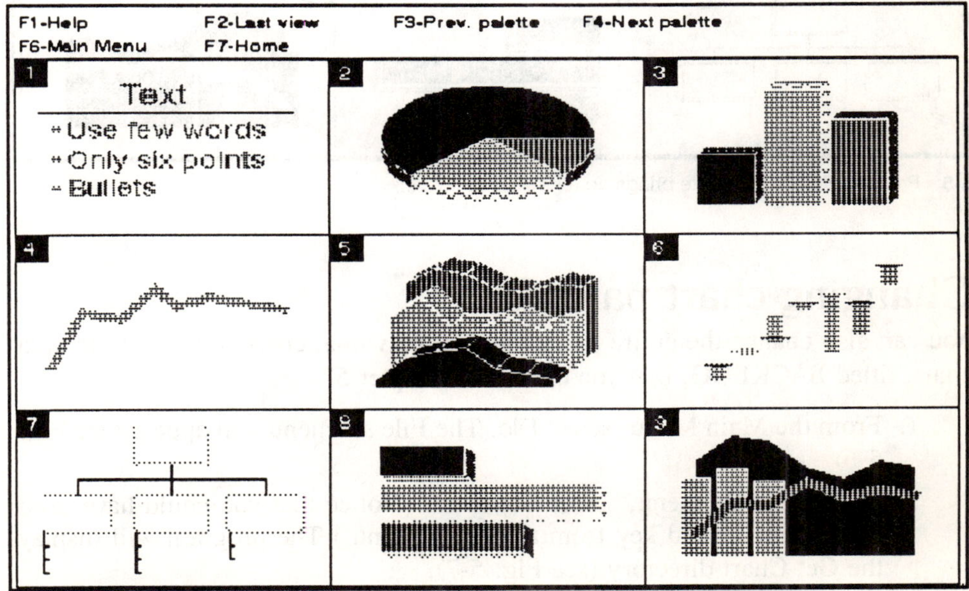

5-4 The Gallery home screen.

The colors in this home screen depend on the chart palette you chose during setup. If you chose HG23.PAL and if you're working with a VGA color monitor, the home screen should have a dark blue textured background and the sample charts should be colored in shades of black, gray, cyan, and yellow.

To change the colors in the Gallery home screen, i.e., to display the home screen with different palettes, simply select F4 – Next palette. The home screen will disappear and reappear in a new palette—in this case, the HG.PL3 palette (see Fig. 5-5). So this is one way to make a major color change—simply click on F4 – Next palette from the Gallery home screen.

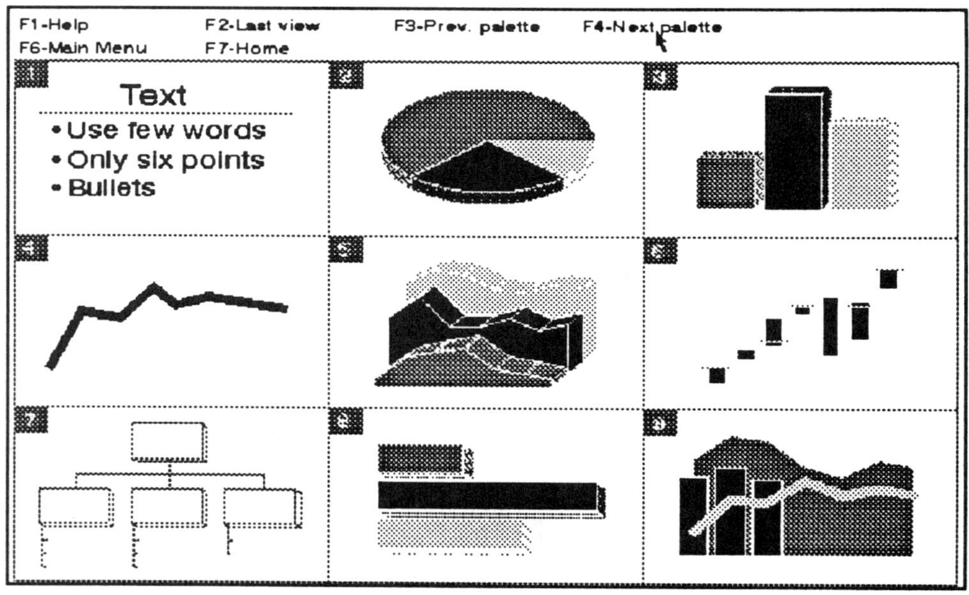

5-5 Pressing F4 – Next palette brings up a new set of colors.

Changing chart palettes

You can also change the entire palette for an individual chart. Let's use the area chart, titled BACKLOG, that you created in chapter 5:

1. From the Main Menu, select File. The File submenu will appear (see Fig. 5-6).
2. At the File submenu, select Get chart. (Notice that you could have used the Ctrl – G speed key from the Main Menu.) The program will display the Get Chart directory (see Fig. 5-7).

```
▸ Get chart              1  Ctrl G
  Get template           2
  Apply template         3
  ─────────────────────────────────
  Save chart             4  Ctrl S
  Save as template       5
  Save as symbol         6
  ─────────────────────────────────
  Import                 7
  Export                 8
```

5-6 The File submenu.

```
                                  Get Chart
     Directory: C:\HG3\DATA\*.CH*
     Filename:   SYLLABUS.CH3
   ─────────────────────────────────────────────────────────────────────────
   ..            <DIR>
  ▸SYLLABUS.CH3  TABLE    Syllabus: English 11-5803
   BLINDS   .CH3 DRAW     Bkg: Horizontal Bands        Use 4,5,7.PL3
   BLUESKY  .CH3 DRAW     Bkg: Sky & Clouds           Use 9 or 10.PL3
   CYLINDER.CH3  DRAW     Bkg: Cylinder blend         Use 3,4,6,7.PL3
   FLOOR    .CH3 DRAW     Bkg: Checkered floor           Use 12HDW.PL3
   FRAME1   .CH3 DRAW     Bkg: single line frame           Use any PL3
   FRAME2   .CH3 DRAW     Bkg: double line frame           Use any PL3
   LEAVES   .CH3 DRAW     Bkg: Leaves               Use 7 or 7SHD.PL3
   LOGOBKG1.CH3  DRAW     Bkg: Use your own logo.pcx       Use any PL3
```

5-7 The directory of available charts.

3. Try out the file sorting utility by selecting F8 – Sort files. When the list has been resorted alphabetically, select the BACKLOG.CH3 file. The chart will appear, as shown in Fig. 5-8.
4. Press Esc to go to the chart data sheet (see Fig. 5-9). Select F8 – Options, and the Options menu will be displayed (see Fig. 5-10).
5. Select Appearance, the third item on this menu. When the Appearance Options menu shows up, it shows that the current chart palette (in this example) is 16COLOR.PL3 (see Fig. 5-11).
6. Click on chart palette. The filename will be highlighted, and the diamond preceding the filename indicates that you have some choices.
7. Select F3 to see the choices. Your screen should display the Get Chart Palette directory that you saw in Fig. 5-3 (see Fig. 5-12). Select HG3.PL3 as your new chart palette.

When you're returned to the Appearance Options menu, the filename for the new palette will appear opposite the chart palette. Select F10 – Continue to return to the chart data screen, and F2 – Show chart. The BACKLOG chart, in all its glorious new palette colors, will fill the screen (see Fig. 5-13). By selecting a new palette, you've changed every element on your original chart: background, text labels, and area indicators.

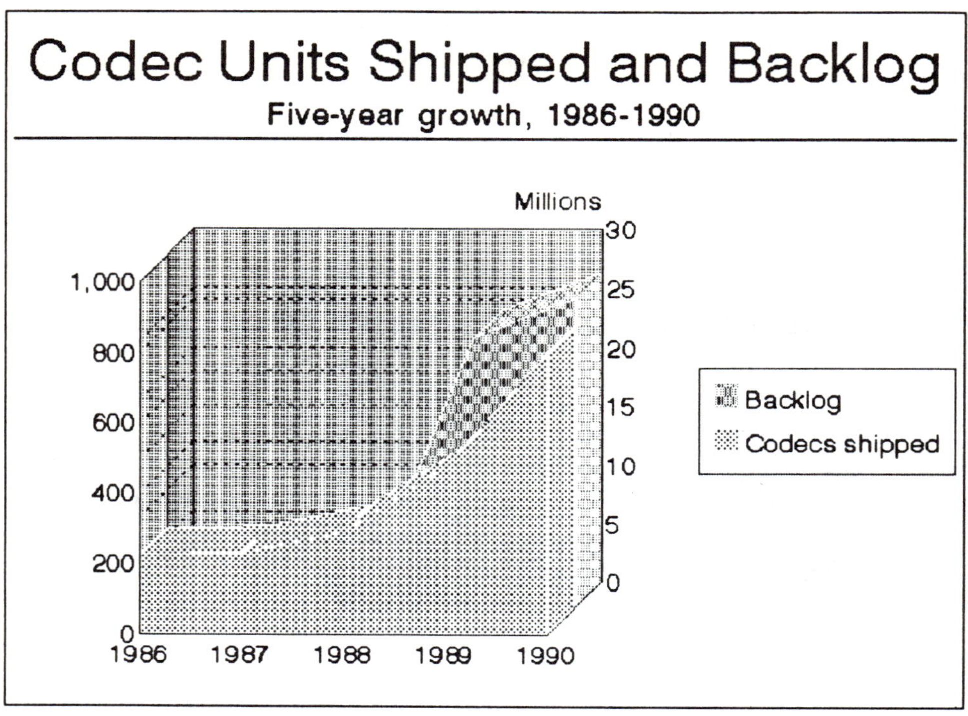

5-8 The area chart named BACKLOG.

BACKLOG.CH3 XY Chart

F1-Help F2-Show chart F4-Draw F5-Mark
F6-Main Menu F7-Spell/Text F8-Options F9-XY data F10-Continue

Title: Codec Units Shipped and Backlog
Subtitle: Five-year growth, 1986-1990
Footnote:

Data Pt	X Axis Year	1 Codecs shi	2 Backlog	3 Series 3	4 Series 4
1	1986	225	363000		
2	1987	231	1762000		
3	1988	292	2200000		
4	1989	478	2.31E+07		
5	1990	802	2.64E+07		
6					
7					
8					
9					
10					
11					
12					

5-9 The data sheet for the Backlog chart.

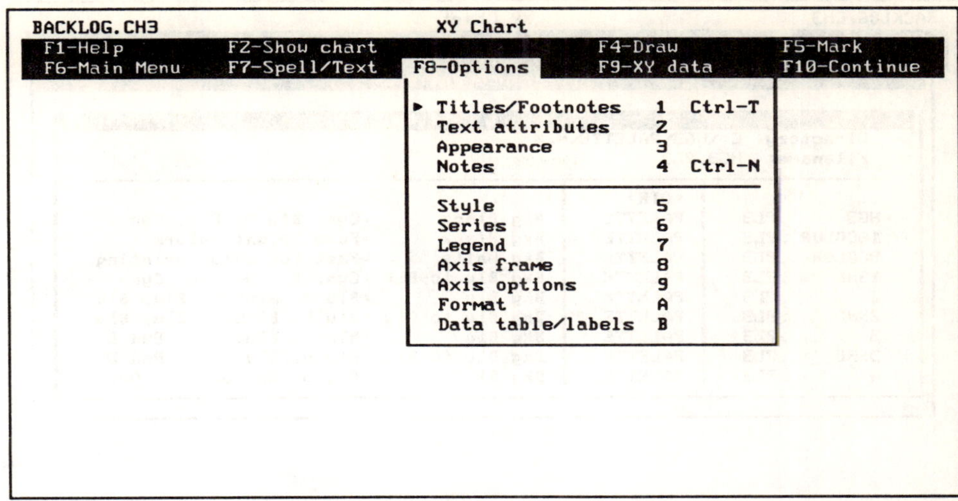

5-10 The Options menu.

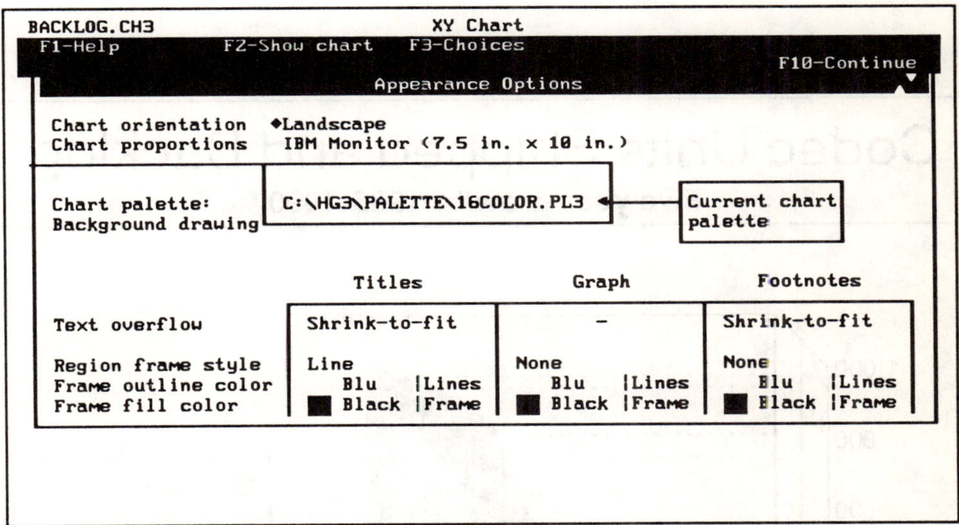

5-11 The Appearance Options menu with the current chart palette.

Changing individual colors in charts

You don't have to change all the colors in a chart by switching to a new palette; you can change individual colors, for instance, of a bar, of a pie slice, of a title, etc. Let's illustrate with that pie chart you created in chapter 4:

1. At the Main Menu, press Ctrl–G to go to the Get Chart menu, i.e., the directory of available charts.

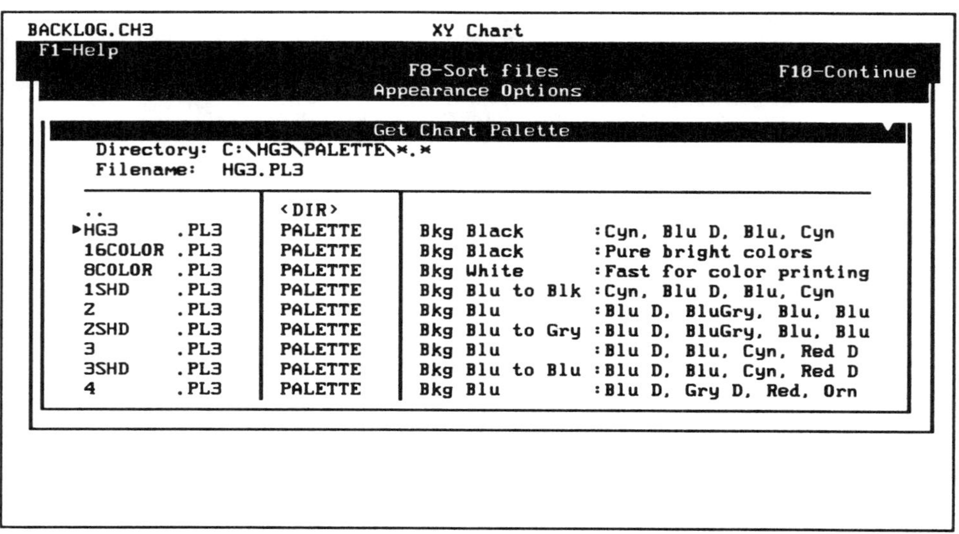

5-12 The Get Chart Palette directory.

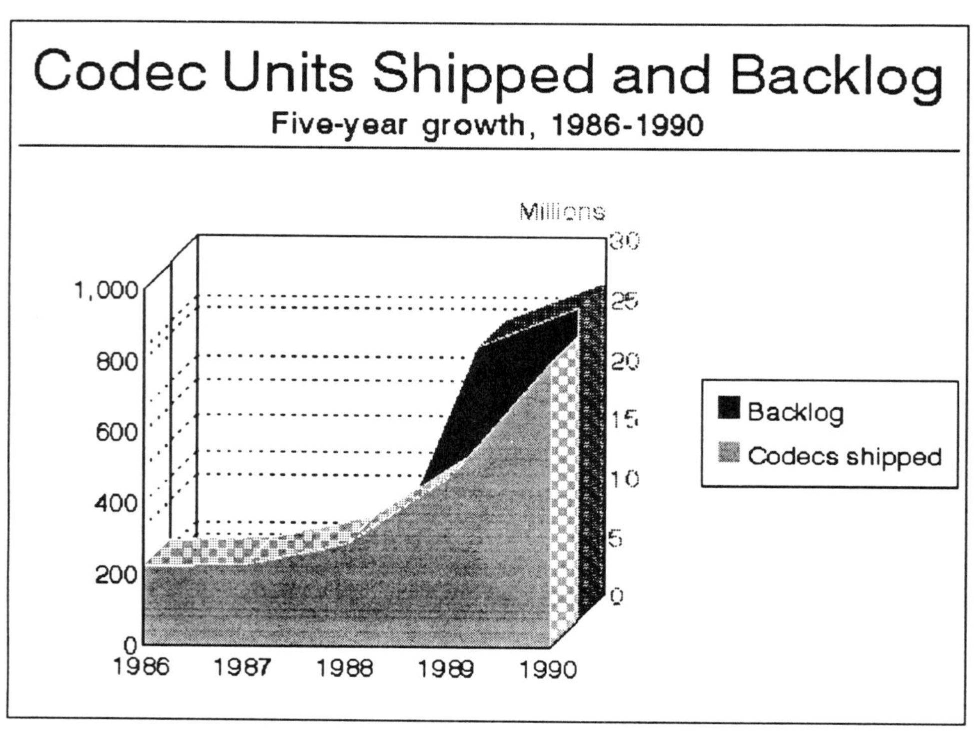

5-13 The Backlog chart in the HG3.PL3 palette colors.

2. Select F8 – Sort files; after the files are resorted, choose COSTS-Q4, the name you gave to the Costs and Expenses pie chart (see Fig. 5-14).
3. Press Esc to go to the chart data screen. Note the slice colors displayed in the Color column. In this case, the cost of sales slice is shown as Cyn D (dark cyan), although the illustration doesn't pick up all the color swatches in this black-and-white rendering (see Fig. 5-15). The chart was originally created with the HG3.PL3 palette.
4. Click on the color in the Slice 1 row. The color is highlighted and preceded by a diamond—which tells you that you have choices.
5. Select F3 – Choices, and the color choice box will appear (see Fig. 5-16).

Because you're working with Slice 1, the program should have assigned the Series 1 color to that slice. Click on the Series 6 color. You'll be returned to the chart data screen, and the Slice 1 color should be the same as the Slice 6 color (see Fig. 5-17). In the case of this illustration, the color is white. Select F2 – Show chart, and the color of your big cost-of-sales slice should now be changed (see Fig. 5-18).

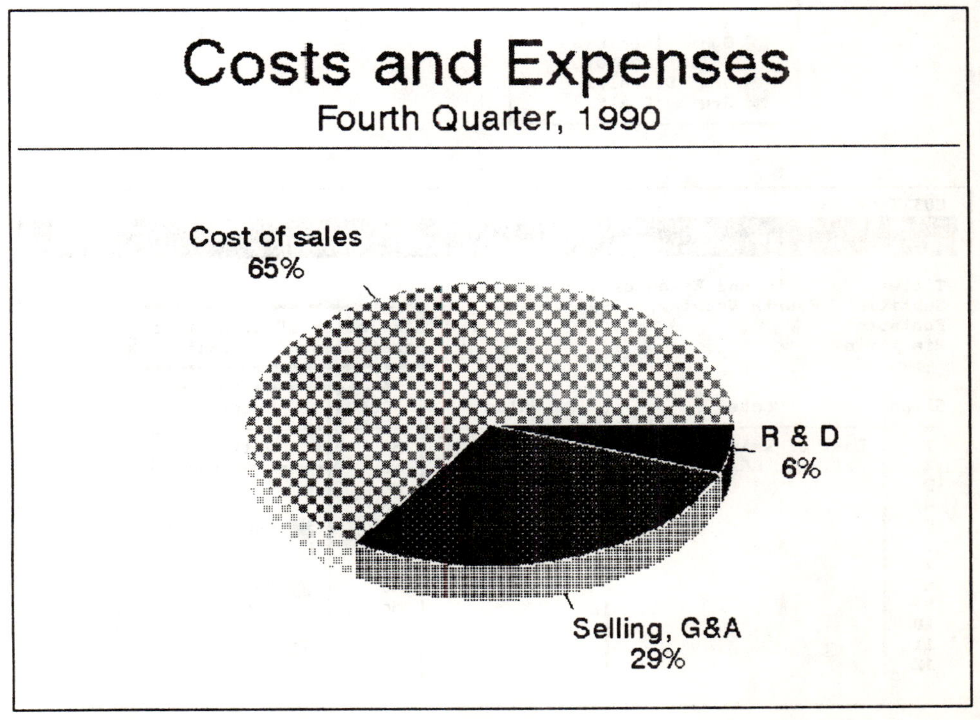

5-14 The Costs and Expenses pie chart.

```
COSTS-Q4.CH3                    Pie Chart 1
 F1-Help        F2-Show chart   F3-Choices      F4-Draw         F5-Mark
 F6-Main Menu   F7-Spell/Text   F8-Options      F9-Pie data     F10-Continue

Title:     Costs and Expenses
Subtitle:  Fourth Quarter, 1990
Footnote:
Pie title:
```

Slice	Label	Value	Cut	Color	Pattern
1	Cost of sales	10134	No	Blu |S	0
2	Selling, G&A	4472	No	Orn |S	1
3	R & D	871	No	Grn |S	2
4			No	Red |S	3
5			No	Cyn |S	4
6			No	White |S	5
7			No	Blu |S	6
8			No	Orn |S	7
9			No	Grn |S	8
10			No	Red |S	9
11			No	Cyn |S	10
12			No	White |S	11

5-15 The chart data screen; slice 1 is shown as blue.

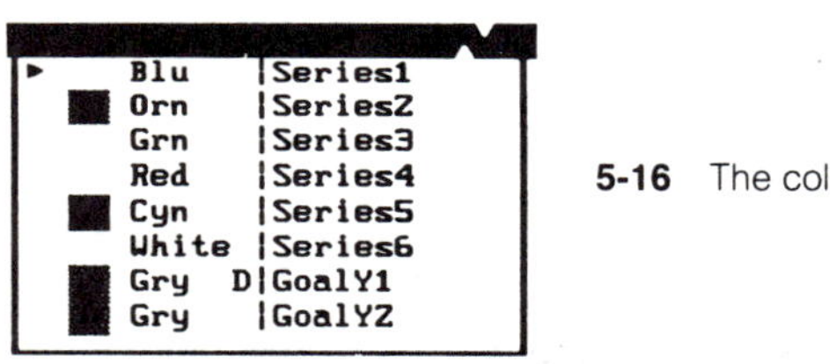

5-16 The color choice box.

```
COSTS-Q4.CH3                    Pie Chart 1
 F1-Help        F2-Show chart   F3-Choices      F4-Draw         F5-Mark
 F6-Main Menu   F7-Spell/Text   F8-Options      F9-Pie data     F10-Continue

Title:     Costs and Expenses
Subtitle:  Fourth Quarter, 1990
Footnote:
Pie title:
```

The color of Slice 1 has been changed to White.

Slice	Label	Value	Cut	Color	Pattern
1	Cost of sales	10134	No	◆ White |S	0
2	Selling, G&A	4472	No		1
3	R & D	871	No	Grn |S	2
4			No	Red |S	3
5			No	Cyn |S	4
6			No	White |S	5
7			No	Blu |S	6
8			No	Orn |S	7
9			No	Grn |S	8
10			No	Red |S	9
11			No	Cyn |S	10
12			No	White |S	11

5-17 The slice-1 color is now the same as the slice-6 color.

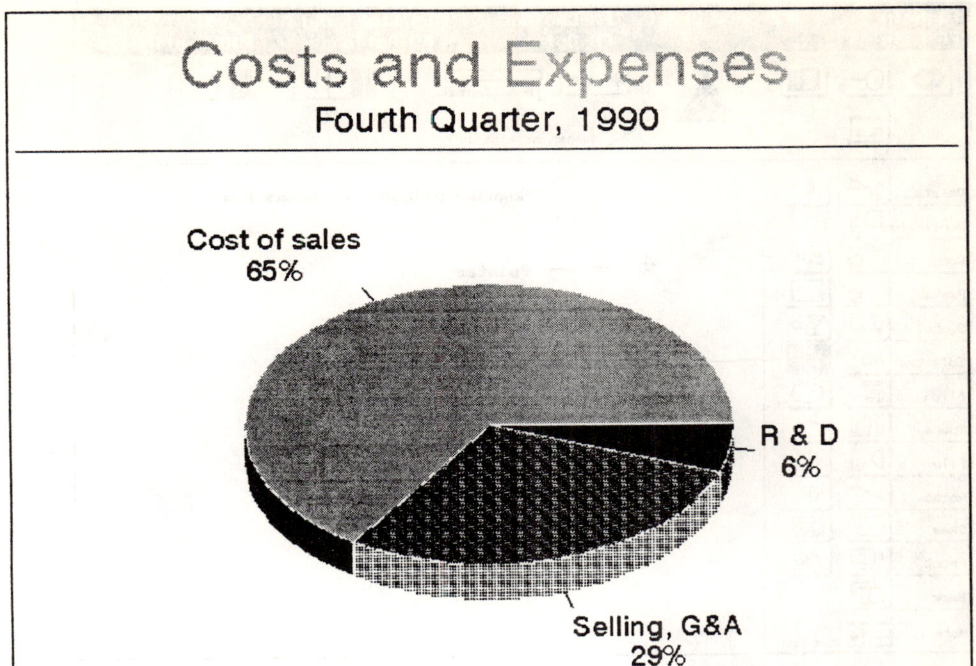

5-18 The Costs of sales slice in its new color.

Changing colors in Draw

In chapter 6, you dealt briefly with the process of changing the color of a Draw object. I'll explain that process in a bit more detail right here:

1. From the Main Menu, select Draw.
2. When the Draw screen appears, select the regular polygon and position the cross-hair pointer in the upper left-hand corner of your canvas, ready to mark the center of the regular polygon you're going to draw (see Fig. 5-19).
3. Click left to set the center of your polygon, then move the pointer downward on your canvas to draw the triangle. (The triangle is the default choice for the regular polygon.)
4. If you want a regular polygon with more sides, change the number in the Number of sides box at the top of your Draw screen.
5. Click right to complete the triangle, which will be filled with the default Fill color. In the screens on which the figures for this chapter are based, the selected Chart palette is MONOCHRW.PL3, and the default fill color is gray (see Fig. 5- 20).

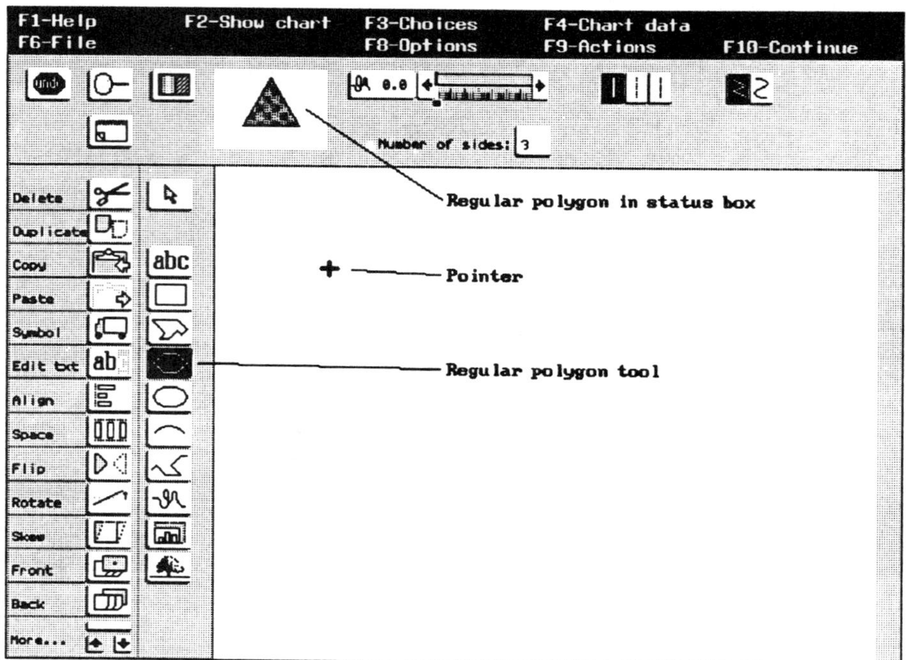

5-19 The regular polygon tool is selected.

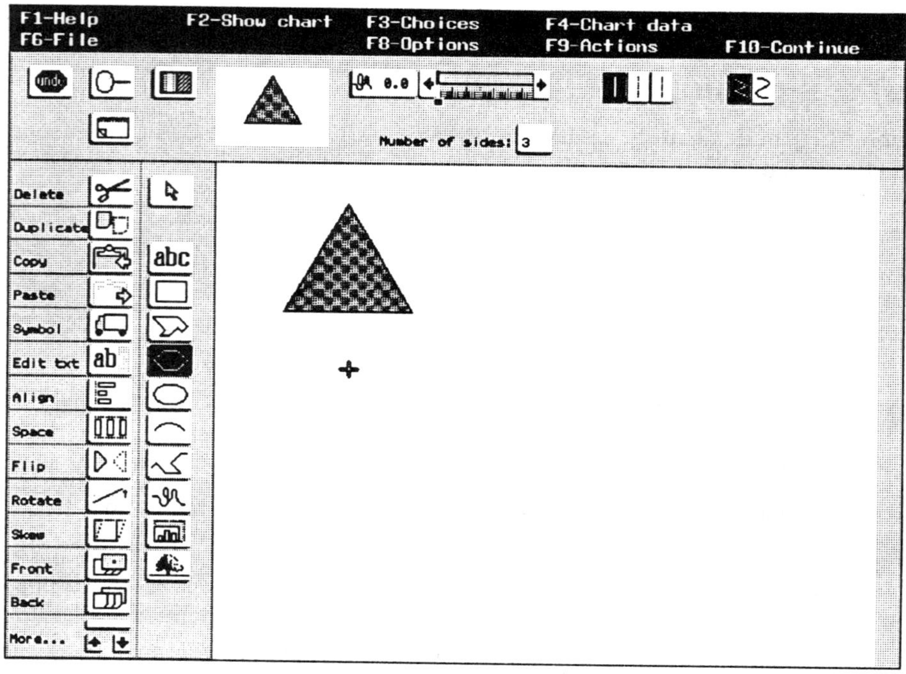

5-20 The first triangle, filled with gray.

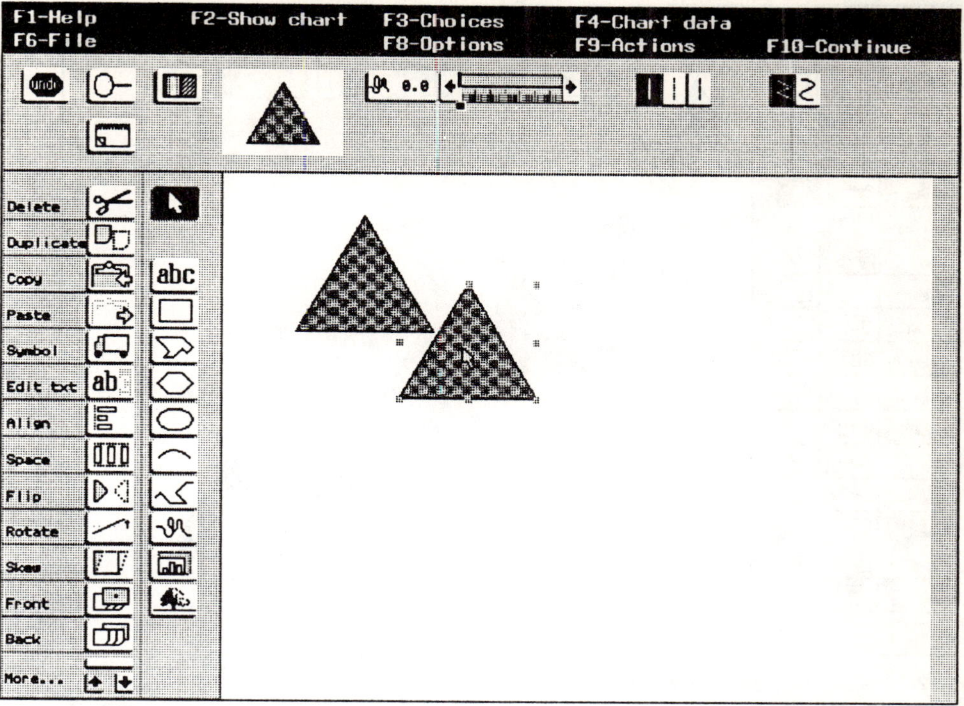

5-21 The duplicated triangle, moved away from the original.

6. Click on the Duplicate tool to create a clone of your triangle, then drag the new triangle diagonally down and to the right of the original (see Fig. 5-21). This determines that the next duplicate will be placed at the same diagonal distance.
7. Make three more duplicates of the triangle. There should now be five, arranged approximately as in Fig. 5-22.

Now you can change the color of these five triangles. Click on the first triangle to select it, then select the color icon. The color panel will appear. The colors arrayed under Chart colors are the colors of your current chart palette. In Fig. 5-23, you can see that there are two rows of colors in the chart colors palette, and that gray is highlighted as the default fill color. (This applies to the MONOCH RW.PL3 palette, which is being used for this demo.) Note that the color is described in words: Gry¦TextDim. That means that the color description is gray, and that in this palette it's the color assigned to text of diminished intensity.

Let's assign some new colors to these triangles. (In these illustrations, unfortunately, you're limited to shades of gray.) Select the black in the top left corner on the top row for the first triangle. Note that, when you click on the color tile, it's

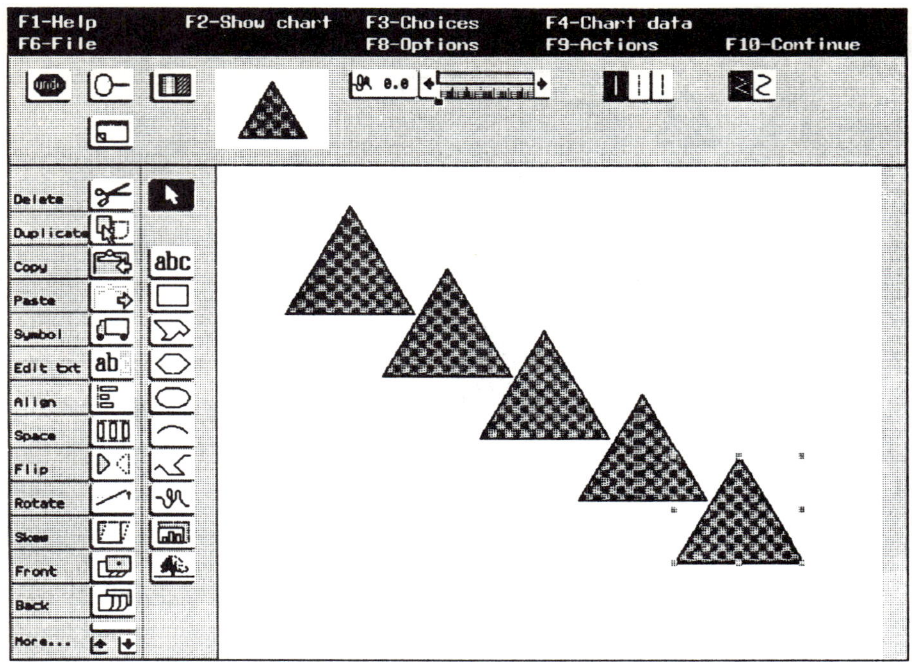

5-22 The original triangle and four copies.

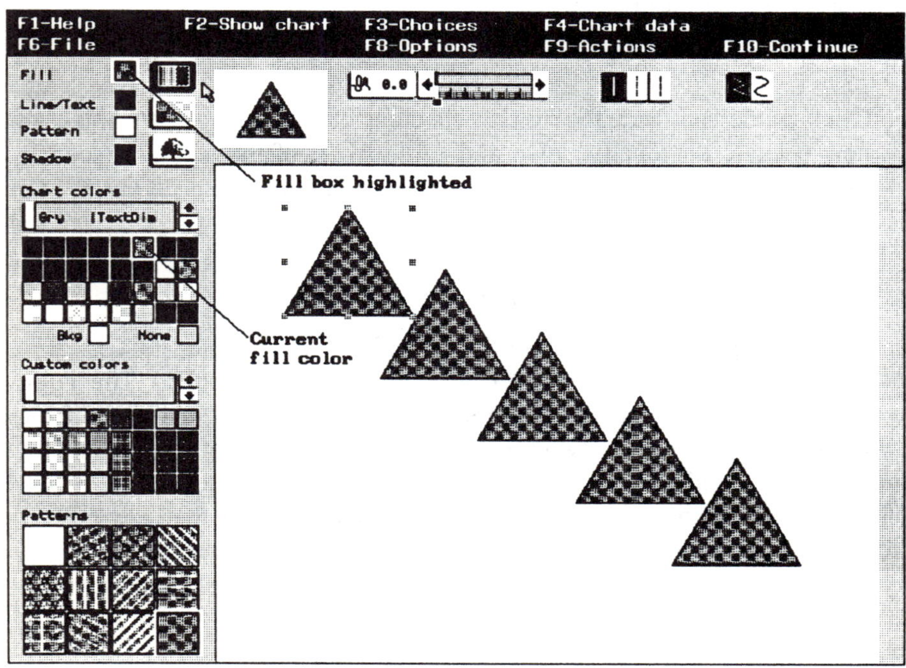

5-23 The color panel, with gray (Gry) highlighted.

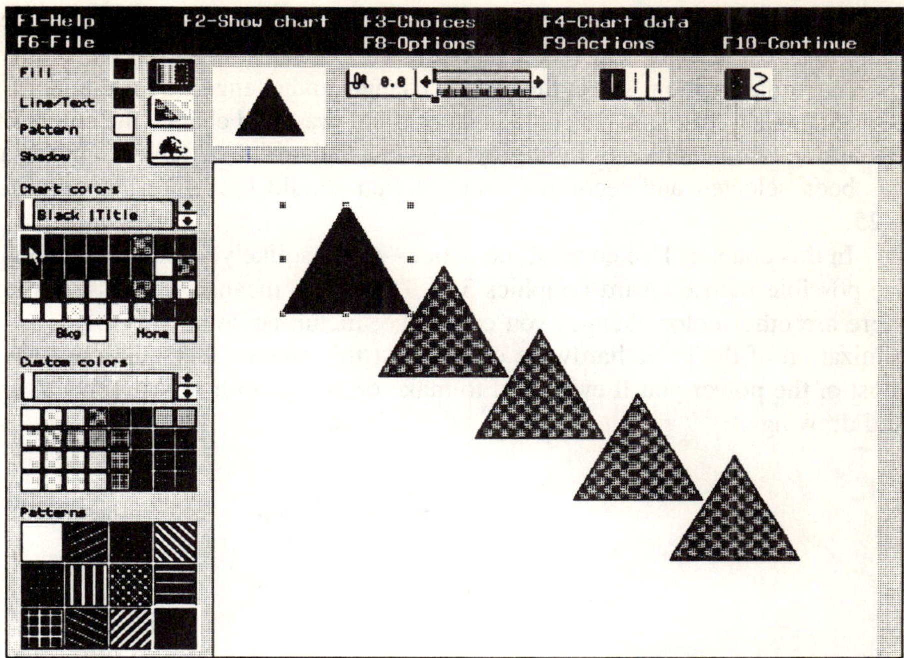

5-24 Black is highlighted and the triangle color is changed.

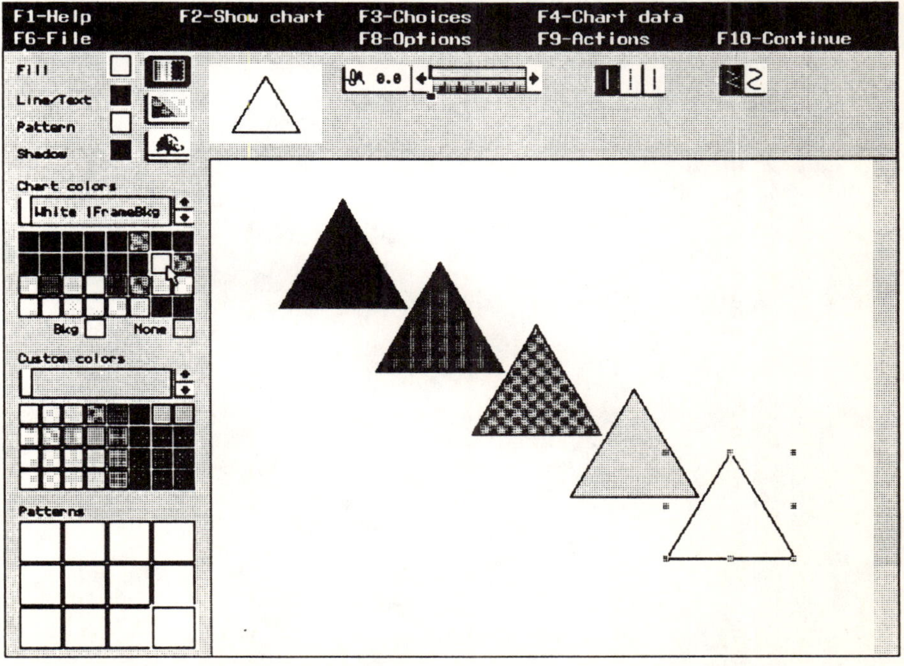

5-25 The five triangles with new colors.

highlighted, the name of the color is displayed in the text block, and the selected triangle takes on that color (see Fig. 5-24).

In similar fashion, select the second triangle and change its color to dark gray (Gry DD). Leave the third triangle in its original gray, and change the colors of the remaining two triangles to light gray (Gry LL) and white. After the final triangle has been selected and recolored, your screen should look like the one in Fig. 5-25.

In this chapter, I've covered the major—or most likely—color alterations that are possible with Harvard Graphics 3.0. This by no means exhausts the subject; there are other color changes you can make, including some very personal customization of the basic hardware colors. But this chapter's discussion gives you most of the power you'll ever need to make ordinary color adjustments to charts and drawings.

6
CHAPTER

Quick presentations

One of the most useful and powerful features of Harvard Graphics 3.0 is the ability it gives you to organize charts and drawings into presentations. You might want graphics to accompany a talk you're making; text screens, product photos, and performance charts for a stand-alone sales presentation; or financial data in graphic form as a sort of electronic annual or quarterly report to send to the money managers and securities analysts who follow your company. All of this (and more!) is possible with the Presentation function of Harvard Graphics 3.0.

In this chapter, you're going to get an introduction to the basics of the Presentation function—enough to make it possible for you to put together, quickly, a very professional-looking presentation. You'll take the charts you created in chapters 2–5, all based on the Compression Labs, Inc. 1990 annual report, and arrange them into a presentation of financial data that could form the core of, say, the CEO's discussion with a group of securities analysts.

Begin, as usual, at the Main Menu. From the Main Menu, select Presentation, item 6, and the Presentation submenu will appear (see Fig. 6-1). From the Presentation submenu, select Create presentation, or press 1. Your monitor should display the Edit Presentation data screen. This is your sheet for a listing of the files (charts or drawings) that will go into your presentation—their sequence, filenames, types (XY, bullet, org, draw, etc.), descriptions, and the directories in which they're found (see Fig. 6-2).

Begin by adding the charts that will comprise your presentation to the listing. Select F7–Add/Edit. The Add/Edit menu will pop up (see Fig. 6-3). As you'll probably have guessed, because most of Harvard Graphics 3.0 operates by intui-

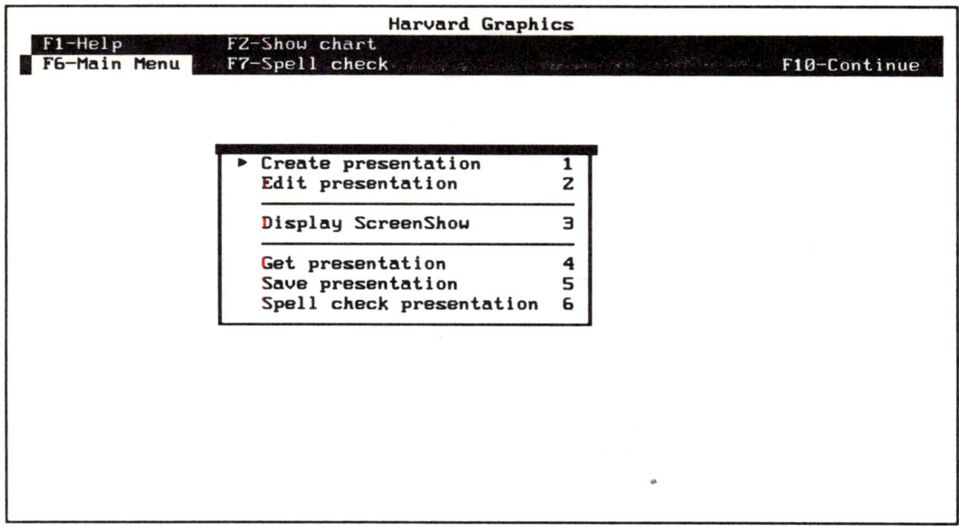

6-1 The Presentation submenu.

Edit Presentation

F1-Help F2-Preview F4-Effects F5-Mark block
F6-Main Menu F7-Add/Edit F8-Options F9-HyperShow F10-Continue

#	Filename	Type	Description/Directory
▶		DRAW	Background drawing for presentation
1			
2			
3			
4			
5			
6			
7			
8			
9			
10			
11			
12			
13			
14			
15			
16			

6-2 The Edit Presentation data sheet.

tive common sense and a good menu system, you should select the first item, Add file. Note that there are four ways to do this:

- Because Add file was highlighted when the Add/Edit menu popped up, you can summon that function simply by pressing Enter.
- You can move the mouse pointer to any point on the Add file line and click the left button.

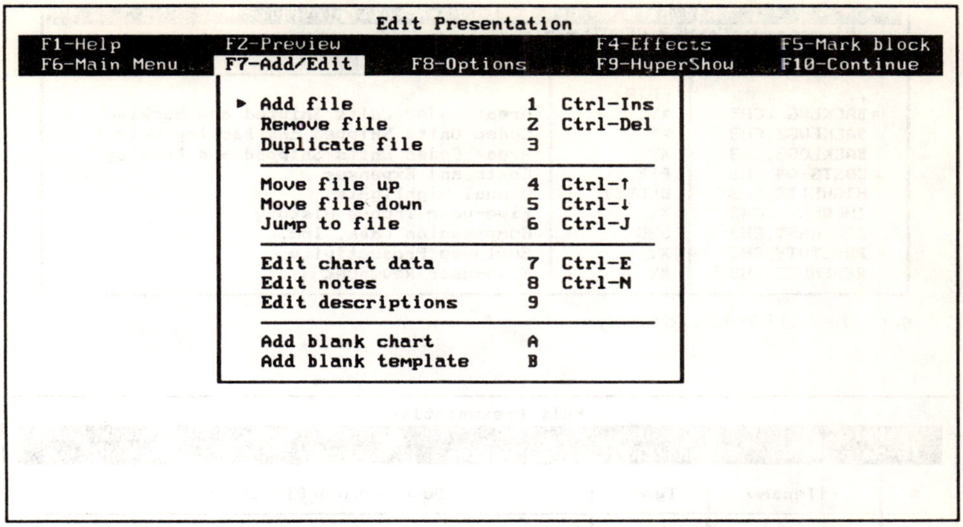

```
                         Edit Presentation
F1-Help        F2-Preview                     F4-Effects     F5-Mark block
F6-Main Menu   F7-Add/Edit    F8-Options      F9-HyperShow   F10-Continue

               ► Add file               1  Ctrl-Ins
                 Remove file            2  Ctrl-Del
                 Duplicate file         3

                 Move file up           4  Ctrl-↑
                 Move file down         5  Ctrl-↓
                 Jump to file           6  Ctrl-J

                 Edit chart data        7  Ctrl-E
                 Edit notes             8  Ctrl-N
                 Edit descriptions      9

                 Add blank chart        A
                 Add blank template     B
```

6-3 The Add/Edit menu.

- You can press 1.
- Ctrl–Ins is indicated as the speed-key combination, so you can press Ctrl–Ins at the Edit Presentation data screen and bypass the Add/Edit menu altogether.

Once you make your selection with any of these four options, the Add File menu, looking very much like your old friend the Chart file directory, will appear (see Fig. 6-4). Note: This directory might look different from your own; I've set up a special directory, called C:\HG3\DEMOS, specifically for the charts and drawings created in the exercises of this book.)

1. Press F8–Sort files. The first file you come to in your directory listing should be BACKLOG.CH3, the area chart you created showing codec units shipped and backlog.
2. Click on this file to select it for your presentation. It will instantly appear as the first file in your listing on the Edit Presentation sheet (see Fig. 6-5).
3. Press Ctrl–Ins to return to the Add File directory.
4. Notice that the top bar of this directory tells you to Press F5 to mark multiple files. Do that now to save a bunch of steps. Use the down arrow key to move to the COSTS-Q4 file and press F5.
5. Move on down to the HIGHLITE file, noting that the COSTS-Q4 file listing remains highlighted. Press F5 again.
6. Follow same procedure for INCOME, ORGCHART, PRDCTVTY, REVENUES, and STOCKS files. You should now have seven files highlighted.

```
                    Add File (Press F5 to mark multiple files)
   Directory: C:\HG3\DEMOS\*.*
   Filename:  BACKLOG.CH3

 ..           <DIR>
►BACKLOG .CH3  XY        Area: Codec Units Shipped and Backlog
 BACKLOG2.CH3  XY        Codec Units Shipped and Backlog w/text
 BACKLOG3.CH3  XY        Area: Codec Units Shipped and Backlog
 COSTS-Q4.CH3  PIE       Costs and Expenses
 HIGHLITE.CH3  BULLET    Annual Highlights
 INCOME  .CH3  XY        Five-year Income History
 ORGCHART.CH3  ORG       Compression Labs, Inc.
 PRDCTVTY.CH3  XY        Employee Productivity
 REVENUES.CH3  XY        Five-year Revenues
```

6-4 The Add File menu/directory.

```
                         Edit Presentation
 F1-Help        F2-Preview                    F4-Effects     F5-Mark block
 F6-Main Menu   F7-Add/Edit    F8-Options     F9-HyperShow   F10-Continue

 #  | Filename     | Type  | Description/Directory
    |              | DRAW  | Background drawing for presentation
►1  | BACKLOG .CH3 | XY    | Area: Codec Units Shipped and Backlog
 2
 3
 4
 5
 6
 7
 8
 9
 10
 11
 12
 13
 14
 15
 16
```

6-5 The first file listed on the Presentation data sheet.

7. Select F10 – Continue. You'll be immediately returned to the Edit Presentation screen, where all eight of the files you selected for your presentation are listed (see Fig. 6-6).

You could run the presentation right now—but you might not like the order. Let's come up with an order that makes a bit more sense. Here's a possibility: Begin with the text chart that lists the highlights; then show revenues, income, costs, backlog, employee productivity, and stock prices; and end with the organization chart.

So now you have all those files to move around, right? Not to worry; simply highlight the file you want to move and use either Ctrl – up arrow or Ctrl – down arrow to move it.

```
                                 Edit Presentation
 F1-Help            F2-Preview                      F4-Effects        F5-Mark block
 F6-Main Menu       F7-Add/Edit      F8-Options     F9-HyperShow      F10-Continue

 #  | Filename     | Type    |         Description/Directory
----|--------------|---------|------------------------------------------------
    |              | DRAW    | Background drawing for presentation
----|--------------|---------|------------------------------------------------
 1  | BACKLOG .CH3 | XY      | Area: Codec Units Shipped and Backlog
►2  | COSTS-Q4.CH3 | PIE     | Costs and Expenses
 3  | HIGHLITE.CH3 | BULLET  | Annual Highlights
 4  | INCOME  .CH3 | XY      | Five-year Income History
 5  | ORGCHART.CH3 | ORG     | Compression Labs, Inc.
 6  | PRDCTVTY.CH3 | XY      | Employee Productivity
 7  | REVENUES.CH3 | XY      | Five-year Revenues
 8  | STOCKS  .CH3 | XY      | Quarterly Stock Prices
 9  |              |         |
 10 |              |         |
 11 |              |         |
 12 |              |         |
 13 |              |         |
 14 |              |         |
 15 |              |         |
 16 |              |         |
```

6-6 The presentation listing now has eight files.

1. Click on HIGHLITE.CH3, hold down Ctrl, and press the up arrow until the file is in the number 1 slot.
2. Click on REVENUES.CH3, and use Ctrl–up arrow to move it up to line 2.
3. In the same way, move INCOME.CH3 into #3, COSTS-Q4.CH3 into #4, BACKLOG.CH3 into #5, PRDCTVTY.CH3 into #6, STOCKS.CH3 into #7, and ORGCHART.CH3 into #8. When you're finished, the Edit Presentation data sheet should look like Fig. 6-7.
4. Click on the first file, HIGHLITE, to highlight it, then press F2–Preview. (The preview will begin with the highlighted file, whatever it is.)

The text chart will appear and stay on the screen until you click the right mouse button, or press the right arrow key (or most other keys). When you do, the chart showing five-year revenues is displayed.

To move ahead, press the right button. To view the previous chart in the sequence, press the left button. To leave the preview mode and return to the Edit Presentation data sheet, press Esc.

Move through the preview until you return to the data screen. Let's add one more touch, then save the presentation for future viewing and editing. One of the choices in the menu bar at the top of the screen is F4–Effects. Press it, and the Edit Presentation screen will be changed. Opposite the file listings are columns devoted to the manner in which charts and drawings are displayed—including Draw direction and speed, time, and erase direction and speed (see Fig. 6-8).

```
CLIXSHOW.SH3                          Edit Presentation
 F1-Help        F2-Preview                          F4-Effects     F5-Mark block
 F6-Main Menu   F7-Add/Edit     F8-Options          F9-HyperShow   F10-Continue

 #  | Filename       | Type    |          Description/Directory
-----------------------------------------------------------------------------
    |                | DRAW    | Background drawing for presentation
-----------------------------------------------------------------------------
 1  |  HIGHLITE.CH3  | BULLET  | Annual Highlights
 2  |  REVENUES.CH3  | XY      | Five-year Revenues
 3  |  INCOME  .CH3  | XY      | Five-year Income History
 4  |  COSTS-Q4.CH3  | PIE     | Costs and Expenses
 5  |  BACKLOG .CH3  | XY      | Area: Codec Units Shipped and Backlog
 6  |  PRDCTVTY.CH3  | XY      | Employee Productivity
►7  |  STOCKS  .CH3  | XY      | Quarterly Stock Prices
 8  |  ORGCHART.CH3  | ORG     | Compression Labs, Inc.
 9  |                |         |
 10 |                |         |
 11 |                |         |
 12 |                |         |
 13 |                |         |
 14 |                |         |
 15 |                |         |
 16 |                |         |
```

6-7 The Edit Presentation data sheet with sequenced charts.

```
CLIXSHOW.SH3                          Edit Presentation
 F1-Help        F2-Preview     F3-Choices     F4-Descriptions F5-Mark block
 F6-Main Menu   F7-Add/Edit    F8-Options     F9-HyperShow    F10-Continue

 #  | Filename       |  Draw    | ←↑↓→ | Speed |Time| Erase   | ←↑↓→ | Speed
-----------------------------------------------------------------------------
    |                | Replace  |      |       |    |         |      |
-----------------------------------------------------------------------------
►1  |  HIGHLITE.CH3  | ◆        |      |       |    |         |      |
 2  |  REVENUES.CH3  |          |      |       |    |         |      |
 3  |  INCOME  .CH3  |          |      |       |    |         |      |
 4  |  COSTS-Q4.CH3  |          |      |       |    |         |      |
 5  |  BACKLOG .CH3  |          |      |       |    |         |      |
 6  |  PRDCTVTY.CH3  |          |      |       |    |         |      |
 7  |  STOCKS  .CH3  |          |      |       |    |         |      |
 8  |  ORGCHART.CH3  |          |      |       |    |         |      |
 9  |                |          |      |       |    |         |      |
 10 |                |          |      |       |    |         |      |
 11 |                |          |      |       |    |         |      |
 12 |                |          |      |       |    |         |      |
 13 |                |          |      |       |    |         |      |
 14 |                |          |      |       |    |         |      |
 15 |                |          |      |       |    |         |      |
 16 |                |          |      |       |    |         |      |
```

6-8 The Effects page of the Edit Presentation data screen.

Time refers to the duration of the chart or drawing on the screen. You can set a time in the row between the two horizontal lines that will apply to every chart, or you can set individual times for each chart.

Click in the top row, immediately under Time, to locate the cursor. Type :05 and Enter (five seconds), and 0:05 will appear in that location. That means that each chart will remain on the screen for approximately five seconds. To test what you've done, select F2 – Preview. Sure enough, the charts are displayed for about five seconds each as the presentation cycles through the charts.

There are many more refinements and enhancements that you can wreak upon presentations—but I'll save those for the chapter on advanced presentations.

1. Select F6 – Main Menu, then Presentation, then Save presentation. The Save Presentation box will appear with the cursor blinking opposite Filename.
2. Because the stock market ticker symbol for Compression Labs is CLIX, name the file CLIXSHOW (no extension needed; the program will provide that) and press the Enter key.
3. Opposite Description type Compression Lab annual report summary. Your screen should now look something like Fig. 6-9.
4. Select F10 – Continue, then F6 – Main Menu.

```
                     Save Presentation
Directory:    C:\HG3\DEMOS
Filename:     clixshow
Description:  Compression Lab annual report summary
```

6-9 The Save Presentation box with the filename entered.

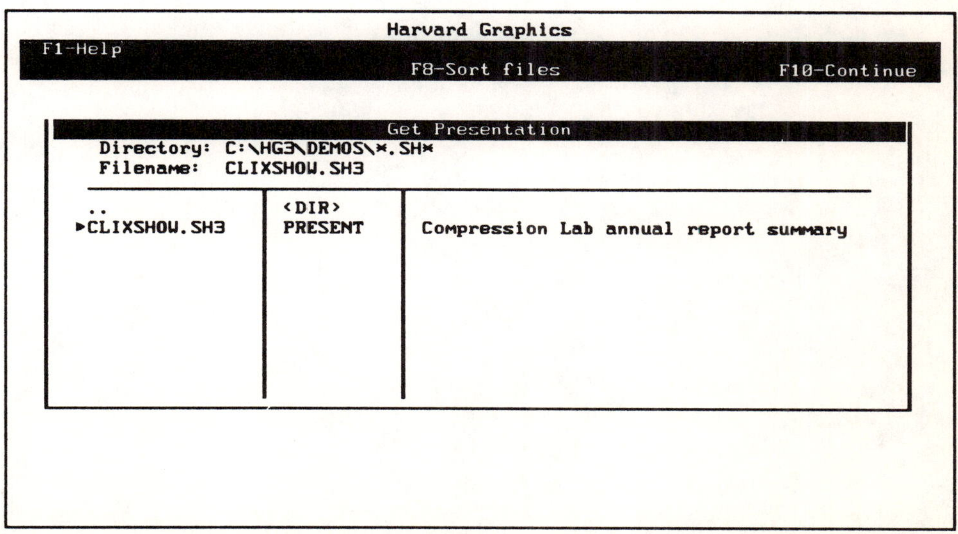

6-10 The Get Presentation box with your new presentation file.

5. From the Main Menu, select Presentation, then Display ScreenShow. The show will begin, running through the entire sequence and returning to the Main Menu when it's through.

You've done it. If you want to look more like a professional designer, there will be ample opportunity later on. For now, however, you should be content with your new status as a producer of presentations.

7
CHAPTER

Using symbols

So you're not an artist—or don't think you are. You can't sit down with pencil and paper and draw a cypress tree, or a hospital, or the flag of Saudi Arabia, or four people sitting at a table. And even if you can, the process of creating good, detailed drawings on a computer screen or tablet is still fairly crude.

But don't despair; Harvard Graphics 3.0 has just what you've been looking for in its Symbol function: over 500 ready-made images, drawings of all kinds, many in color, that you can use by themselves or in conjunction with charts or other drawings.

The Harvard Graphics 3.0 symbols can be sized, colored, and otherwise modified. To illustrate this, you can take one of the off-the-rack symbols, add some text to it, and turn it into a symbol of your own making that might be useful in the presentation you started building in chapter 6.

1. From the Main Menu, select Draw.
2. At the Draw screen, click on the Symbol icon (see Fig. 7-1). Four more Symbol icons or buttons will appear, buttons you can push to get, save, or delete a symbol, plus a button labeled Logo, whose function you'll get to later (see Fig. 7-2).
3. Select Get, and the Get Symbol File directory, a listing of files that are themselves collections of symbols, will pop up (see Fig. 7-3).
4. You're going to extract a symbol from the HUMANS5 file, so click on that filename (all symbol files have the extension .SY3). Your screen will be filled with sixteen symbols, many of them with color, and their names (see Fig. 7-4).
5. You're going to use the symbol named Presenter, in row 3, column 3. Click on that symbol and its name will be highlighted (see Fig. 7-5).

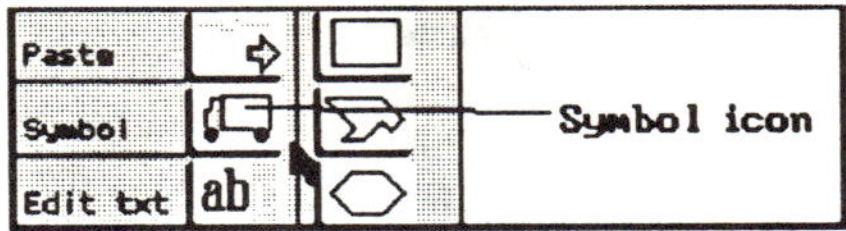

7-1 The Symbol icon.

7-2 The four symbol buttons.

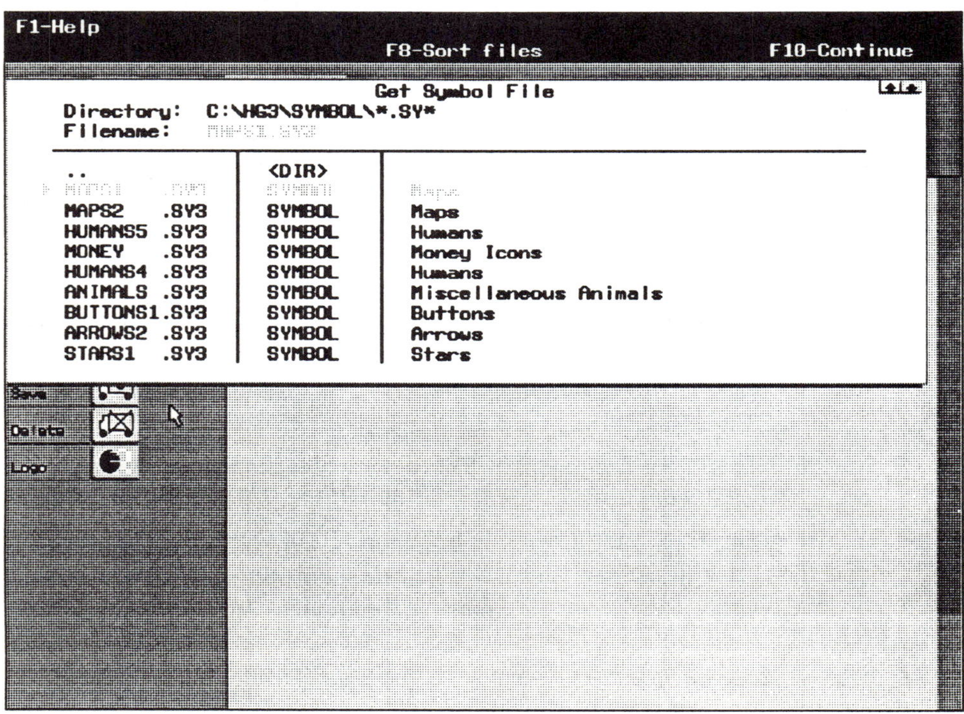

7-3 The Get Symbol File directory.

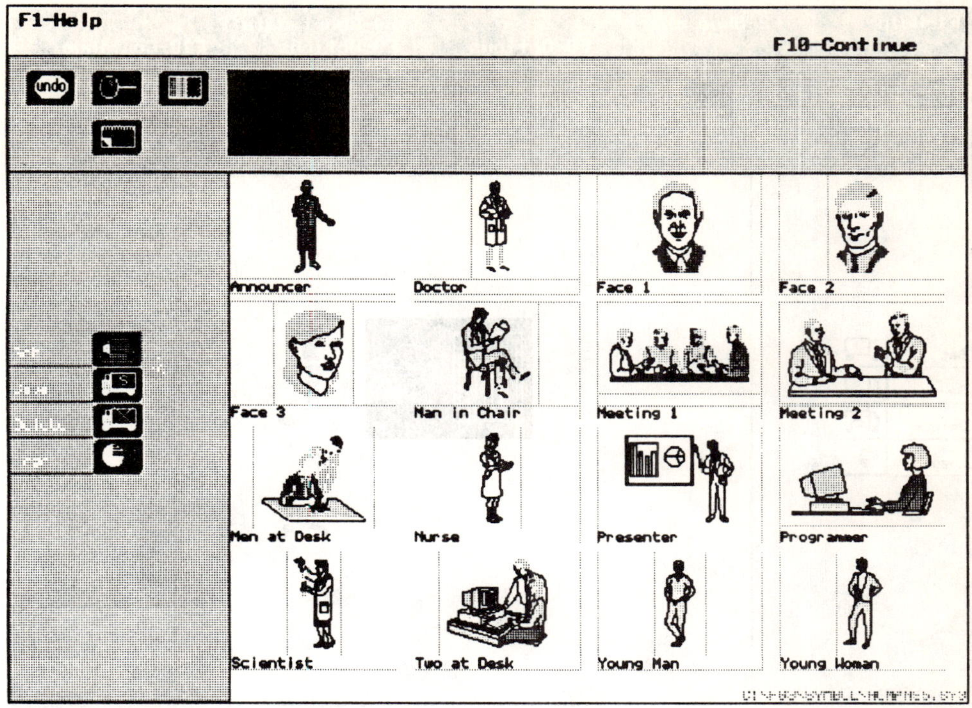

7-4 The 16 symbols in the HUMANS5 file.

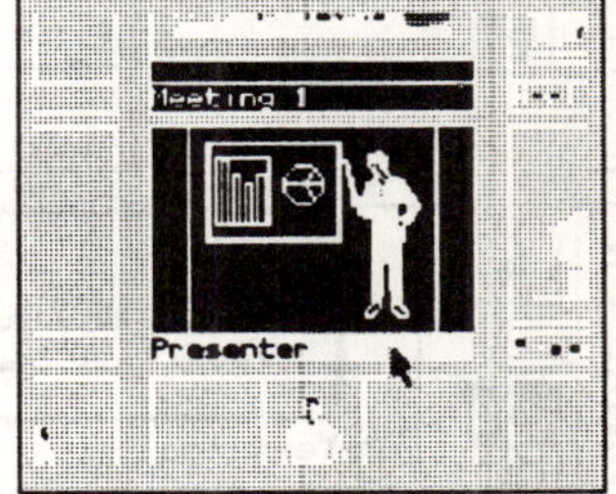

7-5 The selected Presenter symbol with its name highlighted.

6. Press F10 – Continue, and the Presenter symbol will appear alone on your canvas and in the status box (see Fig. 7-6).
7. Click the right mouse button to bring back the Drawing tools, and you're ready to manipulate this symbol.

Now you're going to create a line of text and group it with the Presenter symbol to create a new symbol. Click on the Text tool. After a couple of seconds a message will appear telling you to drag a box or click on a point in the drawing area where you want the text to appear (see Fig. 7-7).

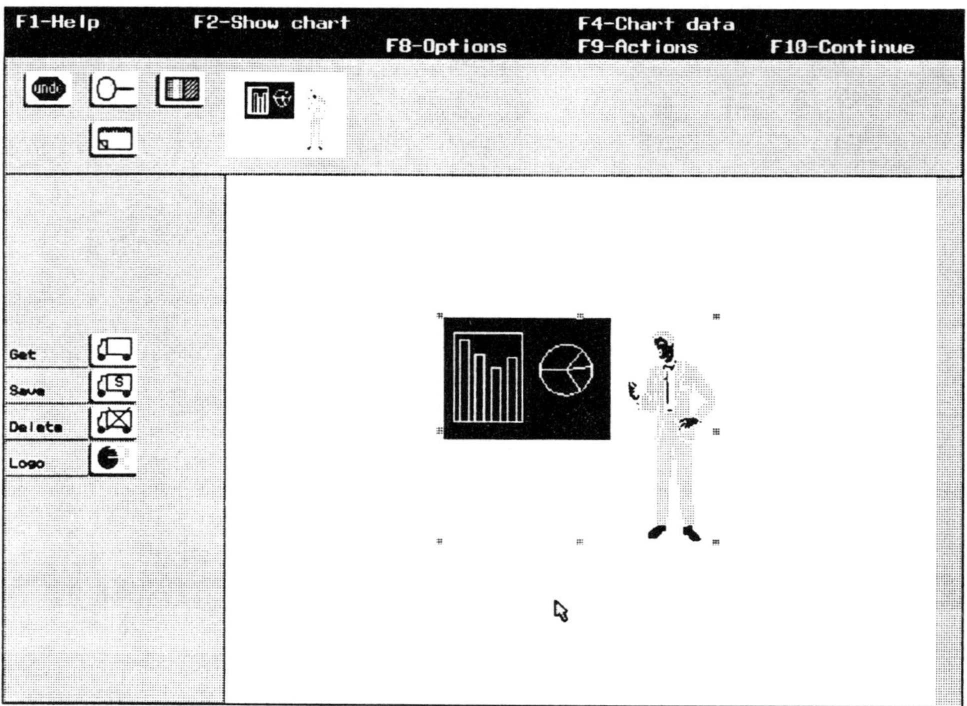

7-6 The Presenter symbol on your canvas and in the status box.

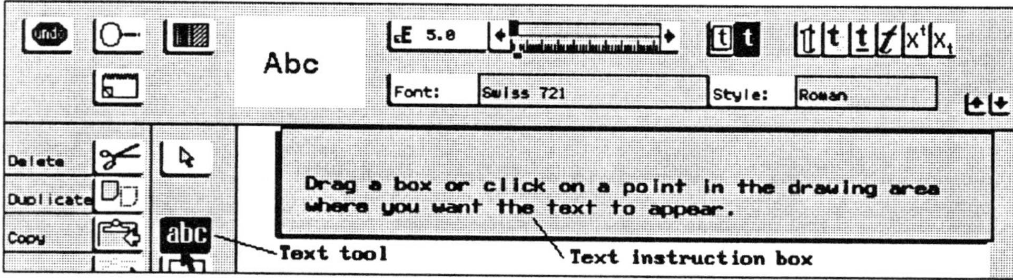

7-7 The Text tool and instruction box.

To *drag a box* means to locate the cross-hair pointer where you want one corner of the text box to be, press and hold the left mouse button, and then slide the mouse until you've drawn a box on your canvas that's the shape you want your text area to be.

Drag a text box under the Presenter symbol. When you release the left mouse button, the box will stay in position and the text pop-up will appear (see Fig. 7-8). Note, too, that the various paraphernalia for editing text attributes have also appeared at the top of the screen (see Fig. 7-9).

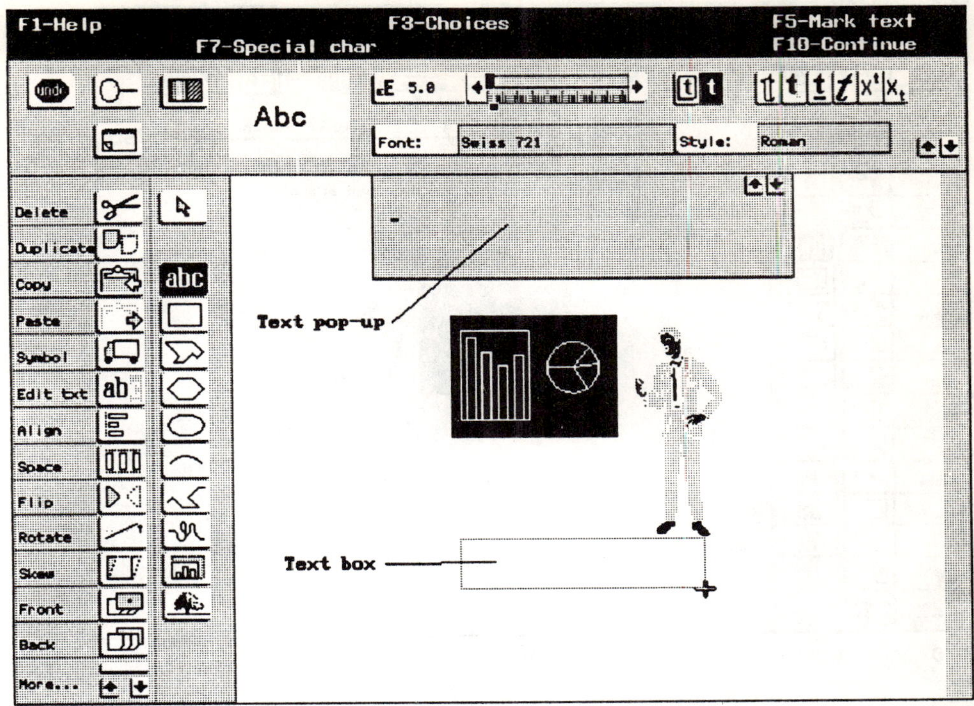

7-8 The text box on the canvas and the text pop-up.

7-9 The selection devices for type size, font, and style.

Accept the default text attributes: your program is probably set for text size 5 (meaning 5% of the vertical size of the chart), font Swiss 721, and style Roman. The text you type will first appear in the text pop-up box.

Type Presentations by The Yorktown Group, Inc., and your text pop-up will look like Fig. 7-10. If the text is correct, press F10–Continue. The line of text will be fitted into the box you drew under the Presenter symbol, probably as two lines, about the way you see it in Fig. 7-11.

This line of text lines up well with the symbol above it. If you want a better fit, click on the selection tool, then, with the pointer somewhere in the middle of your text block on the canvas, press and hold the left mouse button and drag the text box until it fits the Presenter symbol the way you want it to (see Fig. 7-12).

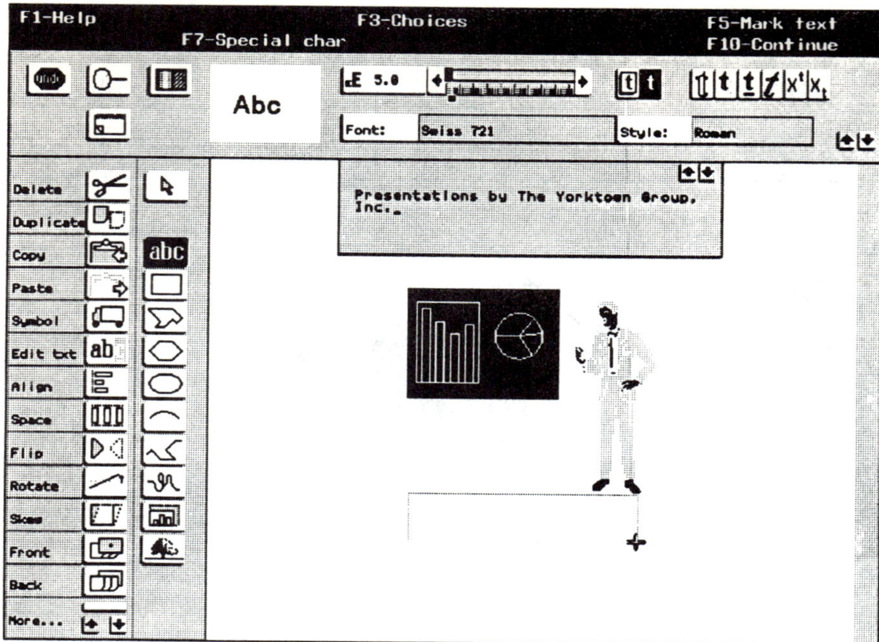

7-10 Your line of text in the text pop-up.

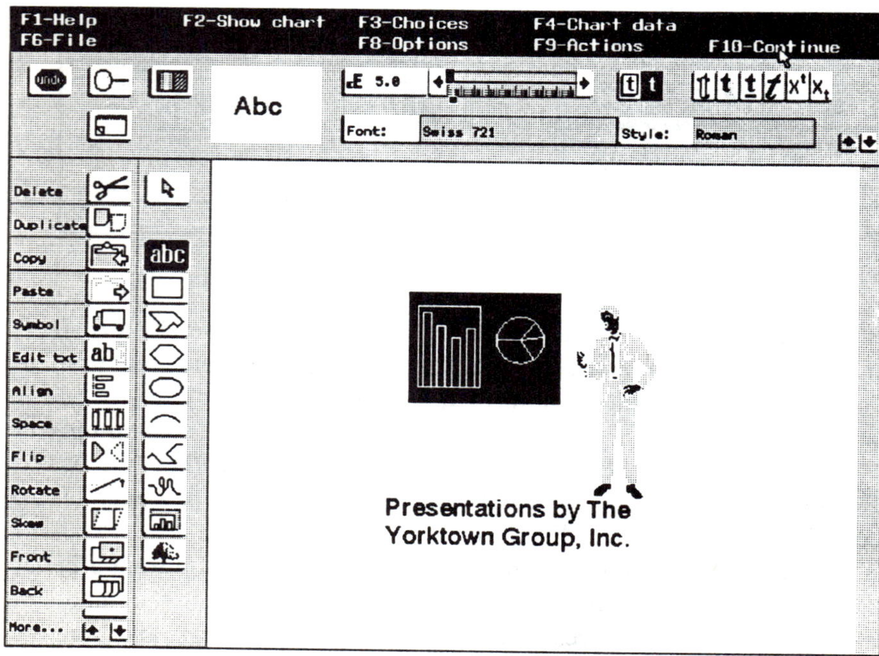

7-11 Your text line on the canvas.

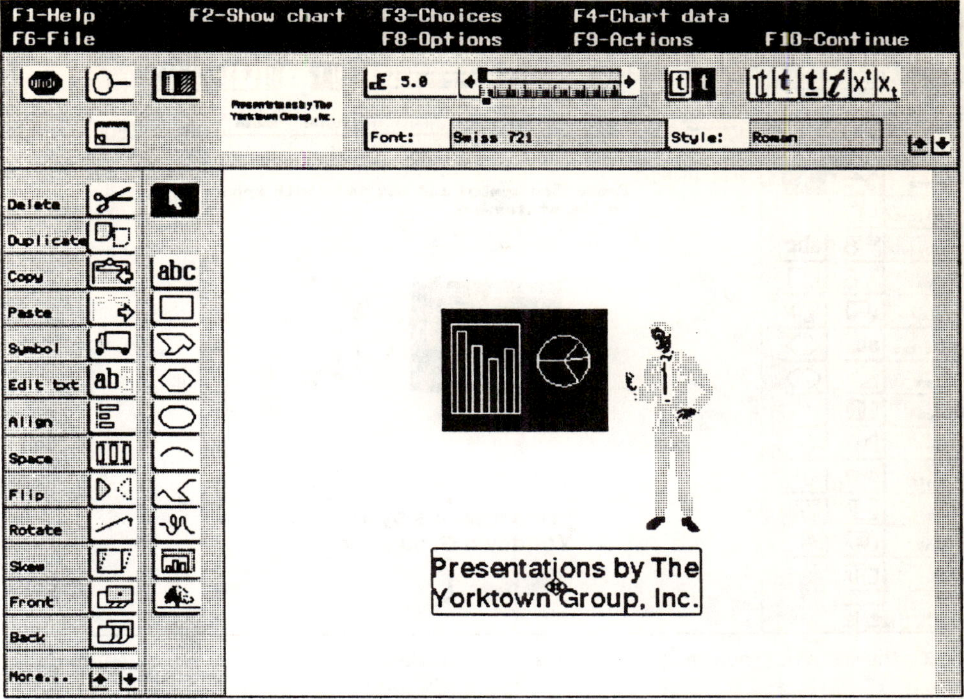

7-12 The text box being adjusted for a better fit.

Next, you want to combine the text and the Presenter symbol into a new symbol. To do this, use the Group tool. First, you have to select every element on your Draw canvas that you want to be included in the new group. Then use the Group tool to fuse those various elements into a single element or group.

Your text block should already be selected (you can tell by the presence of the selection handles). To select the Presenter symbol while keeping the text block selected, hold down the Shift key and click on the Presenter symbol. Selection handles now surround the symbol as well as the text block, and both screen elements appear in your status box (see Fig. 7-13).

If the Group tool isn't visible among your Draw tools, click on the down arrow at the bottom of the tools column and an additional set of tools, including Group, will appear. Click on Group, and the canvas figures will be redrawn with a single set of selection handles surrounding them (see Fig. 7-14).

Now save the new figure, which combines the Presenter with your added text, as a new symbol. Click on the Symbol icon again; the four Symbol icons will reappear. Select the Save icon, the truck with the S on its side. The Save Symbol File box will pop up at the top of the screen (see Fig. 7-15).

The Save Symbol File box will now ask for three items of information: a filename, a description of the symbol (which will appear next to the filename in

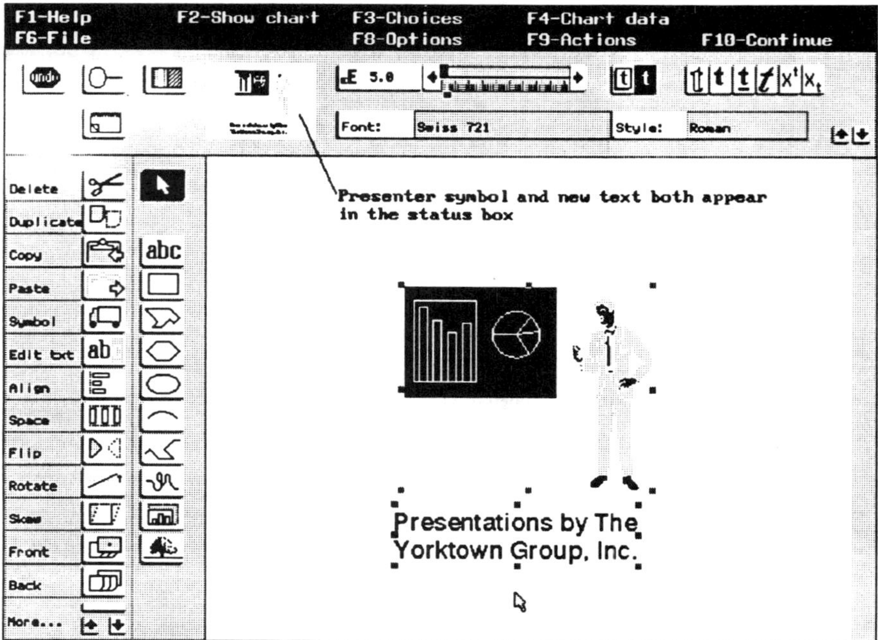

7-13 The status box shows that all screen elements are selected.

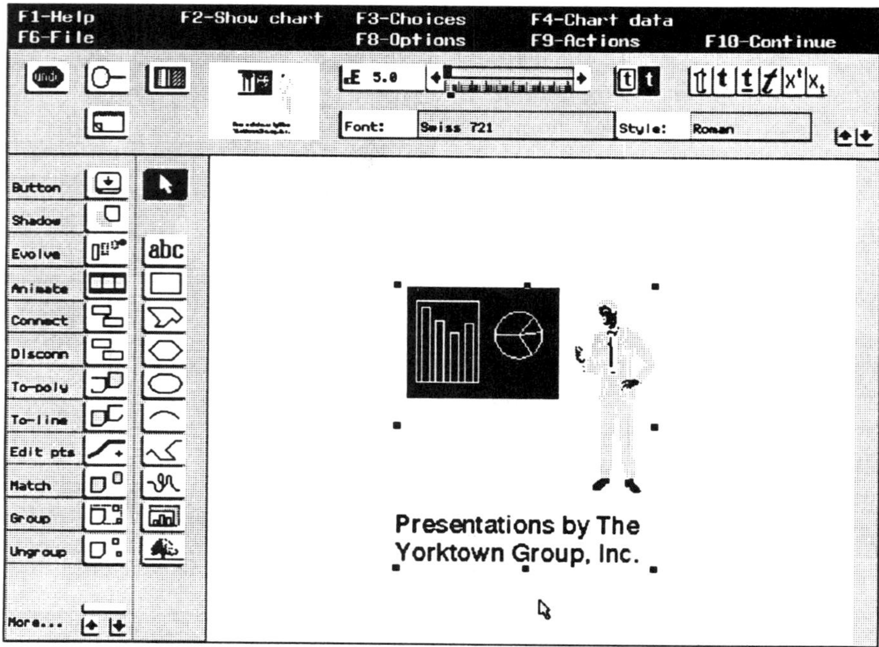

7-14 The new group has a single set of selection handles.

7-15 The Save Symbol File box.

the directory), and a symbol name. The symbol name is the name that appears under the symbol when it's first displayed on the screen. (The original symbol name of the figure you've been working with is Presenter.)

The filename currently indicated is HUMANS5, the original symbol file that contained the Presenter symbol. We can choose to keep this filename and add your new symbol to it, or you can create a new file to contain the new symbol. For this introductory exercise, simply add your new figure to the HUMANS5 file.

1. Press Enter twice to accept HUMANS5 as the filename and Humans as the description.
2. Opposite Symbol name, type TYG Logo. Select F10–Continue. The file is saved with your new symbol on it, and you're returned to the canvas.
3. Press Esc to return to the drawing tools display, then click on the Delete tool (the pair of scissors), as shown in Fig. 7-16. Your canvas is now erased.
4. Select the Symbol icon, then Get. The Get Symbol File will pop up again.
5. Select the HUMANS5 file once more. When the symbols from this file are arrayed on your canvas, you see that there are now 17—the newest being your TYG Logo symbol (see Fig. 7-17).
6. Click on your new logo symbol to highlight its name, then select F10–Continue. It will reappear on your canvas just as you remember it.

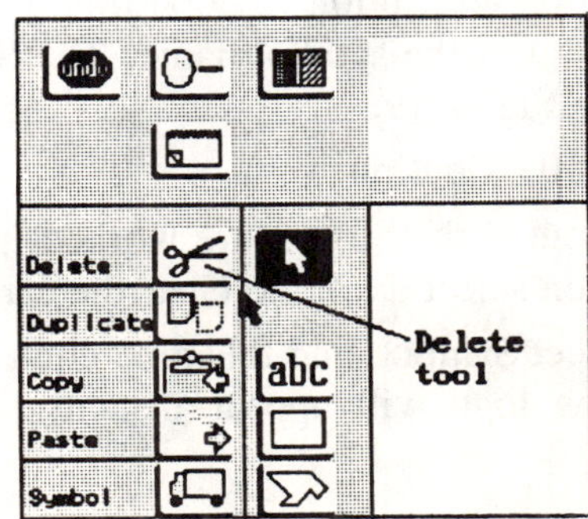

7-16 The Delete tool.

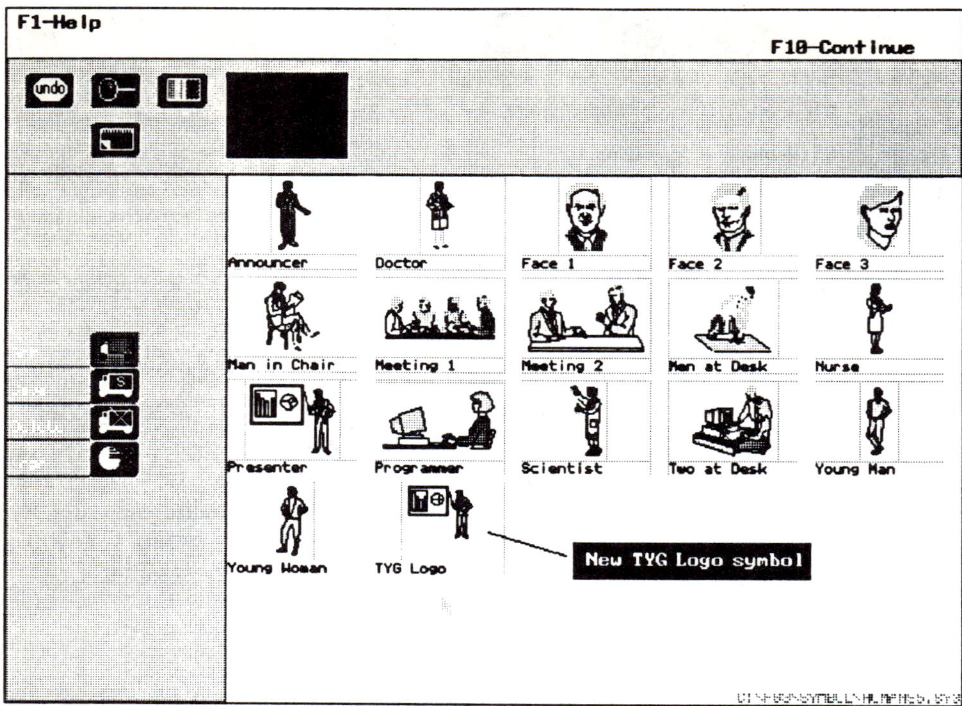

7-17 The new HUMANS5 file, with your TYG Logo at the bottom.

Let's try one more thing; you still haven't dealt with the Logo icon over there on the left. That function lets you create a symbol-logo that can be recalled easily and immediately—it's assumed that the logo is something you'll want quick and frequent access to.

1. Click once more on the Save symbol icon—the truck with an S on its side. The Save Symbol File box will appear with the appropriate directory, filename, and description listings, as shown in Fig. 7-18.
2. Change the directory to C:\HG3; change the filename to HG3LOGO; change the description to Yorktown Group presentations logo; and enter TYG LOGO as the symbol name. The Save Symbol File box should now look like Fig. 7-19.
3. Select F10–Continue.
4. To find out if that procedure worked, press Esc to bring back the Draw tools, then select Delete to clear the canvas.
5. Now select Symbol, and this time click on the Logo icon (see Fig. 7-20). Your new logo will appear instantly, without your having to select a

7-18 The Save Symbol File box, with symbol directory listings.

7-19 The revised Save Symbol File box.

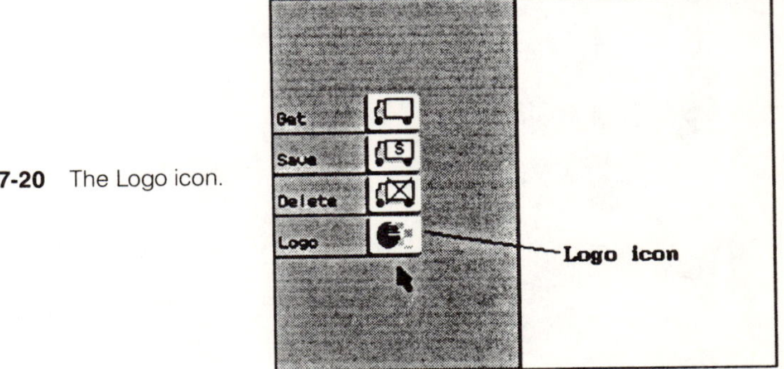

7-20 The Logo icon.

filename from the file directory. The image selected by the Logo icon will always be the first one in the HG3LOGO file.

You now have a good working idea of the procedures and possibilities of the Symbol function contained in Harvard Graphics 3.0. Advanced maneuvers will be discussed in a later chapter.

8
CHAPTER

The spelling checker

Just as if you were working with a good word processing program, Harvard Graphics 3.0 makes it possible for you to check your spelling in text that you put into charts and presentations. You can check and correct an individual chart, or you can check a whole list of charts in a presentation. You can also check the spelling in blocks of text that you added to a chart via the Draw function.

Look first at that bullet chart called HIGHLITE that you created in chapter 4. To begin, call up the chart. At the Main Menu, select File. The File submenu will appear (see Fig. 8-1). From the File submenu, select Get chart. (You could also have pressed Ctrl−G at the Main Menu.) If you like, you can press F8 to sort the files alphabetically (see Fig. 8-2). Select the chart named HIGHLITE.CH3. It will appear in the full-screen mode; click the right mouse button or press Esc to go to the Edit screen (see Fig. 8-3).

Because you were so impeccable in your spelling the first time around, you'll have to insert a couple of artificial mistakes in order to see how the spelling checker works. Change the spelling of vertical to verticle, and in the next-to-last

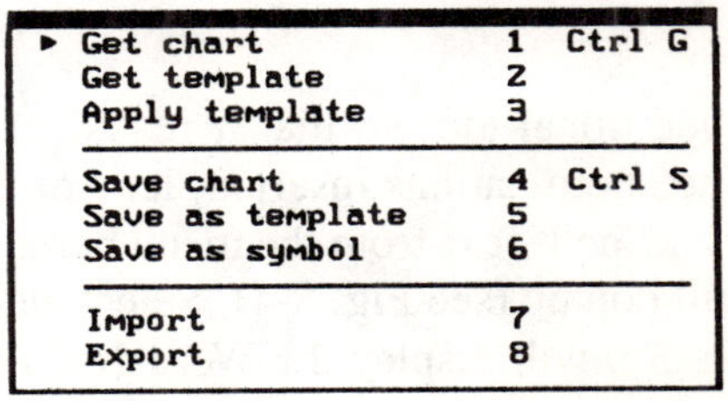

```
► Get chart          1  Ctrl G
  Get template       2
  Apply template     3
  ------------------------------
  Save chart         4  Ctrl S
  Save as template   5
  Save as symbol     6
  ------------------------------
  Import             7
  Export             8
```

8-1 The File submenu.

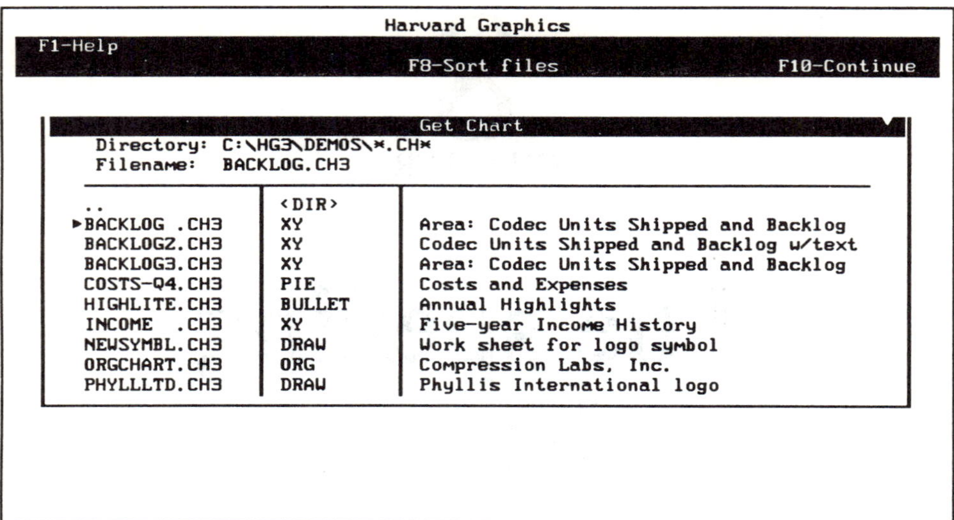

8-2 The Get Chart directory, with files sorted alphabetically.

```
HIGHLITE.CH3                       Bullet Chart
 F1-Help       F2-Show chart                   F4-Draw       F5-Mark
 F6-Main Menu  F7-Spell/Text  F8-Options       F9-Edit bullet  F10-Continue

Title:    Annual Highlights
Subtitle:
Footnote:
----------------------------------------------------------------------
         •  Growing revenues and earnings

         •  Delivering complete solutions

         •  Penetrating vertical markets

         •  Forging strategic partnerships

         •  Building for the future

         •  Looking ahead
```

8-3 The Edit screen for the Annual Highlights bullet chart.

line add an additional the, so that it reads Building for the the future. Now that there are some abominations inserted, let's proceed with the spell checker.

Select F7 – Spell/Text from the menu bar at the top of your screen. The Spell/Text menu will pop up (see Fig. 8-4). Select the first item, Spell check chart. Harvard Graphics 3.0 will display the Word Not Found In Dictionary menu. It cites

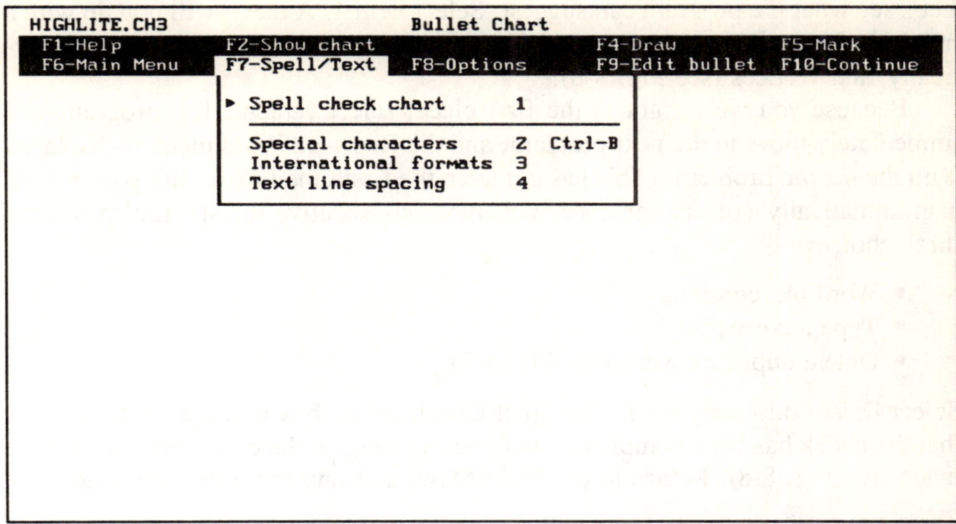

8-4 The Spell/Text menu.

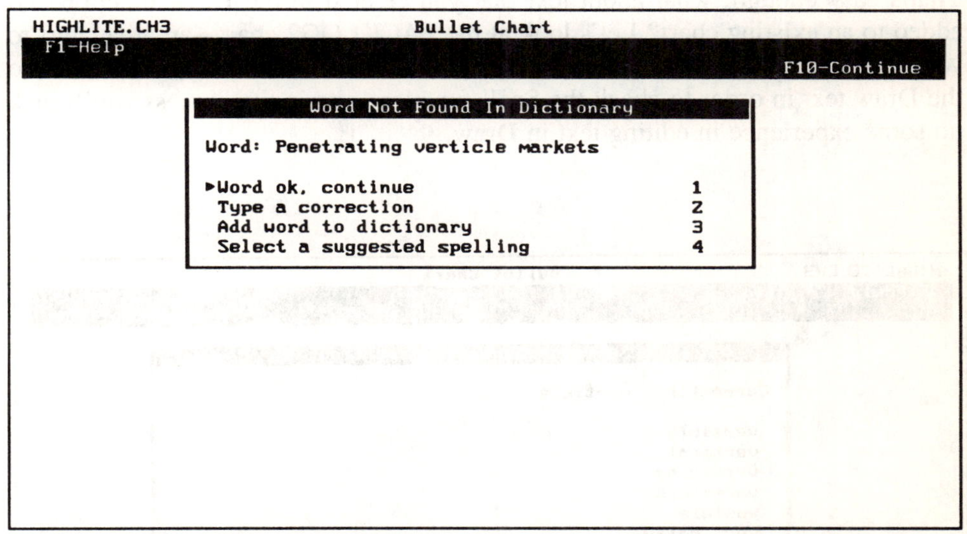

8-5 The Word Not Found In Dictionary menu.

the problem word, in a brief context, and then offers you four remedies:

- Word ok, continue
- Type a correction
- Add word to dictionary
- Select a suggested spelling (see Fig. 8-5)

Let's see what the program can suggest. Select item 4. A menu will pop up with a number of interesting choices: versicle, vertical, versicles, verticals, vesicle, vertically, and vertices (see Fig. 8-6).

Because you were right in the first place, select vertical. The program will immediately move to the next problem, and the Repeated Word menu is displayed with the *the the* problem. (This has got to be the first time in your life you've seen a grammatically correct sentence with three consecutive the's!) You're offered three choices:

- Word ok, continue
- Type a correction
- Delete duplicate word (see Fig. 8-7)

Select Delete duplicate word. The Spell Check Status box will appear to tell you that the check has been completed, and you can see that the corrections have been made (see Fig. 8-8). Return to the Main Menu and save the corrected chart.

Checking spelling in a Draw-created text block

That's easy enough; what about text that you created in the Draw function and added to an existing chart? Let's look at the BACKLOG2 chart—an area chart to which you added a text annotation. First, you'll have to add a couple of errors to the Draw text in order to check the Spell function, and in the process you'll pick up some experience in editing text in Draw.

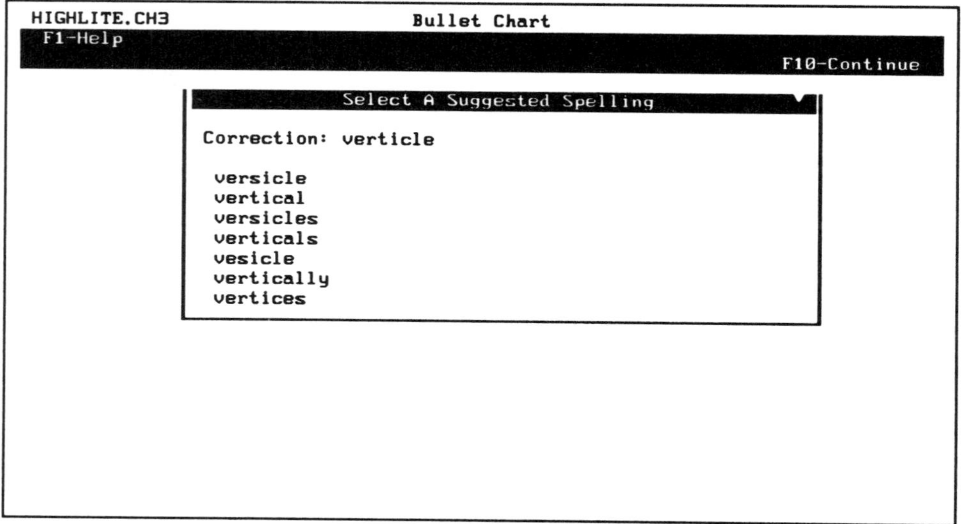

8-6 The pop-up menu for suggested spellings.

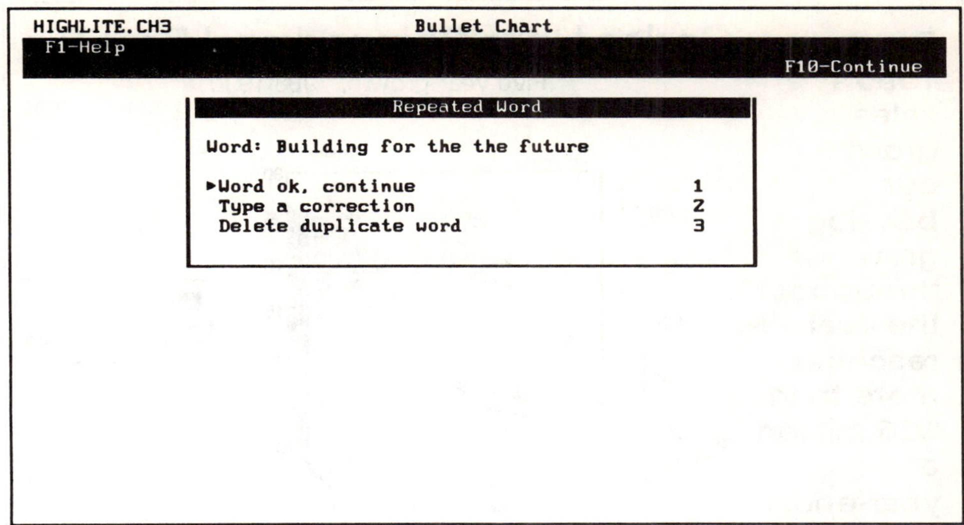

8-7 The Repeated Word menu.

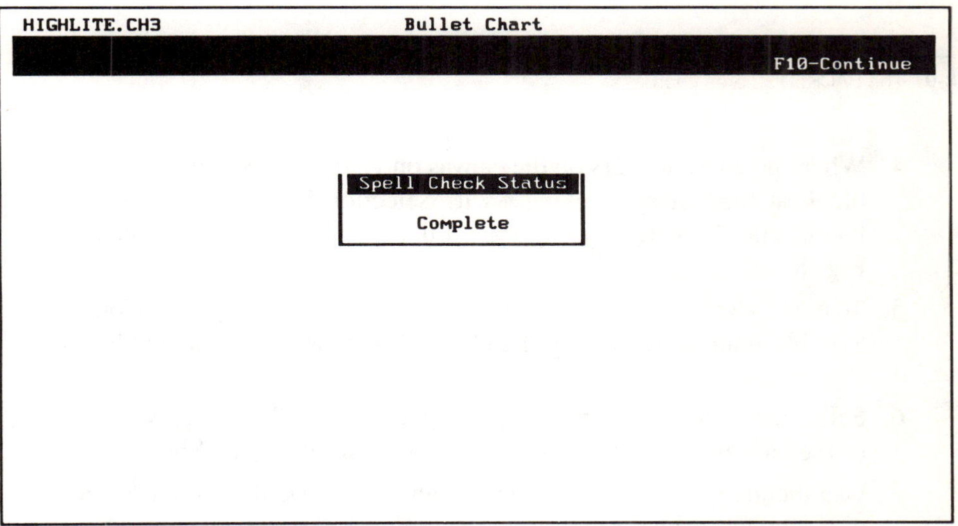

8-8 The Spell Check Status box.

1. At the Main Menu, select File; at the submenu, select Get chart.
2. When the Get Chart directory appears, select the BACKLOG2.CH3 file. The chart, which contains a text annotation at the left side of the screen, looks like Fig. 8-9.
3. Press Esc, then at the chart data screen select F4–Draw.

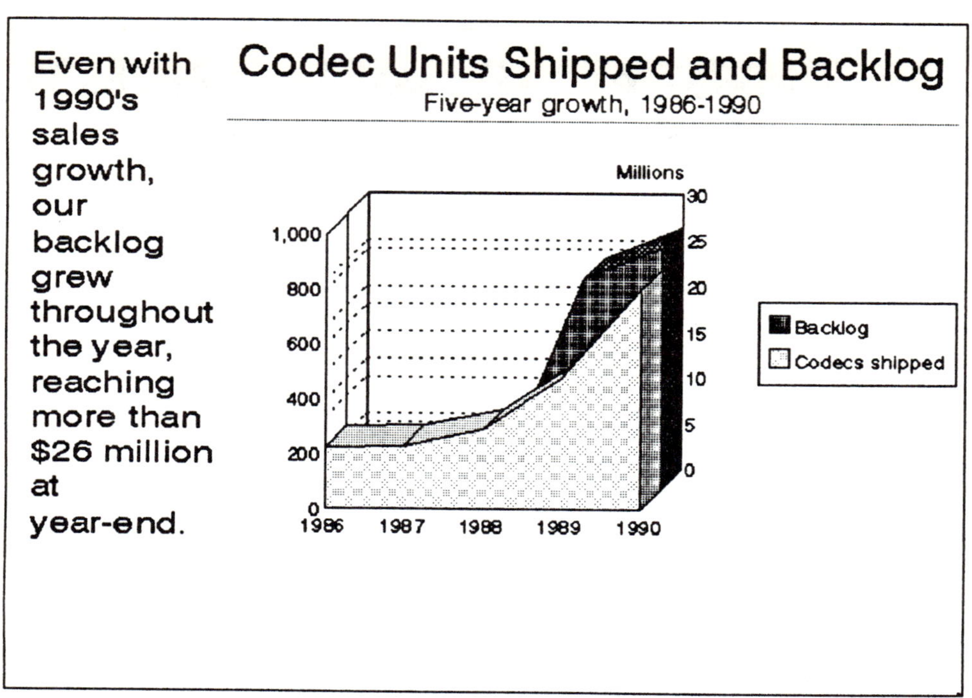

8-9 The BACKLOG2 area chart.

4. When the chart appears on the canvas on your Draw screen, select the text block at the left by clicking on it. Selection handles will surround the block, and its image will appear in the Status box above the canvas (see Fig. 8-10).
5. To edit the text block, press the Edit txt icon. It will reappear, along with a Size blk icon, for changing the physical dimensions of the text block (see Fig. 8-11).
6. Select the Edit txt button. The pop-up text box will be displayed at the top of the canvas, with the cursor under the first letter (see Fig. 8-12).
7. Use the arrow keys or the mouse pointer to move the cursor to the word throughout; change it to threwout (see Fig. 8-13).
8. Select F10—Continue and the chart will be redrawn with the misspelled word.
9. Select F4—Chart data, and your monitor should display the chart's data sheet.

Now you're ready to do your spell check; can you believe that you did all that work to misspell a word? Don't despair; in the process, you learned how the Edit text function works in Draw.

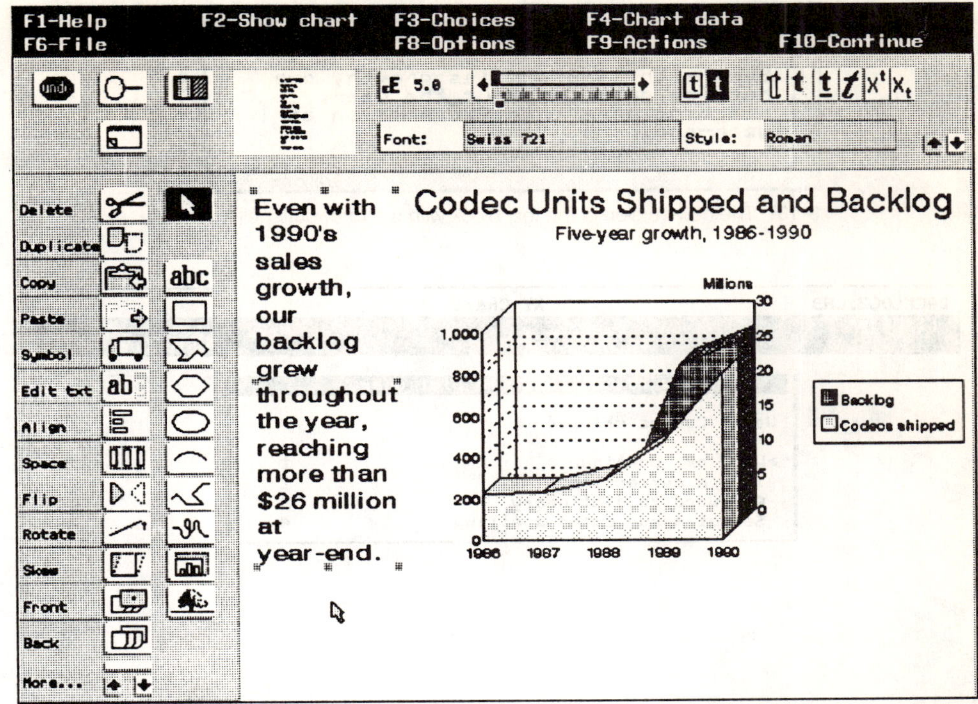

8-10 The Draw screen, with the text block selected.

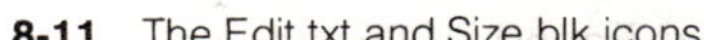
8-11 The Edit txt and Size blk icons.

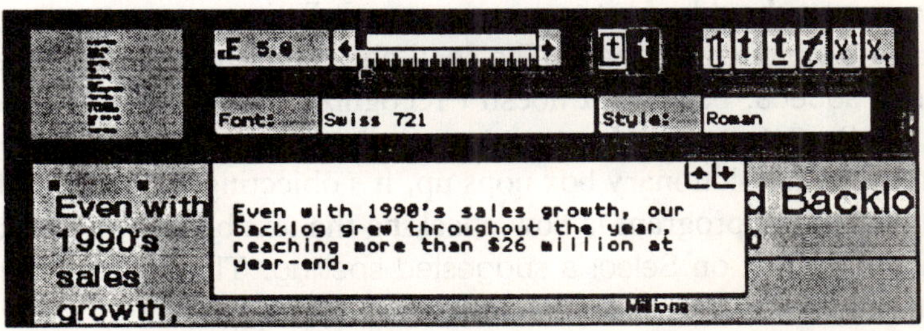

8-12 The pop-up text box.

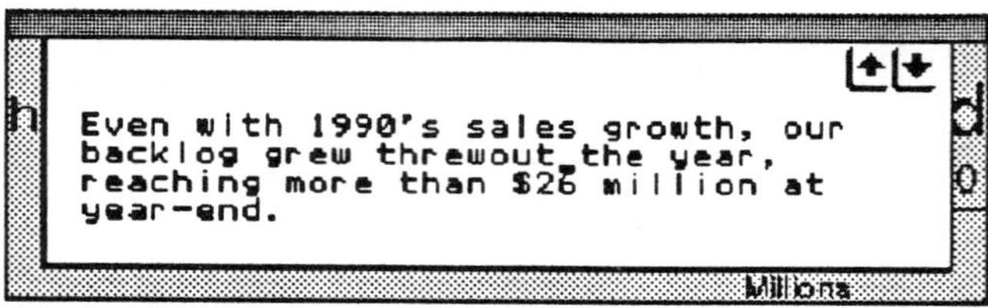

8-13 The new version of the text block with the *threwout* spelling.

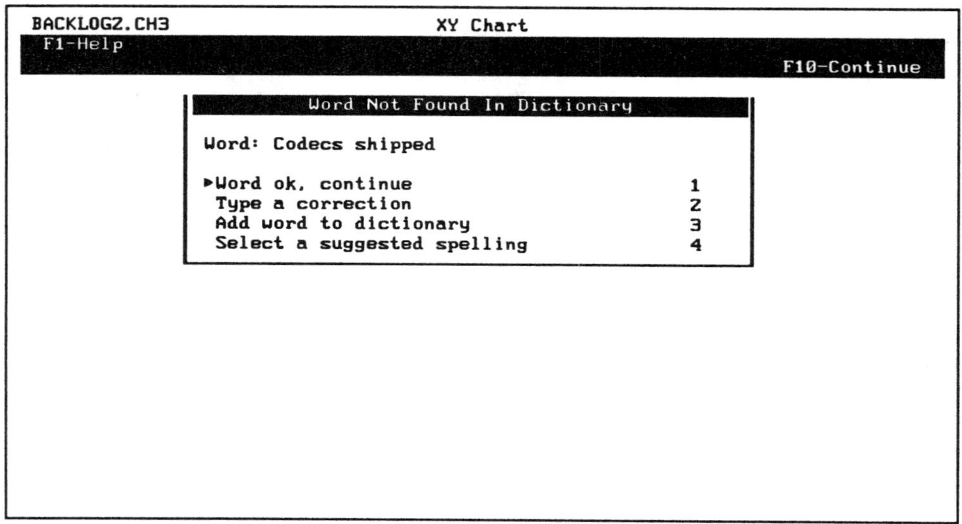

8-14 The Word Not Found In Dictionary box, balking at *Codecs*.

At the data sheet, select F7—Spell/Text. When the Spell/Text menu appears, select Spell check chart. The Word Not Found In Dictionary box will pop up, and it's bothered about the word codec. In this case, the word is spelled correctly; it's just a high-tech coinage that the dictionary doesn't recognize. You have two choices: You can check Word ok, continue, or you can instruct the program to Add word to dictionary. If you simply check Word ok, Harvard Graphics 3.0 will stop at codec the next time it occurs. Let's assume you'll be using the word with some frequency, so you should add it to your personal dictionary.

Select Add word to dictionary. The spell checking proceeds, and the program stops next at codecs, because it doesn't recognize the plural of the word either (see Fig. 8-14). Select Add word to dictionary once more. This time when the Word Not Found In Dictionary box pops up, it's objecting to the word threwout—so you know that the program is now checking the text block you added with the Draw function. Click on Select a suggested spelling. The program will suggest thereabout and trews (?!), neither of which will do (see Fig. 8-15).

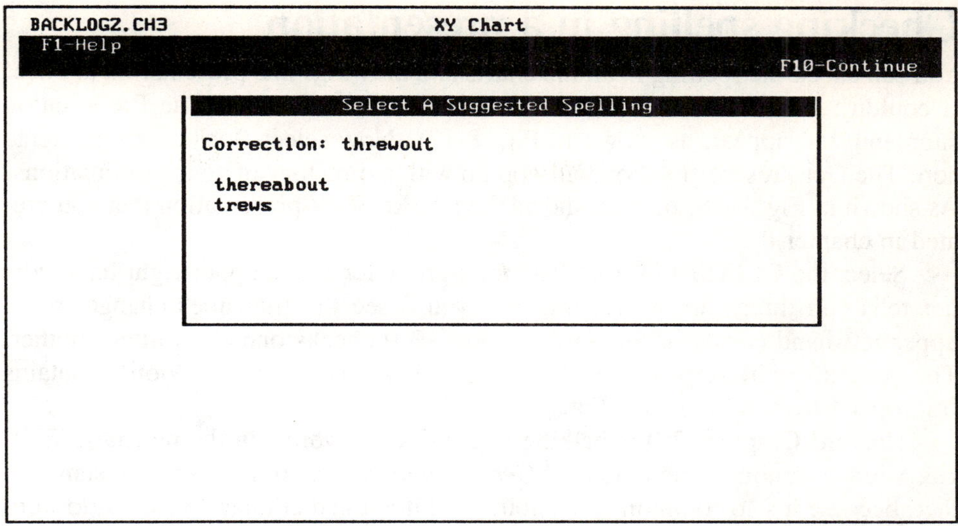

8-15 *Thereabout* and *trews* are suggested in place of *threwout*.

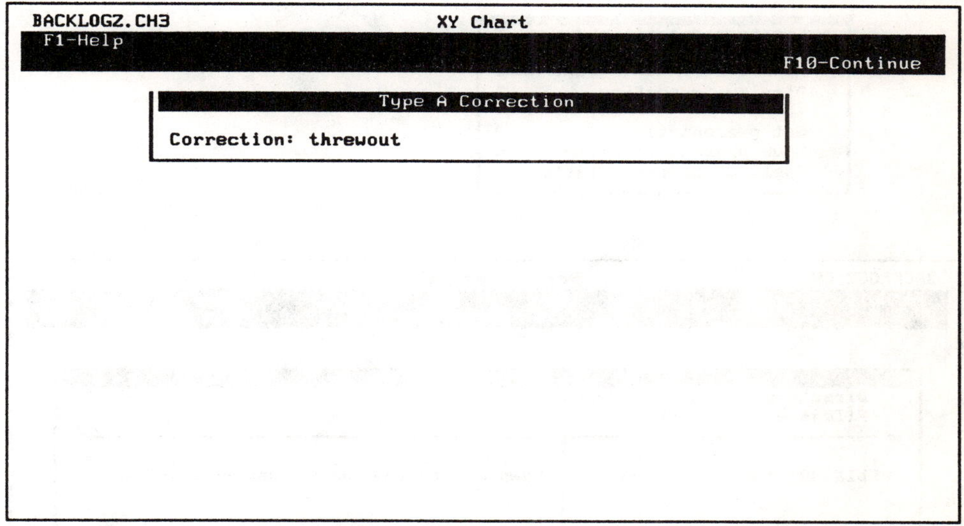

8-16 The Type A Correction box asks you to correct threwout.

Select F10–Continue, and you'll be returned to the Word Not Found In Dictionary box. Because the program won't give you any help, you'll have to struggle with the spelling correction by yourself. Select Type a correction. The (guess what?) Type A Correction box pops up, waiting for you to type in the correct version of the word (see Fig. 8-16). Type throughout, then select F10–Continue. In a twinkling, the Spell Check Status box will tell you that the job is complete.

Checking spelling in a presentation

You can check the spelling in all the charts and drawings in a presentation at once. It couldn't be easier. At the Main Menu, select Presentation. The Presentation submenu will appear, as shown in Fig. 8-17). Now select Spell check presenta tion. The Get Presentation box will pop up with a directory of your presentations. As shown in Fig. 8-18, the box shows the CLIXSHOW presentation that you created in chapter 8.

Select the CLIXSHOW file. The little propeller in the upper right-hand corner tells you things are happening, and you'll see the filenames change in the upper left-hand corner as Harvard Graphics 3.0 checks one chart after another. The program will stop at the COSTS-Q4 chart and display a Word Contains Improper Character box (see Fig. 8-19).

Harvard Graphics 3.0 is balking at the G&A "word" in the piechart. Well, G&A is a common abbreviation for *General and Administrative*, so let it stand. In fact, because it's so common, you should add it to the dictionary. Select Add word to dictionary. The program will keep working through the charts in the presenta-

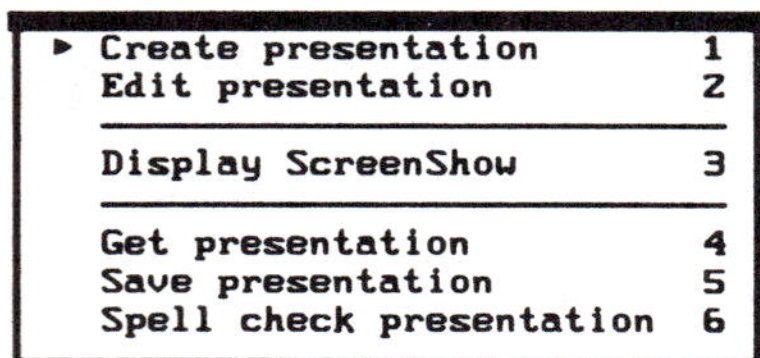

8-17 The Presentation submenu.

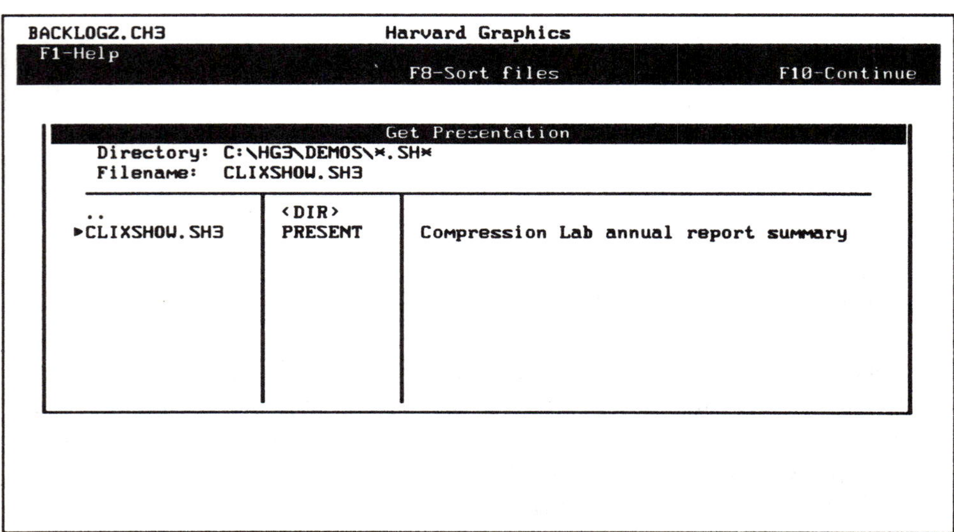

8-18 The Get Presentation box listing the CLIXSHOW presentation.

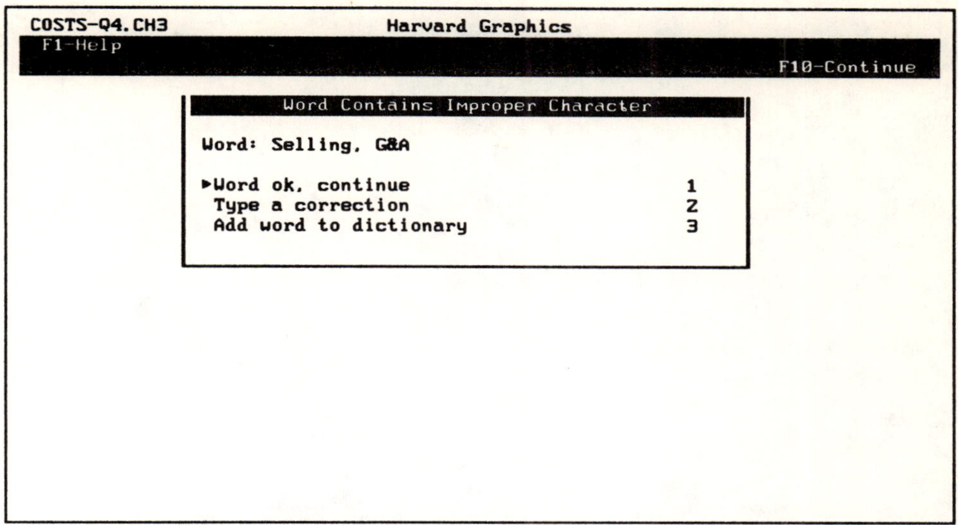

8-19 The Contains Improper Character box.

tion until it comes to the organization chart, ORGCHART.CH3. You're going to get stopped several times here because of proper names that aren't in the dictionary.

In each case, simply select Word ok, continue. Harvard Graphics 3.0 will run you through the whole list of names, and finally signal that the spell check status is complete. Select F10–Continue, the program will return you to the Main Menu, and you've mastered the Spell Check function.

In a future chapter, you'll learn how to print a number of charts at once by putting them onto a presentation listing. Keep in mind that when you do that, you'll also be able to check the spelling of all of those charts at the same time as well.

9
CHAPTER

Printing with Harvard Graphics

When you get one of your Harvard Graphics 3.0 graphics completed, edited, dressed up, and ready to go out into the world, you'll probably be anxious for somebody to see it. There are several ways you can prepare a chart for viewing by an audience—whether you're addressing an audience of one or hundreds.

First, you can output Harvard Graphics 3.0 creations to your computer screen and view them as part of a presentation or ScreenShow. You might want to review chapter 6 for basic instruction on the preparation and presentation of ScreenShows.

It's likely, however, that you'll want paper copies of the charts and graphics you create; in other words, you want to know how to get printed output from Harvard Graphics 3.0. This chapter will guide you through the process.

The first step in getting printed output from Harvard Graphics 3.0 is to tell your program what kind of printers you're using. That's done during the installation process, and you can review that procedure in appendix A. The second step is to be sure that you've loaded the chart or drawing you want to print. You can print one of the samples you already created.

1. From the Main Menu, select File. The File submenu will appear, as shown in Fig. 9-1.
2. From the File submenu, select Get chart. Your Get Chart directory will pop up (see Fig. 9-2).
3. From the Get Chart directory, select the chart named BACKLOG2.CH3 that you created in chapter 8. The program will display your chart full-screen (see Fig. 9-3).

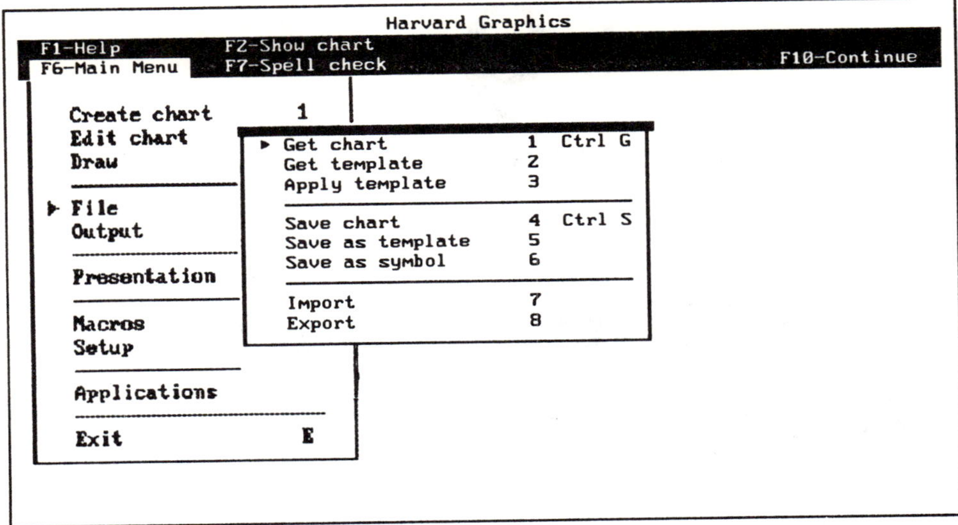

9-1 The File submenu.

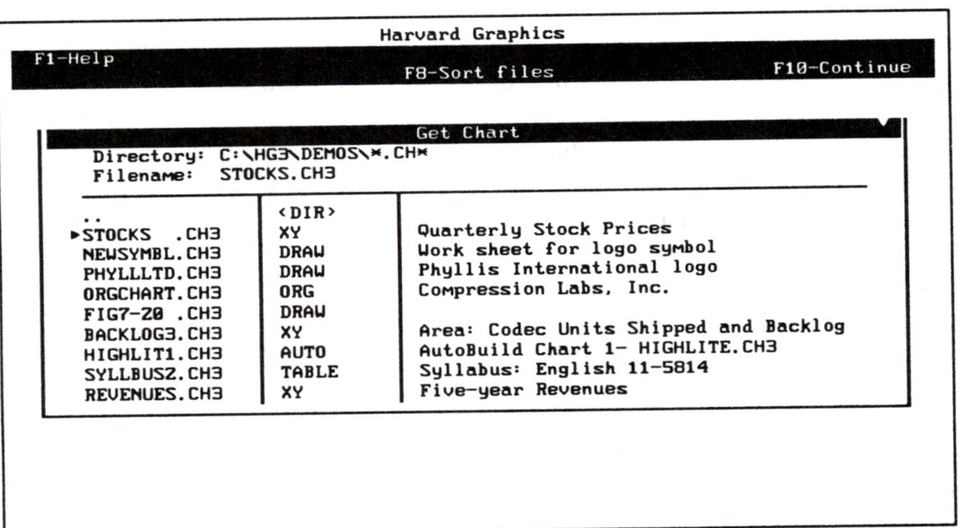

9-2 The Get Chart directory.

4. Click the right mouse button to go to the data screen for BACK LOG2.CH3, then press F6–Main Menu (see Fig. 9-4).
5. At the Main Menu, select Output, item 5. The Output submenu is displayed (see Fig. 9-5).

When you installed Harvard Graphics 3.0, you had the opportunity to install two printer drivers, represented on the Output submenu as Printer 1 and Printer 2.

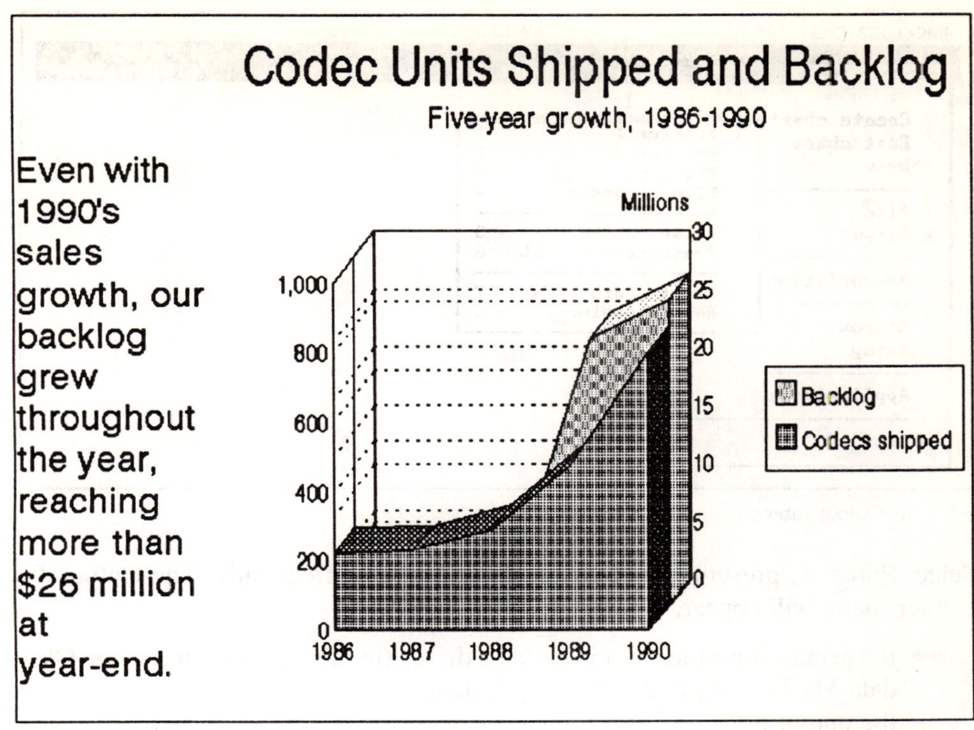

9-3 The screen display of the BACKLOG2 chart.

```
BACKLOG2.CH3                      XY Chart
 F1-Help          F2-Show chart                   F4-Draw          F5-Mark
 F6-Main Menu     F7-Spell/Text   F8-Options      F9-XY data       F10-Continue

   ▸ Create chart        1     ed and Backlog
     Edit chart          2      1986-1990
     Draw                3
                                ---- 1 ------------ 2 ------------ 3 ------------ 4 ----
     File                4
     Output              5
                               Codecs shi    Backlog        Series 3       Series 4
     Presentation        6
                               225           363000
     Macros              7     231           1762000
     Setup               8     292           2200000
                               478           2.31E+07
     Applications        9     802           2.64E+07

     Exit                E
 9
 10
 11
 12
```

9-4 The Main Menu superimposed on the chart data screen.

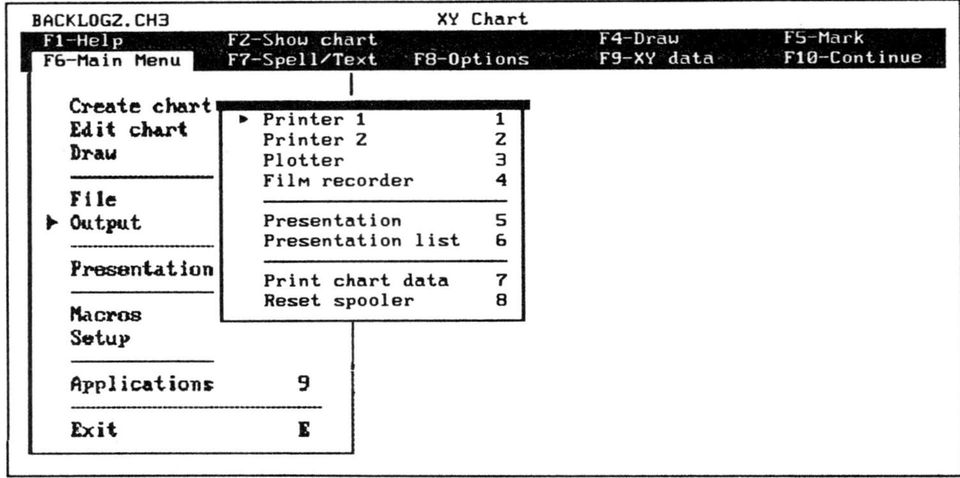

9-5 The Output submenu.

Select Printer 1, presumably the printer you use most frequently. The Output To Printer menu will appear, listing:

- the printer for which you installed a driver (in this illustration it is the Okidata ML393 24-pin dot matrix printer);
- the output port;
- the print quality you prefer (the choices are High, Medium, and Draft);
- the size of the paper you are printing on;
- the size of the chart you wish to print—full size or half size;
- the number of copies you want printed;
- whether you want the output directed to a disk file; and
- the output filename (see Fig. 9-6).

Before you actually make the commitment to print the file, however, you can get a pretty accurate preview of your document by selecting F2–Preview (see Fig. 9-7). If that preview screen looks about the way you want it to, click the right mouse button to return to your Output To Printer menu, then select F10–Continue to print the chart.

Your finished result should look something like Fig. 9-8. When you press F10–Continue, an Output to Printer menu pops up to tell you what's going on, and you'll see a little line rotating like a propeller in the upper right-hand corner of your screen. The rotating propeller tells you that the data is being sent to a print spooler. When that process is complete, the Output To Printer menu will disappear, and you can continue to work in the program while the chart is being printed (see Fig.9-9).

And that's how you produce printed output from Harvard Graphics 3.0. Some other forms of output are discussed in a later chapter.

```
BACKLOGZ.CH3                         XY Chart
 F1-Help          F2-Preview        F3-Choices
                                    F8-Options                  F10-Continue
                                 Output To Printer

        Device             | Okidata ML393 (LQ Module)
        Port               | LPT1
        Quality            |◆High
        Paper size         | A  (8.5 in. x 11 in.)
        Chart size         | Full
        Copies             | 1
        Output to disk     | No
        Output filename    | C:\HG3\OUTPUT\BACKLOGZ.OUT
```

9-6 The Output to Printer menu.

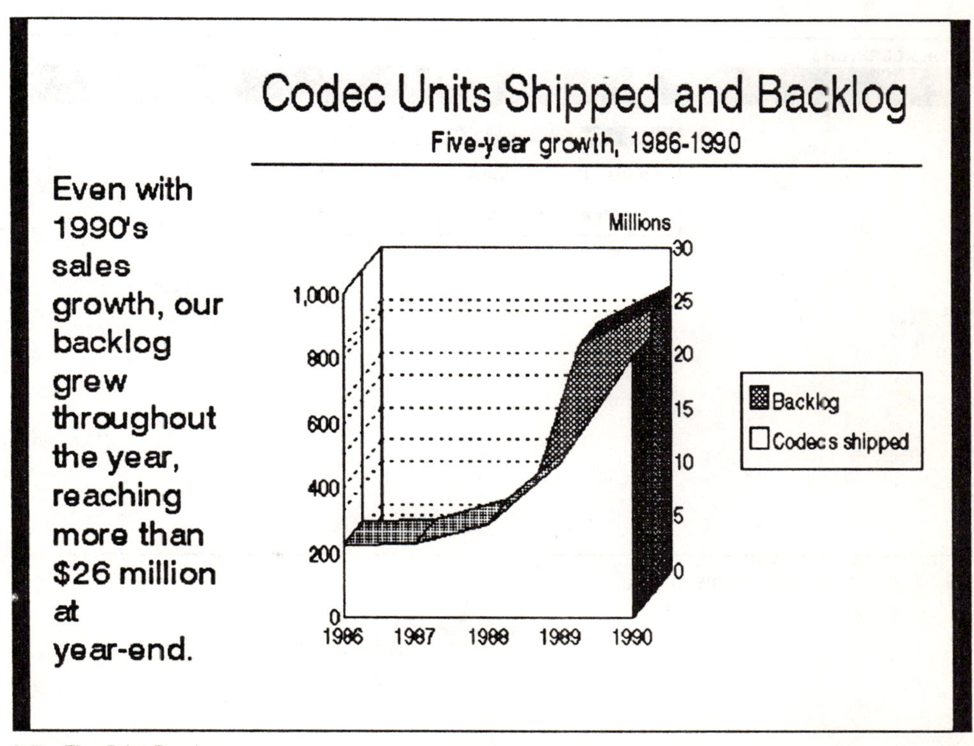

9-7 The Print Preview screen.

Even with 1990's sales growth, our backlog grew throughout the year, reaching more than $26 million at year-end.

Codec Units Shipped and Backlog

Five-year growth, 1986-1990

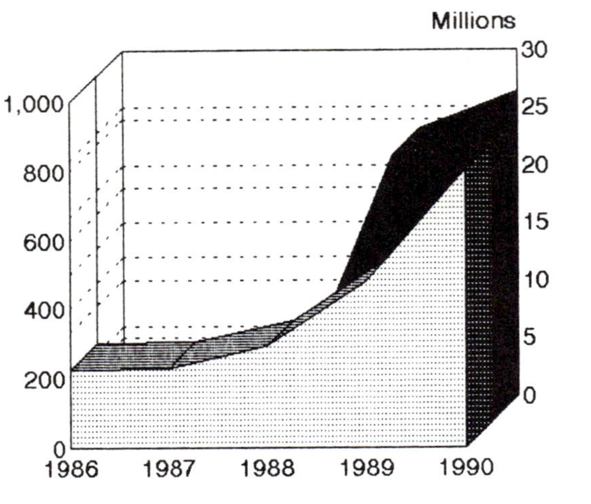

Backlog

Codecs shipped

9-8 The printed version of the BACKLOG2 chart.

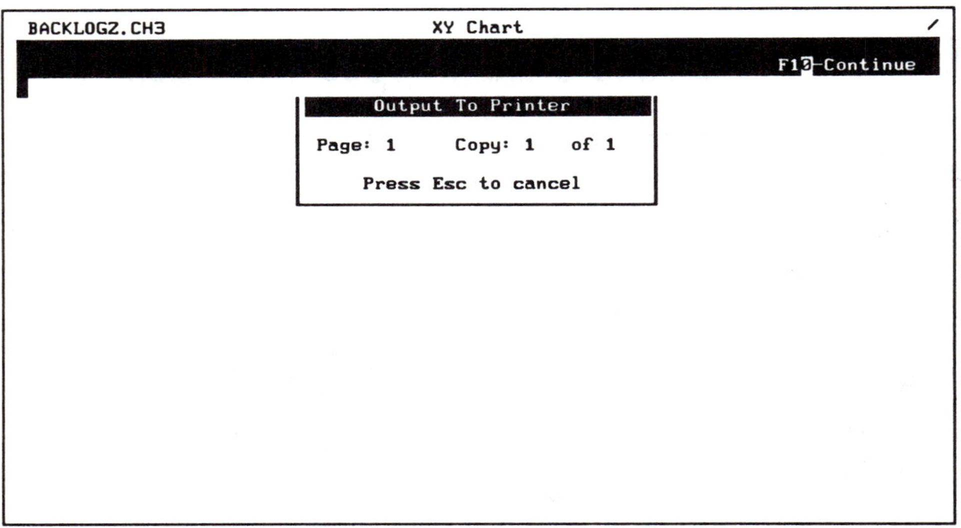

9-9 The Output to Printer menu.

Part 2
Becoming a power user

10 CHAPTER

Advanced text charts

In chapter 4 you created a basic text chart—sort of a common garden variety chart using the settings that came with one of the Gallery charts. Now that you've moved beyond the novice stage, however, you're ready for grander stuff. Well, in Harvard Graphics 3.0, grander stuff is there for the asking. There are numerous ways you can tinker with—er, enhance—a text chart. You'll see most of them in this chapter.

Adding subtitles and footnotes

Let's retrieve the text chart you created in chapter 4 and dress it up a little:

1. At the Main Menu, click on File, then in the File submenu select Get chart.
2. From the Get Chart directory, select the file named HIGHLITE.CH3. That text chart, with highlights from the Compression Labs 1990 annual report, appears in Fig. 10-1.
3. Press Esc or the right mouse button to go to the Bullet Chart data screen (see Fig. 10-2).

Notice the menu bar at the top of the screen—most of the choices for editing this chart will be found under the F8−Options selection. Make that selection now, and the Options menu will pop up (see Fig. 10-3). The first chart element you can edit or alter here is Titles/Footnotes.

Annual Highlights

- Growing revenues and earnings
- Delivering complete solutions
- Penetrating vertical markets
- Forging strategic partnerships
- Building for the future
- Looking ahead

10-1 The Annual Highlights chart you created in chapter 2.

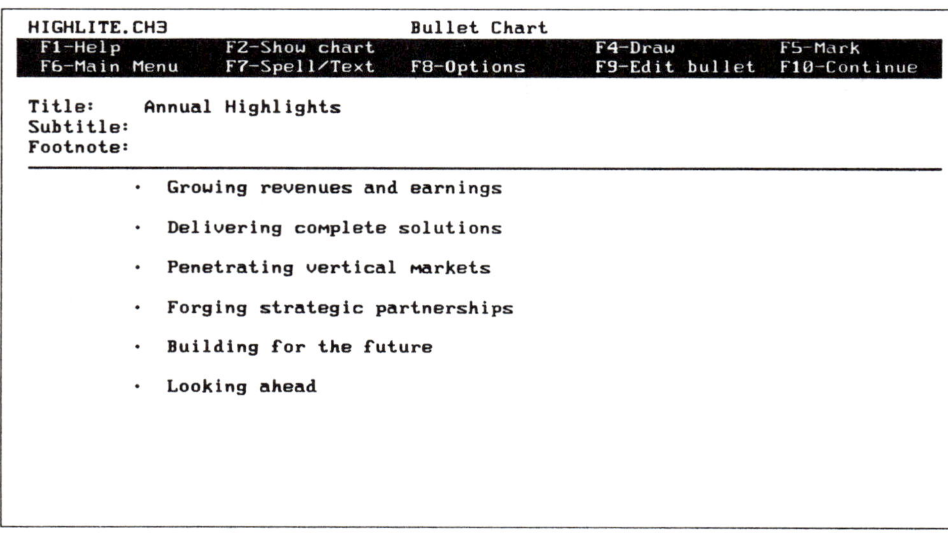

10-2 The Bullet Chart data screen for the Annual Highlights chart.

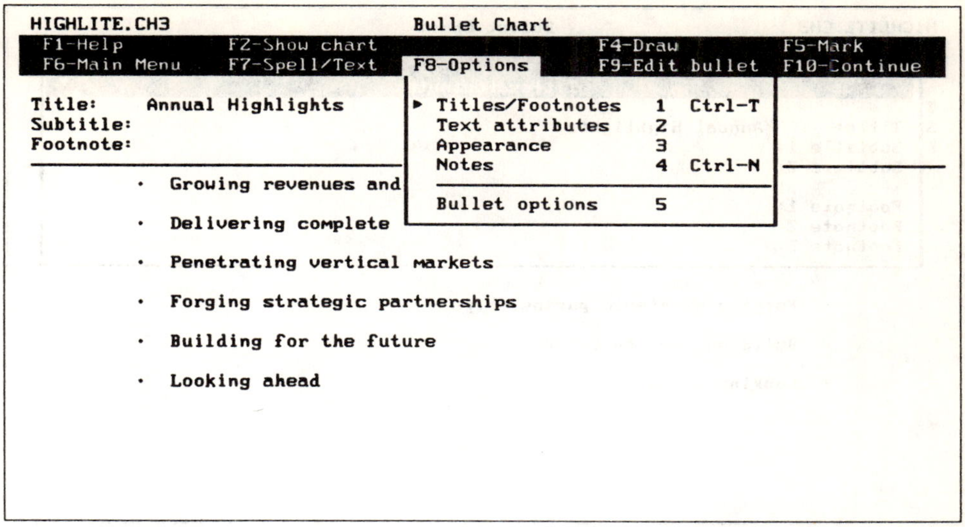

```
HIGHLITE.CH3                          Bullet Chart
 F1-Help          F2-Show chart                          F4-Draw          F5-Mark
 F6-Main Menu     F7-Spell/Text    F8-Options            F9-Edit bullet   F10-Continue

Title:     Annual Highlights       ▸ Titles/Footnotes    1   Ctrl-T
Subtitle:                            Text attributes     2
Footnote:                            Appearance          3
                                     Notes               4   Ctrl-N
          · Growing revenues and   ──────────────────────────────
                                     Bullet options      5
          · Delivering complete

          · Penetrating vertical markets

          · Forging strategic partnerships

          · Building for the future

          · Looking ahead
```

10-3 The Options menu.

1. Click on item 1 or press Ctrl – T, and the Titles/Footnotes box will pop up (see Fig. 10-4).
2. You'll need to add a subtitle and a footnote, so press Tab to move down to the Subtitle 1 line.
3. Opposite Subtitle 1, type Compression Labs Report to Stockholders, 1990, and then press Tab twice. The cursor will move to the line opposite Foot note 1.
4. Type Condensed for oral presentation. The Titles/Footnotes box will now look like Fig. 10-5.
5. Press F2 to view your progress; the chart should look like Fig. 10-6.

Changing the text attributes

The second item on the Options pop-up menu is Text attributes. That term refers to the size, color, alignment, font name, and font style of the text you elect to use in the various sections of a text chart. In order to monkey with the text attributes, press Esc to leave the Show chart screen and return to the Bullet Chart data screen.

Select F8 – Options to bring up the Options pop-up menu. Press 2 or click on Text attributes. The Text Attributes menu will be displayed (see Fig. 10-7). Notice that text size, color, alignment, font name, and font style are given for titles, subtitles, bullet text, and footnotes.

```
HIGHLITE.CH3                           Bullet Chart
 F1-Help          F2-Show chart                          F5-Mark
                                                         F10-Continue
                                   Titles/Footnotes
T
S  Title:       Annual Highlights
F  Subtitle 1:
-  Subtitle 2:

   Footnote 1:
   Footnote 2:
   Footnote 3:

         •  Forging strategic partnerships

         •  Building for the future

         •  Looking ahead
```

10-4 The Titles/Footnotes box.

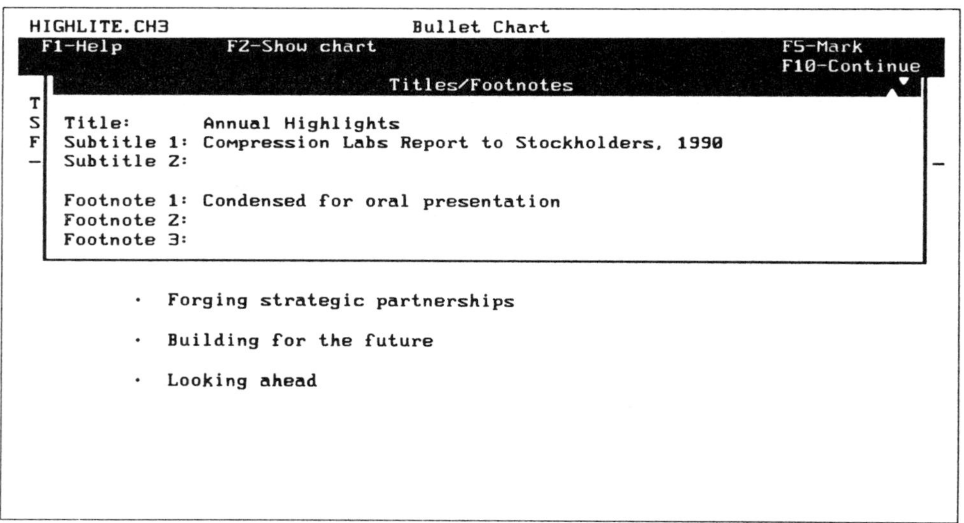

10-5 The completed Titles/Footnotes box.

Text size

The numbers under size signify, according to the gurus at Software Publishing Corporation (publishers of Harvard Graphics 3.0), a percentage of the shortest side of the screen. In other words, because the title size is indicated as 9, the height of the characters in the title would be approximately 9% of the height of the

Annual Highlights

Compression Labs Report to Stockholders, 1990

- Growing revenues and earnings
- Delivering complete solutions
- Penetrating vertical markets
- Forging strategic partnerships
- Building for the future
- Looking ahead

Condensed for oral presentation

10-6 The first stage of your enhanced chart.

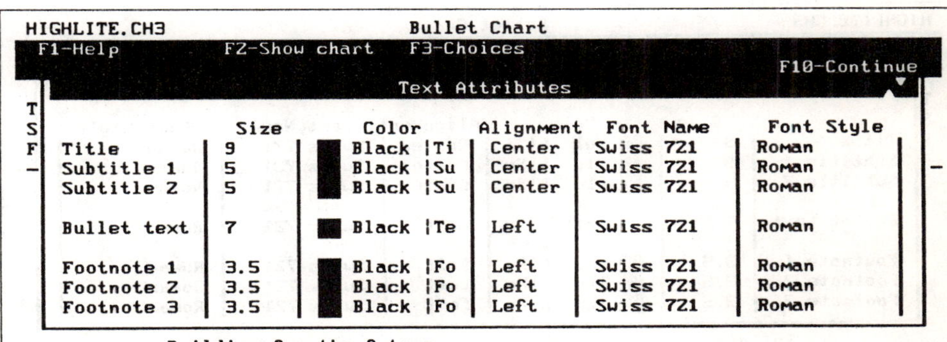

10-7 The Text Attributes menu.

screen. The height of the subtitle characters would be 5%, the height of the bullet text characters 7%, etc.

You are also told that there are limits on the size of the text, that text in the title region and footnote region of the chart is limited to size 25, while text in the bullet text region of the chart can be as large as size 100. You will find, however, that these are only very rough guidelines, and that the actual size of the text on the screen or printout can vary greatly, depending upon how many lines of text there are, whether you have instructed the program to shrink text to fit available space, etc. Your expertise in this area will have to come through exploration and experimentation.

Text color

The available text color options depend on the color palette you're working with. In Fig. 10-7, you see only blacks listed because the MONOCHRW.PL3 palette is being used to create the gray-shade illustrations for this book. If you're using the HG3.PL3 palette, your Text Attributes screen should look like Fig. 10-8.

You can change the color of any text element on your text chart. Let's demonstrate with the title color. Click on the color in the Title row; the color will be highlighted, and a diamond will appear to the left, indicating that choices are available (see Fig. 10-9). When the title color is selected, it's highlighted and the choice diamond appears. Select F3—Choices and the color choices box will pop up (see Fig. 10-10). Click on the hue of your choice to change the color of the title text, then press F2 to see the change in your chart. It's that simple.

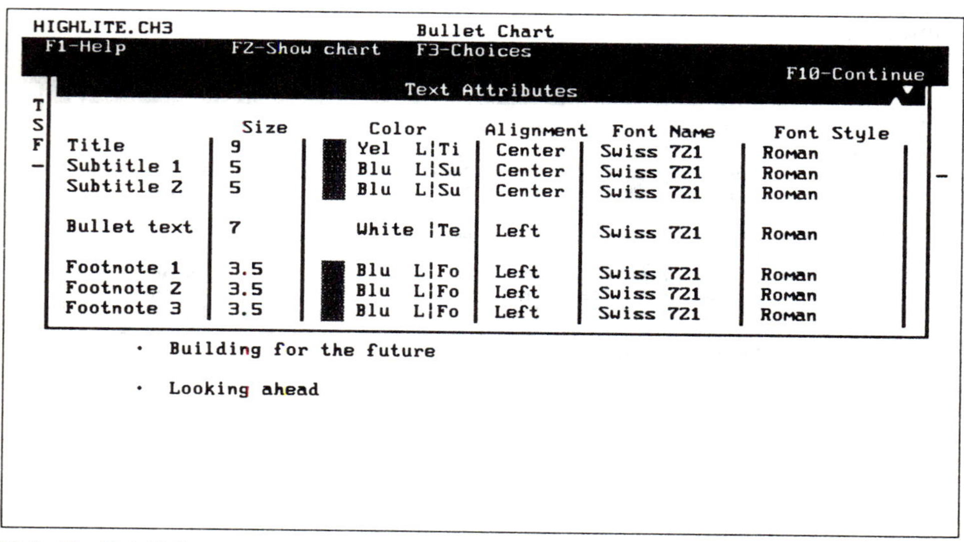

10-8 The Text Attributes screen when the HG3.PL3 color palette is selected.

```
HIGHLITE.CH3                          Bullet Chart
 F1-Help          F2-Show chart     F3-Choices
                                                        F10-Continue
                                Text Attributes
T
S                 Size       Color      Alignment  Font Name      Font Style
F Title           9        ◆ Yel  L|Ti   Center    Swiss 721      Roman
- Subtitle 1      5          Blu  L|Su   Center    Swiss 721      Roman
  Subtitle 2      5          Blu  L|Su   Center    Swiss 721      Roman

  Bullet text     7          White |Te   Left      Swiss 721      Roman

  Footnote 1      3.5        Blu  L|Fo   Left      Swiss 721      Roman
  Footnote 2      3.5        Blu  L|Fo   Left      Swiss 721      Roman
  Footnote 3      3.5        Blu  L|Fo   Left      Swiss 721      Roman

           •  Building for the future

           •  Looking ahead
```

10-9 When the Title color is selected, it is highlighted and the choice diamond appears.

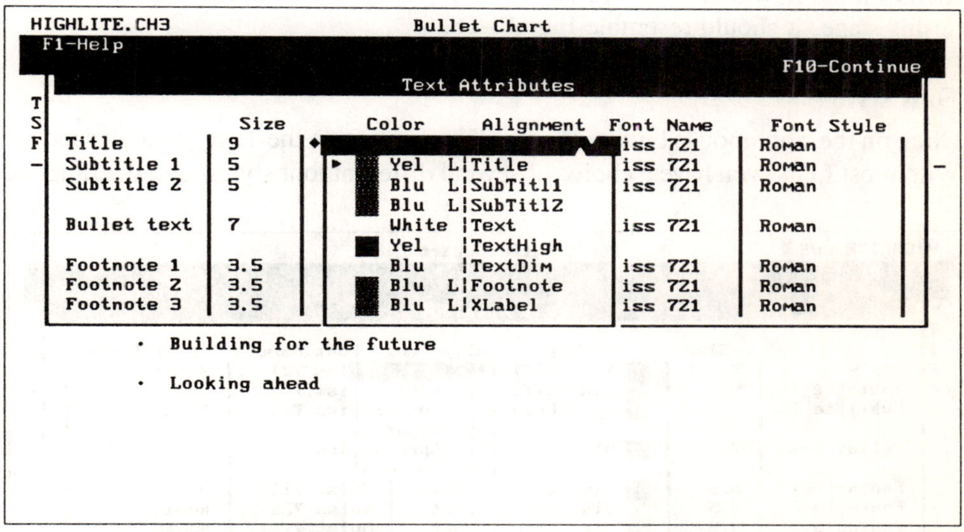

10-10 The box of color choices for title text.

Text alignment

You can elect to align each element of your text chart. There are four choices: left, center, right, and spread. Move to the Alignment column. Current alignment for the title is indicated as Center. Click on Center, and the word will be highlighted with the now-familiar diamond, indicating that there are choices to be made.

Select F3 – Choices, and the little alignment options box will pop up (see Fig. 10-11). Click on Left, and you'll be returned to the Text Attributes screen. Repeat the procedure for the Subtitle 1 line, then select F2 – Show chart to see the results (see Fig. 10-12). Press Esc to return to the Text Attributes screen.

Font name

To change the name of the font used in your text chart, move to the Font Name column. The font that should be showing now is Swiss 721. (Note that the same font is used for all text chart elements. This is important for readability and aesthetics. Start mixing up fonts and you'll end up with a cluttered, tacky chart.)

Click on Swiss 721 in the Title row, then select F3 – Choices to see a listing of the available font names that are standard offerings with Harvard Graphics 3.0 (see Fig. 10-13). You'll want to experiment with typefaces; the eight fonts listed in Fig. 10-13 are illustrated in Fig. 10-14. Different jobs will dictate different fonts. In general, you want to strive for readability and simplicity.

For a good, sturdy, readable font, select Dutch 801. Do the same for Subtitle 1, Bullet text, and Footnote 1. The Font Name column of your Text Attributes menu should now look like Fig. 10-15, and when you press F2 to view your chart at this stage, it should resemble Fig. 10-16.

Font style

Click on the right mouse button or press Esc to return to the Text Attributes menu. With most fonts, you have a choice of several different font styles, and the range of

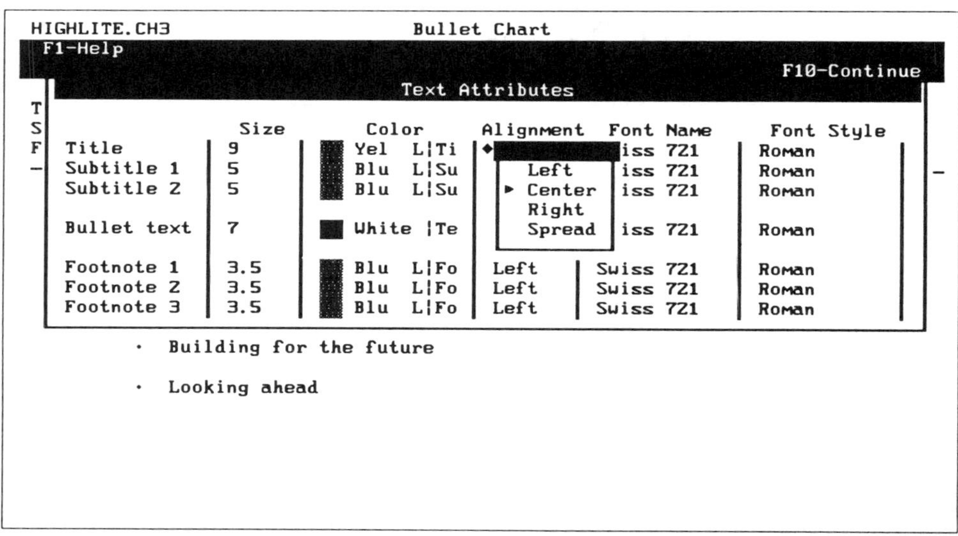

10-11 The alignment options pop-up box.

Annual Highlights

Compression Labs Report to Stockholders, 1990

- Growing revenues and earnings
- Delivering complete solutions
- Penetrating vertical markets
- Forging strategic partnerships
- Building for the future
- Looking ahead

Condensed for oral presentation

10-12 The text chart with title and subtitle aligned left.

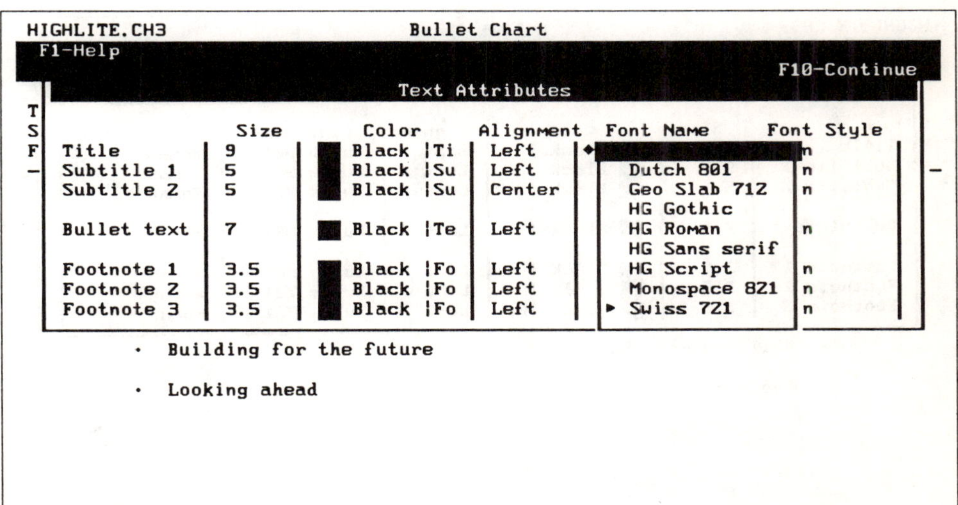

10-13 The Font Name pop-up box.

Eight Harvard Graphics 3.0 Fonts

- This is Dutch 801
- *This is Geo Slab 712*
- This is HG Gothic
- This is HG Roman
- This is HG Sans serif
- *This is HG Script*
- This is Monospace 821
- This is Swiss 721

10-14 The eight standard Harvard Graphics 3.0 fonts.

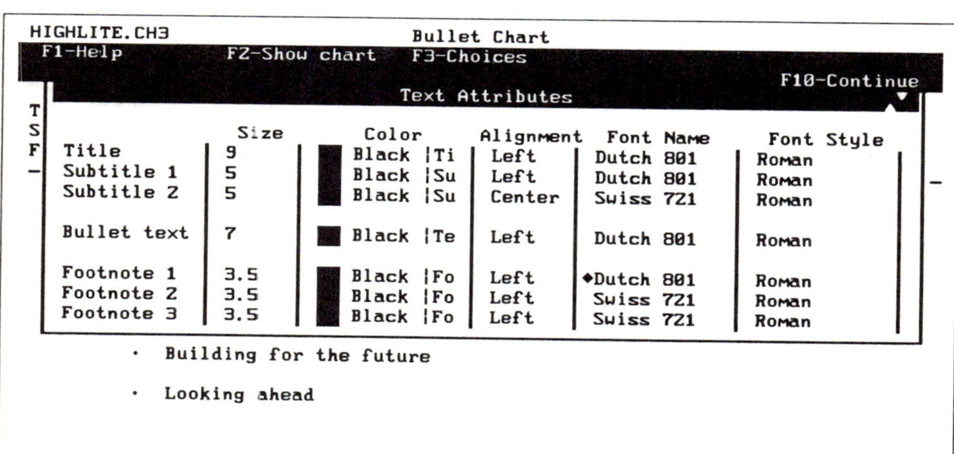

	Size	Color	Alignment	Font Name	Font Style
Title	9	Black ¦Ti	Left	Dutch 801	Roman
Subtitle 1	5	Black ¦Su	Left	Dutch 801	Roman
Subtitle 2	5	Black ¦Su	Center	Swiss 721	Roman
Bullet text	7	Black ¦Te	Left	Dutch 801	Roman
Footnote 1	3.5	Black ¦Fo	Left	◆Dutch 801	Roman
Footnote 2	3.5	Black ¦Fo	Left	Swiss 721	Roman
Footnote 3	3.5	Black ¦Fo	Left	Swiss 721	Roman

10-15 The Font Name column, with our fonts changed to Dutch 801.

Annual Highlights

Compression Labs Report to Stockholders, 1990

- Growing revenues and earnings
- Delivering complete solutions
- Penetrating vertical markets
- Forging strategic partnerships
- Building for the future
- Looking ahead

Condensed for oral presentation

10-16 The chart in progress, with fonts changed to Dutch 801.

choices will vary depending on the font you choose. The current font style listed in your Title row is probably Roman.

If you click on Roman, then press F3 for Choices, you'll see that the Font Style options are Bold, Bold Italic, Italic, and Roman (see Fig. 10-17). To get a sense of the difference in appearance of the four font styles, select Bold for the title, Bold Italic for the bullet text, Italic for Footnote 1, and Roman for Subtitle 1. Your Font Style column will look like Fig. 10-18, and when you press F2 to see your chart it will look like Fig. 10-19.

That completes the range of modifications available in text attributes. Next, let's investigate the Appearance selections.

Working with the Appearance options

If you press Esc or the right mouse button to return to the Bullet Chart data screen, then select F8–Options once again, you'll see that the third of these options is Appearance. Select Appearance, and the Appearance Options menu is displayed (see Fig. 10-20). There are several possibilities for altering the appearance of a text chart on this menu:

```
HIGHLITE.CH3                          Bullet Chart
 F1-Help
                                                                      F10-Continue
                                   Text Attributes
T
S                  Size        Color    Alignment  Font Name       Font Style
F  Title          | 9      |  Black |Ti | Left   | Dutch 801  |◆Roman
-  Subtitle 1     | 5      |  Black |Su | Left   | Dutch 801  | Roman           -
   Subtitle 2     | 5      |  Bla                | Swiss 721  | Roman
                  |        |      Bold
   Bullet text    | 7      |  Bla  Bold Italic   | Dutch 801  | Roman
                  |        |       Italic
   Footnote 1     | 3.5    |  Bla ▸ Roman        | Dutch 801  | Roman
   Footnote 2     | 3.5    |  Bla                | Swiss 721  | Roman
   Footnote 3     | 3.5    |  Black |Fo | Left   | Swiss 721  | Roman

         •  Building for the future

         •  Looking ahead
```

10-17 The Font Style choices for Dutch 801.

```
HIGHLITE.CH3                          Bullet Chart
 F1-Help           F2-Show chart   F3-Choices
                                                                      F10-Continue
                                   Text Attributes
T
S                  Size        Color    Alignment  Font Name       Font Style
F  Title          | 9      |  Black |Ti | Left   | Dutch 801  | Bold
-  Subtitle 1     | 5      |  Black |Su | Left   | Dutch 801  | Roman           -
   Subtitle 2     | 5      |  Black |Su | Center | Swiss 721  | Roman

   Bullet text    | 7      |  Black |Te | Left   | Dutch 801  | Bold Italic

   Footnote 1     | 3.5    |  Black |Fo | Left   | Dutch 801  |◆Italic
   Footnote 2     | 3.5    |  Black |Fo | Left   | Swiss 721  | Roman
   Footnote 3     | 3.5    |  Black |Fo | Left   | Swiss 721  | Roman

         •  Building for the future

         •  Looking ahead
```

10-18 The Font Style column with some new selections.

Landscape or Portrait Orientation

To change the orientation of a chart from landscape (horizontal) to portrait (vertical), click on the Chart Orientation line to highlight it. When the little diamond appears next to Landscape, select F3–Choices and the small box with the Landscape/Portrait option will appear (see Fig. 10-21). Click on Portrait, then press F2

Annual Highlights

Compression Labs Report to Stockholders, 1990

- ***Growing revenues and earnings***
- ***Delivering complete solutions***
- ***Penetrating vertical markets***
- ***Forging strategic partnerships***
- ***Building for the future***
- ***Looking ahead***

Condensed for oral presentation

10-19 The new font styles as they appear in the current chart.

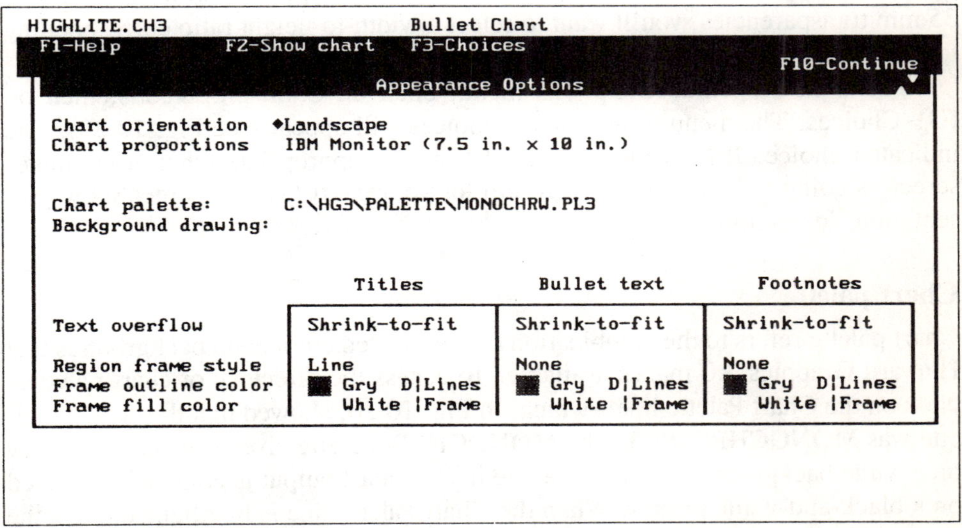

10-20 The Appearance Options menu.

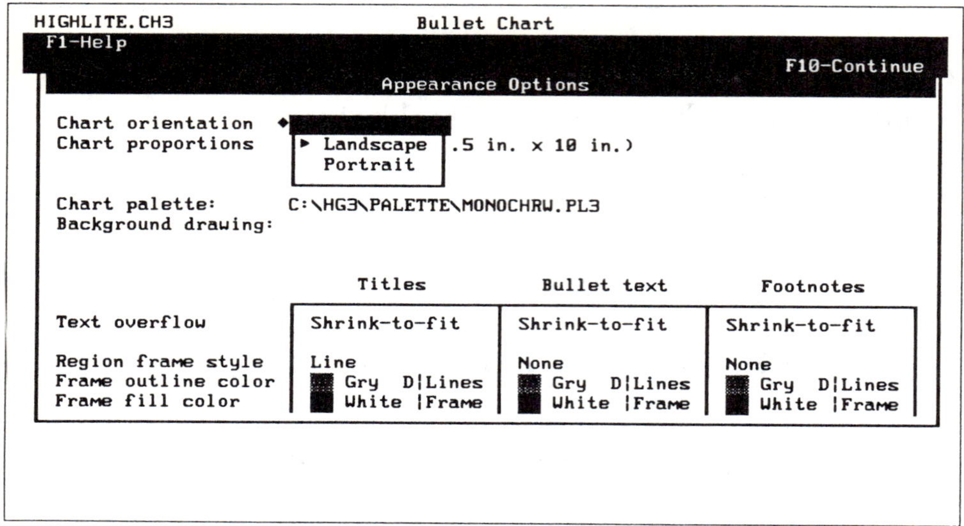

10-21 The Chart Orientation option box.

to see what your chart would look like in the vertical format (see Fig. 10-22). If your chart is going to be inserted into text printed out on standard $8^1/_2 \times 11$ sheets, you will probably want to use the portrait orientation.

Chart proportions

The Chart proportions settings allow you to prepare charts that are sized in proportion to the output format you plan. For example, if you plan to show the charts on 35 mm transparencies, you'll want to select a width-to-height ratio corresponding to that of 35 mm slides.

From the Appearance Options menu, click on Chart proportions, then on F3–Choices. The menu of proportion choices will appear (see Fig. 10-23). The indicated choice, IBM Monitor (7.5×10 in.), is appropriate when a computer screen is going to be the output medium for your chart (as in a ScreenShow presentation, for example).

Chart palette

Chart palette refers to the combination of preselected colors and backgrounds that Harvard Graphics 3.0 makes available. To access the directory of chart palettes, click on the Chart Palette line—which, in Fig. 10-20, showed that the current palette was MONOCHRW.PL3. The MONOCHRW palette gives you shades of gray on a white background—a useful palette if your chart output is going to be printed on a black-and-white printer. When the Chart Palette line is highlighted, with the choice diamond in front of the filename, select F3–Choices to bring up the Get Chart Palette directory (see Fig. 10-24).

Annual Highlights

Compression Labs Report to Stockholders, 1990

- *Growing revenues and earnings*
- *Delivering complete solutions*
- *Penetrating vertical markets*
- *Forging strategic partnerships*
- *Building for the future*
- *Looking ahead*

Condensed for oral presentation

10-22 The text chart in the Portrait or vertical orientation.

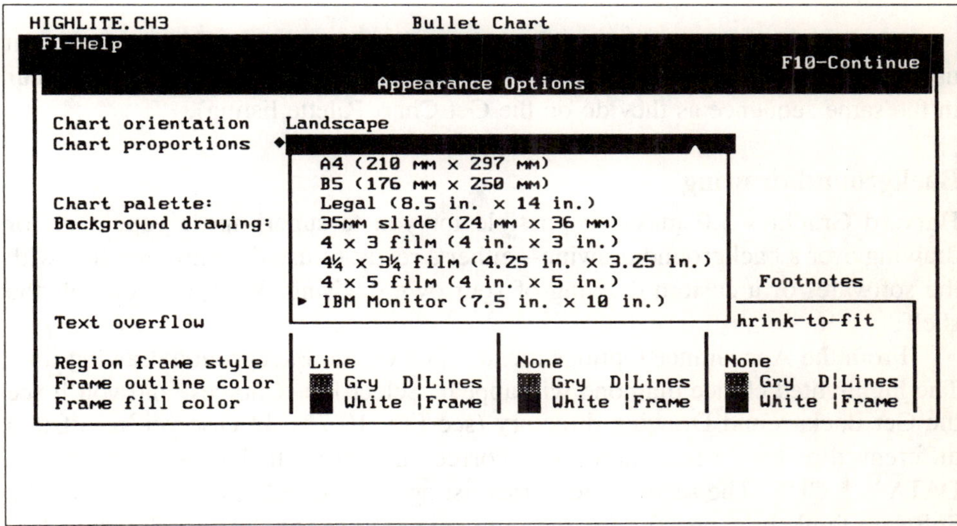

10-23 The partial menu of available chart proportions.

This directory lists filenames, the background color, and the dominant hues. For example, the first palette in the directory listing, HG3.PL3 (the default palette), uses a black background, and the dominant colors are cyans and blues. To change the palette for the current chart, simply locate the cursor on the filename of the palette you want to use and click the right mouse button. You are then returned to the Appearance Options menu.

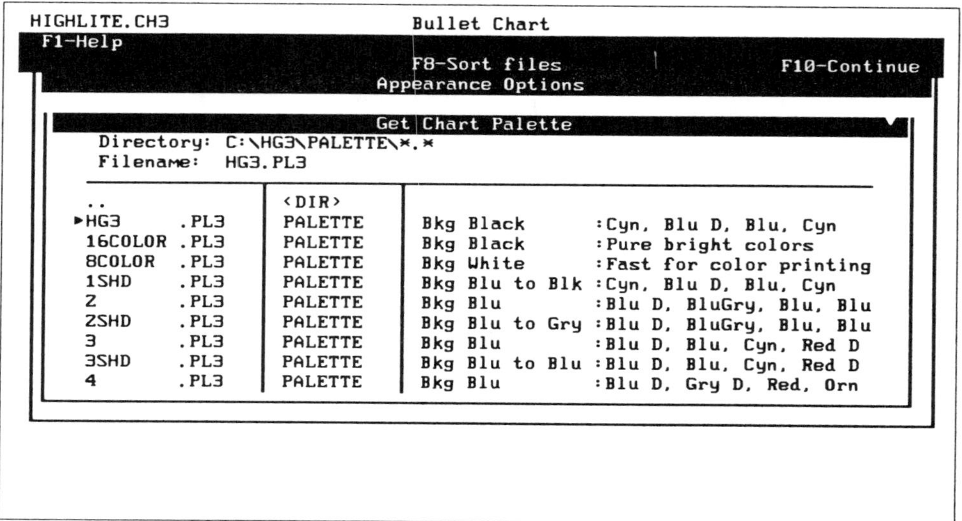

10-24 The Get Chart Palette directory.

The best way to learn about color palettes is trial and error. You might find it useful to go the Gallery home screen and browse through the palettes (they occur in the same sequence as they do on the Get Chart Palette listing).

Background drawing

Harvard Graphics 3.0 makes it possible for you to superimpose your chart or drawing over a background drawing—either a ready-to-use drawing supplied with the software, or a custom drawing of your own devising. We'll take one off the shelf.

From the Appearance Options menu, click on the Background drawing line. The highlighted choice diamond will appear. Select F3–Choices, and you'll see the Get Background Drawing directory (see Fig. 10-25). In case you're off in a different directory somewhere, the correct directory listing is C:\HG3\DATA*.CH*. The second file in this listing, BLUESKY.CH3, is one that the Software Publishing people like to use in their promos for Harvard Graphics 3.0, so we'll try it out.

Click on BLUESKY.CH3. You'll be returned to the Appearance Options menu, and the file you selected will now be listed as the background drawing (see Fig. 10-26). Select F2–Show Chart, and the background of blue skies and white clouds will be drawn first, then your bullet chart superimposed on it. Except for the fact that the gray bullets are disappearing into the sky, this is actually a pretty jazzy, readable graphic, as shown in Fig. 10-27. (We'll take care of those gray bullets later.)

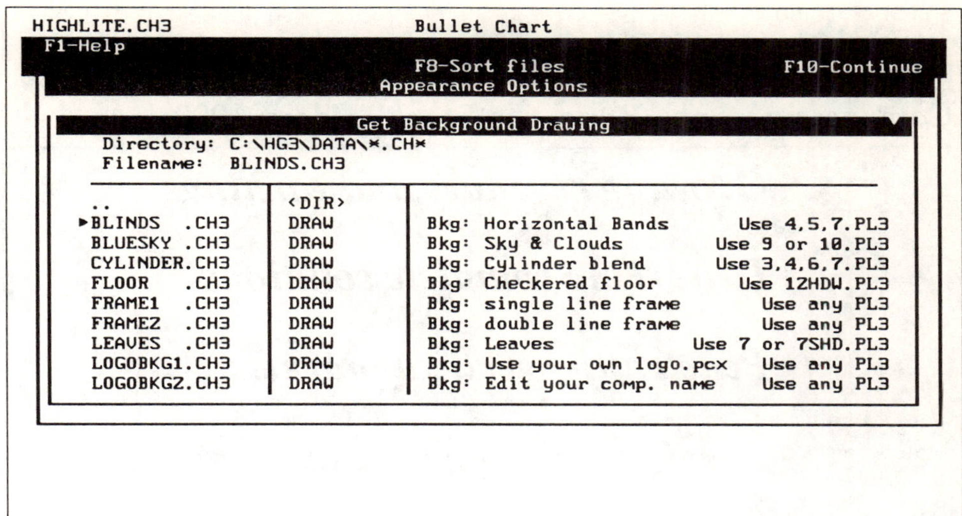

10-25 The Get Background Drawing directory.

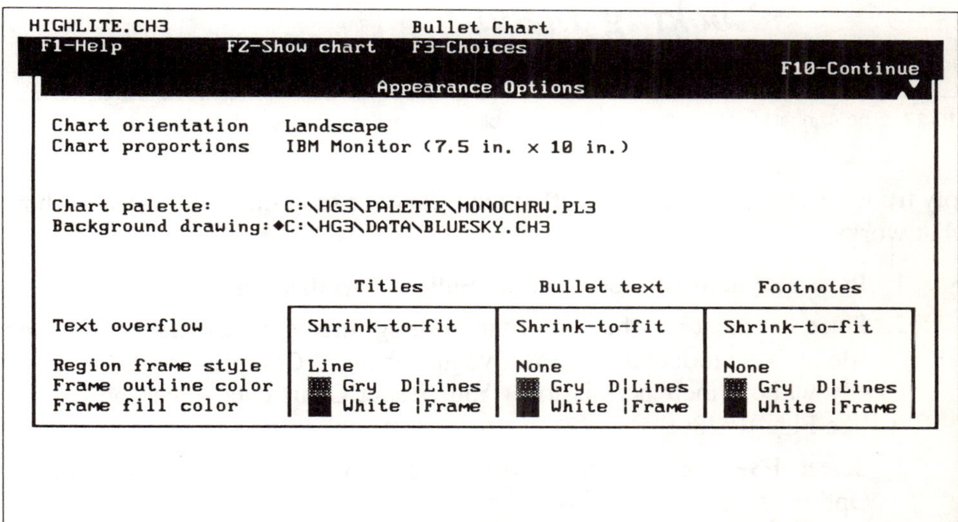

10-26 The Appearance Options menu now shows BLUESKY.CH3 as the background drawing.

Text overflow

Yet another of the remaining options on the Appearance Options screen is Text overflow. This option lets you choose one of three solutions when you have lines of text that threaten to run off the side or the bottom of the screen. You can choose to shrink the text to fit your screen, wrap the text by creating additional lines, or sim-

10-27 The Annual Highlights bullet chart with a blue sky background (use your imagination).

ply truncate the text by cutting it off at the right edge or at the bottom. Here's how that works:

1. Press Esc until you return to the Bullet Chart data screen.
2. Place the cursor at the end of the Forging Strategic Partnerships line and add in new product areas. (You've just changed Compression Labs' strategy without their permission.) Your Bullet Chart data screen now looks like Fig. 10-28.
3. Select F8–Options, then Appearance, to return to the Appearance Options screen.
4. Delete the Background drawing file by clicking on that line, then pressing Ctrl–Del.

You see that the default setting for text overflow is Shrink-to-fit. Press F2 to see what your chart looks like with the new text added (see Fig. 10-29). The text size has been shrunk so that the long line of bullet text will fit on the screen as a single line.

Click the right mouse button, then click on Shrink-to-fit under Bullet text. Select F3–Choices, and your three options will appear: Truncate, Shrink-to-fit,

```
HIGHLITE.CH3                       Bullet Chart
 F1-Help          F2-Show chart                         F4-Draw          F5-Mark
 F6-Main Menu     F7-Spell/Text    F8-Options           F9-Edit bullet   F10-Continue

Title:     Annual Highlights
Subtitle:  Compression Labs Report to Stockholders, 1990
Footnote:  Condensed for oral presentation
------------------------------------------------------------------------------------
           •  Growing revenues and earnings

           •  Delivering complete solutions

           •  Penetrating vertical markets

           •  Forging strategic partnerships in new product areas

           •  Building for the future

           •  Looking ahead
```

10-28 The added text in the fourth bullet line.

Annual Highlights

Compression Labs Report to Stockholders, 1990

- ***Growing revenues and earnings***
- ***Delivering complete solutions***
- ***Penetrating vertical markets***
- ***Forging strategic partnerships in new product areas***
- ***Building for the future***
- ***Looking ahead***

Condensed for oral presentation

10-29 The bullet chart with text size adjusted to fit in the new line.

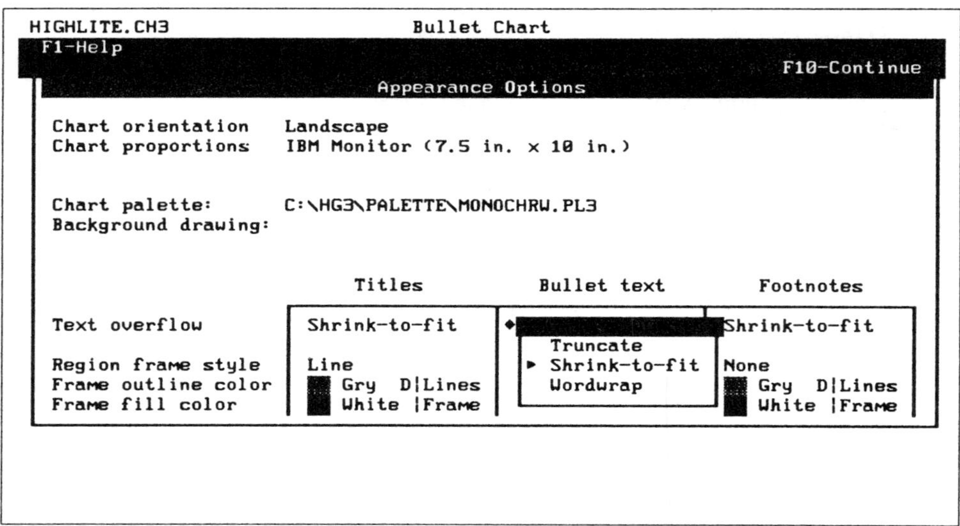

10-30 The Text overflow options box.

Annual Highlights

Compression Labs Report to Stockholders, 1990

- ***Growing revenues and earnings***
- ***Delivering complete solutions***
- ***Penetrating vertical markets***
- ***Forging strategic partnerships in new produ***
- ***Building for the future***

Condensed for oral presentation

10-31 The bullet chart with truncated text.

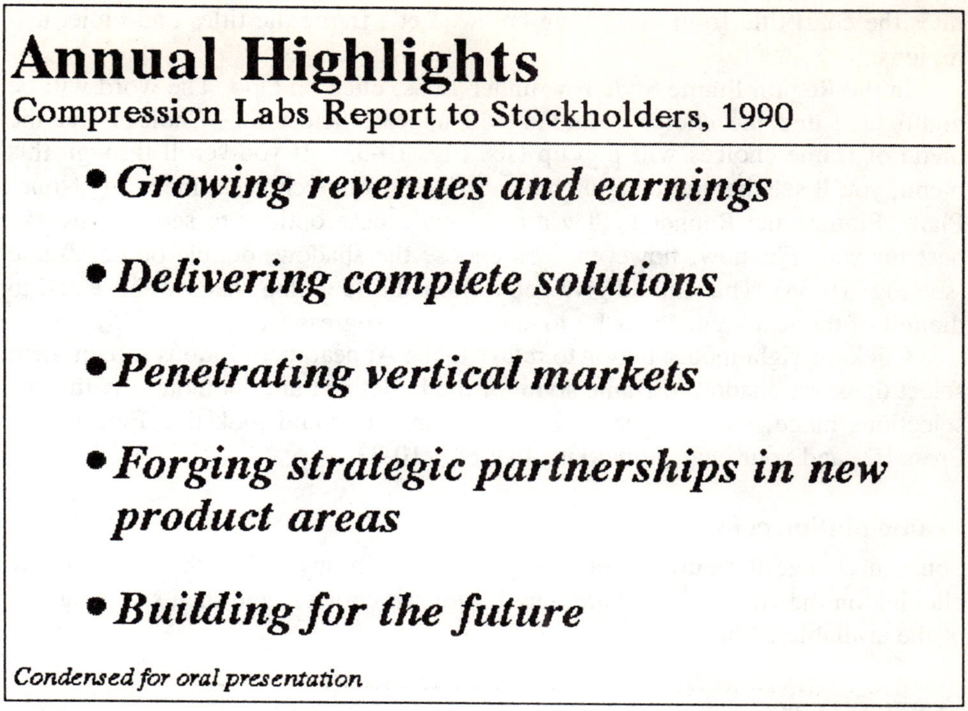

Annual Highlights

Compression Labs Report to Stockholders, 1990

- *Growing revenues and earnings*
- *Delivering complete solutions*
- *Penetrating vertical markets*
- *Forging strategic partnerships in new product areas*
- *Building for the future*

Condensed for oral presentation

10-32 The fourth bullet text is wrapped into a second line, but the final bullet item is missing.

and Wordwrap (see Fig. 10-30). Now click on Truncate, and it will appear in the Text Overflow line. The truncate option will display text in its specified size, and anything that doesn't fit on the screen—either horizontally or vertically—will simply be cut off. Press F2 to see the results of your truncation (see Fig. 10-31).

Press Esc to return to the Appearance Options menu, select F3 – Choices once more, and this time choose Wordwrap. When you press F2 to view this latest alteration of your chart, you'll see that the text in the fourth bullet line has been wrapped into a second line, but that the final bullet item—Looking ahead—is off the screen (see Fig. 10-32). Click the right mouse button to return to the Appearance Options menu, and change the text overflow setting back to Shrink-to-fit.

Region frame style

You can also choose to put frames around your bullet chart. The next option is called Region frame style because you can elect to separately frame the three regions of the chart: the title region, the bullet text region, and the footnotes region.

The current chart settings indicate no frame in the bullet text and footnotes regions, and a line in the titles region. That refers to the horizontal line that separates the chart title from everything below. Let's frame the titles and bullet text regions.

In the Region Frame Style row under Titles, click on Line. The word will be highlighted and the choice diamond will appear. Select F3—Choices and the menu of frame choices will pop up (see Fig. 10-33). If you scroll through this menu, you'll see that there are eighteen different frame choices, including None, Plain, Frame, and Rounded. Play around with these options to see what works best for you. For now, however, let's choose the shadow, double-border frame (see Fig. 10-34). That should give you a framed title with a shadow above and to the left of the text area. Press F2 to check your progress (see Fig. 10-35).

Click the right mouse button to return to the Appearance Options screen, then select the same shadowed frame style for the bullet text and footnotes. With your selections made, your Appearance Options menu should look like Fig. 10-36. Press F2, and your chart now looks like Fig. 10-37.

Frame outline color

You can change the outline color of your frame in any of the three regions by clicking on the current color, pressing F3 for the choices, and then selecting one of the available colors.

Frame fill color

The frame fill color refers to the area inside the frame boundaries. To change that color, click on the right mouse button to return to the Appearance Options menu,

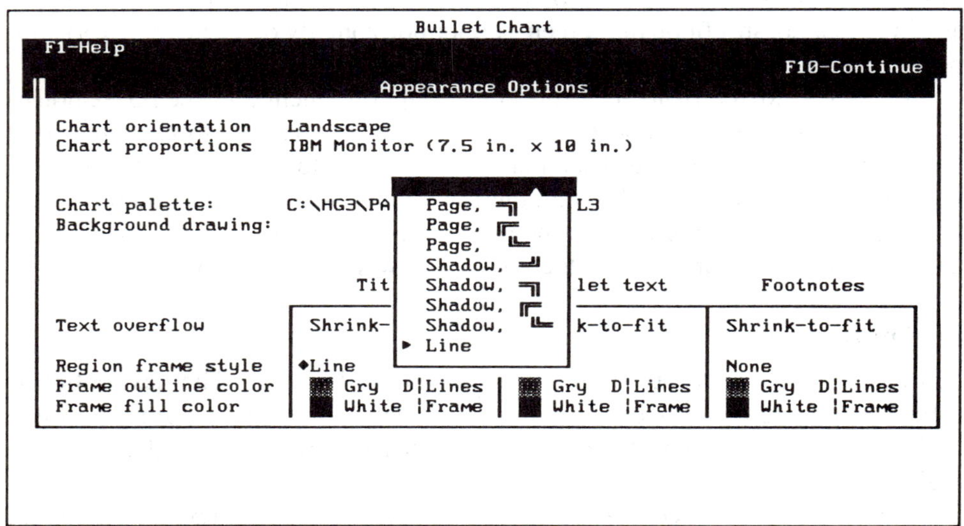

10-33 The partial menu of frame choices.

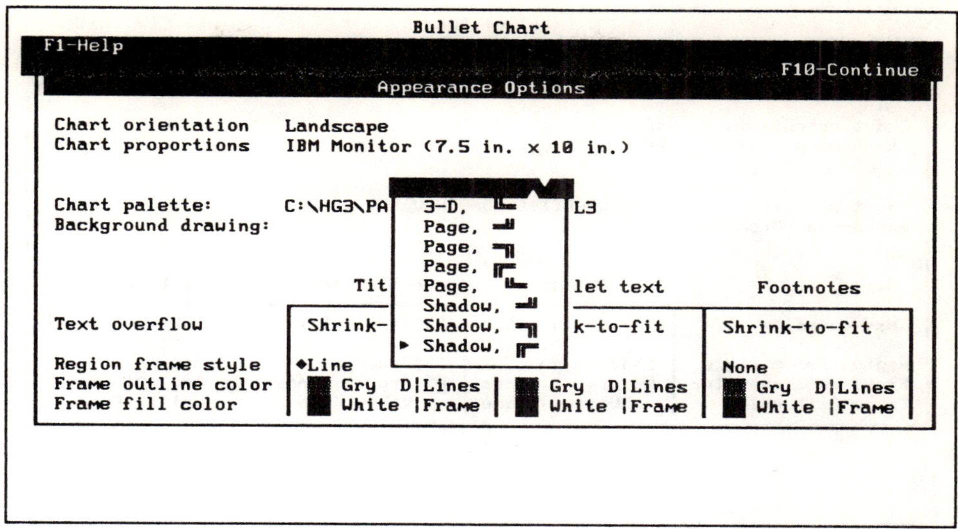

10-34 The double-border, shadow choice in the Frame Style menu.

Annual Highlights

Compression Labs Report to Stockholders, 1990

- ***Growing revenues and earnings***
- ***Delivering complete solutions***
- ***Penetrating vertical markets***
- ***Forging strategic partnerships in new product areas***
- ***Building for the future***
- ***Looking ahead***

Condensed for oral presentation

10-35 The chart in progress with a shadowed title region.

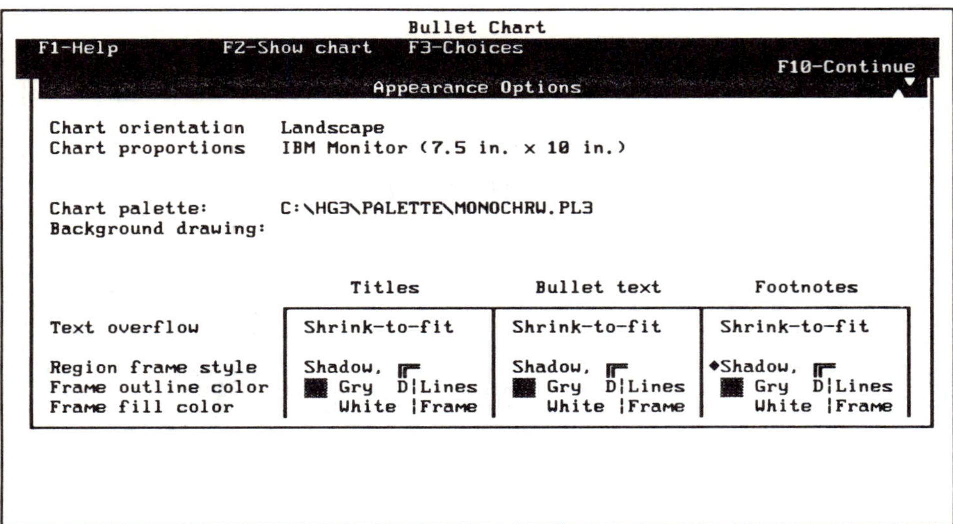

10-36 The Appearance Options menu after you select the shadowed frame style for all three regions.

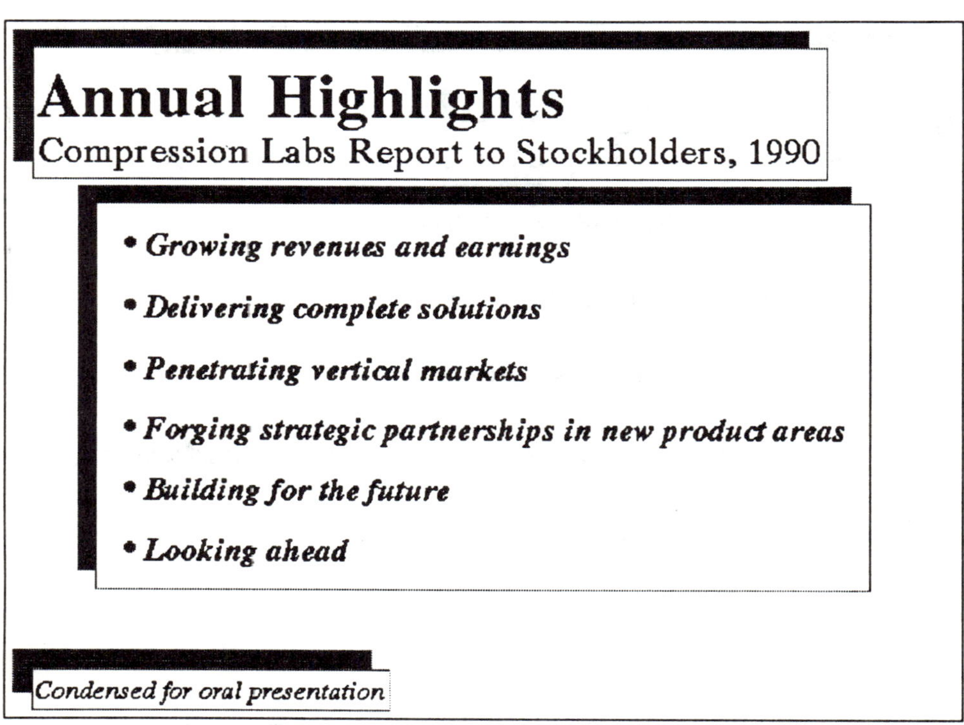

10-37 The fully framed chart.

then click on Frame fill color in the Titles column. Select F3 – Choices, and the Frame Fill Color Options menu will pop up (see Fig. 10-38).

Pick a color that strikes your fancy. (I'm currently working with the MONOCHRW.PL3 palette, so I'll choose the lightest gray, indicated on the menu as Gry LL¦Series5. In similar fashion, choose a color (good aesthetics will probably dictate the same color) to fill the bullet text and footnotes frames. With that accomplished, your Appearance Options menu will resemble Fig. 10-39, and when you press F2 the latest version of this increasingly-enhanced chart will look something like Fig. 10-40.

That covers the range of alterations you can make to a chart via the Appearance Options menu. But there are more possible enhancements waiting in the wings, and you don't even have to pause for a commercial message.

Adding notes to your text chart

You can add notes—up to 11 lines of text—to your charts. From the Bullet Chart data screen, select F8 – Options, and then, when the Options menu appears, select Notes. You can also get to the Notes menu from the Bullet Chart data screen by pressing Ctrl – N (see Fig. 10-41). Let's add a note to this chart, then get a printout. Type the following:

> The data in this chart is based upon the Compression Labs (Enter)
> 1990 annual report to shareholders. For updated figures, (Enter)
> refer to the quarterly reports for fiscal 1991. (Enter)

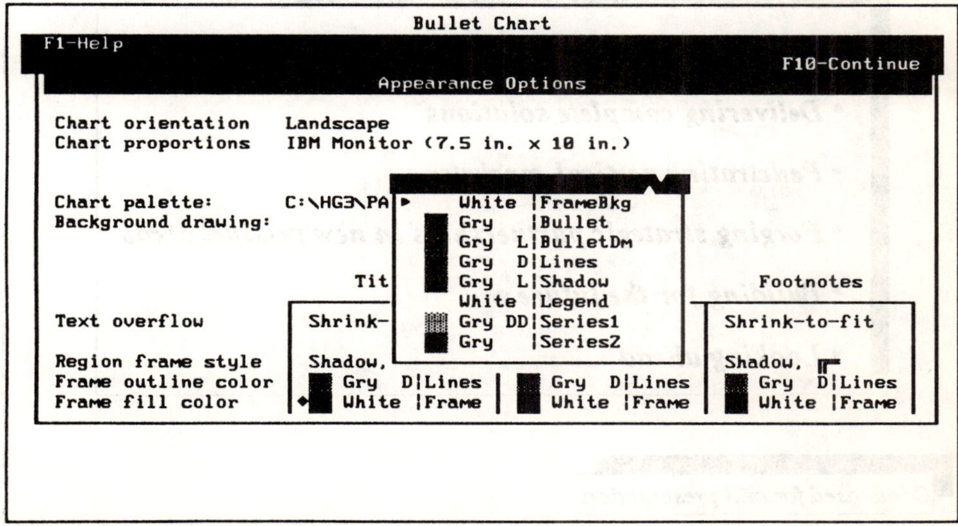

10-38 The Frame fill color options menu.

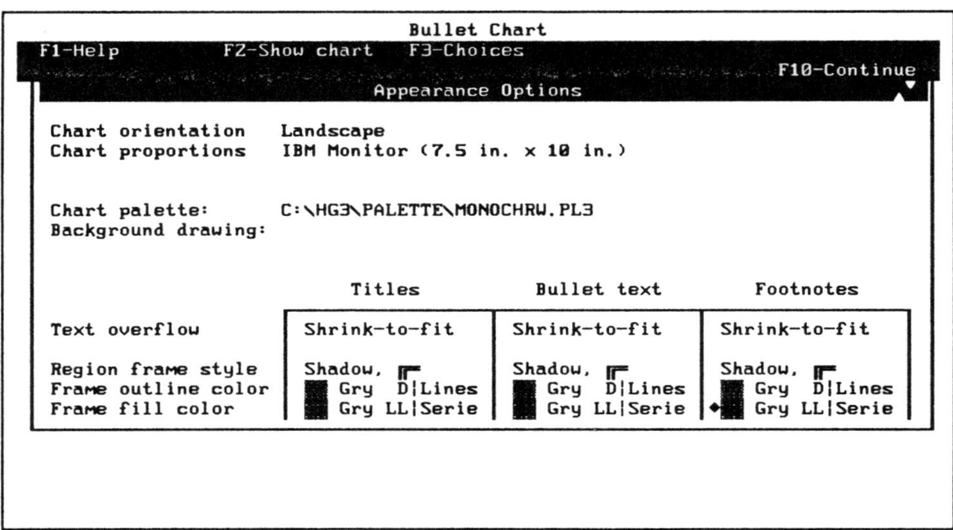

10-39 The Appearance Options menu with new fill colors chosen.

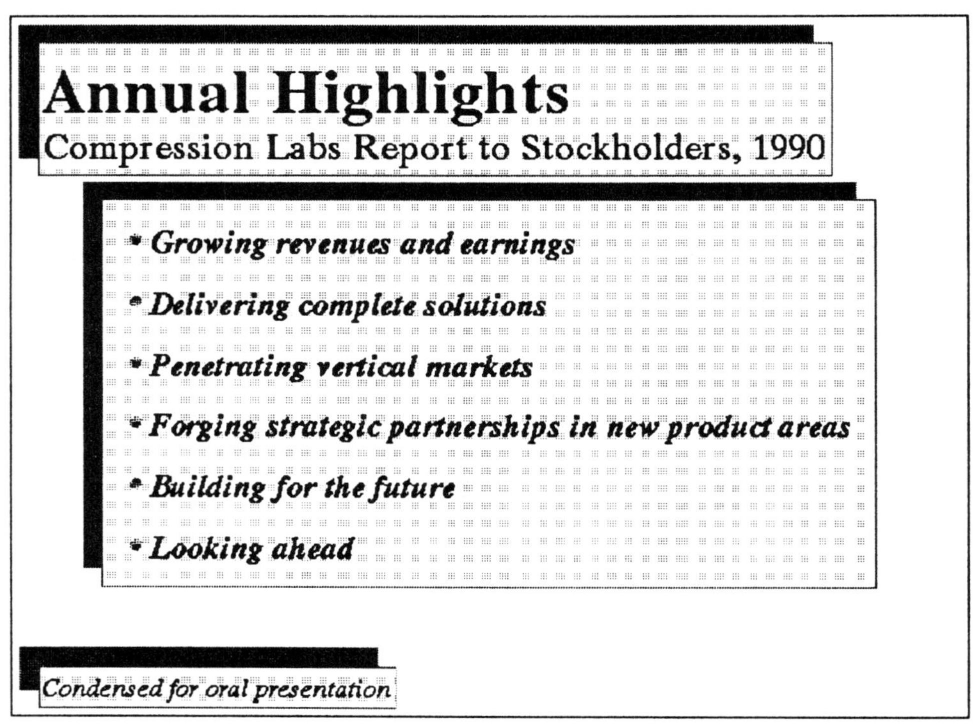

10-40 The bullet chart with a frame fill color in all regions.

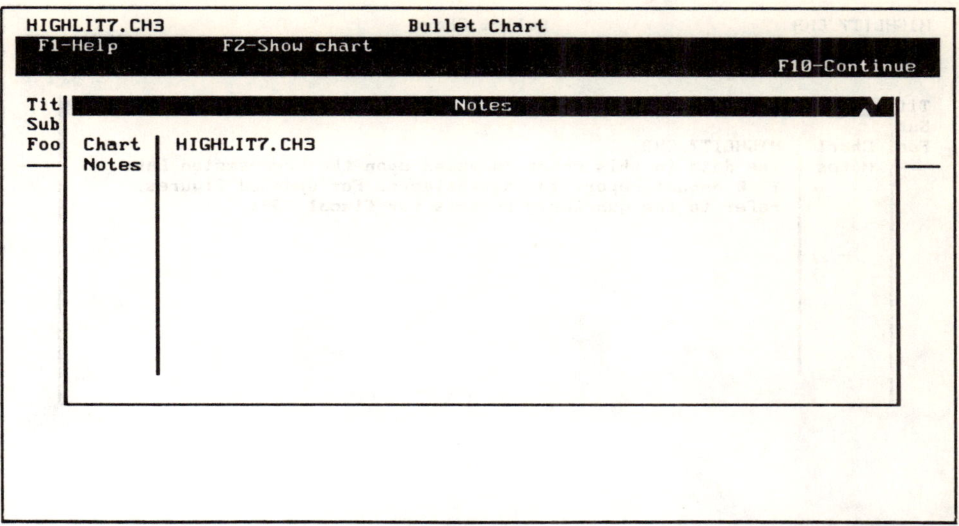

10-41 The Notes menu for appending comments to your chart.

You need to press the Enter key at the end of each line because text isn't wrapped to the next line in the Note function (see Fig. 10-42). Press F10 to record your note and return to the Bullet Chart data screen. To save this chart with the note, press Ctrl–S and type highlit7 for the filename. Select F10–Continue and you're finished.

Changing the bullet options

Harvard Graphics 3.0 gives you a bit of latitude about the way bullets look. To change all of the bullets, select F8–Options, then, from the Options menu, select Bullet options, item 5. The Bullet Options menu will pop up (see Fig. 10-43). You can make changes in a number of bullet-related features. From this menu you can change the type, size, color, numbering, indentation, and vertical alignment. Let's change some of those features:

1. Select Bullet type, then press F3 for choices. A partial menu of bullet choices will be displayed (see Fig. 10-44). Click on the arrowhead symbol (►).
2. Select Bullet size, then F3–Choices. The little size options box will pop up (see Fig. 10-45). Click on Large.
3. Select Bullet color, then F3–Choices. When the Color pop-up menu appears, scroll through it and select a color (the grays and whites in Fig. 10-46 represent the MONOCHRW.PL3 palette; my bullet color selection was black).

HIGHLIT7.CH3
Bullet Chart
F1-Help
F2-Show chart
F10-Continue
Tit
Sub
Foo
Notes
Chart
Notes
HIGHLIT7.CH3
The data in this chart is based upon the Compression Labs
1990 annual report to shareholders. For updated figures,
refer to the quarterly reports for fiscal 1991.

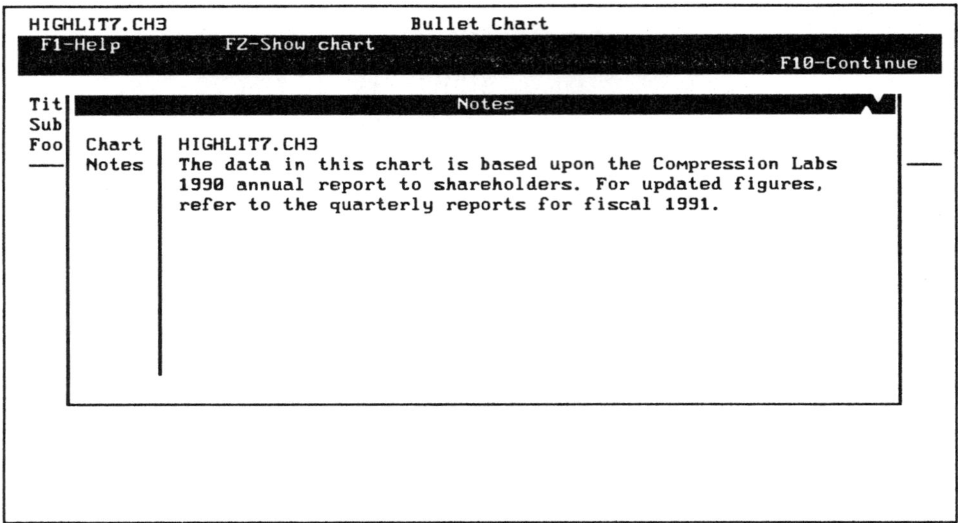

10-42 The Notes pop-up with your notes for the Highlite chart.

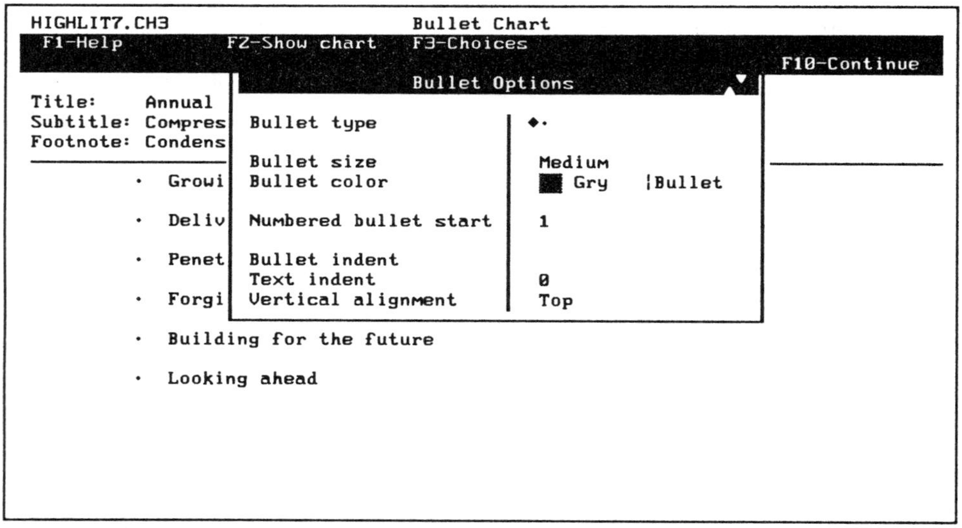

HIGHLIT7.CH3
Bullet Chart
F1-Help
F2-Show chart
F3-Choices
F10-Continue
Bullet Options
Title: Annual
Subtitle: Compres
Footnote: Condens
Bullet type
♦•
Bullet size
Medium
Bullet color
Gry
Bullet
• Growi
• Deliv
Numbered bullet start
1
• Penet
Bullet indent
Text indent
0
• Forgi
Vertical alignment
Top
• Building for the future
• Looking ahead

10-43 The Bullet Options menu.

Because you're using bullets instead of numbers, the Numbered bullet start option doesn't apply. But if you choose to number the items on your chart, you can start the numbering with any number from 0 to 100. Select Bullet indent. The number that you enter here is a measure of the space from the left edge of your screen or paper to the bullet. Typing 0 gives you left justification, 100 gives right justification. If there's no number, the text will be centered.

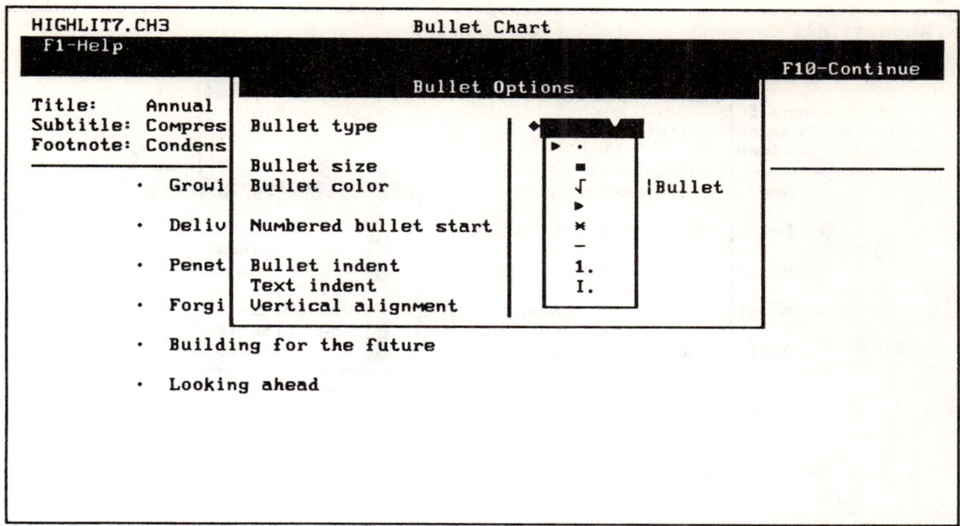

10-44 The menu choices pop-up.

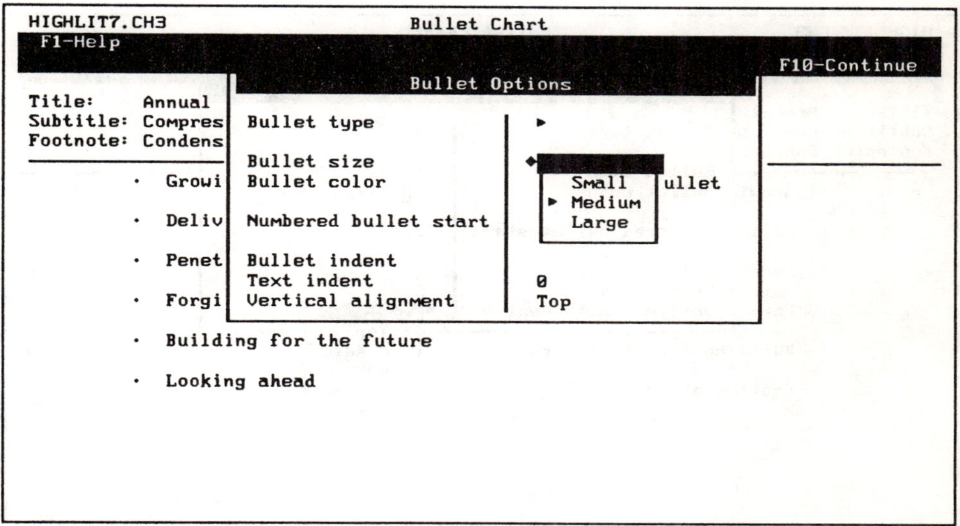

10-45 The bullet size options box.

Type 0 and hit Enter for left justification. The cursor will move down to the Text Indent line. Text indent is a measure of the distance between the bullet and the beginning of the first word in the line of text. You can enter a number between 0 and 90. Type 5 and Enter. The cursor will move to the Vertical Alignment line. Select F3–Choices, and your Vertical Alignment Options menu will pop up (see Fig. 10-47).

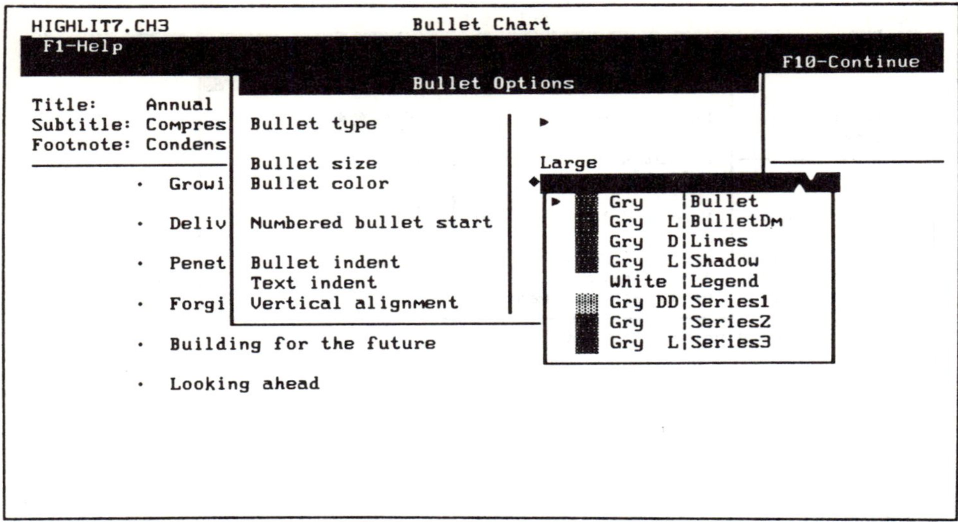

10-46 The Bullet Color pop-up menu.

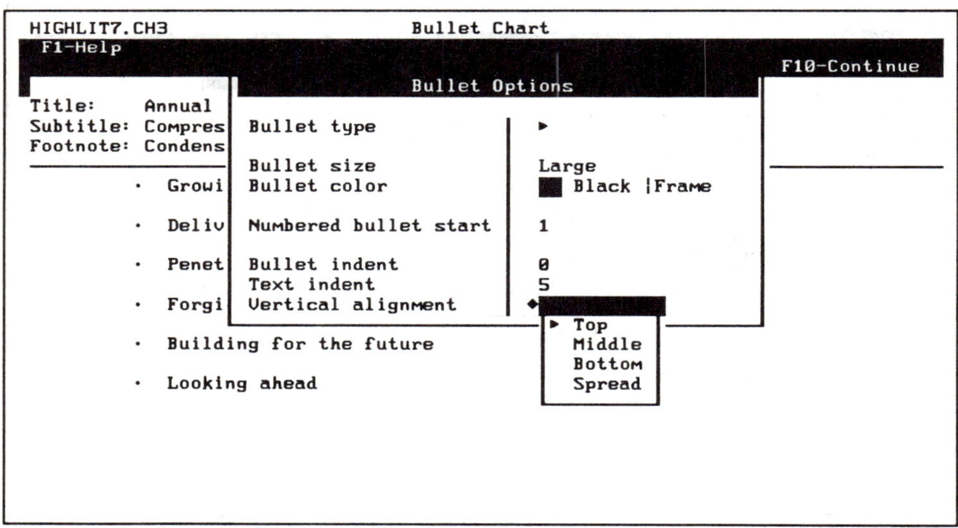

10-47 The Vertical Alignment options.

Your choices are Top, Middle, Bottom, and Spread. In other words, your bulleted text items can be bunched at the top, middle, or bottom, or they can be spread evenly over the page from top to bottom. Select Spread.

You have now completed all the choices in the Bullet Options box, which should look like Fig. 10-48. To see what changes you've wrought in the appearance of the bullet chart, press F2. That's not a bad-looking chart (see Fig. 10-49).

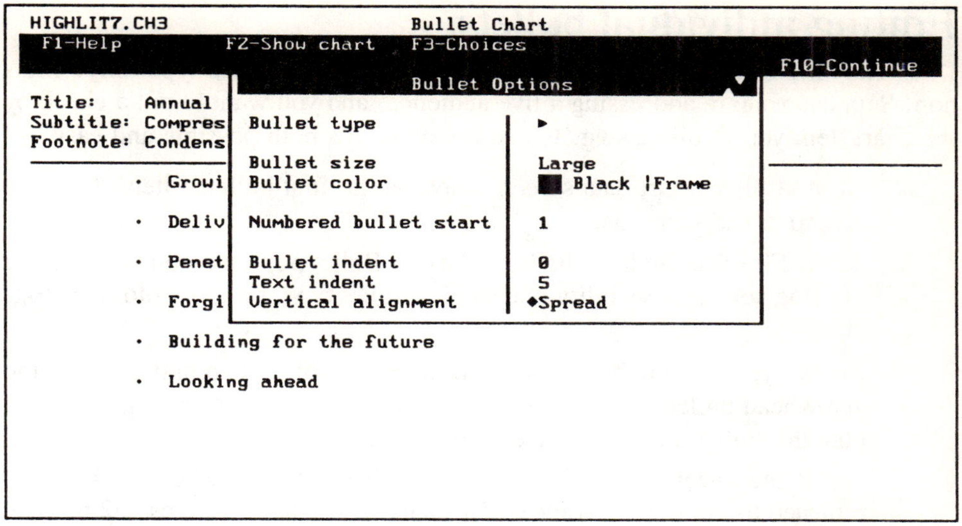

```
HIGHLIT7.CH3                      Bullet Chart
 F1-Help          F2-Show chart   F3-Choices
                                                      F10-Continue
                                  Bullet Options
Title:     Annual
Subtitle:  Compres   Bullet type                    ►
Footnote:  Condens
                     Bullet size                    Large
          • Growi    Bullet color                   █ Black |Frame

          • Deliv    Numbered bullet start          1

          • Penet    Bullet indent                  0
                     Text indent                    5
          • Forgi    Vertical alignment            ◆Spread

          • Building for the future

          • Looking ahead
```

10-48 The Bullet Options box, with your new selections.

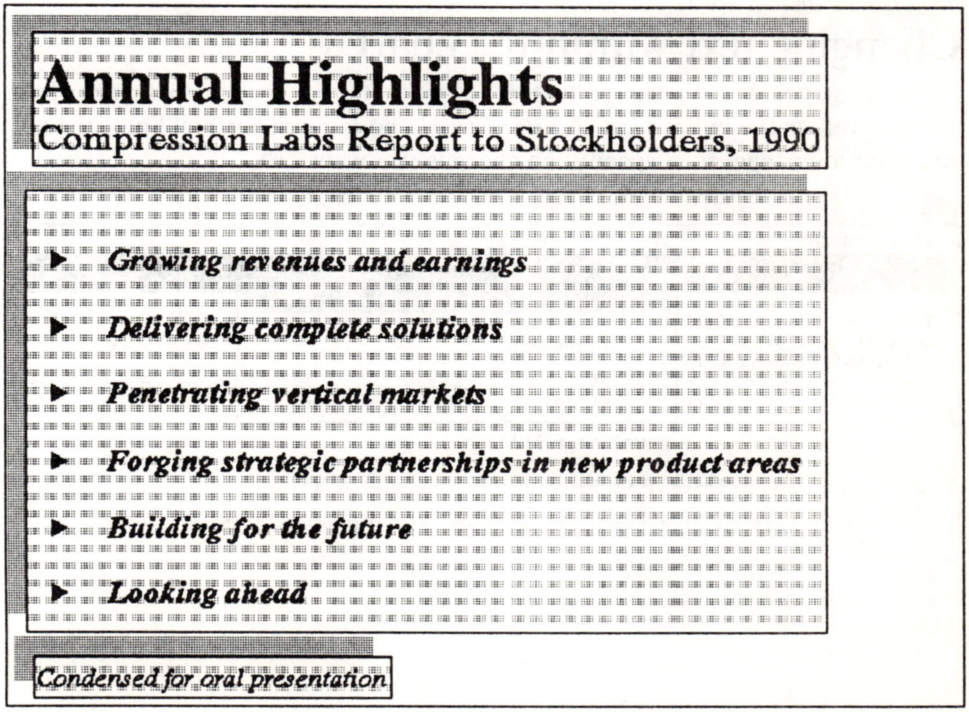

Annual Highlights

Compression Labs Report to Stockholders, 1990

- ► *Growing revenues and earnings*
- ► *Delivering complete solutions*
- ► *Penetrating vertical markets*
- ► *Forging strategic partnerships in new product areas*
- ► *Building for the future*
- ► *Looking ahead*

Condensed for oral presentation

10-49 The Highlights chart with the new bullet options.

Editing individual bullets

Does Harvard Graphics 3.0 require you to have bullets of one type only? Mais non! Suppose you are addressing a live audience, and you want to put a check by the chart item you're discussing. Is that possible? It's both possible and easy.

1. At the Bullet Chart data screen, click on the first bulleted item, Growing revenues and earnings.
2. Select F9 – Edit bullet. The Edit Current Bullet pop-up menu will appear, offering you the possibility of changing bullet type, size, or color (see Fig. 10-50).
3. Bullet type should be highlighted with a choice diamond next to the arrowhead bullet. Select F3 – Choices or click on Bullet type again to display the Bullet Type menu (see Fig. 10-51).
4. Select the checkmark bullet type (just above the arrowhead). You'll be returned to the Edit Current Bullet menu, and when you press F2 to view the altered chart it now displays the checkmark, as shown in Fig. 10-52.
5. Press Esc twice to return to the data screen and close the Edit Current Bullet pop-up menu.

Changing text within the chart

But suppose you want to change the text of that first item, or the appearance of the text, as well as the bullet type. All you have to do is mark, or highlight, the text you want to change, then specify the changes you want.

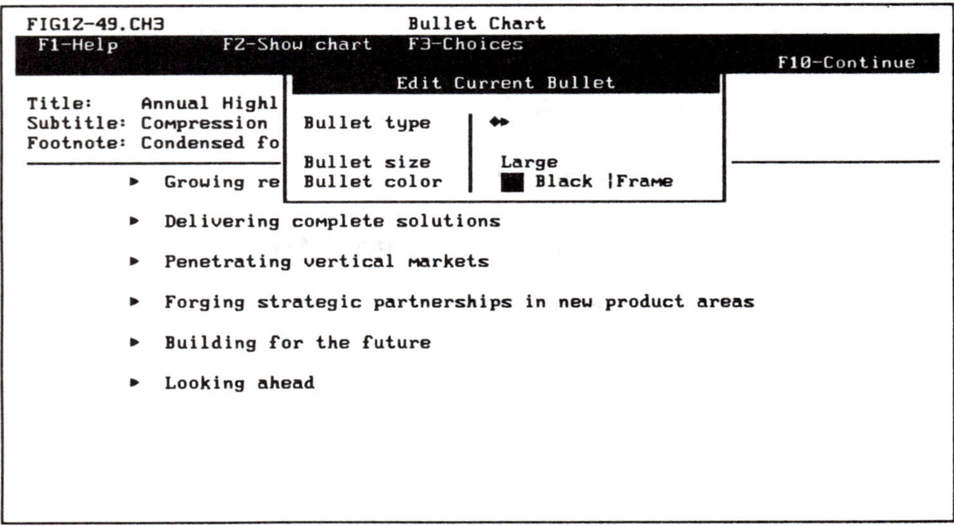

10-50 The Edit Current Bullet pop-up menu.

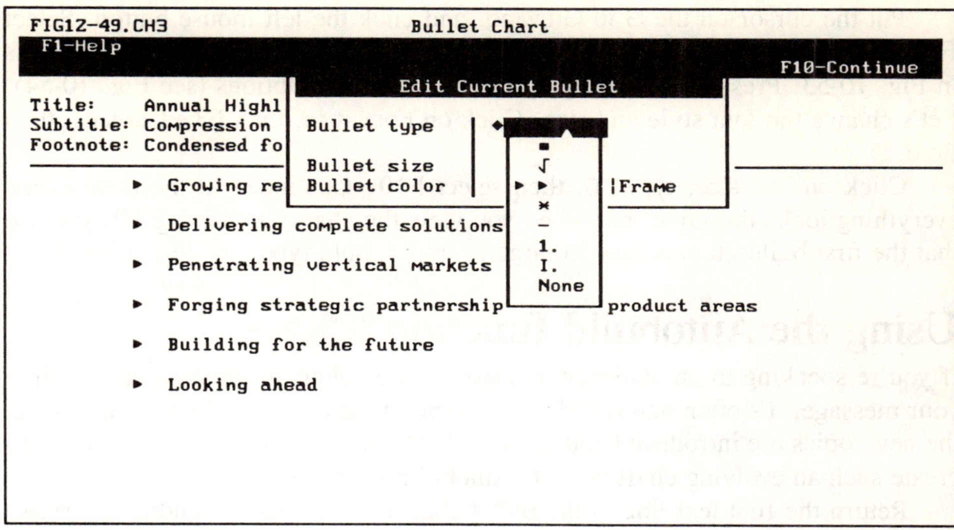

10-51 The Bullet Type menu.

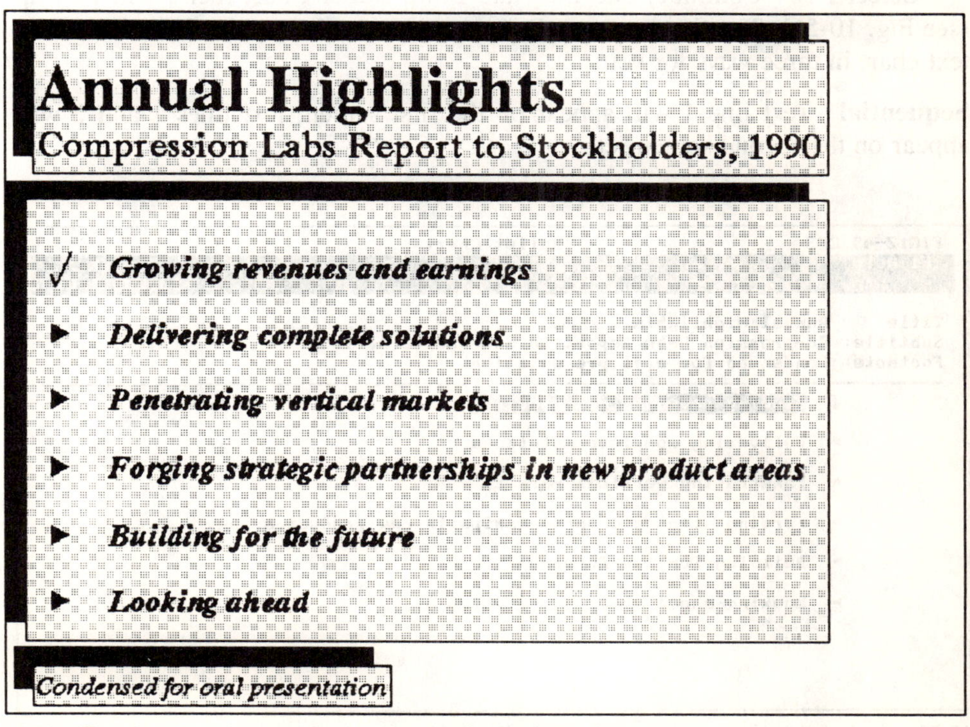

10-52 The chart now shows a checkmark opposite the first bullet item.

Put the cursor on the G in Growing, and click the left mouse button. Select F5 – Mark, then click on the final s in earnings. The line of text is highlighted, as in Fig. 10-53. Press F10 to bring up the Marked Text Options (see Fig. 10-54). Let's change the font style and size. Click on Font style, then F3 – Choices, then Bold.

Click on Text size, type 10, then select F10 – Continue. At the data screen everything looks the same, but when you view the chart by pressing F2, you see that the first bullet item is now in larger, regular, bold type (see Fig. 10-55).

Using the Autobuild function

If you're speaking to an audience and using a text chart to illustrate and outline your message, it's often handy to be able to build the chart one item as a time, as the new topics are introduced and discussed. Harvard Graphics 3.0 allows you to create such an evolving chart with its Autobuild function.

Return the first text line in the bullet chart to its previous condition: arrowhead bullet, size 7 text, in the Dutch 801 bold italic text. Press Ctrl – S to go to the Save Chart menu. When it pops up, type highlitz as the filename, then press Enter three times to go to the Auto-Build line. With No highlighted in the Auto-Build line, press the space bar to change the answer to Yes.

Select F10 – Continue, and the Auto-Build Bullet Chart menu will pop up (see Fig. 10-56). The first option is Build type. Harvard Graphics 3.0 will build a text chart in three ways for you:

Sequential Text line 1 will appear on the first screen, text lines 1 and 2 will appear on the second screen, etc.

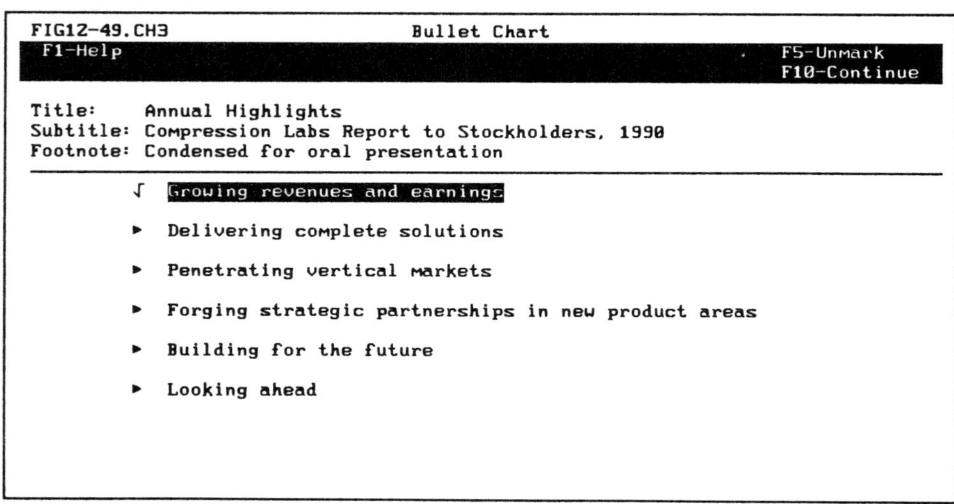

10-53 The text of the first bullet item is highlighted with *Mark*.

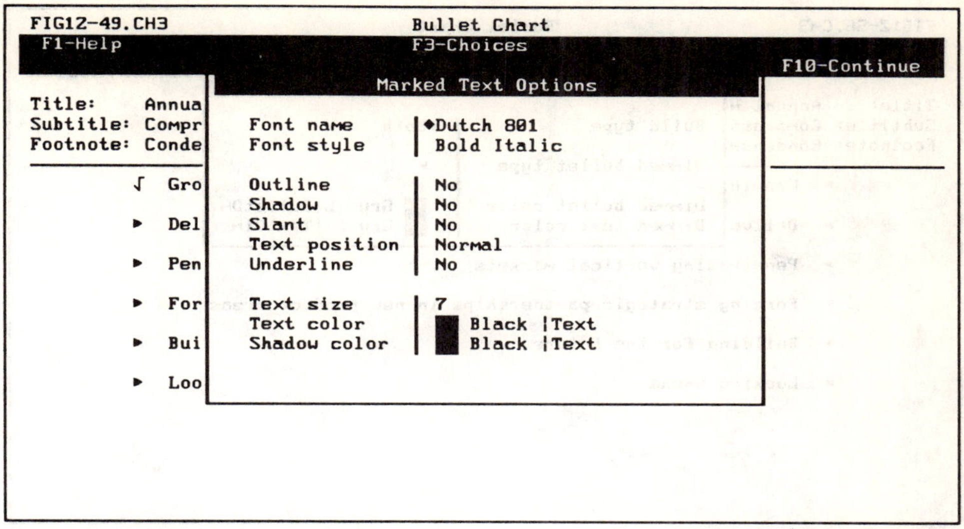

```
FIG12-49.CH3                         Bullet Chart
 F1-Help                             F3-Choices
                                                               F10-Continue
                                  Marked Text Options
Title:      Annua
Subtitle:   Compr     Font name       |◆Dutch 801
Footnote:   Conde     Font style      | Bold Italic

         √  Gro       Outline         | No
                      Shadow          | No
         ▸  Del       Slant           | No
                      Text position   | Normal
         ▸  Pen       Underline       | No

         ▸  For       Text size       | 7
                      Text color      |  █  Black |Text
         ▸  Bui       Shadow color    |  █  Black |Text

         ▸  Loo
```

10-54 The Marked Text Options menu.

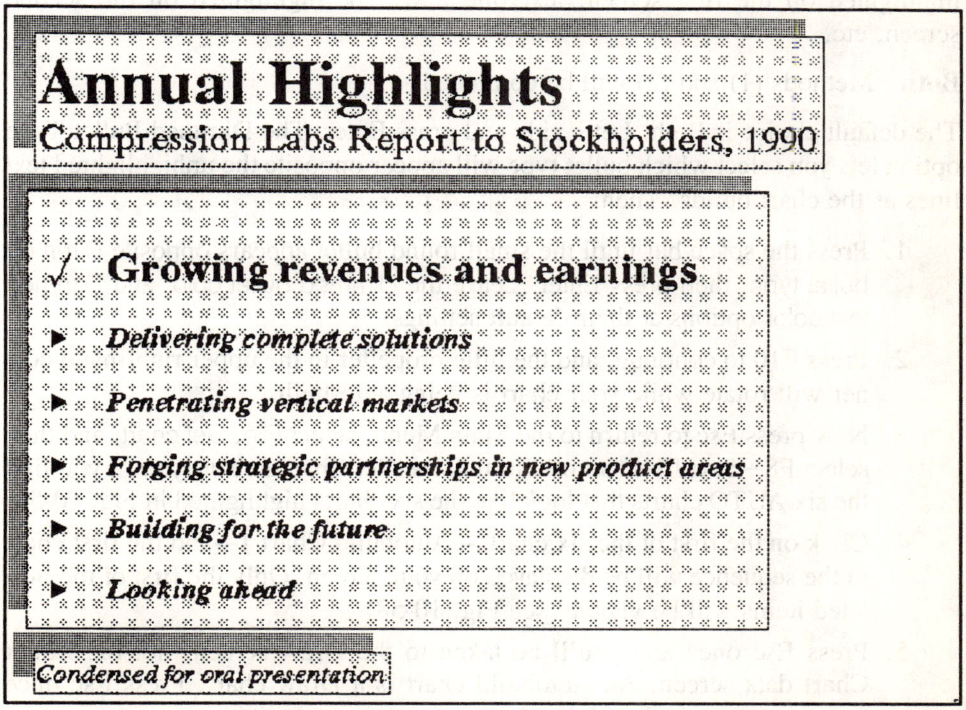

Annual Highlights

Compression Labs Report to Stockholders, 1990

√ **Growing revenues and earnings**

▸ ***Delivering complete solutions***

▸ ***Penetrating vertical markets***

▸ ***Forging strategic partnerships in new product areas***

▸ ***Building for the future***

▸ ***Looking ahead***

Condensed for oral presentation

10-55 The chart with the redesigned first line.

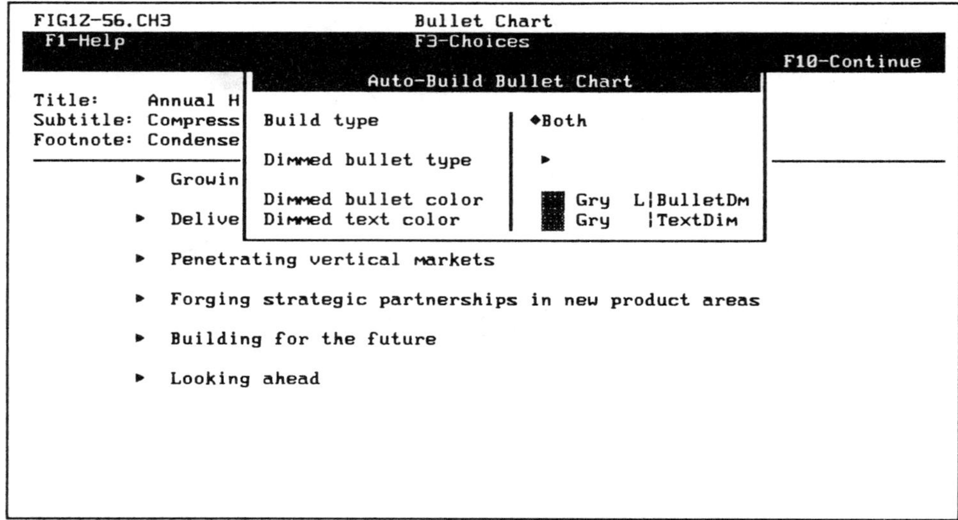

10-56 The Auto-Build bullet chart.

Highlighted All lines of text will appear on all screens, but text line 1 will be highlighted on the first screen, text line 2 will be highlighted on the second screen, etc.

Both Methods (1) and (2) will be combined.

The default choice is Both. Let it ride and press Enter. The Dimmed Bullet Type option lets you select which bullet type will appear opposite the unhighlighted text lines as the chart builds. Then:

1. Press the space bar until the small round bullet appears opposite Dimmed bullet type, then press Enter. Leave the Dimmed bullet color and Dimmed text color options at their default settings.
2. Press F10 to continue, and the little propeller in the upper right-hand corner will rotate while your chart is being auto-built.
3. Now press Esc to return to the Main Menu, select File, Get chart, and then select F8 – Sort files. Scroll through the Get Chart directory until you find the six AUTO charts that look like the six charts highlighted in Fig. 10-57.
4. Click on the first of the six charts—Autobuild Chart 1—and the first chart in the sequence will be displayed on your screen. Only the first of the bulleted items will be visible (see Fig. 10-58).
5. Press Esc once and you'll be taken to the Draw screen, not the Bullet Chart data screen. An Autobuild chart is a Draw chart. Press Esc once more to return to the Main Menu.

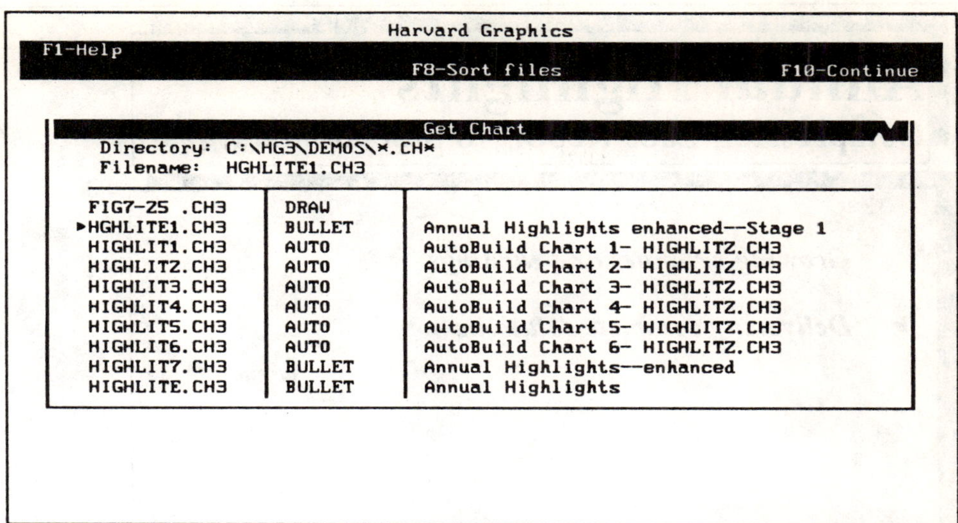

10-57 The six Autobuild charts in the Get Chart directory.

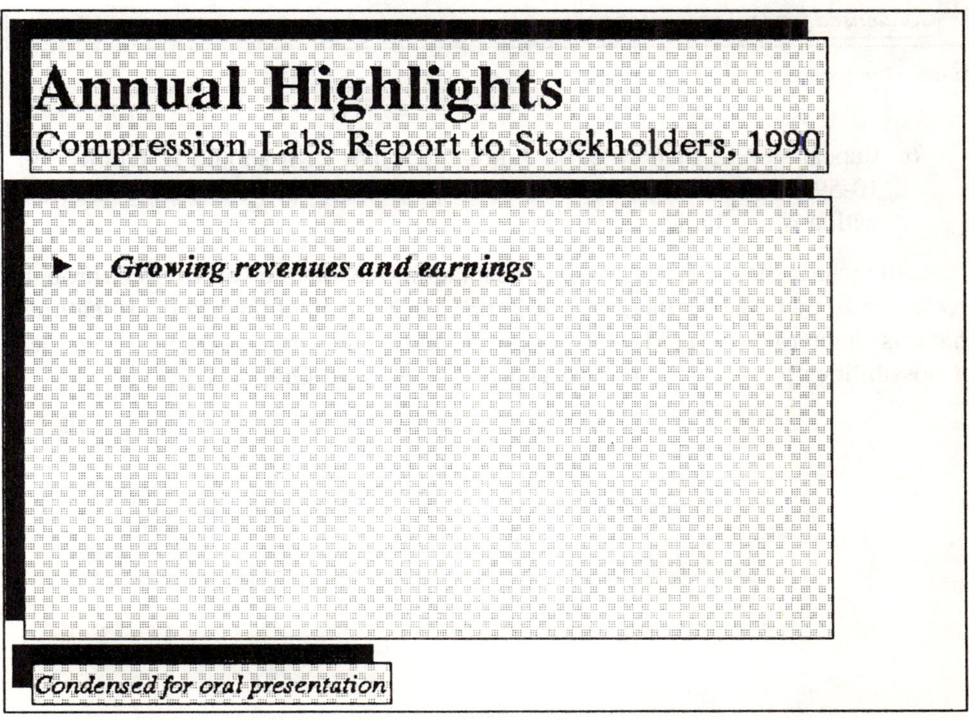

10-58 The first of the Autobuild chart series, showing the first bulleted item.

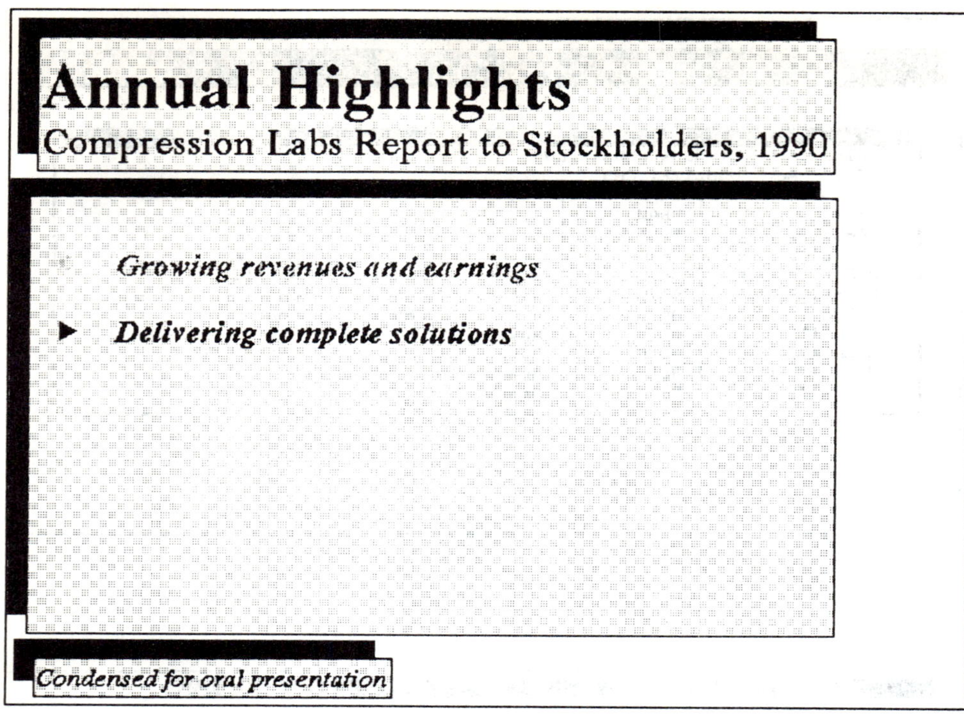

10-59 The second of the Autobuild charts.

6. Repeat step 2, then click on Autobuild Chart 2. It should resemble Fig. 10-59. The second bullet item is emphasized, while the first is dimmed with a round bullet.

You can include these six charts in a presentation like the one you worked through in chapter 6, then display them in a ScreenShow. With all of the text chart features that this chapter has covered, you've only skimmed the surface of the vast number of possibilities for presentation text charts that Harvard Graphics 3.0 provides.

11
CHAPTER

Advanced organization charts

When you first created an organization chart in chapter 5, you used a common garden variety organization chart selected from the Gallery. The closest thing to an enhancement that you allowed yourself was the 3-D appearance of the boxes on the chart—and that indulgence was also built into the Gallery model you chose.

You could have gone farther, however. If you really want to get your organization chart all tricked out and gussied up, Harvard Graphics 3.0 certainly gives you the tools. Let's get out the original version and make some changes.

From the Main Menu, select Ctrl−G. (Remember? That's the fast key combo that takes you right to the Get Chart directory.) When the chart listing pops up, find the organization chart you named ORGCHART.CH3 and click on it. The chart will fill your screen (see Fig. 11-1).

The right mouse button (or Esc) will take you to the Organization Chart data screen. You're going to be looking at two selections in the menu bar at the top of the screen: F8−Options and F9−Organization. The Options menu is concerned primarily with the appearance of the elements of the chart, and the Organization menu is concerned primarily with the arrangement of the elements.

The Options menu

Select F8−Options, and the Options pop-up menu will appear (see Fig. 11-2). The first four items in this menu—Titles/Footnotes, Text Attributes, Appearance,

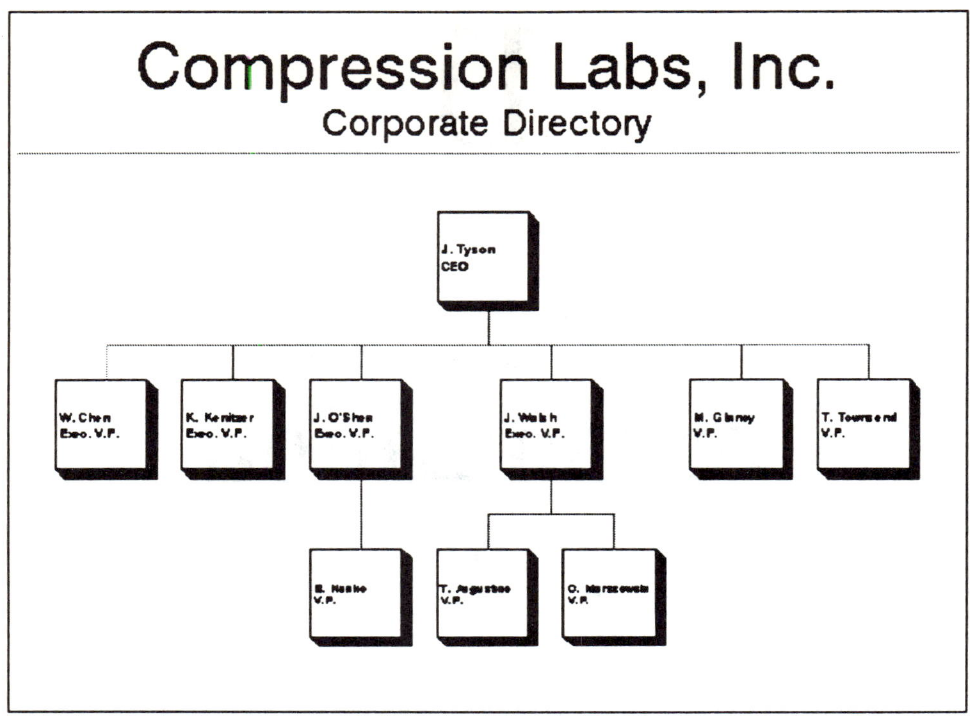

11-1 The plain brown version of the organization chart.

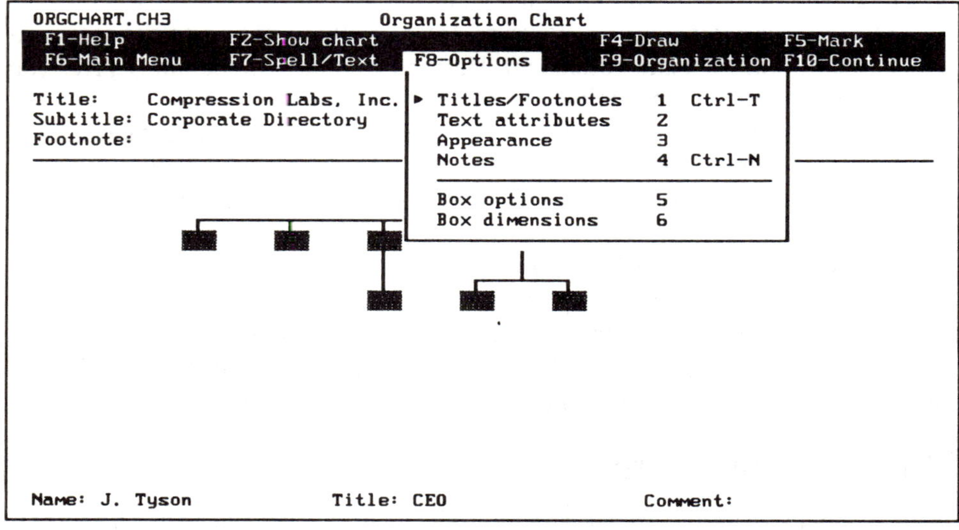

11-2 The Options menu.

and Notes—are identical to the items of the same name on the Bullet Chart data screen. Review chapter 10 for a more detailed tutorial on these items. Make the following changes:

1. Select item 2, Text attributes (see Fig. 11-3). Change the title size to 6, and the subtitle 1 size to 4.
2. Change the font name to Geo Slab 712 (How do you match the sheer poetry of a name like Geo Slab 712?) for the title, subtitle 1, box name, and box title.
3. Change the font style to Medium for the title, subtitle 1, box name, and box title.
4. Change the text color to anything you like. Your Text Attributes screen should now look like Fig. 11-4 (except for the color choices).
5. Press F2 to see the changes in text size and style (see Fig. 11-5). Press Esc twice to return to the data sheet.
6. Select F8 – Options, and this time choose item 3, Appearance (see Fig. 11-6).

This menu is virtually identical to the Appearance Options menu you worked through in chapter 10—which you should review now if you haven't seen it already. The only difference here is that there's no text overflow option under Organization; the program takes over text management in the organization boxes. Don't do anything here right now. Press Esc, then F8 – Options again.

Item 4, Notes, is also identical to the same item on the Bullet Chart data screen. If you want to add a note here, review chapter 10 for instructions. Select

ORGCHART.CH3 Organization Chart

F1-Help F2-Show chart F3-Choices F10-Continue

Text Attributes

	Size	Color		Alignment	Font Name	Font Style
Title	9	Black	Ti	Center	Swiss 721	Roman
Subtitle 1	5	Black	Su	Center	Swiss 721	Roman
Subtitle 2	5	Black	Su	Center	Swiss 721	Roman
Box name	–	Black	Te	Left	Swiss 721	Roman
Box title	–	Black	Su	Left	Swiss 721	Roman
Box comment	–	Black	Su	Left	Swiss 721	Roman
Footnote 1	3.5	Black	Fo	Left	Swiss 721	Roman
Footnote 2	3.5	Black	Fo	Left	Swiss 721	Roman
Footnote 3	3.5	Black	Fo	Left	Swiss 721	Roman

Name: J. Tyson Title: CEO Comment:

11-3 The Text Attributes pop-up menu.

```
ORGCHART.CH3                      Organization Chart
 F1-Help           F2-Show chart   F3-Choices
                                                            F10-Continue
                              Text Attributes
T
S                   Size        Color    Alignment  Font Name     Font Style
F  Title           | 6      |  Black |Ti | Center | Geo Slab 71 | Medium    |
-  Subtitle 1      | 4      |  Black |Su | Center | Geo Slab 71 | Medium    |  -
   Subtitle 2      | 5      |  Black |Su | Center | Swiss 721   | Roman     |

   Box name        |   -    |  Black |Te | Left   | Geo Slab 71 | Medium    |
   Box title       |   -    |  Black |Su | Left   | Geo Slab 71 |♦Medium    |
   Box comment     |   -    |  Black |Su | Left   | Swiss 721   | Roman     |

   Footnote 1      | 3.5    |  Black |Fo | Left   | Swiss 721   | Roman     |
   Footnote 2      | 3.5    |  Black |Fo | Left   | Swiss 721   | Roman     |
   Footnote 3      | 3.5    |  Black |Fo | Left   | Swiss 721   | Roman     |


Name: J. Tyson              Title: CEO                Comment:
```

11-4 The Text Attributes screen after some modifications.

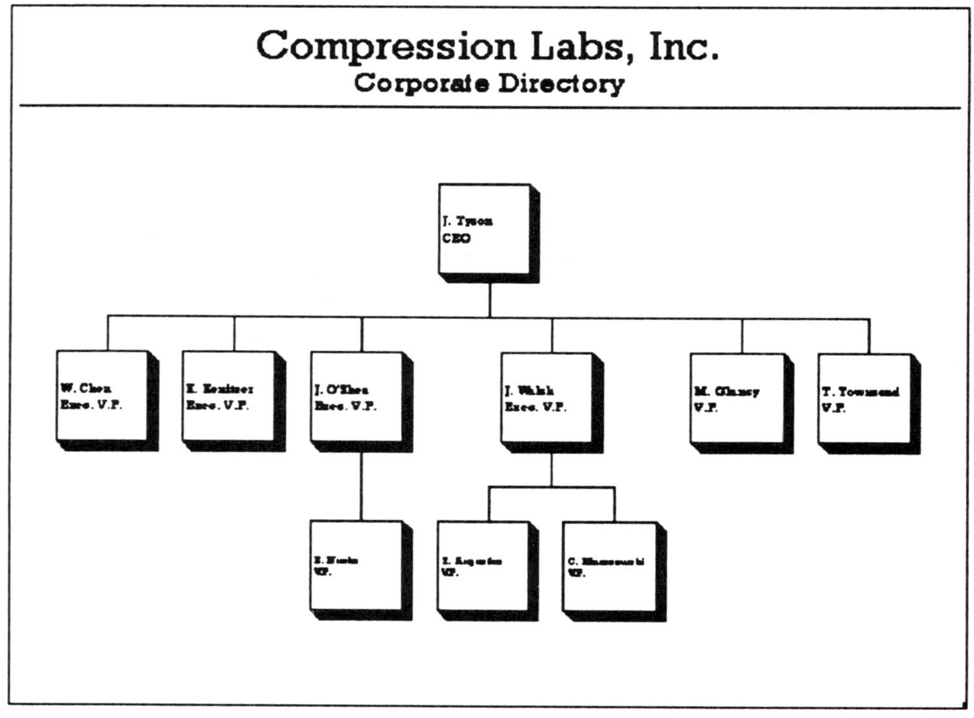

11-5 The chart in progress after you change text sizes and styles.

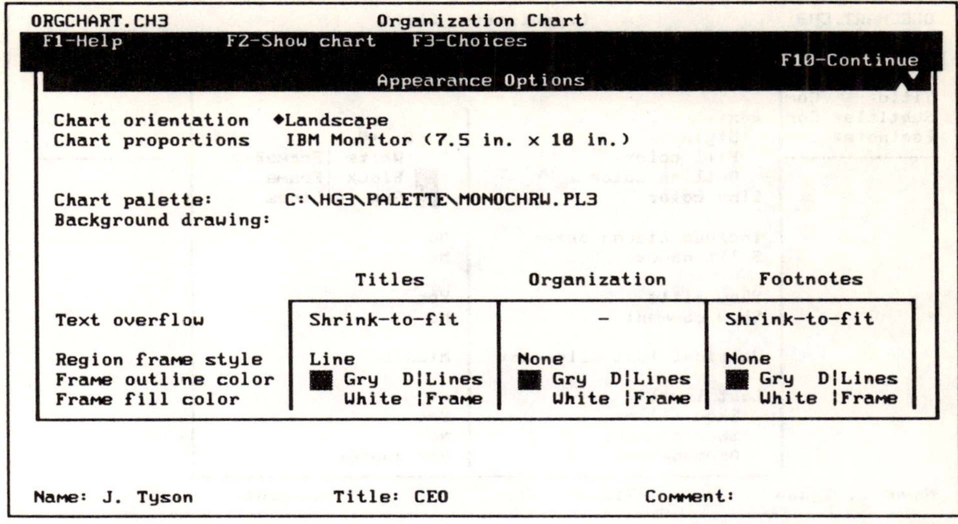

11-6 The Appearance Options menu.

Box options, item 5. When the pop-up menu appears, you'll see that there are some new and unfamiliar options here (see Fig. 11-7). I'll explain some of them.

Box style

Click on Style (under Box), then press F3 – Choices. A partial view of the Box Style menu will appear (see Fig. 11-8). If you scroll through this menu, you'll see that the basic choices of box style are None, Plain, Frame, Rounded, Octagonal, 3-D, Page, and Shadow. You'll want to experiment with these to see which you find the most attractive.

Box colors

Fill color is the background color for the text within the boxes; outline color is the color with which the boxes are outlined.

Line color

The color of the lines that connect the boxes on your organization chart is the line color.

Select 3-D, double-border for the style, and a fill, outline, and line color of your choice. In the demonstration example illustrated here, the choices are the lightest gray (Gry LL ¦ Series 5) for the fill color, light gray (Gry L ¦ Shadow) for the outline color, and dark gray (Gry D ¦ Lines) for the line color. Press F2, and your progress so far is shown in Fig. 11-9. Click the right mouse button to return to the Box Options menu.

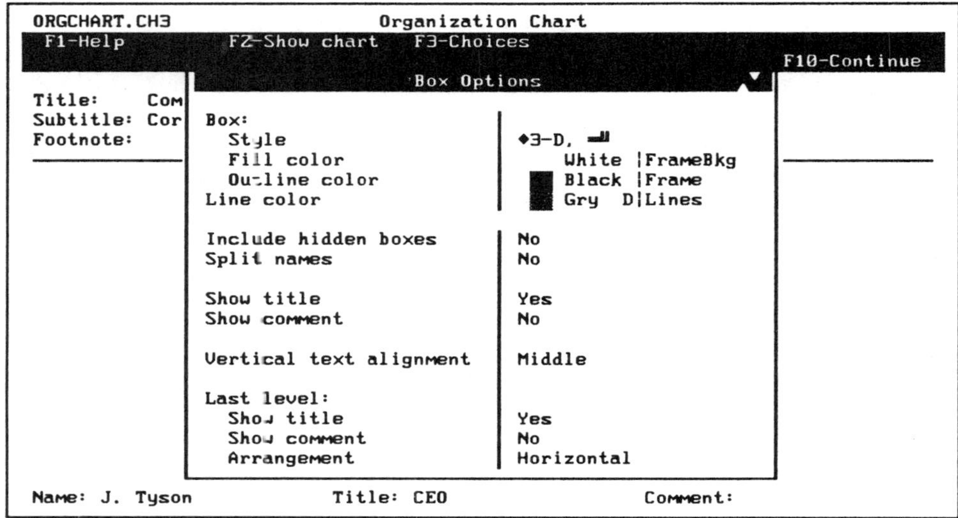

11-7 The Box Options pop-up menu.

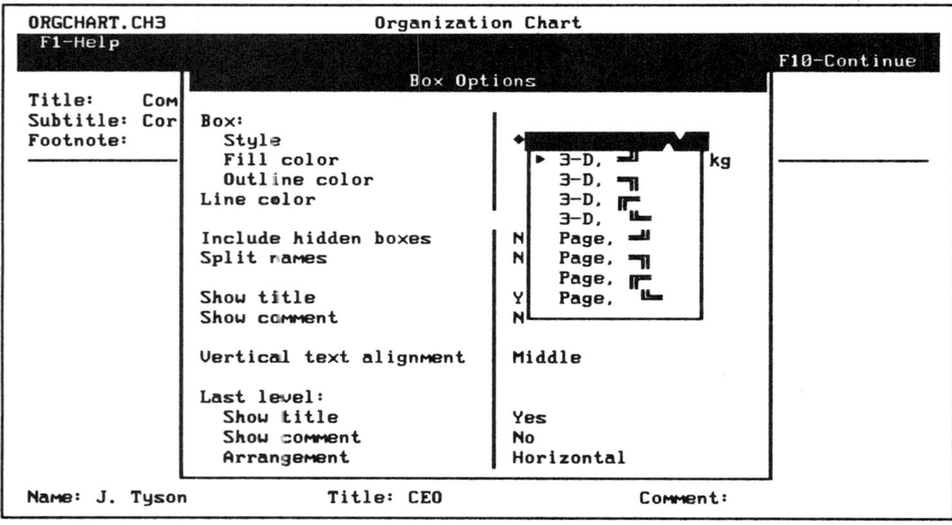

11-8 The Box Style menu.

Include hidden boxes

Under the Organization menu, you can opt to hide the subordinates of any box or person. If you have hidden them in that manner, you can make them visible again by selecting Yes under this option.

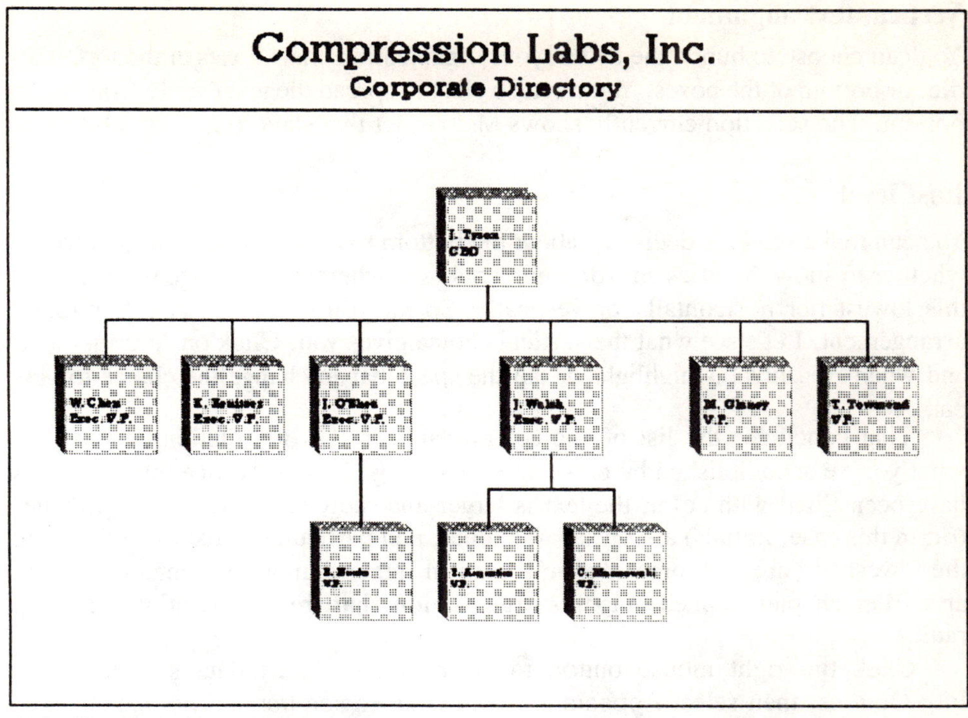

11-9 The chart with new color selections.

Split names

You can elect to put first and last names on separate lines by selecting Yes here. The advantage of this maneuver is that the size of the text in the names doesn't have to be shrunk so much to fit into the boxes, and is therefore more readable. Select Split names, then press the space bar until the option says Yes.

Show title

This option allows you to choose to display a person's title in the chart or not.

Show comment

Do you want to be able to show any additional responsibilities, titles, or reporting assignments a person has? You can do it by selecting Yes at this point. Remember, however, that you do so at the cost of filling up your chart with more detail, which can make it harder to read.

Vertical text alignment

You can choose to bunch the text in your organization chart boxes at the top, middle, or bottom of the boxes. You can also elect to spread the text evenly from top to bottom. The selection currently shows Middle; let that stand (see Fig. 11-10).

Last level

You can make separate decisions about the bottom row in the organization chart—whether to show the titles and/or comments, and whether to arrange the names in this lowest tier horizontally or vertically. So far you've looked at a horizontal arrangement. Let's see what the vertical choice gives you. Click on Arrangement, and when Horizontal is highlighted, tap the space bar to change the choice to Vertical.

That concludes the list of choices available in the Box Options menu. See what you've accomplished by pressing F2 (see Fig. 11-11). Notice that the boxes have been filled with color, the text is larger and more readable, the first names (or, in this case, initials) are on separate lines, and particularly that the officers on the lowest tier are now presented in a vertical rather than a horizontal array. (As an earlier chapter pointed out, this organization chart reports relationships, not rank.)

Click the right mouse button to return to the chart data screen, select F8–Options, then select Appearance. Click on Region frame style under Titles, and press the space bar until the title frame style option is None. This action removes the horizontal line under the title and subtitle, and the chart now looks like Fig. 11-12.

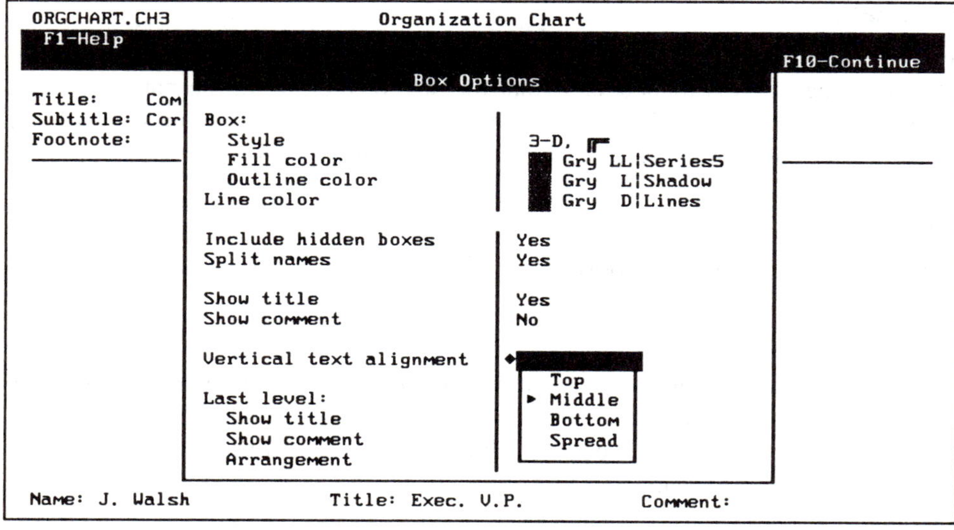

11-10 The Vertical Text Alignment choices.

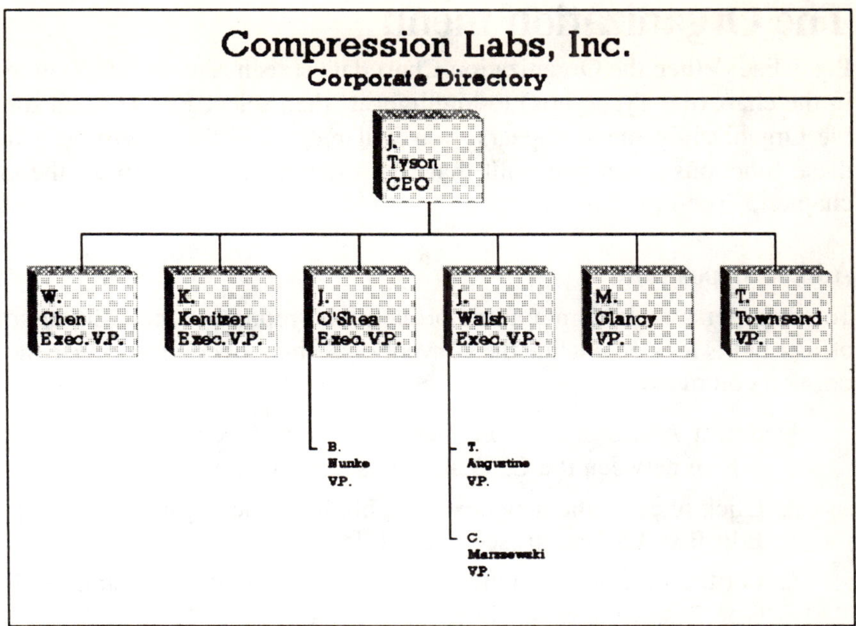

11-11 The organization chart with your latest box option selections.

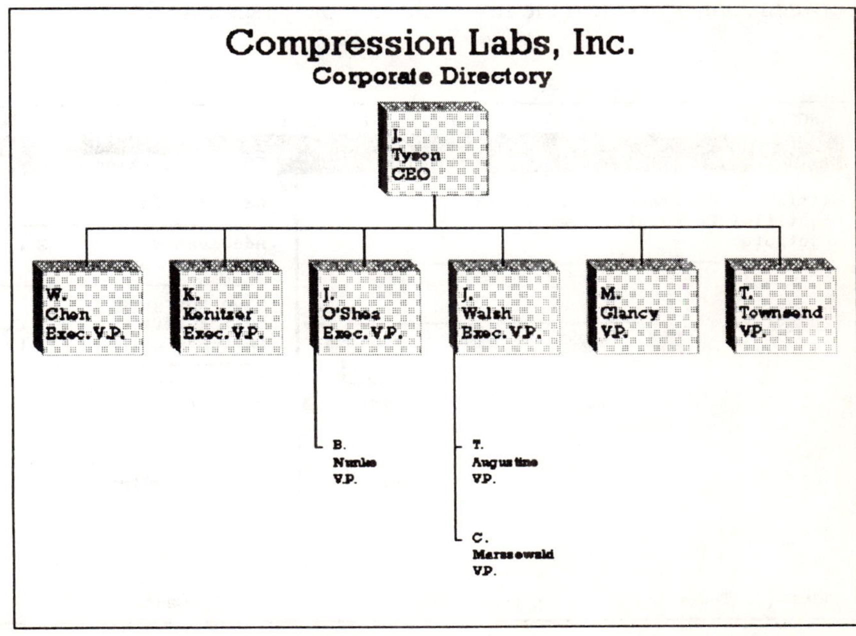

11-12 The chart with the horizontal line removed.

The Organization menu

Press Esc. When the Organization Chart data screen returns, click on the top box in the chart (the Tyson box) to highlight it, then select F9 – Organization. When the Organization menu appears, you will recognize that you used a number of these functions when you built that first organization chart from the Gallery in chapter 3 (see Fig. 11-13).

Add staff position

To add a person who is not a line officer, who reports to the CEO or some other officer but is located outside the conventional chain of command, use the Add staff position command.

1. Select Add staff position, item 3. A new box will appear on your data screen between the CEO and the second tier (see Fig. 11-14).
2. Click once on the new box to highlight it, then again to bring up the Add/Edit Box Text menu (see Fig. 11-15).
3. For the sake of simplicity, simply type Staff opposite Name, hit Enter, and type Position opposite Title.
4. Press F10 to confirm this action, then F2 to see what you've accomplished.

Sure enough, there's that new staff position, hanging precariously on that line between John Tyson and the rest of the company (see Fig. 11-16).

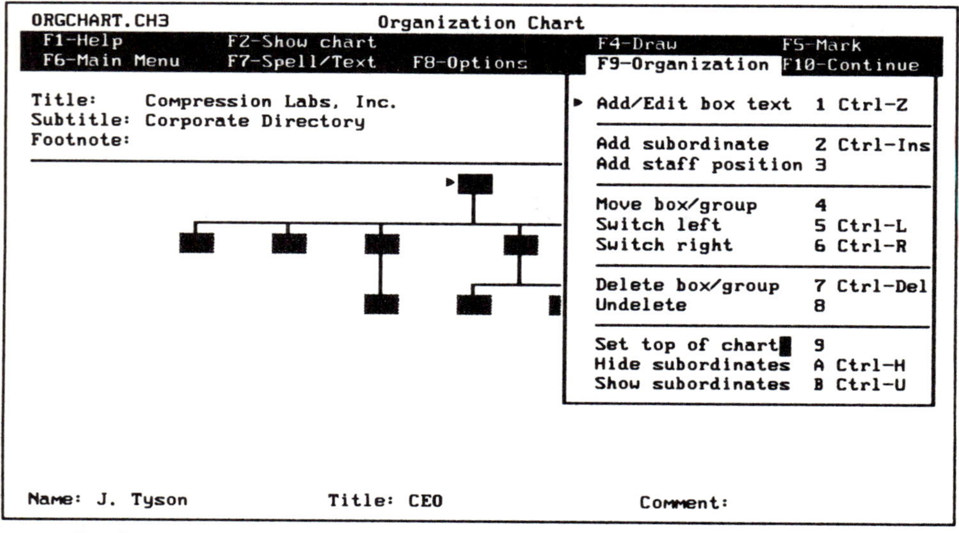

11-13 The Organization pop-up menu.

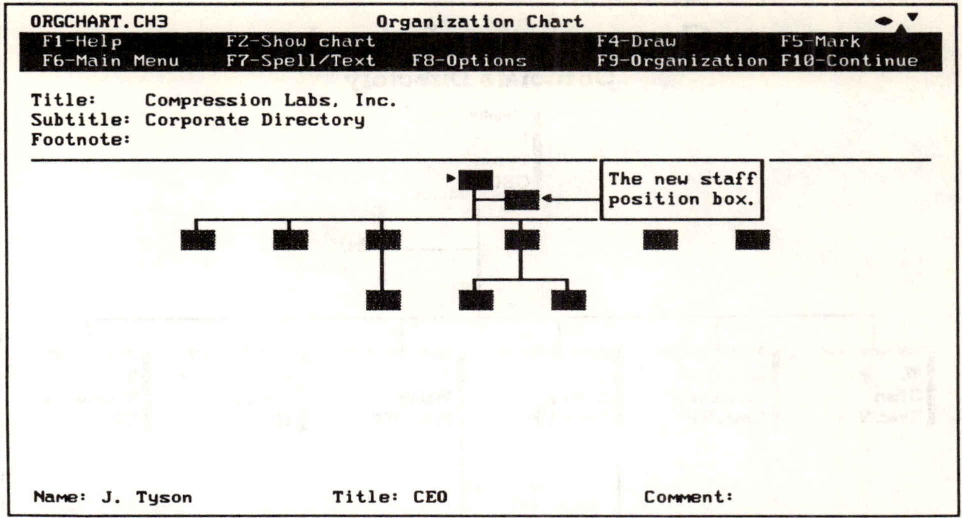

11-14 The new staff position box.

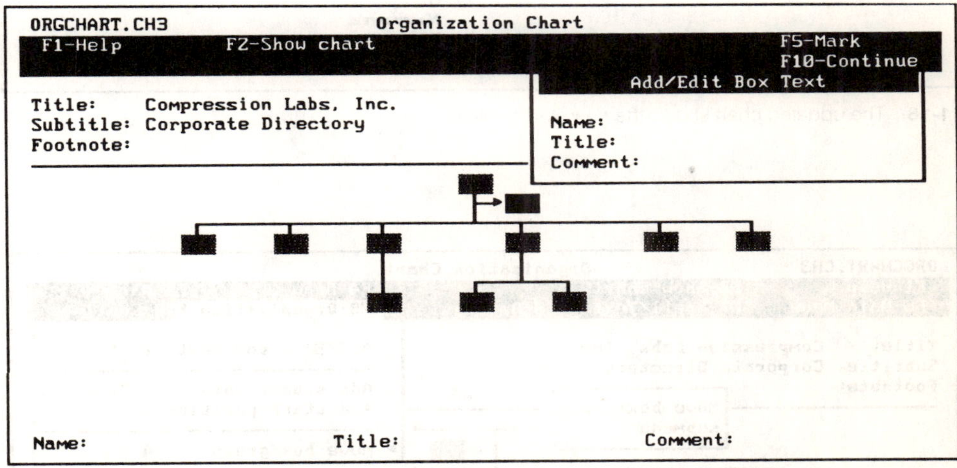

11-15 The Add/Edit Box Text menu.

Move box/group

What if there's a change in reporting assignments and you need to move people to another location? Suppose, for example, that Augustine and Marszewski are assigned to report to Chen rather than Walsh? Here's how to do that:

1. At the data screen, click on Walsh to highlight his block.
2. Select F9 – Organization.

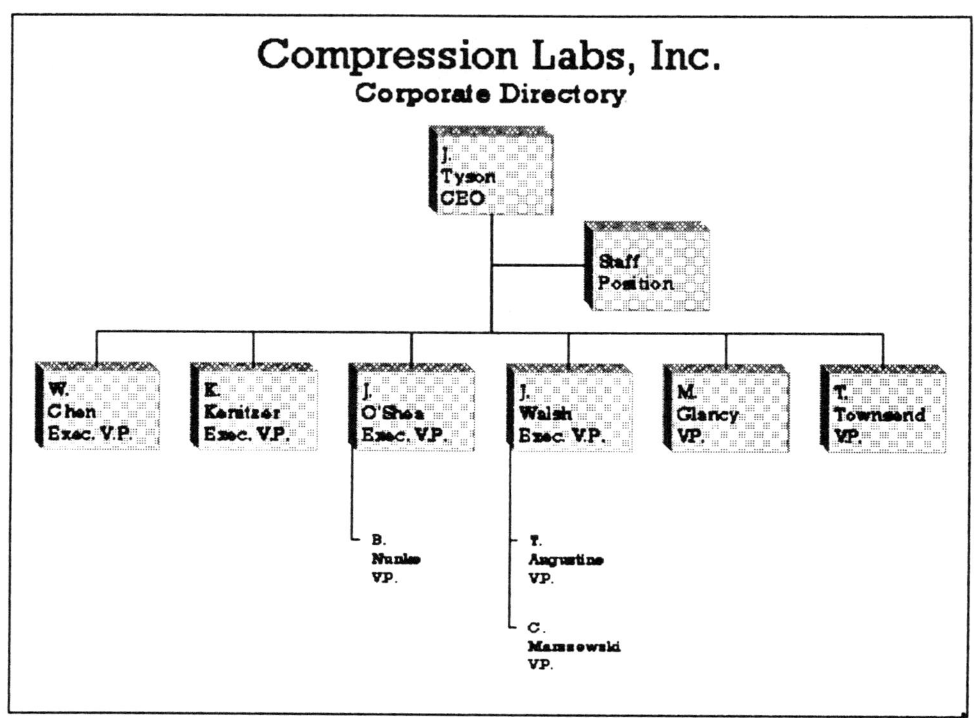

11-16 The updated chart shows the new staff position.

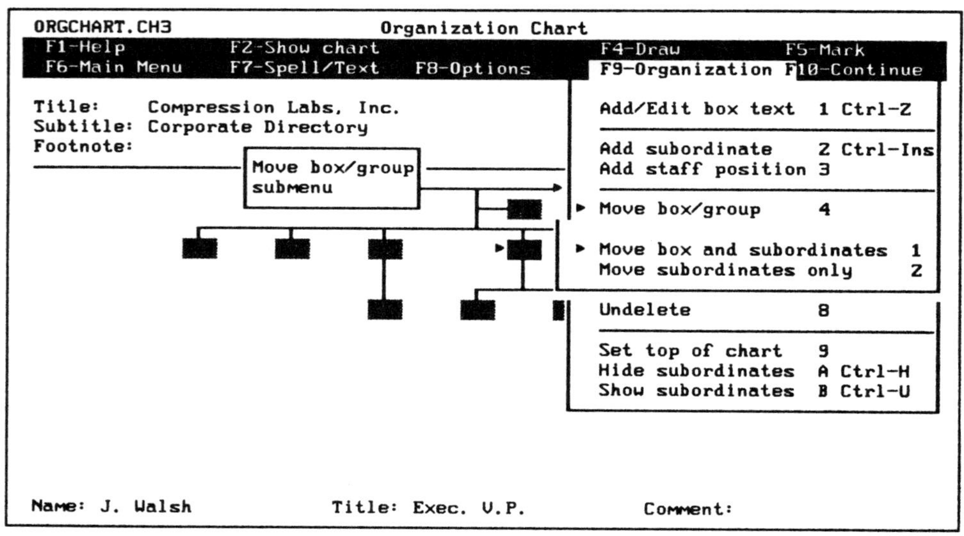

11-17 The Move box/group submenu.

3. From the Organization menu, click on Move box/group, item 4. A small submenu will appear, offering you two choices: Move box and subordi nates, or Move subordinates only (see Fig. 11-17).
4. Click on Move subordinates only, item 2 of the submenu.

Walsh's subordinates will disappear from the data screen, with four little arrows in the upper right-hand corner of the screen indicating that you should use the arrow keys to move the two subordinates to their new location (see Fig. 11-18).

Tap the left arrow key three times; an arrowhead should now be pointing at the Chen position (see Fig. 11-19). Select F10–Continue. The two subordinates will attach themselves to the Chen position, and pressing F2 shows the altered chart. The arrangement of the bottom level has also been changed from vertical back to horizontal (see Fig. 11-20). Finally, press Esc to return to the data screen.

Switch left/Switch right

Select F9–Organization again, and you'll see that items 5 and 6 are Switch left and Switch right. To exchange a box with the box immediately to its right, click on the first box, then either press Ctrl–R or select Switch right from the Organization menu. To illustrate, let's switch Chen and Kenitzer.

At the Organization Chart data screen, click on the Chen box. The box will be highlighted, and Chen's name and title will appear at the bottom of your screen (see Fig. 11-21). Press Ctrl–R. The Chen box now appears in Kenitzer's former position. Note that Chen's subordinates moved with him (see Fig. 11-22). Select F2–Show chart, and you'll see the result on your graphics screen (see Fig.

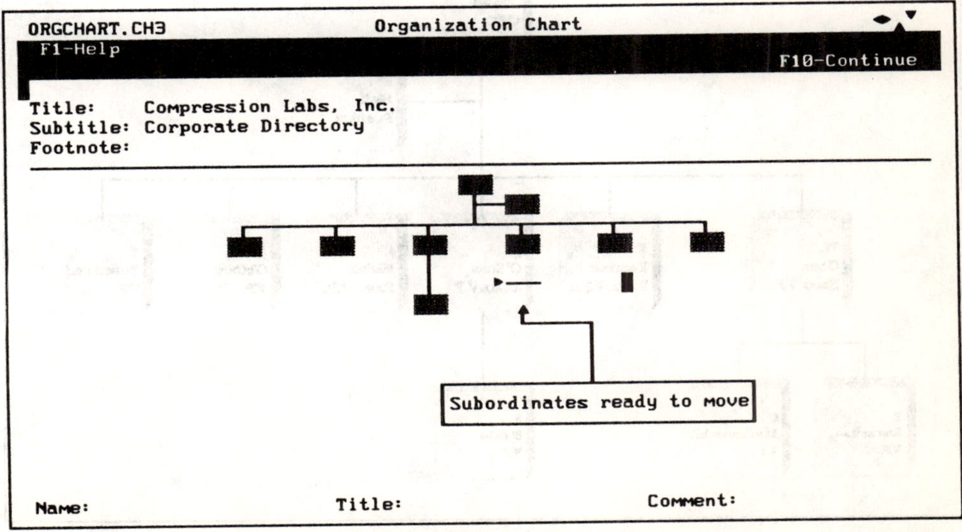

11-18 The data screen shows the Walsh subordinates ready to be moved.

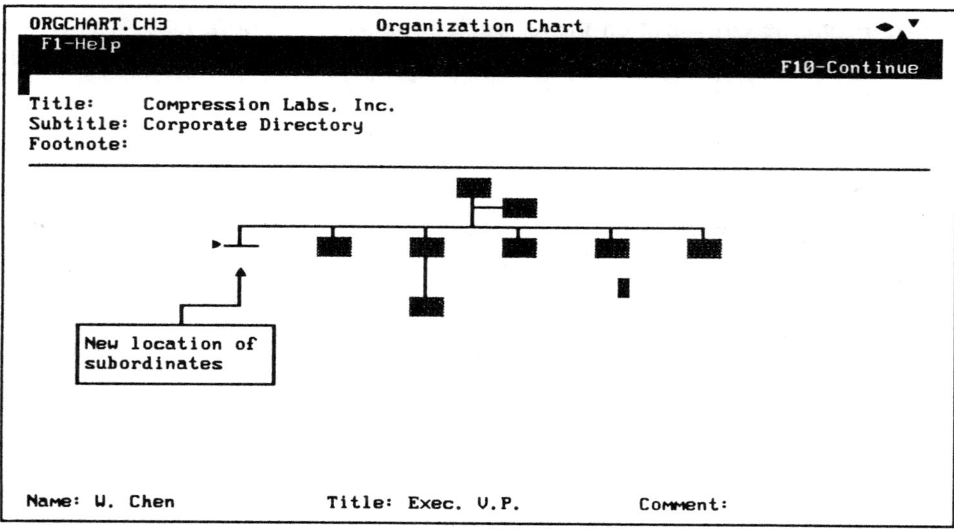

11-19 The arrowhead indicates that the subordinates will be attached to the Chen position.

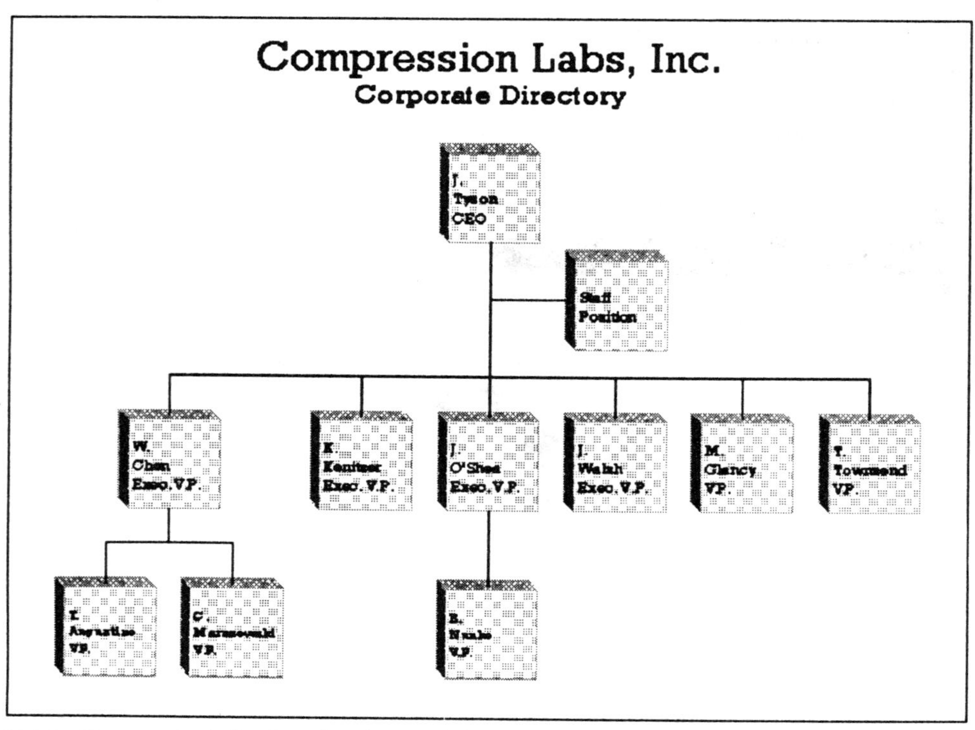

11-20 The new chart after the subordinate switch.

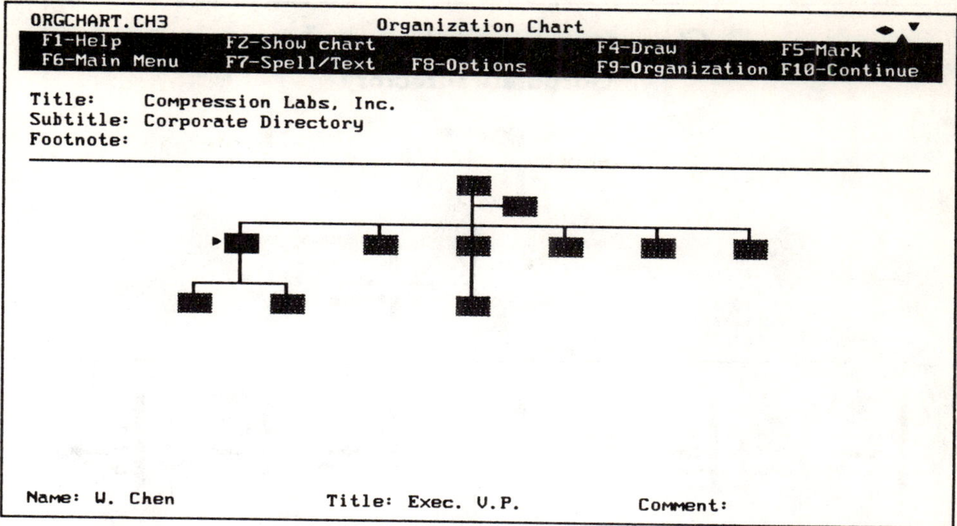

11-21 The data screen with the Chen box selected.

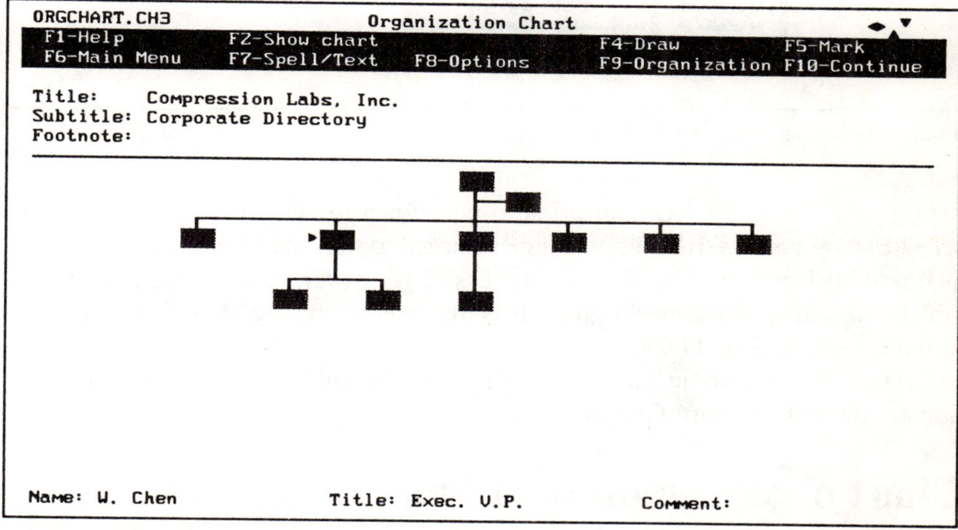

11-22 The new configuration after the Chen-Kenitzer switch.

11-23). Press Esc to return to the data screen. Repeat the move box/group maneuver you learned above, and return Mr. Chen's subordinate group to Mr. Walsh, where it belongs.

Set top of chart

Now that John Walsh has his little group back, let's assume that you want to isolate that group from the rest of the organization chart. Click on the Walsh box to

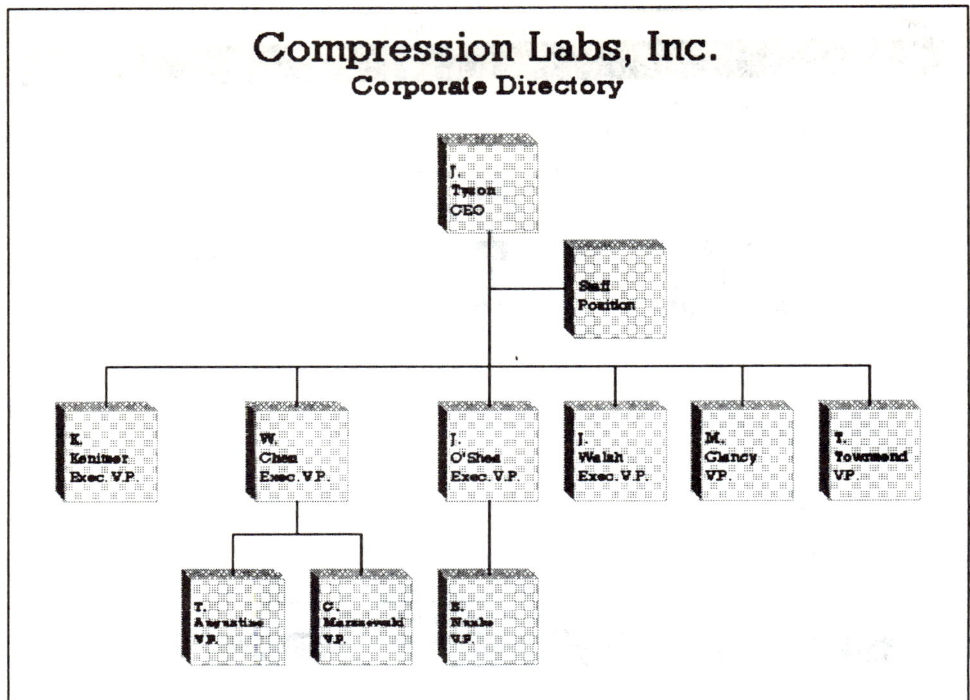

11-23 The finished chart after the left-right switch.

highlight it. Select F9—Organization to pull down the Organization menu, then select Set top of chart, item 9. You'll be returned to the data screen, and it appears as if nothing has happened. When you press F2, however, it's a different story: the Walsh/Augustine/Marszewski group fills the screen, and Walsh is now at the top of the chart (see Fig. 11-24).

And that's the whole truth and nothing but the truth about creating organization charts with Harvard Graphics 3.0.

Chart organization with Draw

Don't forget that, when you're through adding all the buttons and the bows available through the data screen menus, there's an infinite amount of fiddling and fancying-up that's possible via the Draw function. Here's just one quick example:

1. Reset the Tyson box as the top of the chart, then press F4 to display the chart on the Draw canvas (see Fig. 11-25).
2. Click on the Symbol icon, then on the Get icon. The Get Symbol File box will pop up (Fig. 11-26).
3. Select the HUMANS4.SY3 file (see Fig. 11-27).

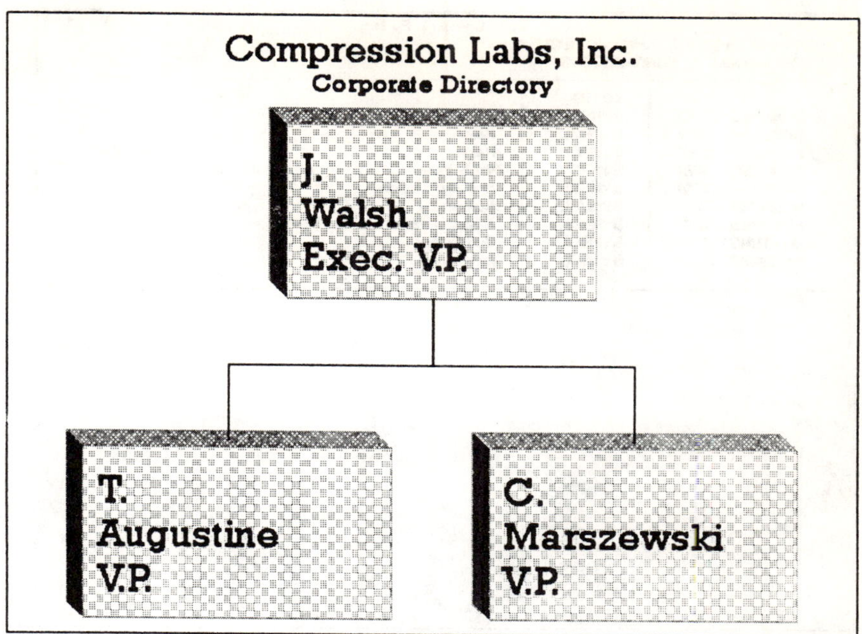

11-24 The Walsh group is isolated after the top-of-chart selection.

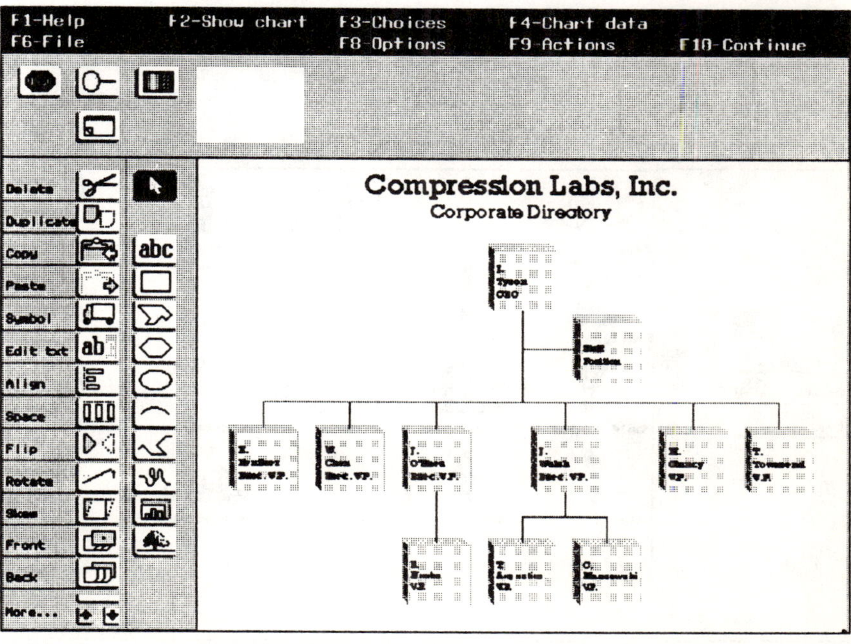

11-25 The organization chart displayed on the Draw canvas.

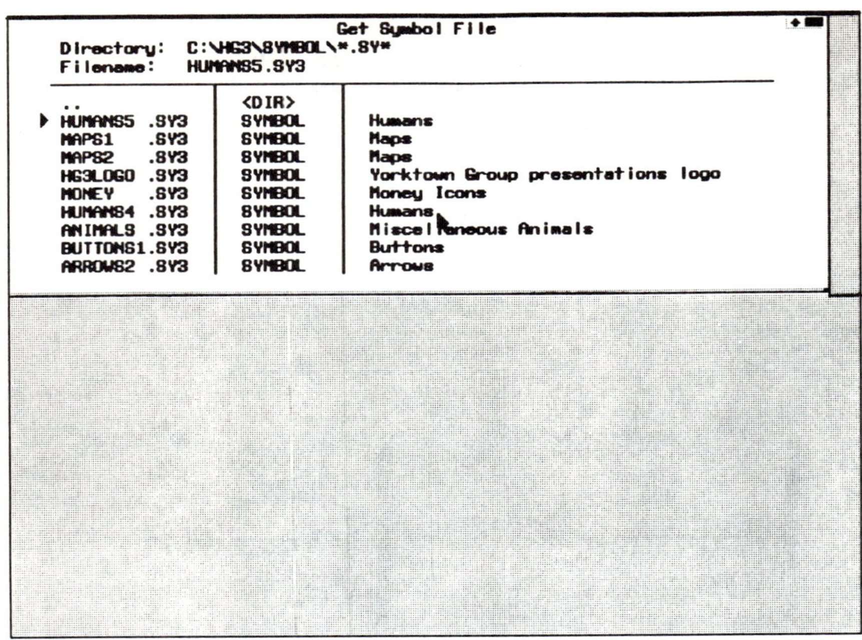

11-26 The Get Symbol File box.

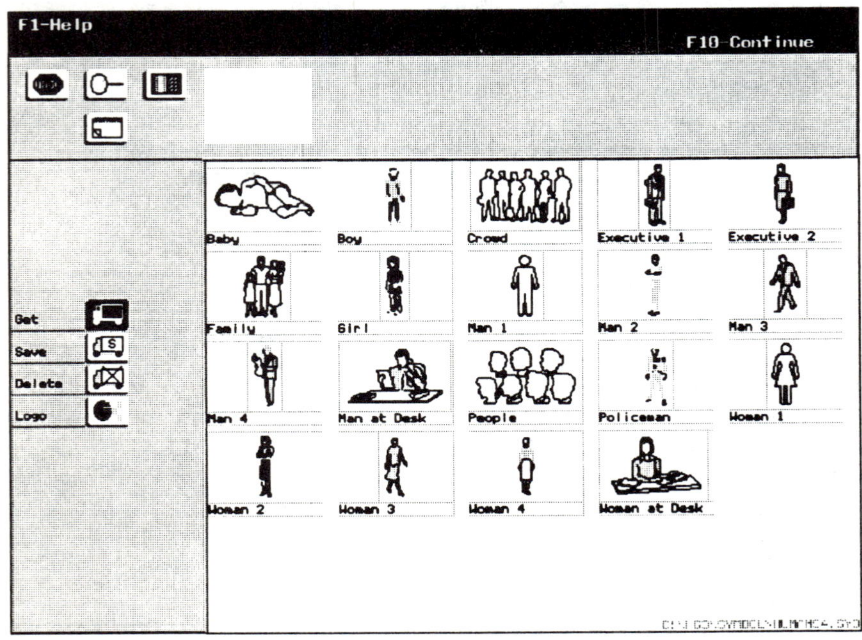

11-27 The 19 symbols in the HUMANS4.SY3 file.

4. Click on the Crowd symbol in the top row, then select F10–Continue. The crowd will appear in the center of your organization chart (see Fig. 11-28).
5. Click the right mouse button to bring back the tool panel, then stretch the symbol by touching the pointer to the selection handles and dragging the sides out until the symbol fills the Draw canvas (see Fig. 11-29).
6. Click on the Color icon to bring up the colors and patterns. (The color maneuvers that follow will succeed only if you are working with the MONOCHRW.PL3 palette.)
7. Click on the Fill icon at the top left-hand corner of the screen, then select white from the chart colors. The crowd figures disappear, but their white silhouettes still loom over the organization chart boxes (see Fig. 11-30).
8. Next, click on the Line/Text icon. Select black, and the shadowy figures will be outlined (see Fig. 11-31).
9. One more move—you have to get this crowd into the background so you can see the chart. Click the right mouse button to bring back the tool panel, select the Back icon, and, when the Back and Back 1 icons appear, click on the Back button.

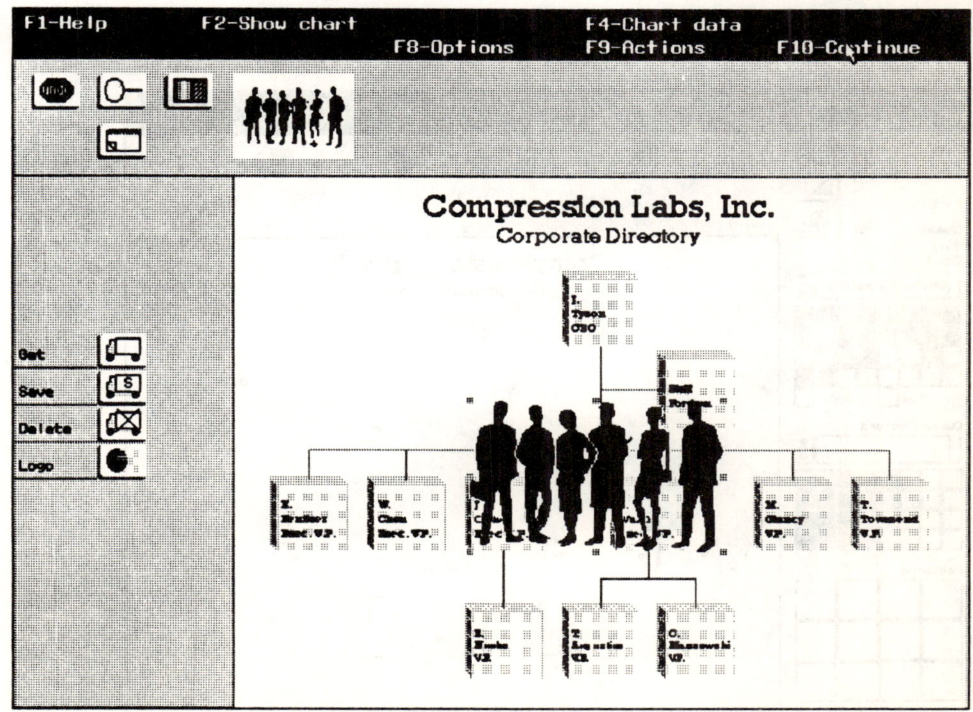

11-28 The Crowd symbol superimposed on the organization chart.

11-29 The Crowd symbol expanded to fill the canvas.

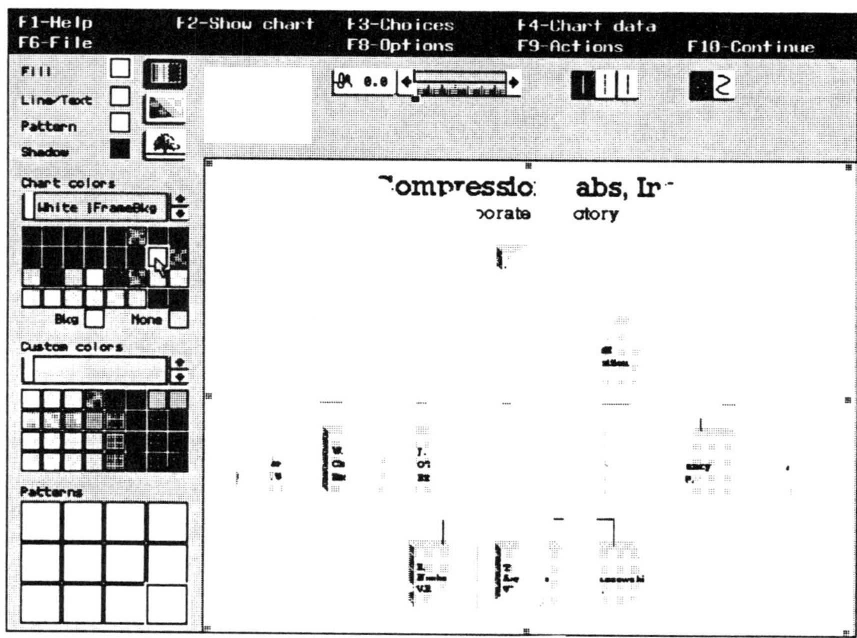

11-30 The Crowd figures have been filled with white.

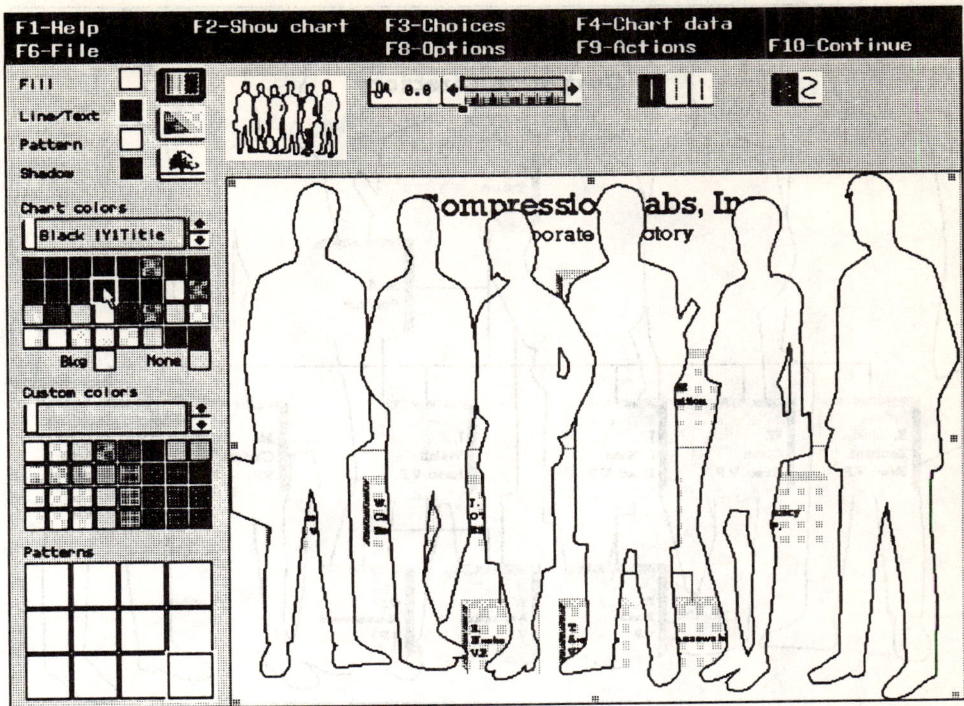

11-31 The white silhouettes now have black outlines.

The silhouettes, representing the employees of Compression Labs, Inc., retreat to the background, and the chart is fully visible in the foreground. Press F2, and your crowning achievement of this chapter is realized (see Fig. 11-32).

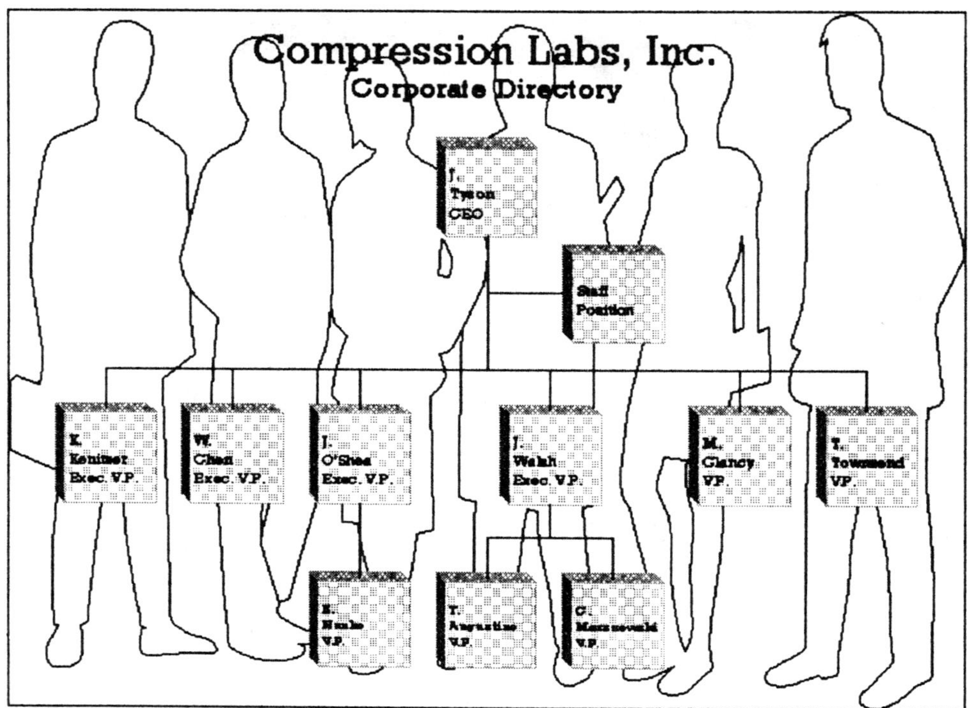

11-32 The ultimate chart, on a background of shadowy figures.

12
CHAPTER

Advanced pie charts

In chapter 2, you created a pie chart using one of the generic, or off-the-shelf, charts from the Gallery. In this chapter, I will show you the arsenal of pie-chart variations, modifications, and decorations that Harvard Graphics 3.0 makes available. Let's use that first chart as a jumping-off point.

1. From the Main Menu, press Ctrl – G to go right to the Get Chart directory (see Fig. 12-1).
2. Select the COSTS-Q4.CH3 file, and the chart will appear full-screen (see Fig. 12-2).
3. Click the right mouse button to go to the Pie Chart 1 data screen (see Fig. 12-3).

Multiple pies

As you begin to be more creative in your use of pie charts, one of the first Harvard Graphics 3.0 features you'll want to take advantage of is the multiple chart feature—the ability to compare two or more pie charts and to display them on the screen simultaneously.

In order to demonstrate this feature, let's get data for two more pies entered into the program. First, I'll show you the feature of Harvard Graphics 3.0 that lets you subdivide a single slice of a pie and view it as a second pie or as a column (a stacked bar). Then you'll add a third pie that looks at the same categories as pie 1, but at a different point in time.

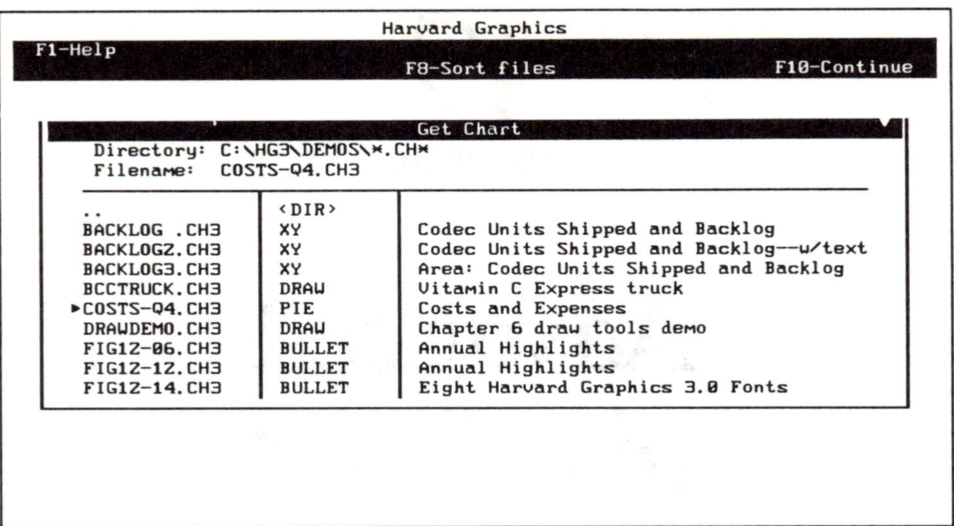

12-1 The Get Chart directory with COSTS-Q4.CH3 highlighted.

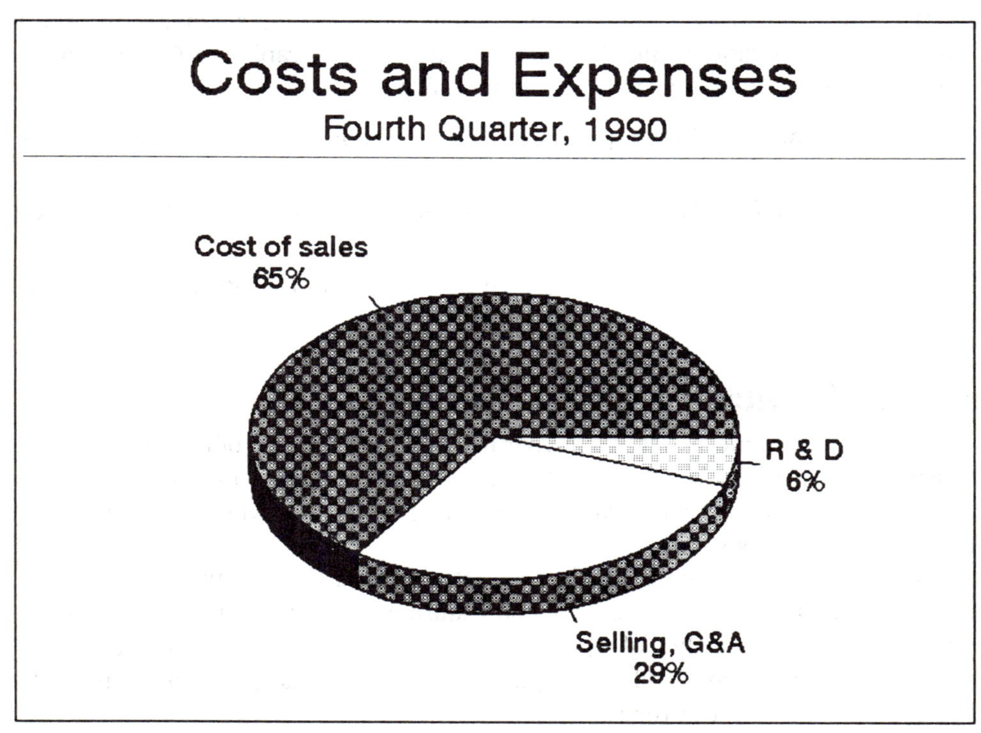

12-2 The Costs and Expenses chart.

```
COSTS-Q4.CH3                              Pie Chart 1
 F1-Help          F2-Show chart    F3-Choices       F4-Draw          F5-Mark
 F6-Main Menu     F7-Spell/Text    F8-Options       F9-Pie data      F10-Continue

Title:      Costs and Expenses
Subtitle:   Fourth Quarter, 1990
Footnote:
Pie title:

Slice          Label              Value          Cut       Color       Pattern

 1     Cost of sales           10134            No       Gry    |S      0
 2     Selling, G&A            4472             No       White  |S      1
 3     R & D                   871              No       Gry LL |S      2
 4                                              No       Gry  L |S      3
 5                                              No       Gry LL |S      4
 6                                              No       White  |S      5
 7                                              No       Gry DD |S      6
 8                                              No       Gry    |S      7
 9                                              No       Gry  L |S      8
10                                              No       Gry  L |S      9
11                                              No       Gry LL |S      10
12                                              No       White  |S      11
```

12-3 The Pie Chart 1 data screen.

To be more specific, the first pie that you created in chapter 2 looked at the major cost and expense categories for Compression Labs, Inc., for the fourth quarter of 1990. The categories are Cost of Sales; Selling, G&A (General and Administrative); and R & D (Research and Development). In the second pie, or column, you're going to break one slice—Cost of Sales—into its two largest components, videoconferencing products and research and development contracts. In pie 3, you'll create a chart representing the same three cost and expense categories as pie 1, but for the fourth quarter of 1989.

At the Pie Chart 1 data screen, select F9 – Pie Data and the Pie Data menu will pop up (see Fig. 12-4). Select item 2, Pie 2 data. The Pie Chart 2 data screen will appear (see Fig. 12-5). Notice that, while the Label and Value columns are empty of data, the title and subtitle are retained because there will still be a single heading for this multiple-pie chart. For the moment, the title and subtitle are OK.

Your cursor should be blinking under the C of Costs and Expenses. Press the Tab key five times to move the cursor down into the Label column opposite Slice 1. Then:

1. Type VC products and Enter. (VC is an abbreviation for videoconferencing; the whole thing won't fit into a label.)
2. Type R & D contracts, and then hit Tab and the up arrow. The cursor should now be in the Value column, opposite Slice 1.
3. Type 8727 and Enter.
4. Opposite R & D contracts, type 1407. Your Pie Chart 2 data screen should now look like Fig. 12-6.

```
COSTS-Q4.CH3                              Pie Chart 1
 F1-Help          F2-Show chart   F3-Choices     F4-Draw       F5-Mark
 F6-Main Menu     F7-Spell/Text   F8-Options     F9-Pie data   F10-Continue

Title:      Costs and Expenses                   ▸ Pie 1 data     1
Subtitle:   Fourth Quarter, 1990                   Pie 2 data     2
Footnote:                                          Pie 3 data     3
Pie title:                                         Pie 4 data     4
                                                   Pie 5 data     5
                                                   Pie 6 data     6
Slice          Label             Value             Next pie       7  Ctrl-PgDn
                                                   Previous pie 8    Ctrl-PgUp
 1    Cost of sales          10134          N
 2    Selling, G&A           4472           No         White  |S       1
 3    R & D                  871            No         Gry LL|S        2
 4                                          No         Gry  L|S        3
 5                                          No         Gry LL|S        4
 6                                          No         White  |S       5
 7                                          No         Gry DD|S        6
 8                                          No         Gry    |S       7
 9                                          No         Gry  L|S        8
 10                                         No         Gry  L|S        9
 11                                         No         Gry LL|S        10
 12                                         No         White  |S       11
```

12-4 The Pie data menu.

```
COSTS-Q4.CH3                              Pie Chart 2
 F1-Help          F2-Show chart   F3-Choices     F4-Draw       F5-Mark
 F6-Main Menu     F7-Spell/Text   F8-Options     F9-Pie data   F10-Continue

Title:      Costs and Expenses
Subtitle:   Fourth Quarter, 1990
Footnote:
Pie title:

Slice          Label             Value          Cut        Color       Pattern

 1                                              No      Gry DD|S        0
 2                                              No      Gry    |S       1
 3                                              No      Gry  L|S        2
 4                                              No      Gry  L|S        3
 5                                              No      Gry LL|S        4
 6                                              No      White  |S       5
 7                                              No      Gry DD|S        6
 8                                              No      Gry    |S       7
 9                                              No      Gry  L|S        8
 10                                             No      Gry  L|S        9
 11                                             No      Gry LL|S        10
 12                                             No      White  |S       11
```

12-5 The Pie Chart 2 data screen.

If you're curious about what you've accomplished so far, press F2 to view the graphics screen. It should look something like Fig. 12-7. Press Esc to return to the data screen. Let's move right on to the data for pie 3 before doing any tinkering. Pie 3 will illustrate the costs and expenses for the fourth quarter, 1989.

1. Press F9—Pie data, then select Pie 3 data.

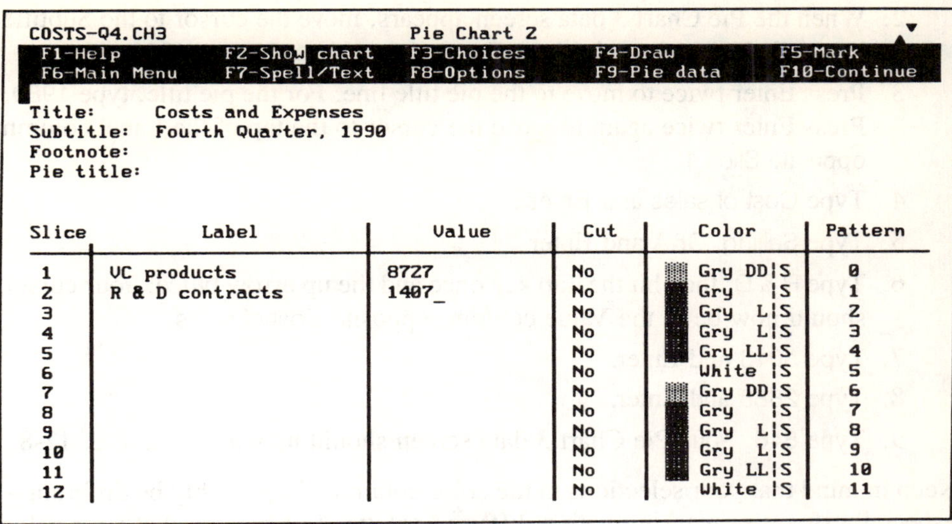

12-6 The Pie Chart 2 data screen with data entered.

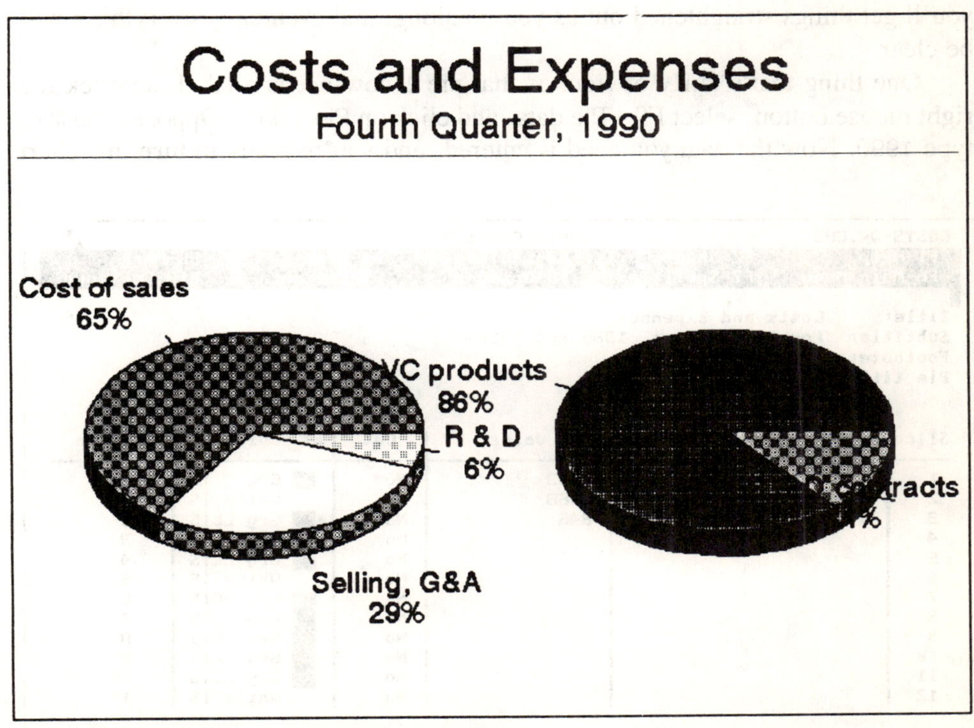

12-7 The first stage of your multiple-chart project.

2. When the Pie Chart 3 data screen appears, move the cursor to the Subtitle line and change the subtitle to Fourth Quarters, 1989 and 1990.
3. Press Enter twice to move to the pie title line. For the pie title, type 1989. Press Enter twice again to move the cursor to the top of the Label column opposite Slice 1.
4. Type Cost of sales and Enter.
5. Type Selling, G&A and Enter.
6. Type R & D, then hit the Tab key once and the up arrow twice. Your cursor should now be in the Value column, opposite Cost of sales.
7. Type 5013 and Enter.
8. Type 2888 and Enter.
9. Type 846. Your Pie Chart 3 data screen should now look like Fig. 12-8.

Keep in mind that your selections in the color column will probably be different—especially if you're working with a different palette. Just be sure that your color selections for Slices 1, 2, and 3 are identical to those for Pie Chart 1.

Press F2 to check your progress. The three charts should appear as shown in Fig. 12-9. This is a rather jumbled and uninformative screen at the moment, but you'll get things straightened out as you go along, and eventually everything will be clear.

One thing that's fairly obvious is that pie 1 now needs a label, so click the right mouse button, select F9 – Pie data, and click on Pie 1 data. Opposite Pie title, type 1990. Now the data you need is entered, and you're ready to turn this chart

```
COSTS-Q4.CH3                          Pie Chart 3
 F1-Help          F2-Show chart    F3-Choices      F4-Draw          F5-Mark
 F6-Main Menu     F7-Spell/Text    F8-Options      F9-Pie data      F10-Continue

Title:      Costs and Expenses
Subtitle:   Fourth Quarters, 1989 and 1990
Footnote:
Pie title:  1989
```

Slice	Label	Value	Cut	Color	Pattern
1	Cost of sales	5013	No	Gry |S	0
2	Selling, G&A	2888	No	White |S	1
3	R & D	846	No	Gry LL|S	2
4			No	Gry L|S	3
5			No	Gry LL|S	4
6			No	White |S	5
7			No	Gry DD|S	6
8			No	Gry |S	7
9			No	Gry L|S	8
10			No	Gry L|S	9
11			No	Gry LL|S	10
12			No	White |S	11

12-8 The Pie Chart 3 data screen with new data entered.

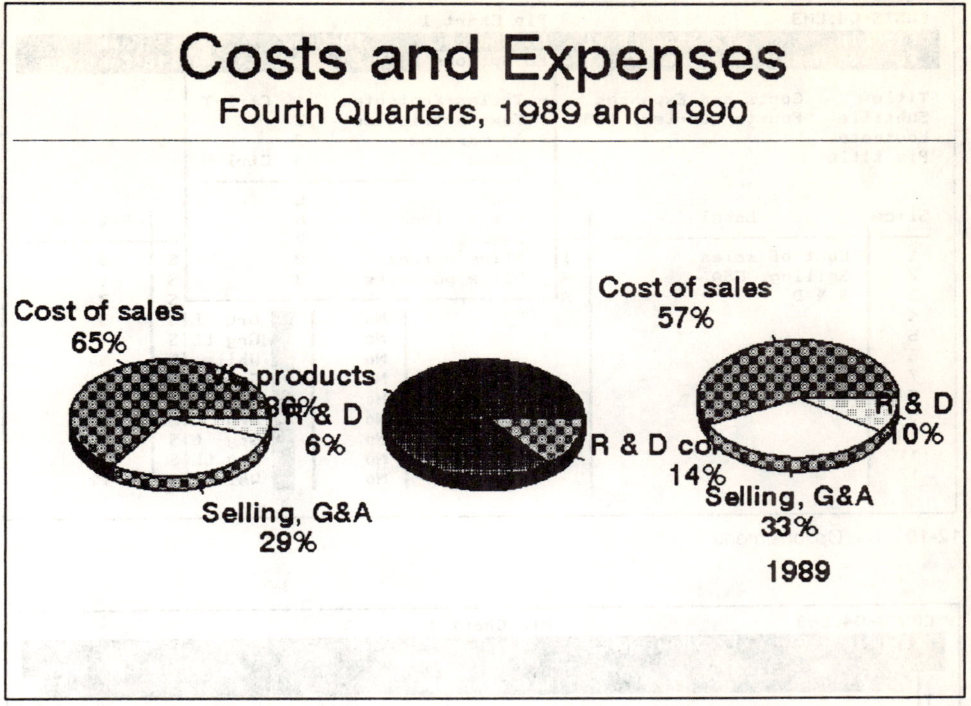

12-9 The charts in progress.

into a thing of beauty. The menu item that offers you the greatest number of opportunities for modifying your pie chart is F8–Options, shown in Fig. 12-10.

Titles and footnotes

If you select the first item, Titles/Footnotes, you'll see a menu similar to the Titles/Footnotes menu discussed in chapter 10 (see Fig. 12-11). There's one new element, however—the legend title line. If you choose to make the legend visible and want to give it a heading, here's where you enter that heading. For your first pair of charts, change the subtitle back to read Fourth Quarter, 1990.

Text attributes

Press Esc, then F8 to return to the Options menu. Select Text attributes, item 2. A submenu will be displayed that lets you choose between text attributes for the titles and footnotes (item 1) and text attributes for the pie labels (item 2) (see Fig. 12-12).

Selecting item 1 leads you to the Text Attributes Titles/Footnotes menu. (To review, see chapter 10.) Selecting item 2 brings up the Text Attributes Labels

```
COSTS-Q4.CH3                               Pie Chart 1
 F1-Help          F2-Show chart    F3-Choices       F4-Draw          F5-Mark
 F6-Main Menu     F7-Spell/Text    F8-Options       F9-Pie data      F10-Continue

Title:      Costs and Expenses    ▸ Titles/Footnotes    1  Ctrl-T
Subtitle:   Fourth Quarter, 1990    Text attributes     2
Footnote:                           Appearance          3
Pie title:                          Notes               4  Ctrl-N
                                    ─────────────────────────────
                                    Style               5
Slice        Label               │  Pie options         6       │ Pattern
─────┬───────────────────────────   Legend              7       ──┬────────
 1   │ Cost of sales            1   Slice values        8      S │  0
 2   │ Selling, G&A             4   Slice percents      9      S │  1
 3   │ R & D                    8                              S │  2
 4   │                         │          │ No  │ Gry   L│S │  3
 5   │                         │          │ No  │ Gry  LL│S │  4
 6   │                         │          │ No  │ White  │S │  5
 7   │                         │          │ No  │ Gry  DD│S │  6
 8   │                         │          │ No  │ Gry    │S │  7
 9   │                         │          │ No  │ Gry   L│S │  8
 10  │                         │          │ No  │ Gry   L│S │  9
 11  │                         │          │ No  │ Gry  LL│S │  10
 12  │                         │          │ No  │ White  │S │  11
```

12-10 The Options menu.

```
COSTS-Q4.CH3                               Pie Chart 1
 F1-Help          F2-Show chart                                F5-Mark
                                                               F10-Continue
                              Titles/Footnotes
T
S  Title:          Costs and Expenses
F  Subtitle 1:     Fourth Quarter, 1990
P  Subtitle 2:

   Footnote 1:
S  Footnote 2:
-  Footnote 3:

   Legend title:

 4   │                         │          │ No  │ Gry   L│S │  3
 5   │                         │          │ No  │ Gry  LL│S │  4
 6   │                         │          │ No  │ White  │S │  5
 7   │                         │          │ No  │ Gry  DD│S │  6
 8   │                         │          │ No  │ Gry    │S │  7
 9   │                         │          │ No  │ Gry   L│S │  8
 10  │                         │          │ No  │ Gry   L│S │  9
 11  │                         │          │ No  │ Gry  LL│S │  10
 12  │                         │          │ No  │ White  │S │  11
```

12-11 The Titles/Footnotes menu.

menu (see Fig. 12-13). This menu controls the labels for the pie slices in your chart, and is just like previous text attributes menus, with one exception: you can't control the alignment (left, center, right) of the labels. You can, however, determine their placement, as you will see shortly.

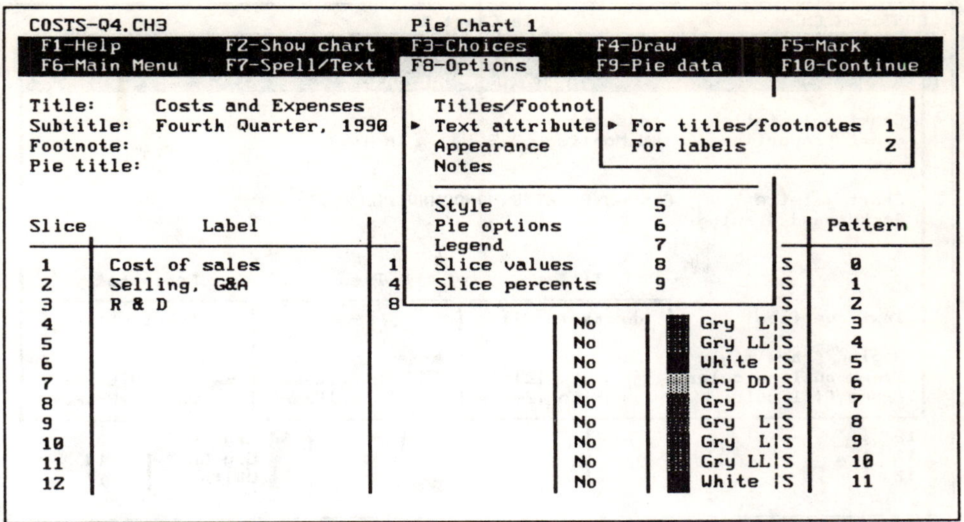

12-12 The Text Attributes submenu.

```
COSTS-Q4.CH3                              Pie Chart 1
 F1-Help           F2-Show chart           F3-Choices
                                                               F10-Continue
                                  Text Attributes Labels
                    Size     Color        Alignment    Font Name    Font Style
  Pie 1 labels    | 4     |  Black |XL |     -     | Swiss 721  | Roman
  Pie 2 labels    | 4     |  Black |XL |     -     | Swiss 721  | Roman
  Pie 3 labels    | 4     |  Black |XL |     -     | Swiss 721  | Roman
  Pie 4 labels    | 4     |  Black |XL |     -     | Swiss 721  | Roman
  Pie 5 labels    | 4     |  Black |XL |     -     | Swiss 721  | Roman
  Pie 6 labels    | 4     |  Black |XL |     -     | Swiss 721  | Roman

  Legend labels   | 3.5   |  Black |XL |     -     | Swiss 721  | Roman
 3  | R & D                 | 871        | No  | Gry LL|S | 2
 4  |                       |            | No  | Gry  L|S | 3
 5  |                       |            | No  | Gry LL|S | 4
 6  |                       |            | No  | White |S | 5
 7  |                       |            | No  | Gry DD|S | 6
 8  |                       |            | No  | Gry   |S | 7
 9  |                       |            | No  | Gry  L|S | 8
 10 |                       |            | No  | Gry  L|S | 9
 11 |                       |            | No  | Gry LL|S | 10
 12 |                       |            | No  | White |S | 11
```

12-13 The Text Attributes Labels menu.

Appearance

Select Appearance, item 3, from the Options menu (see Fig. 12-14). This is the same Appearance menu you worked with in chapter 10, except that there is a Pies column that has no text overflow option. (To review, see chapter 10.)

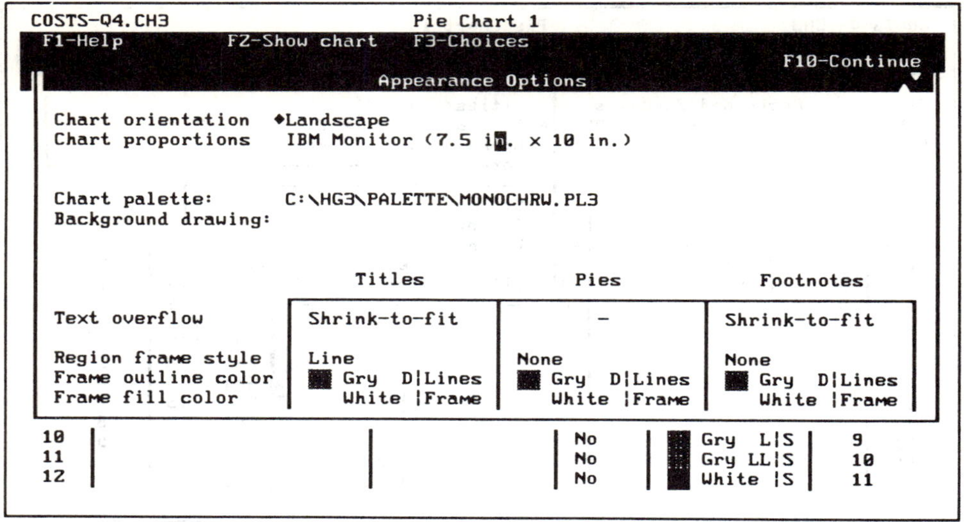

12-14 The Appearance Options menu.

Notes

If you want to add notes to a pie chart (that might be handed out with printed copies during a presentation, for example), use the Notes function. (To review, see chapter 10.)

Style

Item 5 on the Options menu is Style. Click on Style, and the Style Options menu will pop up (see Fig. 12-15). The first style option is Share Pie 1 labels. This is handy if you are displaying several pies, all of which measure the same parameters. In the present example, the second pie is a breakdown of one slice of the first—so the appropriate setting is No. The second style option lets you choose two-dimensional or three-dimensional pies. Leave it at 3D for now.

Next, you are asked whether you want to link pies 1 and 2. This option applies to your current example, where pie 2 is a breakdown of one slice in pie 1. Click on Link Pies 1&2, then press the space bar until the setting is Yes. For the present exercise you don't want proportional pies, but we'll come back to that.

The last three items on the Style Options menu let you stipulate whether to fill your slices with colors, patterns, or both; the outline color for your slices; and the color of the lines that link two pies (if you have selected linking).

At this point, your Style Options menu should look like Fig. 12-16. If you press F2, you'll see that nothing has changed from Fig. 12-9. But what happened to that linkage between pies 1 and 2? The link can't be made until you tell the

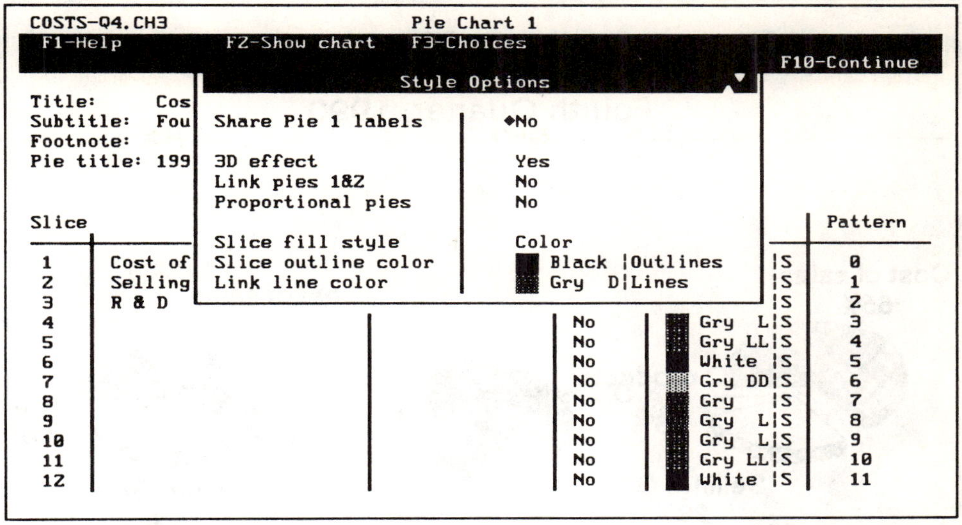

```
COSTS-Q4.CH3                          Pie Chart 1
 F1-Help          F2-Show chart    F3-Choices
                                                                  F10-Continue
                                 Style Options
Title:      Cos
Subtitle:   Fou  Share Pie 1 labels       |   ♦No
Footnote:
Pie title:  199  3D effect                |    Yes
                 Link pies 1&2            |    No
                 Proportional pies        |    No
Slice                                                                 | Pattern
                 Slice fill style         |    Color
 1     Cost of   Slice outline color      |    Black |Outlines   |S   0
 2     Selling   Link line color          |    Gry  D|Lines      |S   1
 3     R & D                                                     |S   2
 4                                     No      Gry  L|S   3
 5                                     No      Gry LL|S   4
 6                                     No      White |S   5
 7                                     No      Gry DD|S   6
 8                                     No      Gry   |S   7
 9                                     No      Gry  L|S   8
10                                     No      Gry  L|S   9
11                                     No      Gry LL|S   10
12                                     No      White |S   11
```

12-15 The Style Options menu.

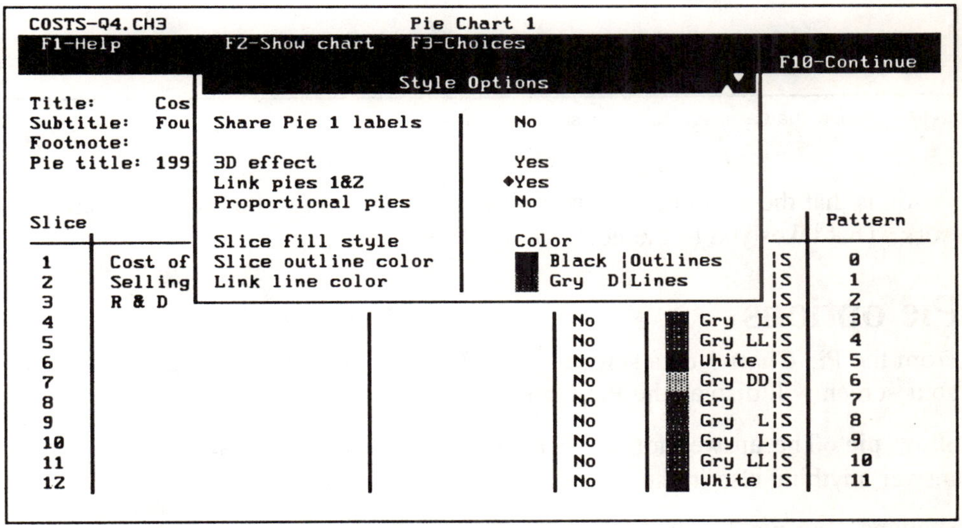

```
COSTS-Q4.CH3                          Pie Chart 1
 F1-Help          F2-Show chart    F3-Choices
                                                                  F10-Continue
                                 Style Options
Title:      Cos
Subtitle:   Fou  Share Pie 1 labels       |    No
Footnote:
Pie title:  199  3D effect                |    Yes
                 Link pies 1&2            |   ♦Yes
                 Proportional pies        |    No
Slice                                                                 | Pattern
                 Slice fill style         |    Color
 1     Cost of   Slice outline color      |    Black |Outlines   |S   0
 2     Selling   Link line color          |    Gry  D|Lines      |S   1
 3     R & D                                                     |S   2
 4                                     No      Gry  L|S   3
 5                                     No      Gry LL|S   4
 6                                     No      White |S   5
 7                                     No      Gry DD|S   6
 8                                     No      Gry   |S   7
 9                                     No      Gry  L|S   8
10                                     No      Gry  L|S   9
11                                     No      Gry LL|S   10
12                                     No      White |S   11
```

12-16 The Style Options menu with the latest settings.

program which slice of pie 1 is to be linked to pie 2. You do that by "cutting" a slice.

Press Esc to return to the Pie Chart 1 data screen, then click on the No in the Cut column in the Slice 1 row. Press the space bar to change the setting to Yes. Select F2 – Show chart to view your progress (see Fig. 12-17). Well, you did succeed in slicing that first pie, but there's still no linkage between pies 1 and 2. The

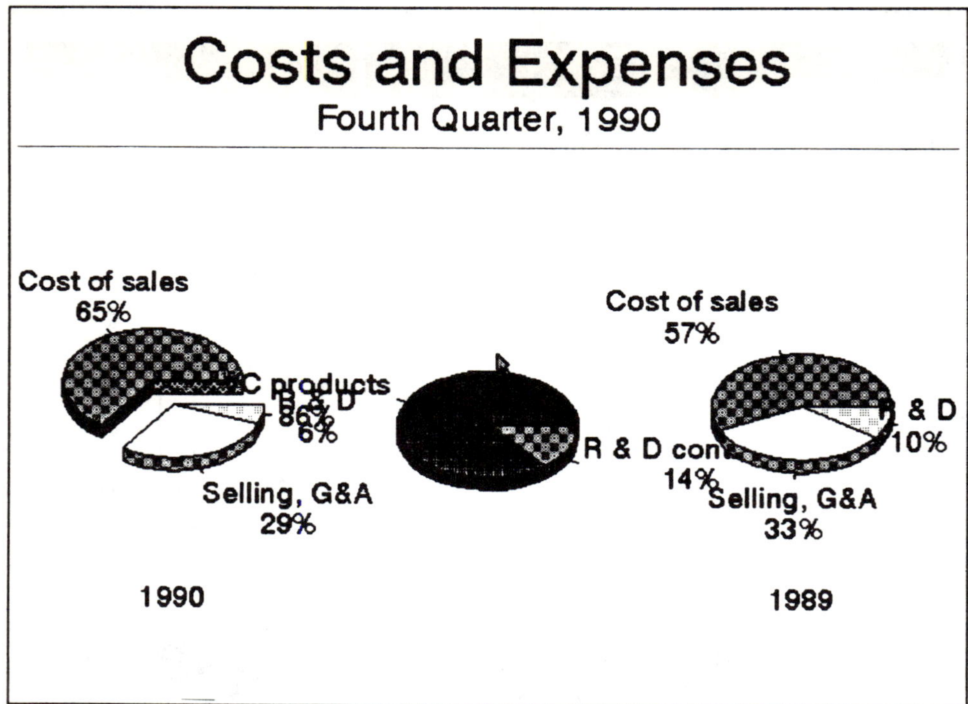

12-17 The pie chart after you cut the cost-of-sales slice.

reason is that there can be only two pies on the screen for the linkage function to work. That takes you to the next feature. Press Esc.

Pie options

From the Pie Chart 1 data screen, select F8 – Options, then Pie options, item 6. Your screen will display the Pie Options menu (see Fig. 12-18).

Show pie The answer for pie 3 is No—which means that you won't need to answer anything else in the Pie 3 column.

Show as For pie 2, select Column.

Pie size You can make the pie, or column, smaller by entering a number less than 100. Assume that the numbers represent a percentage of full size. For now, leave it at 100.

Starting angle You can rotate the pies so that the slices point in different directions. When two pies are linked, however, this option is removed; the linked slice is pointed toward the second pie, or column.

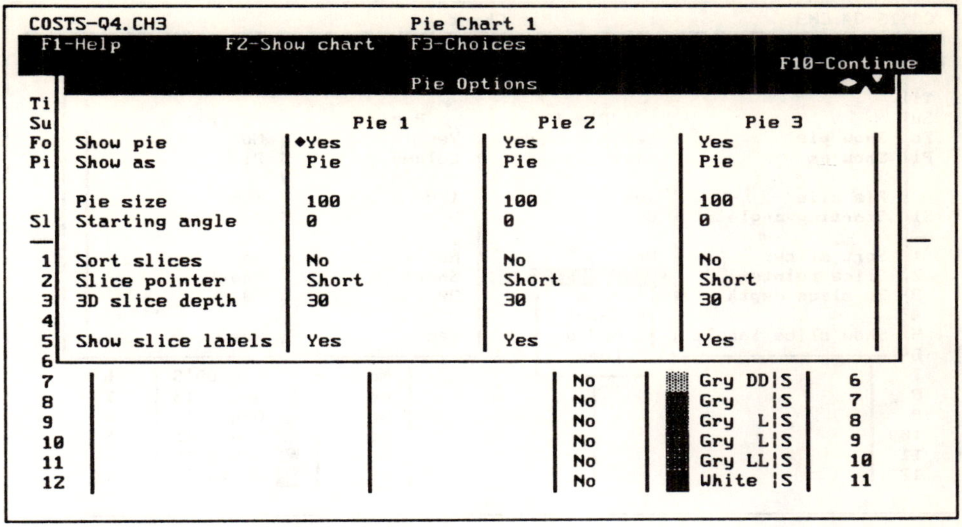

```
COSTS-Q4.CH3                         Pie Chart 1
 F1-Help          F2-Show chart      F3-Choices
                                                                 F10-Continue
                                     Pie Options
Ti
Su                              Pie 1            Pie 2            Pie 3
Fo  Show pie              |♦Yes          | Yes           | Yes
Pi  Show as               | Pie          | Pie           | Pie

    Pie size              | 100          | 100           | 100
Sl  Starting angle        | 0            | 0             | 0

 1  Sort slices           | No           | No            | No
 2  Slice pointer         | Short        | Short         | Short
 3  3D slice depth        | 30           | 30            | 30
 4
 5  Show slice labels     | Yes          | Yes           | Yes
 6
 7  |              |              | No  |  Gry DD|S  | 6
 8  |              |              | No  |  Gry   |S  | 7
 9  |              |              | No  |  Gry  L|S  | 8
10  |              |              | No  |  Gry  L|S  | 9
11  |              |              | No  |  Gry LL|S  | 10
12  |              |              | No  |  White |S  | 11
```

12-18 The Pie Options menu.

Sort slices You can instruct the program to arrange the slices according to size, with the largest slice at 3 o'clock and the slice sizes getting smaller as you move counter-clockwise. Leave the setting at No.

Slice pointer You have four options here: None, Short, Medium, and Long (see Fig. 12-19). Stay with the Short pointer.

3D slice depth The question here is, "Do you prefer a shallow or a deep pie?" I like it deeper, so type 90. Pressing F2 shows that you have a much fatter pie. Actually, it should probably be called a cake chart now (see Fig. 12-20). Return to the data screen by pressing Esc.

Show slice labels You can elect to eliminate the slice labels and explain the chart via a legend instead. You'll do that a little later; for now, the answer remains Yes.

That takes you through the Pie Options menu, which now looks like Fig. 12-21. You're getting there, but you can see in Fig. 12-20 that you still have a problem with overlapping slice labels. There are a number of solutions at this point, and most of the time you'll want to do some trial-and-error to see what gives you the most satisfactory results. You can reduce the size of the labels; you can switch to 2D, you can eliminate the labels, etc. There's no best solution for all cases; you'll have to decide what works best and what looks best to you.

Let's reduce the size of the labels in this case. Press Esc twice to return to the Pie Chart 1 data screen, then select F8–Options, Text attributes, and For labels. The Text Attributes Labels menu will appear, and you see that the default label

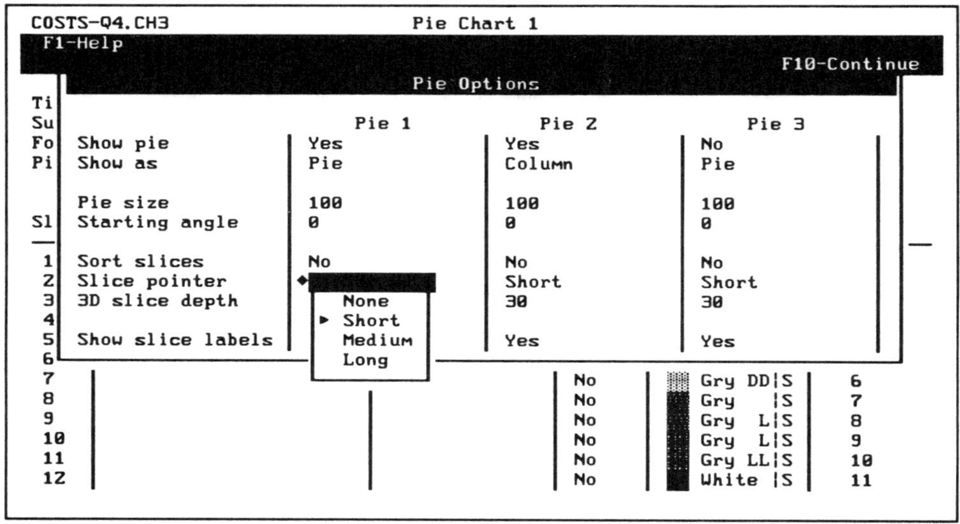

12-19 The Slice Pointer options.

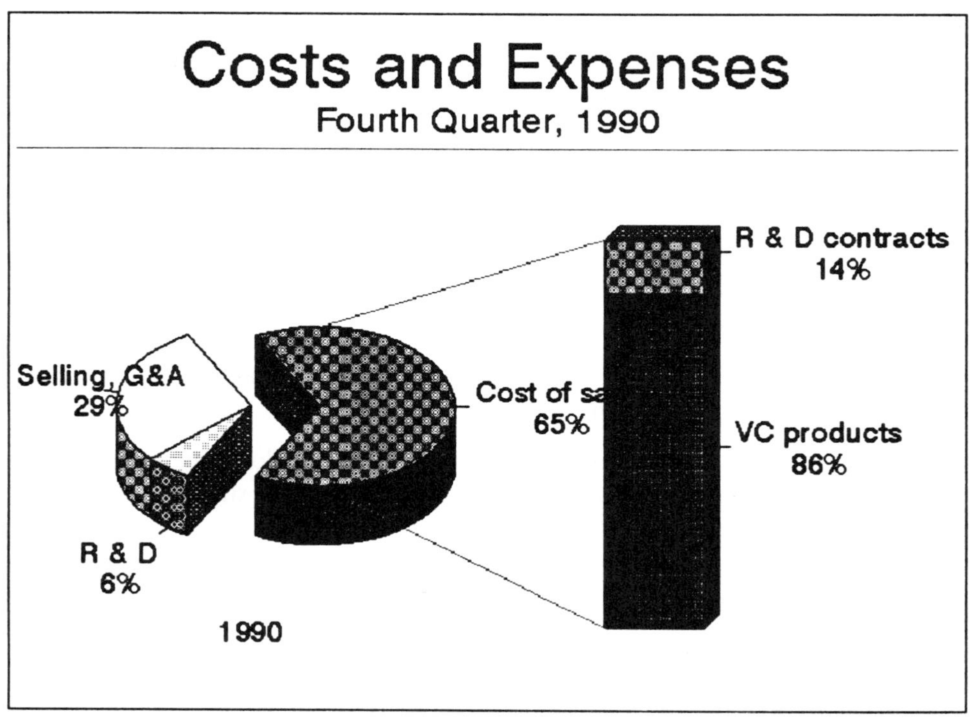

12-20 The pie chart with a 3D slice depth of 90.

```
COSTS-Q4.CH3                      Pie Chart 1
 F1-Help          F2-Show chart   F3-Choices
                                                      F10-Continue
                                  Pie Options
Ti
Su                          Pie 1           Pie 2             Pie 3
Fo  Show pie              | Yes           | Yes             | No
Pi  Show as               | Pie           | Column          | Pie

    Pie size              | 100           | 100             | 100
Sl  Starting angle        | 0             | 0               | 0

 1  Sort slices           | No            | No              | No
 2  Slice pointer         | Short         | Short           | Short
 3  3D slice depth        | 90            | 30              | 30
 4
 5  Show slice labels     |♦Yes           | Yes             | Yes
 6
 7                                       No    Gry DD|S   6
 8                                       No    Gry   |S   7
 9                                       No    Gry  L|S   8
10                                       No    Gry  L|S   9
11                                       No    Gry LL|S   10
12                                       No    White |S   11
```

12-21 The completed Pie Options menu.

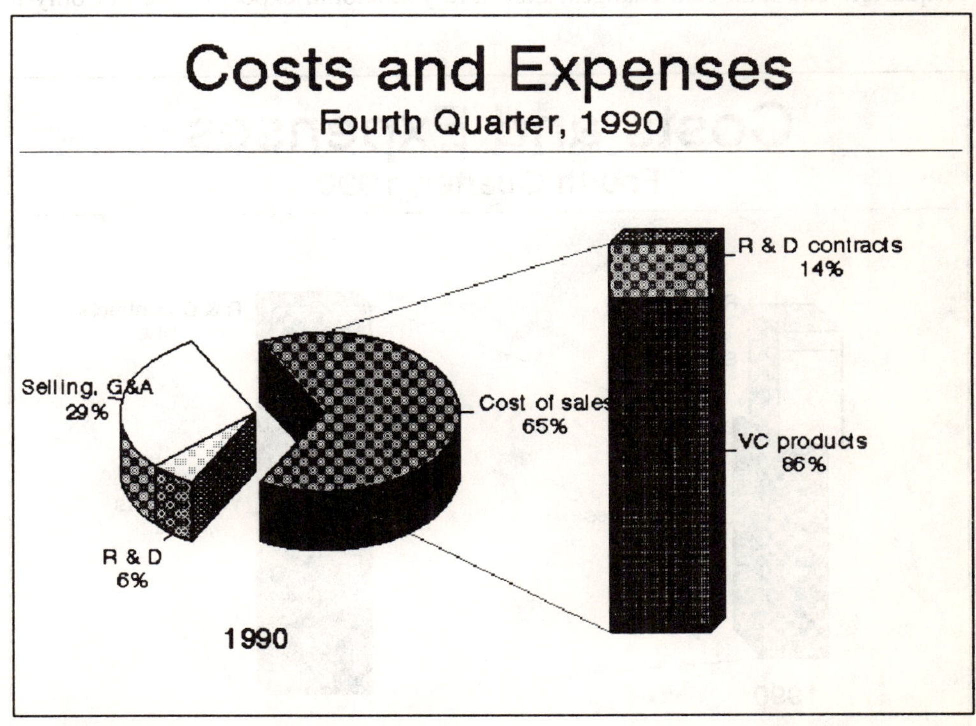

12-22 The chart with reduced label text.

size is 4. Change the label size to 3 for pies 1, 2, and 3. Press F2 to see the results (see Fig. 12-22).

This is now a decent-looking chart. The labels are legible, and the label-text doesn't look quite as "horsey," as graphics designers say.

There's one more step you could take, however, to unclutter the screen. Press Esc twice to return to the data screen, click on F8—Options and Pie options, and change the Pie 1 Show as setting to Column. When you view the chart once more, you'll see that you have achieved a readable, uncluttered chart. The cut slice of pie 1 has become an offset column; the total effect is clean and easy to understand (see Fig. 12-23).

Proportional pies

When you have multiple pies with identical slice labels, you can size the pies to represent the total amounts they represent. For example, you have been looking at data representing quarterly costs and expenses for a single company. Those costs and expenses have been subdivided into three areas: cost of sales, selling, G & A, and R & D. The contribution that each area makes to the total varies from quarter to quarter. The total also changes, therefore you should expect to see not only a

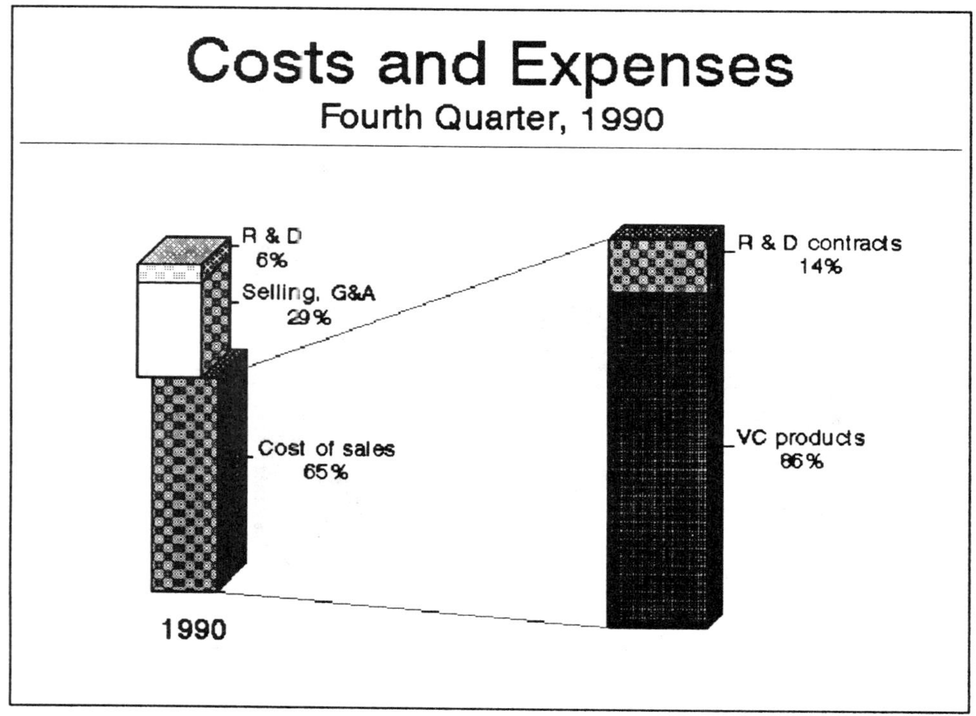

12-23 The final version of the linked-pie chart.

change in the size of the slices, but in the total size of the pies as well. Let's put that into concrete terms—which is what charts are all about.

1. Return to the Pie Chart 1 data screen and select F8 – Options.
2. From the Options menu, select item 6, Pie options.
3. In the Show Pie row, change Pie 2 to No and Pie 3 to Yes.
4. In the Show As row, Pie 1 and Pie 3 should both say Pie.
5. In the 3D Slice Depth row, change the pie 3 depth to 90.
6. In the Show Slice Labels row, Pie 1 and Pie 3 should both read No.

Your Pie Options menu should now be set up as in Fig. 12-24. Click on F2 – Show chart, and you can see you're making progress (see Fig. 12-25). Three things remain to be done. You have to identify the slices (because you removed the labels), uncut that big slice in the 1990 pie, and make the pies proportional.

1. Click the right mouse button to return to the Pie Options menu, and click it again to return to the Pie Chart 1 data screen.
2. In the Slice 1 row, change the Cut column from Yes to No.
3. Select F8 – Options again. When it appears, click on Style, item 4.
5. In the Style options menu, change the Proportional pies setting to Yes. That menu should then look like Fig. 12-26. (The Link pies 1&2 setting doesn't matter, because pie 2 isn't being displayed.)
6. Press Esc to close the Style Options menu, and click again on F8 – Options.

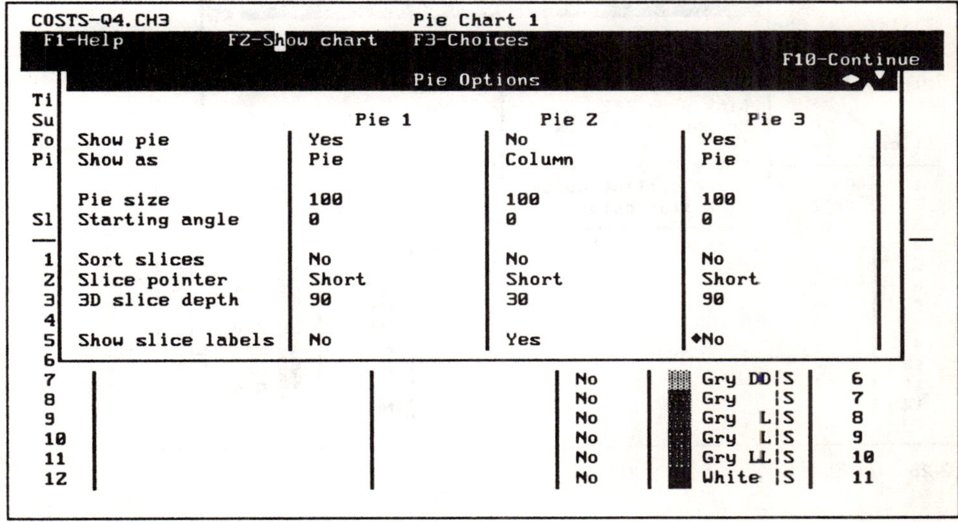

12-24 The Pie Options menu set up for the comparison of Pies 1 and 3.

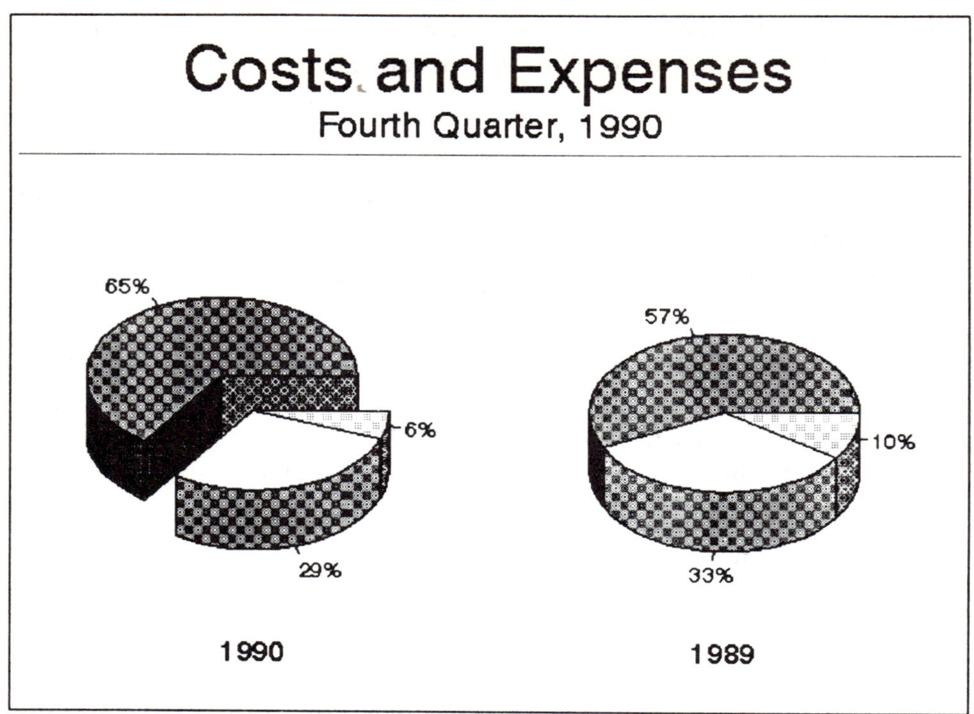

12-25 First stage of the two-pie chart.

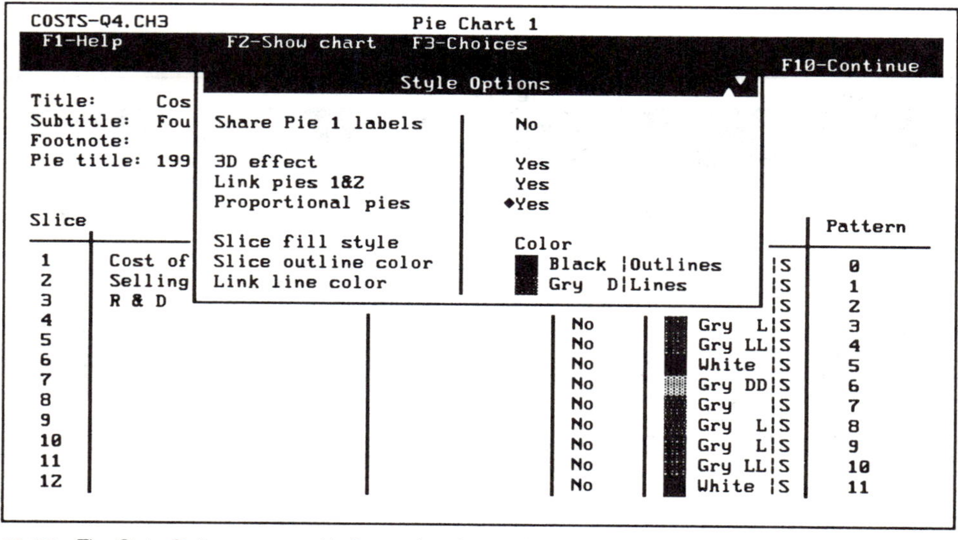

12-26 The Style Options menu with Proportional set to *Yes*.

Legend

You removed the slice labels earlier, so you'll need to insert a legend into the chart to identify the slices of the two pies. From the Options menu, select item 7, Leg end (see Fig. 12-27). In this Legend Options menu, you can instruct the computer to display a legend, where to put it on the chart, how to frame it, and how to color it. Click on Show legend, and press the space bar to change the setting to Yes.

You should now be able to view the legend on your chart with the default settings of location, frame style, outline color, and fill color. To verify this, press F2 (see Fig. 12-28). Note, also, that the two pies are proportionally sized for the first time.

Return to the Legend Options menu, click on Location, and then press the space bar repeatedly until the pointer is at the six o'clock position, midway at the bottom of the page (see Fig. 12-29). When you select F2 – Show chart to view the results, you'll see the legend in its new location—and new horizontal configuration—at the bottom of the screen (see Fig. 12-30). This location works well with the two-pie chart.

Because you're working with 3D pies, let's put the legend in a 3D frame. Click on Legend frame style, press F3 for choices, then select 3 – D and a double-border frame. Leave the frame outline color and frame fill color as is. That takes care of your legend options. Click on the right mouse button to return to the Pie Chart 1 data screen, then select F8 – Options again.

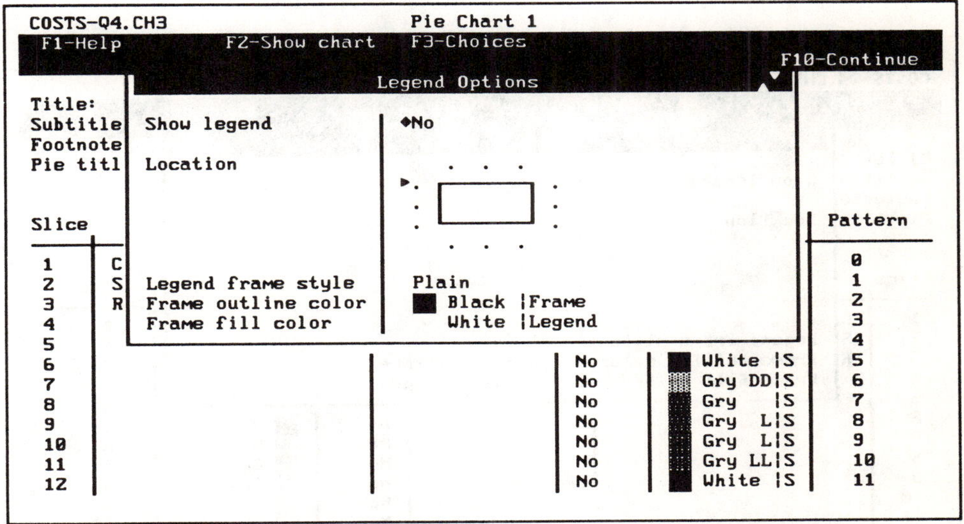

12-27 The Legend Options menu.

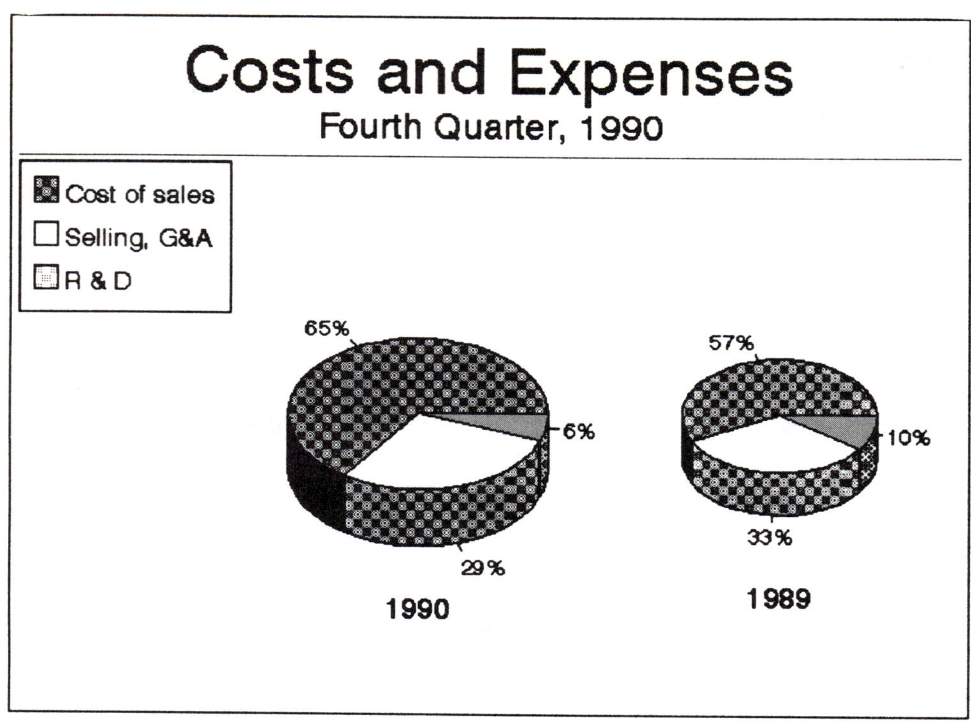

12-28 The chart legend displayed with its default settings.

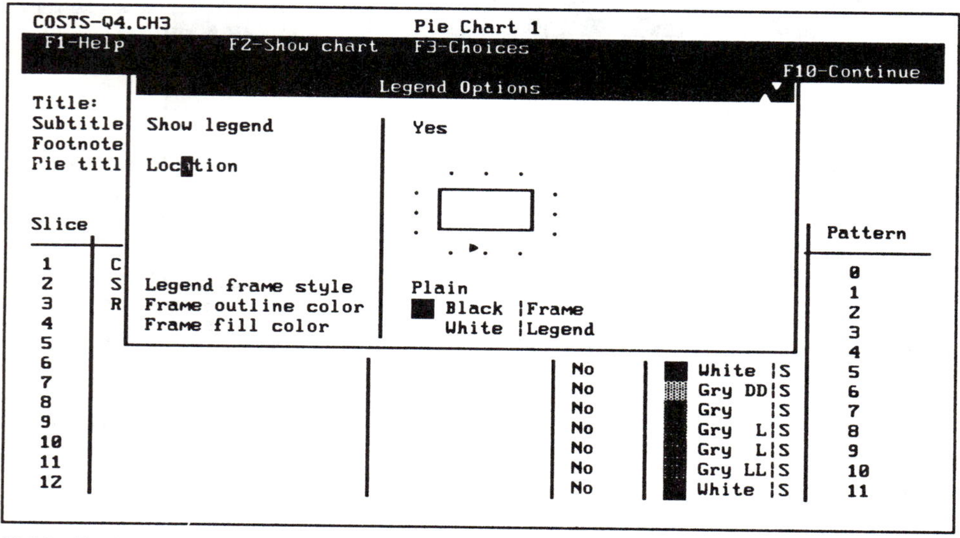

12-29 The location pointer indicating a position at the bottom center of the chart.

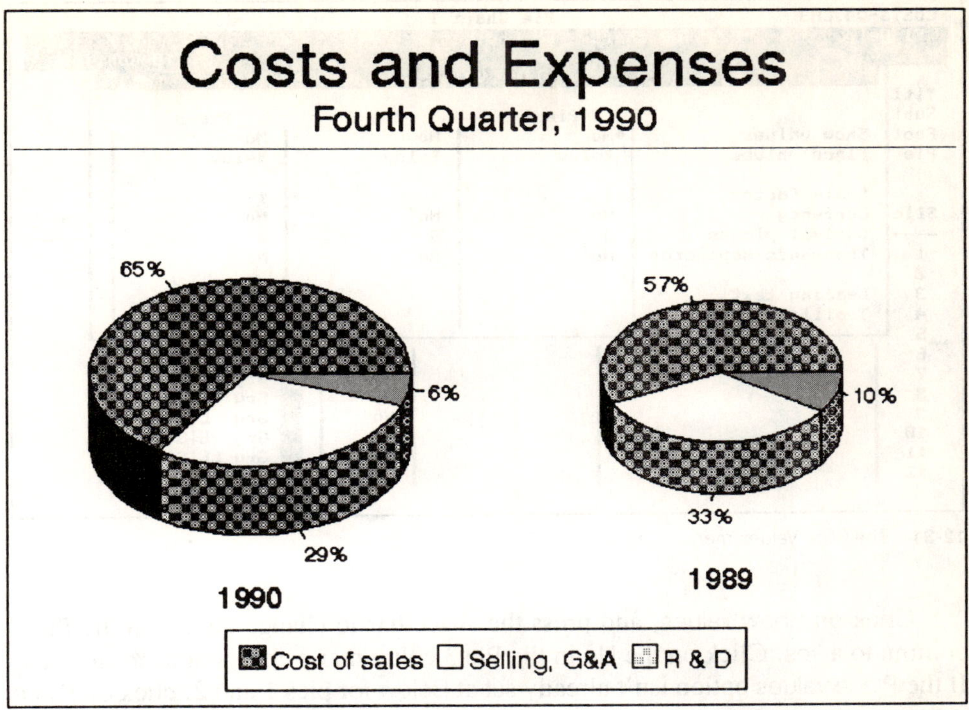

12-30 The legend in its new location and configuration.

Slice values

Right now the chart is short of information—you know what percentage of the whole pie is represented by each slice and you know that the 1990 pie is larger than the 1989 pie, but you don't know what kind of numbers are involved. You can remedy that situation with the Slice values option on the Options menu.

Click on Slice values (or press the number 8), and you'll suddenly get more choices than you might have imagined (see Fig. 12-31). From this menu, you can select:

- whether or not to display the values
- where to place the values: below, adjacent to, or inside the slices
- the scale factor (a constant value by which all the slice values are divided)
- whether to denote the values as currency
- the number of decimal places to use
- whether to separate units of thousands in the values
- any text that you want to lead—or trail—the values

For pies 1 and 3, let's elect to display the values below the slices and denote them as currency.

```
COSTS-Q4.CH3                         Pie Chart 1
 F1-Help          F2-Show chart      F3-Choices
                                                          F10-Continue
                                     Slice Values
Titl
Subt                               Pie 1        Pie 2        Pie 3
Foot  Show values                 ♦No          No           No
Pie   Place values                 Below        Below        Below

      Scale factor                 1            1            1
Slic  Currency                     No           No           No                rn
      Decimal places               0            0            0
 1    Thousands separator          No           No           No
 2
 3    Leading text
 4    Trailing text
 5
 6                                          No       White |S      5
 7                                          No       Gry DD|S      6
 8                                          No       Gry   |S      7
 9                                          No       Gry  L|S      8
 10                                         No       Gry  L|S      9
 11                                         No       Gry LL|S      10
 12                                         No       White |S      11
```

12-31 The Slice Values menu.

Click on Show values, and press the space bar to change the No in the Pie 1 column to a Yes. Click on the No in the Pie 3 column and change it to Yes as well. If the Place values option isn't already set at Below for pies 1 and 2, click on Place values and press the space bar to change the location of the pie 1 values to Below. Click on the location in the Pie 3 column and change it to Below as well.

Click on Currency and press the space bar to change the No in the Pie 1 column to Yes. Click on the No in the Pie 3 column and change it to Yes as well. In the Thousands separator row, change the option to Yes for pies 1 and 3. Your Slice Values menu should now look like Fig. 12-32. Press F2 to view the results (see Fig. 12-33).

As you look at this latest draft of the Costs and Expenses multiple-pie chart, you should recognize that there are a couple of things still to be done—clarify what those currency values mean, put the title/subtitle group in a 3D frame that goes with the rest of the chart, and change the subtitle to reflect the fact that you're presenting results from the fourth quarters of two different years.

1. Click the right mouse button twice to return to the Pie Chart 1 data screen.
2. Select F8–Options, then item 3, Appearance.
3. Click on Region frame style, then select F3–Choices to reveal all of the frame style options (see Fig. 12-34).
4. Scroll through the pop-up menu until you find the 3-D double-border frame, and then click on that choice.

```
COSTS-Q4.CH3                            Pie Chart 1
 F1-Help          F2-Show chart         F3-Choices
                                                            F10-Continue
                                        Slice Values
Titl
Subt                                  Pie 1          Pie 2          Pie 3
Foot  Show values                 |  Yes        |  No         |  Yes        |
Pie   Place values                |  Below      |  Below      |  Below      |
                                  |             |             |             |
      Scale factor                |  1          |  1          |  1          |
Slic  Currency                    |  Yes        |  No         |  Yes        |  rn
      Decimal places              |  0          |  0          |  0          |
 1    Thousands separator         |  Yes        |  No         | ♦Yes        |
 2                                |             |             |             |
 3    Leading text                |             |             |             |
 4    Trailing text               |             |             |             |
 5
 6                                               No    White |S    5
 7                                               No    Gry DD|S    6
 8                                               No    Gry   |S    7
 9                                               No    Gry  L|S    8
10                                               No    Gry  L|S    9
11                                               No    Gry LL|S   10
12                                               No    White |S   11
```

12-32 The Slice Values menu with new selections.

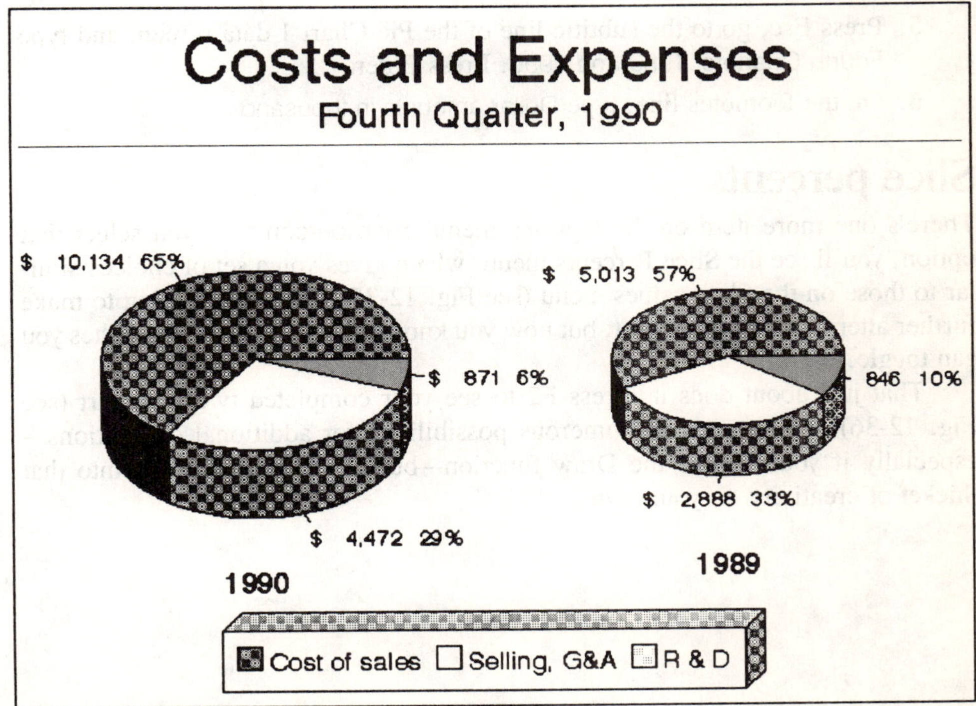

12-33 The pie charts with currency values displayed.

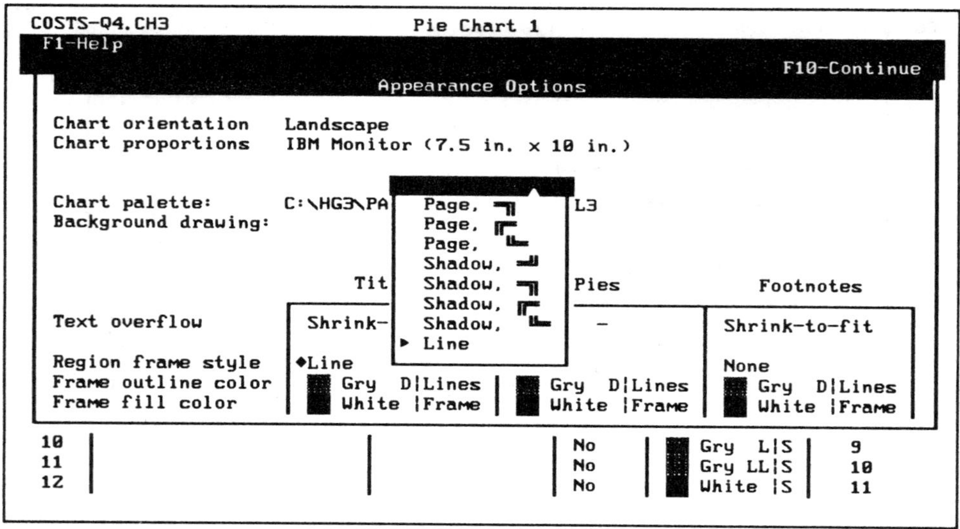

12-34 A partial menu of the frame style options.

5. Press Esc, go to the subtitle line of the Pie Chart 1 data screen, and type Fourth Quarters, 1989 and 1990. Press Enter.
6. On the footnotes line, type Dollar amounts in thousands.

Slice percents

There's one more item on the Options menu: Slice percents. If you select that option, you'll see the Slice Percents menu, which gives you a set of choices similar to those on the Slice values menu (see Fig. 12-35). You're not going to make further alterations to your chart, but now you know about a few more switches you can toggle.

That just about does it. Press F2 to see your completed two-pie chart (see Fig. 12-36). There are still numerous possibilities for additional decorations—especially if you get into the Draw function—but you can wander off into that thicket of creativity on your own.

```
COSTS-Q4.CH3                            Pie Chart 1
 F1-Help          F2-Show chart   F3-Choices
                                                              F10-Continue
                                    Slice Percents
Tit
Sub                              Pie 1             Pie 2             Pie 3
Foo  Show percents      |♦Yes            | Yes             | Yes            |
Pie  Place percents     | Below          | Below           | Below          |

     Decimal places     | 0              | 0               | 0              |
Sli                                                                           n
───  Leading text                                                            ───
 1   Trailing text      |                |                 |                |
 2
 3  | R & D                 | 871             | No   | Gry LL|S |   2
 4  |                       |                 | No   | Gry  L|S |   3
 5  |                       |                 | No   | Gry LL|S |   4
 6  |                       |                 | No   | White |S |   5
 7  |                       |                 | No   | Gry DD|S |   6
 8  |                       |                 | No   | Gry   |S |   7
 9  |                       |                 | No   | Gry  L|S |   8
10  |                       |                 | No   | Gry  L|S |   9
11  |                       |                 | No   | Gry LL|S |  10
12  |                       |                 | No   | White |S |  11
```

12-35 The Slice Percents menu.

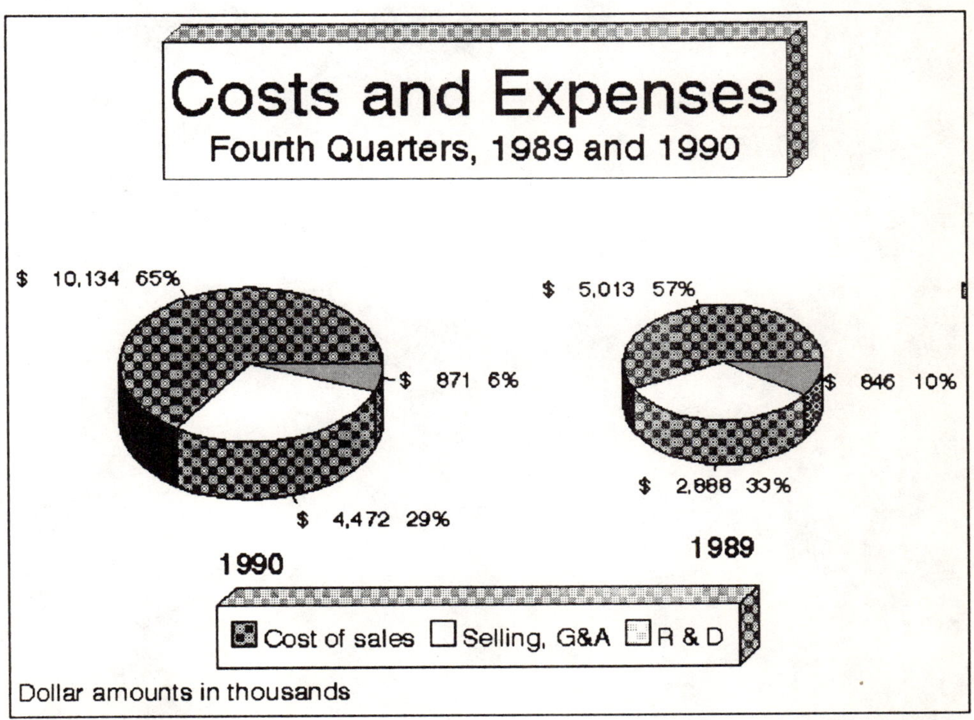

12-36 The completed two-pie chart.

13
CHAPTER

Advanced XY charts

Harvard Graphics 3.0 includes several kinds of charts that are plotted on an X-Y axis: bar charts (including stacked and overlapped bar charts), bar/line charts, line charts, area charts, high/low/close charts, and point charts.

You worked with generic or Gallery versions of these charts in chapters 2 and 3. Many of the possible enhancements to XY charts are the same as those with other types of charts, and were already discussed in chapters 10 through 12. In this chapter, we'll look at those refinements specific to XY charts.

Begin by loading the combination bar/line chart you created in chapter 3. From the Main Menu, press Ctrl – G, the speed key combo that takes you directly to the Get Chart directory. This time, rather than scrolling through the directory looking for your file, simply type INCOME.CH3 and Enter (see Fig. 13-1).

This is a rather busy chart, with the horizontal grid lines and data table. You could elect to demonstrate the XY enhancements by making the income chart even busier and fancier; instead, I'll have you work toward a simpler, more stylized result. Click the right mouse button to go to the XY Chart data screen (see Fig. 13-2). The menus you'll work with here are the F8 – Options menu and the F9 – XY data menu.

Select F8 – Options. When the Options menu drops down, you'll see that most of the items are familiar—you have already worked through them in chapters 10 through 12. In particular, the four items above the horizontal line—Titles/Footnotes, Text attributes, Appearance, and Notes—have all been covered (see Fig. 13-3). For a review, see chapter 10. We'll make some minor changes in those four areas, then move on to cover the items below the line in more detail.

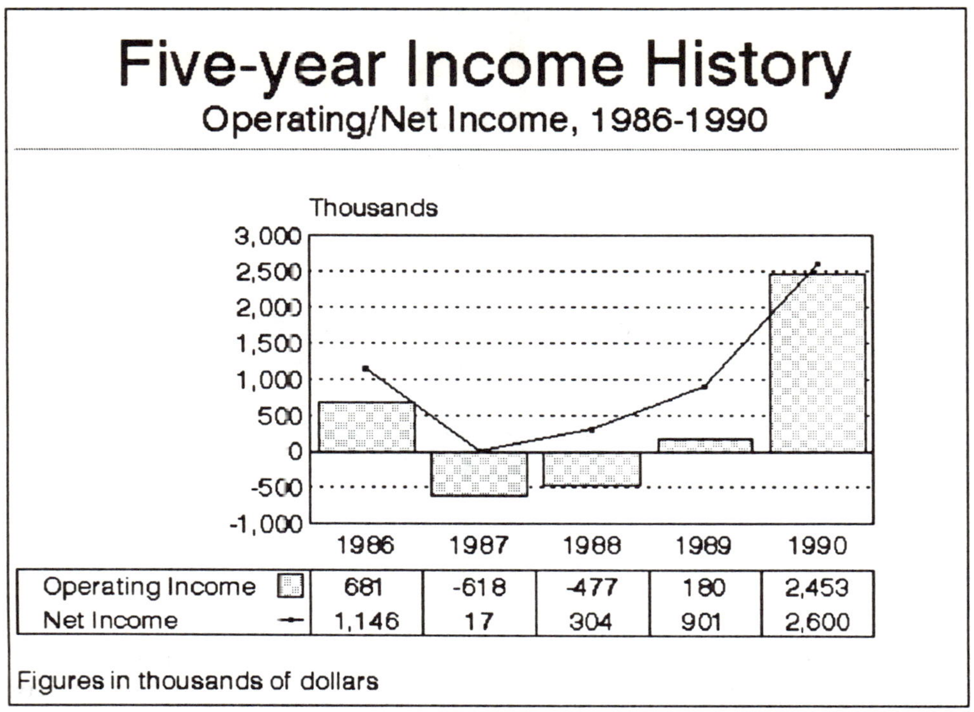

13-1 The income bar/line chart from chapter 3.

```
INCOME.CH3                         XY Chart
 F1-Help        F2-Show chart                   F4-Draw        F5-Mark
 F6-Main Menu   F7-Spell/Text   F8-Options      F9-XY data     F10-Continue

Title:      Five-year Income History
Subtitle:   Operating/Net Income, 1986-1990
Footnote:   Figures in thousands of dollars

                                    1            2            3            4
Data         X Axis
Pt            Year            Operating    Net Income    Series 3     Series 4

1    1986                     681000       1146000
2    1987                     -618000      17000
3    1988                     -477000      304000
4    1989                     180000       901000
5    1990                     2453000      2600000
6
7
8
9
10
11
12
```

13-2 The XY Chart data screen.

```
INCOME.CH3                              XY Chart
 F1-Help          F2-Show chart                       F4-Draw          F5-Mark
 F6-Main Menu     F7-Spell/Text    F8-Options         F9-XY data       F10-Continue

Title:      Five-year Income Hist ▸ Titles/Footnotes      1  Ctrl-T
Subtitle:   Operating/Net Income,   Text attributes       2
Footnote:   Figures in thousands    Appearance            3
                                    Notes                 4  Ctrl-N
                                                                       4
Data         X Axis                 Style                 5
Pt           Year            Oper   Series                6        Series 4
                                    Legend                7
1     1986                   6810   Axis frame            8
2     1987                   -618   Axis options          9
3     1988                   -477   Format                A
4     1989                   1800   Data table/labels     B
5     1990                   2453
6
7
8
9
10
11
12
```

13-3 The Options menu.

Titles/Footnotes

Select Titles/Footnotes from the Options menu. When the Titles/Footnotes menu appears, delete the Y1 axis title (Thousands). That title isn't necessary because Footnote 1 specifies Figures in thousands of dollars. The modified menu should now look like Fig. 13-4. Press Esc to return to the XY Chart data screen.

Text attributes

Press F8 again for the Options menu, then select item 2, Text attributes. From the submenu, select For titles/footnotes. When the Text Attributes Titles/Footnotes menu pops up, change the title size to 6 and the subtitle 1 size to 4. Let the footnote size remain at 3.5. This menu should now resemble Fig. 13-5. Select F10 – Continue.

Appearance

Select F8 – Options, then Appearance. This menu should be familiar to you by now; you'll make only two changes. Click on Background drawing and, when the highlighted choice diamond appears, press F3 for Choices. Scroll through the C: \ HG3 \ DATA directory until you arrive at the FRAME2.CH3 file (see Fig. 13-6). Select F10 – Continue.

Back at the Appearance Options menu, find Region frame style at the bottom of the menu. Under the Titles column, that style is indicated as Line. Click on Line twice to bring up the frame style menu, then scroll through that menu until you

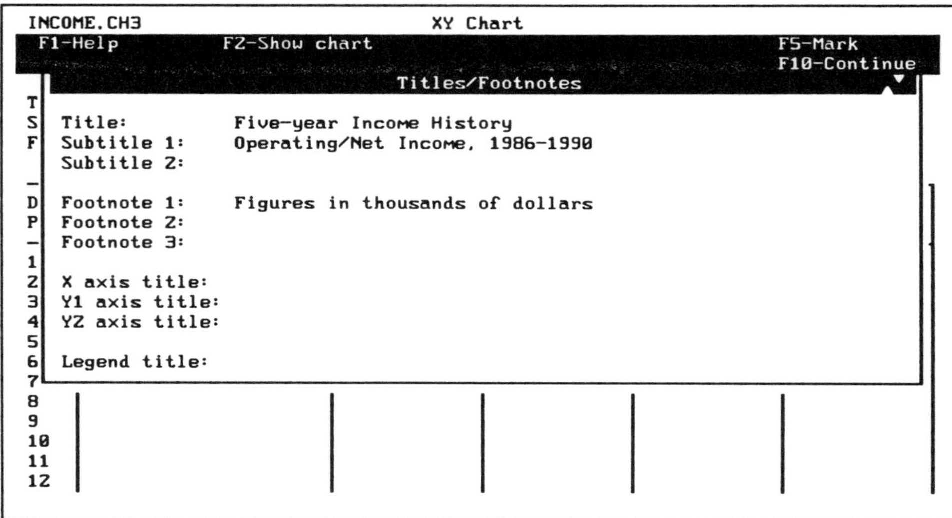

13-4 The modified Titles/Footnotes menu.

INCOME.CH3 XY Chart

F1-Help F2-Show chart F3-Choices F10-Continue

Text Attributes Titles/Footnotes

	Size	Color	Alignment	Font Name	Font Style
Title	6	Black |Ti	Center	Swiss 721	Roman
Subtitle 1	4	Black |Su	Center	Swiss 721	Roman
Subtitle 2	5	Black |Su	Center	Swiss 721	Roman
Footnote 1	3.5	Black |Fo	Left	Swiss 721	Roman
Footnote 2	3.5	Black |Fo	Left	Swiss 721	Roman
Footnote 3	3.5	Black |Fo	Left	Swiss 721	Roman
X axis title	3.5	Black |XT	Center	Swiss 721	Roman
Y1 axis title	3.5	Black |Y1	Top	Swiss 721	Roman
Y2 axis title	3.5	Black |Y2	Top	Swiss 721	Roman
Legend title	3.5	Black |XT	Center	Swiss 721	Roman

8
9
10
11
12

13-5 The Text Attributes Titles/Footnotes menu after the text size changes.

find None (at the very top of the menu). Click on None. The Appearance Options menu will now resemble Fig. 13-7.

To get a view of your progress to this point, press F2. The Five-year Income History chart in progress, with recent alterations, will appear (see Fig. 13-8).

```
INCOME.CH3                              XY Chart
 F1-Help
                                      F8-Sort files                    F10-Continue
                                   Appearance Options

                                 Get Background Drawing
     Directory:  C:\HG3\DATA\*.CH*
     Filename:   FRAME2.CH3

    ..               <DIR>
    BLINDS   .CH3    DRAW       Bkg: Horizontal Bands         Use 4,5,7.PL3
    BLUESKY  .CH3    DRAW       Bkg: Sky & Clouds           Use 9 or 10.PL3
    CYLINDER.CH3     DRAW       Bkg: Cylinder blend         Use 3,4,6,7.PL3
    FLOOR    .CH3    DRAW       Bkg: Checkered floor          Use 12HDW.PL3
    FRAME1   .CH3    DRAW       Bkg: single line frame          Use any PL3
   ►FRAME2   .CH3    DRAW       Bkg: double line frame          Use any PL3
    LEAVES   .CH3    DRAW       Bkg: Leaves                Use 7 or 7SHD.PL3
    LOGOBKG1.CH3     DRAW       Bkg: Use your own logo.pcx      Use any PL3
    LOGOBKG2.CH3     DRAW       Bkg: Edit your comp. name       Use any PL3

10
11
12
```

13-6 The Background Drawing directory with FRAME2.CH3 selected.

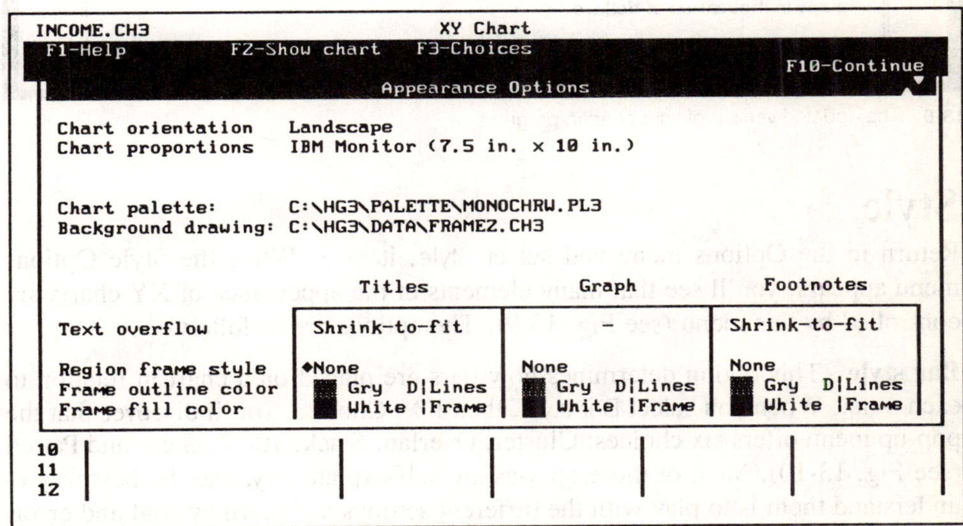

13-7 The Appearance Options menu with new changes.

Notes

If you want to add notes to your chart you can do so at this point, as discussed in chapter 12.

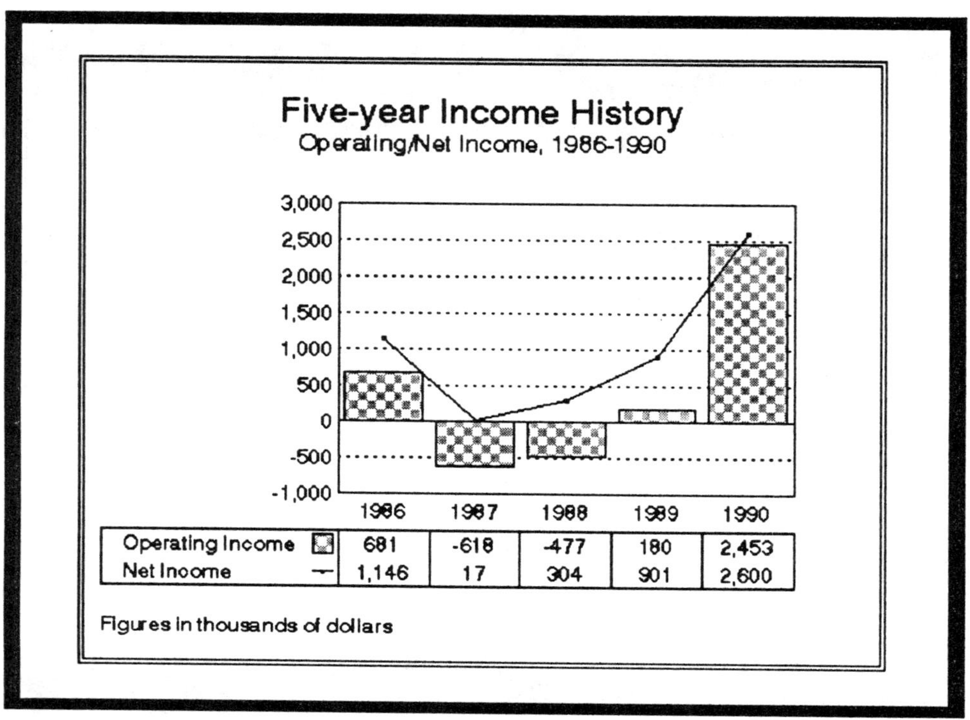

13-8 The updated version of your chart in progress.

Style

Return to the Options menu and select Style, item 5. When the Style Options menu appears, you'll see that many elements of the appearance of XY charts are controlled by this menu (see Fig. 13-9). The options are as follows:

Bar style This option determines how bars are placed on a chart in relation to each other. When you select Bar style, then F3 – Choices, you'll discover that the pop-up menu offers six choices: Cluster, Overlap, Stack, 100%, Step, and Paired (see Fig. 13-10). Most of these options are self-explanatory, and the best way to understand them is to play with the different settings and learn by trial and error. Don't forget that you can call for help on almost any item of any menu by highlighting that item and pressing F1. For example, to get an explanation of bar style, click on that menu option and select F1 – Help. A Help menu will drop down with explanations for the six types of bar styles (see Fig. 13-11). They are:

Bar shape Click twice on Bar shape to view the bar shape choices: Rectangle, Pyramid, Octagon, and Cylinder (see Fig. 13-12). Don't forget that, in two dimensions, rectangles, octagons and cylinders all look the same. For a change of pace, select Pyramid.

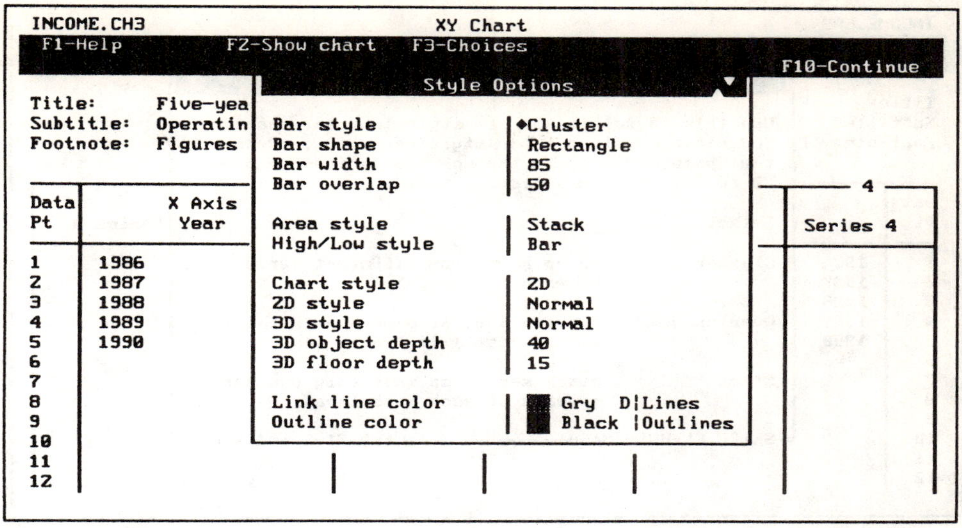

```
INCOME.CH3                              XY Chart
 F1-Help          F2-Show chart   F3-Choices
                                                             F10-Continue
                                Style Options
Title:     Five-yea
Subtitle:  Operatin  Bar style           |◆Cluster
Footnote:  Figures   Bar shape           | Rectangle
                     Bar width           | 85
                     Bar overlap         | 50                      4
Data      X Axis
Pt         Year      Area style          | Stack              Series 4
                     High/Low style      | Bar

1    1986            Chart style         | 2D
2    1987            2D style            | Normal
3    1988            3D style            | Normal
4    1989            3D object depth     | 40
5    1990            3D floor depth      | 15
6
7
8                    Link line color     |   Gry  D|Lines
9                    Outline color       |   Black |Outlines
10
11
12
```

13-9 The Style Options menu.

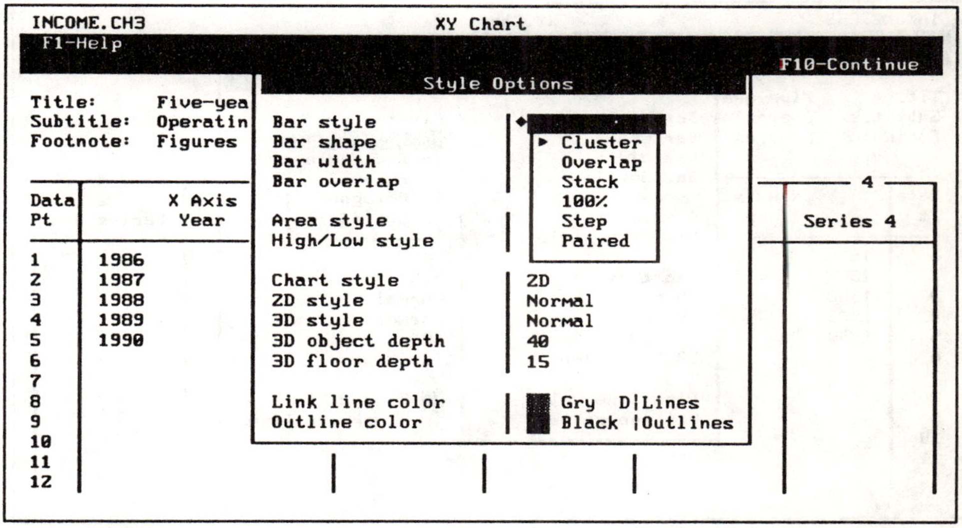

```
INCOME.CH3                              XY Chart
 F1-Help
                                                             F10-Continue
                                Style Options
Title:     Five-yea
Subtitle:  Operatin  Bar style           |◆
Footnote:  Figures   Bar shape           |   ▸ Cluster
                     Bar width           |     Overlap
                     Bar overlap         |     Stack               4
Data      X Axis                               100%
Pt         Year      Area style          |     Step           Series 4
                     High/Low style      |     Paired

1    1986            Chart style         | 2D
2    1987            2D style            | Normal
3    1988            3D style            | Normal
4    1989            3D object depth     | 40
5    1990            3D floor depth      | 15
6
7
8                    Link line color     |   Gry  D|Lines
9                    Outline color       |   Black |Outlines
10
11
12
```

13-10 The Bar Style pop-up menu.

Bar width The number here controls the distance between bars or axis points and the width of the bars. In other words, 100 means that the bar occupies all of the space from one axis point to the next, and that there is, therefore, no space between the bars. A bar width of 50 means that the width of the bar and the width of the space between bars are equal. Leave this number at 85.

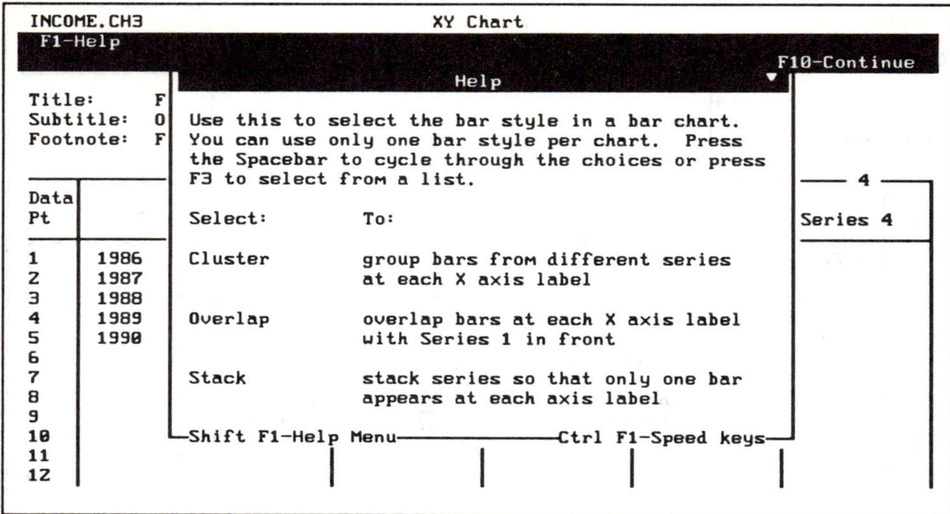

13-11 The Help menu with explanations of the six bar styles.

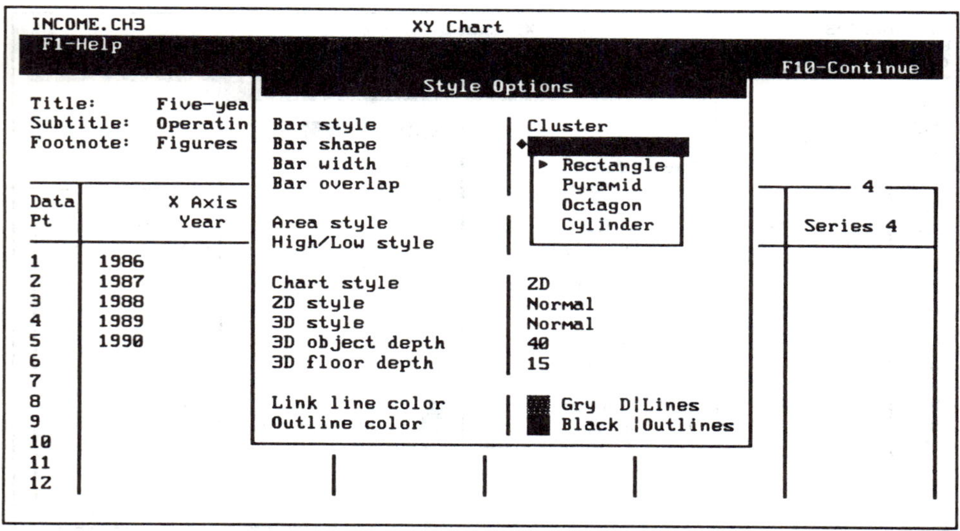

13-12 The menu of bar shape choices.

Bar overlap When overlap bar style is chosen, this number determines the amount of overlap. A number of 50 means that a bar overlaps, or covers, 50% of the bar behind it.

Area style When you are working with an area chart, you can select whether the chart of one data series overlaps the next series, stacks on top of the next series to

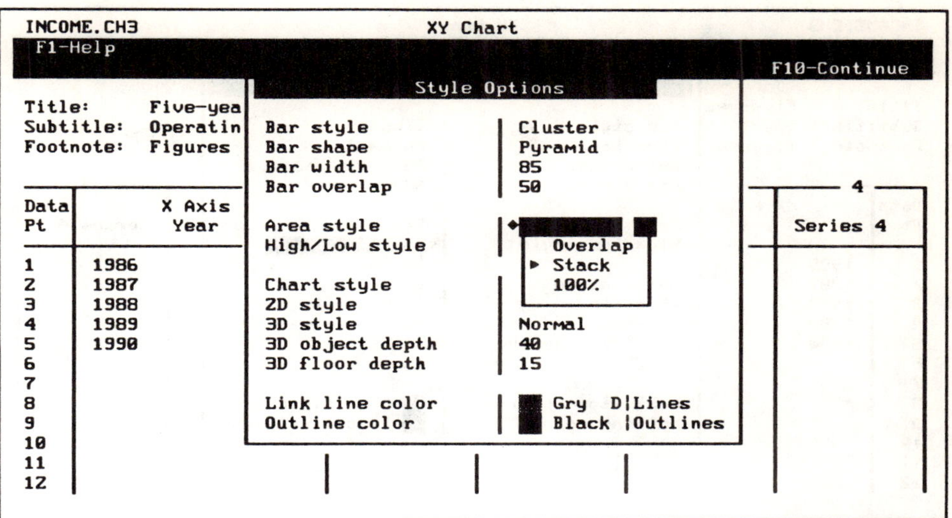

13-13 The Area Style menu.

add up to the sum of the two, or stacks in such a way as to add up to a constant 100% (see Fig. 13-13).

High/Low style In high/low/close/open charts, you have three style choices: Bar, which represents the difference between high and low values as a vertical bar; Area, which represents that difference as a solid area moving across the chart; and Error bar, which uses small horizontal bars to indicate high and low values (see Fig. 13-14).

Chart style You can choose between 2D (two-dimensional) or 3D (three-dimensional) charts.

2D style In 2D charts, you can elect the Normal style (no connecting lines or shadows); Shadow (displays a shadow for bars and areas); Link (connects stacked and 100% bars with a line); and Horizontal (makes the X axis the vertical axis and displays bars horizontally). See Fig. 13-15.

3D style In 3D charts, you can display bars in either the Normal or Horizontal modes (see Fig. 13-16).

3D object depth Enter a number here, from 0 to 100, that will determine the apparent depth of an object. One-hundred is the maximum depth; a setting of 0 means that the object is, in fact, two-dimensional. A setting of 50 means that an object is taking up about half of its available floor depth.

3D floor depth The term *floor depth* is an indicator of the amount of front-to-back space that is allotted for an object. The maximum depth means a setting of 100; minimum depth, or two-dimensions, is achieved with a 0.

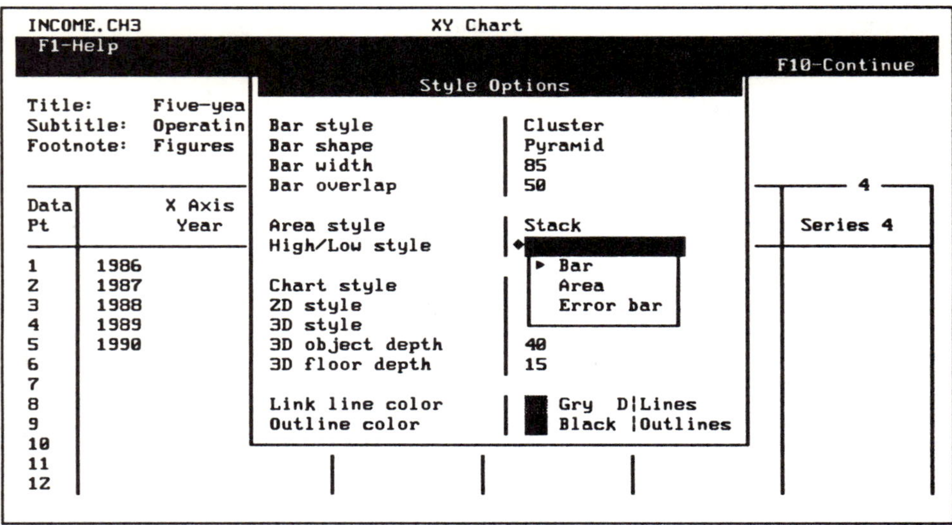

13-14 The high/low style choices.

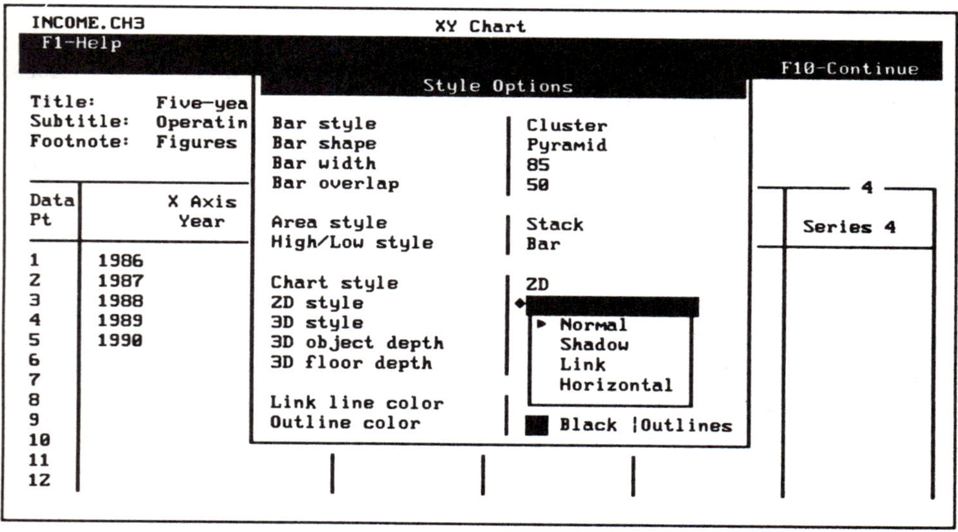

13-15 The 2D Style pop-up menu.

Link line color If you choose to link bars together with lines, here is where to choose the color of the lines (see Fig. 13-17).

Outline color Here's where you select the color to outline bars, areas, and shadows.

At this point, you have covered the Style Options menu, which should look like

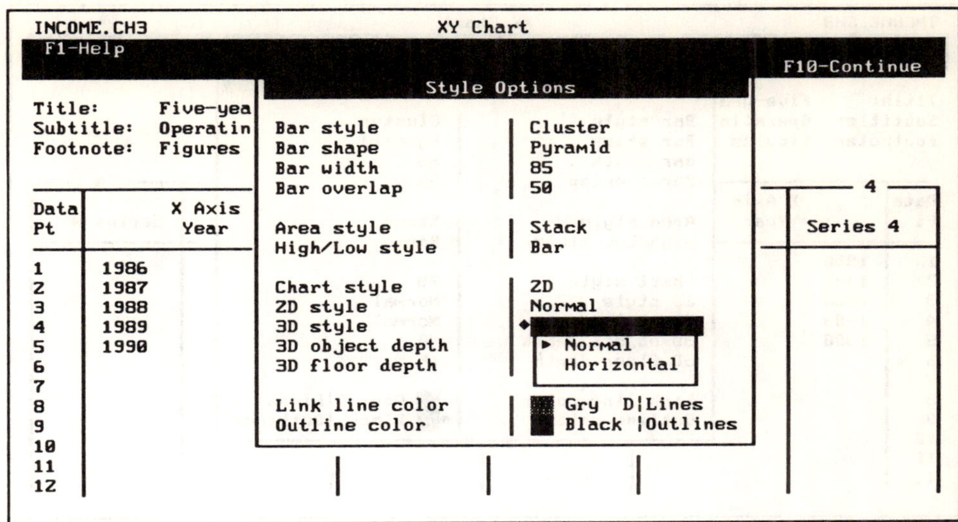

13-16 The 3D Style pop-up menu.

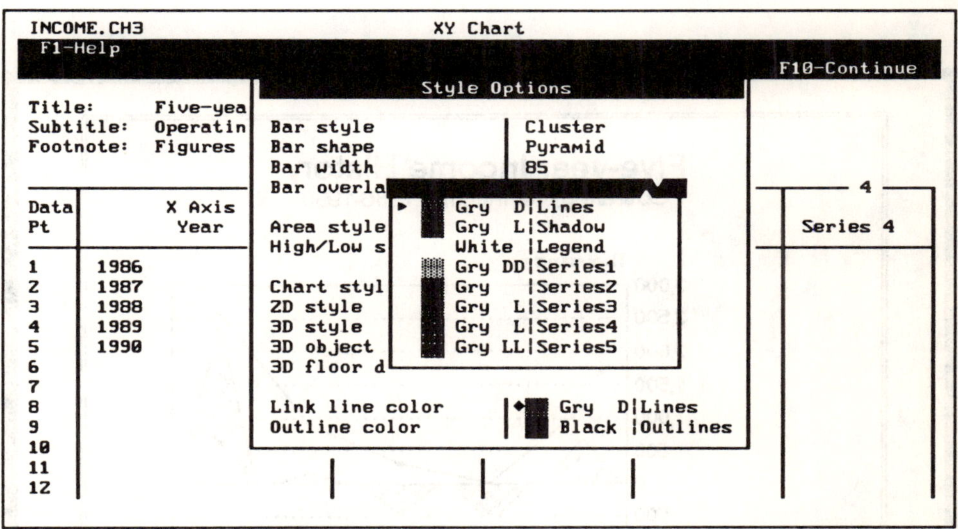

13-17 The Link Line Color pop-up menu.

Fig. 13-18. Press F2 to see the progress of your chart (see Fig. 13-19). Click the right mouse button twice to return to the XY Chart data screen.

Series

At the data screen, select F8–Options, then Series, item 6. The Series Options menu is displayed, with more options than you ever dreamed of (see Fig. 13-20).

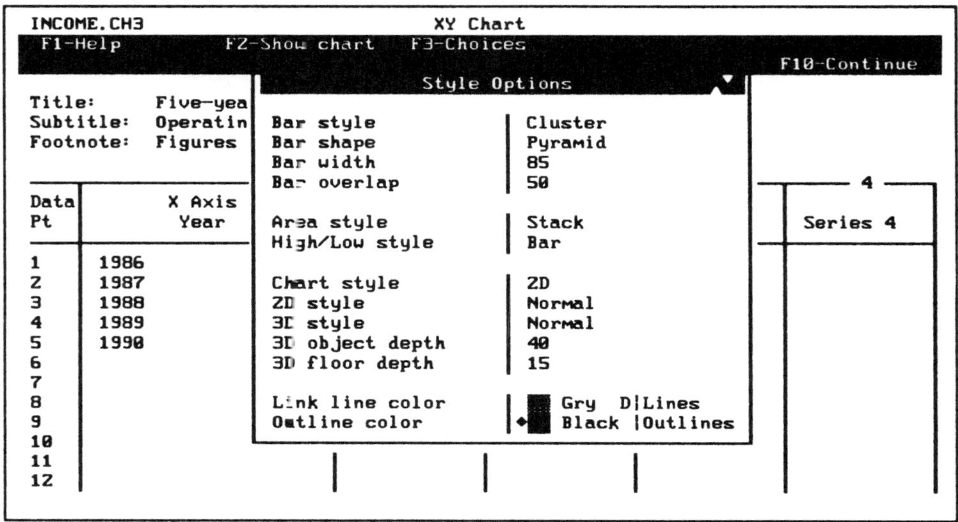

13-18 The Style Options menu with updated entries.

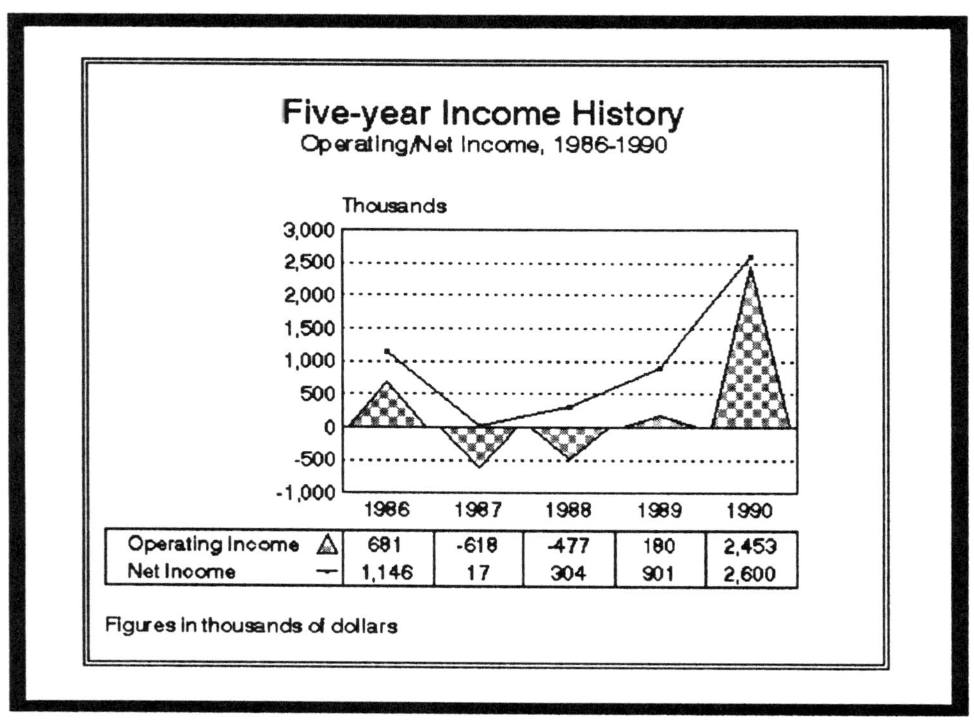

13-19 Your chart with the latest Style Options menu entries.

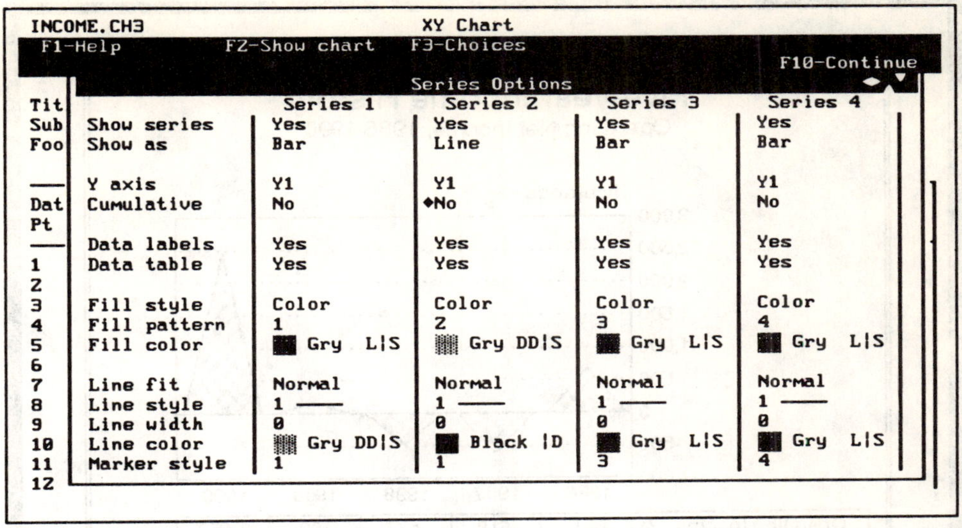

```
INCOME.CH3                              XY Chart
 F1-Help          F2-Show chart   F3-Choices
                                                             F10-Continue
                                 Series Options
Tit                          Series 1       Series 2       Series 3       Series 4
Sub  Show series           | Yes          | Yes          | Yes          | Yes
Foo  Show as               | Bar          | Line         | Bar          | Bar
                           |              |              |              |
---  Y axis                | Y1           | Y1           | Y1           | Y1
Dat  Cumulative            | No           | ♦No          | No           | No
Pt                         |              |              |              |
---  Data labels           | Yes          | Yes          | Yes          | Yes
1    Data table            | Yes          | Yes          | Yes          | Yes
2                          |              |              |              |
3    Fill style            | Color        | Color        | Color        | Color
4    Fill pattern          | 1            | 2            | 3            | 4
5    Fill color            | █ Gry  L|S   | ▒ Gry DD|S   | █ Gry  L|S   | █ Gry  L|S
6                          |              |              |              |
7    Line fit              | Normal       | Normal       | Normal       | Normal
8    Line style            | 1 ———        | 1 ———        | 1 ———        | 1 ———
9    Line width            | 0            | 0            | 0            | 0
10   Line color            | ▒ Gry DD|S   | █ Black  |D  | █ Gry  L|S   | █ Gry  L|S
11   Marker style          | 1            | 1            | 3            | 4
12
```

13-20 The Series Options menu.

Because your current chart involves only two series, you need be concerned only with the Series 1 and Series 2 columns. Most of the items on this menu require only minimal explanation:

Show series You can elect to make any series invisible by selecting No. Figure 13-21 shows the current INCOME.CH3 chart without Series 2 displayed.

Show as If you click on this item and then press F3, you will see a menu listing eight ways to display a series (see Fig. 13-22). Figure 13-23 shows the current chart with Series 2 shown as an area.

Y axis If you are dealing with a series involving values of greatly differing magnitudes—if, for example, Series 1 involves data in millions of dollars and Series 2 involves data in billions—you might need to use a double Y axis, one for each series. In that case, you would click on Y1 in the appropriate series and change it to Y2.

Cumulative You can choose to add the value for each point to the sum of the values for previous points by selecting Yes for any series. In the current chart, for example, you could select Yes in the Net Income series (Series 2), and the 1987 point on the chart would represent the sum of the net incomes from 1986 and 1987. The 1990 point would represent the sum of the net incomes for five years. (This isn't particularly useful for a five-year chart, but might be very appropriate for a quarterly chart.)

Data labels If you want data values displayed above the bars or points on your chart, choose Yes here. (Note: To display the labels, you must also have selected

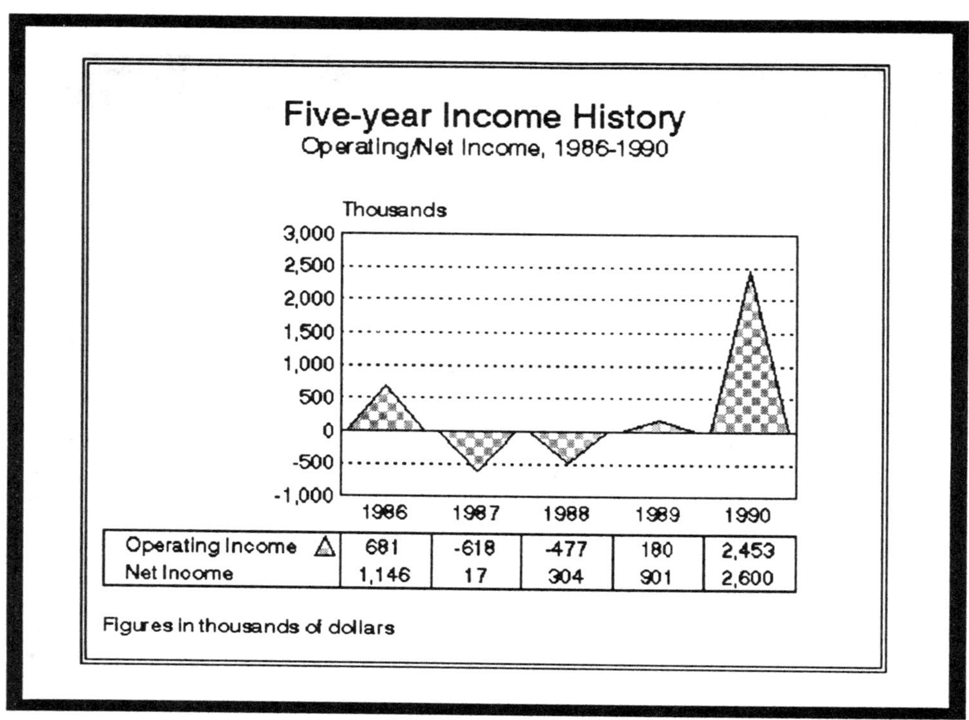

13-21 The INCOME.CH3 chart with Series 2 not shown.

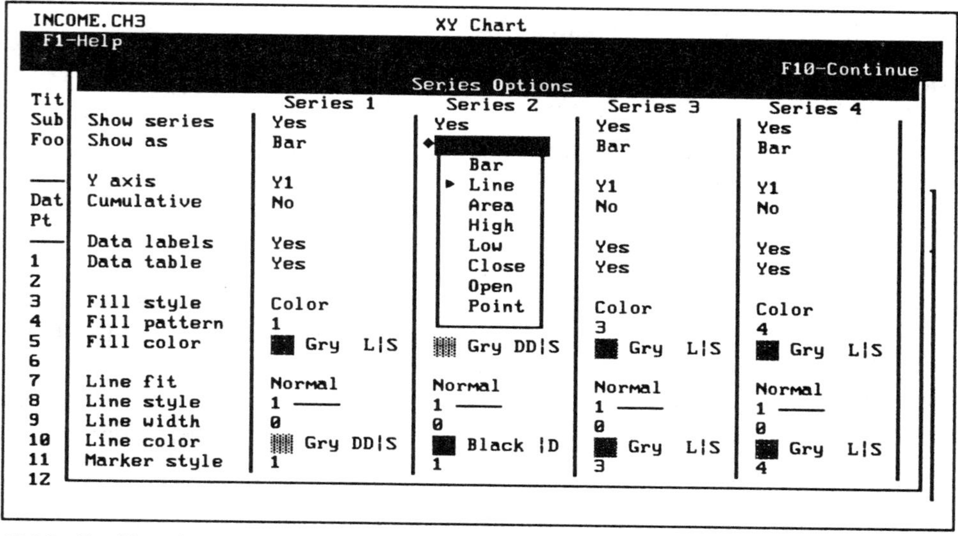

13-22 The Show As pop-up menu.

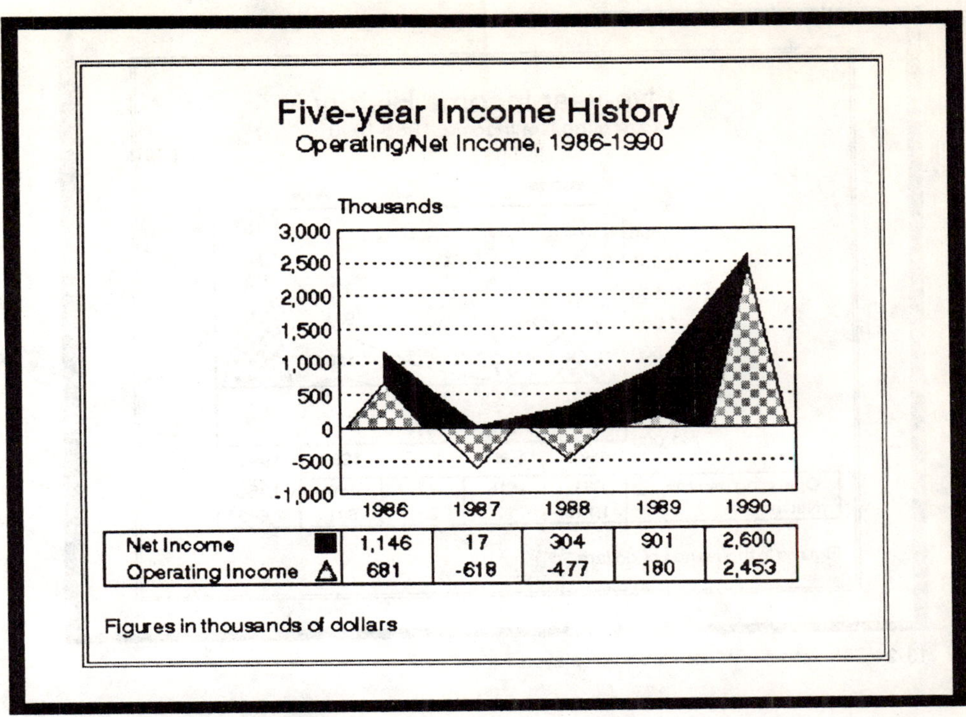

13-23 The current chart with Series 2 shown as an area.

Yes for Show data labels on the Data Table/Data Labels menu—the last item on the Style Options menu.) Figure 13-24 shows data labels displayed for both series. This makes for a cluttered chart, and these numbers are redundant with the data table, but you get the point.

Data table You can choose to display a data table for any or all series on your chart. In the case of the chart you've been working with, a data table for both series comes with the chart. Let's make a change, in the interest of simplicity. Under Series 1 in the Data Table row, click on Yes and press the space bar to change it to No. Do the same for Series 2. Press F2 to view the results (Fig. 13-25). Click on the right mouse button to return to the Series Options menu.

Fill style You can elect to fill your bars, areas, etc. with a color, a pattern, or both. Simply click on the Fill Style row in the appropriate Series column and use the space bar to cycle through the options.

Fill pattern If you want to fill your bars or areas with a pattern of dots or lines, enter a number from 1 to 12. If you haven't selected Both opposite Fill style, the pattern will be white (which means it will be invisible on a white background). If

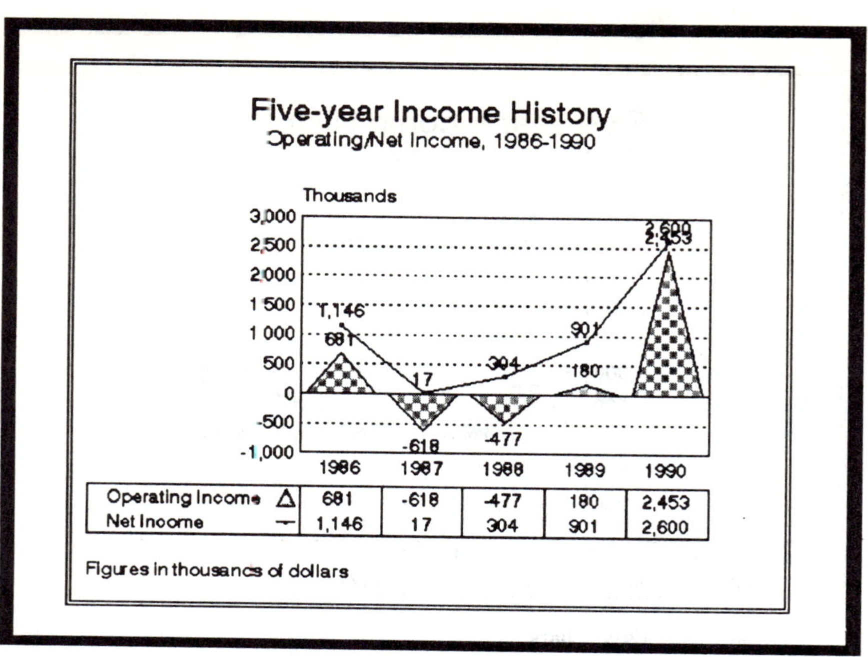

	1986	1987	1988	1989	1990
Operating Income △	681	-618	-477	180	2,453
Net Income —	1,146	17	304	901	2,600

13-24 The chart with data labels displayed.

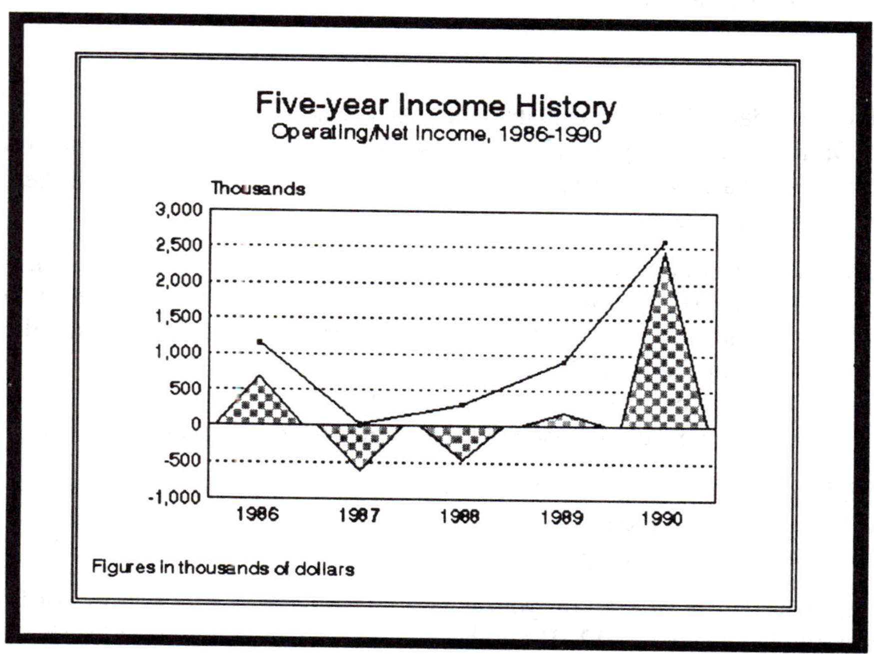

13-25 The current chart without data tables.

```
INCOME.CH3                          XY Chart
 F1-Help
                                                                 F10-Continue
                                   Series Options
Tit                         Series 1        Series 2        Series 3        Series 4
Sub  Show series          Yes             Yes             Yes             Yes
Foo  Show as              Bar             Line            Bar             Bar

     Y axis               Y1                                              Y1
Dat  Cumulative           No             ▸ Normal                         No
Pt                                          Trend
     Data labels          No                Curve                         Yes
1    Data table           No                Average                       Yes
2                                           Step line
3    Fill style           Color             Exponential        or         Color
4    Fill pattern         1                 Log regression                4
5    Fill color           ■ Gry  L|         Power regression  Gry   L|S   ■ Gry  L|S
6
7    Line fit             Normal          ♦Normal         Normal          Normal
8    Line style           1 ——            1 ——            1 ——            1 ——
9    Line width           0               0               0               0
10   Line color           ▒ Gry DD|S      ■ Black |D      ■ Gry  L|S      ■ Gry  L|S
11   Marker style         1               1               3               4
12
```

13-26 The Line Fit pop-up menu.

you have selected Both, the pattern will appear in the color you select opposite Fill color.

Fill color To choose the color or the pattern color, you want to fill your bar or area, click twice on the series color in the Fill Color row, then select a color from the pop-up menu.

Line fit Harvard Graphics 3.0 can do a statistical analysis of the data in any series that you are representing with a line. If you click twice on the Line Fit row in the Series 2 column (it should now say Normal), a pop-up menu with eight types of line fits is displayed (Fig. 13-26). A detailed discussion of statistical line-fitting is beyond the scope of this introductory book, but a brief comment on each item might be useful:

- Normal simply connects the data points with straight lines.
- Trend approximates a straight line to the series of points. The formula is $y = ax + b$.
- Curve finds the best curve that connects all points in the series.
- Average calculates the average of all points in the series with the formula $g_y = \Sigma y_{(i)}/n$, where g is the average, $y_{(i)}$ are the series values, and n is the number of points in the series.
- Step line is very much like a bar graph or histogram. It treats the data points as a series of steps rather than as points in a smooth continuum.
- Exponential fits to the data points a curve with the equation $\ln(y) = a + bx$, where ln is the natural log of y.

- Log regression fits to the data points a curve with the equation $y = a + b \times \ln(x)$.
- Power regression fits to the data points a curve with the equation $ln(y) = a + b \times \ln(x)$.

For our purposes here, leave the setting at Normal for both series.

Line style Click twice on Line style, and you'll see that there are three line styles: solid, dotted, and dashed. For your current chart, stay with a solid line.

Line width You can set the width of a line chart to any value from 0 to 250. To give you an idea of the range you have to play with, Fig. 13-27 shows the current chart with the Series 2 line width set to 250. It's sort of fun, resembling an abstract painting, but it doesn't mean a lot. Let's get serious and set the Series 2 line width to 3.

Line color Click twice on the Line Color row to bring up the pop-up menu. Change to any color you like. One advantage of this option is that, if you're creating a chart with several series represented by lines, using a different color for each line will make it easier to tell them apart.

Marker style In a line or point chart, the series values are represented by mark-

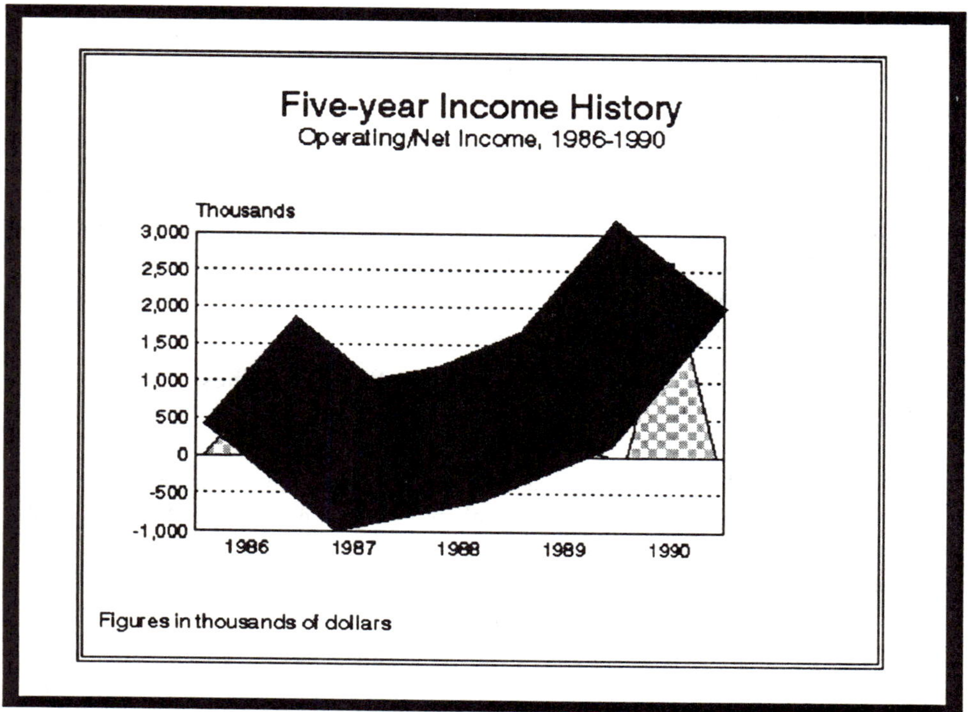

13-27 The income chart with a Series 2 line width of 250.

ers. Choose any number from 0 (no marker) to 13 to select from the arsenal of dots, stars, crosses, etc. that are used as markers. Change the number in the Marker Style row, Series 2 column to 7.

You have now covered all the options in the Series Options menu, which looks like Fig. 13-28. Press F2 to view your accomplishments; you'll see the chart with the wider Net Income line and the new markers (see Fig. 13-29).

Legend

The next item on the Options menu is Legend, item 7. From the XY Chart data screen, select F8 – Options and then Legend, item 7 (see Fig. 13-30). You have seen the elements of this menu before; for a review, go to chapter 12. For now, simply make some entries to help the current INCOME.CH3 chart:

1. Because there is no longer a data table, you need to explain the two chart series. For Show legend, select Yes.
2. For Placement, select Inside. This allows for maximum expansion of the chart, and you can tuck the legend into a corner of the chart where it won't take up any valuable space.
3. Next, click on Location, then use the space bar to move the location indicator clockwise until it is positioned in the lower right-hand corner.
4. For Legend frame style, select None.

That takes care of the legend selections for this chart; the Legend Options menu should now look like Fig. 13-31. Press F2 to check your results, and you'll see the

```
INCOME.CH3                              XY Chart
 F1-Help          F2-Show chart     F3-Choices
                                                                  F10-Continue
                                     Series Options
Tit                      Series 1       Series 2        Series 3        Series 4
Sub  Show series         Yes            Yes             Yes             Yes
Foo  Show as             Bar            Line            Bar             Bar
---
     Y axis              Y1             Y1              Y1              Y1
Dat  Cumulative          No             No              No              No
Pt
---  Data labels         No             No              Yes             Yes
1    Data table          No             No              Yes             Yes
2
3    Fill style          Color          Color           Color           Color
4    Fill pattern        1              2               3               4
5    Fill color          ■ Gry  L|S     ▒ Gry DD|S      ■ Gry  L|S      ■ Gry  L|S
6
7    Line fit            Normal         Normal          Normal          Normal
8    Line style          1 ——           1 ——            1 ——            1 ——
9    Line width          0              3               0               0
10   Line color          ▒ Gry DD|S     ■ Black |D      ■ Gry  L|S      ■ Gry  L|S
11   Marker style        1              7               3               4
12
```

13-28 The completed Series Options menu.

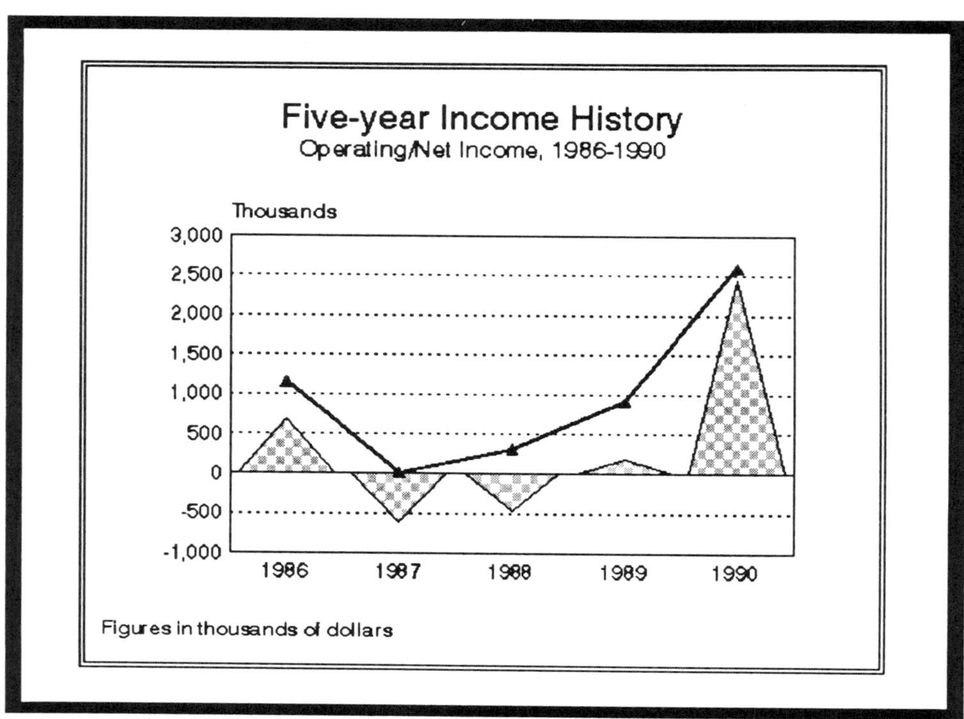

13-29 The income chart updated with new markers and a wider line.

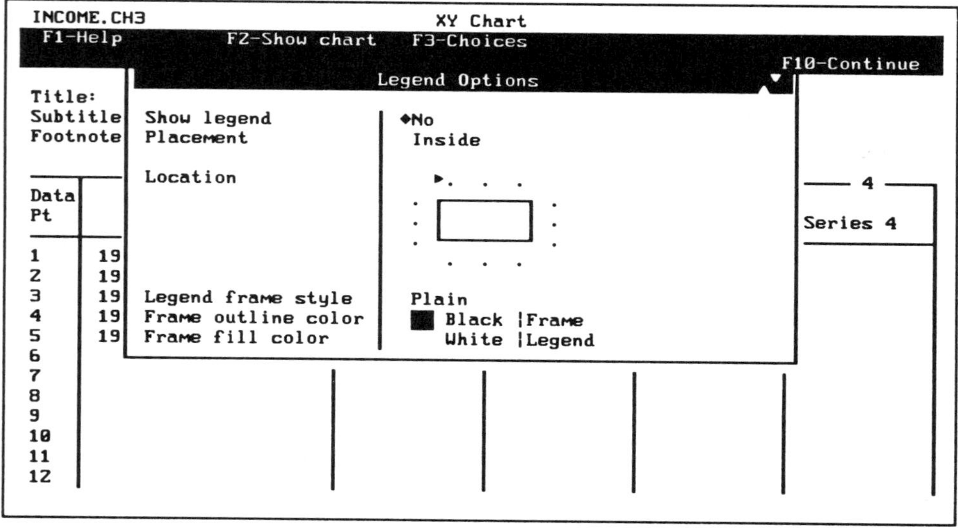

13-30 The Legend Options menu.

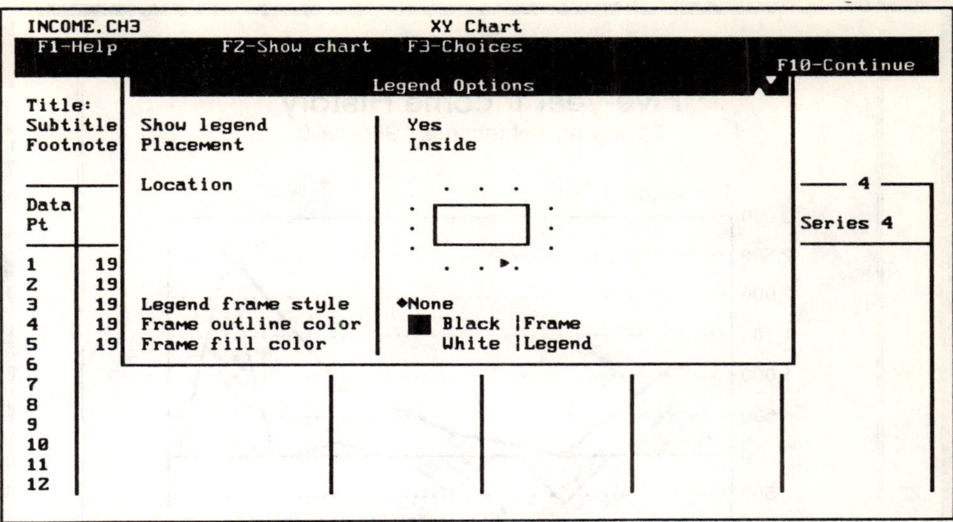

13-31 The Legend Options menu with settings for the current chart.

legend placed inconspicuously in the bottom right-hand corner of the chart (see Fig. 13-32). Click the right mouse button twice to return to the XY Chart data screen.

Axis frame

Select F8–Options once more, and this time click on item 8, Axis frame. This option lets you dictate the appearance of your chart's axis frame: the extent of the frame, its outline color, and the color (if any) with which to fill it (see Fig. 13-33).

Click twice on Axis frame style, and a pop-up menu will appear (see Fig. 13-34). This menu gives you five choices: Full, which frames the chart with a complete rectangle (that's what you've been working with so far); XY, which displays the horizontal X axis at the bottom and the vertical Y axis at the left (unless you're using a horizontal bar format, in which case the X axis will be the vertical one); X, which displays only the horizontal X axis at the bottom; Y, which displays only the vertical Y axis at the left (unless you're using a dual Y axis format, in which case Y1 will be left and Y2 will be right; and None. Select None. (We're from the minimalist school of chart design; less is more.) Press F2, and you'll see that the chart has gotten one step plainer—er, simpler (see Fig. 13-35). Click the right mouse button twice to return to the XY Chart data screen.

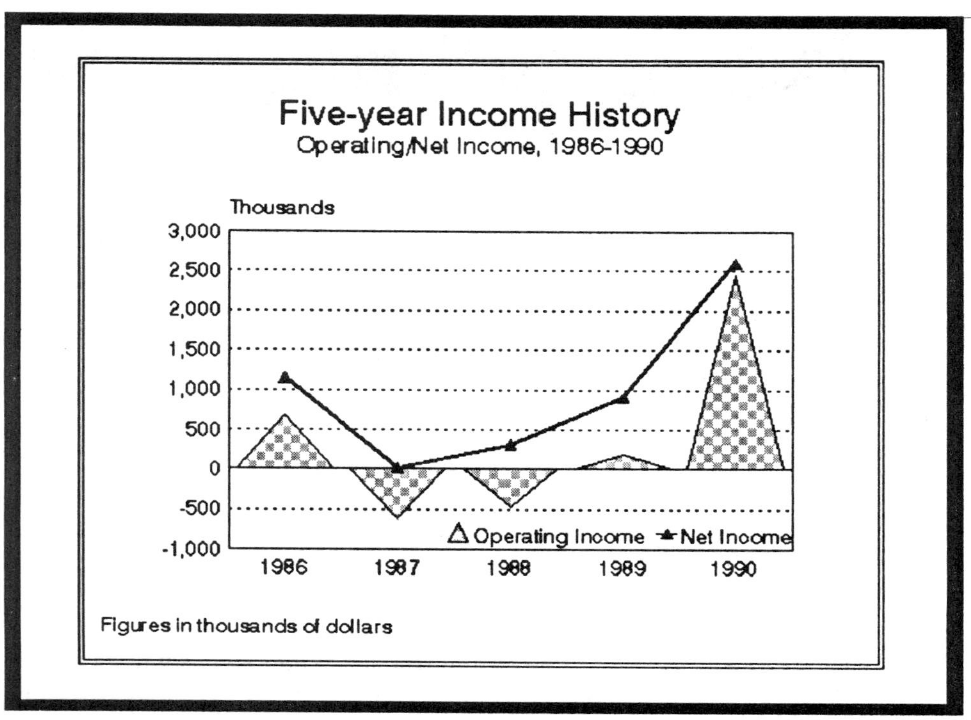

13-32 The updated chart with the legend in the corner.

```
INCOME.CH3                            XY Chart
 F1-Help          F2-Show chart   F3-Choices
                                                          F10-Continue
                                  Axis Frame
Title:      Fiv
Subtitle:   Ope  Axis frame style      ♦Full
Footnote:   Fig  Frame outline color   ■ Black  |Frame
                 Frame fill color        White  |FrameBkg
                                                             4
Data       X Axis
Pt          Year           Operating     Net Income    Series 3     Series 4

1     1986                 681000        1146000
2     1987                 -618000       17000
3     1988                 -477000       304000
4     1989                 180000        901000
5     1990                 2453000       2600000
6
7
8
9
10
11
12
```

13-33 The Axis Frame menu.

```
INCOME.CH3                          XY Chart
 F1-Help
                                                              F10-Continue
                                    Axis Frame
Title:      Fiv
Subtitle:   Ope   Axis frame style           ◆
Footnote:   Fig   Frame outline color        ▶ Full   |Frame
                  Frame fill color             XY     |FrameBkg
                                               X                       4
Data     X Axis                                Y
Pt         Year            Operating           None   ome    Series 3      Series 4

1        1986              681000         1146000
2        1987              -618000        17000
3        1988              -477000        304000
4        1989              180000         901000
5        1990              2453000        2600000
6
7
8
9
10
11
12
```

13-34 The Axis Frame Style pop-up menu.

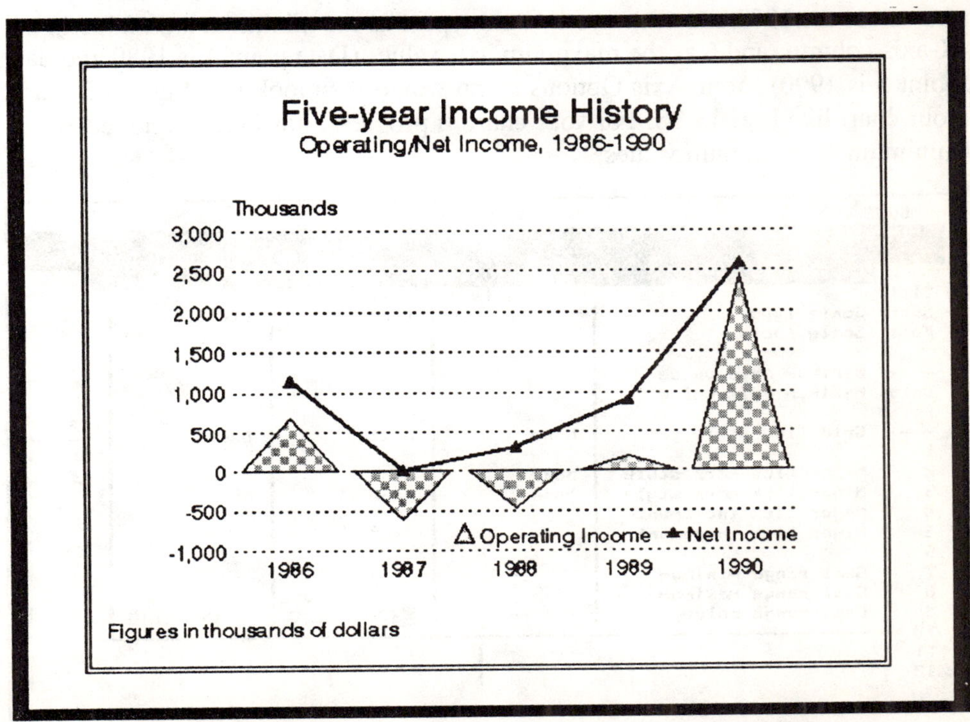

13-35 The income chart, sans frame.

Axis options

Select F8 – Options, then item 9, Axis options (see Fig. 13-36). Options on this menu include:

Scale type You can choose either Linear or Logarithmic.

Scale factor You can designate a factor by which all data values in the series are to be divided. This is commonly done to reduce the size of the numbers to be displayed. Where values are in the millions, for example, you might designate 1,000,000 as the factor so that 1,200,000 could be displayed as 1.2. If you leave this option blank, Harvard Graphics 3.0 will automatically scale the data for you and indicate the scale factor in the axis title. In the current chart, for example, Harvard Graphics 3.0 has entered a Y-axis scale factor of 1,000 and specified the Y-axis title in thousands.

Minimum/Maximum axis value You can determine the minimum and maximum values you want to be displayed on your chart by setting limiting values for either the X axis or Y axis. If you want to set the range on the X axis, and your X-axis labels are nonnumeric (such as the year labels on the current chart), then indicate the range by using the data point numbers from the Data Pt column at the far left of the XY Chart data screen. For example, if you wanted to display only the values for 1989 and 1990, you would type 4 as the minimum axis value in the X-axis column, and 5 as the maximum axis value. (Data point 4 is 1989 and data point 5 is 1990). Your Axis Options menu would then look like Fig. 13-37, and your chart like Fig. 13-38. For your chart in progress, however, do not enter any minimum or maximum values.

```
INCOME.CH3                       XY Chart
 F1-Help          F2-Show chart   F3-Choices
                                                        F10-Continue
                                 Axis Options
Titl                              X Axis       Y1 Axis       Y2 Axis
Subt  Scale type                 ♦Linear       Linear        Linear
Foot  Scale factor

      Minimum axis value
Data  Maximum axis value
Pt                                                                        4
      Grid line style             None         Dotted        Dotted
1
2     Major tick mark style       None         None          None
3     Minor tick mark style       None         None          None
4     Major tick increment
5     Minor tick increment
6
7     Goal range minimum            -
8     Goal range maximum            -
9     Goal range color              -          █ Gry LL|G    Gry LL|G
10
11
12
```

13-36 The Axis Options menu.

```
INCOME.CH3                           XY Chart
 F1-Help          F2-Show chart    F3-Choices
                                                          F10-Continue
                                     Axis Options
Titl                                X Axis        Y1 Axis        Y2 Axis
Subt  Scale type                  | Linear      | Linear       | Linear
Foot  Scale factor                |             |              |
                                  |             |              |
----  Minimum axis value          | 4           |              |
Data  Maximum axis value          | 5           |              |
Pt                                |             |              |             4
----  Grid line style             | None        | Dotted       | Dotted
1                                 |             |              |
2     Major tick mark style       | None        | None         | None
3     Minor tick mark style       | None        | None         | None
4     Major tick increment        |             |              |
5     Minor tick increment        |             |              |
6                                 |             |              |
7     Goal range minimum          |    -        |              |
8     Goal range maximum          |    -        |              |
9     Goal range color            |    -        | ▆ Gry LL¦G   | ▆ Gry LL¦G
10
11
12
```

13-37 The Axis Options menu with minimum and maximum values entered.

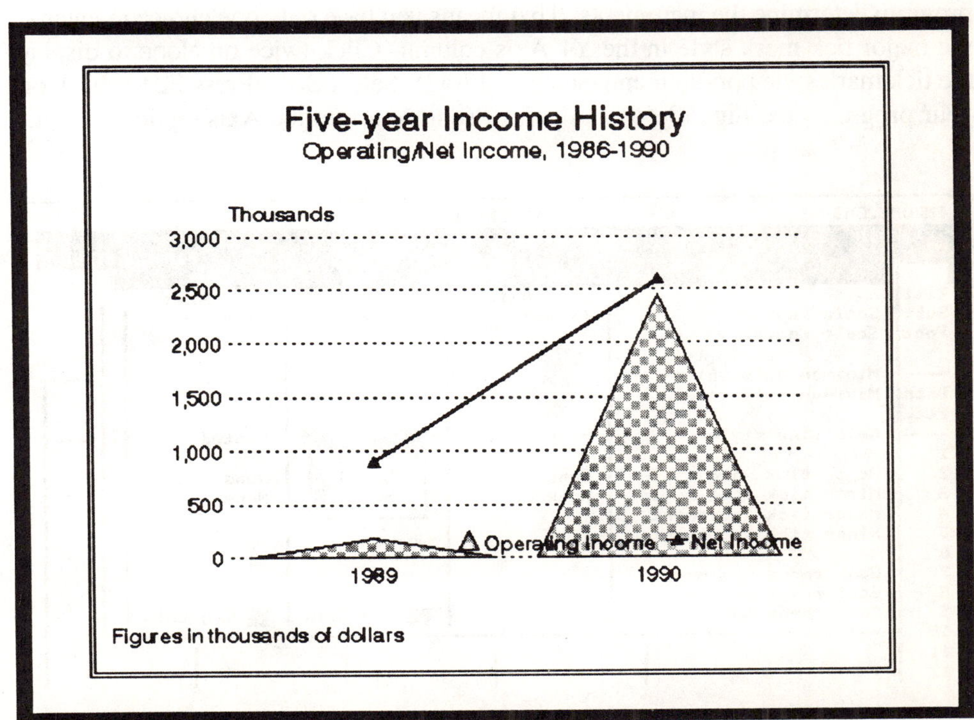

13-38 The chart showing only the values in the range from 1989 to 1990.

Grid line style You can have both X-axis grid lines (which will be vertical) and Y-axis grid lines (which will be horizontal), and you can choose to display them as either dotted or solid lines. Because you are pressing on in quest of a minimalist design, eliminate all grid lines. In order to do so, follow these steps: In the Grid Line Style row and Y1 Axis column, click twice on the word Dotted. The little Grid Line Style pop-up menu will appear; click on None (see Fig. 13-39). Press F2 to see your chart; it's starting to look very clean (see Fig. 13-40). Click the right mouse button to return to the Axis Options menu.

Goal range Suppose that, for some weird reason, Compression Lab's goal was to keep both their operating and net incomes between $1 million and $3 million. You could display that range on your chart by entering 1000000 as the goal range minimum in the Y1 axis column, and 3000000 as the goal range maximum in the same column. You could then select a goal range color in the bottom row. Your Axis Options menu would look like Fig. 13-41, and your chart with its new goal range display would look like Fig. 13-42.

Tick marks Harvard Graphics 3.0 lets you place tick marks on the X axis or on the Y axis, and to set the intervals between any marks. Because you got rid of the grid lines, you'll probably need some indicator of the value points along the two axes. Place tick marks at the major increments along the X and Y axes, and let the program determine the increments. That means you have only one choice to enter—the major tick mark style in the Y1 Axis column. Click twice on None to display the tick mark style pop-up menu (see Fig. 13-43). Select Both. Press F2 to check on your progress (see Fig. 13-44) and press Esc to return to the Axis Options menu.

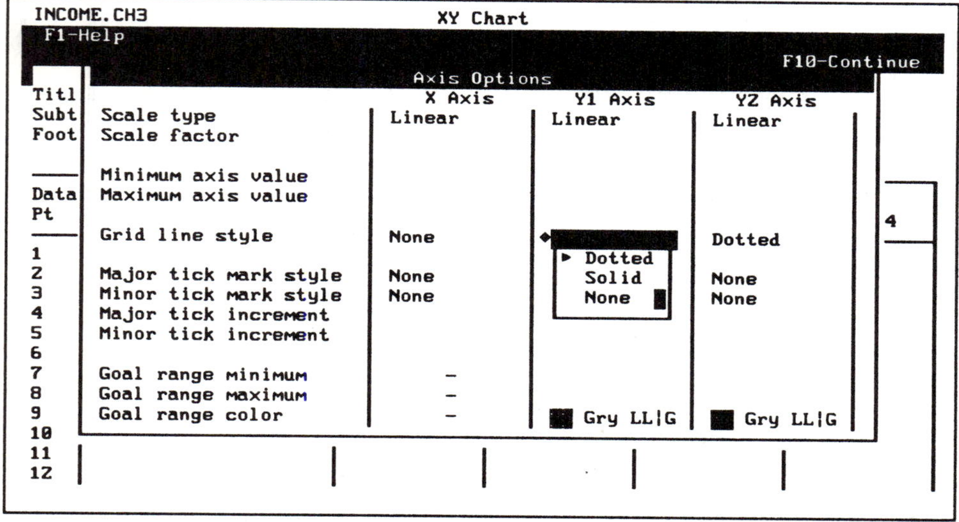

13-39 The Grid Line Style pop-up menu.

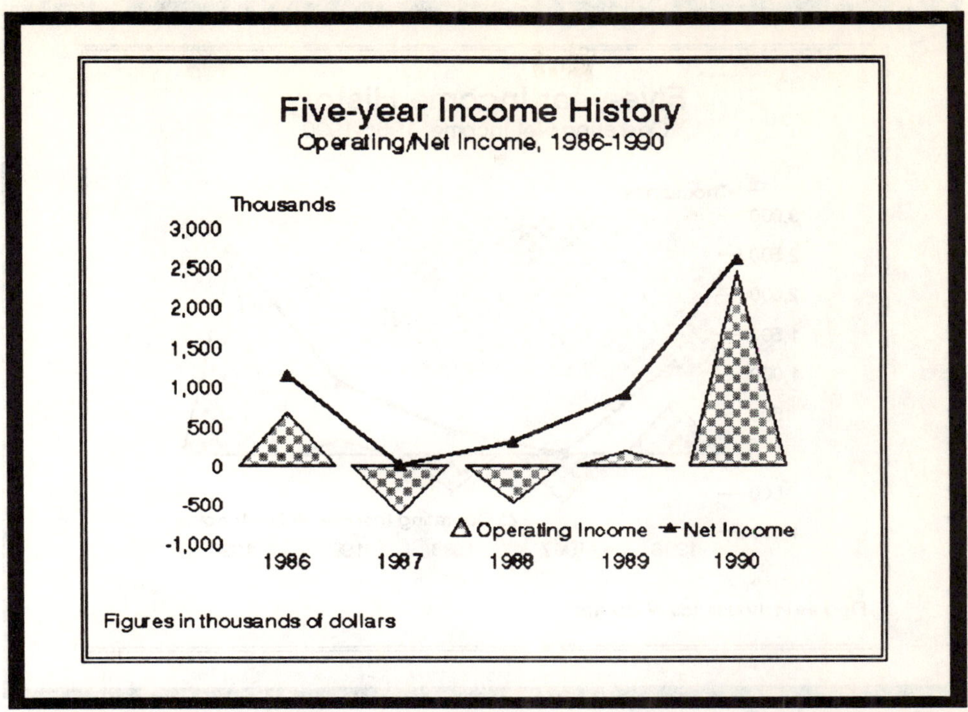

13-40 Your chart without grid lines.

```
INCOME.CH3                          XY Chart
 F1-Help        F2-Show chart     F3-Choices
                                                       F10-Continue
                                  Axis Options
Titl                                X Axis        Y1 Axis      Y2 Axis
Subt  Scale type                   Linear        Linear       Linear
Foot  Scale factor

      Minimum axis value
Data  Maximum axis value
Pt                                                                        4
      Grid line style              None          None         Dotted
1
2     Major tick mark style        None          Both         None
3     Minor tick mark style        None          None         None
4     Major tick increment
5     Minor tick increment
6
7     Goal range minimum             -           1000000
8     Goal range maximum             -           3000000
9     Goal range color               -           ■ Gry LL|G   ■ Gry LL|G
10
11
12
```

13-41 The Tick Mark Style pop-up menu.

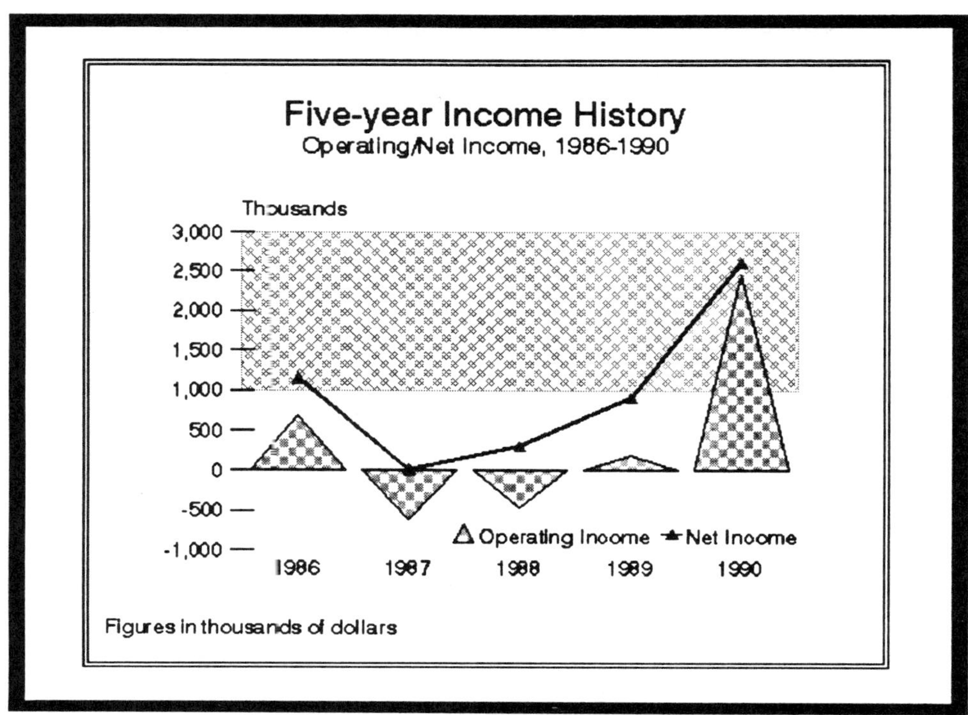

13-42 Your income chart, sporting new tick marks on the Y axis.

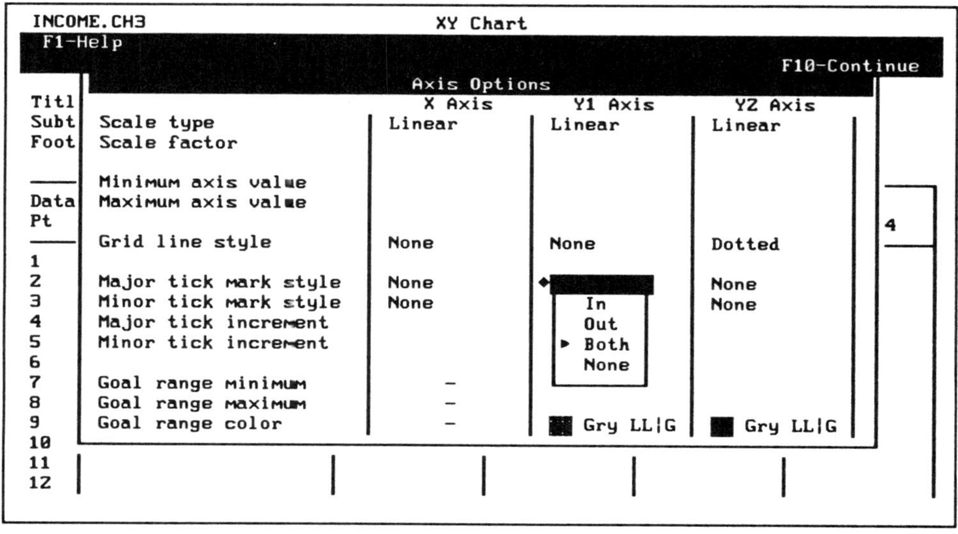

13-43 The income chart displaying a goal range.

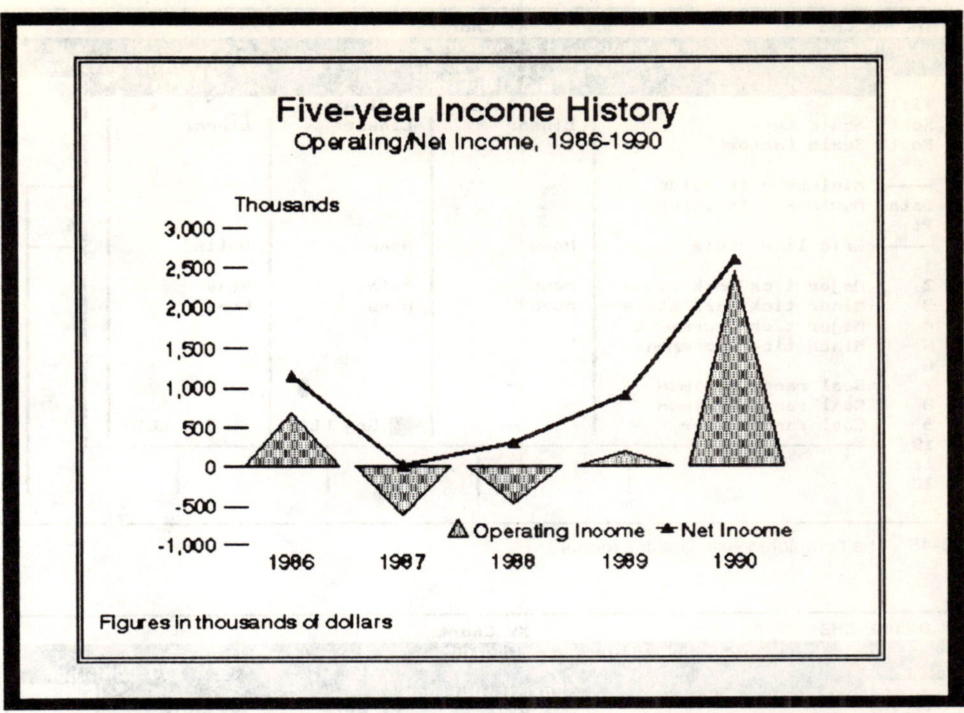

13-44 The Axis Options menu with the goal range minimum and maximum values entered.

That concludes the Axis Options menu. Remove any numbers you might have entered when experimenting with the goal range minimum/maximum settings, and the final version of this menu should look like Fig. 13-45.

Format

Press Esc to return to the XY Chart data screen, then F8 to return to the Options menu. This time, select Format, item A (see Fig. 13-46).

Show axis labels You can choose to label the points along the X and Y axes or not.

Percent A Yes in any column here would cause the corresponding axis labels to be displayed as percentages.

Currency To display figures as monetary amounts using the currency symbol you selected previously, choose Yes.

Scientific notation If you select Yes, Harvard Graphics 3.0 will enter all numbers for the corresponding axis as powers of 10. For example, 3,000 would be entered as 3E+03, or 3×10^3.

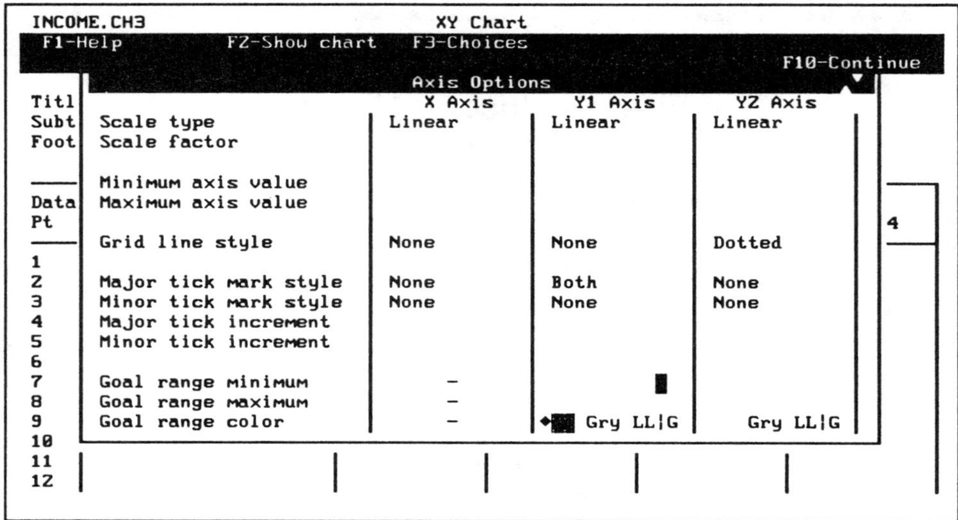

13-45 The completed Axis Options menu.

```
INCOME.CH3                                    XY Chart
 F1-Help           F2-Show chart    F3-Choices
                                                                F10-Continue
                                        Format Options
Title                                 X Axis          Y1 Axis          Y2 Axis
Subti   Show axis labels            ♦Yes            Yes              Yes
Footn
        Percent                      No              No               No
        Currency                     No              No               No
Data
Pt      Scientific notation          No              No               No              4
        Decimal places
1       Thousands separator          Yes             Yes              Yes
2
3       Leading text
4       Trailing text
5
6
7
8
9
10
11
12
```

13-46 The Format Options menu.

Decimal places Enter the number of decimal places at which you want all values displayed.

Thousands separator Enter Yes if you want units of thousands separated by commas (or by whatever separator you've previously chosen).

Leading text Enter any text you want to precede your axis labels.

Trailing text Enter any text you want to follow your axis labels.

You've made no changes in this menu, so your current chart still looks the same. Press Esc, then F8, to return to the Options menu.

Data table/labels

Select Data table/labels, item B, to display the final menu of choices (see Fig. 13-47).

Show data table Click twice on this item to display the data table options (see Fig. 13-48). You can elect not to show a data table at all, to show a data table along with the chart, or to show only the data table. Select No; you don't want to display the data table.

Table grid lines Click on this item to see your options. You can display vertical or horizontal grid lines, both, or none.

Show data labels Indicate with Yes or No whether you want to display values at each data point. Click on this item and press the space bar to change the setting to No. Then press the right mouse button to return to the XY Chart data screen.

You've done almost all of the enhancing you need to do to this chart, but one nagging detail remains: Harvard Graphics 3.0 automatically put a Thousands label on the Y axis when it inserted a scale factor of 1,000. That label is redundant, however, with the footnote that reads Figures in thousands of dollars. So get rid of it,

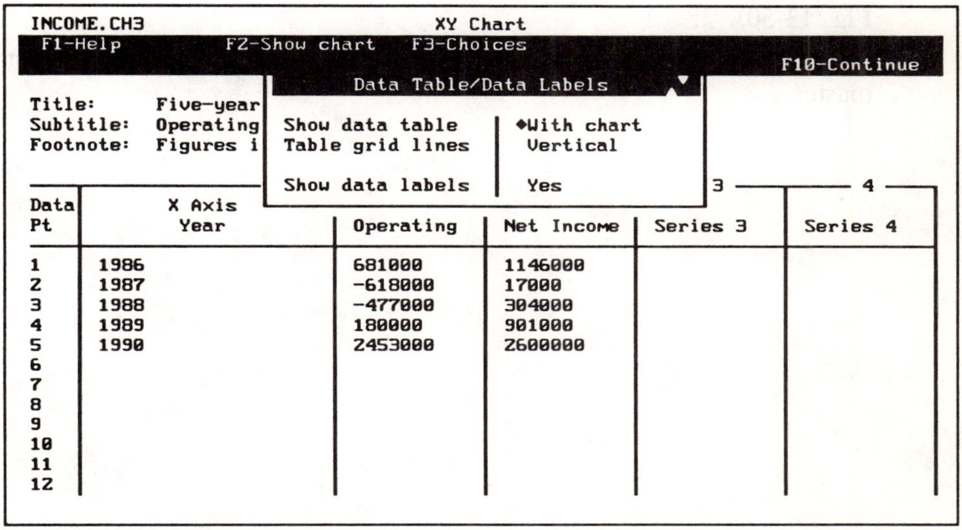

```
INCOME.CH3                          XY Chart
 F1-Help        F2-Show chart   F3-Choices
                                                       F10-Continue
                         Data Table/Data Labels
Title:     Five-year
Subtitle:  Operating  Show data table      ♦With chart
Footnote:  Figures i  Table grid lines      Vertical

                      Show data labels      Yes          3 ——— 4 ———
Data        X Axis
Pt           Year             Operating   Net Income   Series 3   Series 4

1     1986                    681000      1146000
2     1987                    -618000     17000
3     1988                    -477000     304000
4     1989                    180000      901000
5     1990                    2453000     2600000
6
7
8
9
10
11
12
```

13-47 The Data Table/Data Labels menu.

```
INCOME.CH3                         XY Chart
 F1-Help
                                                                  F10-Continue
                          Data Table/Data Labels
Title:      Five-year
Subtitle:   Operating   Show data table      ◆
Footnote:   Figures i   Table grid lines      No
                                            ▸ With chart
                        Show data labels      Table only    3 ---------- 4 ---
Data        X Axis
Pt          Year              Operating   Net Income   Series 3    Series 4

1     1986                    681000      1146000
2     1987                    -618000     17000
3     1988                    -477000     304000
4     1989                    180000      901000
5     1990                    2453000     2600000
6
7
8
9
10
11
12
```

13-48 The data table options.

and let your chart expand a little bit more:

1. At the XY Chart data screen, press Ctrl – T (don't forget the fast keys!) to display the Titles/Footnotes menu (see Fig. 13-49).
2. Delete the Y1 axis title (Thousands).
3. Select F2 – Show chart to see the final result you've been working toward in this chapter—a masterpiece of uncluttered simplicity and clarity (see Fig. 13-50).
4. Save the completed work as INCOME2.CH3. You're now an XY chart master.

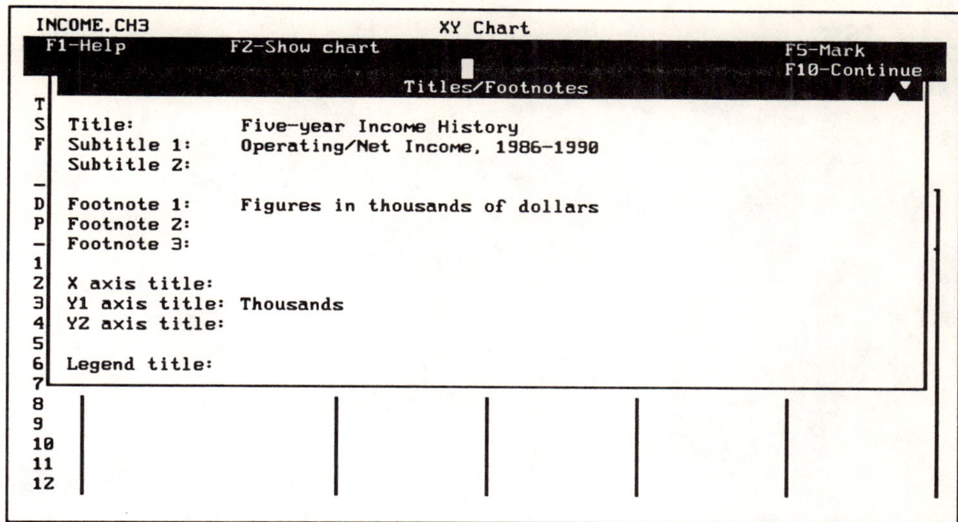

13-49 The Titles/Footnotes menu.

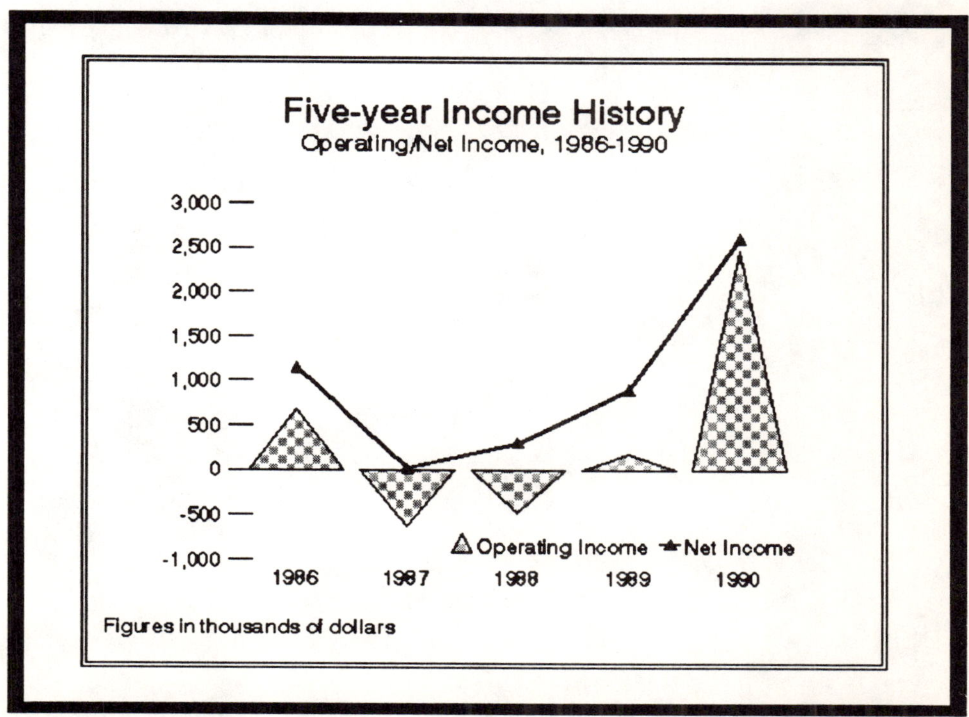

13-50 The completed income chart.

14
CHAPTER

Advanced Draw techniques

The Draw function of Harvard Graphics 3.0 has a mind-boggling array of features and tricks you can do with figures and text that will make you look like a professional designer. In chapter 6, you took an introductory stroll through the gardens of Draw; in this chapter you'll explore those paths in more detail, and you'll be an expert navigator by the time you get to the end.

You're going to step through an extensive tutorial exercise that will allow you to examine almost every corner of the Draw function. Begin from the Main Menu, select Draw, item 3, and the now-familiar Draw screen will appear—a blank canvas (the color depends on which palette you're working with) and two panels of tools at the left and top of the screen, which display an intriguing array of icons or buttons (see Fig. 14-1).

Grid

First, you might want to be able to locate objects very specifically on the canvas. That's done via the grid. Select F8–Options and click on Grid, the second item on the Options menu (see Figs. 14-2 and 14-3). There are six elements on this menu: You can elect to display a grid or not; to set the units for the grid in inches, centimeters, or percentages; to set the horizontal and/or vertical spacing of the grid; to instruct the program to snap objects to the nearest grid horizontally, the nearest vertically, both, or neither; and to select a snap handle for the grid—i.e., the point on an object that you want to connect to a point on the grid.

14-1 The Draw screen.

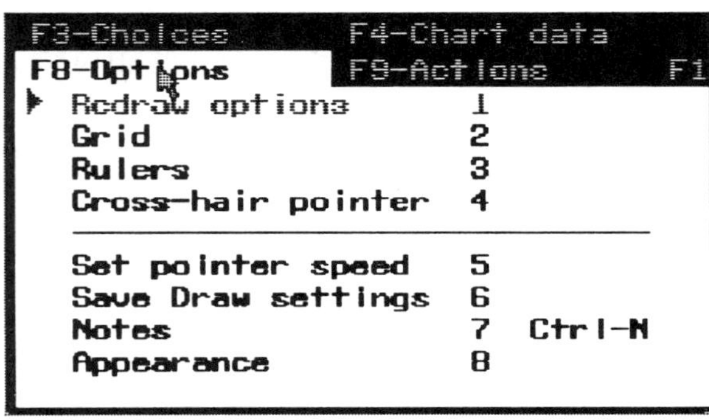

14-2 The Options menu in the Draw function.

1. Click on Show grid, and press the space bar until the setting is Yes.
2. Click on Horizontal spacing, type .5, and press Enter.
3. For vertical spacing, type .5, and press Enter.
4. Opposite Snap to, press the space bar until the setting is All, then press Enter.

The Snap handle option offers nine locations to attach objects to grid points, eight around the periphery of the objects and one at the center. Click on the small cross that indicates the center handle. Your Grid menu should now look like Fig. 14-4.

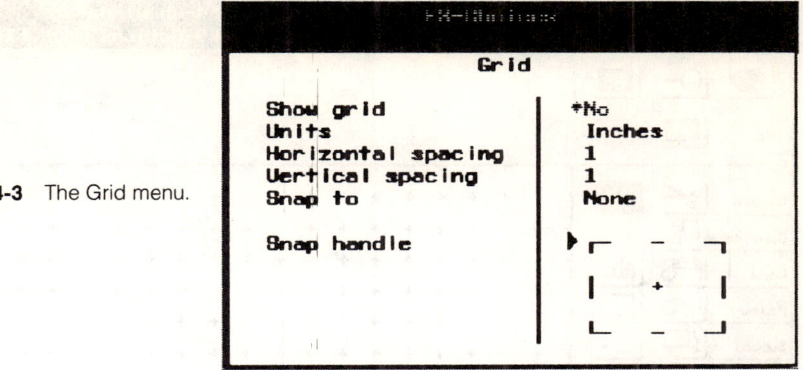

14-3 The Grid menu.

Grid

Show grid — Yes
Units — Inches
Horizontal spacing — 0.5
Vertical spacing — 0.5
Snap to — All
Snap handle

14-4 The Grid menu with your new settings.

Select F10 – Continue. The Draw canvas will be covered with little crosses at half-inch intervals, as shown in Fig. 14-5. (If you had elected Horizontal as the Snap to setting, they would be little horizontal lines; if you had elected Vertical, they would be little vertical lines; and if you had elected None, the grid markers would be dots.)

Rulers

Select F8 – Options once more, and this time click on item 3, Rulers. When the Rulers pop-up menu appears, press the space bar until the Show rulers setting is Yes (see Fig. 14-6). Select F10 – Continue and rulers will appear at the top and left sides of the canvas (see Fig. 14-7).

Help

Next, you're going to draw a couple of figures, then play with them to demonstrate a number of the Draw tools. Before you go any further, however, you should

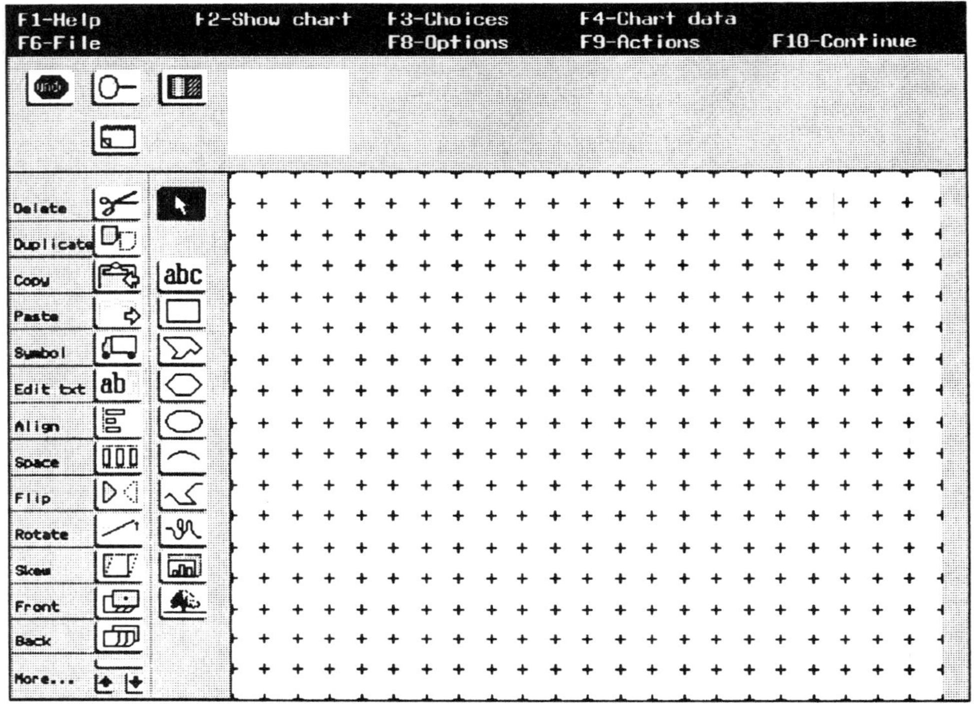

14-5 The grid with snap handles set to *All*.

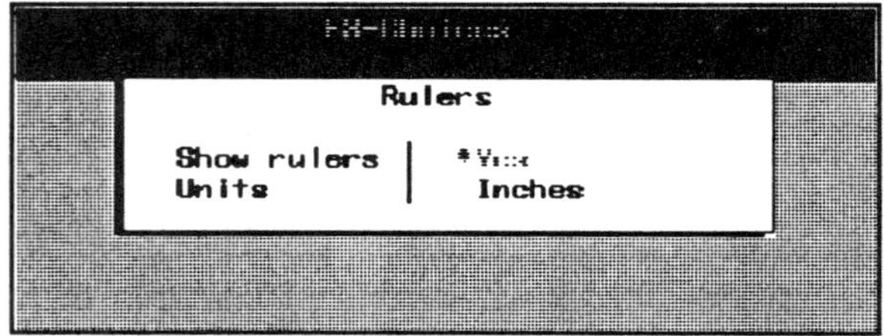

14-6 The Rulers pop-up menu with Show Rulers set to *Yes*.

be sure to fix in your mind the great usefulness of the Help function in Harvard Graphics 3.0. Take a look at that collection of tool icons in the panel at the left side of the canvas. In order to get information about using any one of them, you simply position the mouse pointer over the one you're interested in (don't press or click anything, just put the arrow on the icon) and press F1. For example, if you put the arrow on the Box icon and press F1, a Help screen will drop down and explain how to use the Box tool (see Fig. 14-8).

Box

With that handy Help guide fresh in your mind, let's draw a box. Press Esc to close the Help screen, then select the Box tool by pressing Ctrl–B. (Just to

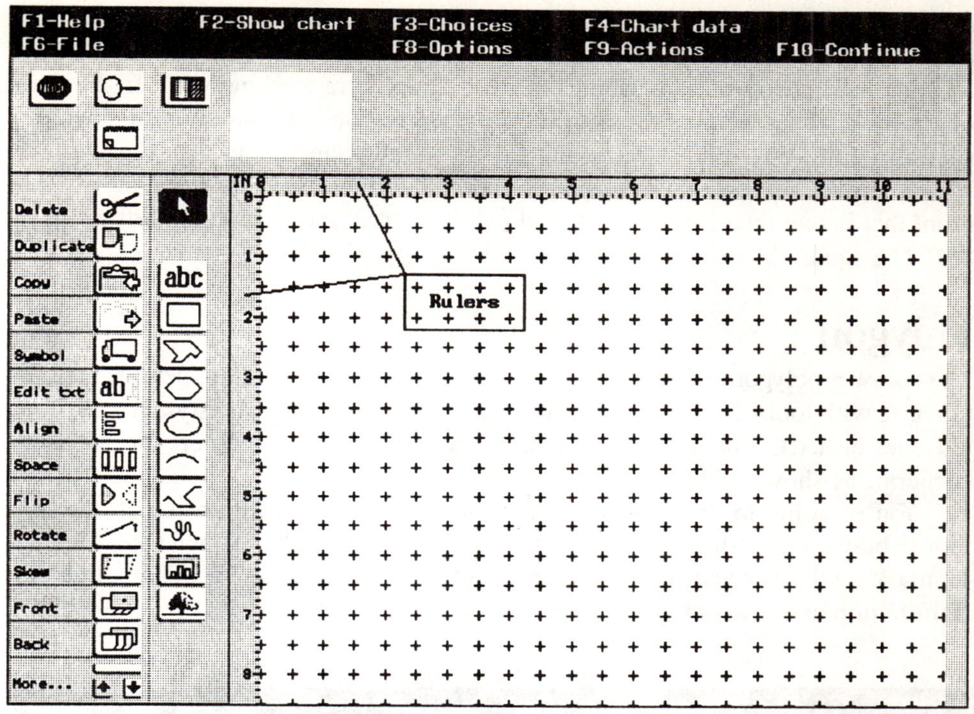

14-7 The canvas with rulers showing.

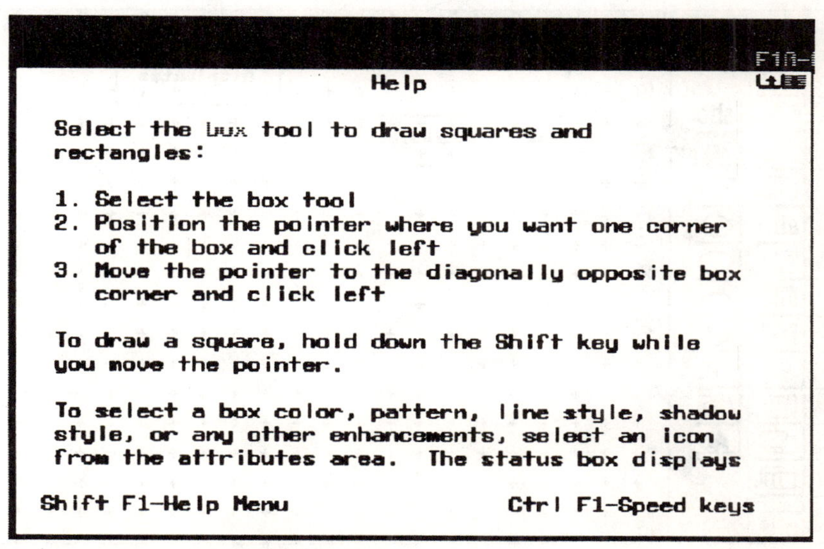
Help

Select the box tool to draw squares and rectangles:

1. Select the box tool
2. Position the pointer where you want one corner of the box and click left
3. Move the pointer to the diagonally opposite box corner and click left

To draw a square, hold down the Shift key while you move the pointer.

To select a box color, pattern, line style, shadow style, or any other enhancements, select an icon from the attributes area. The status box displays

Shift F1-Help Menu   Ctrl F1-Speed keys

14-8 The Help screen for the Box tool.

remind you about using the speed keys.) The strip along the top of your screen above the canvas is called the *attributes area*, and it contains tools and icons that let you determine specific attributes of the figure you're working with. In the case of the box, for example, the attributes area lets you set line style and width, shadow depth, box style, outline and fill color and pattern, etc. (see Fig. 14-9).

To draw a box two inches square, click the left mouse button first at 1,1 (the point that is one inch from the left and one inch from the top). Click left again at 3,3. The square box shown in Fig. 14-10 will appear.

Polygon

Next draw a polygon. Click on the Polygon icon; a polygon will appear in the status box, with tools displayed in the attributes area for setting line style (solid, dotted, or dashed), line thickness, and corner style (sharp corners or rounded corners), as shown in Fig. 14-11.

You're going to draw an irregular, somewhat random figure. Click the left mouse button at 3,1 (the point opposite the 3″ mark on the horizontal ruler and the 1″ mark on the vertical ruler), at 4,3, at 5,1, at 3.5,2, and at 5,2. Then click the right button at 3,3 to complete the figure (see Fig. 14-12).

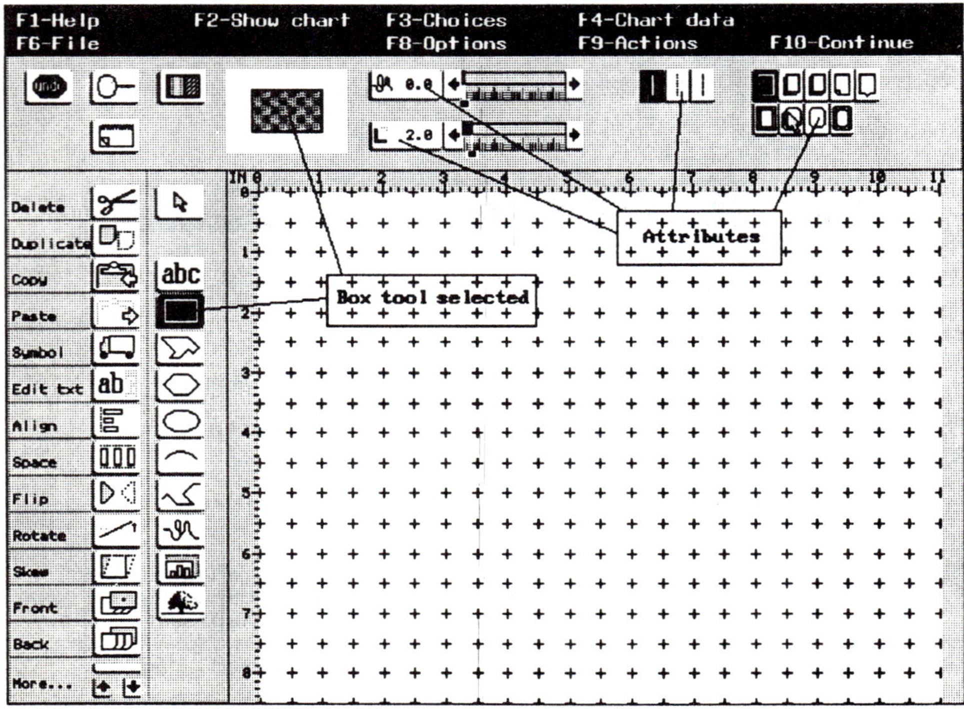

14-9 With *Box* selected, the box attributes appear in the attributes area.

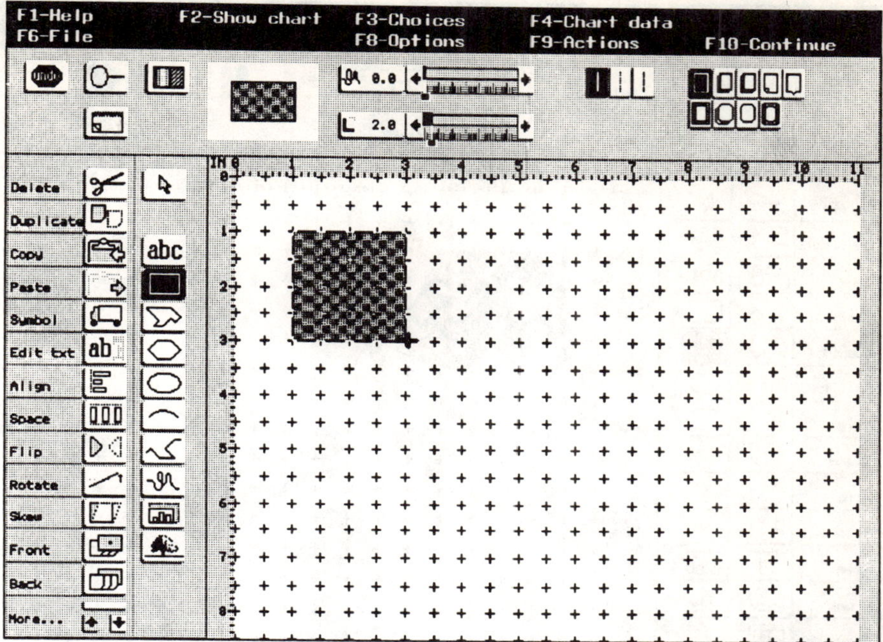

14-10 The two-inch square box.

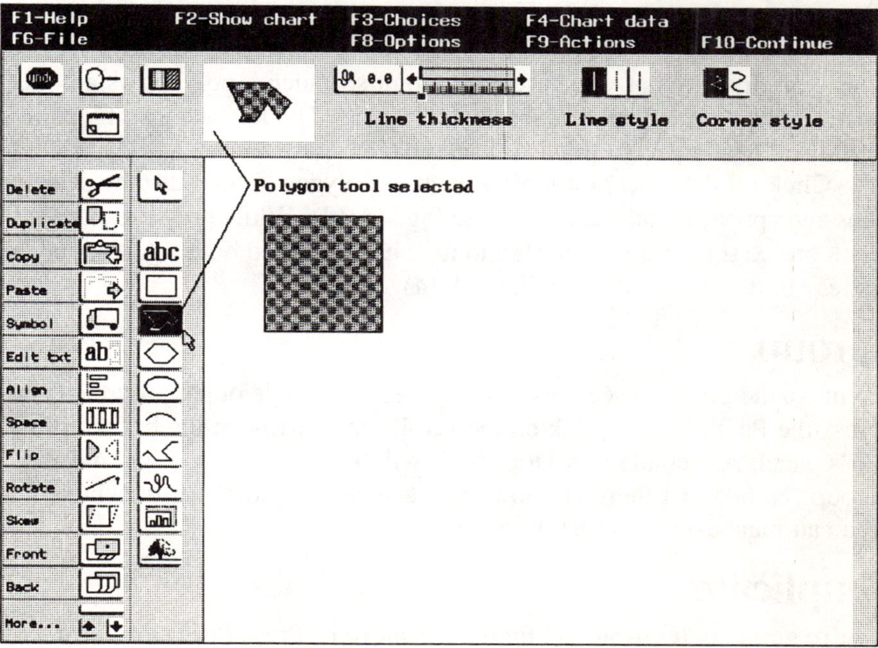

14-11 The Polygon tool selected.

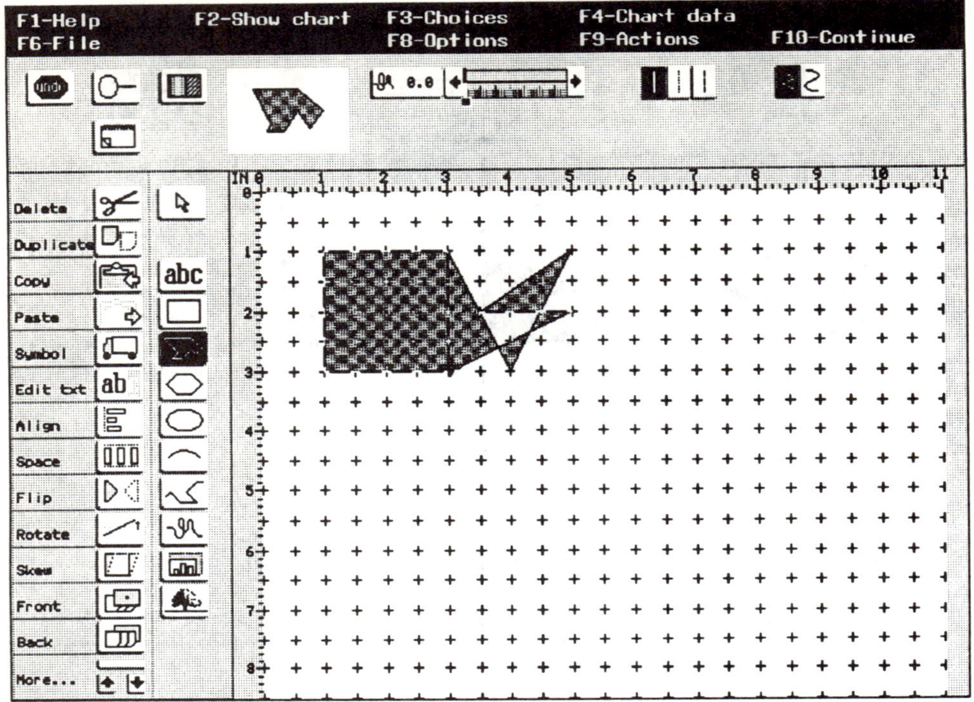

14-12 The completed polygon.

Harvard Graphics 3.0 will fill in any closed area that has been created by the lines you draw. What you have here is not so much a polygon as a collection of small triangles attached to your original square. The figure doesn't look like much so far, but you're about to work some magic.

Click on the Selection tool; your new polygon should display selection handles and appear in the status box (see Fig. 14-13). While pressing either Shift key, click on the square box. You should now have selected both figures, and both will appear in the status box (see Fig. 14-14).

Group

To make the program see these two figures as a single object, use the Group tool. Press the PgDn key, or click on the scroll down arrow at the bottom of the Draw tools panel. A second set of Draw tools will be revealed (see Fig. 14-15). Click on Group. Notice that there are now eight selection handles for the entire figure, so you can maneuver it as one object.

Duplicate

You're going to duplicate the figure and move it. Press PgUp to return to the first panel of Draw tools. Click on the Duplicate tool. A second box will appear, offset

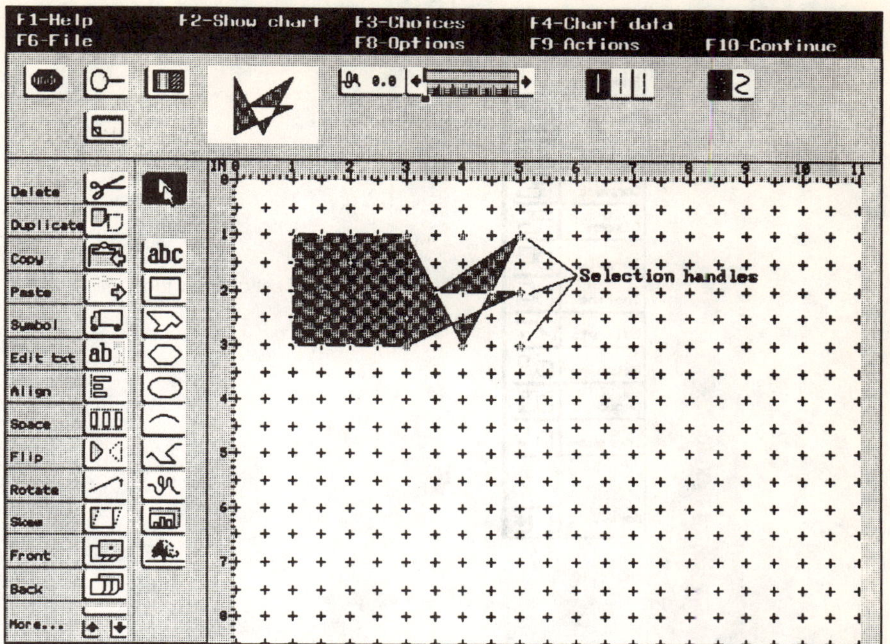

14-13 The new selected "polygon" appears in the status box.

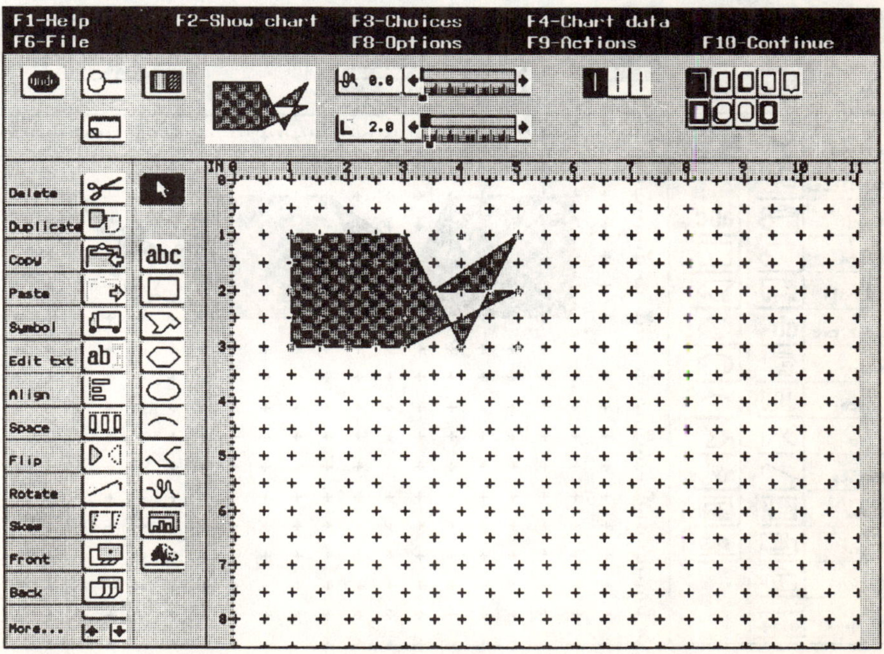

14-14 Both figures are selected and appear in the status box.

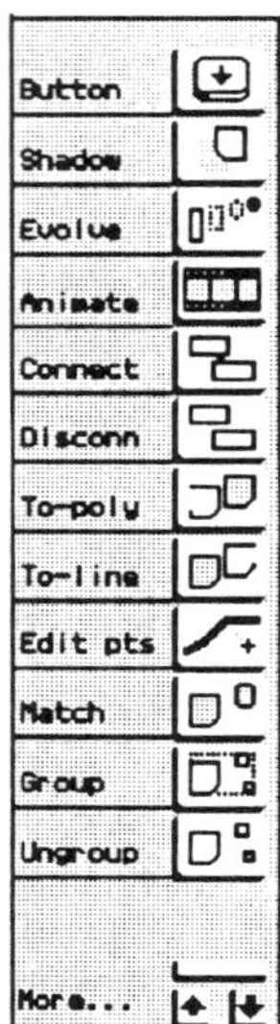

14-15 The second set of Draw tools.

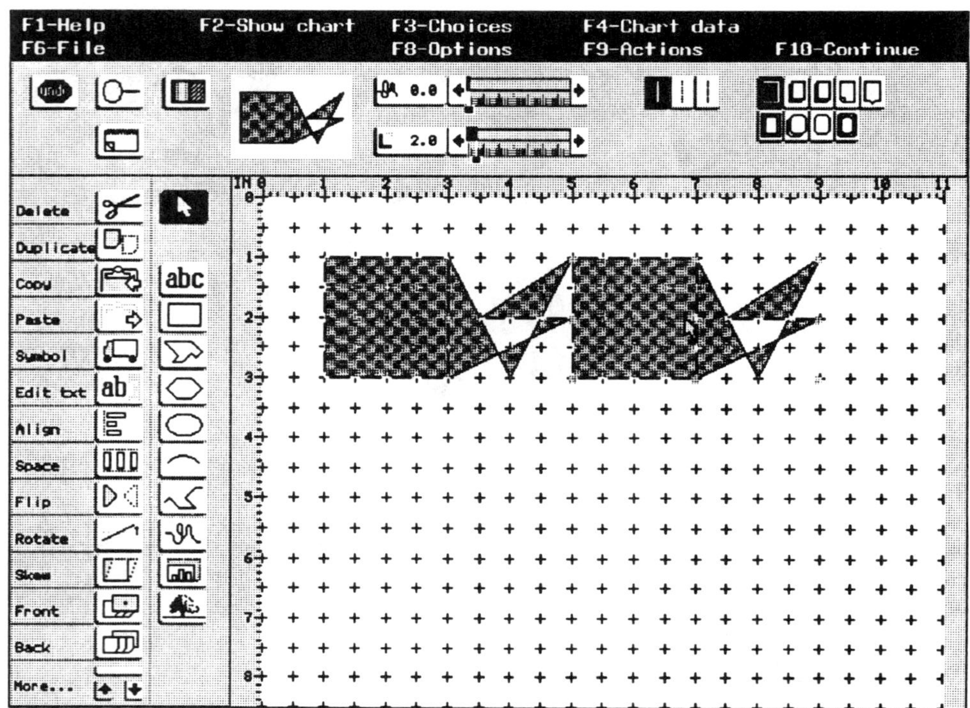

14-16 The duplicate of your developing figure.

slightly from the first. Drag this box to the right end of the figure under construction, as shown in Fig. 14-16.

Flip horizontally

Next, in order to make your duplicate a mirror image of the original figure, you're going to use the Flip tool. Click on the Flip icon; another pair of icons will appear in the tool panel, offering you the option of flipping horizontally or vertically (see Fig. 14-17).

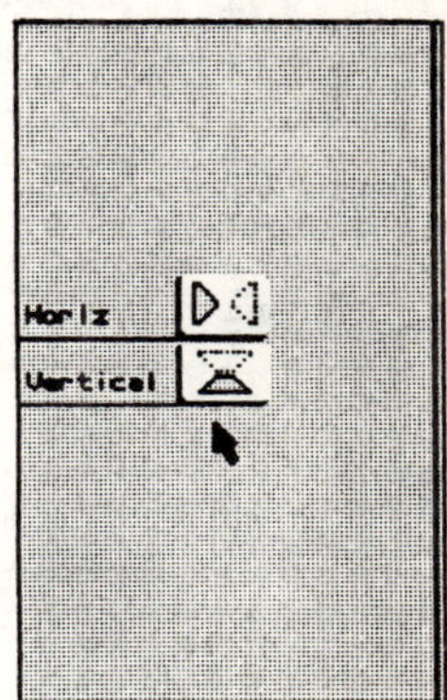

14-17 The Flip Horizontal and Flip Vertical icons.

Click on the Horiz button; the marvel of symmetry will reveal itself, and your figure suddenly doesn't look so random (see Fig. 14-18). Now you're going to (you guessed it!) turn this whole contraption into a single object again by using the Group tool. But first, a new selection trick. There are at least three different ways to simultaneously select all the objects on the screen. Here's a new one:

Select all objects

To select all objects on the canvas, just use the Selection tool to drag a rectangle around all objects.

1. Click on the Selection tool.
2. Position the pointer at one end, top or bottom, of the figure. Press the left mouse button and hold it down.
3. Drag the mouse diagonally to form a rectangle that completely encloses the figure(s) you want to select (see Fig. 14-19).

When you release the mouse button, all figures will be selected—as you can confirm by looking at the status box. You're now going to define the entire figure as a single object. Press PgDn and select Group. The eight selection handles that identify your symmetrical object as a single group will appear.

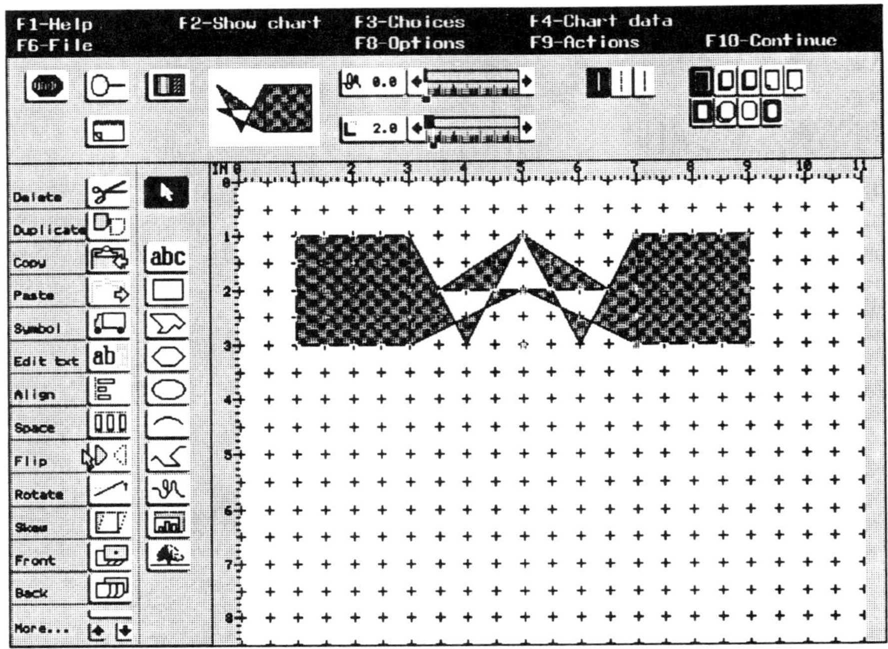

14-18 Your figure in transit after the horizontal flip.

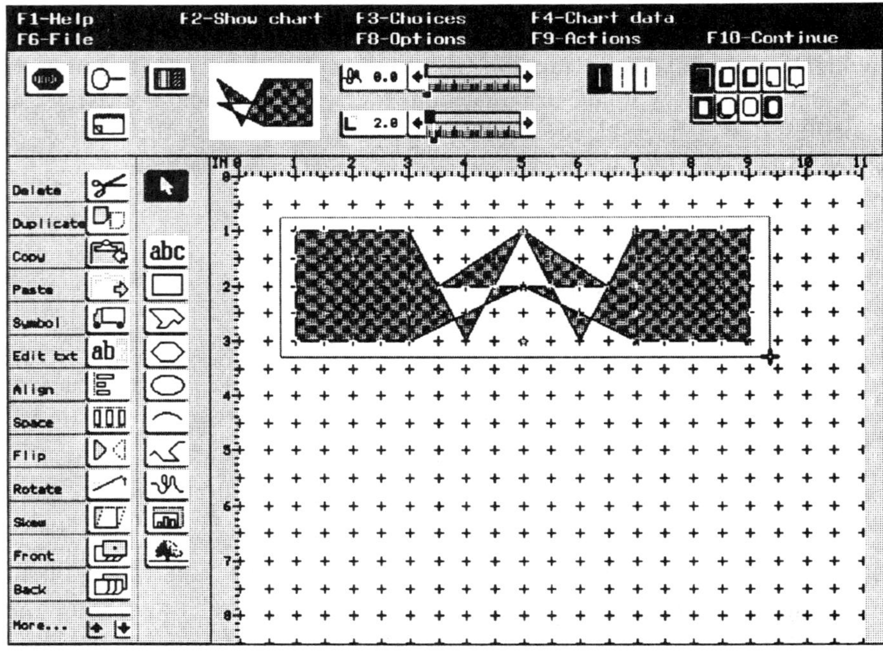

14-19 The rectangle you dragged around the figures.

Now move this group out to the center of the canvas to give you some working room. Simply click in the middle of the figure and drag it to the center, so that the coordinates of the upper left-hand corner are 1.5,2.

You'll repeat a couple of the maneuvers you just practiced. With the new group-figure selected, click on Duplicate again and drag the duplicated figure down to a position adjacent to its original (see Fig. 14-20). Select Flip, and this time choose Vertical. Ecco! Ain't symmetry grand? You've just designed a jazzy new logo for someone—maybe for a new automobile model (see Fig. 14-21).

You can have a lot of fun and get some amazing results playing around with the geometric figures you create with Harvard Graphics 3.0. Using your new-found expertise, select the entire figure and turn it into a group. Duplicate this new group and place it exactly on top of its original.

Rotate

You're going to rotate the new duplicate 90 degrees clockwise. With the new duplicate still selected, click on Rotate. The Rotate options will appear; you have to stipulate the number of degrees to rotate and the direction. Reverse means counterclockwise and Forward means clockwise (see Fig. 14-22).

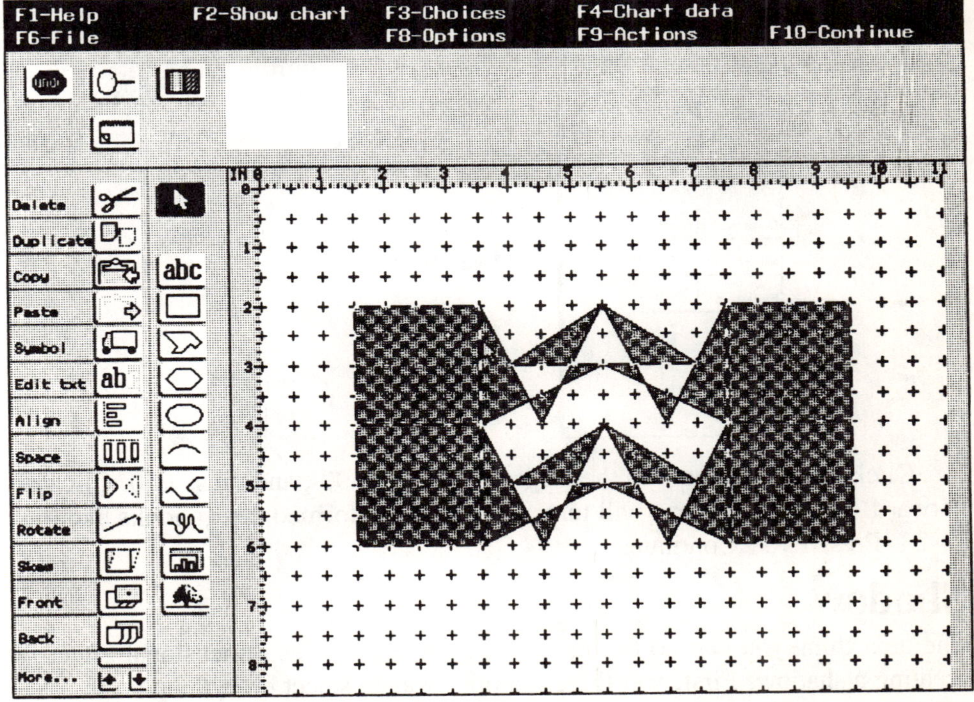

14-20 The new duplicate, positioned below the original.

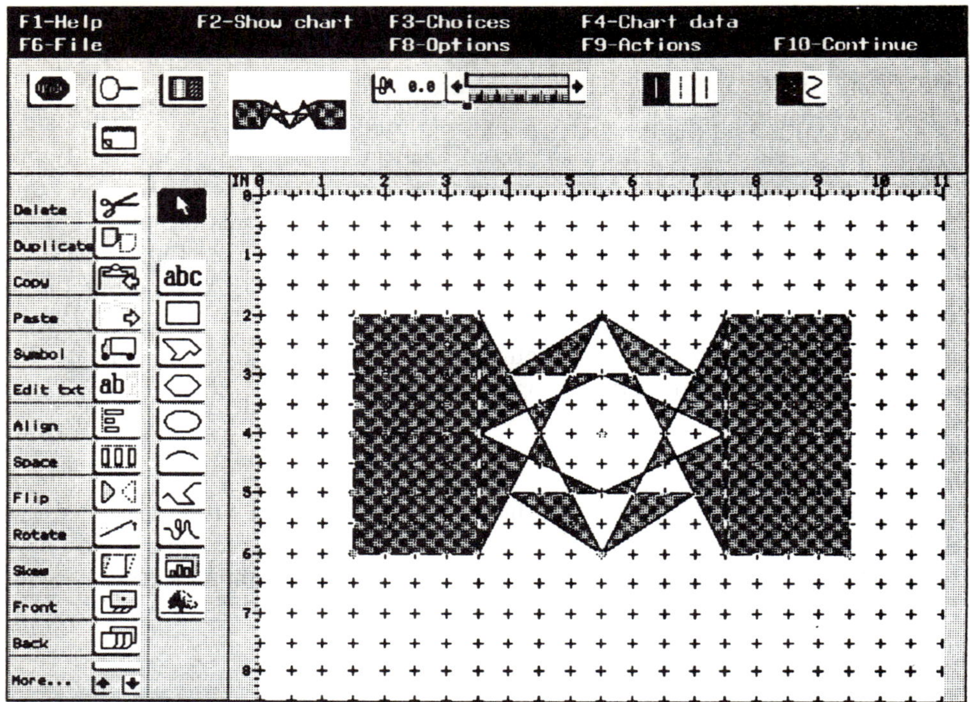

14-21 Your new logo.

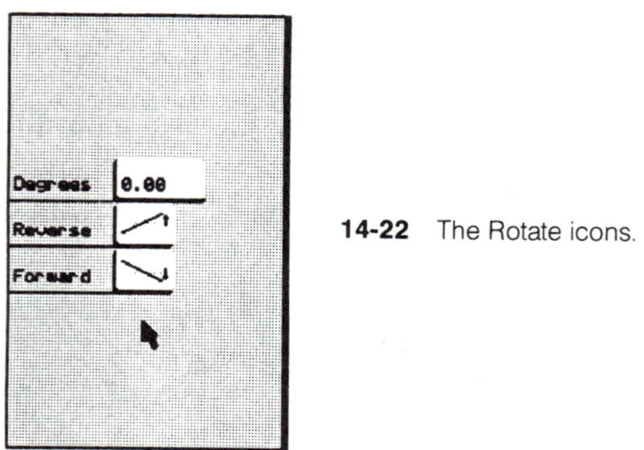

14-22 The Rotate icons.

Click on the first zero in the Degrees box, type 90., and press F10. Click on Forward. The kaleidoscope will turn, and your transformed design looks like Fig. 14-23. Press F10–Continue.

Shadow

The next thing you can do to this figure is to add a three-dimensional effect by creating a shadow. First, you'll learn a third way to select everything on the canvas.

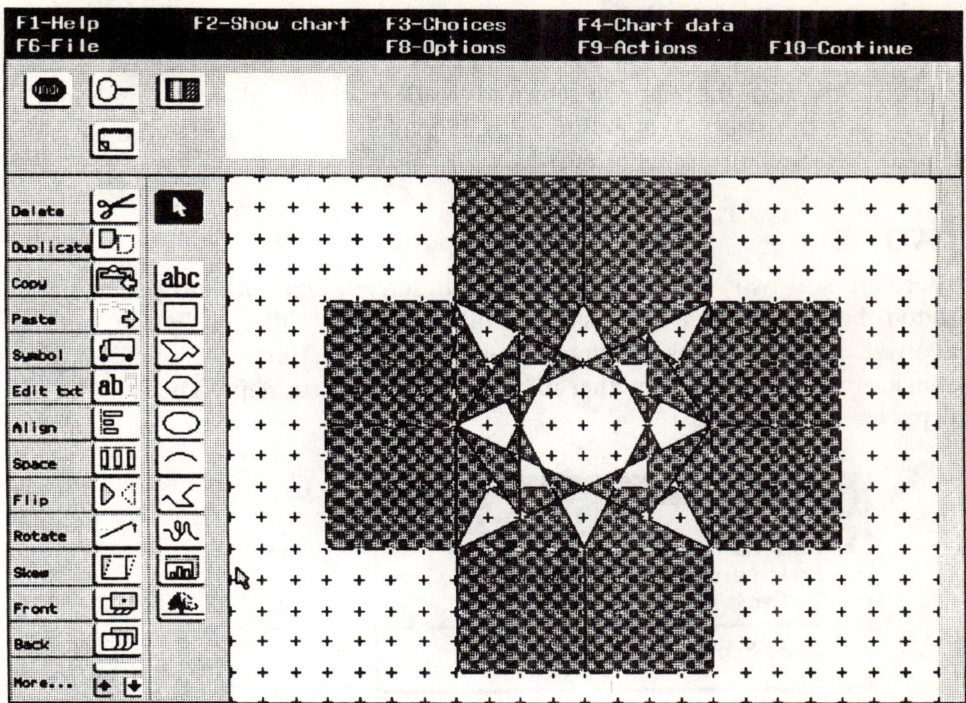

14-23 Your design after the duplicate is rotated 90 degrees.

1. Select F9—Actions.
2. From the Actions menu, select item 3, Select objects (see Fig. 14-24). A Select Objects box appears, and, if you press F3, you'll discover that your choices are All, None, Similar, and Buttons (see Fig. 14-25).
3. Click on All, and you have selected every object on the canvas. Press F10 to continue, noting that the status box now shows that all figures are selected.
4. Press PgDn, or click on the scroll down arrow to reveal the second panel of Draw tools.
5. Click on the Shadow tool. A group of Shadow attributes will appear in the tool panel, from which you can choose the location of the shadow (four choices), the depth of the shadow, and the familiar scissors icon that lets you cancel the shadow (see Fig. 14-26).
6. Select the upper left-hand icon for shadow location (this puts the shadow above and to the left of the figure), and change the shadow depth controller to 2.0 by clicking on the first digit and typing 2.
7. Click on the right mouse button to see the shadowed figure (see Fig. 14-27).

8. To get the full effect, press F2 to view your accomplishment as a full-screen drawing (see Fig. 14-28).
9. Click the right button to return to the Draw screen, then be sure both figures are selected. Now you're ready to observe some of Harvard Graphics 3.0's snazzier functions.

Evolve

There are still two separate figures on your screen, and both are selected. The bottom half of the tool panel should still be visible. Click on Evolve, and the Evolve tools or attributes will appear (see Fig. 14-29). Harvard Graphics 3.0 can transform one object into another in a number of discrete steps. The default is 10 steps; let's change it to 18.

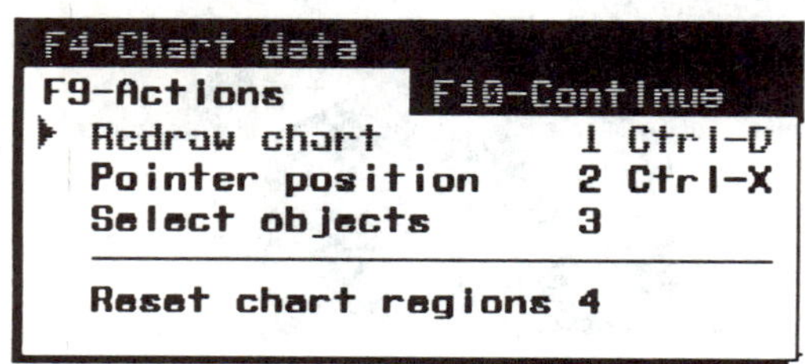

14-24 The Actions menu.

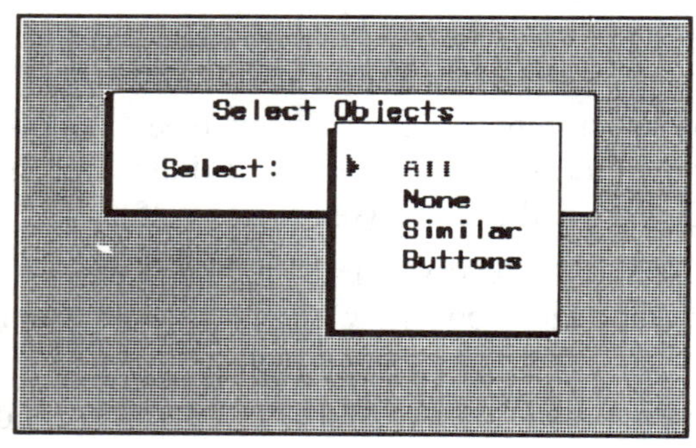

14-25 The Select Objects box with choices.

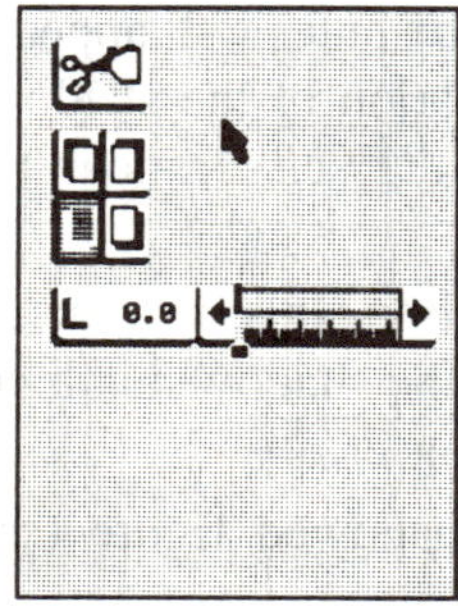

14-26 The Shadow attributes.

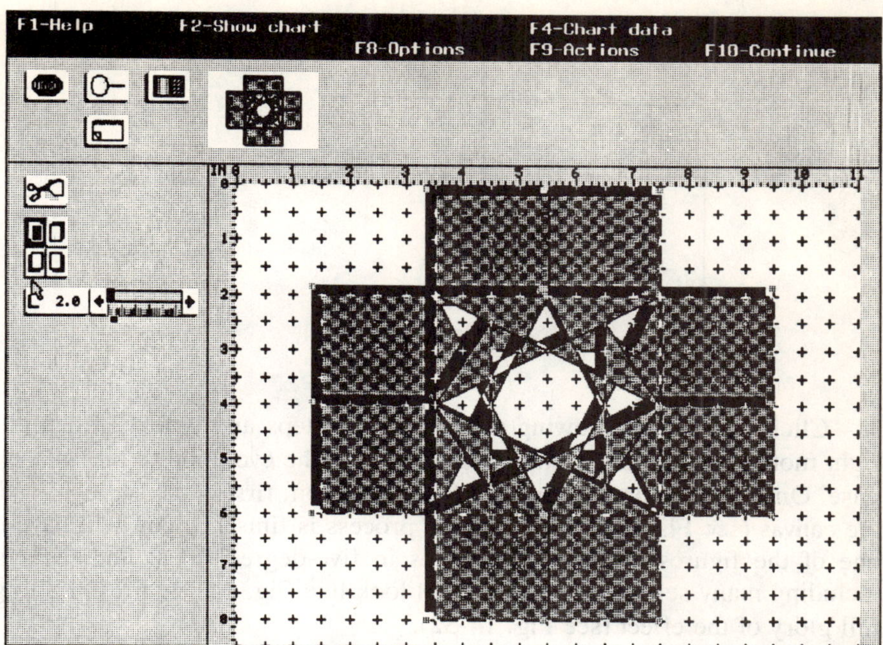

14-27 Your new figure enhanced by a shadow.

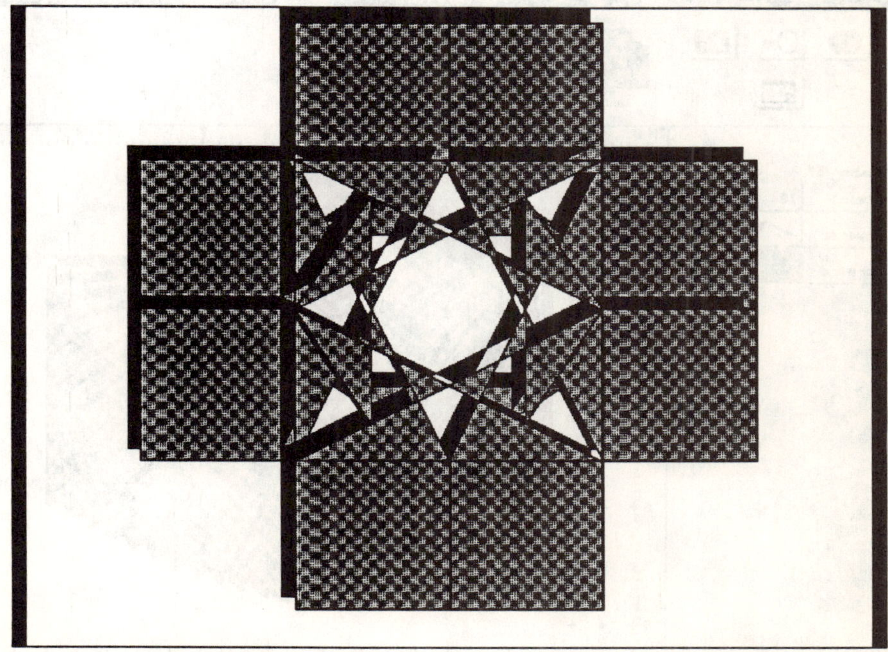

14-28 The new creation shown full-screen.

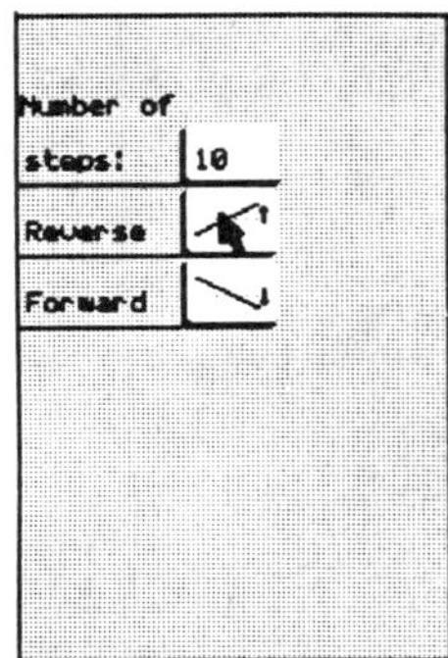

14-29 The Evolve tools or attributes.

Click on the box showing the number of steps and type 18, then click the right mouse button. Click on Forward to cause the evolution to take place clockwise. One of the figures begins an 18-step rotation, first in the status box, then on the canvas (see Fig. 14-30). When the process is finished, you will have rotated one of the figures through 90 degrees in five-degree steps, and the results—including many selection handles—will look like Fig. 14-31. Press F2 to get the full glory of the effect (see Fig. 14-32).

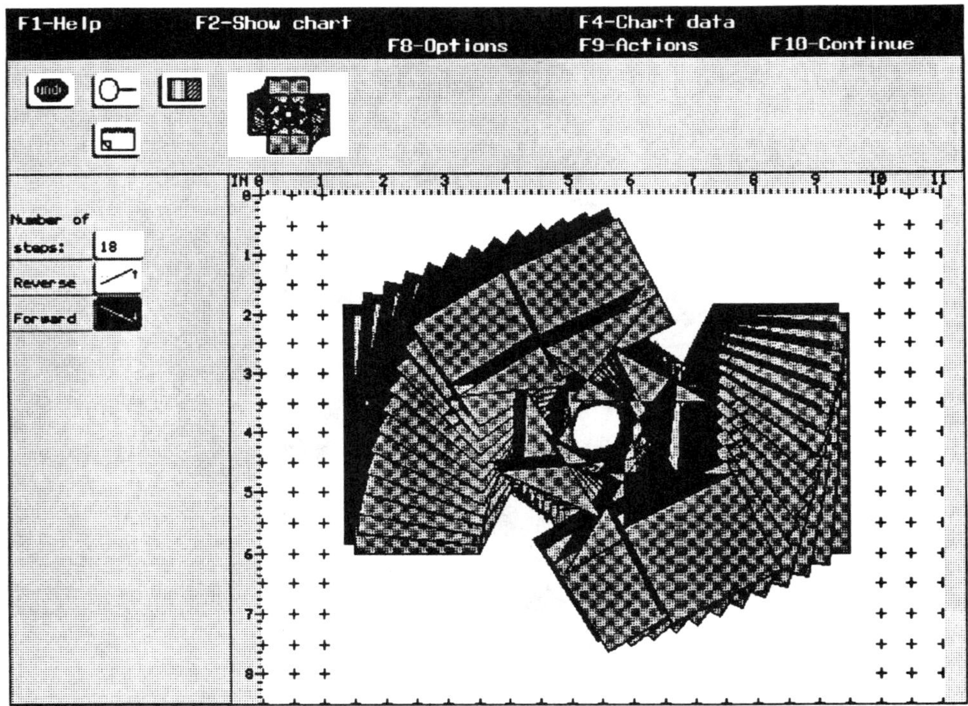

14-30 The evolution stopped in transit.

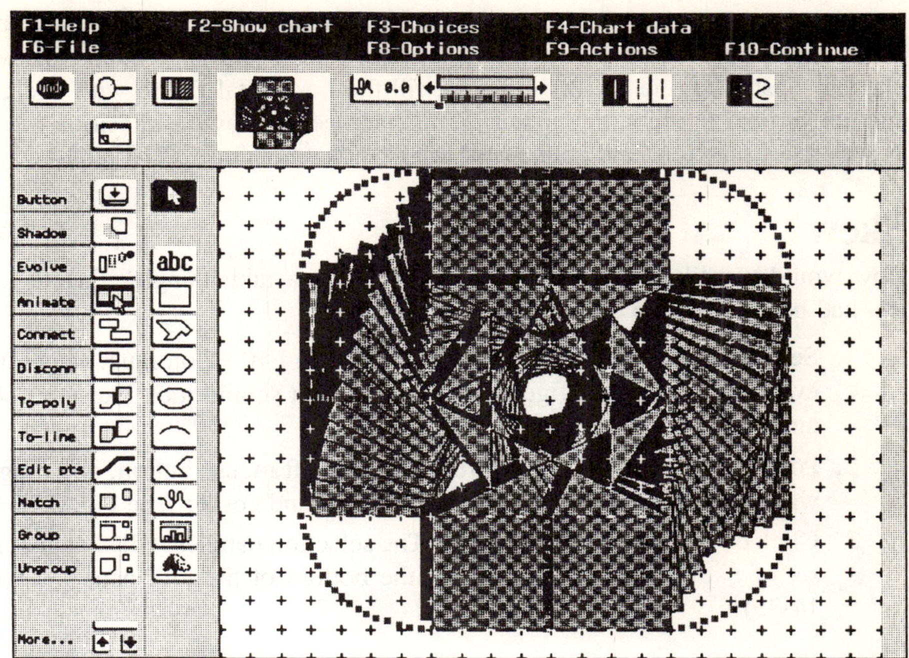

14-31 The completed evolution on the canvas.

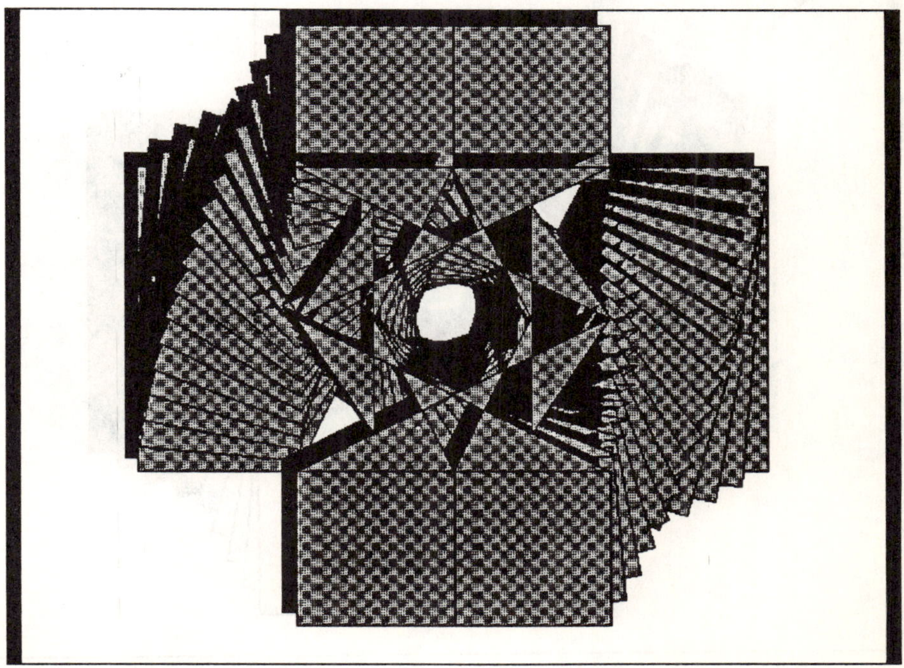

14-32 Big-screen evolution.

Here's an exercise you can get some spectacular results with: go back to the beginning of the process and, before you perform the evolution (sounds like we're playing Masters of the Universe here!), fill the horizontal figure with one color and the vertical figure with another. You'll then get a stepwise transition of color as well as of position, and your result might look something like Fig. 14-33.

Skew

How would you like to set this whole whirligig at a rakish angle? Exactly what you had been hoping to do, right? Here's how:

1. Select F9—Actions, then Select objects, then F10—Continue. This selects every element of the figure, and your screen should look like Fig. 14-31 again.
2. Point to the center of the figure, press the left mouse button, and drag the whole assemblage down to the lower left-hand corner (see Fig. 14-34).
3. Click on Skew in your tool panel. The selection handles will change, and a set of Skew icons will appear at the bottom of the tool panel (see Fig. 14-35).

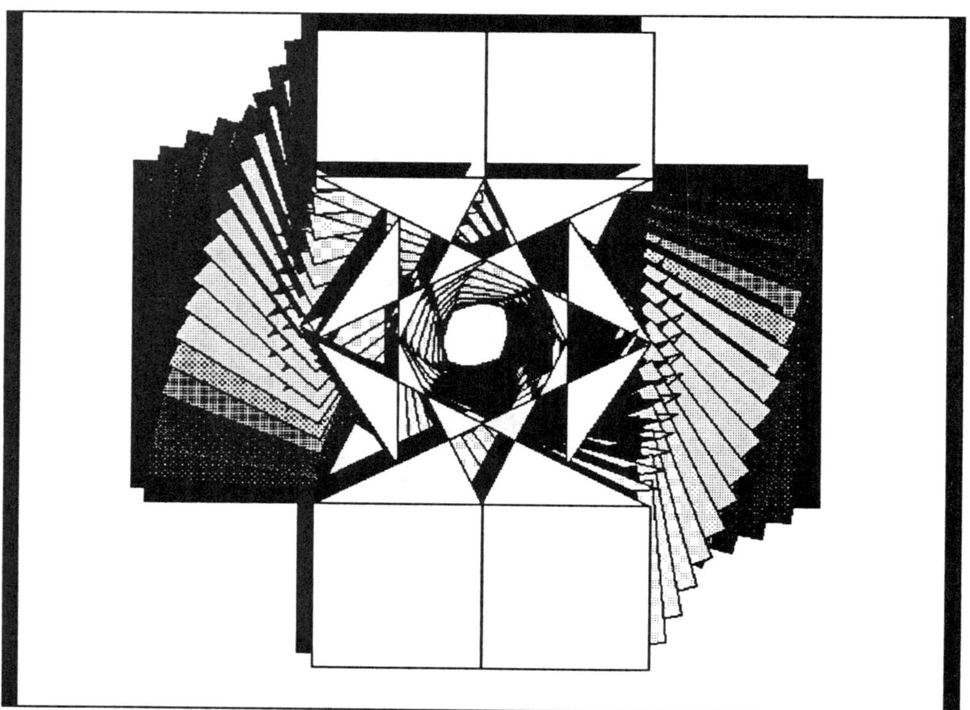

14-33 The same evolution performed when the horizontal figure is black and the vertical figure is white.

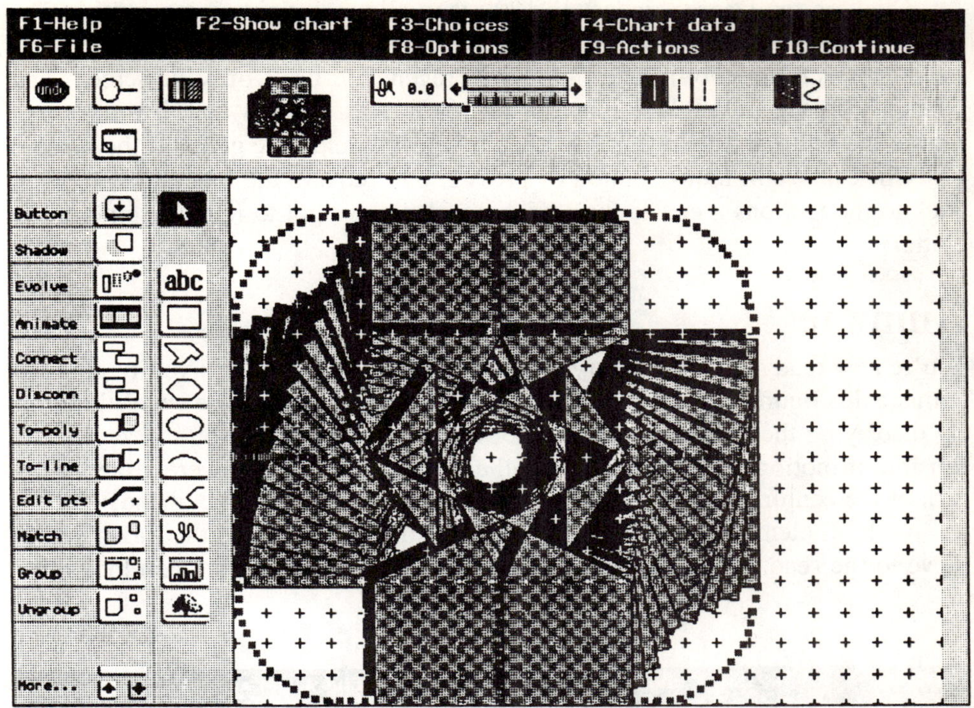

14-34 The evolved figure moved to the lower left-hand corner.

14-35 The Skew icons.

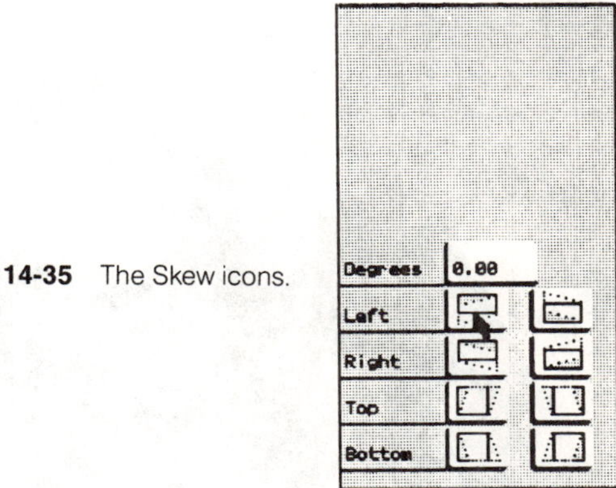

These Skew icons let you determine the direction and amount of the skew (skewage?). The pictures on the little icons illustrate what will happen, with the solid rectangles representing the original figure and the dotted parallelograms representing the figure after it has been skewed. For your tutorial exercise, you're going to skew the top of the figure 30 degrees to the right.

Click on the Degrees icon, type 30., then click the right mouse button. The Degrees icon should now say 30.0. Click on the left-hand Top icon (there are two icons for each direction). The figure will regenerate itself on your screen, and when it's finished it will look like Fig. 14-36. You can see now that, if you had not moved the figure to the lower left-hand corner, it would have gone off the screen.

Click the right mouse button or press Esc to retrieve the tool panel, then go back to the Options menu to turn off the grid (you've got to remove some of the clutter).

Animate

You're now ready for one of Harvard Graphics 3.0's cutest tricks: you're going to animate this figure, using the 18 separate images that comprise the evolved figure. By displaying the images one at a time, in quick succession, you can create the illusion of motion. (This takes you to the point where movies were at about the turn of the century, except that you don't have to crank the reel by hand.)

With all elements of the evolved figure still selected, press the PgDn key to move to the second part of the tool panel. Click on Animate (the icon looks like

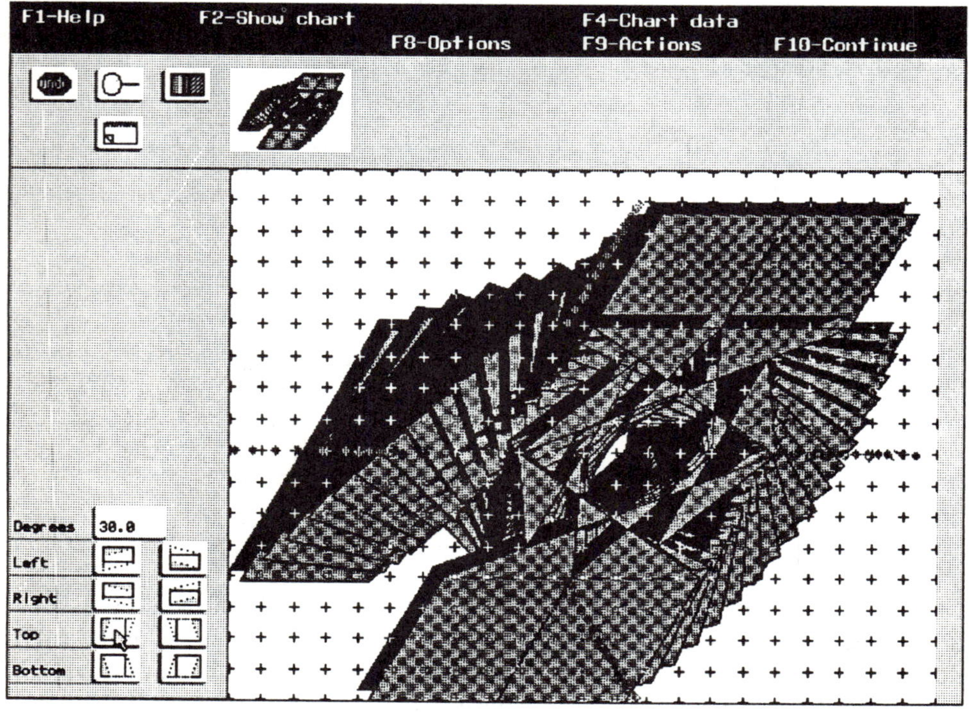

14-36 The figure with its top skewed 30 degrees to the right.

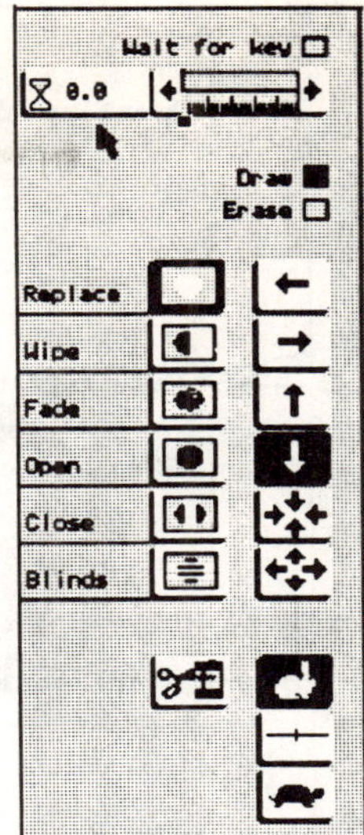

14-37 The Animation controls.

three frames of motion picture film), and a whole panel of animation controls will appear (see Fig. 14-37).

The animation controls allow you to determine the duration of each image on the screen, the manner in which each image is drawn and erased, the direction, and the speed. For example, if you choose the Wipe technique of drawing figures on the screen, you can elect to have the figure revealed from left to right, top to bottom, etc. You can also elect to have the wipe proceed quickly (by selecting the rabbit at the bottom of the panel), slowly (by selecting the turtle), or at medium speed. If you choose Replace as the draw technique, the direction and speed settings are irrelevant and can be ignored.

By setting the ruler at the top of the animation tools panel, you can govern the length of time each figure stays on the screen, from 0 to 100 seconds. You set the time either by pointing to the small rectangle below the ruler and dragging it to the right or left, or by clicking on the arrows at either end of the ruler. One click on either arrow changes the time by 0.1 second. Above the ruler is the Wait for key option; click on this little box if you want to hold any figure on screen until you press a key. The icon with the scissors cutting a frame of film is used to cancel the animation effects.

For now, set the duration at 0.3 seconds, the draw technique as Wipe, the erase technique as Fade, the wipe direction as left to right, and the change speed as Turtle. Here you go:

1. Click three times on the right arrow at the end of the ruler. The setting should now read 0.3.
2. Click on the Draw box. It will be highlighted.

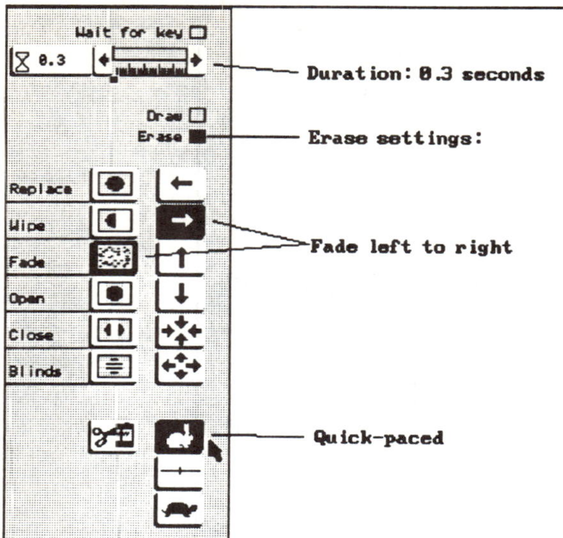

14-38 The animation tool panel with your new settings.

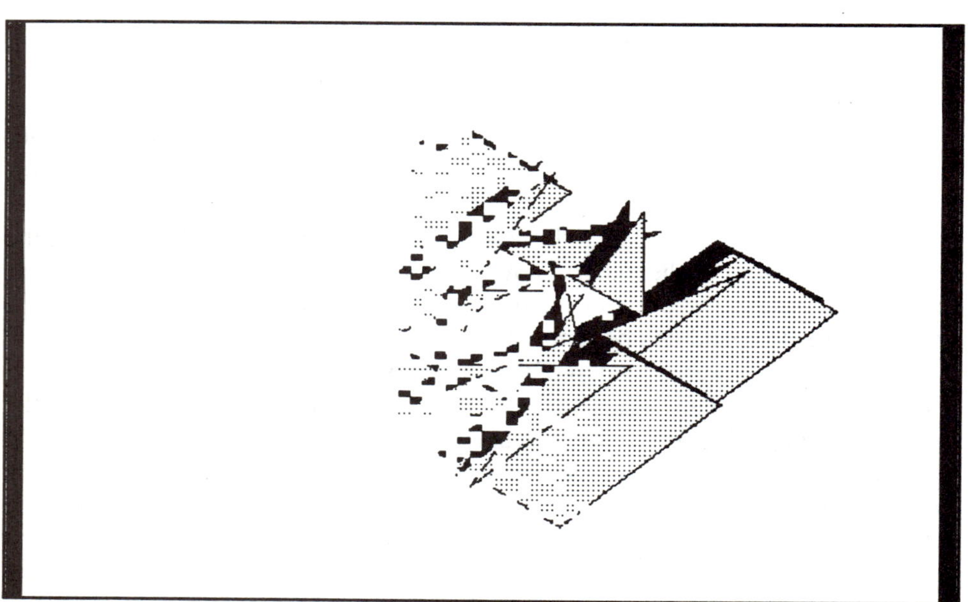

14-39 A figure as it fades from the screen in the middle of the animation sequence.

3. Click on the Wipe icon, and then on the left-to-right arrow just next to it.
4. Click on the Turtle.
5. To set the erase method, click on the Erase box.
6. Click on the Fade icon, then on the left-to-right arrow.

7. Click on the rabbit. Your animation tool panel should now be set up like Fig. 14-38.
8. Click on F2 – Show chart to test your results (see Fig. 14-39).

And that's just the beginning. You'll want to play with this function to be able to tap the full range of possibilities. In fact, that's good advice for the Draw function overall. Experiment with every function in all of its options; you'll be astounded to discover the artistic powers you can summon up.

15
CHAPTER

Advanced presentations

In chapter 6 you learned how to put together a basic presentation, or Screenshow. The presentation you created, saved as CLIXSHOW.SH3, is a generic presentation: eight charts, each replacing the preceding one after an on-screen appearance of five seconds.

You learned how to rearrange the order of the slides or charts, and how to check the spelling for the whole presentation. There are other effects you can create, especially those that you enter in the Draw column of the Edit Presentation data screen; they include Replace, Overlay, Wipe, Scroll, Fade, Open, Close, and Blinds. You saw most of these effects in connection with the Animate feature of the Draw function, and the best way to become acquainted with them is through trial and error. Just remember to "KISS" (Keep it simple, Señorita!) and don't let the graphical pyrotechnics and special effects obscure your message.

The real excitement and power that Harvard Graphics 3.0 brings to presentations, however, is in the Hypershow functions. These functions, which can involve the use of keys or "buttons" you create, allow you to move freely among charts and graphs in almost any direction and manner you choose. For example, if you're discussing a pie chart in a presentation and someone raises a question about one slice of the pie, you can—if you've defined the slice as a button—click on the slice and go directly to another chart that provides information specifically about that slice. You're going to step through a tutorial in which I illustrate that procedure, plus some others that turn presentations into very flexible, interactive tools.

Begin by loading the CLIXSHOW.SH3 presentation to make it the current presentation. Next, you'll create three quick text charts that you'll need in order to experiment with the Hypershow functions. Finally, you'll create the necessary buttons that will make the whole megillah work.

Loading a presentation

To load the presentation you created in chapter 6, begin at the Main Menu. Select Presentation, and then from the Presentation submenu select Get presentation, item 4. The Get Presentation file directory will appear (see Fig. 15-1).

Select CLIXSHOW.CH3, the presentation you created in chapter 6. (If you need to review presentation basics, you might want to go back to chapter 6 and review or work through that tutorial again.) The Edit Presentation data screen will appear with eight charts listed (see Fig. 15-2).

Now that you've established a current presentation, press F6 to return to the Main Menu. You're going to create three quick text charts here as samples of charts that might be used in conjunction with the COSTS-Q4 pie chart. The three slices of that pie are labeled Cost of Sales, R & D, and Selling, G & A, so you're going to create three text charts to correspond to those slices.

Select Create chart, then Text, and then Title to begin creating a text chart, as shown in Fig. 15-3 (you're using the Title chart format because you're not going to be putting real data into the chart). With the cursor blinking in the top section of the chart, type Cost of Sales and press Enter four times. With the cursor in the middle section of the chart, type Data and commentary about cost of sales.

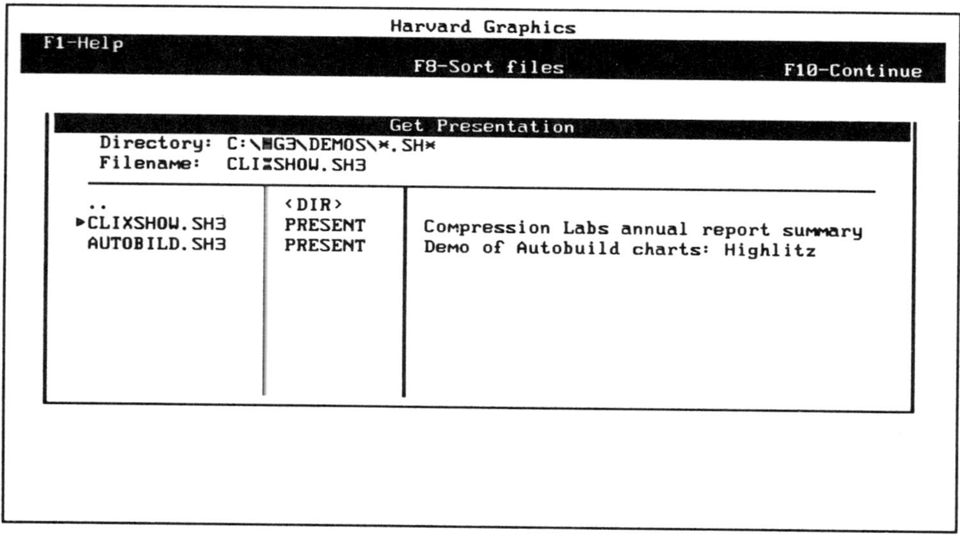

15-1 The Get Presentation file.

```
CLIXSHOW.SH3                          Edit Presentation
 F1-Help          F2-Preview       F3-Choices       F4-Descriptions F5-Mark block
 F6-Main Menu     F7-Add/Edit      F8-Options       F9-HyperShow    F10-Continue

 #  |   Filename    |    Draw    |  ←↑↓→  |  Speed  | Time |  Erase  |  ←↑↓→  |  Speed
 ▶  |               | ♦Replace   |        |         | 0:05 |         |        |
 1  |  HIGHLITE.CH3 |
 2  |  REVENUES.CH3 |
 3  |  INCOME  .CH3 |
 4  |  COSTS-Q4.CH3 |
 5  |  BACKLOG .CH3 |
 6  |  PRDCTVTY.CH3 |
 7  |  STOCKS  .CH3 |
 8  |  ORGCHART.CH3 |
 9  |
 10 |
 11 |
 12 |
 13 |
 14 |
 15 |
 16 |
```

15-2 The Edit Presentation data screen with the eight-chart presentation from chapter 6.

```
                                 Title Chart
 F1-Help          F2-Show chart                      F4-Draw          F5-Mark
 F6-Main Menu     F7-Spell/Text    F8-Options                         F10-Continue
 ------------------------------------ Top ------------------------------------

 ---------------------------------- Middle -----------------------------------

 ---------------------------------- Bottom -----------------------------------

 -----------------------------------------------------------------------------
```

15-3 The Title Chart data screen.

Your Title Chart data screen should now look like Fig. 15-4, and if you press F2 to view the chart it will resemble Fig. 15-5. Now:

1. At the Title Chart data screen, press Ctrl−S to save the chart.
2. For filename, type salecost and Enter.
3. For description, type Cost of Sales and Enter.

4. In the line that says Add to current presentation:, press the space bar so that the response is Yes.
5. Press F10—Continue twice to return to the Main Menu.
6. Select Presentation, then Edit presentation, and you'll see that the SALE COST.CH3 chart has been added to your presentation list as item 9 (see Fig. 15-6).

As you just did, create two more text/title charts. The first will say R & D in the top section and Data and commentary about R & D expenses in the middle section. It will be saved as R&DCOST. The chart will look like Fig. 15-7, and will appear on your presentation list as item 10.

The second text/title chart will say G & A in the top section and Data and com mentary about G & A expenses in the middle section. It will be saved as G&ACOST. The chart will look like Fig. 15-8, and will appear on your presentation list as item 11. Your Edit Presentation data screen should now look like Fig. 15-9, with the three new charts appearing as items 9 through 11. Save the expanded presentation under the original name, CLIXSHOW.

Adding buttons to charts

You now have all of the charts you need, but in order to link them together you need buttons. In the case of the COSTS-Q4 pie chart, you'll actually transform (before your very eyes!) the individual slices into buttons. With the three new text charts, you'll need to install new buttons onto the charts.

```
                          Title Chart
F1-Help         F2-Show chart                  F4-Draw         F5-Mark
F6-Main Menu    F7-Spell/Text   F8-Options                     F10-Continue
──────────────────────────────── Top ─────────────────────────────────
Cost of Sales

─────────────────────────────── Middle ───────────────────────────────
Data and commentary about cost of sales

─────────────────────────────── Bottom ───────────────────────────────

──────────────────────────────────────────────────────────────────────
```

15-4 The Title Chart data screen with text entered for the Cost of Sales chart.

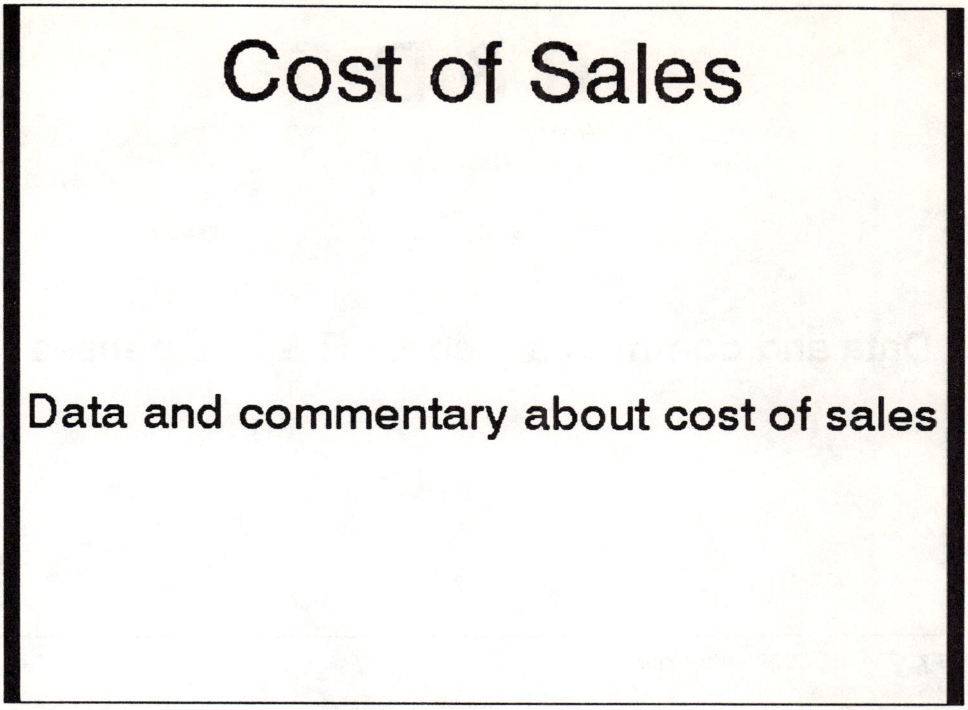

Cost of Sales

Data and commentary about cost of sales

15-5 The full-screen version of the Cost of Sales chart.

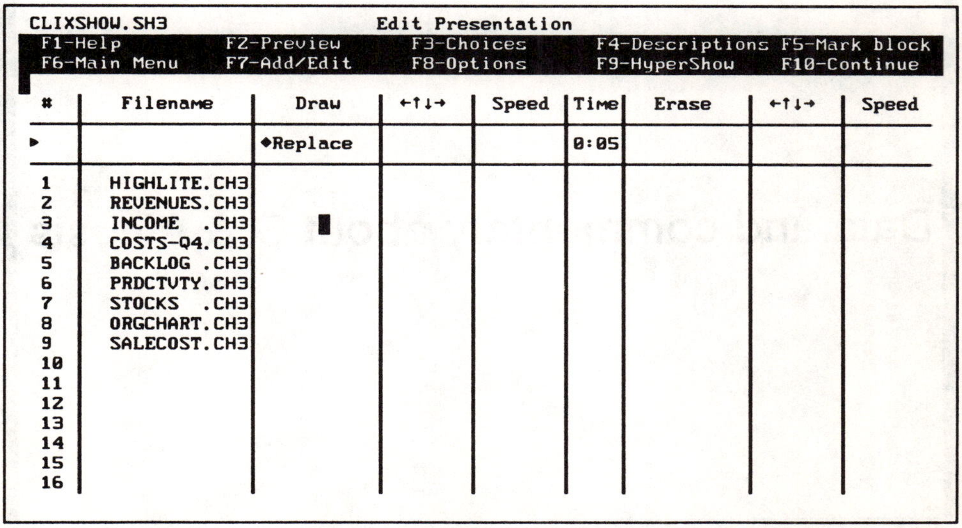

```
CLIXSHOW.SH3                          Edit Presentation
 F1-Help          F2-Preview       F3-Choices       F4-Descriptions F5-Mark block
 F6-Main Menu     F7-Add/Edit      F8-Options       F9-HyperShow    F10-Continue
```

#	Filename	Draw	←↑↓→	Speed	Time	Erase	←↑↓→	Speed
▶		♦Replace			0:05			
1	HIGHLITE.CH3							
2	REVENUES.CH3							
3	INCOME .CH3							
4	COSTS-Q4.CH3							
5	BACKLOG .CH3							
6	PRDCTVTY.CH3							
7	STOCKS .CH3							
8	ORGCHART.CH3							
9	SALECOST.CH3							
10								
11								
12								
13								
14								
15								
16								

15-6 The Edit Presentation data screen with the SALECOST chart added.

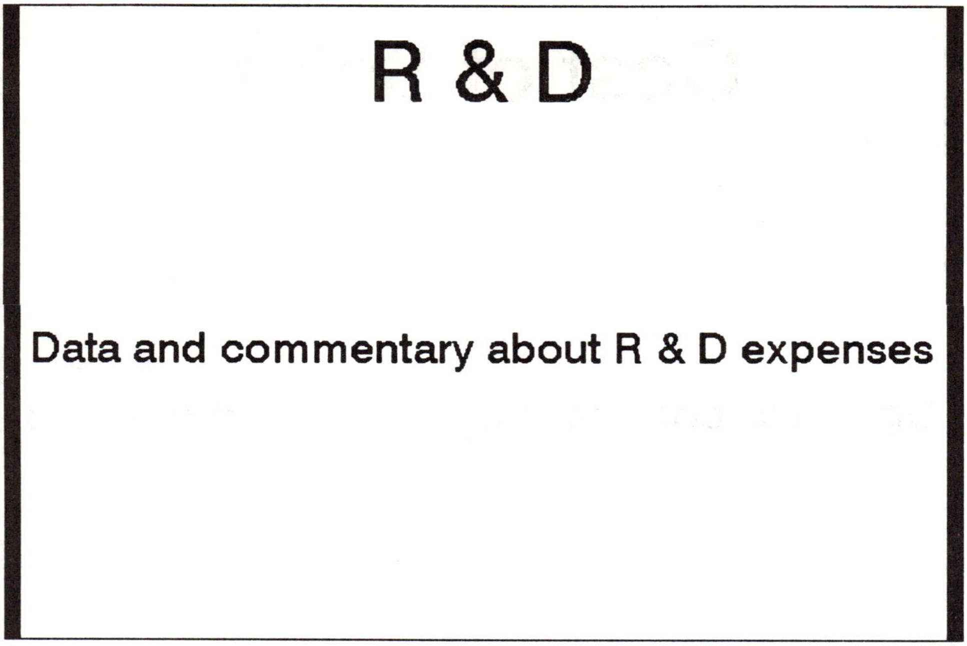

R & D

Data and commentary about R & D expenses

15-7 The R&DCOST text/title chart.

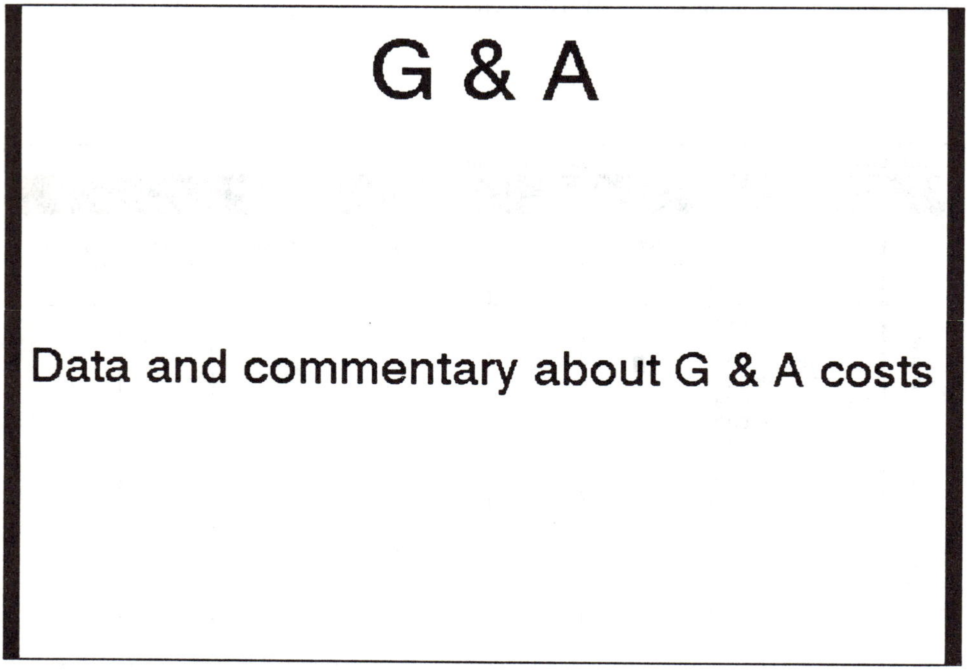

G & A

Data and commentary about G & A costs

15-8 The G&ACOST text/title chart.

Turning chart components into buttons

Installing new buttons on a chart is a fairly straightforward process, which I'll come to shortly. Transforming chart elements into buttons, however, requires a few extra steps. To begin with, a chart has to be saved as a symbol before its individual elements (bars, slices, etc.) can be isolated or separated.

1. Return to the Main Menu and select Draw.
2. When the Draw screen appears, select F6 – File and Get chart for the Get Chart directory. Then select the chart named COSTS-Q4 from that directory (see Fig. 15-10).
3. Press Esc, then F4 – Draw to display the chart on the Draw canvas (see Fig. 15-11).
4. Select F6 – File, then Save as symbol, item 4. The Save Symbol File box will pop up (see Fig. 15-12).
5. Remember that there are already a number of symbol files, containing several symbols each. You can assign this new symbol to one of those files, or create a new file; let's assign it to an existing buttons file. Opposite Filename, type buttons1 and Enter.
6. Opposite Description, type COSTS-Q4 pie chart as buttons and Enter.
7. Opposite Symbol name, type COSTS-Q4 pie. Your Save Symbol File box should now look like Fig. 15-13.
8. Select F10 – Continue.

CLIXSHOW.SH3 Edit Presentation

F1-Help	F2-Preview	F3-Choices	F4-Descriptions	F5-Mark block
F6-Main Menu	F7-Add/Edit	F8-Options	F9-HyperShow	F10-Continue

#	Filename	Draw	←↑↓→	Speed	Time	Erase	←↑↓→	Speed
▶		♦Replace			0:05			
1	HIGHLITE.CH3							
2	REVENUES.CH3							
3	INCOME .CH3							
4	COSTS-Q4.CH3							
5	BACKLOG .CH3							
6	PRDCTVTY.CH3							
7	STOCKS .CH3							
8	ORGCHART.CH3							
9	SALECOST.CH3							
10	R&DCOST .CH3							
11	G&ACOST .CH3							
12								
13								
14								
15								
16								

15-9 The Edit Presentation data screen with three new text/title charts.

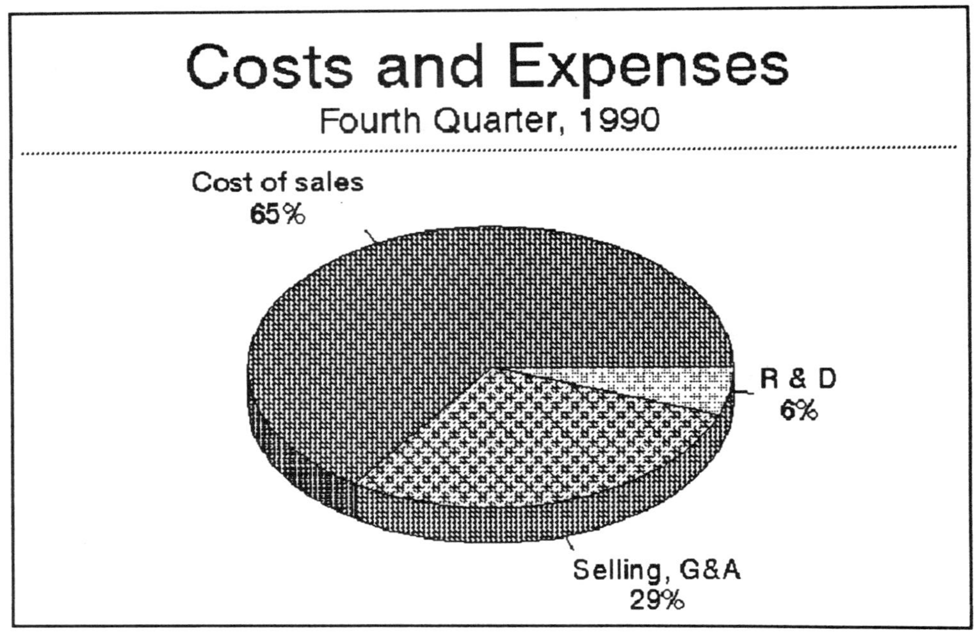

15-10 The COSTS-Q4 chart.

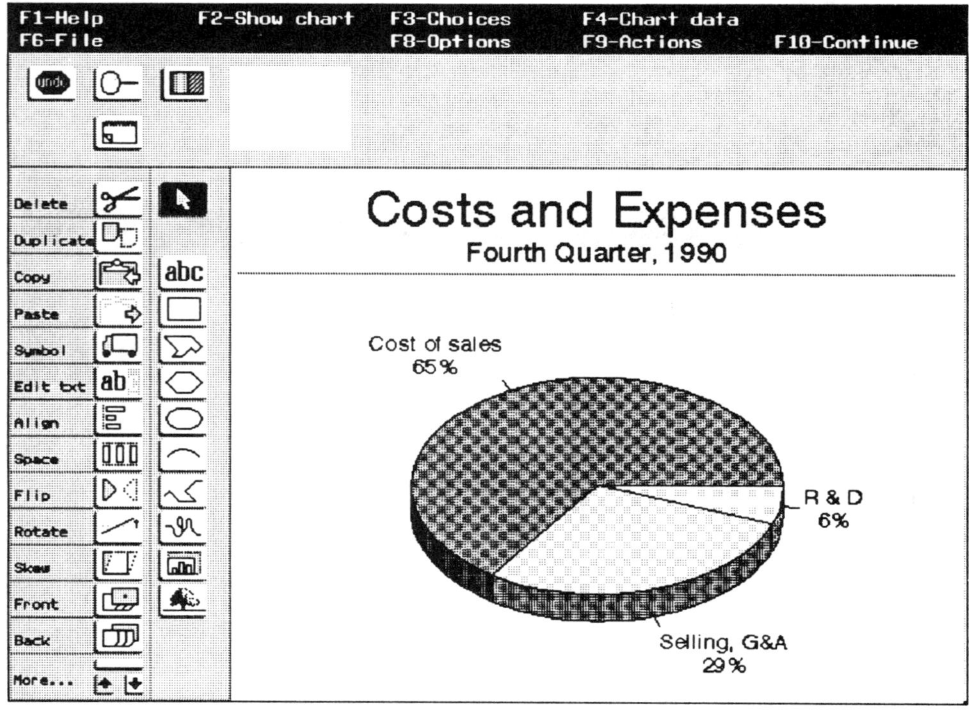

15-11 The Costs and Expenses chart on the Draw canvas.

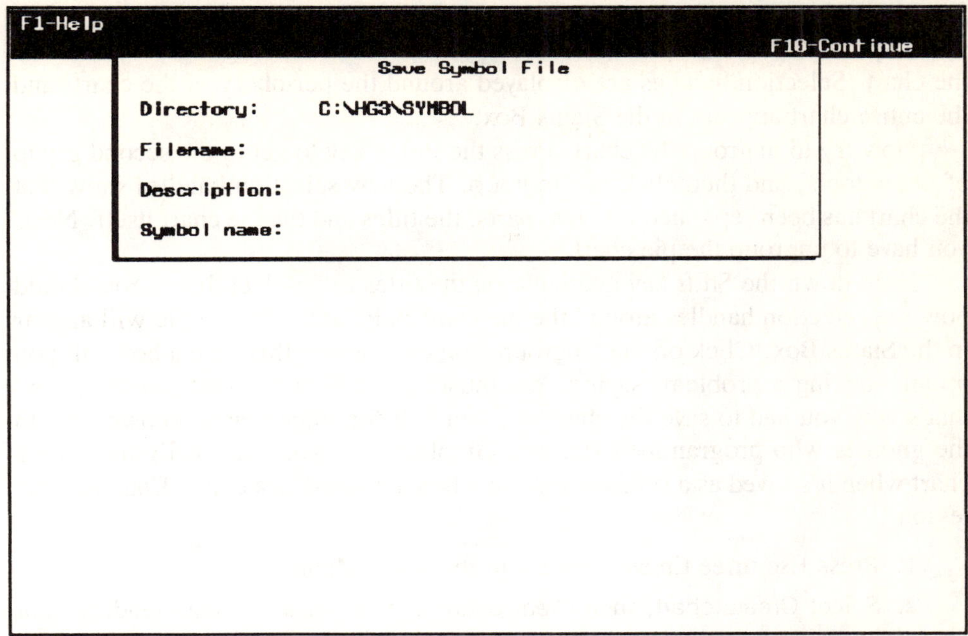

15-12 The Save Symbol File box.

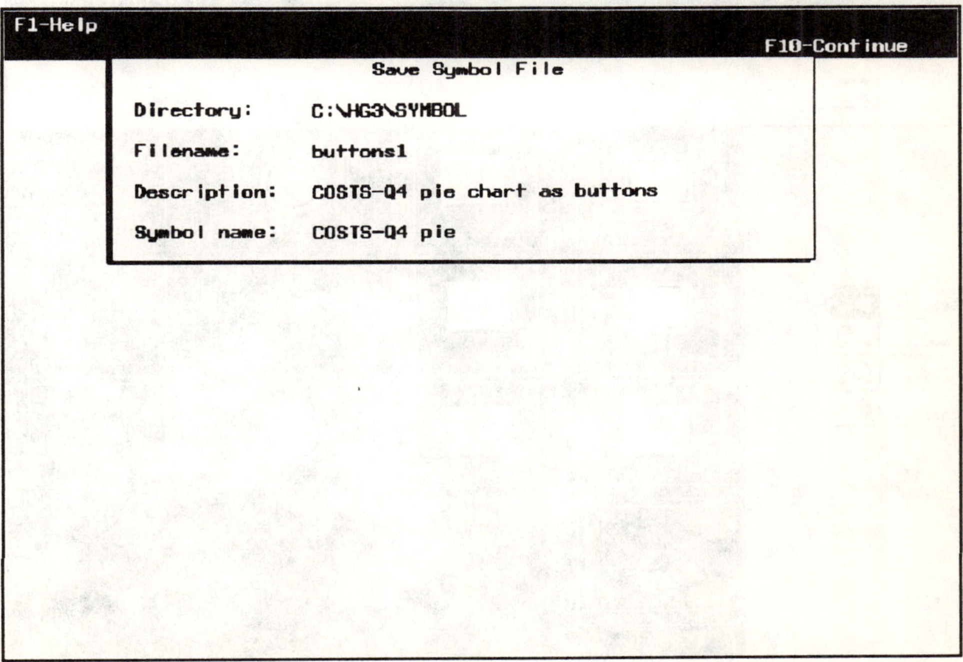

15-13 The completed Save Symbol File box.

I'm now going to interrupt this procedure for a quick object lesson. Your chart is still displayed on the Draw canvas. With the selection tool highlighted, click on the chart. Selection handles are displayed around the periphery of the chart, and the entire chart appears in the Status Box.

Now try to ungroup the chart. Press the PgDn key to get to the second group of Draw tools, and then click on Ungroup. The new selection handles show that the chart has been separated into two parts: the titles and the pie chart itself. Next, you have to ungroup the pie chart.

Hold down the Shift key and click on the titles to deselect them. You should now see selection handles around the pie chart only, and only the pie will appear in the Status Box. Click on the Ungroup icon once more; this time a box will pop up announcing a problem, saying, You must have a Group object selected. And that's why you had to save the chart as a symbol; for some reason known only to the gnomes who programmed Harvard Graphics 3.0, you can totally ungroup a chart when it's saved as a symbol, but not when it's saved as a chart. End of object lesson.

1. Press Esc three times to return to the Main Menu.
2. Select Create chart, then Clear chart. If you get a message reading Your latest changes have not been saved, select F10—Confirm.

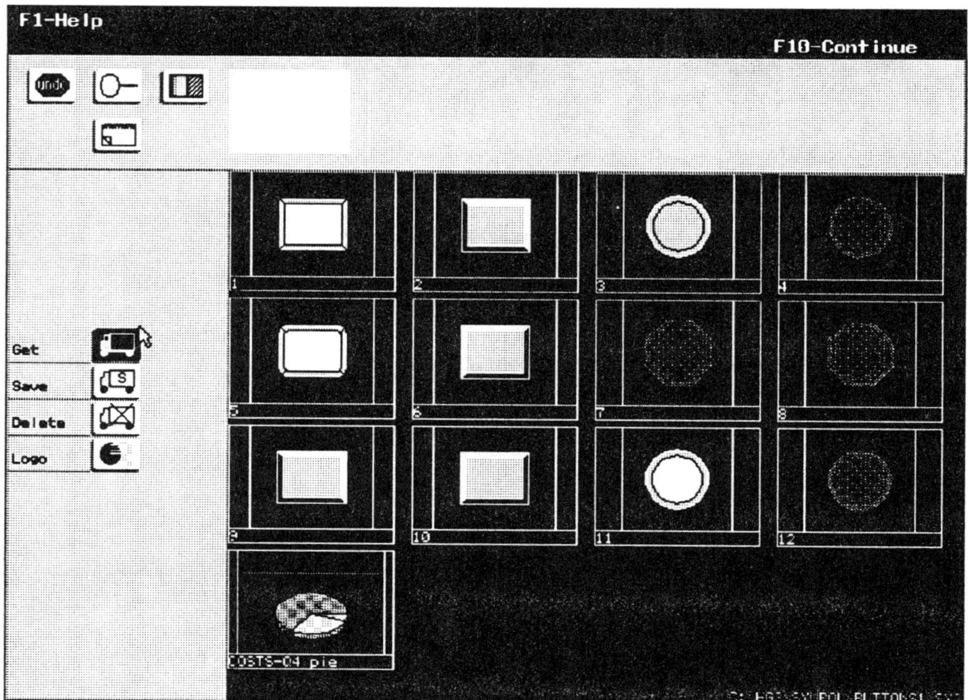

15-14 The button symbols in the BUTTONS1.SY3 file.

3. Select Draw, item 3, to return to the Draw screen.
4. Press the PgUp key if the first panel of Draw tools is not displayed, then click on the Symbol tool.
5. When the Symbol icons appear, click on Get. The Get Symbol File directory will be displayed.
6. Locate and select the file named BUTTONS1.SY3.

Thirteen buttons will appear on the Draw canvas: twelve originals, imaginatively numbered 1 through 12, and your new symbol, labeled COSTS-Q4 pie (see Fig. 15-14). Select your pie symbol, then F10–Continue. Your pie chart will appear once more on the Draw canvas, with eight selection handles. Click the right mouse button to return the Draw tools.

Press the PgDn key to display the second panel of Draw tools, then select the Ungroup icon. The new selection handles show the chart to be divided into two parts: the titles and the pie. While pressing the Shift key, click on the title area to deselect it. Selection handles should now appear only around the pie area, and only the pie is shown in the Status Box (see Fig. 15-15).

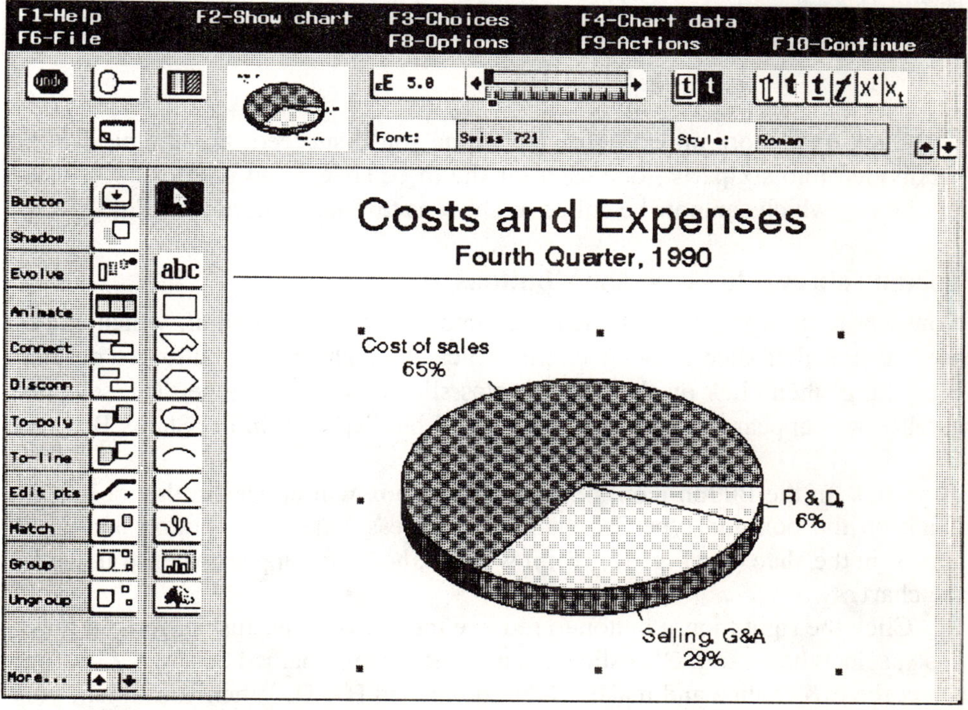

15-15 The pie region of the chart selected.

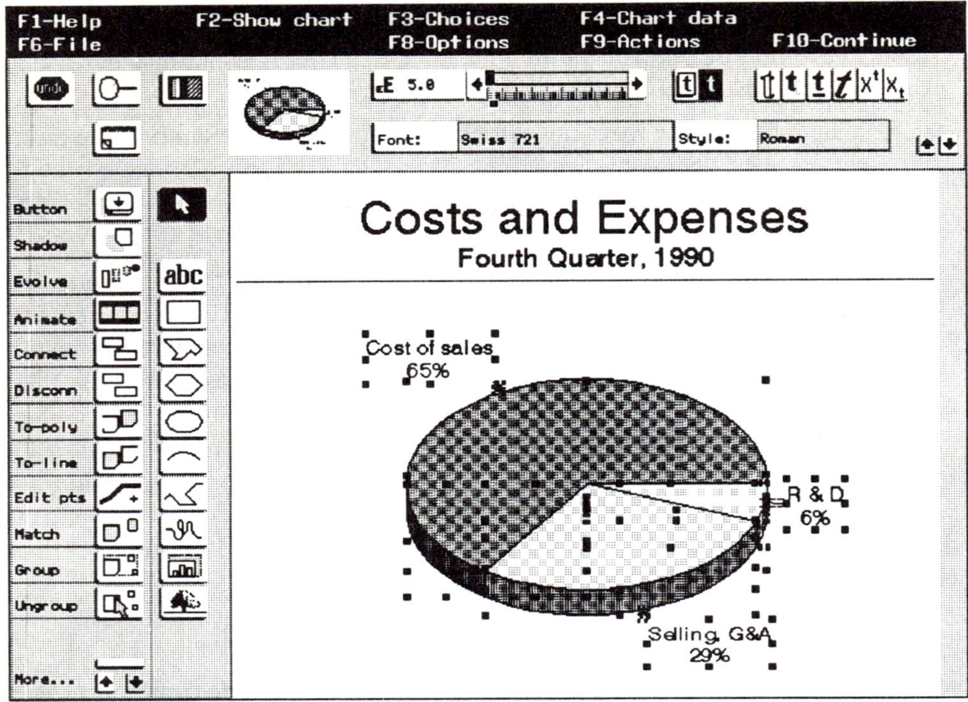

15-16 The pie ungrouped into several parts.

Click once more on Ungroup. This time you'll succeed, and the pie will be subdivided into six parts—one each for the three slices, and one for each of the text labels, which can now be edited in Draw as text annotations (see Fig. 15-16).

Turning slices into Hypershow buttons

Now you're going to convert each slice into a Hypershow button, which can be used to link that slice to other charts. Click the right mouse button to deselect everything, then click on the Cost of sales slice to select it alone. The selection handles will appear, and the single slice will be displayed in the Status Box (see Fig. 15-17).

Click on the Button icon; a Button Name box will appear in the tool panel. Click on the box and type Sales cost, then press Enter. The button name will appear in the slice (see Fig. 15-18); it will not, however, appear when you display the chart.

Click the right mouse button to retrieve the Draw tools. Just as you did previously, select the Selling, G&A slice and make it a button named Selling, G&A. Then select the R & D slice and make it a button named R & D. When you finish, your chart will look like Fig. 15-19. Save the chart under its original name, COSTS

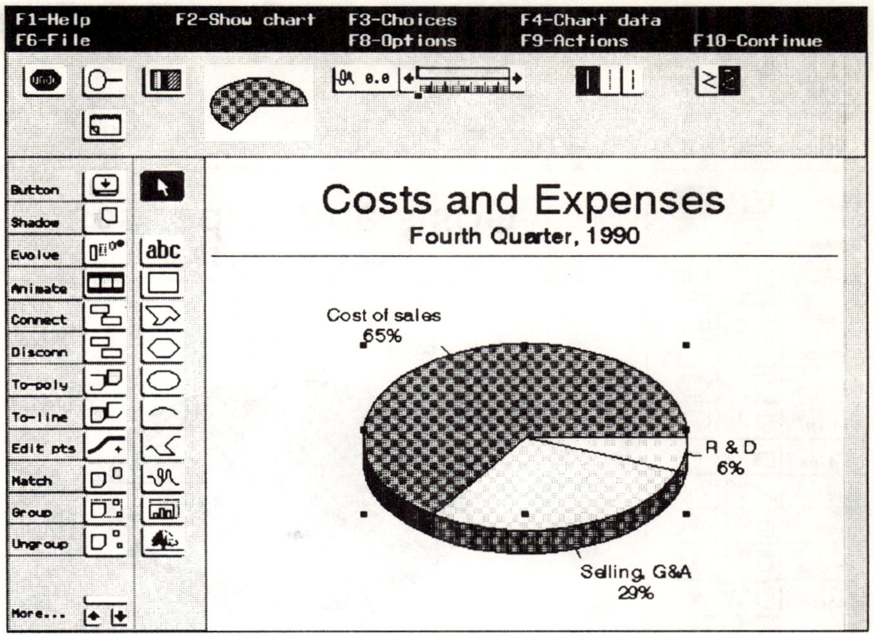

15-17 The Cost of Sales slice selected.

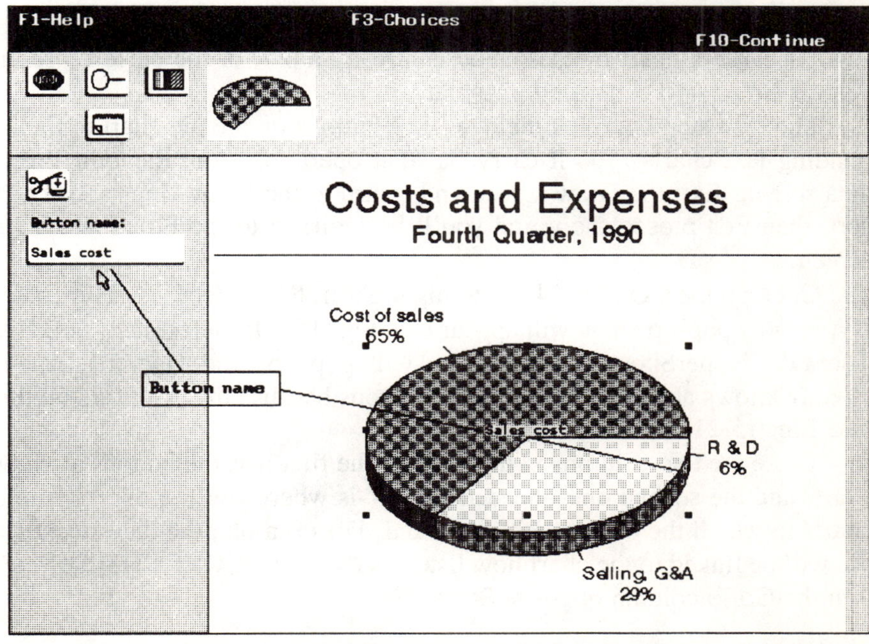

15-18 The Button Name box, with the button name entered in the box and on the slice.

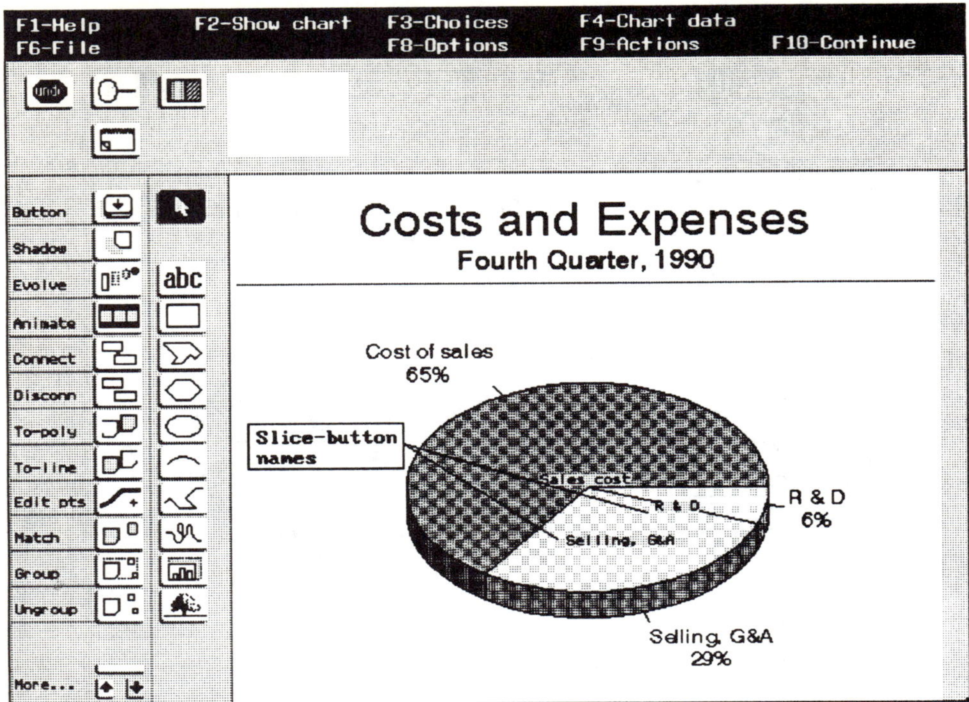

15-19 The pie chart with the three slices named as buttons.

-Q4. Because a chart by that name is already a part of the current presentation, answer No to Add to current presentation.

The next step is to link the new slice buttons on the pie chart to their corresponding text charts. You'll carry out that operation from the Edit Presentation data screen. Exit the Draw screen and return to the Main Menu. Select Presenta tion, then Edit presentation, and you'll be returned to the Edit Presentation data screen.

Click on the COSTS-Q4 file to highlight it, then select F9 – Hypershow. The Hypershow pop-up menu will appear (see Fig. 15-20). Select item 2, Edit buttons. The Edit HyperShow Buttons menu will pop up, and Harvard Graphics 3.0 already knows about those three slice buttons because they're listed on this menu (see Fig. 15-21).

There are two columns in this menu: The first lists the buttons already on the chart, and the second one—headed Go To—is where you'll enter, by number, the charts to which the buttons will be linked. For example, the Sales Cost slice button will be linked to the chart now listed as #9, SALECOST.CH3. So you'll enter 9 in the Go To column opposite Sales cost.

```
CLIXSHOW.SH3                     Edit Presentation
 F1-Help         F2-Preview       F3-Choices      F4-Descriptions F5-Mark block
 F6-Main Menu    F7-Add/Edit      F8-Options      F9-HyperShow    F10-Continue

 #    Filename       Draw     ←↑↓→    Speed   ▸ Edit keys              1  peed
                                                Edit buttons           2
                    Replace                     Set recalculation      3

 1    HIGHLITE.CH3
 2    REVENUES.CH3
 3    INCOME  .CH3
▸4   ·COSTS-Q4.CH3
 5    BACKLOG .CH3
 6    PRDCTVTY.CH3
 7    STOCKS  .CH3
 8    ORGCHART.CH3
 9    SALECOST.CH3
10    R&DCOST .CH3
11    G&ACOST .CH3
12
13
14
15
16
```

15-20 The Hypershow menu.

```
CLIXSHOW.SH3                     Edit Presentation
 F1-Help
                                                               F10-Continue

 #    Filename          Edit HyperShow Buttons   Erase    ←↑↓→    Speed
                         Button         Go To
                   Re
                      ▸Sales cost
 1    HIGHLITE.CH3     Selling, G&A
 2    REVENUES.CH3     R & D
 3    INCOME  .CH3
▸4   ·COSTS-Q4.CH3 ◆
 5    BACKLOG .CH3
 6    PRDCTVTY.CH3
 7    STOCKS  .CH3
 8    ORGCHART.CH3
 9    SALECOST.CH3
10    R&DCOST .CH3
11    G&ACOST .CH3
12
13
14
15
16
```

15-21 The Edit HyperShow Buttons menu with your three slice buttons listed.

1. Opposite Sales cost, type 9 and Enter.
2. Opposite Selling, G&A, type 11 and Enter to link that button to the G&ACOST chart.
3. Opposite R & D, type 10 and Enter to link that button to the R&DCOST

chart. Your Edit HyperShow Buttons menu should now look like Fig. 15-22.

4. Select F10 – Continue.

You can run a test later; however, you should now have solved the first part of your challenge—linking the slices and the corresponding text charts so that you can summon the text charts by clicking on the slice buttons. The second part of your challenge is to create a link that returns you to the original COSTS-Q4 chart from the text charts. To accomplish that, you're going to put a button on each text chart.

Installing buttons on charts

1. Return to the Main Menu and select Draw.
2. Press Ctrl – G to go to the Get Chart directory, and select the text chart named SALECOST.CH3. Display the chart on the Draw screen canvas.
3. At the tool panel, click on Symbol, then Get, then select the Symbol file named BUTTONS1.SY3 (see Fig. 15-23).
4. Click on button #1, then select F10 – Continue. Button 2, with selection handles, will appear on your chart (see Fig. 15-24).
5. Click the right mouse button to bring back the tool panel, then drag the button down to the lower left-hand corner of the chart (see Fig. 15-25).

With the new button still selected, press the PgDn key to bring up the second group of Draw tools. Click on the Button icon. Then click in the button name box, type costs-q4 and Enter, and the name will be superimposed on your new button.

```
CLIXSHOW.SH3                    Edit Presentation
 F1-Help
                                                          F10-Continue

 #  | Filename      |   | Edit HyperShow Buttons |Erase | ←↑↓→ | Speed
    |               |Re |  Button        Go To   |      |      |
 1  | HIGHLITE.CH3  |   |▸Sales cost      9      |      |      |
 2  | REVENUES.CH3  |   | Selling, G&A    11     |      |      |
 3  | INCOME  .CH3  |   | R & D           10     |      |      |
▸4  |·COSTS-Q4.CH3  |◆  |                        |      |      |
 5  | BACKLOG .CH3  |   |                        |      |      |
 6  | PRDCTVTY.CH3  |   |                        |      |      |
 7  | STOCKS  .CH3  |   |                        |      |      |
 8  | ORGCHART.CH3  |   |                        |      |      |
 9  | SALECOST.CH3  |   |                        |      |      |
 10 | R&DCOST .CH3  |   |                        |      |      |
 11 | G&ACOST .CH3  |   |                        |      |      |
 12 |               |   |                        |      |      |
 13 |               |   |                        |      |      |
 14 |               |   |                        |      |      |
 15 |               |   |                        |      |      |
 16 |               |   |                        |      |      |
```

15-22 Your Edit HyperShow Buttons menu with all the links entered.

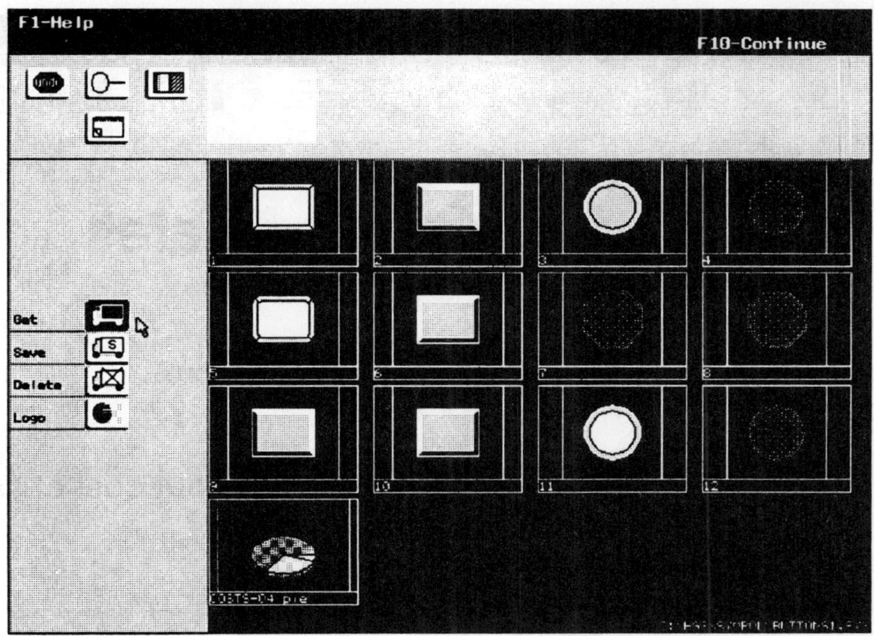

15-23 The BUTTONS1 assortment again.

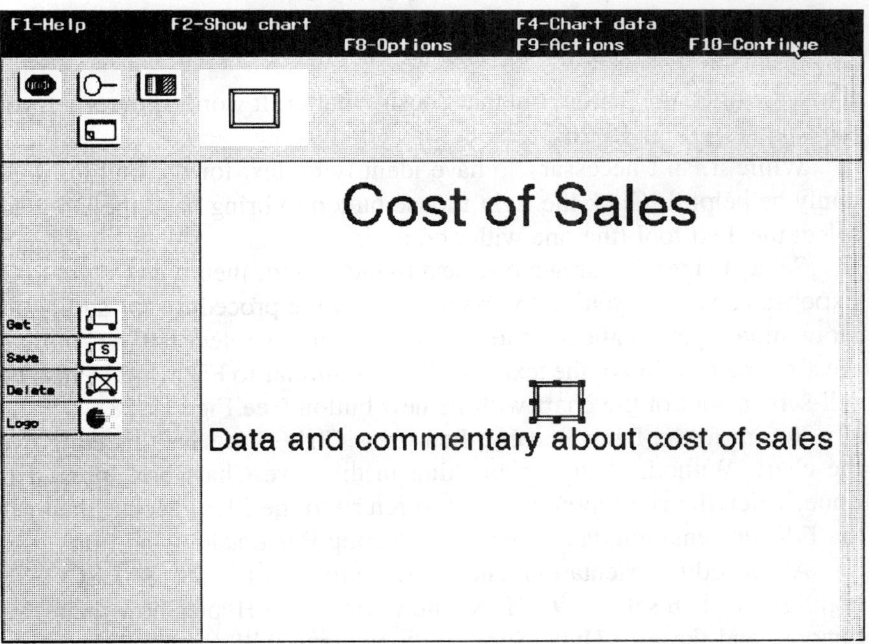

15-24 Button #1 in the middle of your text chart.

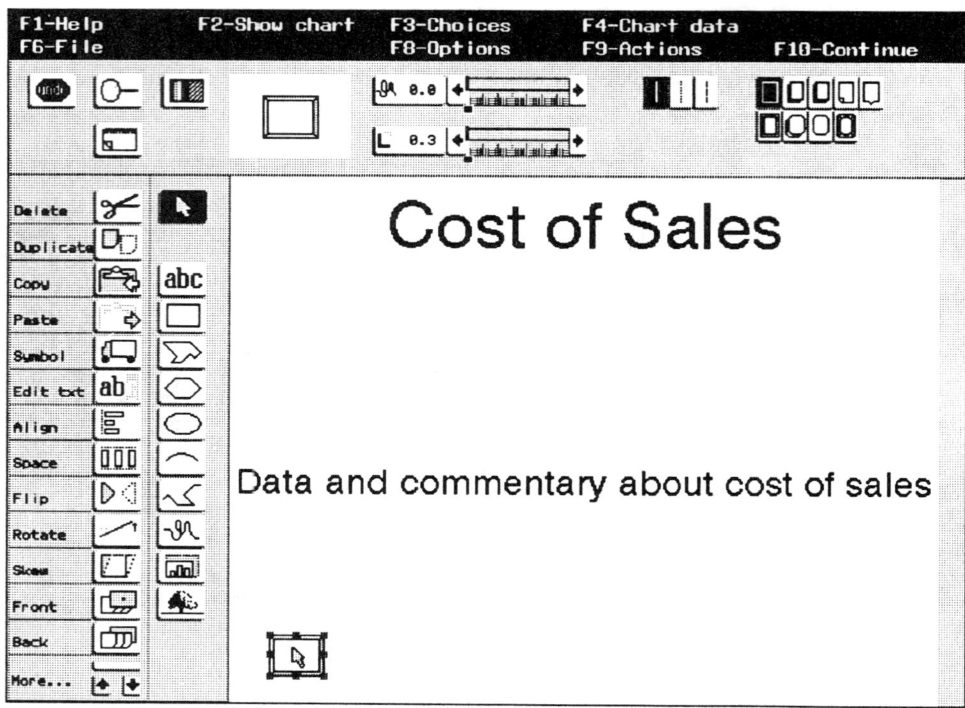

15-25 The new button in position on the Cost of Sales chart.

It's bigger than the button, but that doesn't matter. It won't show when you display the chart (see Fig. 15-26).

While it isn't necessary to have identifying text for the button, it could certainly be helpful. Click the right mouse button to bring back the Draw tools, and select the Text tool (the one with abc on it).

Set text size at 3, drag a box next to the button, then type Return to Costs and Expenses chart. (If you've forgotten some of the procedure for adding text in the Draw mode, you might want to review chapter 4.) Select F10—Continue. Adjust the size and position of the text until it looks similar to Fig. 15-27 Press F2 to get a full-screen shot of the chart with its new button (see Fig. 15-28).

Return to the Draw screen, then press Ctrl—S to save this edited version of the chart. Without changing anything in the Save Chart box, press F10—Continue. Click the right mouse button to return to the Main Menu, then get back to the Edit Presentation data screen by selecting Presentation and Edit presentation.

At the Edit Presentation data screen, click on file #9, SALECOST.CH3, to highlight it, then select F9—Hypershow. From the HyperShow menu, select Edit buttons, and the Edit HyperShow Buttons menu will display the costs-q4 button waiting to be linked (see Fig. 15-29).

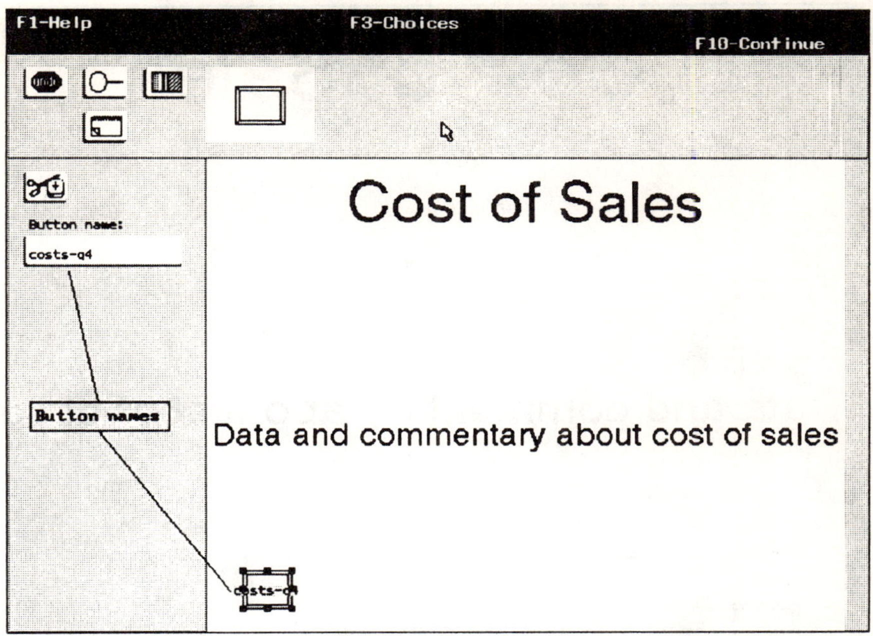

15-26 The new button with its new name.

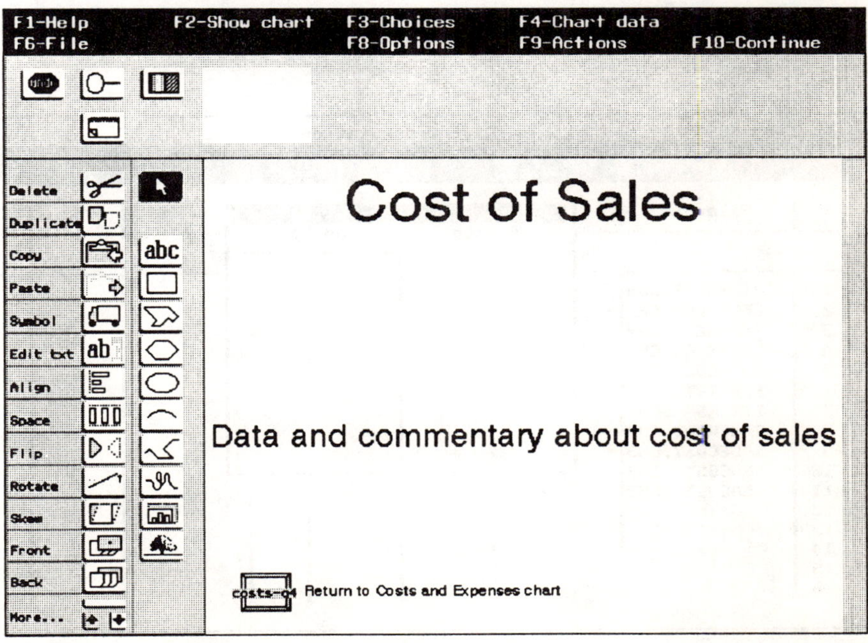

15-27 The identifying text for the HyperShow button.

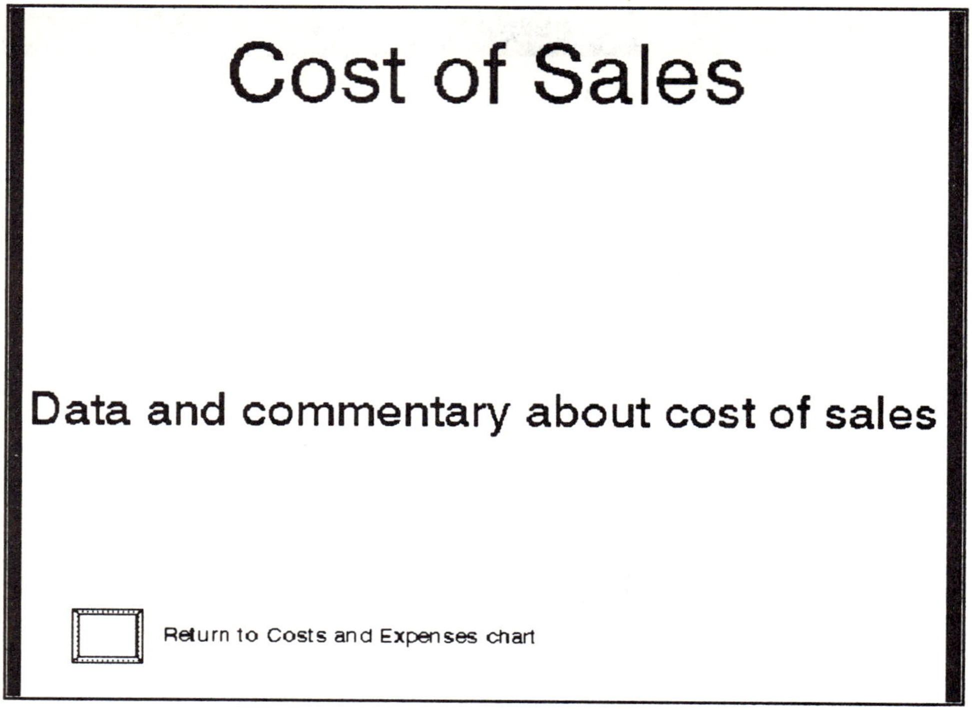

Cost of Sales

Data and commentary about cost of sales

Return to Costs and Expenses chart

15-28 A full-screen view of the chart and its new button.

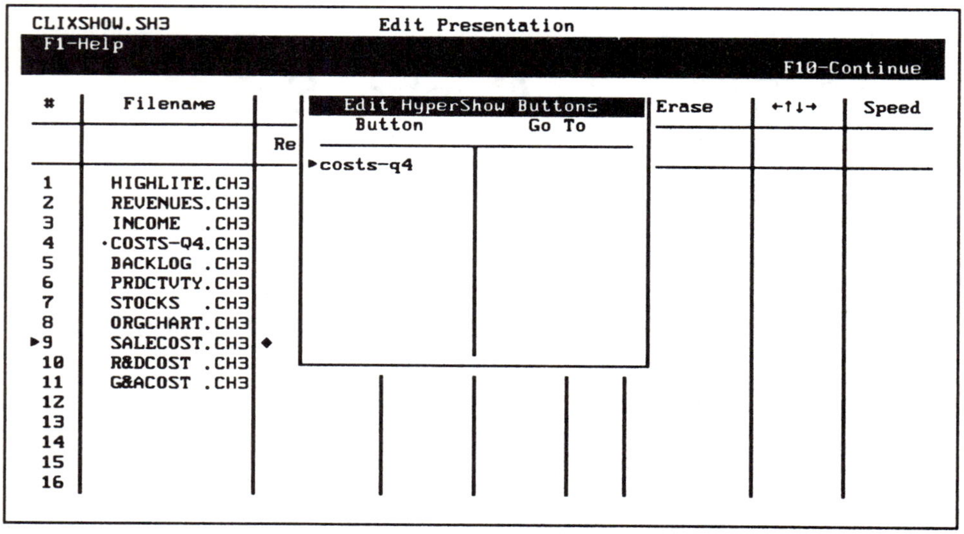

```
CLIXSHOW.SH3                    Edit Presentation
F1-Help
                                                          F10-Continue

 #  | Filename      |   | Edit HyperShow Buttons |  Erase | ←↑↓→ | Speed
                    |Re | Button         Go To   |
                        |▸costs-q4               |
 1  | HIGHLITE.CH3  |
 2  | REVENUES.CH3  |
 3  | INCOME  .CH3  |
 4  |·COSTS-Q4.CH3  |
 5  | BACKLOG .CH3  |
 6  | PRDCTVTY.CH3  |
 7  | STOCKS  .CH3  |
 8  | ORGCHART.CH3  |
▸9  | SALECOST.CH3  | ◆
 10 | R&DCOST .CH3  |
 11 | G&ACOST .CH3  |
 12 |
 13 |
 14 |
 15 |
 16 |
```

15-29 The Edit HyperShow Buttons menu displays the costs-q4 button, ready to be linked.

Opposite costs-q4, type 4 to link this chart back to the COSTS-Q4.CH3 chart. Select F10 – Continue to complete the procedure. (Notice that a bullet denoting the presence of linked buttons now appears in front of the SALE COST.CH3 chart as it already had in front of the COSTS-Q4.CH3 chart.)

You should be finished. To check out your results, click on the first chart to highlight it, then select F2 – Preview. The first chart will appear, then be replaced by the succeeding chart after five seconds. When you get to the fourth chart, Costs and Expenses, click on the Cost of Sales slice to move to the Cost of Sales chart. Then click on the button on the Cost of Sales chart to return to the Costs and Expenses chart. Like magic, ain't it?

Congratulations! You've just mastered a technique, made possible by Harvard Graphics 3.0, that is revolutionizing the interactive capabilities of many new software applications. You can expect that, in a new release that will be coming along not too far down the road, Harvard Graphics will make it possible for you to create a button in a chart or drawing that will take you into another medium—such as stereo sound or video. For now, however, you have a tool for creating powerful, versatile presentations over which you have virtually total control.

16 CHAPTER

Advanced work with symbols and templates

It's customary for a company or organization to develop, or even acquire overnight, a distinctive look and style. Corporations pay huge sums for the design of corporate identities, which are spelled out in thick books of specifications. Logos, typefaces, colors, and corporate symbols and artwork are all specified in the most minute detail. Every visible manifestation of the organization, from the letterhead on the stationery to the signs on the restroom doors, must appear in strict accordance with the rules in that corporate identity book.

Consequently, charts, graphs, and presentations that you prepare for audiences inside and outside the organization are likely to have a standard "look and feel," as they say. Even if yours is a solo operation, you are likely to develop a visual style that identifies you or that you are comfortable with. Charts and presentations that you create will have the same look. You'll probably settle on a palette, font, bullet style, and line width that you use in almost every chart. You might also want to include your logo and possibly some identifying symbol on most or all of the slides you show.

In short, there is probably going to be a significant amount of duplication in your graphics, and the challenge is to automate the duplicated portions of your charts so that you don't have to go through the same batch of keystrokes and mouse maneuvers every time. How do you meet that challenge and jack up your productivity? The answer is templates.

A *template* is a set of chart specifications that you can save and call up every time you want to create a new chart. Elements of a template can be text attributes (size, color, font style, etc.), chart orientation and proportions, color palette, background drawing, frame style, outline and fill colors, bullet type and size, and more. You can also save symbols and drawings as part of a template. When you've entered all of the specifications and then save the chart as a template, you can then use that template over and over as you design subsequent charts.

Let's get down to specifics—you're going to create a template for all text charts that are to be part of presentations on behalf of your company, Gothic Transport Ltd. The charts will all have the same text attributes, bullet styles, etc. (which you'll specify presently), and in addition they will all have an identifying logo/symbol which you will forge from a symbol in the symbol library and some text.

Using a symbol to create a logo

You'll need to put that logo together first. Because you've already worked with symbols and text on the Draw screen, it shouldn't be necessary to walk through this procedure step by minute step. Here's a rough outline:

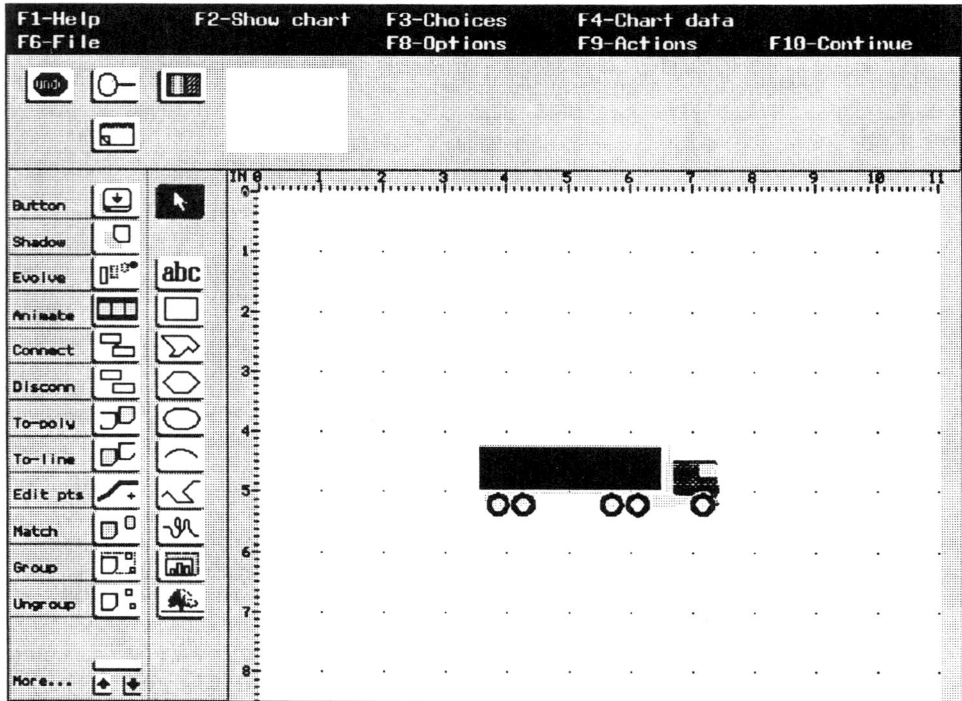

16-1 The Semi 1 symbol.

From the Main Menu, go to the Draw screen. Go to the symbol file named TRANSPT2.SY3, and retrieve the symbol named Semi 1, as shown in Fig. 16-1. (Feel free to do whatever fiddling you want to do with the colors in the truck.) Move the truck to the lower right-hand corner of your canvas, and size it down a bit. Use the text tool to create a text block that says Gothic Transport Ltd. Select the HG Gothic font (what else?), bold style, and size it to correspond to the size of the truck. Position the text in the lower left-hand corner, something like Fig. 16-2.

Add some streamlines to connect the text and the truck, select everything, convert it into a single group, and save the new group as a symbol named GOTHIC LOGO in the TRANSPT2 file. The full-screen version should look like Fig. 16-3.

Creating a background drawing

You can now consider this blank screen with the logo at the bottom as the standard background drawing for the template you're creating. Before you go further, however, you need to specify the area of the canvas where any chart will appear. If a chart is superimposed on the logo, the whole thing will get muddied up.

Select the Canvas tool. The tool will be highlighted, and the colors reversed on the drawing area (see Fig. 16-4). You're now going to define the area of the

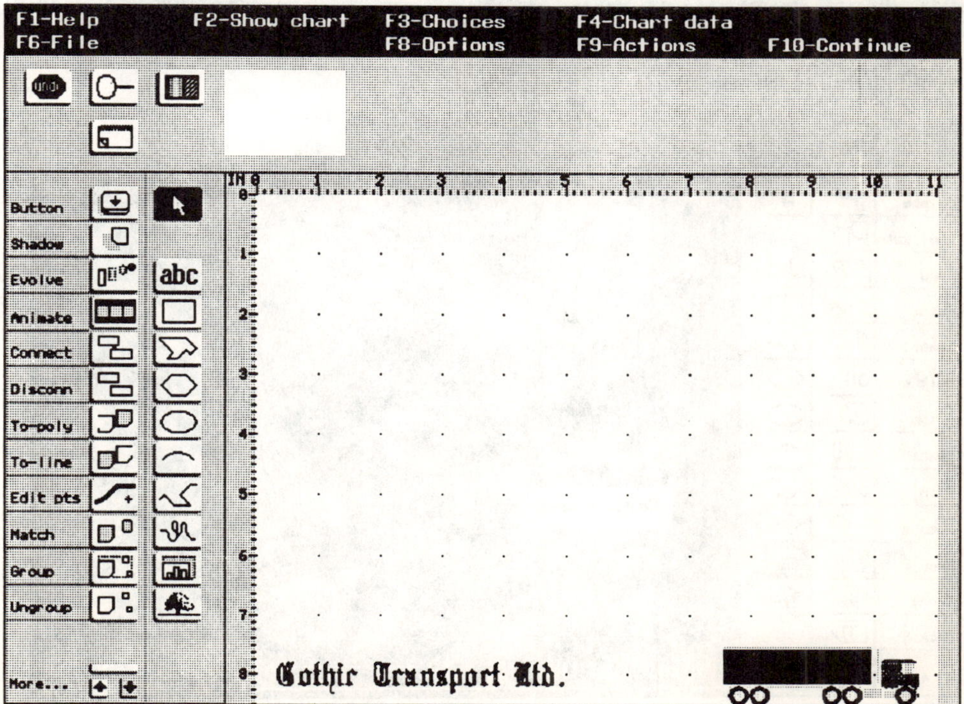

16-2 The logotext in the lower left-hand corner.

16-3 The full-screen version of your new logo.

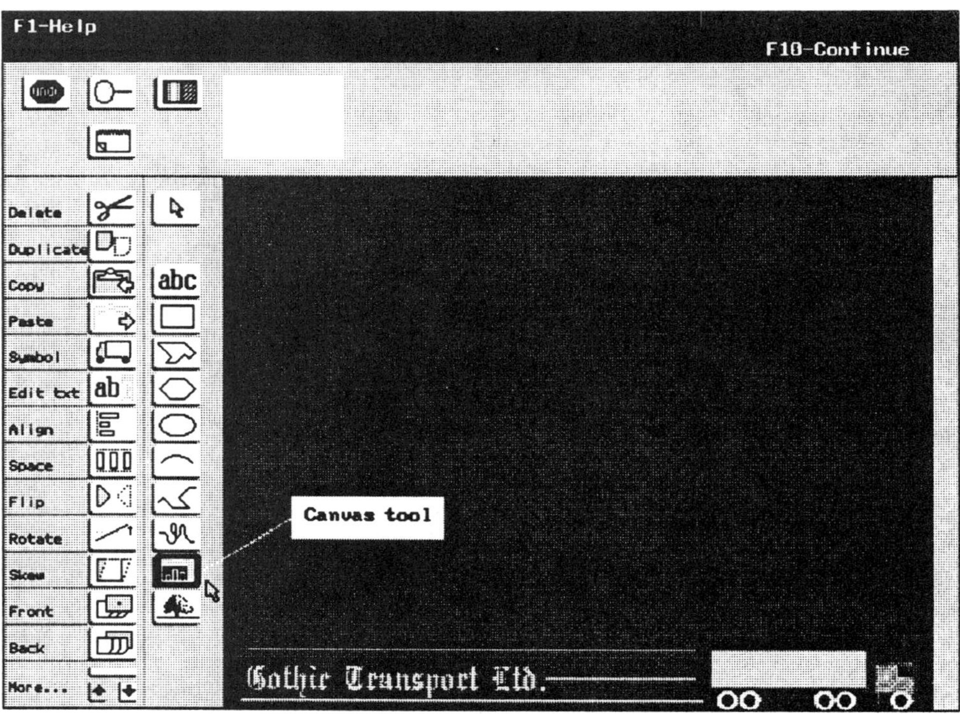

16-4 The drawing area in reversed colors with the Canvas tool selected.

canvas where charts will appear—in this case, the entire area above the logo at the bottom of the screen. Move the crosshair to the upper left-hand corner of the screen and press the left mouse button. Move the pointer diagonally down and to the right until the canvas area is defined above the Gothic Transport logo. Click the left mouse button again, and your screen will look like Fig. 16-5.

You now need to save this background drawing; it will shortly become part of the template you're concocting. Save this drawing as GOTHLOGO.

Creating a template

1. Clear the drawing screen and return to the Main Menu.
2. Select Create chart, then Text, then Bullet. The Bullet Chart data screen will appear (see Fig. 16-6).
3. Opposite Title, type This Is the Title and Enter.
4. For the subtitle, type This is the subtitle and Enter.
5. For the footnote, type This is the footnote and Enter.
6. You're getting the idea. Opposite the first bullet, type First bulleted item and two Enters.
7. Opposite the second bullet, type Second bulleted item.

16-5 The canvas defined above the logo.

```
                              Bullet Chart
 F1-Help        F2-Show chart                F4-Draw        F5-Mark
 F6-Main Menu   F7-Spell/Text   F8-Options   F9-Edit bullet F10-Continue

Title:
Subtitle:
Footnote:
________________________________________________________________________
```

16-6 The Bullet Chart data screen.

That's enough of that silliness. The Bullet Chart data screen should now look like Fig. 16-7. Press F2 to verify that your chart looks all right so far (see Fig. 16-8). Click the right mouse button to return to the data screen.

To create the template for your Gothic Transport charts, proceed to the Options menu. Press F8 – Options, then select Text attributes, item 2. Leave the text sizes the same. Do what you want with the colors; perhaps they should be black, blue, and blood red. Alignment is OK. For font name, select (of course!) HG Gothic5 all the way down. When you select Gothic, you'll notice that Font Style will change to Bold, which is fine. (It's got to be; you don't have a choice.) When you're finished, the Text Attributes menu will resemble Fig. 16-9.

Click the right mouse button, then select F8 – Options to retrieve the Options menu. This time click on Appearance, item 3. On this menu, enter the name of the background drawing you created earlier, including the path: C:\HG3\DATA\GOTHLOGO.CH3. Change the region frame style to None across the board. Make your own choices for the frame fill color. The completed Appearance Options menu will look something like Fig. 16-10.

Return to the Bullet Chart data screen, then select the Options menu one more time. There's one more item you need to deal with: bullet options. Select item 5 and change the bullet type to the square solid bullet, bullet size to Large, and bullet color to Black. The completed Bullet Options menu will look like Fig. 16-11. That does it. Your Gothic Transport template is now fully specified; all you have to do is save it for future use.

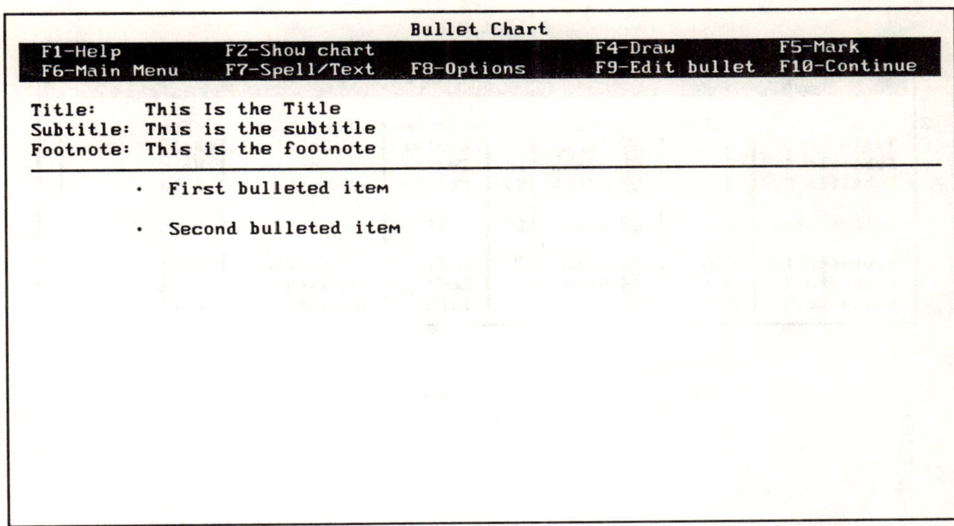

16-7 The Bullet Chart data screen with sample text entered.

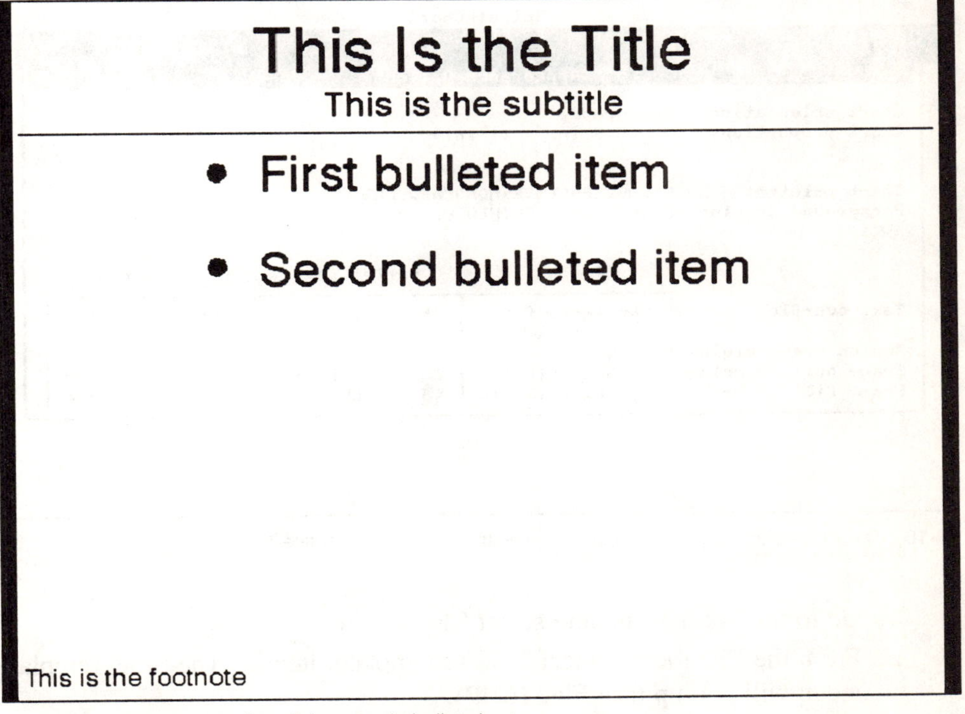

16-8 The full-screen version of the sample bullet chart.

Bullet Chart

F1-Help F2-Show chart F3-Choices F10-Continue

Text Attributes

	Size	Color	Alignment	Font Name	Font Style
Title	9	Black ¦Ti	Center	HG Gothic	◆Bold
Subtitle 1	5	Black ¦Su	Center	HG Gothic	Bold
Subtitle 2	5	Black ¦Su	Center	HG Gothic	Bold
Bullet text	7	Black ¦Te	Left	HG Gothic	Bold
Footnote 1	3.5	Black ¦Fo	Left	HG Gothic	Bold
Footnote 2	3.5	Black ¦Fo	Left	HG Gothic	Bold
Footnote 3	3.5	Black ¦Fo	Left	HG Gothic	Bold

16-9 The Text Attributes menu with settings for the Gothic Transport template.

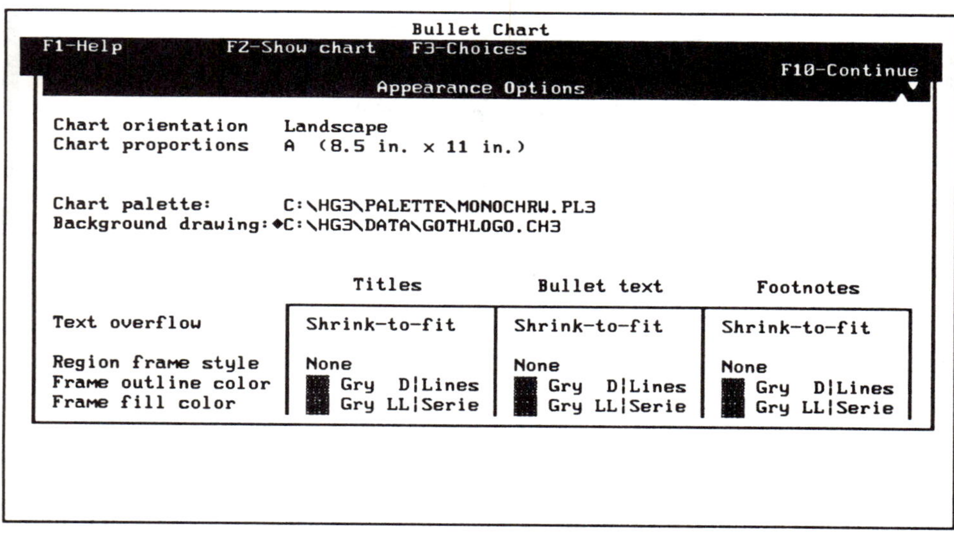

16-10 The Appearance Options menu for the Gothic Transport template.

1. Go to the Main Menu and select File, item 4.
2. From the File menu, select Save as template, item 5. The Save Template menu will pop up (see Fig. 16-12).
3. For the filename, type gothtext and Enter.
4. For the description, type Gothic Transport bullet template and Enter.

```
                          Bullet Chart
 F1-Help       F2-Show chart  F3-Choices
                                                   F10-Continue
                          Bullet Options
Title:     This Is
Subtitle:  This is  Bullet type                ■
Footnote:  This is
                    Bullet size                Large
      •  First      Bullet color               ◆█ Black |Frame

      •  Secon      Numbered bullet start      1

                    Bullet indent
                    Text indent                3
                    Vertical alignment         Top
```

16-11 The completed Bullet Options menu.

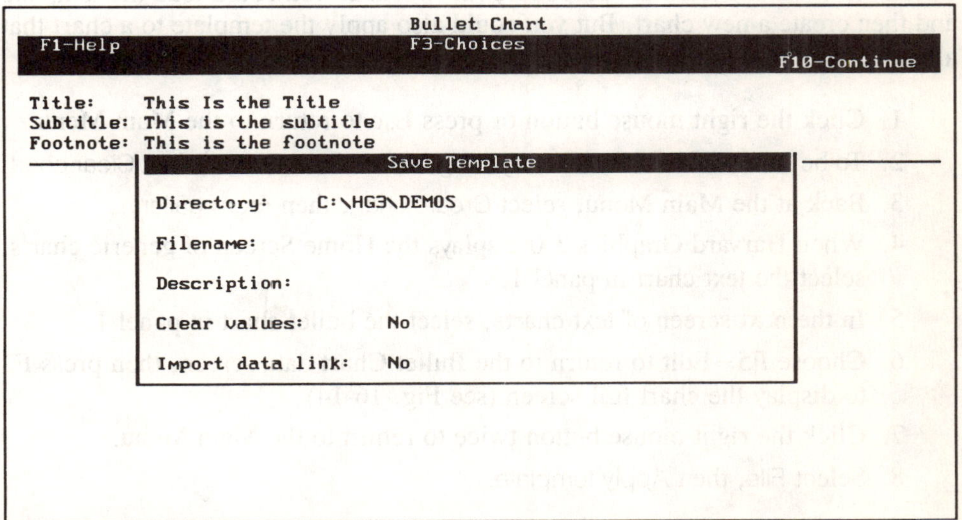

16-12 The Save Template menu.

5. For Clear values, press the space bar to change the setting to Yes. Your Save Template menu now looks like Fig. 16-13.
6. Press F10 – Continue to finish saving the template, then press F10 again to confirm that your data have not been saved. You'll be returned to a blank Bullet Chart data screen.

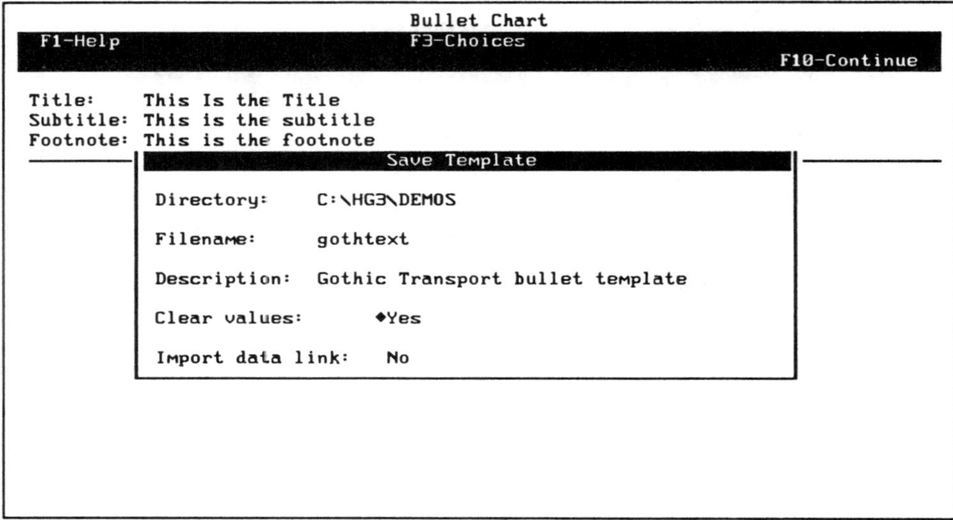

16-13 The completed Save Template menu.

Let's find out if the template procedure has worked. You could load the template and then create a new chart. But you could also apply the template to a chart that already exists. Go to the Chart Gallery in order to do this.

1. Click the right mouse button or press Esc to return to the Main Menu.
2. To be sure you've cleared everything, select Create chart, then Clear chart.
3. Back at the Main Menu, select Create chart, then From gallery.
4. When Harvard Graphics 3.0 displays the Home Screen of generic charts, select the text chart in panel 1.
5. In the next screen of text charts, select the bullet chart in panel 1.
6. Choose F5—Edit to return to the Bullet Chart data screen, then press F2 to display the chart full-screen (see Fig. 16-14).
7. Click the right mouse button twice to return to the Main Menu.
8. Select File, then Apply template.

When the Apply Template menu appears, select the template you just created (GOTHTEXT.TLP3). You will be returned to the Bullet Chart data screen, and it looks the same. But is it really the same? Select F2—Show chart, and, lo and behold, that generic bullet chart has gone Gothic (see Fig. 16-15).

You've just mastered a powerful tool. With templates, you can improve productivity and give your presentations a consistent, professional look. Stay tuned for yet another productivity tool—the macro.

Bullet Chart

- Use short phrases
- Not too many of them
- Break up into two slides
- Use pictures

16-14 The generic bullet chart from the Gallery.

Bullet Chart

- Use short phrases
- Not too many of them
- Break up into two slides
- Use pictures

Gothic Transport Ltd.

16-15 The Gothic Transport template applied to the generic bullet chart.

17 CHAPTER

Increasing your productivity with macros

People are always looking for ways to save time and energy. The promise of computers has always been that they would allow us to do more work in less time. Too often, however, the reality has been that we simply do more work. The boss buys a terrific presentation software package called Harvard Graphics 3.0 and then fires the designer, which means that you now have to design the charts as well as gather the data. If that's the case, you need to know every available trick to increase your productivity—to turn out more work per hour or day or week.

The template you created in chapter 16 is a great labor-saving device. It acknowledges the fact that, at Gothic Transport Ltd. (where your main business is probably shipping werewolf coffins, black satin capes, things like that), you need to create charts over and over in the same basic format. You created a template, therefore, that has all of the parameters of that basic format built in, and when you're ready to create a new chart you simply go get that template.

In this chapter we're going to go even one step further. In the process of learning what macros are and how they are created and used, you're going to automate the process of calling up that Gothic Transport text chart template. You're even going to go a couple of steps beyond that; because many of the charts you generate have identical titles and subtitles, you're going to build those text items into your macro.

A macro is a small—or not so small—program that allows you to record a great many keystrokes or commands, then recall them in the same sequence with a mere handful of keystrokes (sometimes as few as one). A macro is something like a batch file, if you've ever created a batch file in DOS. If you repeat certain procedures frequently, and those procedures involve a fair number of keystrokes, program them into a macro.

First of all, a cautionary remark: macros don't follow mouse movements, so you'll have to do everything from the keyboard. Whenever you're creating a macro, forget about pointing and clicking. Use only keyboard commands, just as you're going to do in the example below.

1. At the Main Menu, press 7 for Macros. You'll be offered three choices: Select macro file, Run macro, and Record macro (see Fig. 17-1).
2. Press 3 for Record macro. The Start Recording menu will pop up, asking for a Filename, a macro name, and the designation of a speed key, i.e., any letter or number that will be used in combination with the Alt key. (The designation of a speed key is optional.)
3. Opposite Filename, type macros and press Enter.
4. For Macro name, type template and then press Enter.
5. For Speed key, type 1 and press Enter.

You'll be returned to the Main Menu and, at the upper left-hand corner of the screen, it will now say Recording. Every keystroke you make from now on will be recorded as part of this macro. Macros should always be run from the same point

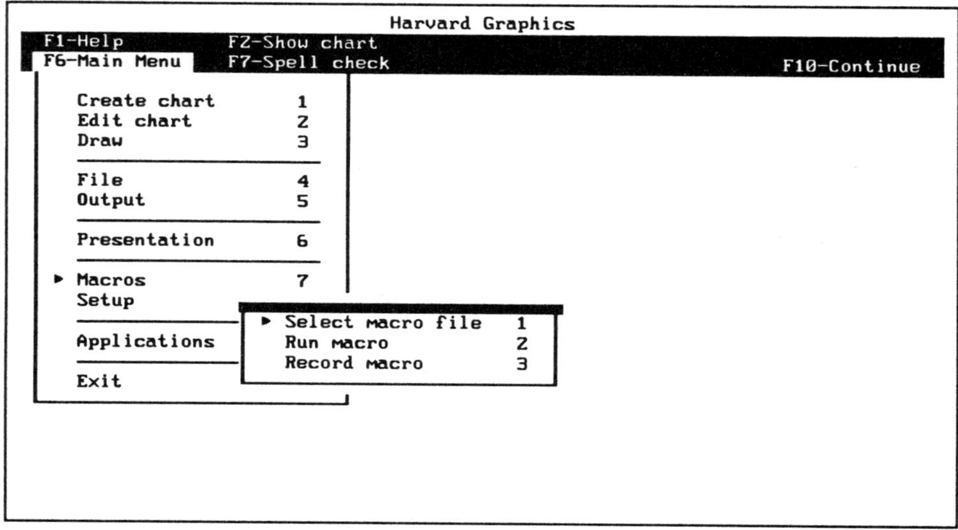

17-1 The Macros pop-up menu.

in the program. The Main Menu is a good starting point for most macros, so:

1. Begin the macro by pressing Esc about six times.
2. Press 4 for File, then 2 for Get template. The Get Template menu will be displayed, with a directory of existing templates (see Fig. 17-2).
3. The cursor should be blinking opposite Filename. Type gothtext.tp3, then press F10 to continue. The Bullet Chart data screen will appear. Assume that you frequently produce a bullet chart headed Marketing Activities, Current Quarter, and that the subtitle is always the company name.
4. Opposite Title, type Marketing Activities, Current Quarter and Enter.
5. Opposite Subtitle, type Gothic Transport Ltd. and Enter. Your Bullet Chart data sheet should now look like Fig. 17-3.
6. Press Alt−0 for the Recording Options menu (see Fig. 17-4).
7. Press the down arrow twice to highlight Stop recording, then press F10 to continue. The Recording message will disappear from the upper left corner.

To see what you've accomplished to this point, press F2. Your Gothic Transport template with title and subtitle should appear on the screen, as shown in Fig. 17-5. Now clear the chart and see if you can get back to Fig. 17-5 with just one keystroke.

Press Esc twice to return to the Main Menu. Select Create chart, then Clear chart. If you get a message saying Your latest changes have not been saved, press F10 to confirm that you know it and you want to proceed anyway. To be sure that

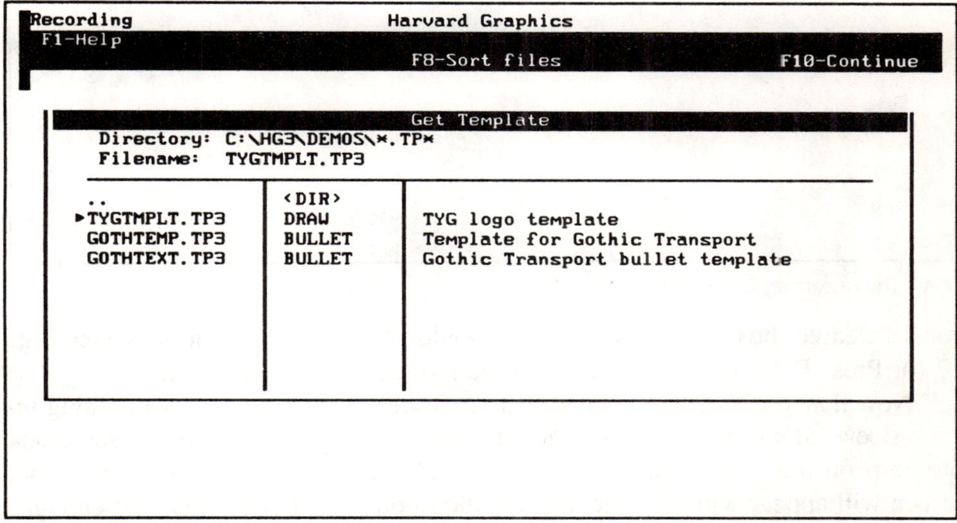

17-2 The Get Template directory.

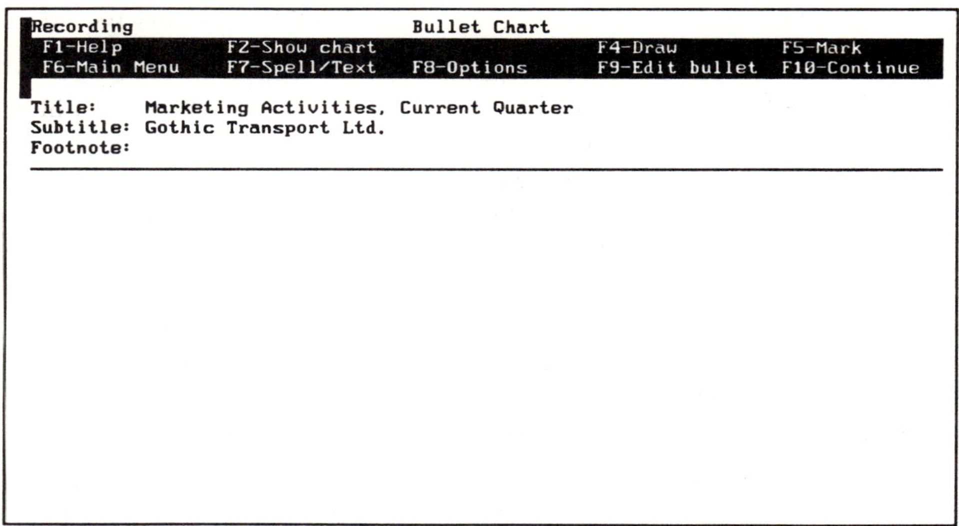

17-3 The Bullet Chart data sheet with title and subtitle entered.

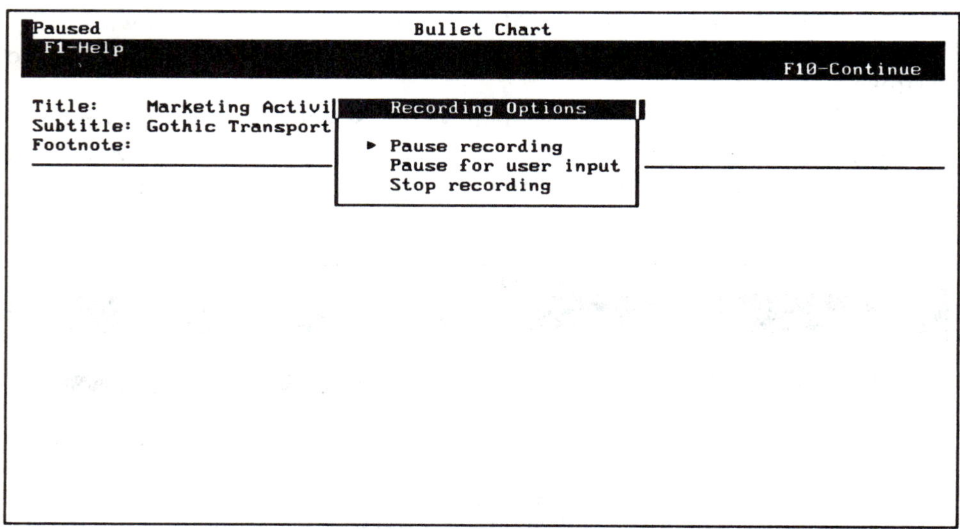

17-4 The Recording Options menu.

you've cleared the chart, press F2. You should get the Problem message (see Fig. 17-6). Press F10–Continue and you'll be returned to the Main Menu.

Now that you've demonstrated that you have no chart loaded and nothing up your sleeve, it's time to test-run the new macro. Press Alt–1. You'll see quick program on the screen for a few milliseconds, and then the Bullet Chart data screen will appear with the title and subtitle in place. Press F2 and sure enough, it's all there, just as in Fig. 17-5.

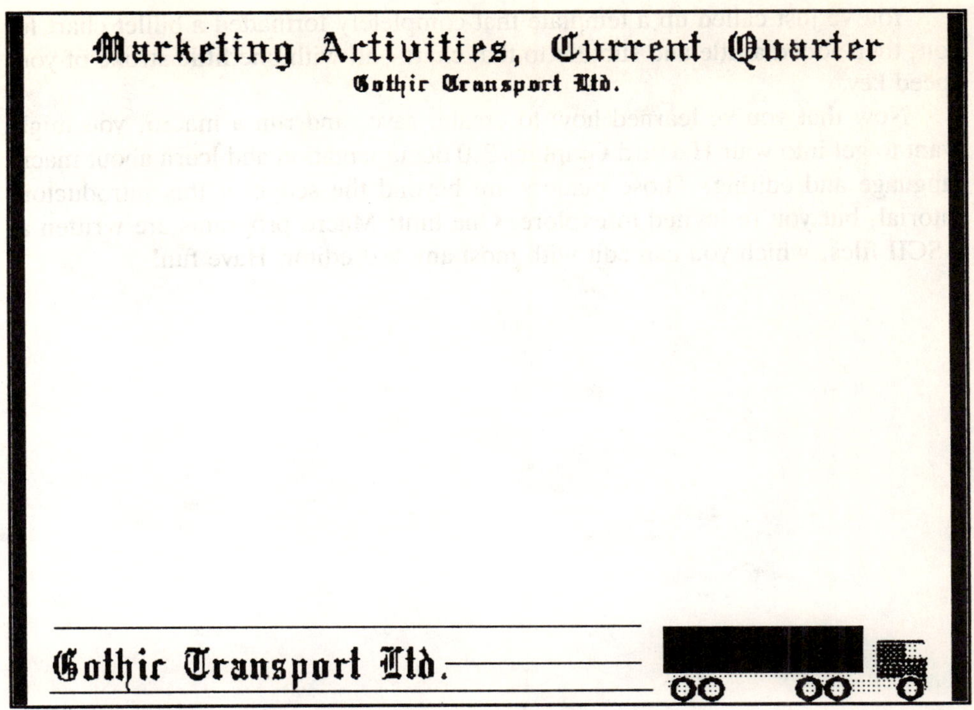

17-5 The basic Gothic Transport template with title and subtitle.

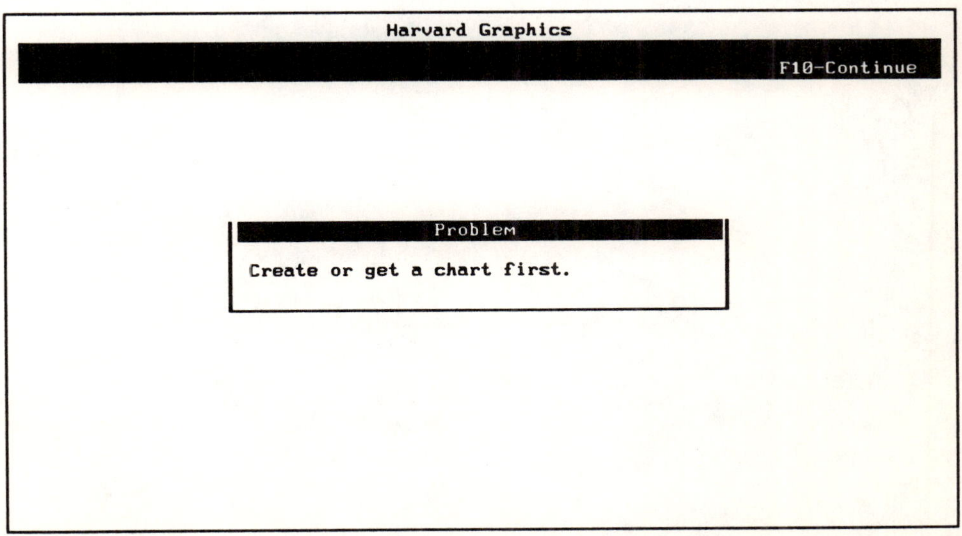

17-6 The Problem message telling you there is no chart available to display.

You've just called up a template that completely formatted a bullet chart for you, then added a title and subtitle to that chart—all with one little stroke of your speed key.

Now that you've learned how to create, save, and run a macro, you might want to get into your Harvard Graphics 3.0 documentation and learn about macro language and editing. Those matters are beyond the scope of this introductory tutorial, but you're invited to explore. One hint: Macro programs are written as ASCII files, which you can edit with most any text editor. Have fun!

18 CHAPTER

Importing spreadsheet data and graphs

Harvard Graphics 3.0 is a program that gives you great versatility. It allows you not only to design and present a wide variety of charts and graphs from scratch (that all-purpose generic ingredient), but also to import data and graphs from other programs and present them with all the modifications and enhancements that Harvard Graphics 3.0 makes possible. The chapter illustrates a few combinations that are available; you can discover many more on your own.

Spreadsheet programs are an obvious source of data and graphs that you might want to work with. Because Lotus 1-2-3 is one of the most widely used spreadsheet programs, I'll have you work through a couple of exercises using Lotus 1-2-3. Note: As of this writing, Harvard Graphics 3.0 works only with files from Lotus 1-2-3 Releases 1.A, 2.0, and 2.2. The folks at Software Publishing Corporation say that the next release of Harvard Graphics 3.0 will support files from later releases of Lotus 1-2-3.

Importing data from Lotus 1-2-3

You can import data in its raw spreadsheet form into Harvard Graphics 3.0 data screens and create new charts, or you can import charts already created with a program such as Lotus 1-2-3, then glamorize those charts with the enhancements provided by Harvard Graphics.

Let's start with spreadsheet data. You're going to take a sample Lotus spreadsheet provided as part of a tutorial with Lotus 1-2-3 Release 2.2. The spreadsheet is the 1989 income statement from a company called Goodwin's Sports Supply (Montreal), filename MONTREAL.WK1. As displayed in Lotus, the spreadsheet looks like Fig. 18-1. (If you don't have this spreadsheet, you can reproduce it on your own version of Lotus 1-2-3.)

Whether you're importing either data or graphs into Harvard Graphics 3.0 from some external source, you must first select a chart type. It doesn't matter if the type you select is not the one you ultimately decide to use; you just need a place to put the data that is coming in, and you can change chart types later.

At the Main Menu, select Create chart; then select XY from the Create Chart submenu. A bar chart is a likely form for an income statement, so select Bar from the XY submenu. The X Data Type menu will appear, superimposed on the XY Chart data screen (see Fig. 18-2). Select F3–Choices and, because you're dealing with a quarterly income statement, click on Quarter. The rest of the information for the X data will come from the Lotus chart, so press F10–Continue.

You now have a data sheet set up to receive the imported data. Select F6–Main Menu, then File, and then Import, item 7. The Import submenu will pop up (see Fig. 18-3). Select Import Lotus data, item 2, and the Select Lotus Worksheet directory will be displayed (see Fig. 18-4). Type in the correct disk drive, directory, and filename; in my case, it's c:\123r2.2\montreal.wk1. Press F10–Continue. You'll now see a new screen, headed Import Lotus Data Into XY Chart (see Fig. 18-5). Let's get familiar, however, and call this the Import Data screen for short.

A1: 'INCOME STATEMENT 1989: Goodwin's Sports Supply (Montreal) READY

	A	B	C	D	E	F
1	INCOME STATEMENT 1989: Goodwin's Sports Supply (Montreal)					
2						
3		Q1	Q2	Q3	Q4	YTD
4	------------	------------	------------	------------	------------	------------
5	Net Sales	$19,500.00	$24,700.00	$19,200.00	$19,700.00	$83,100.00
6	------------	------------	------------	------------	------------	------------
7						
8	Operating Expenses:					
9	Payroll	3,900.00	4,940.00	4,160.00	3,952.00	16,952.00
10	Utilities	2,925.00	3,705.00	3,120.00	2,964.00	12,714.00
11	Rent	1,300.00	1,300.00	1,300.00	1,300.00	5,200.00
12	Ads	1,560.00	1,976.00	1,664.00	1,580.00	6,780.00
13	COG Sold	6,825.00	8,645.00	7,280.00	6,916.00	29,666.00
14	------------	------------	------------	------------	------------	------------
15	Tot Op Exp	16,510.00	20,566.00	17,524.00	16,712.00	71,312.00
16	------------	------------	------------	------------	------------	------------
17	Op Income	$2,990.00	$4,134.00	$1,676.00	$2,988.00	$11,788.00
18						
19						
20						

19-Dec-91 03:40 PM UNDO NUM

18-1 The Lotus worksheet MONTREAL.WK1, as displayed in Lotus 1-2-3 Release 2.2.

```
XY Chart
F1-Help                    F3-Choices
                                                F10-Continue
Title:          X Data Type
Subtitle:
Footnote:       X data type       ♦Name

                Starting with                    4
Data   X Ax     Ending with
Pt     Nam      Increment                 Series 4
1
2
3
4
5
6
7
8
9
10
11
12
```

18-2 The X Data Type menu.

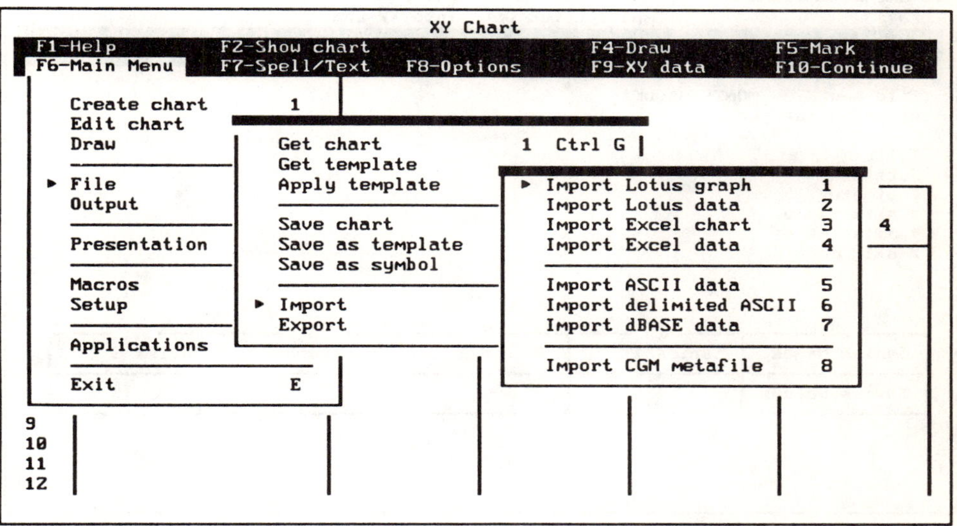

18-3 The Import submenu.

One convenient feature about this screen is that it allows you to move quickly back and forth between it and the spreadsheet, and to mark cells or ranges on the spreadsheet. (Assuming that, because you're interested in this chapter you're familiar with spreadsheet functions and terminology, you won't pause here for a Lotus 1-2-3 tutorial or explanation of terms such as *cells* or *ranges*.)

```
                         Harvard Graphics
 F1-Help
                         F8-Sort files                 F10-Continue

                     Select Lotus Worksheet
     Directory: C:\HG3\IMPORT\*.W*
     Filename:  c:\123r2.2\montreal.wk1

   ..                 <DIR>
  ▸FILMS    .WK1      OTHER
```

18-4 The Select Lotus Worksheet directory with MONTREAL.WK1 typed in as the filename.

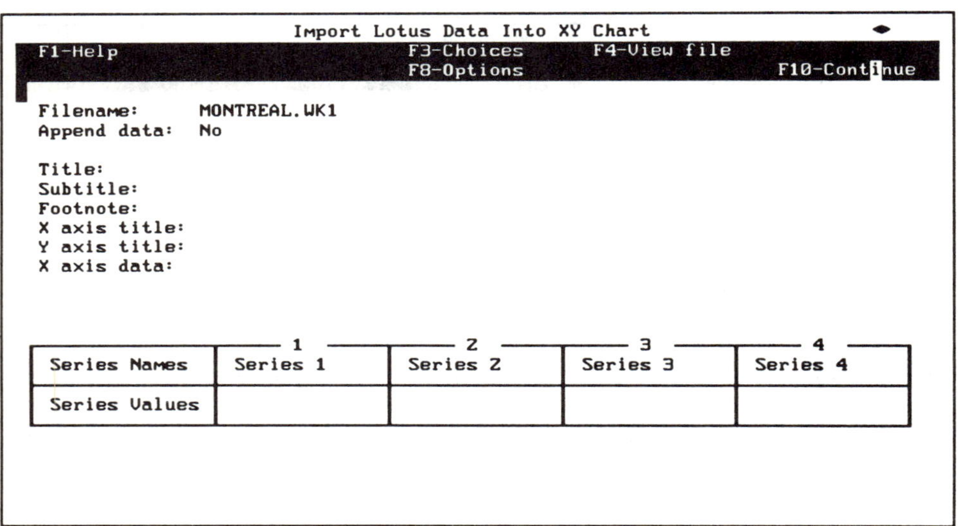

18-5 The Import Lotus Data Into XY Chart screen.

1. The cursor should be blinking opposite Title. Type Net Sales and Operating Income, 1989 and Enter.
2. For the subtitle, type Goodwin's Sports Supply—Montreal and Enter.
3. For the footnote, type Figures in $thousands and Enter.

4. For the X-axis title, type Quarter and Enter.
5. Leave the Y-axis title blank. Press Enter to move on.

For X-axis data, you'll go to the spreadsheet for the first time. Select F4 – View file, and a slightly squeezed version of the spreadsheet will appear on your screen (see Fig. 18-6).

In row 3, you'll see the X-axis data points: Q1 through Q4. (You're not going to include the YTD (year to date) figures in your chart.) Use your mouse or the arrow keys to move the cursor to cell B3. The current location indicator in the upper left-hand corner tells you that you are at cell B3, and the content of the cell is Q1 (see Fig. 18-7).

Press F5 – Mark to mark cell B3; it should now be highlighted. Click on Q4; all four quarters will be highlighted and the current location indicator will read B3..E3: Q4 (see Fig. 18-8). Select F4 – Import form; you'll be returned to the Import Data screen, where the X-axis data is shown to be the range B3..E3 (see Fig. 18-9).

Move down to the table at the bottom of the screen. Click on Series 1 (in the Series Names row) to highlight it, then select F4 – View file again. The name of Series 1 will be Net Sales, which you'll see in cell A5. Click on A5 (left mouse button), then go back to the Import Data form by selecting F4. Series 1 has now been replaced with \A5.

Click on Series 2 in the Series Names row, then jump back to the spreadsheet by pressing F4. Series 2 will represent the operating income, so click on cell A17, which says Op Income. Press F4 again, and Series 2 on the Import Data screen has been replaced by \A17 (see Fig. 18-10).

```
                                View Lotus Worksheet
 F1-Help                                            F4-Import form  F5-Mark
                                                    F9-Jump to      F10-Continue

Current location: A1: INCOME STATEMENT 1989: Goodwin's Sports Supply (Montrea

          A         B         C         D         E         F         G         H
 ►1    INCOME ST
  2
  3             Q1        Q2        Q3        Q4        YTD
  4    --------------------------------------------------------
  5    Net Sales$19,500.0$24,700.0$19,200.0$19,700.0$83,100.0
  6    --------------------------------------------------------
  7
  8    Operating
  9      Payroll3,900.00 4,940.00 4,160.00 3,952.00 16,952.00
 10      Utiliti2,925.00 3,705.00 3,120.00 2,964.00 12,714.00
 11      Rent   1,300.00 1,300.00 1,300.00 1,300.00 5,200.00
 12      Ads    1,560.00 1,976.00 1,664.00 1,580.00 6,780.00
 13      COG Sol6,825.00 8,645.00 7,280.00 6,916.00 29,666.00
 14    --------------------------------------------------------
 15      Tot Op 16,510.0020,566.0017,524.0016,712.0071,312.00
 16    --------------------------------------------------------
 17    Op Income$2,990.00$4,134.00$1,676.00$2,988.00$11,788.0
```

18-6 The View Lotus Worksheet screen.

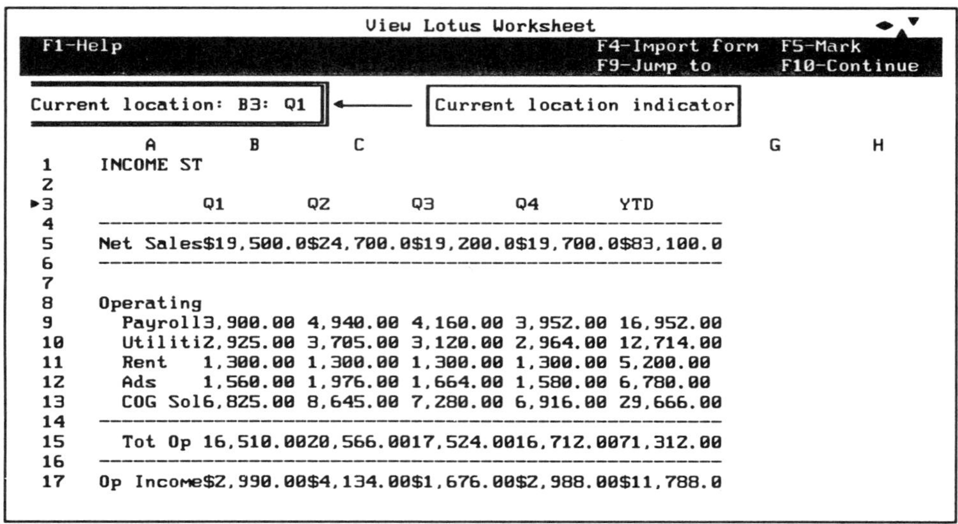

18-7 The current location indicator, showing the cursor at B3, which contains Q1.

```
                          View Lotus Worksheet
 F1-Help                                       F4-Import form  F5-Unmark
                                               F9-Jump to      F10-Continue

Current location: B3..E3: Q4

        A        B        C        D        E        F        G        H
1    INCOME ST
2
►3               Q1       Q2       Q3       Q4       YTD
4    -------------------------------------------------------
5    Net Sales$19,500.0$24,700.0$19,200.0$19,700.0$83,100.0
6    -------------------------------------------------------
7
8    Operating
9      Payroll3,900.00 4,940.00 4,160.00 3,952.00 16,952.00
10     Utiliti2,925.00 3,705.00 3,120.00 2,964.00 12,714.00
11     Rent    1,300.00 1,300.00 1,300.00 1,300.00 5,200.00
12     Ads     1,560.00 1,976.00 1,664.00 1,580.00 6,780.00
13     COG Sol6,825.00 8,645.00 7,280.00 6,916.00 29,666.00
14   -------------------------------------------------------
15     Tot Op 16,510.0020,566.0017,524.0016,712.0071,312.00
16   -------------------------------------------------------
17   Op Income$2,990.00$4,134.00$1,676.00$2,988.00$11,788.0
```

18-8 With all four quarters highlighted, the current location indicator shows the highlighted range (B3...E3) and the cursor location (Q4).

You now need to indicate which ranges of cells contain the values that will be plugged into the two series. In the table at the bottom of the Import Data screen, click on the box opposite Series Values in the Series 1 column, then select F4 – View file to return to the spreadsheet.

The values for four quarters of net sales are found in row 5, in cells B5, C5,

```
                    Import Lotus Data Into XY Chart
 F1-Help                          F3-Choices      F4-View file
                                  F8-Options                    F10-Continue

 Filename:      MONTREAL.WK1
 Append data:   No

 Title:         Net Sales and Operating Income, 1989
 Subtitle:      Goodwin's Sports Supply--Montreal
 Footnote:      Figures in $thousands
 X axis title:  Quarter
 Y axis title:
 X axis data:   B3..E3
```

	1	2	3	4
Series Names	Series 1	Series 2	Series 3	Series 4
Series Values				

18-9 The Import Data screen with B3..E3 entered as X-axis data.

```
                    Import Lotus Data Into XY Chart
 F1-Help                          F3-Choices      F4-View file
                                  F8-Options                    F10-Continue

 Filename:      MONTREAL.WK1
 Append data:   No

 Title:         Net Sales and Operating Income, 1989
 Subtitle:      Goodwin's Sports Supply--Montreal
 Footnote:      Figures in $thousands
 X axis title:  Quarter
 Y axis title:
 X axis data:   B3..E3
```

	1	2	3	4
Series Names	\A5	\A17	Series 3	Series 4
Series Values				

18-10 The headings for Series 1 and 2 have been replaced by cell addresses.

D5, and E5. Click on cell B5. Check the current location indicator to be sure you've selected the right cell (value $19,500.00), then select F5–Mark to designate B5 as the beginning of the range. Press the right arrow three times to highlight cells Q2 through Q4 (or click on Q4), then return to the Import Data screen by pressing F4. The Series Values box for Series 1 will now show the range B5..E5.

Click on the Series Values box in the Series 2 column and return to the spreadsheet. Series 21 is the four quarters of the operating income, so click on B17 and select F5 – Mark. Press the right arrow key three times to highlight cells C17, D17, and E17, then return to the Import Data form by pressing F4. The range B17..E17 will appear as the Series Values for Series 2, and your work on this Import Data form is complete (see Fig. 18-11).

Select F10 – Continue, and you'll jump back to the XY Chart data screen. Et voilà! All the values and headings have been neatly entered (see Fig. 18-12). To verify that you have actually created a chart, press F2, and there it is, as shown in Fig. 18-13). Press Esc to return to the data screen, and save the chart as montreal. Obviously, you can now perform all manner of Harvard Graphics 3.0 legerdemain to glorify this chart; meanwhile, I'll move on to demonstrate the process of importing charts directly.

Importing charts from Lotus 1-2-3

Lotus 1-2-3 is, of course, capable of producing charts. Those charts are limited, however, and simply not capable of all the rococo ornamentation possible with Harvard Graphics 3.0 charts. But don't despair; you can take any of those pristine graphs from Lotus 1-2-3 and turn them into a production that would have gladdened the heart of Louis XV.

Another of the sample files that comes with Release 2.2 of Lotus 1-2-3 has the filename TUTOR10X.WK1. The spreadsheet looks like Fig. 18-14; if you don't have this file and want to reproduce the worksheet, go to it.

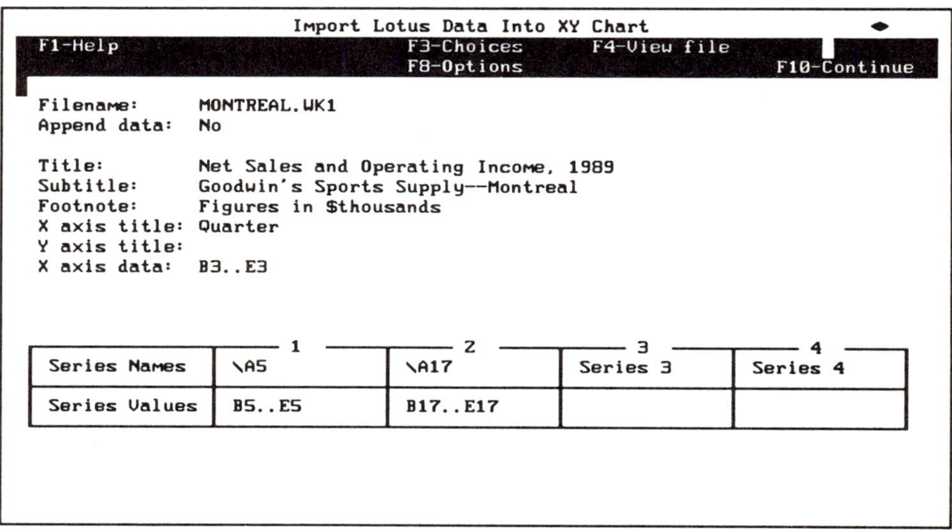

18-11 The completed Import Data form.

XY Chart

F1-Help	F2-Show chart		F4-Draw	F5-Mark
F6-Main Menu	F7-Spell/Text	F8-Options	F9-XY data	F10-Continue

Title: Net Sales and Operating Income, 1989
Subtitle: Goodwin's Sports Supply--Montreal
Footnote: Figures in $thousands

Data Pt	X Axis Quarter	1 Net Sales	2 Op Income	3 Series 3	4 Series 4
1	Q1	19500	2990		
2	Q2	24700	4134		
3	Q3	19200	1676		
4	Q4	19700	2988		
5					
6					
7					
8					
9					
10					
11					
12					

18-12 The XY Chart data screen with all of the spreadsheet values entered.

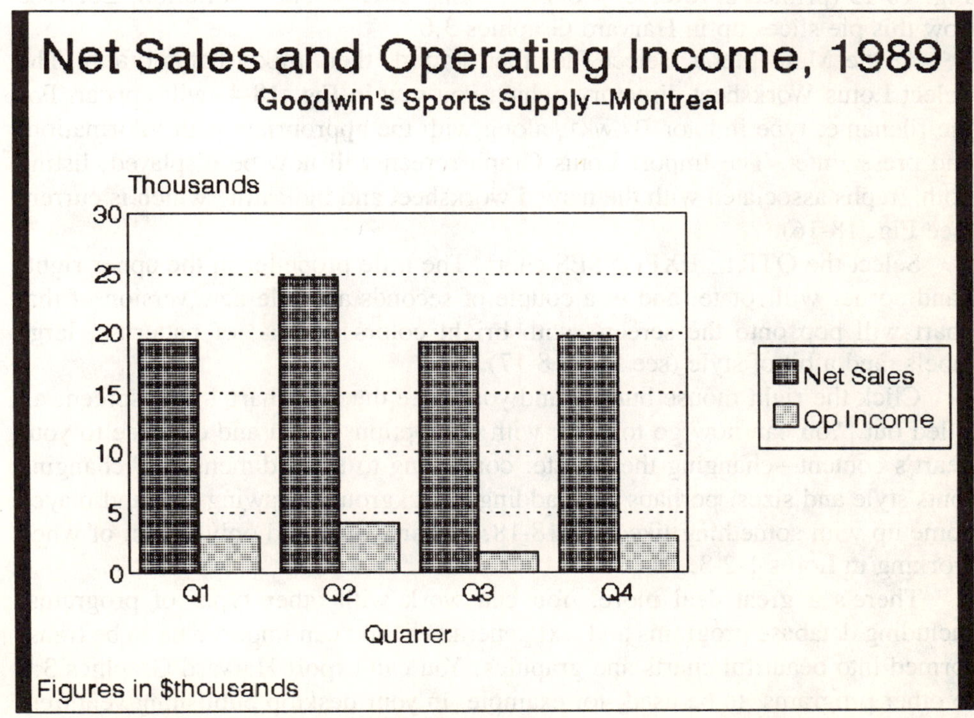

18-13 The bar chart from the Lotus spreadsheet data.

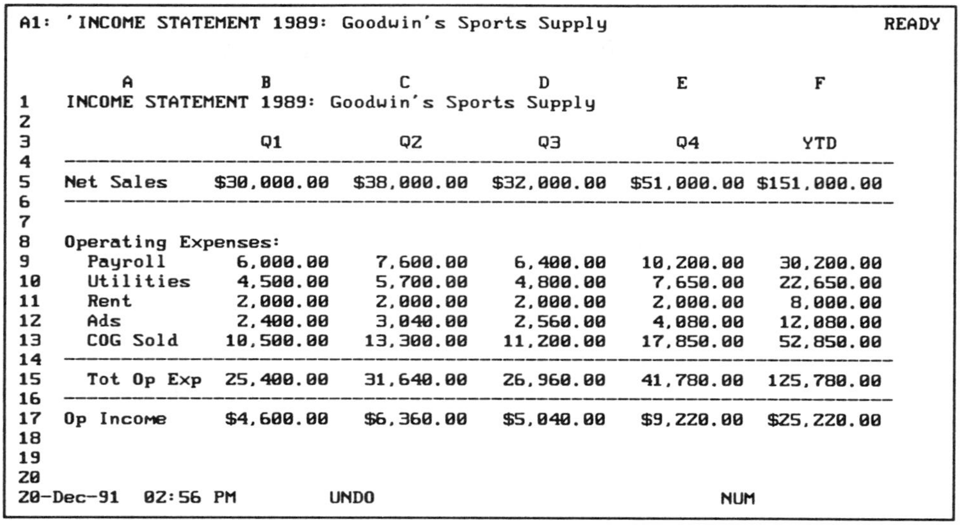

```
A1: 'INCOME STATEMENT 1989: Goodwin's Sports Supply                          READY

         A            B            C            D            E            F
1   INCOME STATEMENT 1989: Goodwin's Sports Supply
2
3                     Q1           Q2           Q3           Q4          YTD
4   --------------------------------------------------------------------------
5   Net Sales    $30,000.00   $38,000.00   $32,000.00   $51,000.00  $151,000.00
6   --------------------------------------------------------------------------
7
8   Operating Expenses:
9     Payroll      6,000.00     7,600.00     6,400.00    10,200.00    30,200.00
10    Utilities    4,500.00     5,700.00     4,800.00     7,650.00    22,650.00
11    Rent         2,000.00     2,000.00     2,000.00     2,000.00     8,000.00
12    Ads          2,400.00     3,040.00     2,560.00     4,080.00    12,080.00
13    COG Sold    10,500.00    13,300.00    11,200.00    17,850.00    52,850.00
14  --------------------------------------------------------------------------
15    Tot Op Exp  25,400.00    31,640.00    26,960.00    41,780.00   125,780.00
16  --------------------------------------------------------------------------
17  Op Income     $4,600.00    $6,360.00    $5,040.00    $9,220.00   $25,220.00
18
19
20
20-Dec-91  02:56 PM          UNDO                          NUM
```

18-14 The spreadsheet named TUTOR10X.WK1 in Lotus 1-2-3.

There are two ready-made graphs that came with TUTOR10X.WK1, 89_EXPENSES and QTR1_EXPENSES. The latter, a five-slice pie, looks like Fig. 18-15 (printed in reverse)—totally lacking in verve and inspiration. Let's see how this pie slices up in Harvard Graphics 3.0.

At the Main Menu, select File, then Import, then Import Lotus graph. The Select Lotus Worksheet directory, which you saw in Fig. 18-4, will appear. For the filename, type in tutor10x.wk1, along with the appropriate path information, and press Enter. The Import Lotus Graph screen will now be displayed, listing both graphs associated with the named worksheet and indicating which is current (see Fig. 18-16).

Select the QTR1_EXPENSES chart. The little propeller in the upper right-hand corner will rotate, and in a couple of seconds a whole new version of that chart will pop onto the screen—with bright colors (instead of patterns), large labels, and a bit of style (see Fig. 18-17).

Click the right mouse button, and you'll see the Pie Chart 1 data screen, all filled out. You can now go to work with the Options menu and enhance to your heart's content—changing the palette, converting to three dimensions, changing fonts style and sizes, perhaps even adding a background drawing . . . and maybe come up with something like Fig. 18-18, a chart you could only dream of when working in Lotus 1-2-3.

There's a great deal more. You can work with other types of programs, including database programs and text generators. You can import data to be transformed into beautiful charts and graphics. You can export Harvard Graphics 3.0 to other programs, to be used, for example, in your desktop publishing ventures. You'll want to experiment with some of these options.

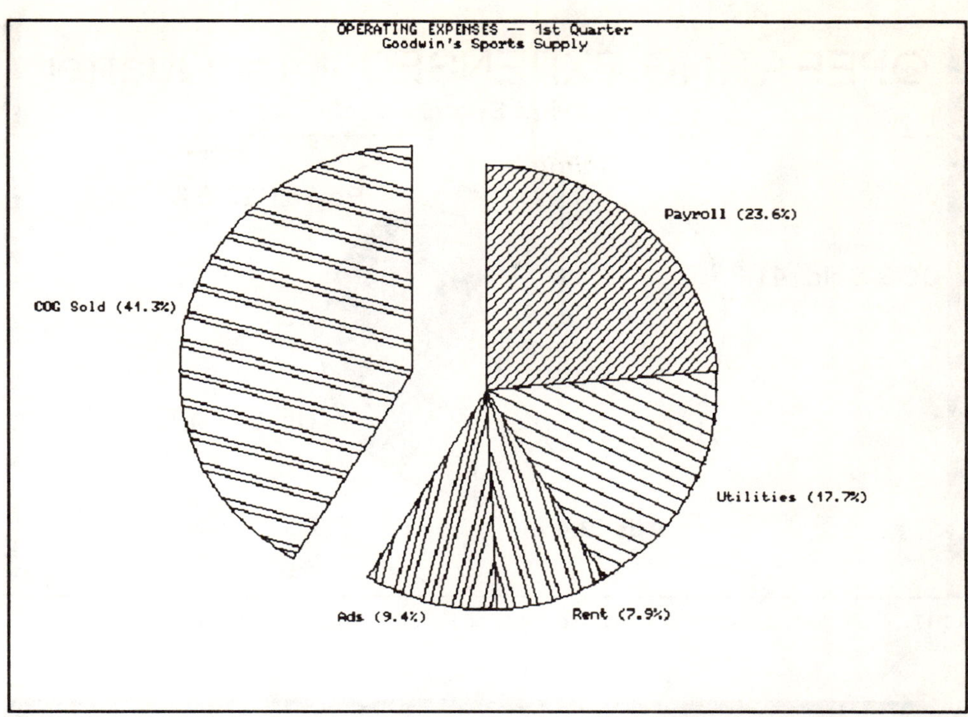

18-15 The QTR1__EXPENSES chart from the Lotus 1-2-3 worksheet TUTOR10X.WK1.

Import Lotus Graph

F1-Help F3-Choices F8-Worksheet F10-Continue

Worksheet: TUTOR10X.WK1
Named graph: CURRENT
Import data only: No

Named Graph	Type	Title
▸CURRENT	PIE	OPERATING EXPENSES -- 1st Quarter / Good
89_EXPENSES	BAR	OPERATING EXPENSES 1989 / Goodwin's Spor
QTR1_EXPENSES	PIE	OPERATING EXPENSES -- 1st Quarter / Good

18-16 The Import Lotus Graph data screen, listing the graphs associated with worksheet TUTOR10X.WK1.

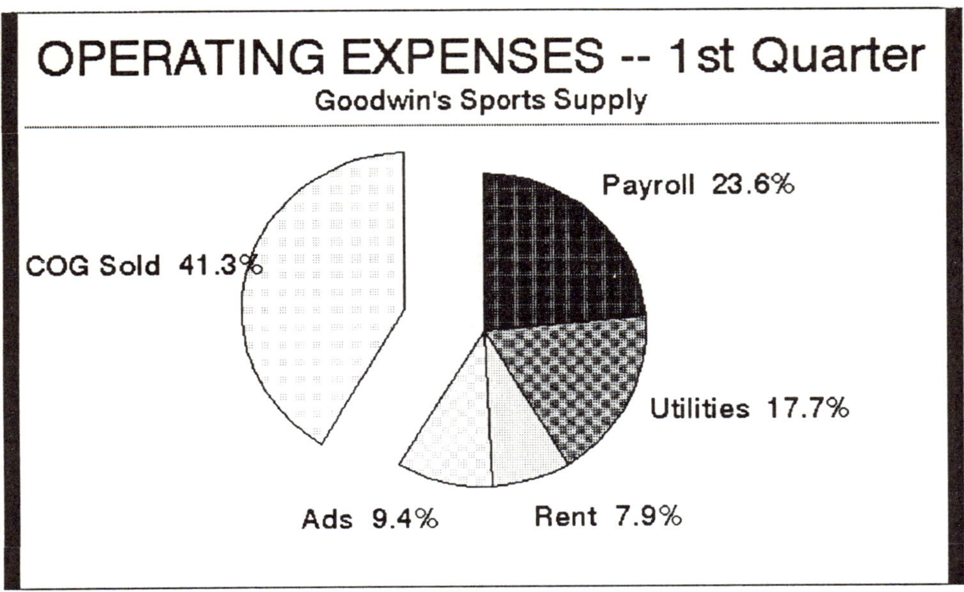

18-17 The Lotus 1-2-3 chart converted into a generic Harvard Graphics 3.0 format.

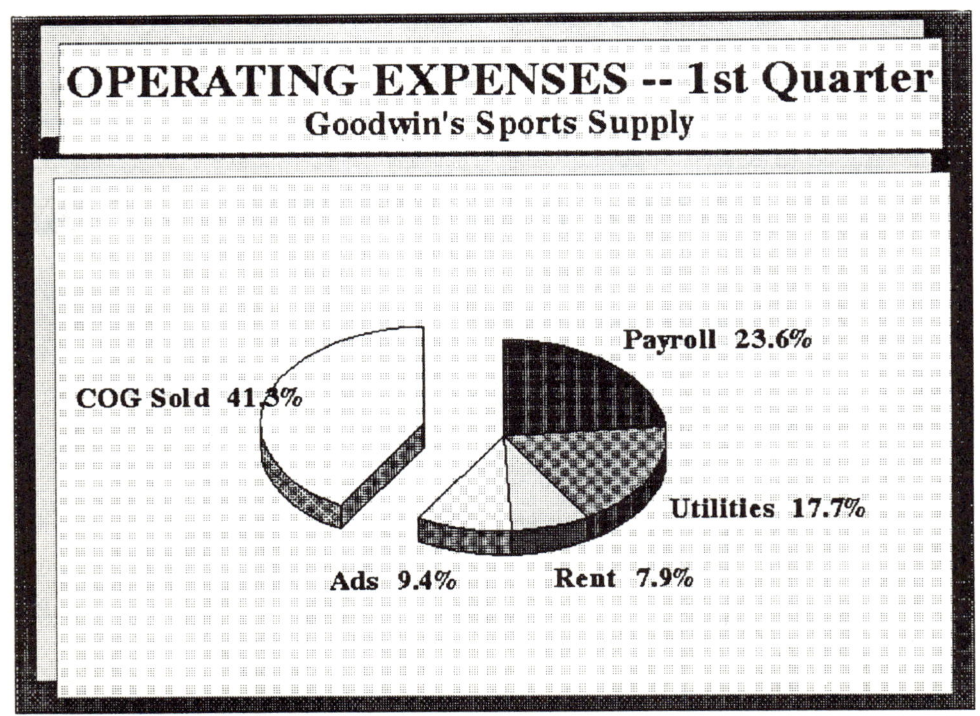

18-18 A considerably enhanced version of the Lotus pie chart.

For now, however, you're well equipped to turn out graphic work of a sophistication that, in the very recent past, was associated only with the work of good commercial artists and graphic designers. Your imagination is your only limit. And your budget. And maybe your corporate identity manual. And your boss's aesthetic judgment . . . .

APPENDIX

Installing Harvard Graphics 3.0

Harvard Graphics 3.0 comes in compressed files on four $3^1/_2$″ disks or five $5^1/_4$″ disks. The fact that the files are compressed means that you cannot install Harvard Graphics 3.0 simply by copying files from the original disks onto your hard disk drive; you must use the Install program, which decompresses the files as it goes along.

1. Insert the Installation Disk, Disk 1, into either the A or B drive of your computer.
2. At the DOS prompt, type A: (or B:) and press Enter.
3. Type install and Enter. The first thing that will appear on your screen is a message estimating the amount of time and disk space required for installing the program (see Fig. A-1).
4. Press Enter. The next screen will ask you to select the hard disk on which to install the program. Change the indicated drive if necessary, and press Enter (see Fig. A-2).
5. Next, the screen message tells you that the program will be installed on directory \HG3 unless you designate otherwise. When the directory you want is on the screen, press Enter (see Fig. A-3).

The Main Menu will now be displayed. You can elect to install all files, or you can

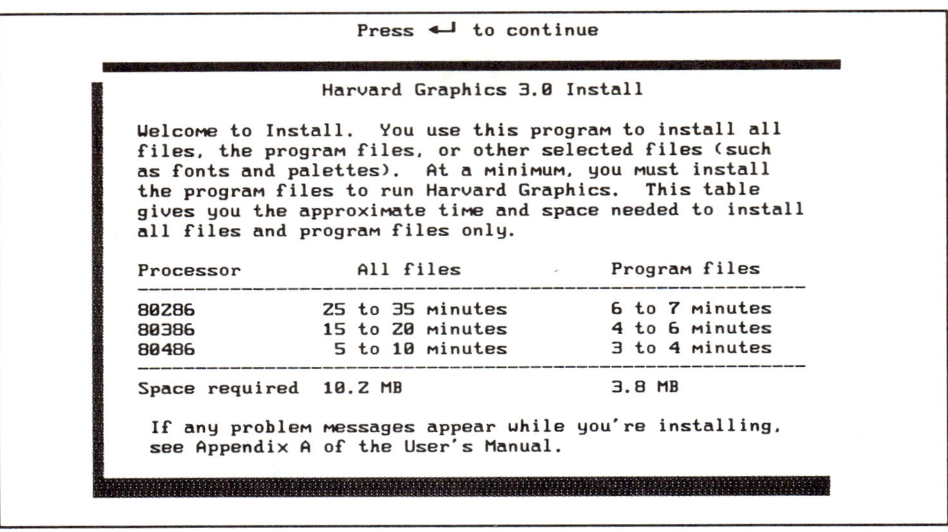

A-1 The first screen, with estimates of time and disk space needed for installation.

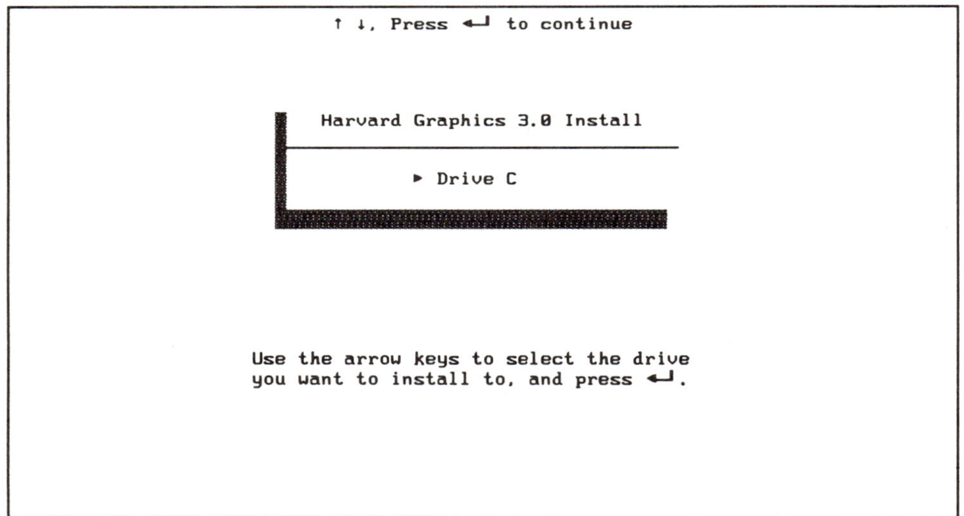

A-2 This screen prompts you to select the hard disk drive on which you want the program installed.

choose among a list of files to install. For example, if you want to omit the tutorial files to save disk space, you can do so by installing selectively from this list. The minimum installation is the program files.

Proceed under the assumption that you are installing all files. With All files highlighted, press Enter. You'll get a Please wait... message as the disk starts to whir, then the message Writing files to C:\HG3 (or the directory you stipulated)

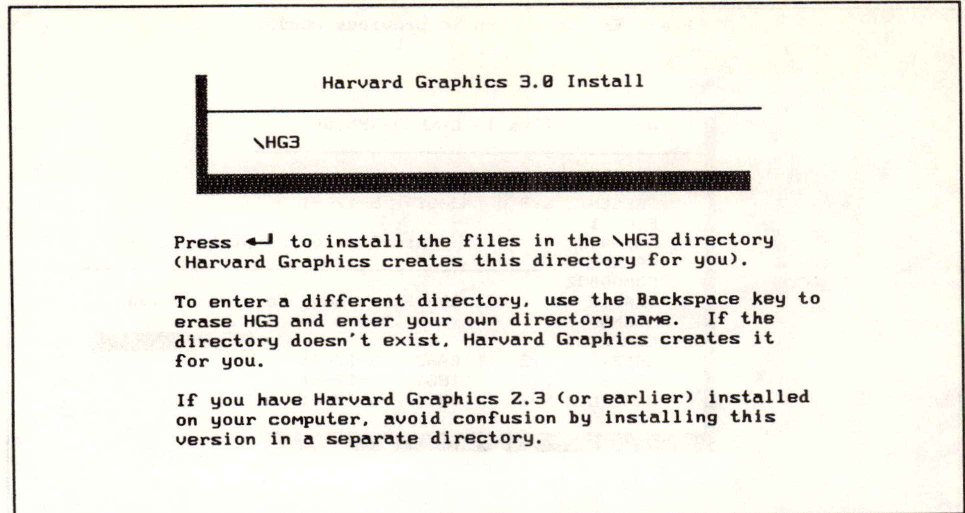

A-3 The designated directory for installing Harvard Graphics 3.0.

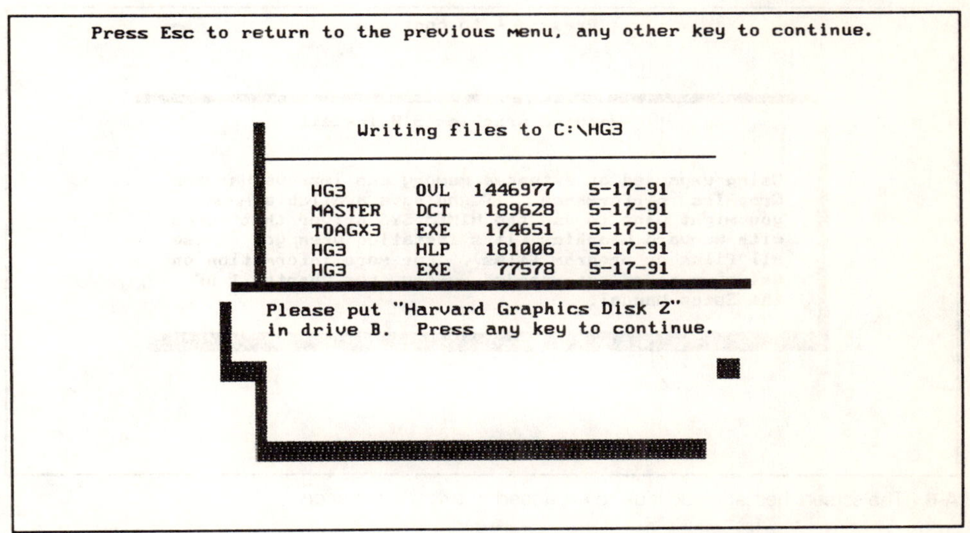

A-4 After listing the files copied from Disk 1, the program prompts you to insert Disk 2.

and a listing of the files as they are decompressed and copied to your hard disk drive.

When all files have been copied from the first disk, you'll be prompted to insert the next disk (see Fig. A-4). Insert Disk 2 and press any key. The copying and listing will resume; simply follow the screen prompts until the files have been copied from all four (or five) disks. When that happens, you'll get an Installation

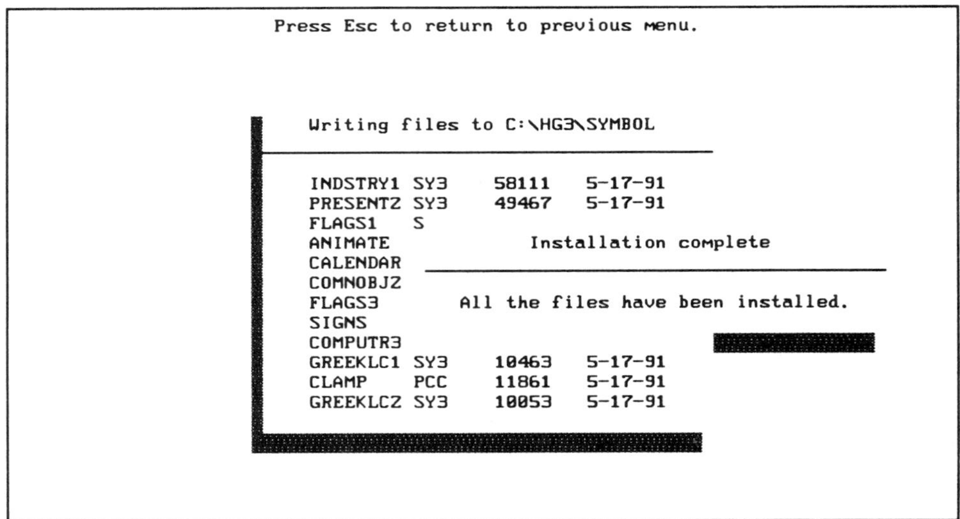

A-5 The *Installation complete* message.

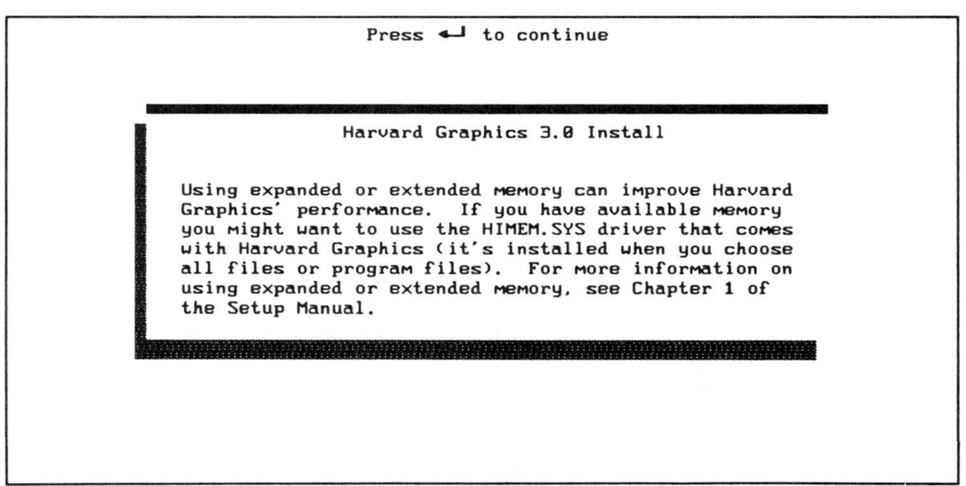

A-6 The screen message about using expanded or extended memory.

complete message, and you should press Esc to return to the Main Menu (see Fig. A-5). Use the down arrow to move down to Exit and press Enter. The screen will display a message about using expanded or extended memory; read it and press Enter (see Fig. A-6).

Your next screen prompt will read, To start Harvard Graphics, type HG3 at the DOS prompt and press <Enter>. Press Enter to return to the DOS prompt, then type HG3 and press Enter. After a few seconds, the Harvard Graphics 3.0 logo will appear, and then the Main Menu (see Fig. A-7). You're on your way.

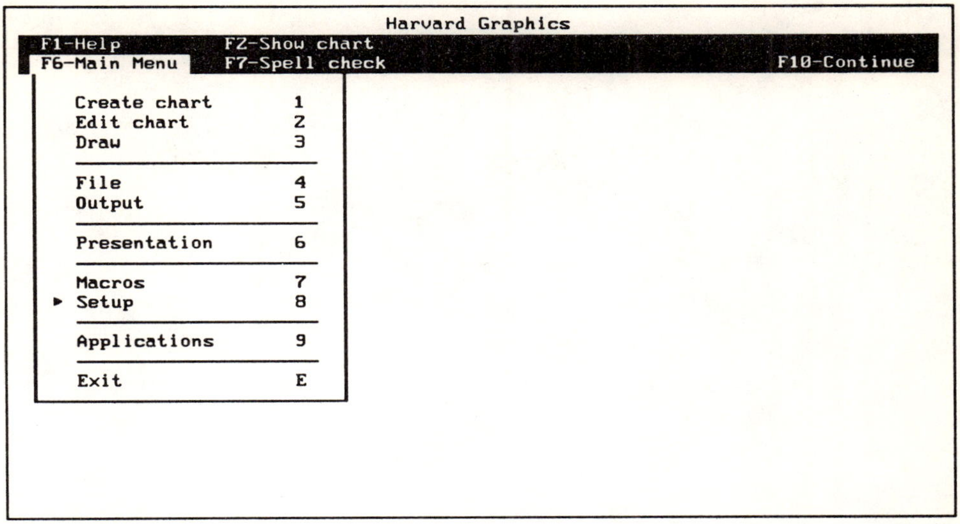

```
                              Harvard Graphics
 F1-Help           F2-Show chart
 F6-Main Menu      F7-Spell check                          F10-Continue

     Create chart        1
     Edit chart          2
     Draw                3

     File                4
     Output              5

     Presentation        6

     Macros              7
   ► Setup               8

     Applications        9

     Exit                E
```

A-7 The Main Menu of Harvard Graphics 3.0.

APPENDIX

Configuring output devices

Before you can produce output with Harvard Graphics 3.0, you need to configure the program for the specific devices you plan to use. In other words, you have to tell the program that you're sending output to a Hewlett-Packard LaserJet printer, or an Okidata Microline 393 printer, so that Harvard Graphics 3.0 can download the data in a form that will be understood and correctly handled by the output device.

There are many possible output devices that Harvard Graphics 3.0 can work with. For now, because most people will be printing Harvard Graphics 3.0 charts, we'll step through the procedure of setting up the program for the right printer(s).

At the Main Menu, select Setup, item 8, and the Setup menu will pop up on your screen (see Fig. B-1). Select Printer 1, item 5 (see Fig. B-2). The printer that is highlighted has been selected; to change it, select F3 – Choices. The Printer Choices menu will appear (see Fig. B-3).

Scroll through the Printer Choices menu until you find the printer you plan to use as your primary printer. In the example illustrated here, the Okidata ML393 (LQ Module), a 24-pin dot-matrix printer, has been selected (see Fig. B-4). There are other options on this menu that you might want to consider, but we're just stepping through a generic setup. You can experiment with the options after you get into the program a bit more.

Select F10 – Continue. You'll be returned to the Setup menu, where you can go on to set up the program for another printer, a film recorder, etc.

It's that easy. Now you're ready to create smashing charts and graphics and print them out. Press Esc to return to the Main Menu and go to work.

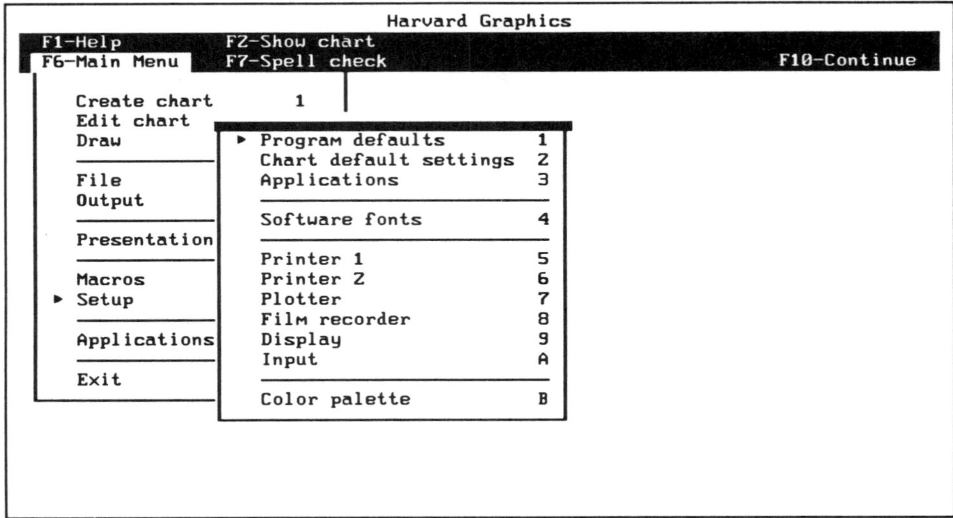

B-1 The Setup menu.

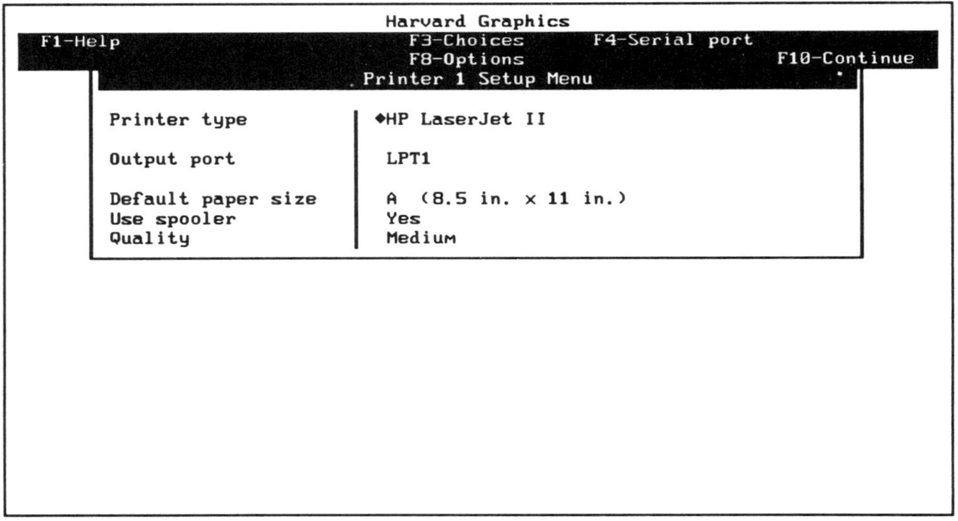

B-2 The Printer 1 Setup Menu.

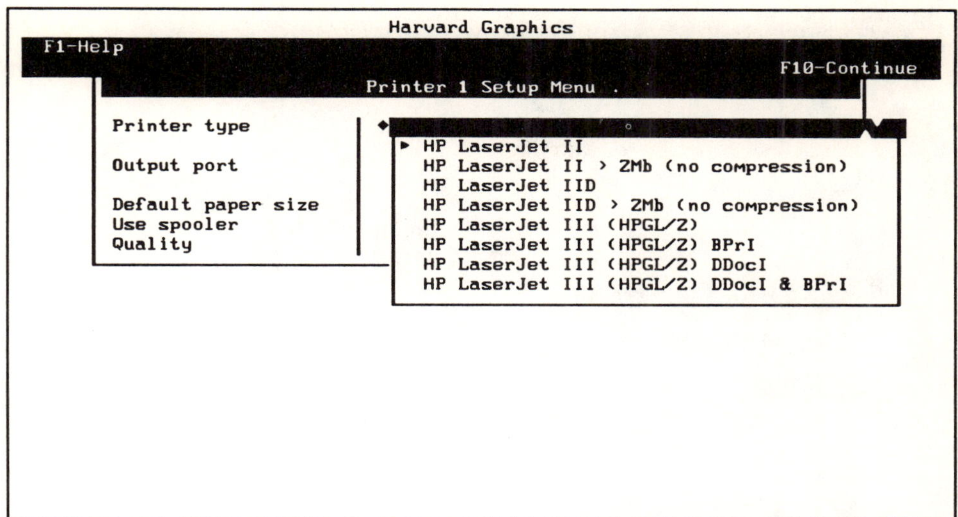

B-3 The Printer Choices menu.

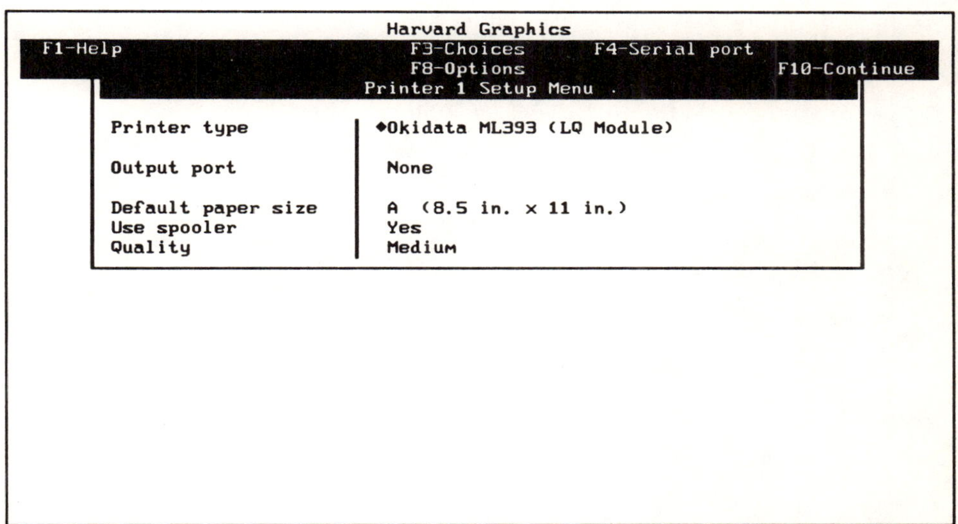

B-4 The Okidata ML393 printer chosen as Printer 1.

Index

D

Other Bestsellers of Related Interest

BUILD YOUR OWN 386/386SX COMPATIBLE AND SAVE A BUNDLE —2nd Edition—*Aubrey Pilgrim*

Now, with the latest in Pilgrim's best-selling Build Your Own series, you can assemble an 80386 microcomputer at home using mail-order parts that cost a lot less today than they did several years ago. Absolutely no special technical know-how is required—only a pair of pliers, a couple of screwdrivers, and this detailed, easy-to-follow guide. 248 pages, 79 illustrations. **Book No. 4089, $18.95 paperback, $29.95 hardcover**

BIT-MAPPED GRAPHICS—*Steve Rimmer*

This is one of the first books to cover the specific graphic file formats used by popular paint and desktop publishing packages. It shows you how to pack and unpack bit-map image files so you can import and export them to other applications. And, it also helps you sort through available file formats, standards, patches, and revision levels, using commercial-quality C code to explore bit-mapped graphics and effectively deal with image files. 504 pages, 131 illustrations. **Book No. 3558, $26.95 paperback, $38.95 hardcover**

MACINTOSH SYSTEM 7: The Complete Sourcebook—*Gordon M. Campbell*

Campbell shows off some of the exciting new features of System 7 and offers tips for upgrading your hardware and software. This is your best guide to the first major development in the Macintosh since its introduction in 1984. With this book by your keyboard, you can count on clear skies and smooth sailing, for either upgrade or installation. 320 pages, Illustrated. **Book No. 4074, $29.95 paperback only**

MS-DOS® BATCH FILE PROGRAMMING —3rd Edition—*Ronny Richardson*

Now updated to cover DOS 5.0, this book explores the power of .BAT—the PC user's key to total system control. Richardson shows how to boost productivity dramatically with simple step-saving programs. He discusses two of the most often customized system batch files, AUTOEXEC.BAT and CONFIG.SYS. You can then progress to creating your own batch files in order to make your computer run more smoothly and do exactly what you want it to do. 440 pages, 186 illustrations, 5.25″ disk included. **Book No. 3916, $26.95 paperback, $36.95 hardcover**

MS-DOS® BATCH FILE UTILITIES —*Ronny Richardson*

Featuring more than 200 of the best batch file programs available for the PC, this is the most complete source of documentation available for batch file utilities currently offered as shareware or in the public domain. Arranged alphabetically and meticulously cross-referenced by category, this valuable reference features detailed descriptions and instructions for ALL commercial batch files on the DOS market today. 368 pages, 275 illustrations, 5.25″ disk included. **Book No. 3915, $26.95 paperback, $36.95 hardcover**

FOXPRO®: The Master Reference —2nd Edition—*Robin Stark and Shelley Satonin*

Design and run powerful, customized databases in no time using all the exciting new features of FoxPro. This alphabetical guide to every FoxPro command and function covers all versions through 2.0—more than 350 entries in all. Its innovative three-part indexing system leads you quickly to all commands, functions, and examples found in the book. 512 pages, 135 illustrations. **Book No. 4056, $24.95 paperback only**

NORTON UTILITIES® 6.0: An Illustrated Tutorial—*Richard Evans*

Richard Evans shows you how to painlessly perform the most dazzling Norton functions using the all-new features of Norton Utilities 6.0. He also reviews the best from previous releases, providing clear, easy-to-follow instructions and screen illustrations reflecting Norton's new developments. You'll also learn about NDOS, a new configuration and shell program that replaces COMMAND.COM. 464 pages, 277 illustrations. **Book No. 4132, $19.95 paperback, $29.95 hardcover**

101+ FOXPRO® AND dBASE® IV USER-DEFINED FUNCTIONS—*Philip Steele*

Whether you've already written many lines of database code and just want to improve your code or you want to develop more complex applications for distribution in the corporate marketplace, this book's for you. It contains professional guidelines for developing and writing UDFs that will eliminate repetitive database programming tasks. A companion disk, offered on an order form at the end of the book, contains all the UDFs used in the book. 368 pages, 159 illustrations. **Book No. 3951, $18.95 paperback only**

COMPUTER SECURITY HANDBOOK —2nd Edition—*Richard H. Baker*

This edition emphasizes practical, affordable measures that protect networks and database servers, featuring all-new coverage of virus control methods, the 1986 Computer Fraud and Abuse Act, and recent case studies of security problems. You'll find complete information on prevention and cure of viruses, electronic eavesdropping, personnel controls, identifying your most vulnerable points, password perils, security planning, and how a computer can protect itself. 432 pages, 70 illustrations. **Book No. 3592, $24.95 paperback, $34.95 hardcover**

GRAPHICAL USER INTERFACE PROGRAMMING—*Steve Rimmer*

Graphical user interfaces are one of the hottest topics in PC software technology today. Creating and using GUIs requires a delicate combination of graphics programing skill and an ability to organize multiple graphic objects. This book shows you how to combine these skills to create images through bitmapping graphics. Rimmer shows you how to write tight code menus, screen fonts, mouse interfaces, icons, and more. 440 pages, 176 illustrations. **Book No. 3875, $34.95 hardcover only**

THE RELATIONAL DATABASE ADVISOR: Elements of PC Database Design —*Kimberly Maughan Saunders*

Kimberly Saunders gives you easy-to-follow guidelines for every phase in the database design process, providing specific suggestions for building databases that fit a variety of business needs and software environments. You'll soon create sophisticated libraries of database files with common informational links. 248 pages, 128 illustrations. **Book No. 3944, $16.95 paperback only**

SQL: Structured Query Language —2nd Edition—*Dr. Carolyn J. Hursch and Dr. Jack L. Hursch*

Carolyn J. Hursch and Dr. Jack L. Hursch present a complete overview of SQL, tracing its mathematical structure from its basis in first-order logic to its present-day role and the efforts of the American National Standards Institute (ANSI) to develop a standard SQL language. They cover all the components of conventional SQL language; SQL commands, keywords and data types; and value expressions supported by SQL. 216 pages, Illustrated. **Book No. 3803, $21.95 paperback, $32.95 hardcover**